LIBRARY OF HEBREW BIBLE/
OLD TESTAMENT STUDIES

524

Formerly Journal for the Study of the Old Testament Supplement Series

Editors
Claudia V. Camp, Texas Christian University
Andrew Mein, Westcott House, Cambridge

Founding Editors
David J. A. Clines, Philip R. Davies and David M. Gunn

BREAKING BOUNDARIES

Female Biblical Interpreters Who Challenged the Status Quo

edited by

Nancy Calvert-Koyzis
and
Heather Weir

t&t clark

NEW YORK • LONDON

Published by T & T Clark International
A Continuum imprint
80 Maiden Lane, New York, NY 10038
The Tower Building, 11 York Road, London SE1 7NX

www.continuumbooks.com

Visit the T & T Clark blog at www.tandtclarkblog.com

Library of Congress Cataloging-in-Publication Data
A catalog record for this book is available from the Library of Congress.

ISBN: 978-0-567-59503-4 (hardback)

Typeset and copy-edited by Forthcoming Publications Ltd. (www.forthpub.com)
Printed in the United States of America by Thomson-Shore, Inc

CONTENTS

CONTRIBUTORS

Beth Bidlack is Bibliographer for Religion and Philosophy at the University of Chicago Library.

Nancy Calvert-Koysis is adjunct faculty in the religious studies department at McMaster University.

Kristin Kobes Du Mez is assistant professor of History, Calvin College.

Rebecca G. S. Idestrom is associate professor of Old Testament at Tyndale Seminary, Toronto, Canada.

Bernon Lee is assistant professor of biblical and theological studies at Bethel University in St. Paul, Minnesota.

Caryn A. Reeder is assistant professor of New Testament at Westmont College.

Brian Sowers is visiting assistant professor, Washington and Lee University.

J. Glen Taylor is associate professor of Old Testament and Biblical Proclamation at Wycliffe College, University of Toronto.

Heather E. Weir is an instructor at Wycliffe College, University of Toronto and Tyndale University College, Toronto.

ABBREVIATIONS

AJP	*American Journal of Philology*
ANRW	*Aufstieg und Niedergang der Romischen Welt*
AQ	*American Quarterly*
BBC	Blackwell Bible Commentaries
BDAG	Bauer, W., F. W. Danker, W. F. Arndt, and F. W. Gingrich. *Greek–English Lexicon of the New Testament and Other Early Christian Literature*. 3d ed. Chicago, 1999
ByzF	*Byzantinische Forschungen*
CH	*Church History*
CSCO	Corpus scriptorum christianorum orientalium
HTR	*Harvard Theological Review*
HTS	Harvard Theological Studies
ICS	*Illinois Classical Studies*
IEJ	*Israel Exploration Journal*
JAAR	*Journal of the American Academy of Religion*
JAH	*The Journal of American History*
JBL	*Journal of Biblical Literature*
JÖB	*Jahrbuch der Österreichischen Byzantinistik Gesellschraft*
JTS	*Journal of Theological Studies*
LCL	Loeb Classical Library
LSJ	Liddell, H. G., R. Scott, H. S. Jones, *A Greek–English Lexicon*. 9th ed. with revised supplement. Oxford, 1996
NIGTC	New International Greek Testament Commentary
RAr	*Revue Archéologique*
RE	*Paulys Realencyclopädie der Classischen Altertumswissenschaft*
SBLSymS	SBL Symposium Series
SWR	Studies in Women and Religion
WBC	Word Biblical Commentary
YCS	Yale Classical Studies

INTRODUCTION:
BOUNDARIES BROKEN, VOICES HEARD

Heather E. Weir and Nancy Calvert-Koyzis

The concept of boundaries, defined as "the marking off of a delimited space," is widely used metaphorically in feminist theory and discourse for the ideas related to "going beyond or exceeding identities of various kinds."[1] This metaphor is related to the concept of marginality: certain groups of people are envisioned at the edge of a society rather than at its center. People could be marginalized because of such characteristics as gender, socio-economic class, race, ethnicity, or any combination of these and other factors. As people attempt to move from the margin to the centre, they cross boundaries placed upon them by society, boundaries that mark out their marginal identity. The women discussed in the essays that make up this volume all crossed boundaries in some way. All of them published works that interpreted the Bible; this act in itself is outside of the bounds of what was expected of women in the past. Many of these women also broke other societal boundaries in their work, including theological, educational, methodological, and genre boundaries.

We chose to use the boundaries metaphor for the title of this volume since that idea expresses a theme that ties the various essays together. We do acknowledge, however, that the metaphor of boundaries, and the associated metaphors around marginality, may contribute to a misreading of the past. The assumptions and metaphors we use to frame history influence both the questions we ask and the answers we find in historical documents. It may be that an examination of the work of the women discussed in these essays, and others like them, will shift the way we see the past. It is possible that our placement of women at the margins of the Christian religion, or even of society, may be a misunderstanding. This is the thesis of Kimberly Anne Coles with regard to the position of women

---

1. Sonya Andermahr, Terry Lovell, and Carol Wolkowitz, eds., *A Glossary of Feminist Theory* (London: Arnold, 2000), 27.

in literary culture in early modern England.[2] Future studies of the history of biblical interpretation might fruitfully examine past dialogues between women and men around hermeneutical issues and theology.

There are two aspects to the social boundaries that the women represented in this book encountered. First, each of their social contexts had a particular system for structuring the relationships between the sexes; this structure has often been called patriarchal. Second, societies often distinguished between the public and private spheres of life. Women's social roles were bounded by the way their particular context structured both the relation between the sexes and the distinction between public and private life.

The term "patriarchy" can refer quite specifically to a particular structure of family or clan life led by the father or patriarch—the most senior male member of the household or group. Metaphorically, kings were seen as fathers to the larger household of their kingdom, and in the church, clergy of various ranks fathered households of faith. In feminist theory, the term often refers more broadly to any "over-arching system of male dominance."[3] The women interpreters represented in this volume lived in societies that practiced some form of patriarchy. We must note that in the Victorian era, the idea of patriarchy extending to the country or kingdom was nuanced as the reigning monarch was a woman. This would have similarly been true in the (first) Elizabethan era.

The concept of separate public and private spheres, with women's actions confined to the private sphere, is a common representation in feminist theory. Pinning down precisely what constitutes the separate spheres, as well as when and how these distinctions played a role in any society, is much more difficult to do. There is no clearly demarcated boundary between the two spheres.[4] When women of the past spoke of

---

2. Kimberly Anne Coles, *Religion, Reform, and Women's Writing in Early Modern England* (Cambridge: Cambridge University Press, 2008), 1: "The critical charting of women's texts within sixteenth-century English culture itself has still operated on the (however tacit) assumption that their literary products were devalued in this context. This book posits a different view of English literary history: that rather than the standard narrative of women writers as marginal within the operations of sixteenth-century English culture, some women writers were instead central to the development of a Protestant literary tradition." See also the similar argument made by Barbara Kiefer Lewalski in *Writing Women in Jacobean England* (Cambridge, Mass.: Harvard University Press, 1993).

3. Andermahr, Lovell, and Wolkowitz, eds., *Glossary*, 193. In the "Patriarchy" entry, the authors note that feminists dispute how the term should be used.

4. Ibid., 219: "Feminist scholarship has uncovered the extent to which this division [between public and private] continues into the topology of the home:

separate spheres for women and men, it is not clear that they know what the boundaries were between those spheres. The rather abstract and theoretical boundary between public and private spaces is one of the social boundaries broken by the women discussed in these essays.

The women discussed in these essays all worked within the Christian tradition. As such, there were theological aspects to the way they understood and identified themselves as women, often in opposition to their male contemporaries' theologies of womanhood. Questions around the full humanity of women reappeared throughout the history of the church, including questions about whether women were made in the image of God and whether women had a soul. Women could be either demonized as temptresses like Eve, or exalted as saintly, like the Virgin Mary. Many of the women interpreters discussed in this book explicitly redeemed Eve in their writings, and proposed alternate theological understandings of what it meant to be a woman.

Boundaries were often placed around the educational opportunities women had. The women discussed in this volume were all privileged in that they had access to some kind of education, whether from family instruction, or schooling outside the home. Most of them knew more than one language; many knew biblical languages, and this knowledge influenced their interpretation of the Bible. The women who attended colleges and did post-graduate studies, such as Olympia Brown and Elizabeth MacDonald, broke boundaries around who could attend and graduate from these institutions so that later other women could also study. Some of the women discussed, for example Sarah Trimmer, taught others; Trimmer used her own education to teach her own children, the poor children of her parish, and other parents and teachers. She broke boundaries set up around which social classes could learn to read. The women represented here all took responsibility for learning what they could—and in their writing, particularly their interpretation of the Bible, they passed that learning on to others.

As the women discussed in these essays interpreted the Bible, they questioned the methodologies of their male contemporaries. They questioned the translation of the Hebrew and Greek text into English; they questioned the assumptions made by male interpreters; they brought new questions to the biblical text, breaking the methodological and hermeneutical boundaries others had set up around the text. The women respected some boundaries: most wanted to be considered orthodox in

---

private houses have their public rooms which allow entrances from the outside, and their more private quarters. Conversely, attention has been drawn to privileged and powerful private spaces within the public sphere, such as men's clubs."

their understanding of the Bible. At the same time, they argued that orthodoxy did not require a traditional theology of women.

Women did not always choose to write in typical interpretive genres, such as commentaries. For example, Eudocia and Lanyer wrote poetry that interpreted the Gospels. Trimmer wrote educational works for children, an acceptable genre for a woman to write; however, her work for children is clearly a work of natural theology. Trimmer's intended audience made it acceptable for her to write and publish the book; this is a subtler example of boundary breaking. Greswell and MacDonald wrote traditional scholarly works: Greswell a textbook, and MacDonald a doctoral dissertation. In so doing, these women broke boundaries around who could write in a particular genre. All of these women authored works that interpreted the Bible, but did so in ways that broke the boundaries of the genre of biblical interpretation.

Female Interpreters in their Contexts

Each woman's particular historical context meant some of the above boundaries were more pronounced than others. Each era had its own particular way of setting boundaries around acceptable gender roles/ identities. While most of the women discussed in this volume published their works during the nineteenth century, others wrote during the fifth, seventeenth and eighteenth centuries. While each author in this volume provides background appropriate to the particular women, in this section we will consider some of the boundaries emphasized in each period.

Women in Late Antiquity

The location of earliest Christianity was in the private sphere, which allowed women to have measures of authority and participation therein; however, by the fifth century women's leadership in the church became unimaginable. This change in the roles of women was due, in a large degree, to the more public face of the church with its "pomp of public ceremonial rites and architectural monuments" and its increasingly patriarchal structure.[5] According to Kenneth G. Holum,

> [W]omen...occupied a secondary position in Christian society from the outset. Encouraged to labor in charitable occupations such as care for the sick, destitute, and aged, they had been categorically excluded from the priesthood and any office of teaching or leadership. Their subordination found concrete expression when the people of Constantinople gathered in

5. Virginia Burris, *Late Ancient Christianity* (ed. Denis R. Janz; A People's History of Christianity 2; Minneapolis: Fortress, 2005), 10.

the Great Church; women were physically separated from men and generally restricted to the galleries or *gynaikeia*, the "women's section," and
no female might ever enter the sanctuary. Whatever the origins of these
attitudes or practices, dogma had a convenient explanation: woman was
the daughter of Eve, and through Eve sin had entered the world.[6]

One of the ways in which women could pursue a religious vocation was
within ascetic communities. For example, Melania the Younger (ca. 385–
429), who is perhaps the best known among Roman senatorial women
who joined the ascetic movement in the fourth and early fifth centuries,
and founded her own religious communities.[7]

Unless a woman devoted herself to God through ascetic or other
religious communities (where women were often seen to be brides of
Christ), marriage was the most central aspect of a woman's life. Her
marriage was arranged and she could divorce her husband, but her
husband could divorce her much more easily and for a wider variety of
claims.[8] The major role for a married woman was to produce legitimate
children. For this reason, laws for extramarital relationships differed for
men and women. A man might have extramarital sexual relationships
with prostitutes or slaves without penalty, but "if a married or marriage-
able woman had an extramarital sexual relationship with a man, she and
her partner were severely condemned, since any doubt about her chastity
also cast doubt on the legitimacy of her children."[9] During this time, the
Church attempted to redefine adultery as infidelity by either spouse,
although many Christian wives still pretended not to notice her husband's infidelity.[10]

The example of a woman from Late Antiquity in this volume is
Eudocia, wife of Theodosius II. Originally from Athens, Eudocia (previously Athenais) was not from a noble family, but she was the daughter of
a philosopher. She appears to have been married to Theodosius II for
political reasons.[11] It was during Eudocia's reign that the position of the
empress underwent striking changes from being seen primarily as a child

6.   Kenneth G. Holum, *Theodosian Empresses: Women and Imperial Dominion
in Late Antiquity* (Berkeley: University of California Press, 1982), 140.

7.   Kate Cooper, "The Household and the Desert: Monastic and Biological
Communities in the Lives of Melania the Younger," in *Household, Women, and
Christianities in Late Antiquity and the Middle Ages* (ed. Anneke B. Mulder-Bakker
and Jocelyn Wogan-Browne; Turnhout: Brepols, 2005), 11–36.

8.   Gillian Clark, *Women in Late Antiquity: Pagan and Christian Life-Styles*
(Oxford: Clarendon, 1994), 21–27.

9.   Ibid., 29–29.

10.   Ibid., 38–41.

11.   Holum, *Theodosian Empresses*, 120–21.

bearer who would continue the dynasty, to embodying a sacred character. This sacred character was called *basileia*, and referred to the imperial dominion of women, which was a precursor to the European ideology of sacred kingship. Yet this status did not prevent her from being exiled permanently to Jerusalem in 441, when her husband accused her of having an affair.[13]

Women in Late Antiquity were also under-educated and lacked the experiences of life that men had; "they were dependent, both for property and for advice, on their male relatives rather than on colleagues and contacts; they were emotionally vulnerable."[14] Even if women were to receive the same moral training as men, they might be just as capable of virtue as men, but this training was to be used in the traditional sphere of wife and mother.

Eudocia, however, used her academic training to write copious amounts of poetry, at a time when women poetesses were seen as second class. As Brian Sowers shows in his article, this poetry included biblical interpretation, and was written in part from the perspective of fifth-century ascetic theology. It is also likely that Eudocia had an interest in stabilizing academic life, particularly at the so-called university of Constantinople that was originally founded in 425 C.E., during her husband's reign, and in honoring successful teachers. It is also probably that her presence at the imperial court after being crowned Augusta benefited ambitious men of literary distinction, who could then display the "culture they had attained through hard work."[15] Of course, it was because of her political influence that she could leave her mark on poetic and religious landscape of fifth-century Byzantium.

Women in Early Stuart England
The second era represented by a woman discussed in this volume is the early seventeenth century. Amelia Lanyer published her book of poetry, *Salve Deus Rex Judaeorum*, in 1611, the same year that the King James Version of the Bible was first published. King James, who authorized the translation of the Bible, succeeded his cousin Elizabeth I to the English throne. The period following Elizabeth's reign has been portrayed as difficult for women, not least because the king himself held a traditional theory of patriarchy, one in which the power of God was "imaged in the

---

12. Ibid., 3.
13. Many aspects of the story of Eudocia's affair are questionable. See ibid., 176–78.
14. Clark, *Women in Late Antiquity*, 56.
15. Holum, *Theodosian Empresses*, 127.

absolute monarch of the state, and in the husband and father of the family."[16] A woman's role was to be subject to her father, then her husband; she "imaged the subjection of all English people to their monarch, and of all Christians to God."[17] Certainly this era saw "an outpouring of antifeminist or overtly misogynist sermons, tracts, and plays detailing women's physical and mental defects, spiritual evils, rebelliousness, shrewishness, and natural inferiority to men in the hierarchy of being."[18]

Despite this apparently hostile environment to women, during this time period in England there was "a breakthrough in female authorship," and Lanyer was a key figure in this group of women writers.[19] These women resisted the patriarchal values of English society in their poetry, drama, and prose. As Caryn Reeder shows in her essay, Lanyer opposed interpretations of the Bible which supported patriarchy, and proposed her own understanding of the biblical narrative of the Fall.

Understanding the biblical text was vital to breaking any of the boundaries imposed upon women in early seventeenth-century England. The authority of Scripture was paramount in shaping ideas about the world and relations between people. Protestant England, like the rest of Protestant Europe, placed a high value on reading the Bible and following what it said.[20] This meant that a high value was placed on literacy for all, so that all could read the Bible. Women benefited by this emphasis on literacy, though many understandings of the Bible did not benefit them. Through her poetry, Lanyer not only advocated for a woman-friendly understanding of the Bible, but also for communities of women to gather in order to pursue true Christianity.

Women in Eighteenth-Century England

In the late eighteenth century, as in the early seventeenth century, English society was shaped by theology, and "the main challenge to established religion and its social consequences came from heterodox theology."[21] Sarah Trimmer, the representative of this time period examined in this

16. Lewalski, *Writing Women in Jacobean England*, 2.
17. Ibid.
18. Ibid.
19. Ibid., 3.
20. Diarmaid MacCulloch, *The Later Reformation in England 1547–1603* (London: Macmillan, 1990), 164. As noted already, the most-remembered result of James's reign was the translation and publication of the King James Bible, underlining the importance of Scripture in society at this time.
21. J. C. D. Clark, *English Society 1660–1832: Religion, Ideology and Politics During the Ancient Regime* (rev. ed.; Cambridge: Cambridge University Press, 2000), 30.

volume, defended orthodox theology from these challenges. While women did not generally write theological works in the eighteenth century, Trimmer wrote children's educational books, a more acceptable genre for women to pursue.

During the eighteenth century, two shifts in the understanding of children and childhood occurred that allowed women to write educational books for children. First, the proper occupation of children became learning instead of work.[22] Second, there was a shift in the perceived responsibility for rearing children from the father to the mother.[23] By the late eighteenth century, women had become the designated teachers of children, so women could properly write books for children. Children's books became a flourishing new area of publishing because of these changes. These changes in the view of children expanded the boundaries around women's place in society, providing women such as Trimmer with more opportunities than existed previously.

The Church of England had no official roles for women in the late eighteenth century. Women, such as Sarah Trimmer, who wanted to serve God had to find unofficial ways to do so. Within their families and households, women could teach their children, and instruct their servants in the Christian faith, and many carried out these responsibilities diligently. Women also attended the sick, and assisted the poor of their parishes. In the late eighteenth century, Sunday schools began to appear in many parishes. Many women found an outlet for their energies in organizing these new schools, seeing them as an extension of the work they did in their own homes. By influencing the young, women, including Trimmer, sought to influence the future of their society.

By the end of the eighteenth century, the boundaries around women's place in society and the church had expanded. Women such as Trimmer, along with her contemporary Hannah More, stepped into the newly defined area of work with children. In so doing, these women continued to put pressure on the boundaries placed upon women, stretching them further, making room for women of the nineteenth century, who followed.

22. Peter N. Stearns, *Childhood in World History* (Themes in World History; New York: Routledge, 2006), 55.

23. Hugh Cunningham, *Children and Childhood in Western Society Since 1500* (Studies in Modern History; Harlow: Pearson Education, 2005), 64–65: "In the thought patterns which dominated from the Renaissance through to the Enlightenment fathers played the key role in the rearing of children. With Romanticism, mothers regained the predominance they had held in the middle ages; child-rearing became a female occupation, and fathers were relegated to a subordinate position."

Women in Nineteenth- and Early Twentieth-Century Britain and North America

The majority of contributors in this volume address nineteenth- and early twentieth-century North American and British women. Those who published in the nineteenth century include Scotswoman Eliza Smith (fl. 1848–1850), Englishwomen Elizabeth Rundle Charles (1828–1896) and Joana Julia Greswell (1838–1906); Americans Harriet Beecher Stowe (1811–1896), Sarah Towne Martyn (1805–1870), Katharine Bushnell (1855–1946), Lee Anna Starr (1853–1937) and Olympia Brown (1835–1926). Finally, early twentieth-century interpreter Elizabeth Mary MacDonald (1897–1984), who was a Canadian, completes the list. All were from the white middle classes and all saw themselves as members of the Christian tradition.

Prior to the mid-eighteenth century, families often worked together at home, with little separation between domestic and work life. With the changes in manufacturing practices that occurred in the late eighteenth and early nineteenth centuries, men's work lives became separated from the household. Increasingly through the nineteenth century, the home became a place of leisure and sociability where men could escape from the competition of the outside world.[24] A woman's sphere was thought to be private and limited to the household, while men operated in the public sphere.[25]

The consignment of women into the domestic sphere was based on nineteenth- and early twentieth-century perceptions of women as inferior to men physically and mentally. If women had literary and intellectual interests, these pursuits were not to interfere with their domestic responsibilities.[26] Wives were encouraged to cultivate the qualities of piety, purity, submissiveness, and domesticity, thus modeling themselves after the ideal of the "True Woman."[27] According to de Groot and Taylor, middle-class women in both England and North America aspired to the ideal of separate spheres:

24. Rachel G. Fuchs and Victoria E. Thompson, *Women in Nineteenth-Century Europe* (Basingstoke: Palgrave Macmillan, 2005), 45; Christiana de Groot and Marion Ann Taylor, eds., *Recovering Nineteenth-Century Women Interpreters of the Bible* (SBLSymS 38; Atlanta: Society of Biblical Literature, 2007).

25. In the nineteenth century, the idea of separate spheres for men and women was widespread, which, in turn, influenced the way historians reconstructed their own research. See Linda K. Kerber, "Female Worlds, Woman's Place: The Rhetoric of Women's History," *The Journal of American History* 75 (1988): 9–39.

26. Barbara Welter, "The Cult of True Womanhood: 1820–1860," *American Quarterly* 18 (1966): 151–74 (154).

27. Ibid., 152.

It was a sign of status if women were maintained at home, busy with the
work of educating their children and supervising the domestic help, free
from daily chores. For middle-class women, the image of being delicate,
of not being able to handle difficult decisions, and of having an inferior
intellect was cultivated.[28]

While the ideal of the delicate woman was promoted, the reality of the
life and work of the women portrayed in this volume displays resistance
to this ideal.

Except for a few segments of Christianity such as the Salvation Army,
women's leadership in the church was officially forbidden.[29] For example, when author, pastor and preacher Antoinette Brown Blackwell was a
student at Oberlin College in Ohio, her professor, James H. Fairchild,
stated, "Take the pulpit and the bar. Can woman occupy these stations to
an equal extent with man? The answer must be, No, for two general reasons: it is improper and impossible."[30] While women's leadership in the
church continued to be officially forbidden for theological reasons, the
social construct of true womanhood both reinforced and was reinforced
by a theology of womanhood.

The middle-class women examined in this book pushed the boundaries
that constrained them. In spite of living in a society in which women's
intellectual gifts were demeaned, Joanna Greswell, an accomplished
Hebraist, published a Hebrew grammar on the Psalms that was used by
Oxford students. Harriet Beecher Stowe turned the theory of the two
spheres on its head by arguing for the maternalization of American society. In contrast to traditional interpretations in which Mary Magdalene
was little more than a prostitute, Sarah Towne Martyn interpreted biblical texts in ways that gave more significance to Magdalene's part in the
Gospels. Katherine Bushnell and Lee Anna Starr, trained in the biblical
languages, agued against faulty translations and interpretations of the
Bible that subjugated women in the nineteenth century. In the twentieth
century, Elizabeth Mary MacDonald was the first woman to complete a
doctorate in the Department of Oriental Languages at the University of
Toronto. Many of these women also used their gifts in the public sphere;
for example, Olympia Brown pastored churches in the northeastern and

28. De Groot and Taylor, eds., *Recovering*, 4.
29. Pamela J. Walker, "Gender, Radicalism, and Female Preaching in Nineteenth-Century Britain: Catherine Booth's Female Teaching," in *Strangely Familiar:
Protofeminist Interpretations of Patriarchal Biblical Texts* (ed. Nancy Calvert-
Koyzis and Heather E. Weir; Atlanta: SBL, 2009), 171–84 (181).
30. Quoted in Beth Bidlack, "Antoinette Brown Blackwell: Pioneering Exegete
and Congregational Minister," in Calvert-Koyzis and Weir, eds., *Strangely Familiar*,
151–79 (151).

midwestern United States and Methodist pastor Lee Anna Starr served churches in the American Midwest.

All of the women writers studied in this volume broke boundaries and challenged the status quo of their particular contexts. Each interpreter needs to be heard again with her context in mind in order to gain new appreciation for her work. With other women who interpreted the Bible in the past, these women contribute to a fuller understanding of the reception history of the Bible.

Women Interpreters in the Context of the History of Biblical Interpretation

The history of biblical interpretation has its own boundaries and canon; there are certain ideas about who is important, and how importance can be measured.[31] The boundaries set up around the canon of writings that interpret the scriptural canon exclude women, primarily because women were not educated, nor did they participate in official scholarly circles in their own time. This book is part of a larger project of recovery and analysis of women interpreters; this large project demands that the boundaries that exclude women from consideration as important in the history of biblical interpretation need to be re-thought.

Several other recent published works focus on the recovery and analysis of the work of women who interpreted the Bible. *Let Her Speak for Herself: Nineteenth-Century Women Writing on the Women of Genesis*,[32] edited by Marion Ann Taylor and Heather E. Weir, is an example of recovery work: the book contains excerpts from many books of biblical interpretation written by women, along with the biographies of the authors, where those could be discovered. An earlier work by Marla Selvidge, *Notorious Voices: Feminist Biblical Interpretation 1500–1920*,[33] looks for a feminist consciousness in women writing on the Bible from the time of the Reformation to the early twentieth century. Two edited volumes, one containing papers given at the Canadian Society for

---

31. See particularly the Introduction to Donald K. McKim, *Dictionary of Major Biblical Interpreters* (Downers Grove, Ill.: InterVarsity Press Academic, 2007). See also John Sandys-Wunsch, *What Have They Done to the Bible? A History of Modern Biblical Interpretation* (Collegeville, Minn.: Liturgical Press, 2005).

32. Marion Ann Taylor and Heather E. Weir, eds., *Let Her Speak for Herself: Nineteenth-Century Women Writing on the Women of Genesis* (Waco, Tex.: Baylor University Press, 2006).

33. Marla Selvidge, *Notorious Voices: Feminist Biblical Interpretation 1500–1920* (London: SCM, 1996).

Biblical Studies, the other papers presented at the Society of Biblical Literature meetings, provide analysis of some of the writings of these women.[34] Some church historians have also taken up this work of recovery and analysis.[35] This volume contributes to the ongoing project of the recovery and analysis of women interpreters of the Bible. Some of the women studied in the essays need no recovery in the sense that they are well-known writers; Harriet Beecher Stowe is the most obvious example. Other women, such as Eliza Smith or Joana Julia Greswell, are presently hardly known at all. Whether a woman discussed in these essays is remembered by history or not, her work as an interpreter of the Bible has certainly been forgotten or overlooked, and it is this herme-neutical work that we recover and analyze here.

Because the women who interpreted the Bible did not always write in traditional interpretive genres, they have often been studied by scholars in other fields, such as history or literature.[36] Some of these scholars have appreciated the writings as works of biblical interpretation. Patricia Demers, for example, wrote an entire book on women interpreters of the Bible from her perspective as a literature scholar.[37] Unfortunately, some scholars have either ignored or misunderstood the biblical interpretation in women's writings.[38] The essays in this volume aim to provide a more nuanced understanding of the religious and theological work of the women studied.

The growing and fruitful field of the reception history of the Bible has expanded the understanding of biblical interpretation to include the arts, both visual and written. This expanded understanding provides hope for

34. De Groot and Taylor, eds., *Recovering*; Calvert-Koyzis and Weir, eds., *Strangely Familiar.*

35. See, for example, Timothy Larsen, "Christina Rossetti, the Decalogue, and Biblical Interpretation," *Zeitschrift für Neuere Theologiegeschichte/Journal for the History of Modern Theology* 16, no. 1 (2009): 21–36.

36. The genre of women's interpretive work is often cited as a reason they have been left out of the "canon" of the history of biblical interpretation.

37. Patricia Demers, *Women as Interpreters of the Bible* (Mahwah, N.J.: Paulist, 1992). For another example of a literature scholar who carefully examines the religious aspects of women's writings, see Christine L. Krueger, *The Reader's Repentance: Women Preachers, Women Writers, and Nineteenth-Century Social Discourse* (Chicago: University of Chicago Press, 1992). An example of history which includes a discussion of women's biblical interpretation is Gerda Lerner, *The Creation of Feminist Consciousness: From the Middle Ages to Eighteen-seventy* (New York: Oxford University Press, 1993).

38. For example, Christina Rossetti's religious writings are often ignored or misunderstood. For a discussion of this aspect of Rossetti scholarship, see Larsen, "Christina Rossetti," 23–25.

integrating women into the broader history of biblical interpretation. The Blackwell Bible Commentaries, currently being published, are devoted to the reception history of the Bible.[39] As one example, David Gunn successfully integrates women interpreters into his commentary on Judges in this series. It is our hope that the essays in the present volume will contribute further to the study of these women and their inclusion in histories of biblical interpretation, finally breaking the boundaries placed around that field of study.

39. Several volumes of the Blackwell Bible Commentaries series are in print, including: Jo Carruthers, *Esther Through the Centuries* (Oxford: Blackwell, 2008); Eric S. Christianson, *Ecclesiastes Through the Centuries* (Oxford: Blackwell, 2007); Mark Edwards, *John Through the Centuries* (Oxford: Blackwell, 2004); Susan Gillingham, *Psalms Through the Centuries* (Oxford: Blackwell, 2008); and David M. Gunn, *Judges Through the Centuries* (Oxford: Blackwell, 2005).

RETELLING AND MISREADING JESUS: EUDOCIA'S HOMERIC CENTO

Brian Sowers

Introduction

Recovering ancient exegetes—let alone female ones—is particularly challenging since only a fraction of ancient literature survives, and what does survive frequently tells only one side of the story. When one turns to the recovery of ancient female interpreters of the Bible, even more hurdles stand in the way, a fact evidenced in Methodius's third-century Christian version of Plato's *Symposium*. His eighth speaker, Thecla, the proto-martyr of her sex, says the following about women of her day: "Wise men have said that our life is a festal assembly, and that we have come as though into a theater to show the drama of truth, that is, of righteousness."[1] Ancient women, including Christian women, frequently serve as mirrors for ancient men, who are the best surviving transmitters of stories about women. Methodius's Thecla compares this reflective function to that of an actor on the stage, a wearer of masks and a player of parts. Ancient literature, with the exception of the papyrological record, depends upon readers and copyists, the majority of whom, for at least 1000 years, were men. These two factors result in either the silencing or the distortion of the ancient female; their stories, both those they lived and those they voiced, are either lost or edited by subsequent male editors.

When we turn to the stories of Aelia Eudocia, wife of emperor Theodosius II (408–450 C.E.), the same selective editing and mirroring are evident. The account of Eudocia's life is, as we will see below, one written exclusively by men who indiscriminately weave the legendary with the historical to create a more interesting and, therefore, more "survivable" product. Unraveling fact from fiction in these accounts often leaves us with little to go on; removed from her mythos, we know little of the historical Eudocia. The same can be said of the stories Eudocia voiced. Despite the survival of over 3300 lines of poetry attributed to

1. Methodius of Olympus, *Symposium* 8.1.

Eudocia—considerably more than any other ancient female poet—her writings were subject to considerable revision and her voice, therefore, subject to distortion. As we will see, the majority of her poetry was later rewritten, and the roughly 1000 lines that survive unedited did so accidentally. Moreover, because the 3300 surviving lines represent less than 10 percent of the known literary output of Aelia Eudocia, only a fraction of her stories are recoverable, thereby precluding a complete picture of Eudocia's exegetical program. The historian of ancient Christian women is constantly faced with the unfortunate reality that only a small percentage of the works of antiquity's female authors survives, and, therefore, our understanding of these women is doomed to remain shrouded in mystery and myth.

Despite the difficulties facing ancient historians, the case of Aelia Eudocia is exceptionally promising. After all, 3300 lines survive, so, unlike countless early female readers and interpreters of the Bible whose voices have been silenced altogether, much can be said about Eudocia's approach to the Bible as well as the freedom she felt to retell the narrative and to revise biblical episodes into a more socially relevant product. In the end, Eudocia's *oeuvre*, apart from its fortunate survival, was hardly exceptional; her poetry is consistent with the literary developments of the fourth and fifth centuries. On the other hand, the story of Eudocia's life, what little we can recover, was quite remarkable.

The Story Eudocia Lived

In the year 421 C.E., Aelia Eudocia, born Athenais, married the eastern emperor Theodosius II. The marriage was an unusual one; Eudocia came neither from the Constantinopolitan aristocracy nor from a Christian background. Her father was apparently a pagan teacher of rhetoric from Athens, and, like most late antique pedagoges, he had educated his daughter in the classical curriculum, which began with reading poetry, most commonly Homer's epics and Euripides's tragedies, and ended with rudimentary rhetorical argumentation.[2] At the time of her marriage,

---

2. Our ancient sources are consistent in how they present Athenais's family, but this hardly warrants their wholesale acceptance. The amount of legendary material found in the story suggests instead that soon after Athenais married Theodosius, unreliable stories circulated about Athenais, her origin, and, perhaps most damaging to her reputation, her religious background. For more on the standardization of ancient education, see Raffaella Cribiore, *Writing, Teachers, and Students in Graeco-Roman Egypt* (Atlanta: Scholars, 1996); Teresa Morgan, *Literate Education in the Hellenistic and Roman Worlds* (New York: Cambridge University Press, 1998); and Raffaella Cribiore, *Gymnastics of the Mind: Greek Education in Hellenistic and*

Athenais had already acquired a reputation as an erudite poetess, although our surviving historical sources suggest that her fame as a remarkable beauty was a close second. It is difficult to reconcile how these meager and unsatisfying descriptions of Athenais advanced her candidacy as the future wife of Theodosius. Moreover, the decision regarding whom Theodosius would marry was most likely made by Pulcheria, elder sister of Theodosius and figurehead of the conservative branch of Constantino-politan Christianity, who held tremendous sway over the young emperor, his court, and the Byzantine church throughout much of Theodosius's reign.[3] Despite Athenais's unlikely candidacy as imperial spouse and Pulcheria's equally unlikely hand in the selection process, Athenais and Theodosius were married on June 7th, 421 C.E., at which time Athenais converted to Christianity,[4] changed her name to Aelia Eudocia,[5] and

Roman Egypt (Princeton, N.J.: Princeton University Press, 2001). Although the previous model of a monolithic educational system in antiquity, most commonly attributed to Henri Marrou, *A History of Education in Antiquity* (trans. G. Lamb; New York: Sheed & Ward, 1956); trans. of *Histoire de l'éducation dans l'antiquité* (Paris: Seuil, 1948), is no longer accepted, the other extreme, namely that of a system that had no systematization, is as equally unlikely. Students did learn to read and write, and from the surviving examples of later rhetorical handbooks, there appears to have been some degree of systematization. On the role of early rhetorical exercises, the progymnasmata, see Ronald F. Hock and Edward N. O'Neal, eds., *The Chreia and Ancient Rhetoric: Classroom Exercises* (Leiden: Brill, 2002), and George A. Kennedy, *Progymnasmata: Greek Textbooks of Prose Composition and Rhetoric* (Leiden: Brill, 2003).

   3.   The rise of Pulcheria and her role in the political events from the beginning of Theodosius's reign in 408 until her fall from power in the 440s is part of a centuries long development during which Roman women found themselves privileged to increasing legal and social rights and influences unknown in the Roman republic and early principate. See Kenneth G. Holum, *Theodosian Empresses: Women and Imperial Dominion in Late Antiquity* (Berkeley: University of California Press, 1982), and Gillian Clark, *Women in Late Antiquity: Pagan and Christian Life-styles* (Oxford: Clarendon, 1993). The most difficult aspect of Pulcheria's influence to reconcile with her approval or, most likely, selection of Athenais is her religious conservatism. In a world whose legal codes lumped pagans, heretics, and Jews in the same negative category, it is unlikely that those responsible for the marriage of the empire's most eligible and influential bachelor would have turned a blind eye to Athenais's serious ideological incompatibility simply because she was a beautiful poet. I suspect Athenais's pagan background needs to be re-evaluated.

   4.   As suggested above, this is most likely a vestige of the court intrigue and gossip that doubtless surrounded Eudocia during the early years of her marriage. To the best of my knowledge, there is no verifiable evidence to suggest that Eudocia was a pagan prior to her trip to Constantinople. That her relatives were perhaps pagan hardly clarifies the issue; rather it hides Eudocia's religious identity behind that of her brothers.

directed her poetic talents to the praise and honor of Christ and his church.[6] The early decades of Eudocia's marriage were generally uneventful, with the exception of the ongoing tensions between Eudocia and Pulcheria.[7] The most famous conflict between the two came in the late 430s when Eudocia returned from pilgrimage to the Holy Land with the foot of St. Stephen the Protomartyr. Eudocia intended to display the relic in the newly built basilica of St. Stephen. Since Pulcheria had personally financed the basilica's construction and, as a result, could expect public recognition, Eudocia's decision to provide the church with a relic as significant as the foot of Stephen himself was interpreted as an affront to Pulcheria's prerogative.[8] Not to be outdone, Pulcheria quickly turned to other building programs in the capital.

A few years later, Eudocia fell victim to court intrigue, was exiled from Constantinople, and went on pilgrimage to the Holy Land, where she remained, despite the death of Theodosius in 450, until her own death a decade later.[9] The account of her fall from Theodosius's favor

---

5. Aelia Eudocia's new name places her in a line of Theodosian empresses, including Aelia Flaccilla, wife of Theodosius I, Aelia Eudoxia, mother of Theodosius II, and Aelia Pulcheria, sister of Theodosius II. For a complete discussion on the Theodosian empresses, and for a useful family tree, see Holum, *Theodosian Empresses*, 133.

6. The conversion of pagan poets to Christianity often accompanies a conversion of literary themes as well, from classical to Christian ones. This is a well-known and often-repeated topos in late antique literary traditions. For example, Eudocia's fellow centoist, Faltonia Proba, says in the opening lines of her cento that she originally wrote traditional poems, that is, those with secular topics, but has recently turned to the writing of sacred stories. Although such details are commonly taken as historically reliable, their frequency and predictability in the *vitae* of poets hardly reflects reality and more likely reveals the rhetoric of conversion used in the early centuries of Christianity. Eudocia's own corpus intimates how the story of her conversion contradicted her literary output. By the end of her life, she was best known for her Christian poems, a fact that strongly encouraged later legends about the significance of her conversion, yet early in her marriage to Theodosius she wrote at least one encomion to her husband, as well as an encomion to the city of Antioch— neither of which can be strictly termed Christian poems, although the encomia certainly could, and most likely, did include Christian content. Encomiastic poetry had been and remained viable literary genres of pagan poets well into the sixth century.

7. Holum, *Theodosian Empresses*, 175–216.

8. Ibid., 189.

9. The political atmosphere in Constantinople during the early 440s was not favorable to the Theodosian empresses. Around 440 Pulcheria retired from the Constantinopolitan court to a villa near the city where she set up a monastic community with her sisters. Although previous theories attributed Pulcheria's withdrawal from

deserves mention. According to the sixth-century historian John Malalas, a certain man sold Theodosius a remarkably large apple, which the emperor gave to Eudocia, who in turn gave the apple to Paulinus, her friend in court who held the position of master of offices.[10] Paulinus decided to give the apple to Theodosius and the emperor instantly recognized that this was the same apple he had recently given his wife. Theodosius asked Eudocia what she had done with the apple. When she insisted that she had eaten it, Theodosius produced the apple and caught Eudocia in a lie. The emperor suspected that Eudocia was sexually involved with Paulinus, whom Theodosius then exiled from Constantinople. Once safely removed from the imperial court and its penchant for gossip, Paulinus fell under the executioner's sword. Theodosius, taking a more lenient approach with his wife, allowed Eudocia to live but sent her to the Holy Land as a permanent exile, where she remained until her death in 460.

Although the degree to which the story of Eudocia's fall from favor contains legendary motifs remains unclear, that the narrative should not be taken at face value is without question.[11] The central difficulty of the account is its most prominent element: the apple. Beginning with the Trojan War cycle and continuing well into 1001 Arabian Nights, the "apple of discord" motif is a common legendary *topos*.[12] With the removal of the apple motif, most of the account's details, particularly those describing the relationship between Eudocia's exile and Paulinus's execution, also come into question. Reconstructions of Eudocia's final months in Constantinople understandably differ, ranging from one extreme which depicts the empress as victim only of the political machinations of Theodosius's court eunuch, Chrysaphius, to another extreme

Constantinople to Eudocia, the recent suggestion of Alan Cameron, "The Empress and the Poet: Paganism and Politics at the Court of Theodosius II," *YCS* 27 (1982): 217–89, attributes Pulcheria and Eudocia's fall to the same individual, the court eunuch, Chrysaphius.

10.   John Malalas, *Chronography* 14. The *magister officiorum*, or master of the offices, was the highest non-military position in the later Roman Empire. Among the responsibilities of the *magister officiorum* was the oversight of the imperial guards. See Arnold H. M. Jones, *The Later Roman Empire, 284–602* (3 vols.; Oxford: Blackwell, 1964), 2:575–90.

11.   The standard arguments are outlined in Holum, *Theodosian Empresses*, 176–78, and Cameron, *The Empress and the Poet*, 258–61.

12.   For the use of apple imagery in Byzantine literature, see Antony R. Littlewood, "The Symbolism of the Apple in Byzantine Literature," *JÖB* 23 (1974): 33–59.

which describes an attempted resolution of the charge of infidelity and a power struggle between the Theodosian empresses and Chrysaphius.[13] According to Alan Cameron, rumors regarding Eudocia's involvement with Paulinus must have spread quite rapidly through the empire, since references to the event are found in the works of contemporary authors. If Cameron's model is the preferred one, then the infidelity charges are to some extent historically reliable and should not be thrown out with the apple of legend "bathwater." Of course, this does not remove the possibility that Chrysaphius orchestrated and spread rumors of the affair in Theodosius's Constantinopolitan court; indeed, that is a possibility since Chrysaphius had already moved against Pulcheria a few years earlier and held considerable influence over Theodosius at the time.

Despite her difficulties in Constantinople, Eudocia's life in the Holy Land was not uncomfortable. In fact, Eudocia left Constantinople in 441 with all of the pomp of a Theodosian empress, and it was during these years away from the imperial court that Eudocia wrote many of her best and most controversial poems.[14] A few years after 441, according to the Byzantine historians Marcellinus and Priscus, Eudocia killed an imperial agent sent by Theodosius to spy on her. The agent presumably had killed two members of Eudocia's retinue. Both sources state explicitly that Eudocia killed the agent in person, a detail that is as fascinating as it is unlikely. As a result of this bizarre event, about which we know little, Theodosius mandated that Eudocia be deprived of her retinue in 444. Without the imperial court expected of a Theodosian empress, Eudocia spent the final sixteen years of her life, and the final six of Theodosius's, in relative modesty; her building programs after 444, for example, were without opulent ceremonies. But if Eudocia planned fewer or less conspicuous parties, she was hardly lost in the Jerusalem crowd; she remained a central figure in the events of the 440s and 450s and was particularly active in the monophysite controversy both before and after the Council of Chalcedon in 451. The influence of these events on her poetry can certainly not be underestimated. Although she promoted socially conservative values—at least by today's standards—Eudocia never avoided a controversy as both her life and poetry prove.

13. Holum, *Theodosian Empresses*, 176–78, and Cameron, *The Empress and the Poet*, 258–61.

14. Cameron, *The Empress and the Poet*, 260, discusses the issue of the final divide between Theodosius and Eudocia, although the sources for the account are both fragmentary and contain legendary elements.

The Stories Eudocia Told

As mentioned above, Eudocia's poetic ability was recognized by many of her contemporaries. Unfortunately, like the vast majority of ancient literature, only a fraction of what Eudocia wrote survives and we are forced to rely on summaries of her poetry included in later Byzantine accounts.[15] Eudocia's poetry falls into two broad categories: original compositions and paraphrastic poetry.[16] Of her original poems, little survives. The ecclesiastical historian and Eudocia's contemporary, Socrates, refers to an ode written by Eudocia in honor of Theodosius's victory over the Persians in 422.[17] We also know of another encomiastic work, written in honor of the city of Antioch. According to Evagrius Ponticus, Eudocia recited her work in a speech before the city's Senate, a rare and frequently perilous venture for women in antiquity.[18] Much has been

15. For a convenient summary of Eudocia's poetry, see Peter Van Deun, "The Poetical Writings of the Empress Eudocia: An Evaluation," in *Early Christian Poetry: A Collection of Essays* (ed. J. den Boeft and A. Hilhorst; Leiden: Brill, 1993), 273–82.

16. There is often a divide in recent scholarship between paraphrastic literature, quite common in the fourth and fifth centuries, and what I here call original compositions. The latter refers to a poem that is not primarily a revised version of a prose original.

17. Socrates, *Historia Ecclesiastica* 7.21.

18. Evagrius, *Historia Ecclesiastica* 1.20. There is little evidence for women giving speeches, although there are a few examples from classical Athens (Aspasia of Miletus), from Rome proper (Sempronia, Hortensia), and from elsewhere in the empire (Maesia of Sentinum, Carfania). For more on these women, see the articles in Michelle Ballif and Michael G. Moran, eds., *Classical Rhetorics and Rhetoricians: Critical Studies and Sources* (Westport, Conn.: Praeger, 2005). These examples, as has often been observed, were exceptional, and the behavior of these women, notably in the cases of Maesia and Carfania, elicited harsh criticism. While there is plenty of evidence for female philosophers, particularly associated with the Pythagorean school, most of this evidence relates to the fourth century B.C.E. and does not reflect the situation in the later Roman Empire, although it would be interesting to explore the effect that Neo-Platonism had on educated women in Late Antiquity. Of the Neo-Platonic women, Hypatia is the closest analogue, temporally and socially, to Eudocia. This is not the venue to attempt to untangle the various, convoluted layers from the Hypatian legend. Suffice it to say that from what little we know for certain about this fascinating fifth-century woman, she most likely engaged in semi-public speaking engagements in the course of which she presented either a scientific lecture or a philosophical treatise. That being said, Eudocia's public and perhaps political speech to the Antiochenes was certainly noteworthy. Compare E. D. Hunt, *Holy Land Pilgrimage in the Later Roman Empire: AD 312–460* (Oxford: Clarendon, 1982), and Alan Cameron, *Claudian: Poetry and Propaganda at the Court of Honorius* (Oxford: Clarendon, 1970).

made of the single surviving line from Eudocia's encomiastic speech in Antioch (ὑμετέρης γενεῆς τε καὶ αἵματος εὔχομαι εἶναι, "I claim to be from both your race and blood"), with most of the scholarly focus placed on the line's relevance to Eudocia's ethnicity.[19] Such readings often overlook the line's original Homeric context and the effect it would have on listeners in fifth-century Antioch.[20] Taken in its Homeric and late antique contexts, the line presents Eudocia as an Antiochene benefactor, who were in high demand within many fifth-century cities. Antioch responded in kind by erecting multiple statues in Eudocia's honor. The final original poem, the only one to survive in full, is a seventeen-line encomiastic ekphrasis from the therapeutic bath complex at Hammat Gader.[21] Eudocia's ekphasis brings the reader through the various sections of the bath as she praises it both for its beauty and utility.

Eudocia is best known today as an author of paraphrastic literature, although when Eudocia wrote them remains unclear.[22] The current theory is that most of Eudocia's paraphrastic poems were written during her

19.   Related to the issue of the meaning of the line is the content of the rest of the speech. The assumption, based solely on the single surviving line, is that Eudocia's speech was in dactylic hexameters, a fact hardly proven. See the discussion in Cornelia Horn, "The Empress Eudocia and the Monk Peter the Iberian: Patronage, Pilgrimage, and the Love of a Foster-mother in Fifth-century Palestine," *ByzF* 28 (2004): 197–213, and Cameron, *The Empress and the Poet*. Eudocia could just as easily have ended her speech with a Homeric adaptation. She was, as we will see below, quite adept at manipulating the Homeric epics. Without more information regarding the Eudocia's speech in Antioch, the most we can say regarding its form is that it ended with a Homeric allusion.

20.   For more on the intertextual context of the line and how it might be understood in a late antique, urban setting, see my "Eudocia: The Making of a Homeric Christian" (Ph.D. diss., University of Cincinnati, 2008).

21.   An ekphrasis is a literary description of any object; some of the most famous, such as the shield of Achilles in *Iliad* 18, were descriptions of art. On the bath at Hammat Gader, see Yizhar Hirschfeld and G. Solar, "The Roman Thermae at Hammat Gader: Preliminary Report of Three Seasons of Excavations," *IEJ* 31 (1981): 197–219; J. Green and Y. Tsafrir, "Greek inscriptions from Hammat Gader," *IEJ* 32 (1982): 77–96; A. Scheiber, "Parallels to a Topos in Eudocia's Poem," *IEJ* 34 (1984): 180–81; and L. Di Segni, "The Greek Inscriptions of Hammat Gader," in *The Roman Baths of Hammat Gader* (ed. Y. Hirschfeld; Israel: Israel Exploration Society, 1997), 185–266.

22.   Paraphrastic literature is a broad category of literature, commonly associated with the work of Michael Roberts, *Biblical Epic and Rhetorical Paraphrase in Late Antiquity* (Liverpool: F. Cairns, 1985). Paraphrastic literature should not be limited to late antique Christian authors; the practice was quite common as early as the silver age of Latin. Germanicus, for example, who wrote a Latin paraphrase of Aratus' *Phaenomena*, which still survives.

exile in the Holy Land. Among Eudocia's works, Photius lists verse para-
phrases of the Octateuch (the first eight books of the Hebrew Scripture)
as well as the prophets Zechariah and Daniel.[23] Other than the verses'
composition in dactylic hexameter (Photius cites two lines), little else is
known about the purpose or interpretive methods used by Eudocia in
these poems.[24] Of Eudocia's second paraphrastic project, substantial
sections survive. Eudocia composed a three-book epic on the conversion,
public confession, and martyrdom of a fourth-century magician, Cyprian
of Antioch.[25] All of Book 1 and most of Book 2 survives; the content of
Book 3 can be reconstructed from Photius's summary.[26] Finally, Eudocia
edited a pre-existing versification of the Bible, the so-called Homeric
cento. In the 2300 extant lines, the Homeric cento retells selections from
the Genesis account (creation and fall) as well as episodes from the
Gospels (birth, life, death, and resurrection of Jesus). Since the Homeric
cento is literally a rewriting of the Bible, it provides a window into
Eudocia's interpretive method and, as a result, will be the focus of the
rest of this essay.

The Cento in Context

Simply, a cento is a poem constructed by borrowing and reordering lines
of an existing author, typically Homer or Virgil, to create an innovative

23. Photius, *Bibliotheca* 2 (ed. Henry).

24. The dactylic hexameter was the standard metrical pattern used for epic poetry
and consisted of seven measures made up of dactyls (one stressed syllable followed
by two unstressed syllables) or spondees (two stressed syllables).

25. Arthur D. Nock, "Hagiographica II. Cyprian of Antioch," *JTS* 28 (1927):
411–15; Martin P. Nilsson, "Greek Mysteries in the Confession of St. Cyprian,"
HTR 40 (1947): 167–76; Martin P. Nilsson, "Mantique et mystères antiques d'apres
la Confession de Saint Cyprien," *RAr* 35 (1950): 205–7; Claudio Bevegni,
"Eudociae Augustae Martyrium S. Cypriani I 1–99," *Prometheus* 8 (1982): 249–62;
Enrico Salvaneschi, "De Sancto Cypriano," in Σύγκρισις: *Testi e studi di storia e
filosofia del linguaggio religioso 1* (ed. C. Angelino and E. Salvaneschi; Genova: Il
melangolo, 1982), 11–80; H. M. Jackson, "A Contribution Toward an Edition of the
Confession of Cyprian of Antioch: The *Secreta Cypriani*," *Le Muséon* 101 (1988):
33–41; and Claudio Bevegni, ed., *Eudocia Augusta: Storia di San Cipriano* (Milan:
Adelpho, 2006).

26.   Bevegni, *Eudocia Augusta*, contains the only complete published translation
(Italian). Salvaneschi, "De Sancto Cypriano," remains the only, albeit incomplete,
recent edition of the *Martyrdom*, and contains an Italian translation (also incomplete). In English, I. M. Plant, ed., *Women Writers of Ancient Greece and Rome*
(Norman: University of Oklahoma Press, 2004), 198–209, translated Book 1 (minus
the first 100 lines). My doctoral dissertation, "Eudocia," contains the only complete
English translation of Eudocia's *Martyrdom of Saint Cyprian*.

narrative. That the cento held significant cultural value in the later Roman Empire is evidenced in the nearly twenty examples that survive from the second through sixth centuries C.E., including the Virgilian cento of Faltonia Proba, a copy of which was in the possession of the Theodosian family.[27] When we turn to the Homeric cento attributed to Eudocia, the central difficulty surrounding it is one of authorship. Textual tradition suggests that the evolution of the cento required four hundred years and four authors, each of whom redacted and emended the text he or she received. The first centoist was Patricius, of whom we know nothing save that he lived around the beginning the fifth century, perhaps no more than one generation before Eudocia. Soon after Patricius wrote his cento, Eudocia revised it, and, in turn, the otherwise unknown Optimus revised her version. Finally, the eighth-century poet Cosmas of Jerusalem edited the cento he had received from Optimus. Because the textual tradition blends the products of four different authors, resolving the frequently convoluted manuscripts has been the first challenge, one taken up by three major scholars.[28] Mark Usher was the first to suggest that certain manuscripts evidence Eudocia's cento, and although his thesis has not gained widespread support, Usher's research encouraged others to put their hand to the task of editing the cento.[29] This led to the 2006/2007 three-volume edition, commentary, and Italian translation by Rocco Schembra, who evaluated the tradition more thoroughly than his predecessors.[30] Schembra identified within the manuscript tradition two

27. The standard discussion of the ancient cento remains Giovanni Salanitro, "Osidio Geta e la poesia centonaria," *ANRW* 34.3: 2314–60, but see also O. Crusius, "Cento," *RE* 6:1930–31, and K. H. Schelkle, "Cento," *RAC* 2:972–73. For Faltonia Proba's Virgilian cento, see M. Petschenig et al., eds., *Poetae Christiani Minores.* (Vindobonae: F. Tempsky, 1888), 568–609, and Elizabeth Clark and Diane F. Hatch, *The Golden Bough, the Oaken Cross: The Virgilian Cento of Faltonia Betitia Proba* (Chico, Calif.: Scholars Press, 1981). Clark and Hatch, *The Golden Bough*, 12–13, note that a copy of Proba's cento was in the possession of the Theodosian emperors.

28. André-Louis Rey, ed., *Centons homériques (Homerocentra). Patricius, Eudocie, Optimus, Côme de Jérusalem. Introduction, texte critique, traduction, notes et indexes* (Paris: Cerf, 1998); Mark D. Usher, ed., *Homerocentones Eudociae Augustae* (Stuttgart: Teubner, 1999); Rocco Schembra, *La prima redazione dei centoni omerici: Traduzione e commento* (Alessandria: Edizioni dell'Orso, 2006); and Rocco Schembra, ed., *Homerocentones* (Turnhout: Brepols, 2007).

29. Mark D. Usher, "Prolegomenon to the Homeric Centos," *AJP* 118 (1997): 305–21, and *Homeric Stitchings: The Homeric Centos of the Empress Eudocia* (Lanham, Md.: Rowman & Littlefield, 1998).

30. See the following works by Schembra: *La prima redazione*; *La seconda redazione dei centoni omerici: Traduzione e commento* (Alessandria: Edizioni dell'Orso, 2007); and *Homerocentones*. Rey's *Centons homériques* corresponds to

recoverable authorial moments. Schembra's first "recension" corresponds to the manuscript tradition Usher had attributed to Eudocia and the second to the final revision of Cosmas of Jerusalem.[31] For the first time, therefore, we can more confidently speak of individual pericopes within the cento as emanating from the authorial, or, more conservatively, the editorial hand of Eudocia.[32]

The task of editing another author's work was both laborious and risky, so why did Eudocia feel the need to edit Patricius's cento? Fortunately, Eudocia wrote a verse preface to her cento in which she answers this very question herself, explaining both the literary faults she found in Patricius's cento and her intended role as redactor of the text.[33] Eudocia begins not by identifying herself, but rather by naming her predecessor, Patricius:

> ἥδε μὲν ἱστορίη θεοτερπέος ἐστὶν ἀοιδῆς. /
> Πατρίκιος δ', ὃς τήνδε σοφῶς ἀνεγράψατο βίβλου, /
> ἔστι μὲν ἀενάοιο διαμπερὲς ἄξιος αἴνου, /
> οὕνεκα δὴ πάμπρωτος ἐμήσατο κύδιμον ἔργον. (Usher)[34]

This is the account of a poem pleasing to God.
Patricius, who sagaciously authored this book,
is eternally worthy of ever-flowing praise,
especially since he was the very first to plan the glorious work.
　　　(*Prolegomenon ad Homerocentones Eudociae Augustae* 1–4)

Unfortunately, his poem missed the mark of centonic aesthetics. According to Eudocia, Patricius did not tell everything truthfully, nor did he preserve the harmony of the text or limit his cento exclusively to Homeric verses:

Schembra's as-yet unpublished second "recension" (by which Schembra means the final recension, technically the fourth recension, by Comas of Jerusalem).

31.　See the Introduction in Schembra, *Homerocentones*, for a detailed analysis of the differences between Schembra's first recension text and Usher's.

32.　For the sake of clarity, this is not an argument made by Schembra, who seems less concerned with attributing authorial hands to the texts as he is reconstructing the cento's multiple recensions.

33.　Usher, "Prolegomenon," remains the only scholarly discussion on the poem, but Usher's article only uses the preface piecemeal and focuses instead on the priority of the Iviron manuscript recension in the reconstruction of Eudocia's original cento. This is not the venue for such a discussion, so some of what follows will perforce be a summary of a more general study on the part of the author which compares the literary concerns of the (Christian) Homeric cento with evidence from centos more broadly, that is, both Greek and Latin, Christian and secular.

34.　I follow Usher's Greek text (Usher, Homerocentones). All translations of Eudocia's poetry are my own.

ἀλλ' ἔμπης οὐ πάγχυ ἐτήτυμα πάντ' ἀγόρευεν· /
οὐδὲ μὲν ἁρμονίην ἐπέων ἐφύλαξεν ἅπασαν, /
οὐδὲ μόνων ἐπέων ἐμνήσατο κεῖνος ἀείδων, /
ὁππόσα χάλκεον ἦτορ ἀμεμφέος εἶπεν Ὁμήρου.

On the other hand, he didn't tell everything entirely truthfully,
nor did he preserve the complete harmony of the verses,
nor in his singing did he keep in mind only the verses,
which the brazen heart of blameless Homer sang.

(*Prolegomenon ad Homerocentones Eudociae Augustae* 5–8)

Such literary deficiencies forced Eudocia to extract from the text those elements that were not in good order and to rewrite the cento so that it might achieve harmony:

ἀλλ' ἐγὼ ἡμιτέλεστον ἀγακλεὲς ὡς ἴδον ἔργον /
Πατρικίου, σελίδας ἱερὰς μετὰ χεῖρα λαβοῦσα, /
ὅσσα μὲν ἐν βίβλοισιν ἔπη πέλεν οὐ κατὰ κόσμον, /
πάντ' ἄμυδις κείνοιο σοφῆς ἐξείρυσα βίβλου· /
ὅσσα δ' ἐκεῖνος ἔλειπεν, ἐγὼ πάλιν ἐν σελίδεσσι /
γράψα καὶ ἁρμονίην ἱεροῖς ἐπέεσσιν ἔδωκα.

But when I beheld Patricius's glorious, half-completed project
and took the holy pages in hand,
whatever verses were not in order
I ripped out of that man's clever book,
and whatever he neglected, I
wrote back into the text and I gave harmony to the holy verses.

(*Prolegomenon ad Homerocentones Eudociae Augustae* 9–14)

Therefore, Eudocia's activity as co-author of a Homeric cento was from the outset an interpretive activity—her version was a truthful account of the biblical story that at the same time preserved the poetic harmony of Homer's words. But Eudocia hardly viewed her redacted cento as a completely new product; indeed, she asserts that both Patricius and Eudocia share responsibility for the authorship of the redacted cento:

ἀλλ' ἔμπης ξυνὸς μὲν ἔφυ πόνος ἀμφοτέροισι, /
Πατρικίῳ κἀμοί καὶ θηλυτέρῃ περ ἐούσῃ· /
κεῖνος δ' ἤρατο μοῦνος ἐν ἀνθρώποις μέγα κῦδος. /
ὃς πάμπρωτος ἐπήξατο κλεινὸν ἕδος γε δόμοιο /
καλὴν ἐξανάγων φήμην βροτέοιο γενέθλης.

Nonetheless, the work is shared by both
Patricius and myself, although I am a woman.
But he alone among men received great honor,
who was the first to construct the renowned base of the house
bringing forth good news for the mortal race.

(*Prolegomenon ad Homerocentones Eudociae Augustae* 33–38)

Latent within this section is the notion that women writers, with the exception of a few, select lyric poetesses, were second-class citizens. The role of gender in Eudocia's poetry will be explored briefly in what follows and is part of a broader project by the author. To address briefly the role of gender in Eudocia's preface (and by association in her poetry more generally), she recognizes the place of women among the literary elite (both readers and writers) of her day. By demonstrating that she is a superior, although not necessarily a more orthodox, exegete and poet, Eudocia's nod to Patricius's honor can be taken tongue in cheek. On the other hand, she does mention Patricius by name five times in her preface, while never explicitly naming herself.

With her emphasis on Patricius's failure to tell the true story (l. 5), Eudocia implicitly claims to present an accurate account in keeping with the Bible. This is a tall order considering that the cento must use Homer's words to tell the truth. Many themes central to the Bible are not found in the Homeric corpus, so finding lines to reuse in new contexts would prove to be a more arduous task than Eudocia readily admits. Moreover, the original Homeric context was always hiding beneath the surface, making a biblically accurate reading—whatever that might have looked like for a fifth-century reader—difficult. In his work on paraphrastic literature from Late Antiquity, Scott Johnson suggests that in the act of paraphrasing, particularly during Late Antiquity, an author inevitably interprets.[35] He writes, "Authors often sought, or felt compelled, to reclassify, reorient, and purify the textual past for the sake of their audiences and readers-to-come."[36] Since interpretation and paraphrase go hand in hand, Eudocia's invocation of truth points less to her biblical model than it does to her goal to tell the story more truthfully than Patricius. Joseph Pucci suggests that in order for allusion to function properly, an author depends on a "full-knowing reader," who has the ability to recognize literary intertextuality yet is neither constrained nor compelled by text or author to interpret the text in a particular way.[37] Monolithic interpretations are therefore impossible, or at least extremely unlikely, since each reader responds to and appreciates allusions based on his or her own unique perspective. With unlimited allusive potential, the Homeric cento, more than most other genres, allows for a greater

---

35. Scott J. Johnson, *The Life and Miracles of Thekla: A Literary Study* (Washington, D.C.: Center for Hellenic Studies, Trustees for Harvard University, 2006).
36. Ibid., 106.
37. Joseph Pucci, *The Full-Knowing Reader: Allusion and the Power of the Reader in the Western Literary Tradition* (New Haven: Yale University Press, 1998).

degree of interpretative latitude and demonstrates, in this case, how a literary woman from Late Antiquity was able to transform the biblical narrative into an allusively charged story. In what follows, neither a search for the correct interpretation nor authorial intent takes center stage; rather, I will emphasize the degree to which Eudocia altered the biblical story and presented a Jesus who was as Homeric as he was Christian.

The Samaritan Woman Episode

For the sake of conciseness, we will examine a single biblical pericope, the Samaritan woman at the well episode from John 4, which demonstrates how creative and, perhaps, how controversial Eudocia was. Indeed, Eudocia has not left much of the narrative intact. The Samaritan city of Sychar is transformed into a Homeric polis, complete with poplar groves and agora, and the characters have lost their Semitic flavor and interact according to different social codes. For example, the tension between Jews and Samaritans, central to John's account, is replaced with the obligations of guest and host, a popular Homeric motif.[38] But it is the theme of sexual propriety, which Eudocia alters in stark and surprising ways, that deserves our attention here.

The Gospel account (John 4:4–42) delays any explicit mention of the woman's sexual activity for one third of the story, about thirteen verses. The interim material contains social and theological themes relevant to early Christian communities, such as the spread of the gospel to the Samaritans and the living water metaphor. But with Jesus' seemingly innocent command for the woman to get her husband, the narrative shifts as he prophetically reveals the woman's sordid past.[39] We learn that she has had five husbands and that the one she is currently with, presumably a sixth man, is not her husband. Although multiple marriages

---

38. Usher, *Homeric Stitchings*, 113–26, recognizes each of these differences, to some extent. Whereas Usher focuses on Eudocia's selection of Homeric lines to create the episode, I want to show how Eudocia used those lines to emphasize or undermine the sexual ethic from the Samaritan women scene.

39. In John 4:16–18 we read that Jesus said to the woman: λέγει αὐτῇ· ὕπαγε φώνησον τὸν ἄνδρα σου καὶ ἐλθὲ ἐνθάδε. ἀπεκρίθη ἡ γυνὴ καὶ εἶπεν αὐτῷ· οὐκ ἔχω ἄνδρα. λέγει αὐτῷ ὁ Ἰησοῦς· καλῶς εἶπας ὅτι ἄνδρα οὐκ ἔχω· πέντε γὰρ ἄνδρας ἔσχες καὶ νῦν ὃν ἔχεις οὐκ ἔστιν σου ἀνήρ· τοῦτο ἀληθὲς εἴρηκας ("'Go, call your husband and come here.' The woman answered and said, 'I have no husband.' Jesus said to her, 'You have correctly said, "I have no husband"; for you have had five husbands, and the one whom you now have is not your husband; this you have said truly'" [NASB]).

and extramarital affairs would carry with them deep cultural shame in the first-century world, particularly in Palestine, Jesus proffers no overt criticism. The narrator focuses on Jesus' facility for prophetic revelation, which directs the rest of the narrative. As a result of his proclamation about the Samaritan woman, she first assumes that Jesus must be a prophet and eventually identifies him as the Messiah. Indeed, Jesus' ability to reveal the woman's past becomes the crux of her "evangelistic" message to the rest of the town and the cause for their initial belief.

Unlike her biblical model, Eudocia places rebuke within the first quarter of the narrative (l. 12) and gives Jesus' words an epic tone, particularly because the cento is intrinsically limited only to Homeric lines. Eudocia's Jesus, speaking of himself, says:

> τίφθ' οὕτως ἀνδρὸς νοσφίζεαι, οὐδὲ παρ' αὐτὸν /
> ἑζομένη μύθοισιν ἀνείρεαι ἠδὲ μεταλλᾶς; /
> καὶ δ' ἄλλην νεμεσῶ, ἥ τις τοιαῦτά γε ῥέζοι, /
> ἥ τ' ἀέκητι φίλων πατρὸς καὶ μητρὸς ἐόντων /
> ἀνδράσι μίσγηται πρίν γ' ἀμφάδιον γάμον ἐλθεῖν. /
> οὐ μὲν κ' ἄλλη ὧδε γυνὴ τετληότι θυμῷ /
> ἀνδρὸς ἀποσταίη, ὅς τοι κακὰ πόλλ' ἐμόγησε· /
> σοὶ δ' αἰεὶ κραδίη στερεωτέρη ἐστὶ λίθοιο.

Why do you ignore a man in this way? You neither sit next to him nor question nor inquire after him. I am indignant at any woman who would do this—who, against the will of those dear to her, namely her father and mother, would have intercourse with a man before coming to a public wedding. No other woman, with a stout heart, would stand aloof from a man who has suffered many toils. But your heart is always more unyielding than stone.

(*Homerocentones Eudociae Augustae* 1064–71 [Schembra])

The cento version alters the canonical story substantially and comes from *Odyssey* 23, which will be discussed in further detail below, καὶ δ' ἄλλην νεμεσῶ ἥ τις τοιαῦτά γε ῥέζοι· ἥ τ' ἀέκητι φίλων πατρὸς καὶ μητρὸς ἐόντων, ἀνδράσι μίσγηται πρίν γ' ἀμφάδιον γάμον ἐλθεῖν ("I, too, would blame another maiden who should do likewise, and in spite of her own father and mother, while they still live, should consort with men before the day of public marriage," Homer, *Odyssey* 6.286–88). Jesus' simple request for water has been replaced with an overt and rather harsh criticism of the woman's marital impropriety, highlighted by the speech's ring composition. Jesus' initial observation that the woman has stood distant from him (ll. 1064–65) corresponds to a parallel rebuke in ll. 1069–71, thereby emphasizing the central portion of the speech, an admonition against the woman's sexual conduct (ll. 1066–68). In the cento version, Jesus never refers to the woman's husband as such—he is simply a man.

Moreover, the reference to the lack of a public wedding perhaps explains how the woman's current situation was abnormal and therefore immoral. Jesus' miraculous revelation causes the woman to identify him no longer as a prophet or even the Messiah, but as a god in human form.[40] Like the Gospel account, Jesus' ability to tell the woman about her sordid past and her identification of Jesus as God become the crux for her evangelistic message to the town and their subsequent belief.

As suggested earlier, paraphrastic literature, of which the cento is an example, resists monolithic interpretations. By retelling the biblical episode in Homer's words, Eudocia takes up John's expository prose and charges it with allusive energy. The cento's multivalence is particularly potent when one approaches the Samaritan women at the well episode from the various backgrounds and perspectives of late antique readers in order to explore how individual readers might have understood Jesus' rebuke. The first response to Eudocia's revised narrative would likely occur in light of fifth-century ascetic theology concerning women, with its emphasis on, ideally, a woman's virginity, or, minimally, her chastity. From this perspective, the episode reinforces late antique concerns: women had two viable options, either rejection of marriage, that is, celibacy, or religiously sanctioned marriage.[41] As narrator of the cento,

---

40. This shift from messianic identification to divine begins with the woman's insistence that Jesus meet the local people (l. 1090): ἔρχεο· ἶσον γάρ σε θεῷ τίσουσιν ἅπαντες ("Go [as well] for everyone will honor you as a god"). She repeats this a few lines later (ll. 1095–96): ἔνθα δ' ἄνδρες ναίουσι πολύρρηνες πολυβοῦται, / οἵ κε σε δωτίνῃσι θεὸν ὣς τιμήσουσι ("The oxen- and sheep-rich men who dwell there will honor you with gifts as if to a god"). Finally, when the woman relates her experience with Jesus, she emphasizes his divine nature (ll. 1145–50): οὐκ ἔσθ' οὗτος ἀνὴρ διερὸς βροτὸς οὐδὲ γένηται· / οὐ γάρ πως ἂν θνητὸς ἀνὴρ τάδε μηχανόῳτο / ᾧ αὐτοῦ γε νόῳ, ὅτε μὴ θεὸς αὐτὸς ἐπελθὼν / ῥηιδίως ἐθέλων θείη νέον ἠδὲ γέροντα. / ὥς τέ μοι ἀθάνατός γ' ἰνδάλλεται εἰσοράασθαι, / ἄλλῳ δ' αὐτὸν φωτὶ κατακρύπτων ἤισκεν ("This man is not a living mortal, nor was he born, for a mortal man could not devise such things in his mind. Never could a god coming (to earth) easily take the guise of a young or old man. And he appears to me as a god to behold, but disguising himself, he took the appearance of another" [Schembra]).

41. The dichotomy between marriage and perpetual virginity is an exclusively Christian one. Although Roman and Jewish traditions valued and encouraged virginity, it was not culturally accepted, with the exception of clearly defined religious purposes, as an alternative to marriage. Virginity was therefore appropriate and socially demanded for a defined period of time, that is, before marriage, but was intended to lead up to marriage. See Geoffrey S. Nathan, *The Family in Late Antiquity: The Rise of Christianity and the Endurance of Tradition* (London: Routledge, 2000), 77 and 130–31. For an alternative perspective, see Mary F. Foskett, *A Virgin Conceived: Mary and Classical Representations of Virginity* (Bloomington: Indiana

Eudocia alludes to this teaching when she describes the Samaritan woman as follows: ἡ δ' οὐ ἠρνεῖτο στυγερὸν γάμον οὔτε τελεύτα ("she neither refused marriage as something shameful nor had she brought it about," *Homerocentones Eudociae Augustae* 1072 [Schembra]). Clearly, in the eyes of the narrator, choosing neither, like the woman in the story, was to be caught in the precarious and iniquitous third option between marriage and chastity. The choice between virginity and marriage corresponds neither to Jewish/Samaritan nor classically Roman sexual mores.[42] Although ancient cultures prized virginity, maidenhood was typically restricted to the time between childhood and marriage. Generally, virginity was not a viable option during adulthood. Late antique Christianity, on the other hand, prized virginity more than marriage, and Jerome's *Ad Jovinianum* suggests that there was a growing need for detailed teaching regarding the relationship between the celibate and married lifestyles.[43] Eudocia modifies the biblical account, which recognizes marriage as the only viable option, and allows our first reader to recognize late antique concerns in a story that, by the fifth century, could have become ethically outdated.

Not every reader, however, would approach the text with Christian literature and ethics from Late Antiquity in mind; the abundance of Homeric allusions—every line, by necessity, recalled some Homeric context—opened a multitude of interpretive directions to readers familiar with the epics. If a reader begins with the Homeric texts in mind, he or she recognizes scenes from the *Odyssey* within Jesus' criticism of the Samaritan women and interprets the text accordingly. The first series of lines comes from Book 6, the famous Nausicaa passage. In the narrative, the Phaeacian princess, Nausicaa, has happened upon a ship-wrecked and naked Odysseus, who is in dire need of help. Unfortunately, keeping company with a strange man, and a naked one at that, has the potential to bring dishonor upon Nausicaa and her father's house, so she must exercise caution. Her words to Odysseus, which Eudocia appropriates in ll. 1066–68, reveal the degree to which public shame surrounding sexual

University Press, 2002), who contrasts Jewish and Roman perspectives on virginity, and Will Deming, *Paul on Marriage and Celibacy: The Hellenistic Background of 1 Corinthians 7* (2d ed.; Grand Rapids, Mich.: Eerdmans, 2004), for a general argument for the Hellenic roots of asceticism. Compare also David G. Hunter, ed., *Marriage in the Early Church* (Minneapolis: Fortress, 1992), and Teresa M. Shaw, "Sex and Sexual Renunciation," in *The Early Christian World* (ed. P. F. Esler; London: Routledge, 2000), 401–21.

42. See n. 41, above.

43. David G. Hunter, *Marriage, Celibacy, and Heresy in Ancient Christianity: The Jovinianist Controversy* (Oxford: Oxford University Press, 2007), 30–35.

scandal would have profoundly affected Homeric women: καὶ δ᾽ ἄλλην νεμεσῶ ἥ τις τοιαῦτά γε ῥέζοι· ἥ τ᾽ ἀέκητι φίλων πατρὸς καὶ μητρὸς ἐόντων, ἀνδράσι μίσγηται πρίν γ᾽ ἀμφάδιον γάμον ἐλθεῖν ("I, too, would blame another maiden who should do likewise, and in spite of her own father and mother, while they still live, should consort with men before the day of public marriage," Homer, *Odyssey* 6.286–88 [ed. Murray, LCL]). But Nausicaa's role in the narrative is important; Odysseus successfully obtains her father's aid and returns to his native Ithaca only through Nausicaa's ingenious machinations. The second Homeric scene comes from the end of the *Odyssey*, after Odysseus has returned home, successfully killed his wife's suitors, and has revealed himself to Penelope. With her husband off at war or missing for twenty years, combined with the incessant presence of eager suitors, Penelope errs on the side of suspicion and she neither sits near Odysseus nor speaks to him. Telemachus, son and rightful heir of Odysseus, addresses his mother with what comes to us as Eudocia's ll. 1064–65 and 1069–71: τίφθ᾽ οὕτω πατρὸς νοσφίζεαι, οὐδὲ παρ᾽ αὐτὸν ἑζομένη μύθοισιν ἀνείρεαι ἠδὲ μεταλλᾷς; οὐ μέν κ᾽ ἄλλη γ᾽ ὧδε γυνὴ τετληότι θυμῷ ἀνδρὸς ἀφεσταίη, ὅς οἱ κακὰ πόλλ᾽ μογήσας· σοὶ δ᾽ αἰεὶ κραδίη στερεωτέρη ἐστὶ λίθοιο ("Why do you thus hold aloof from my father, and do not sit by his side and ask and question him? No other woman would harden her heart as you do, and stand aloof from her husband, who has suffered many sad toils...but your heart is always harder than stone," Homer, *Odyssey* 23.98–101, 103 [ed. Murray, LCL]).

That the Homeric context of Jesus' words comes from speeches delivered by or directed to women not only shocks our second reader, it may even undermine the force of Jesus' reproof. Both Penelope and Nausicaa are in extraordinary circumstances that test the limits of their integrity. Despite patriarchal criticism from suitor and son alike, Penelope endures and is reunited with Odysseus. In fact, it is through withdrawal and cunning that the reunion between Odysseus and Penelope is made possible. In the same way, Nausicaa utilizes creativity and deception to preserve her good name and avoid the potential scandal of being with an unknown man.[44] Is it possible that the intertextual presence of these prominent Homeric women undermines or reconstitutes the Samaritan woman's position in the narrative? She might become a more dominant character, like a Homeric heroine, thereby making Jesus' criticism incongruous. Contrariwise, an allusion to virtuous Homeric women has the potential to emphasize further the woman's indecency. Since the

44. This is only half the story. One can just as easily read the Homeric women as negative models, which allows a different reading of the passage.

woman at the well has not intentionally preserved her and her family's honor through an avoidance of morally questionable situations, her behavior appears more negligent. Read in this light, Jesus' words contain rhetorical flair and are entirely apropos—this woman, he suggests, is not like the chaste women of yore.

As I have suggested, the choice between these various interpretations remains with the reader since Eudocia cannot control which allusions a reader recognizes, nor can the poet inhibit interpretative choices that diverge from the biblical account. As a female interpreter of the Bible, Eudocia depends still on subsequent interpreters to make sense, or not, of her poem. Moreover, the exegetical examples discussed above are only two in an endless sea of possible approaches. Some readers might be familiar with only John's account, others a combination of the biblical and Homeric, while others still might be entirely ignorant of all the intertexts and would receive the cento version at face value.

Conclusion

Literature of Late Antiquity evidences much of the political, social, and cultural dynamism taking place during Christianity's dawn and the twilight of the Roman empire. Christian poetry is central to this literary development. With the security brought about by the Edict of Milan, a slowly expanding literary elite manifested their shifting religious identity in new and often bizarre ways. Eudocia, I suggest, was one of such elite. As empress of the eastern empire, and daughter of an Athenian *rhetor*, Eudocia had the cultural pedigree and political influence to leave her mark on both the poetic and religious landscape of the fifth century. And yet, despite Eudocia's status and reputation as the "it girl" of the Con-stantinopolitan literati, her poetry broke in many ways from the tradition of previous generations. Not only did Eudocia compose many of her surviving poems while in exile in the Holy Land, she also chose literary media that were unpopular in the eyes of the Christian establishment. One of these "literary freaks," to borrow the term used by David Bright, was the Homeric cento, a genre explicitly condemned by Jerome as potentially subversive, particularly in the hands of female authors.[45]

Eudocia's revision of the Gospels, as evidenced in the Homeric cento, informs both how literary figures of the period read canonical stories and

45. David F. Bright, "Theory and Practice in the Vergilian Cento," *ICS* 9 (1984): 79–90, attempts, explicitly, to raise the cento above its fellow attractions, as it were, and, I suspect, employs the term "freak" ironically. For Jerome's criticism of Christian centos, see *Epistles* 53.

retold them to a contemporary audience and how Eudocia in particular revised the Bible to suit her unique interpretation. I have suggested that the way an ancient audience could construe Eudocia's interpretation depends on its individual concerns and literary ability. At the same time, this does not change the fact that Eudocia rewrote substantial sections of the Samaritan at the well episode from John 4. In fact, she left little unaltered. The "Samaritan" woman's sexuality receives so much attention and revision from Eudocia that the theme of sexual morality becomes one of the main lessons to be learned from the cento episode, whereas the same theme hardly receives the same airtime in the Gospel account. To complicate matters further, centos are intrinsically intertextual—the Christian cento actually contains multiple intertextual vectors, namely, Homer, the Bible, the early church fathers, and so on. A reader more familiar with one intertextual vector such as the church fathers could read Eudocia's revised sexual ethic as relevant and informative. On the other hand, the Homeric allusions latent within the story have the potential to undermine or reinforce the Samaritan woman's traditional role in the pericope. By selecting a high percentage of Homeric lines about powerful women, Eudocia retells the account with multiple interpretative directions and she leaves it up to her reader to make sense of the intertextual landscape she has created. This freedom of interpretation likely motivated Jerome's invective against Christian centos and is one of the central characteristics of Eudocia's literary legacy. As reteller and misreader of Jesus, Eudocia broke the social and literary boundaries of her day and challenged a world that was quickly becoming increasingly intolerant of religious plurality. Her Homeric cento stands in the face of monolithic interpretations; perhaps this is what makes them so appealing to twenty-first-century readers of the Bible.

Vindicating Womankind:
Aemilia Lanyer's *Salve Deus Rex Judaeorum*

Caryn A. Reeder

As a myth of beginnings, the first three chapters of Genesis have deeply influenced Christian understandings and practices of gender. The Pauline corpus of the New Testament draws on Genesis to define the respective places and roles of men and women in the world and in the body of Christ, and interest in teasing out the implications of Gen 1–3 remains to this day. Until the nineteenth century, the most vociferous interpreters of the biblical presentation of gender roles were men. From Paul to Augustine to John Calvin to John Milton, male readings of Gen 1–3 framed the church's thought on men and women in relation to each other and in relation to God. Within this context of male-dominated commentary on gender roles in the Bible and in the church, Aemilia Lanyer's renarration of Gen 3:1–7 stands out as a reversal of traditional interpretation. Her radical new reading of Gen 1–3 in *Salve Deus Rex Judaeorum* provides the foundational myth for a new sort of society—we might even say a new sort of church.

To understand the radical nature of Lanyer's interpretation of Genesis, we will first explore a few interpretations given by male readers she may have known.[1] We will then turn to *Salve Deus Rex Judaeorum* itself, focusing on the retelling of Gen 3 set inside Lanyer's poem on the passion of Christ. Finally, we will question the implications of Lanyer's version of the Garden of Eden story for the world after the text.

Reading Genesis 1–3 with Churchmen

Perhaps the earliest Christian text to connect a reflection on Gen 1–3 with the construction of gender in the church is found in 1 Timothy. In

---

1. For comprehensive surveys of contemporary interpretation of Gen 1–3, see Arnold Williams, *The Common Expositor: An Account of the Commentaries on Genesis 1527–1633* (Chapel Hill: University of North Carolina Press, 1948), and Philip C. Almond, *Adam and Eve in Seventeenth-Century Thought* (Cambridge: Cambridge University Press, 1999).

1 Tim 2:11–15, the author claims the order of creation and the order of the fall in Eden as factors that determine the place of women in the church; because the woman was created second, yet was deceived and sinned first, women should be subordinate to men. Women cannot teach or be in authority over men, but instead should bear children and live virtuous lives. In Lanyer's day, 1 Tim 2:11–15 was taken as an authoritative reading of Gen 1–3, as the Geneva Bible's marginal notes indicate.[2] The Geneva Bible of 1560 refers the reader of 1 Tim 2:12–15 back to Gen 1:27 and 3:6. The note on 1 Tim 2:14 explains that the woman, deceived herself, became "the instrument of Satan to deceive the man." The notes on 1 Tim 2:12–15 in the Geneva Bible of 1599 go even further. In Gen 2, woman was created after man and, according to the note on 1 Tim 2:13, "for man's sake." Therefore, the subjection of women to men, identified as an "ordinance of God," is determined by creation order. This ordinance is reinforced by the order of deception in Gen 3. Because the woman was deceived and only then deceived her husband, "she is worthily for this reason subject to her husband and ought to be." The influence of the interpretation of Gen 1–3 in 1 Tim 2 can be seen in the Geneva Bible's translation of "your desire will be for your husband" in Gen 3:16 as "thy desire *shal be subject* to thine housband" (italics original). For the scholars of the Geneva Bible, 1 Timothy and Genesis present a unified witness to the necessary subjection of woman to man.

John Calvin's commentaries and sermons also bear witness to the influence of 1 Timothy on Christian interpretations of Eden.[3] In his 1556 commentary on 1 Timothy, Calvin recognizes the controversial nature of 1 Tim 2:11–15; he relies on Gen 1–3 to answer the questions raised by this passage. The order of creation shows that women "are born to obey"; woman "was created after man as a kind of appendage to men for the specific purpose of readily obeying them."[4] Female subservience to men receives further support from Eve's failure to advise her husband wisely

---

2. The Geneva Bible was the most popular English translation before the Authorized Version of 1611; see Benson Bobrick, *The Making of the English Bible* (New York: Simon & Schuster, 2001), 176. Note that "s" and "v" have been regularized in quotations from sixteenth- and seventeenth-century texts.

3. Calvin's influence on the sixteenth- and seventeenth-century Anglican Church is explored by Francis Higman, "Calvin's Works in Translation," in *Calvinism in Europe, 1540–1620* (ed. Andrew Pettegree et al.; Cambridge: Cambridge University Press, 1994). Higman suggests that the many English editions of Calvin's works were intended for and used by everyone, not just the educated authorities of the church (p. 96).

4. John Calvin, *1, 2 Timothy and Titus* (Crossway Classic Commentaries; Wheaton, Ill.: Crossway, 1998), 48.

in the garden. Because of Eve, women have lost their "freedom" willingly (naturally) to serve men. Now this service is demanded by punishment as well as nature.[5] Reference to male headship and female submission in Calvin's commentary on Gen 2:18 and 21 further demonstrates the influence of the letters of Paul on his reading of creation and the fall.[6] In his interpretation of Gen 3:1–7, Calvin condemns the woman as wholly depraved in soul and body.[7] He argues that before her temptation and fall, the woman already doubted God (Gen 3:4, 6). Furthermore, because the woman looks at the tree with desire in v. 6, Calvin suggests she has an impure heart and corrupt senses: she was unholy through and through.[8] Calvin furthermore vehemently denies that the man was with the woman, that is, physically present, during the temptation and fall. Rather, the two met soon after the woman ate the fruit; then the man also ate, their eyes were opened, and they realized their sin (Gen 3:6–7).[9] For Calvin, men and women are equals in sin; but just as man was first in creation, so woman was distinctly first in sin.

In a sermon on 1 Tim 2:12–14, Calvin clearly and explicitly identifies Eve as the forerunner of womankind.[10] The connection between Eve and all women is common in Christian tradition, and the tendency to place the primary guilt of original sin on Eve correlates with a similar tendency to identify her female descendants as temptresses, seducers of innocent men, and also as the weaker half of humanity. In this view, women lack the moral strength needed to withstand the temptation to sin. In conjunction with women's perceived ability to entice men, their perceived inability to withstand sin condemns women as the curse of all men.

---

5. Ibid., 48–49.

6. John Calvin, *Genesis* (Crossway Classic Commentaries; Wheaton, Ill.: Crossway, 2001), 38.

7. Ibid., 43.

8. Ibid., 42–43. Cf. the Geneva Bible's note on Gen 3:3.

9. Calvin, *Genesis*, 43–44. This assumption rests on a (mis)reading of "with her" in Gen 3:6.

10. In a sermon on 1 Tim 2:12–14, Calvin comments, "as God punished mankind for the sin of Adam, so must the fault of Eve's transgression be punished in all women" (*Sermons of M. Iohn Calvin, on the Epistles of S. Paule to Timothy and Titus* [trans. L. T.; London: Printed by Henry Middleton for G. Bishop and T. Woodcoke, 1597], 215). Calvin's views on women swing between progressive and severely conservative. See further Willis P. deBoer, "Calvin on the Role of Women," in *Exploring the Heritage of John Calvin* (ed. David E. Holwerda; Grand Rapids: Baker, 1976), 236–72, and Jane Dempsey Douglas, "Christian Freedom: What Calvin Learned at the School of Women," *CH* 53, no. 2 (1984): 155–73.

This understanding of womankind is represented in John Donne's *The Progress of the Soul (Metempsychosis)*. For Donne, the first woman's fateful decision is echoed by her descendants:

Man all at once was there by woman slain,
And one by one we're here slain o'er again
By them. The mother poison'd the well-head,
The daughters here corrupt us, rivulets;
No smallness 'scapes, no greatness breaks their nets;
She thrust us out, and by them we are led
Astray, from turning to whence we are fled.
Were prisoners Judges, 'twould seem rigorous,
She sinn'd, we bear; part of our pain is, thus
To love them, whose fault to this painful love yok'd us.[11]

For Donne, Adam and Eve symbolize all men and women throughout history. The first woman sins and her daughters follow her example. The first man dies because he gives in to his woman, and his sons likewise die by women's poison. Genesis 3 tells the story of mankind's curse—the insidious influence of womankind.

At approximately the same time Donne condemned women for visiting corruption, pain, and death on men, Aemilia Lanyer rewrote Gen 3 to exonerate Eve and her daughters of the guilt of such wrongdoing.[12] It is highly unlikely that she would have known of Donne's satire; though written in 1601, *The Progress of the Soul* was not published until 1633. It is very likely, however, that Lanyer was familiar with the sentiment and conclusions of Donne's reading of Gen 3:1–7. Since the Geneva Bible was so popular in Elizabethan and Jacobean England, Lanyer would have known its English translation and commentary. She was born only nineteen years after Cranmer encouraged all people, "all manner of persons, men, women, young, old, learned, unlearned, rich, poor, priests, laymen, lords, ladies, officers, tenants, and mean men, virgins, wives, widows, lawyers, merchants, artificers, husbandmen, and all manner of persons of what estate or condition whosoever they be," to study the Bible, an exhortation taken seriously in Reformation England.[13] In her reading, Lanyer may have had access to Calvin's writings (one of his English

11. John Donne, *Poems by John Donne* (ed. Hugh I'anson Fausset; Everyman's Library 867; London: Dent & Sons, 1943), 231 (stanza 10).
12. *Salve Deus Rex Judaeorum*, first published in 1611, has been edited and published by Susanne Woods, *The Poems of Aemilia Lanyer: Salve Deus Rex Judaeorum* (Oxford: Oxford University Press, 1993), which is the edition referenced in this essay.
13. Cranmer's 1540 Preface to the Great Bible is quoted in Bobrick, *The Making of the English Bible*, 151.

translators, Anne Vaughan Lock, was sister to a friend of Lanyer's parents).[14] The very omnipresence of Gen 1–3 in contemporary life and thought, from the church to the farm to the palace, demands a certain level of familiarity with popular translations, commentaries, and interpretations.[15] Lanyer certainly knew what she was up against when she began to write her own, very different, interpretation of this foundational myth of Western society.

Aemilia Lanyer: Rereading Genesis 1–3

Born in London to the Bassanos, an Italian family of court musicians, in 1569, Aemilia Lanyer was (possibly) educated when she served in the household of Susan, Countess of Kent.[16] In her youth, Lanyer was the mistress of Elizabeth's Lord Chamberlain, Henry Carey, Lord Hunsdon, but this relationship was broken when Lanyer became pregnant. She married Alfonso Lanyer, a court musician, in 1592, giving birth to a son in 1593.[17] Some years after her marriage, she became connected with

14.   See Susanne Woods, *Lanyer: A Renaissance Woman Poet* (Oxford: Oxford University Press, 1999), 8–9. In *Salve Deus Rex Judaeorum*, Lanyer comes across as a devout Anglican, perhaps even a supporter of church reform (see further Katherine A. Armstrong, *Blood Lines and Class Boundaries: Aemilia Lanyer's Salve Deus Rex Judaeorum* [Gender Studies Working Papers; Chester: Chester College, 1996], 28). Literary critics sometimes express resistance to Lanyer's faith, claiming she used religion to mask her feminist purpose, as does Suzanne Trill, "Religion and the Construction of Femininity," in *Women and Literature in Britain, 1500–1700* (ed. Helen Wilcox; Cambridge: Cambridge University Press, 1996), 30–55 (42), but a Protestant Christian faith is clearly central to her poetic vision. Confusion over the distinctions between the Catholic tradition, the Lutheran and Reformed Churches in Europe, and the Church of England is also evident in scholarship on Lanyer. Despite the connections between England and Calvin's Geneva, the English church was not Lutheran or Reformed; Anglican tradition and theology is in many ways more akin to Catholicism. The supposed Catholic tendencies in Lanyer's work noted by Catherine Keohane, "'That Blindest Weakenesse Be Not Over-bold': Aemilia Lanyer's Radical Unfolding of the Passion," *English Literary History* 64, no. 2 (1997): 359–90 (365), and Woods, *Lanyer*, 130, 138, are also Anglican.

15.   See Williams, *The Common Expositor*, Chapter 1.

16.   Lanyer implies that Susan Bertie had a role in her education in *Salve Deus*, 18 (cf. Woods, *Lanyer*, 9–14). All we know of Lanyer's life comes from her book, the diaries of Simon Forman, and church and legal records. See Barbara K. Lewalski, "Of God and Good Women: The Poems of Aemilia Lanyer," in *Silent But For the Word: Tudor Women as Patrons, Translators, and Writers of Religious Works* (ed. Margaret Patterson Hannay; Kent, Ohio: Kent State University Press, 1985), 204–7, and Woods, *Lanyer*, 3–41.

17.   Woods, *Lanyer*, 16–18.

Margaret Clifford, Countess of Cumberland, staying with the countess and her daughter at a country estate, Cookham, between 1603 and 1605.[18] Margaret and Anne feature heavily in Lanyer's poetry; both women are presented as paragons of humanity. Lanyer credits her stay with the Cliffords with the original inspiration to write.[19] *Salve Deus Rex Judaeorum*, Lanyer's single extant volume of poetry, was published in 1611. Her muse seems then to have turned to money, itself an important sub-theme in the dedicatory poems of *Salve Deus*, and promotion for her husband, who died in 1613.[20] Aemilia Lanyer died in 1645.

In *Salve Deus*, Lanyer retells the story of the Garden of Eden within the context of the passion of Christ. The poem centers on the figure of Christ, but Lanyer also highlights the virtuous women who weave in and out of his story.[21] The poem's table of contents announces this secondary concern. First on the list is the passion of Christ itself, but the other three issues specially mentioned relate directly to women: "Eves Apologie in defence of Women," "The Teares of the Daughters of Jerusalem," and "The Salutation and Sorrow of the Virgine Mary."[22] Reinforcing this focus, eight of the dedicatory poems that preface *Salve Deus* address various female members of the royalty and nobility.[23] Another poem calls

18. Louise Schleiner, *Tudor and Stuart Women Writers* (Bloomington, Ind.: Indiana University Press, 1994), 23, and Woods, *Lanyer*, 28–32, explore Lanyer's relationship with the Cliffords.

19. *Salve Deus*, 130.

20. Woods, *Lanyer*, 19–21 and 32–33, explores Lanyer's life after 1611 through Forman's diaries and legal records of various enterprises.

21. It is sometimes claimed that Lanyer's subject was only "ostensibly" Jesus, while her real goal was to write about women only, or even to replace Jesus with Margaret Clifford as the center of a new female church; see, for instance, Brenda J. Powell, "'Witnesse Thy Wife (O *Pilate*) Speakes for All': Aemilia Lanyer's Strategic Self-Positioning," *Christianity and Literature* 46, no. 1 (1996): 5–23 (5), or Keohane, "That Blindest Weakenesse," 379–84. Lanyer's primary focus, however, is Christ. She repeatedly tells her readers that she is presenting Jesus for their viewing (*Salve Deus*, 5, 17, 19, etc.; cf. Marie H. Loughlin, "'Fast Ti'd Unto Them in a Golden Chaine': Typology, Apocalypse, and Woman's Genealogy in Aemilia Lanyer's *Salve Deus Rex Judaeorum*," *Renaissance Quarterly* 53, no. 1 [2000]: 133–79 [152]).

22. *Salve Deus*, 1.

23. Lanyer has an uneasy relationship with the aristocracy, sometimes preaching social egalitarianism and nobility based on virtue (*Salve Deus*, 42–44, 134–35, etc.), but also clearly honoring the titled ladies she knows. According to Simon Forman, she wanted a title herself (Woods, *Lanyer*, 21). See further Kari Boyd McBride, "Sacred Celebration: The Patronage Poems," in *Aemilia Lanyer: Gender, Genre, and the Canon* (ed. Marshall Grossman; Lexington: University Press of Kentucky,

on "all vertuous Ladies in general"—a dedication echoed in Lanyer's prose introduction to the passion of Christ, directed even more broadly to the "Vertuous Reader." The virtuous readers in view are women; men are never addressed in the prefatory material.[24]

The women readers addressed in *Salve Deus* are identified as a cohesive group set against "them," the "evil disposed men" who judge women.[25] There is little room for shades of grey; one is either for women or against them. This aspect of Lanyer's work locates her within the Renaissance *querelle des femmes*, an ongoing dispute over the value and virtue of women. The *querelle* began with the publication of *The City of Women* by Christine de Pisan in 1404 and continued into the eighteenth century.[26] In England, the *querelle* was introduced in the early 1540s with the publication of *The Schoolhouse of Women*, an attack on women's sexuality, habit of gossip, and laziness, among other failings. Jane Anger, the first Englishwoman to join the *querelle*, published a response to the misogynist pamphlets of her day in 1589.[27] The *querelle* was exacerbated at the end of Elizabeth I's fifty-year reign by the division of the royal court into male and female spheres under James I, and a veritable flurry of pamphlets was published from 1615 to 1620.[28] Lanyer's work reflects the questions and concerns of her era. She draws a sharp separation between men and women, ably defending women against misogyny and

1998), 60–82; or Kari Boyd McBride and John C. Ulreich, "Answerable Styles: Biblical Poetics and Biblical Politics in the Poetry of Lanyer and Milton," *Journal of English and Germanic Philology* 100, no. 3 (2001): 344–47.

24. *Salve Deus*, 48. The book refers positively to only a few men: Jesus, Lady Katherine's husband (p. 37), several martyrs (pp. 125–28), and "all good Christians and honourable minded men" who are willing to be good to women (p. 50).

25. *Salve Deus*, 48.

26. The *querelle* was influenced by the humanist recognition and education of women, and was joined by such scholars as Cornelius Agrippa and Marguerite de Navarre; see Joan Kelly, "Early Feminist Theory and the 'Querelle des Femmes', 1400–1789," *Signs* 8, no. 1 (1982): 4–28; Douglas, "Christian Freedom," 167–72; and Barbara McManus, "Eve's Dowry: Genesis and the Pamphlet Controversy About Women," in *Women, Writing, and the Reproduction of Culture in Tudor and Stuart Britain* (ed. Mary E. Burke et al.; Syracuse, N.Y.: Syracuse University Press, 2000), 193–206.

27. The English *querelle* is thoroughly discussed by Katherine U. Henderson and Barbara F. McManus, *Half Humankind: Contexts and Texts of the Controversy about Women in England, 1540–1640* (Champaign, Ill.: University of Illinois Press, 1985).

28. See further Achsah Guibbory, "The Gospel According to Aemilia: Women and the Sacred," in *Aemilia Lanyer: Gender, Genre, and the Canon* (ed. Marshall Grossman; Lexington: University Press of Kentucky, 1998), 191–211 (193); Woods, *Lanyer*, 36; and Henderson and McManus, *Half Humankind*, 15–18.

supporting women by envisioning, and inviting her readers to join, an all-female community.[29]

The female readers described by Lanyer abound in virtue, as do the female subjects of her poetry.[30] Susan, Countess Dowager of Kent, "the Sunnes virtue," is praised for fearing the proper authorities, withdrawing from "worldly pleasures," and being patient, faithful, humble, and steadfast in morality.[31] The Countess of Cumberland likewise lights the world with her virtuous learning and "powers divine" ("Salve Deus Rex Judaeorum," ll. 1369–76, 1391).[32] Lanyer honors faithful, wise women like Deborah, Esther, Judith, and Susanna, who displayed their particular virtues in overpowering men, and she also praises what Sharon Cadman Seelig calls the "masculine, martial" qualities of some of her subjects.[33] In *Salve Deus*, these women provide a model for the reader to emulate; Lanyer desires "all increase of virtue" for her readers.[34]

The emphasis on virtue is not unusual in a seventeenth-century text. However, the particular virtues Lanyer finds and praises in her female subjects and readers, including wisdom, learning, and courage, were more commonly associated with men. Traditional feminine virtues were limited to chastity, silence, and obedience.[35] Lanyer does encourage chastity and obedience—but with reference to God in place of the expected husbands, and silence does not fit into her picture of female virtue. In fact, the one figure who maintains virtuous silence in *Salve Deus* is Christ. The virtues Lanyer associates with Jesus, including

29. Lewalski, "Of God," 207, calls Lanyer's poem a "comprehensive 'Book of Good Women'." It is also a book *for* good women.

30. On the use of virtue in Lanyer's work, see Sharon Cadman Seelig, "'To All Virtuous Ladies in Generall': Aemilia Lanyer's Community of Strong Women," in *Literary Circles & Cultural Communities in Renaissance England* (ed. Claude J. Summers and Ted-Larry Pebworth; Columbia: University of Missouri Press, 2001), 44–58.

31. *Salve Deus*, 18–19.

32. From this point forward, I refer to Lanyer's ten dedicatory poems and the epilogue, "The Description of Cooke-ham," by page number in Woods's 1993 edition of *Salve Deus*. For greater precision, line numbers (l. and ll.) refer to the title poem, "Salve Deus Rex Judaeorum."

33. Seelig, "To All Virtuous Ladies," 51. See *Salve Deus*, 3, 23, and 49; Lanyer also praises the muses who avoid violent action (p. 13).

34. *Salve Deus*, 48–50.

35. See Constance Jordan, *Renaissance Feminism: Literary Texts and Political Models* (Ithaca, N.Y.: Cornell University Press, 1990), 21, or Kim Walker, *Women Writers of the English Renaissance* (Twayne's English Authors Series 521; New York: Twayne, 1996), 8.

patience, love, and piety, are traditionally "feminine."[36] By presenting the male Jesus as the ultimate model of what Jacobean society saw as "female" virtues, and the excellence of the women as models of "male" virtues, Lanyer demands that all these virtues be recognized as Christian, common to men and women.[37]

While the women of *Salve Deus* display the virtues of Christ and men, the men in the passion story are distinctly lacking in "masculine" virtues. This characterization of women and men supports Lanyer's intention to praise women. She draws attention to biblical and pagan heroines. Jesus himself was "pleased" to be born of, brought up by, and obedient to, a woman. He included women in his ministry, and his first appearance after his resurrection was to a woman. Women have taken part in the ongoing struggle of the church as faithful Christians and even martyrs; thus, men should respect women.[38] This demand is sustained by Lanyer's novel interpretation of Gen 3.

Lanyer's Defense of Eve
The apology for Eve is foretold in the first dedication, "To the Queenes most Excellent Majestie." Lanyer cheekily asks the queen to determine if her reading of Gen 3:1–7 is correct ("To judge if it agree not with the Text"); she also demands the social consequences of her interpretation— that women should no more be blamed or defamed by men.[39] In "Salve Deus Rex Judaeorum," the apology begins in l. 761. Lanyer deflects the blame for original sin from womankind by identifying Eve as the victim of the serpent's cunning: Eve is a "poore soule," unable to identify the serpent's words as deceit (l. 773), without the "power" to see the end of her action (ll. 765–66). She did not understand that the serpent was trying to trick her (ll. 769–70). Lanyer points out that Eve faithfully gave

---

36. See, e.g., *Salve Deus*, ll. 957–59 and also p. 40. Boyd Berry, "'Pardon… Though I Have Digrest': Digression as Style in 'Salve Deus Rex Judaeorum,'" in *Aemilia Lanyer: Gender, Genre, and the Canon* (ed. Marshall Grossman; Lexington: University Press of Kentucky, 1998), 212–33 (213–15), suggests Jesus is feminized in *Salve Deus*; Seelig, "To All Virtuous Ladies," 57, thinks women are masculinized. Perhaps both Jesus, the ideal "man," and the women are humanized.

37. Elaine V. Beilin, *Redeeming Eve: Women Writers of the English Renaissance* (Princeton: Princeton University Press, 1987), explores similar arguments made by other Renaissance women writers (see pp. xv, 180, and 190–97). See also Janel Mueller, "The Feminist Poetics of 'Salve Deus Rex Judaeorum,'" in *Aemilia Lanyer: Gender, Genre, and the Canon* (ed. Marshall Grossman; Lexington: University Press of Kentucky, 1998), 99–127 (112), and Seelig, "To All Virtuous Ladies," 57.

38. *Salve Deus*, 49–50.

39. Ibid., 6.

God's command about the tree to the serpent; it was the serpent who denied the truth of her words (ll. 775–76). For Lanyer, Eve was truly deceived, just as it says in 1 Tim 2:14. Lanyer sees this deception, resting as it does on Eve's weakness, as reason to excuse Eve from the guilt of original sin.[40]

The picture of Eve as a poor, powerless woman, unable to withstand the temptation to sin, may seem on the surface to be no different from what we have seen in the works of male commentators.[41] According to the traditional interpretation of Gen 3 and 1 Tim 2 represented by Calvin and Donne, morally powerful man rules woman because of woman's moral weakness. In *Salve Deus*, however, power and weakness do not relate to morality. Rather, power is knowledge, and weakness is ignorance. The "weake imagination or wit of man" lacks the ability to understand the "infinite value" of Christ.[42] Lanyer's own lack of learning limits her power to write, so she relies on God for literary empowerment (ll. 273–328 and p. 47).[43] This is the sort of weakness and power we find in the apology for Eve. Lanyer's attribution of original sin to Eve's *mental* weakness sets her interpretation apart from that of her forerunners and contemporaries.[44]

In *Salve Deus*, Eve "[w]as simply good, and had no power to see" what the consequences of her action would be (l. 764). She lived in "undiscerning Ignorance" (l. 769), and her inability to understand the serpent's deception betrayed her into sin. The man's direct knowledge of God's command, on the other hand, should have given him the mental power to withstand the serpent's deception (ll. 785–92; cf. Gen 2:17). Eve sinned for lack of knowledge, but Adam for lack of discretion—he failed to judge their act as wrong, though he had the ability to do so (ll. 795–800): "No subtill Serpents falsehood did betray him / If he would eat it, who had power to stay him?" Lanyer reverses the common assertion of female inferiority on the basis of creation order, instead insisting that the greater moral responsibility rests on Adam, the first created (ll. 780–92).

Lanyer admits that Eve sinned in eating the forbidden fruit. She was at "fault" in the story, and womankind did "fall" in Eden (ll. 762, 768, 778,

---

40. Cf. McBride and Ulreich, "Answerable Styles," 333–34.

41. As is assumed by Beilin, *Redeeming Eve*, 196.

42. *Salve Deus*, 34.

43. Lanyer's self-deprecation represents her apology for her writing, but the attribution of her work to God cleverly reinforces its authority. See further Guibbory, "The Gospel," 192, 194.

44. Cf. Powell, "Witnesse Thy Wife," 8.

and 801). But, because of her ignorance, Eve did not realize her action was wrong. The deception of the serpent had worked. Eve was tricked into thinking good, not evil, would come of eating the fruit:

> That undiscerning Ignorance perceav'd
> No guile, or craft that was by him intended;
> For had she knowne, of what we were bereav'd,
> To his request she had not condiscended.
> But she (poore soule) by cunning was deceav'd,
> No hurt therein her harmelesse Heart intended. (ll. 769–76)

Eve "intended" good in eating the fruit of the forbidden tree; she erred "for knowledge sake" (l. 797). Furthermore, her aim in giving the fruit to Adam was to increase his knowledge. Her fault was

> …onely too much love,
> Which made her give this present to her Deare,
> That what shee tasted, he likewise might prove,
> Whereby his knowledge might become more cleare… (ll. 801–4)

Love and knowledge are virtues in Lanyer's book (ll. 71, 477, 531, etc.). In sharing the fruit with Adam, Eve lovingly desires the increase of his virtue. According to Lanyer's presentation of the Christian story of original sin, then, Adam knew better and should have rebuked Eve. Eve, however, did not know better, and moreover she meant good to come of her actions. Therefore, her sin is less than that of Adam.[45]

This interpretation of Gen 3:1–7 removes the inherent condemnation of women from the traditional identification of women as (morally) weak. A lack of knowledge can be corrected, allowing "weak" women to aspire to the strength of men. In fact, Lanyer exhorts her readers to be wise in the dedication "To all vertuous Ladies in generall." According to Lanyer, the readers should take on the persona of the wise bridesmaids, awaiting Christ the bridegroom who will reveal his truth to them.[46] They are called to travel in the paths of Minerva, goddess of wisdom, and dress in finery surpassing that of wise Solomon (cf. 1 Kgs 10).[47] The virtuous readers should display their virtue in steady, clear minds, overcoming defiling thoughts.[48] As in Lanyer's retelling of Gen 3, sin is here almost equated with lack of knowledge.[49] It is this sin that is Eve's

45. See also ibid., 8–9.
46. *Salve Deus*, 12.
47. Ibid., 12–13.
48. Ibid., 13–14.
49. The connection of sin with ignorance, and wisdom with virtue, is sustained throughout *Salve Deus* (ll. 157–60, 1397, 1489–96, 1737–40, etc., and pp. 19, 32, and 43).

problem in Eden, this sin that led to the disequilibrium between mankind and womankind, this sin that Lanyer calls her readers to redress in becoming wise themselves.[50]

Lanyer's presentation of Eve as woefully ignorant, but loving and well-intentioned, directly challenges the prevailing contemporary interpretation of the story in which the woman tempted (or seduced) the man to sin. The sequence of the two sins becomes the worst part of the story for John Milton. In Book 9 of *Paradise Lost*, Eve willfully separated herself from Adam (ll. 205–386); then, having fallen prey to the serpent, she realizes that her own death may result from her action. Adam, who has not yet eaten the fruit, would live on with another wife, forgetting the first Eve. Eve gives Adam the fruit in order to force him to sin and die with her (ll. 816–83). Milton's Eve is a paragon of wickedness.[51] Lanyer's retelling of Gen 3 does not allow such an interpretation. Nevertheless, Eve and Adam bring suffering onto their offspring because of their actions, both the ignorantly well-intentioned and the knowingly wrong.

The Fall and the Passion
Early Christian tradition identified Jesus' death and resurrection as the restitution of the sin and death brought about by Adam (see, e.g., Rom 5:12–21 and 1 Cor 15:21–22). Likewise for Lanyer, the death of Christ resolves the suffering introduced by Adam and Eve. Moreover, Jesus' story parallels the story of Eden (ll. 257–64 and 839–40, and p. 34). Lanyer draws explicit connections between Adam and Christ. Adam is the "Lord and King of all the earth" and Jesus, the monarch of creation (ll. 783 and 1711). Both men are beautiful and perfect (ll. 786, 791, 893, and 1710, and pp. 38–40). Both lose their "breath" (ll. 264 and 790). Mary and Eve are connected by the similarity of their roles: Mary becomes Christ's wife as well as mother, and Eve, the wife of Adam, is "Mother" (ll. 763, 1087–88). They are tied together by fruit (Eve's fair fruit and Mary's faultless fruit, Jesus, ll. 798, 1025), and poverty (ll. 773, 784, and 1086).

50.   In the Renaissance, education for women was discouraged for fear that they would lose their virtues of chastity, silence, and obedience; see Valerie Wayne, "Some Sad Sentence: Vives' *Instruction of a Christian Woman*," in Hannay, ed., *Silent But For the Word*, 15–29; Hilda L. Smith, "Humanist Education and the Renaissance Concept of Woman," in Wilcox, ed., *Women and Literature in Britain, 1500–1700*, 9–29; and Walker, *Women Writers*, 4–25. Lanyer claims the opposite: learning will increase women's virtue (cf. Beilin, *Redeeming Eve*, 190).

51.   The man, on the other hand, is a paragon of virtue, a sort of twisted representation of Christ, sacrificing his own sinless state to be with his wife (*Paradise Lost* 9.896–999).

In its immediate context, Lanyer's interpretation of Gen 3 also links Adam and Eve with Pilate and his wife.[52] Matthew 27:19 reports that Pilate's wife, disturbed by a dream about Jesus, warns her husband against him. This single reference to Pilate's wife sparked centuries of speculation about her name, her faith, and the source of her dream. In *Salve Deus*, the wife is a worthy Christian woman (ll. 751–52), and her brief message becomes Lanyer's apology for Eve.[53] The wife calls Pilate to "see" the truth and so act in justice and righteousness; he should "view" the holy life of Christ, his "good desert," and protect him rather than condemn (ll. 753–58). Eve's inability to "see" the outcome of her action should be a warning to Pilate (ll. 765–66). Throughout *Salve Deus*, Lanyer equates true, clear sight with wisdom and understanding (e.g. ll. 25, 1549, and pp. 21, 31, and 35). The men in the book rarely see wisely, and therefore they fail to act wisely (Stephen in ll. 1761–68 is the one exception). Men such as Peter, the gang who arrested Jesus, and Caiaphas do not see Jesus clearly, even when he explicitly reveals the truth to them, and therefore they betray and condemn him to death (ll. 341–42, 420, 504–12, and 712). Pilate's wife calls her husband to use the wisdom gained through Eve's sin of ignorance to see the truth of the situation in which he finds himself in order to avoid the trap into which these other (blind) men have fallen.

Pilate's wife's interpretation of Gen 3 is granted authority by her dream, a vehicle of divine revelation. As a woman, one of Eve's daughters, the wife needs this authority: since Eve traditionally gave bad advice to her husband in Eden, women's words were mistrusted in Jacobean England.[54] Lanyer repeatedly expresses anxiety over the acceptability of her own voice as an interpreter of the biblical story.[55] Her own dreams provide some justification for her writing, and Lanyer also claims divine authorization.[56] Through Pilate's wife, a woman who gave good advice to her husband, Lanyer attempts to restore faith in women's

52. The parallel drawn between Pilate and his wife and Adam and Eve has some precedence. See W. Gardner Campbell, "The Figure of Pilate's Wife in Aemilia Lanyer's *Salve Deus Rex Judaeorum*," in *Renaissance Papers 1995* (ed. George Walton Williams and Barbara J. Baines; Southeastern Renaissance Conference, 1996), 5–12.

53. On Lanyer's depiction of Pilate's wife, see Powell, "Witnesse Thy Wife."

54. See ibid., 12; Guibbory, "The Gospel," 194; and Mary Ellen Lamb, "Patronage and Class in Aemilia Lanyer's *Salve Deus Rex Judaeorum*," in Burke et al., eds., *Women, Writing, and the Reproduction of Culture in Tudor and Stuart Britain*, 38–57 (50).

55. E.g. *Salve Deus*, 15, 41, and throughout.

56. Ibid., 21–31, 36, 139.

words.[57] Like Adam, Pilate has the knowledge and understanding to choose wisely, but both choose poorly.[58]

Of course, the reader already knows that Pilate's wife would be unsuccessful in her plea. Lanyer, building on this foreknowledge, issues (through the wife) a stirring call for women to regain equality with men on the basis of the greater sin Pilate is about to commit. This demand reveals a third level of identification with Adam and Eve: Adam, and therefore Pilate, represent all men, while Eve and Pilate's wife stand for all women. The use of the first person plural in the apology for Eve indicates Lanyer's broad characterization of all women as one body: "thy wife (O *Pilate*) speakes for all" (l. 834).[59] When Adam falls, moreover, the man Jesus is no longer identified with him. Adam's sin brings danger and disgrace to the world (l. 792), and in dying, Jesus suffers that disgrace (l. 592). Adam mistreats his wife (ll. 793–95, 805–8), while Jesus is "a Lover much more true / Than ever was since first the world began" (ll. 52–53). Once *man* falls, Jesus is instead identified with the *women* in the story.

As previously noted, Lanyer describes Jesus and her female subjects and readers with the same language. Adam, the "perfect'st man that ever breath'd on earth," loses his perfection (cf. imperfect Peter, l. 350), but the women retain theirs (ll. 41, 1090, 1540, 1562, etc.). Like Eve, Jesus is "poore" (l. 1720), patient (l. 604), and loving (ll. 366, 387). To complete the correlation, both parties suffer from "vipers," men who cruelly attack them.[60] These vipers are associates of the "subtile Serpent" who betrayed womankind in Eden (l. 767).

Lanyer uses the shift in the identification of Jesus with Adam to Eve to great effect. Since women are so virtuous and men so wicked, Lanyer's Pilate's wife demands:

> Then let us have our Libertie againe,
> And challendge to your selves no Sov'raigntie;
> You came not in the world without our paine,
> Make that a barre against your crueltie;
> Your fault beeing greater, why should you disdaine

---

57. Powell, "Witnesse Thy Wife," 12.

58. Compare *Salve Deus*, ll. 777–92, with l. 931. The critique of Pilate is equivocal; he condemned an innocent man, but that innocent man's death is salvific (cf. Campbell, "The Figure," 4). Lanyer recognizes this conundrum (*Salve Deus*, l. 472).

59. See also *Salve Deus*, ll. 759–68, 794, 825–33.

60. Compare ibid., l. 753, with l. 828, and also see pp. 48–49.

> Our beeing your equals, free from tyranny?
> If one weake woman simply did offend,
> This sinne of yours, hath no excuse, nor end. (ll. 825–32)

In Gen 3:16, God announces that, on account of Eve's sin, her pain and trouble in bearing children will be increased. Furthermore, her desire will be for her husband, who will rule over her. The subjection of women to men in the church's understanding of world order thus rests in part on the consequences of the first woman's first sin.[61] Lanyer identifies the curse on Eve in Gen 3:16 as the only reason for male superiority (ll. 760, 825–27).[62] In the voice of Pilate's wife, the representative of all women, she calls on mankind, represented by Pilate, to reverse the traditional inequality of the sexes. The sin Pilate is about to commit is far greater than the sin committed by Eve (see also ll. 761–62 and 815–24). Moreover, while Eve sinned in ignorance, Pilate is fully informed of the wrongness of his decision (ll. 913–36). Lanyer concludes that condemning the Savior of the world to death draws condemnation onto men including Pilate, Judas Iscariot, the Jewish leaders, Jesus' male disciples, and their male descendants. All mankind falls in the actions of those few who abandon, betray, condemn, and crucify Christ.[63]

The argument for the equality of women gains support from the women participants in the passion story who, unlike the men, remain faithful to Jesus. Lanyer's praise of such women resounds in the passage on the women of Jerusalem who wept over Jesus in Luke 23:27–31. These women are steadfast in their faith and love, and their eyes see Jesus' bright eyes (*Salve Deus*, ll. 988–89). Like the Countess of Cumberland, they have "eagle eyes" able to see the "Sunne" (that is, Jesus; l. 991).

> When spightfull men with torments did oppresse
> Th'afflicted body of this innocent Dove,
> Poore women seeing how much they did transgresse,
> By teares, by sighes, by cries intreat, may prove,

61. See, e.g., 1 Tim 2:11–15 and Calvin, *Genesis*, 48.
62. Traditionally, creation order also demonstrated male superiority (see above). Lanyer uses the order of creation to highlight male responsibility (ll. 780–92) and wryly comments, "If any Evill did in [Eve] remaine, / Beeing made of [Adam], he was the ground of all" (ll. 809–10).
63. Guibbory, "The Gospel," 200–201, claims that, for Lanyer, the significance of Jesus' death lies in the salvation of women from social strictures (cf. Keohane, "That Blindest Weaknesse," 368, and Lamb, "Patronage," 49–50). The point of the passion is still salvation from sin, however (*Salve Deus*, ll. 1297–304, 1722–26, etc.); it is man's role in bringing about the passion that liberates woman.

What may be done among the thickest presse,
They labor still these tyrants hearts to move;
In pitie and compassion to forbeare
Their whipping, spurning, tearing of his haire. (ll. 993–1000)

These women see male sin and speak against it (offering another instance of the good, wise words of women). They are the antitype of the men who, like Adam, fail to rebuke sin in themselves or others.

Pilate's wife's message to Pilate and the men he represents demands recognition that they are guilty and deserve judgment. Eve may not have been the wisest woman of all time, but Pilate's wife exemplifies a woman who does know, can reason, and clearly sees the significance of the passion. In the dedicatory poems and in "The Description of Cooke-ham," Lanyer identifies the women of her acquaintance as equally wise, discerning, and far-seeing. These women and all women deserve their "Libertie," equality with men who in the end have no superior character to buttress their superior social position.

The New Eden

Lanyer's declaration of female equality in ll. 825–32 of *Salve Deus* grounds her vision for a new sort of society centered on women within which women are supported, educated, and enabled by other women. At one point in her life, Lanyer was part of such a community gathered around Margaret Clifford at Cookham. The countess, her daughter Anne, and their waiting women retreated to the countryside, leaving men behind in the city. According to Lanyer, they led a life of scholarly study and religious meditation.[64] Lanyer's version of the passion story, the apology for Eve, the praise for Margaret and other women, and the poem on Cookham all support her hope for the formation of a new religious, scholastic community of women.

As already noted, Lanyer calls her women readers to a lifestyle of study and seeking wisdom and knowledge; learning is a key virtue (l. 1391). The wise bridesmaids of Matt 25:1–13 provide a model for the readers. The readers are exhorted to fill their lamps with oil in order to see what Christ has to reveal.[65] They should not let shadows confuse their sight, the object of which is Jesus.[66] The exhortation to learning speaks directly to the problem of Eden. The life Lanyer envisions for her readers reflects purity of devotion to Christ. Jesus is the subject of study, and throughout

64. *Salve Deus*, 133, 135–36.
65. Ibid., 12.
66. Ibid., 14.

Salve Deus, Lanyer expresses a desire for her readers to see Jesus and read his story in her poetry (e.g. ll. 1325–68, and pp. 5, 31).[67]

Female devotion to Jesus extends into marriage. Christ is repeatedly described as the true Lover (ll. 672, 1267, and pp. 32, 38, etc.), and bridegroom imagery appears throughout the dedications "To all vertuous Ladies in generall" and "To the Ladie Anne, Countesse of Dorcet." The depiction of Jesus in *Salve Deus*, ll. 1305–20, is modeled on the Song of Songs, which, according to traditional Christian interpretation, symbolizes the marriage of Jesus with his bride, the church. This metaphorical relationship originates in the New Testament (e.g. Eph 5:22–32 and Matt 22:1–14). Lanyer realizes that the sexual nature of the metaphor is peculiarly applicable to women.[68] She insists on Jesus' identity as Lord, Lover, and King of all women (*Salve Deus*, l. 982; cf. l. 1023). She encourages her audience to be faithful to their Lover, accepting Jesus, the "faire Bridegroom," into their "soules pure bed."[69] Put into practice, Jesus as bridegroom would radically alter traditional social relationships between a wife and her human husband, and Lanyer suggests that virginity or a chaste lifestyle provides the proper arena for living virtuously.[70] In this respect, it is important to note that, although most of the women named in the dedications are married, Lanyer makes reference to only one good husband.[71] Adam and Pilate, men who mistreat or ignore their wives, represent the average husband in *Salve Deus*.[72] Devotion to Jesus provides a time-honored, somewhat socially acceptable path for women to live independently. Celibacy frees women from subjection to a husband—freeing them to be subject only to Christ, a man who respected women and who, in Lanyer's words, is almost a woman himself.

If an ignorant woman and her morally weak husband lost Paradise, wise women married to Christ, Virtue incarnate, can regain Paradise. Lanyer's community of women scholars is the new humanity, reversing the damage done in Eden. Throughout *Salve Deus*, Lanyer reinvents Eden around the Countess of Cumberland and her daughter.[73] "The

67. McBride, "Sacred Celebration," 64–66, and Guibbory, "The Gospel," 206, identify Lanyer as a priest who presents Jesus to her readers, the communicants.

68. Cf. Walker, *Women Writers*, 118, and Woods, *Lanyer*, 142–43.

69. *Salve Deus*, 20.

70. Ibid., 134.

71. Ibid., 37–38.

72. Margaret and Anne Clifford had infamously bad husbands (Lewalski, "Of God," 207, and Seelig, "To All Virtuous Ladies," 44–45). On the other hand, on the title page of *Salve Deus* Lanyer is introduced as "Wife to Captaine Alfonso Lanyer" (p. 1).

73. See, e.g., *Salve Deus*, ll. 17–24 and 257–64, and p. 34.

Description of Cooke-ham" centers on garden imagery; one tree in particular is singled out as glorious and central to the poem. In "To the Ladie Margaret," the tree is Jesus himself.[74] When the countess walked in Cookham's garden, she walked with Christ and his apostles.[75] Even more strikingly, like Eve, the countess is tempted by Satan, but she does not fall prey to his temptations (ll. 36–40, 51). While Eve "had no power to see" the consequences of her action (l. 765), Lanyer repeatedly affirms the countess's eagle-sharp vision (ll. 25, 1365, 1549, etc.). The Countess of Cumberland plays the role of Eve, though without sin and without a merely human Adam, in Lanyer's new garden of Eden.[76]

In addition to representing Eve, Margaret and her daughter also act as a new Peter. Since he abandoned Jesus in Gethsemane, Lanyer takes away Peter's place as the most important disciple. The dedication to Anne Clifford identifies her, instead of Peter, as the shepherd who will feed Jesus' sheep (cf. John 21:15–19). No longer is Peter the foundation of the church (Matt 16:18); Anne will build on Jesus.[77] Finally, Peter's keys are given to the Countess of Cumberland (*Salve Deus*, ll. 1369–70; cf. Matt 16:19). In Lanyer's new Paradise, women form the core of the community.

Conclusion

A strong proto-feminist streak runs through Lanyer's one volume of poetry.[78] She has a vital interest in proving that women are worthy of respect. They cannot be passed over as weak and ignorant; they are just as faithful in their love as men, perhaps even more so. Lanyer identifies the traditional male interpretation of Eve's action in the garden of Eden as the determining factor behind the low view of women in her society, and in *Salve Deus* she carries out a sustained argument for a fresh interpretation of Gen 3:1–7 and its significance for gender relations in the church and world.

74. Ibid., 34.

75. Ibid., 132.

76. Some of the descriptions of Margaret and Anne are redolent of Jesus himself; see ll. 1337–44, 1369–85, and p. 40, etc. However, contra Keohane, "That Blindest Weaknesse," 361–62, Lanyer does not identify Margaret as the Christ figure of a new church. Rather, like Jesus' disciples in the New Testament, Margaret and Anne imitate Jesus in the world.

77. *Salve Deus*, 46.

78. Mueller, "The Feminist Poetics," points out that while Lanyer was no feminist by modern standards, she was radical in her context.

While some of the elements of Lanyer's interpretation may not be persuasive, she rightly challenges the prevailing critique of Eve as the primary sinner in Gen 3. Furthermore, her plea for female wisdom and learning answers the contemporary use made of 1 Tim 2:11–15 to condemn women to silence and ignorance. Lanyer's creative retelling of the passion with a focus on the distinct involvement and responses of men and women addresses the debates and questions she would have faced in Elizabethan and Jacobean society, and her commentary on biblical and theological tradition illuminates the thoughts and struggles of this particular early English female interpreter of scripture. Lanyer's interpretation, however, did not gain adherents. Only nine copies of the book survive, perhaps indicating that few copies were printed in the first place.[79] The influence of Lanyer's radically different interpretation may have been restricted by the prevailing traditional interpretation, which was itself strengthened by the immense popularity of John Milton's *Paradise Lost*, published about fifty years later. Aemilia Lanyer has in recent years re-entered the canon of English literature; and as one of the earliest recorded female interpreters of Gen 3 and the passion of Christ, she deserves to be part of the history of biblical interpretation as well.

79. Woods, *Poems*, xlvii.

READING NATURE BEFORE READING THE BIBLE: SARAH TRIMMER'S NATURAL THEOLOGY

Heather E. Weir

Introduction

Sarah (Kirby) Trimmer (1741–1810) was a prolific English author of religious education books for children and their teachers. She lived and worked in Brentford, just outside of London, and became interested in education as she taught all of her twelve children at home. In order to fulfill this responsibility, she read widely on the subject of education. In 1780, at the encouragement of her friends, she began her writing career, basing her work on her experience teaching her own children. Her first book was entitled *An Easy Introduction to the Knowledge of Nature and Reading the Holy Scriptures.*[1] In this essay I examine this work of Trimmer's to find how the tradition of seeing nature and the Bible as God's two "books" influenced her reading of the Bible.[2] I will describe the work itself, then examine how the worldview constructed in the book serves as an introduction to reading Scripture, and finally, look at how this worldview influenced the way Trimmer interpreted the Bible.

This examination of Trimmer's work led me to think about some implications for the inclusion of *An Easy Introduction,* as well as other works written for children, in the history of ideas. At the end of the essay

---

1. Sarah Trimmer, *An Easy Introduction to the Knowledge of Nature, and Reading the Holy Scriptures* (London, 1780). In the rest of this essay I cite this work using page numbers in brackets. When referring to the work in the text, I use the short title *An Easy Introduction.* A discussion of the term "nature," particularly Trimmer's use of the term in *An Easy Introduction,* is provided later in this essay.

2. For a brief history of the "book" metaphor for nature, see Alister E. McGrath, *A Scientific Theology.* Vol. 1, *Nature* (Grand Rapids, Mich.: Eerdmans, 2001), 103–4. McGrath helpfully notes that this metaphor had its origins in "the desire to set nature alongside Scripture as two distinct, yet related, sources of knowledge of God" (*Nature,* 104). As we shall see, Trimmer saw nature in precisely this way. For a critical discussion of the two-books language, see George L. Murphy, "Reading God's Two Books," *Perspectives on Science and Christian Faith* 58, no. 1 (2006): 64–67.

I will examine how scholars currently understand Trimmer's work, and suggest some ways her book could be engaged as a part of the history of the idea of natural theology.

Description of an Easy Introduction

An Easy Introduction is an educational work written in the form of a fictional conversation between a mother and her two young children, Charlotte and Henry.[3] This "conversation" is actually a monologue: Mother's voice is the only one actually heard, with Charlotte's and Henry's voices present only by implication in Mother's responses to them.[4] The first two-thirds of the book contains lessons on the natural world taught to both children; these make up the introduction to the knowledge of nature promised in the title. The lessons in the final third of the book are the introduction to reading Scripture. In early editions of *An Easy Introduction*, Mother introduces only Charlotte, who is probably about six or seven, to reading Scripture, as Henry, at three or four, is too young to begin to read the Bible. After the tenth edition (1799), Henry is also introduced to reading the Bible.

In the first two parts of the book, Mother gives Charlotte and Henry lessons on the natural world. These lessons are informal, drawing on what the children see as they walk with Mother in fields, gardens, and yards around their house. The first set of lessons focuses on plants (pp. 1–41), and the second set on animals and birds (pp. 41–79). At the beginning of the third set of lessons, Mother introduces the children to a microscope as an aid to observation; the children then use the microscope to learn

3. Bill Marsden suggests that the teacher in *An Easy Introduction* is "at least a mother-figure." See Marsden's "Book of Nature and the Stuff of Epitaphs: Religion, Romanticism and Some Historical Connections in Environmental Education," *Paradigm* 1.24 (1997), n.p. Online: http://faculty.ed.uiuc.edu/westbury/Paradigm/Marsden.html. The teacher's relationship to the children's father indicates that she is indeed their mother, and I refer to her as Mother throughout this essay. (See Trimmer, *An Easy Introduction*, 103, 241.)

4. For example, "What does your brother say Charlotte? That he wishes his eyes were microscopes. Alas! my dear boy, you know not what you wish for" (p. 93). It is not clear why Trimmer did not introduce the children's voices. Some scholars see the missing children's voices as an example of Trimmer's authoritarian style: she suppressed the children's voices. This may be the case, but the book she cited as her example in the introduction to *An Easy Introduction* also contained a monologue from a mother with implied responses from a child. (See Anna Barbauld, *Lessons for Children* [4 vols.; London: J. Johnson, 1778–79].) Trimmer may simply have followed Barbauld's example.

more about insects and the microscopic world (pp. 79–100). Mother introduces a globe at the beginning of the fourth set of lessons. With the globe
as an aid to thinking about the world outside the children's immediate
experience, Mother teaches Charlotte and Henry a little geography (pp.
100–121). The globe also helps Mother discuss the sea and sea creatures
as well as introductory economics in the fifth set of lessons (pp. 121–54).
The sixth set of lessons introduces the children to some ideas of physics
and astronomy, again with the aid of the globe (pp. 154–90).

The final section of *An Easy Introduction* contains two lessons Mother
gives Charlotte on reading Scripture. These two lessons occur on a rainy
day as Mother and Charlotte sit with their needlework (p. 191). This final
section is vital to Trimmer's core purpose in writing this work: it shows
how nature functions as an introduction to reading Scripture. The first
lesson of the final section connects Mother's view of the world to the
Bible. Mother makes the argument that the good, ordered world must
have a designer, and that this designer is God (pp. 207–10). God has not
only revealed himself through his creative work in making the world, but
also in the Bible (p. 212).[5] Through telling the story of Moses, the
assumed author of the Pentateuch, Mother makes a case for the authority
of the Bible (pp. 212–13). The second lesson of the final section occurs
after Mother and Charlotte read Gen 1–3 together. Mother explains the
reading to Charlotte carefully, and encourages Charlotte to ask questions
whenever she has them as she reads Scripture in the future, thus setting
the stage for future discussions on other parts of the Bible. This final
lesson on Gen 1–3 was dropped from *An Easy Introduction* after the first
edition. Trimmer's second work, *Sacred History*, took its place, giving
lessons on the narrative portions of the Bible from Genesis through
Revelation in six volumes.[6] By dropping the final lesson on Gen 1–3,
Trimmer indicated that she thought that discussing the biblical creation
account was not essential to her discussion of Nature as an introduction
to the Bible.

Nature as an Introduction to Scripture

In the introduction to *An Easy Introduction*, Trimmer first noted that the
idea for the book was prompted by Isaac Watts's work on education, in

5. Trimmer used the traditional male pronouns of God in her writing; in order to
represent her more clearly, I have done the same in this essay.
6. Sarah Trimmer, *Sacred History Selected from the Scriptures: With Annota-
tions and Reflections, Suited to the Comprehension of Young Minds* (6 vols.;
London: J. Dodsley, T. Longman and G. Robinson, and J. Johnson, 1782–85).

which he encourages parents to teach children about nature because it is something about which they are already curious.[7] Trimmer then wrote that since parents might find it difficult to engage young children in scientific discussions, a more introductory approach might be appropriate.

> I therefore thought, that a Book containing a kind of general survey of the Works of Providence, might be very useful; as a means to open the Mind by gradual steps to the knowledge of the Supreme Being. For as we need only read the Volume of Nature, in order to discover his *Wisdom* and *Goodness*, a desire of doing his Will might from thence be excited in their minds, before they were permitted to read the *Holy Scriptures*, which they should not begin till they had been previously taught, that they contain the Revelation which he has vouchsafed to make of himself, his gracious Dispensations toward Mankind, and the Duties we are required to perform in order to obtain his Favour. (pp. vii–viii)

This purpose statement outlines exactly what Trimmer attempted in her volume. She introduced her readers to the "Works of Providence" found in the natural world, or the "Volume of Nature," then moved from these natural wonders to a discussion of God the creator and an introduction to God's other book of revelation, the Holy Scriptures.

Trimmer's argument as a whole shows that she was a theologian of her time: like most eighteenth-century thinkers she was a foundationalist. For a foundationalist, a rational belief must be either a properly basic belief, or logically supported by beliefs that are properly basic. Most foundationalists would exclude belief in God as properly basic, so theologians in the Middle Ages and early modern periods often began their work with arguments for the existence of God. Here, Trimmer did not begin with assuming God's existence, but argued for God from basic beliefs founded upon the evidence of the senses.[8] In her first work, she argued to establish the existence of God; in subsequent works she built upon this foundational argument.[9]

---

7.   Trimmer, *An Easy Introduction*, v–vi. See also Isaac Watts, *A Treatise on the Education of Children and Youth* (2d ed.; London: J. Buckland & T. Longman, 1769). Watts (1674–1748) was a dissenting minister and writer; his work on education was first published posthumously in 1753. Trimmer referenced his works for children in several of her books.

8.   See Stephen T. Davis, *God, Reason and Theistic Proofs* (ed. Paul Helm; Reason and Religion; Grand Rapids, Mich.: Eerdmans, 1997), 80–82.

9.   In Murphy's terms, Trimmer took the classical view of the relationship between natural theology and revelation, in which "natural theology provides a foundation upon which distinctively Christian theology—that based upon revelation—can build" (Murphy, *God's Two Books*, 66).

Before beginning to read the Bible, Trimmer thought children must first be instructed that it contains God's self-revelation. Trimmer's introduction to God's self-revelation began with what she called in her title, "Nature." "Nature" is an easily misunderstood term, which is used in a variety of ways.[10] The word can be used to refer to the innate character of someone or something. Most commonly, the word nature is used to refer to some part or the whole of the material universe. Unfortunately, the meaning of nature as it relates to the material universe differs from writer to writer; their particular understanding is not always explained, since to them it is obvious, or "natural."[11]

In the Christian world, nature usually refers to the material universe that God created, so that nature is "distinct from God and also related to him as artifact to artist, or as servant to master."[12] In *An Easy Introduction*, Trimmer used the word "nature" without explaining how she understood the term; the context of the book as a whole as well as the specific contexts in which the term was used do provide some clarity around how she used the word.[13] Trimmer's use of the word in her title does not help us in discovering her meaning; however, her discussion of the purpose of the volume in her introduction does provide some assistance. Nature and Providence are often used together in the introduction, indicating that the two words are closely linked in Trimmer's thought. She set out to "impress the Minds of Children with a devout sense of their Creator, and a *desire of immortal Happiness*, by calling their [children's] early attention to *the Works of His* [the Creator's] *Providence, and the Truths of*

10. The *Oxford English Dictionary* lists fourteen senses of the word "nature." The fourteen senses are grouped into four categories: (1) senses relating to physical or bodily power, strength, or substance; (2) senses relating to mental or physical or bodily power; (3) senses relating to innate character; (4) senses relating to the material world.

11. On nature as a socially constructed concept, see McGrath, *Nature*, 81–133. See also C. S. Lewis, *Studies in Words* (Cambridge: Cambridge University Press, 1960), 24–74.

12. Lewis, *Studies in Words*, 39. Lewis discusses the term "Nature" extensively in this work.

13. Trimmer can be criticized for not defining the term "Nature" as she used it. More recent scholars, however, also make similar assumptions when using this term. For example, Edward Grant, in his *A History of Natural Philosophy from the Ancient World to the Nineteenth Century* (Cambridge: Cambridge University Press, 2007), assumes that nature is a given, not an invented or constructed concept, and so does not explain or define the term. His only attempt at a definition of nature is found in a description of how the first humans would have encountered it: "The first humans must have been aware of nature, which was all around them and which involved everything they did" (p. 1).

His Religion" (p. xiv). If Trimmer's phrase "the Works of His Providence, and the Truths of His Religion" is comparable to the "Knowledge
of Nature and Reading the Holy Scriptures" of her title, then her understanding of "nature" includes the works of the creator God's providence.
In the body of the work, Mother gives Charlotte a reason for their walks:
"[A]t the same time we are benefiting our Health, by Air and Exercise,
might improve our Minds; for every object in Nature, when carefully
examined, will fill us with Admiration, and afford us both Instruction and
Amusement" (p. 1). It is "Nature" that Mother and the children examine
on their walks. Trees, plants in the garden and in cultivated fields, wild
and domesticated animals, insects, stones and minerals, as well as the
sun and other heavenly bodies are all examples of objects studied in the
lessons Mother taught the children. From these observations a provisional definition for nature as Trimmer used the word is "the material
world that God created and providentially sustains."[14]

Trimmer constructed a particular worldview for her readers through
Mother's lessons to her children. Mother presents the world to Charlotte
and Henry as a good, beautiful, diverse, useful, instructive, ordered, and
rational place. Mother often implies the goodness of the world in her
actions and lessons; she is unafraid of the natural world and embraces its
beauty and variety. She takes delight in the beauty of a sunset, as well as
in a variety of plants and animals.[15] The goodness of the world is also
seen in the usefulness of things in the world. People use natural resources
for their benefit, and animals and plants are also useful to one another.[16]
The world is also instructive. Lessons on storing provisions for the

14.   Because Trimmer understood nature as God's creation, and used this understanding in her argument for God's existence, her version of the design argument
was not built only upon sense evidence; it is thus not as logically sound as she might
have thought it was.

15.   On the beauty of a sunset, see *An Easy Introduction*, 157. To teach the children about the variety of plants, Trimmer had both children collect different kinds of
meadow grasses and flowers. "You know that it is call'd a Meadow: See how green
the Grass looks, and what a number of pretty Flowers!—Run about, and try to see
how many different Sorts of Grass you can find, for it is now in Blossom.—One,
two, three—bless me, you have got eight Sorts!—carry them home, that we may
compare them with the Herbal, for they are all described there.—Charlotte has
gathered quite a Nosegay;—Daisies, Cowslips, Buttercups: As for the rest, I do not
know their Names, so we must search the Herbal, and we shall find Prints of them
and learn what they are called" (pp. 4–5).

16.   Mother remarks on the usefulness of things throughout her lessons. To give
one example, Mother observes that the oak produces food for pigs and is also useful
for humans (p. 12).

winter can be learned from the busy ants, for example: "Look at those little busy Ants, they are at work as hard as possible.—Do you know that they get all the Corn they can, and lay it up against the Winter comes?" (p. 84). None of the insects the children observe are idle. "Keep in mind too, that not even the least of these Creatures which I have shewed to you, are Idle; all are employed.—They don't saunter away their Time, but take care of their Families, and build Houses" (pp. 86–87). The organization, or order, of the world is implicit in all of Mother's lessons; she explicitly mentions the order of the world when discussing astronomy (p. 164). The good, beautiful, and well-ordered world may be complex, but it is rational and can be studied and understood. As Mother constructs this worldview for her children, God is never mentioned. God is only introduced into the discussion during Mother's first lesson with Charlotte on reading the Bible.

Before discussing God with Charlotte, Mother first argues for the existence of a human soul beginning from the observations on nature made during the walks she shared with the children. Mother summarizes the nature lessons as follows.

> We have examined a variety of Flowers, Plants, Trees, &c. and find them all most wonderfully formed to answer the purposes they seem to have been designed for; likewise the Elements, Fire, Air, Earth, and Water, and everything that the Earth and Sea contain.—Animals are still more curious, and we have discovered, that they are of a nature superior to Vegetables, or any inanimate production of the Earth; that every one is furnished with what is necessary for its subsistence, and has as much knowledge as it has occasion for, in order to preserve itself from harm, and to take care of its young, as long as they stand in need of assistance. (pp. 192–93)

Mother then argues that no other creature is like a human being, and that "every thing appears to have been made in some measure for our use," (p. 193). Humans are thus the centre and lords of creation. Mother acknowledges that humans are similar to animals in many ways, but claims that humans are superior to animals because they have souls. She claims souls are what allow humans to feel emotions, have memories, make plans, and become wise. Humans also design and invent new things, something animals cannot do. Mother uses a watch as her primary example of human ingenuity (pp. 203–6). She then asks Charlotte the following rhetorical question about the importance of the soul:

> Now if we think it necessary to do what we can to nourish and preserve these Bodies of ours, which are of so perishing a nature that they may be cut off in a moment, or if they escape from being destroyed by Disease or

Accidents, will most certainly decay with old Age and sink into the
Grave,—is it not of infinite consequence to us to study what we can do
for the Soul, which I hope I have convinced you is so much superior to
the former? (pp. 206–7)

Mother informs Charlotte that people are responsible for how their souls
spend eternity. She then shifts her focus from humans to God. God first
explicitly appears in the body of this work on p. 207 of 263.[17] God is
implied in Mother's discussion of the created world; however, only after
Mother has established the reasonableness of discussing God is the deity
mentioned explicitly. This avoidance of mentioning God, or even syno-
nyms for God, like Providence, shows that Trimmer was attempting to
present an argument for God's existence based only upon Charlotte's
sense impressions.[18]

Mother tells Charlotte that while she has often informed her about
God the creator, and has taught her to pray, Mother "forbore to say
much" to Charlotte about God as she knew "the subject was too sublime"
for her "tender Mind" (p. 208). Up to this point, Mother has talked about
God as if God exists, but now Mother thinks that Charlotte is ready to
understand more about God, and desires to teach her. First, Mother says,
she will attempt to convince Charlotte that there is a God (p. 208).

Mother's argument for the existence of God is a version of the design
argument.[19] The design argument begins with the claim that aspects of
the natural world appear to have a purpose; by analogy with objects with
a purpose made by humans, these natural objects must have a designer;
this designer is God.[20] For example, humans construct houses in order to
live in them. Houses take a variety of forms depending upon the materi-
als available, the number of people that will live in them, the climate of
the country in which the house is located, and many other factors. From

17. Trimmer did explicitly mention God in the introduction to *An Easy Introduction*. That part of the work was directed to parents or other educators, not to
children, the primary audience of the rest of the book.

18. While the word "provident" is used once in the body of the text, it is used of
men and women planning for the future. "Providence" as a characteristic of God, or
as a synonym for God, is only found in the introduction to *An Easy Introduction*,
then on p. 236 in the discussion of the creation of the world found in Gen 1–3.

19. For a more detailed discussion of the design argument, see Davis, *Theistic
Proofs*, 97–120.

20. This analogical aspect of the design argument is often glossed over in discussions of the argument. See Frederick Ferré, "Design Argument," in *Dictionary of
the History of Ideas: Studies of Selected Pivotal Ideas* (ed. Philip P. Wiener; New
York: Charles Scribner's Sons, 1973–74), 670–77 (670).

experience, humans know that houses do not spontaneously appear of their own accord; if we see a house we infer that a person designed and built it. By analogy, the design argument says that the complex universe could not have spontaneously appeared of its own accord; since the complex universe exists, we must infer a designer and builder of the universe. This designer and builder is God.

In the version of the argument that Mother presents to Charlotte, Mother first rhetorically asks if a watch or house could make itself, or grow spontaneously from the ground (pp. 208–9).[21] Since these carefully designed items are not spontaneously formed but purposely designed and built by humans, Mother then argues that other natural objects, which humans cannot make, require a designer superior to humans:

> It is not in the power of the wisest man in the World, to make even a blade of grass, and less must be expected from the Animals, which I have shown are inferior to us. It is evident, from the construction of every part of Nature, from the noblest to the most insignificant, that they are admirably formed; they must therefore have been the Work of some wise powerful BEING, infinitely our superior. We can no otherwise account for our Existence, than by supposing that we are likewise the Work of his Hand, for we know that we did not create ourselves, nor have we yet met with any Creature that could form us. (pp. 209–10)

Mother follows her argument for the existence of God with a brief argument that humans are bound to be thankful to God, their creator and benefactor, for the large share of the blessings of creation God gives humans (p. 211). Mother asks Charlotte whether "it would be a happy thing if GOD would vouchsafe to publish his Will to Mankind, and teach us the Duties he requires us to perform" (p. 212). The Bible, Mother tells Charlotte, contains what humans need to know about God, and "it is truely [*sic*] called the *Word of* GOD, tho' penned by Men" (p. 212).

Nature serves as the basis for Trimmer's argument that God exists. Through creation, God can be seen to be the creator and benefactor of humans; God thus deserves humanity's thanks and service. The Bible is God's revelation to humans, informing us what we need to know about

---

21. Comparing the works of humans to naturally occurring objects, or the works of God, was common in the seventeenth and eighteenth centuries. See John Hedley Brooke, "'Wise Men Nowadays Think Otherwise': John Ray, Natural Theology and the Meanings of Anthopocentrism," *Notes and Records of the Royal Society of London* 54, no. 2 (2000): 199–213 (204–5). The most famous example of comparing nature to a watch is found in William Paley, *Natural Theology, or, Evidences of the Existence and Attributes of the Deity: Collected from the Appearances of Nature* (London: R. Faulder, 1802).

God, and how to serve God. In Trimmer's argument, nature introduces
Scripture by showing both the existence of God, and the need for a more
detailed revelation from God.

Reading the Bible as Introduced by Nature

After beginning with an argument from nature for both God's existence
and the need for the Bible, one might expect Mother to continue her
introduction to the Bible with the creation account of Genesis. Instead,
Mother turns to Exodus and the call of Moses in order to show Charlotte
that Moses, the presumed author of the Pentateuch, was divinely
authorized to write the first five books of the Bible (pp. 212–13). Mother
summarizes the situation of the Israelites in Egypt for Charlotte, then
tells her the story of Moses' call, and gives a summary of the story of the
Exodus (pp. 213–30). Mother ends the summary by telling Charlotte why
she has told her this story:

> What I have told you, was with a view to shew you, before you begin to
> read the Holy Scriptures, that the Writer of the first part of them was
> really no common Writer, but was commissioned by GOD to inform the
> Israelites of their original [*sic*], and to communicate a set of Laws which
> they were to obey in order to please him. (pp. 229–30)

Mother then argues for the veracity of the Pentateuch based on Moses'
authorship. She reasons that Moses wrote the works "during the lives of
the Persons who had been so miraculously delivered, therefore had they
not been strictly true, they could not possibly have gained Credit" (p.
231). Mother hopes that her efforts to convince Charlotte that the Bible is
a book inspired by God were not in vain: "I hope, Charlotte, you are
disposed to believe, that Moses was not a Deceiver, but really sent from
God; we will therefore, tomorrow, begin reading the Holy Bible, and I
hope you will daily encrease [*sic*] in the knowledge of God, and ever
continue his true and faithful Servant" (p. 233).

   While Mother tells the Exodus story in order to show the inspiration of
the Pentateuch, she cannot resist some tangential theological and moral
commentary on the story. Mother remarks on Pharaoh as a negative
example and gives theological meaning to the entire Exodus story.

> [God] resolved to make such an example of him [Pharaoh], as should
> serve for a Lesson to all succeeding Generations; and at the same time to
> perform such signal Miracles, as should convince all who heard them
> related, that his Almighty Power is able to do whatsoever pleaseth him;
> and that as he made all things at first, they are still subject to his Will, and
> he can reward the Good, and punish the Wicked in the most astonishing
> manner. (pp. 213–14)

Notice that Mother's theological meaning builds on the idea that God made all things, something she worked hard to establish by using nature as an introduction to the Bible.

Another theological aside that builds on God as the maker of the world reflects on how God appeared to Moses in the burning bush. The burning bush was an unusual sight, and, Mother explains, the extraordinary nature of the sight was what drew Moses to it:

> The great God himself, my dear Charlotte, is of a Nature so infinitely superior to ours, that whilst we are in the body, we cannot possibly see him, but we may know by his Works, (those wonderful Works which I have lately been endeavouring to make you in some measure acquainted with,) that he is present every where, and knows all things. But as they are always before our eyes, we are apt to overlook his Hand, therefore when the *Almighty* had any particular purpose of shewing his Power or Goodness, it was usual for him to make his *Presence evident* by some extraordinary appearance, which should awaken their attention, and prepare them to receive and execute his Commands;—sometimes by a bright and sudden Glory in the Heavens, often by altering the course of Nature;—sometimes by sending his holy Angels, or good Men called Prophets, to make his Will known to Mankind. (pp. 216–17)

The natural world alone is not always sufficiently arresting enough to get human attention—so God used supernatural appearances, like the burning bush, when human attention was urgently required.

These two theological reflections, on Pharaoh's example and the burning bush, use the concept of God as the designer and maker of the natural world introduced by Mother in her connection between the study of the natural world and the Bible. Mother's ideas about God the Creator influence her theology and interpretation of Scripture.

Mother is also concerned for the duties of humans toward God, because she has introduced God as the great benefactor who made the world and blessed humans in creation. Just as people owe duties to human benefactors, so all of humanity owes duty of some kind to God; the Bible tells humans what their duty to God is.[22] For example, when Mother discusses Moses' divine authority to write Scripture, she notes that "the LORD commanded Moses to go up to Mount Sinai, and there he told him to write the two Tables of the Law which are still called the Commandments, and make a part of our Duty at this Time" (p. 230).

22. Trimmer drew her understanding of the relationship between God and humans from the vertical relationships that dominated the society in which she lived. For a discussion of this dominant view of the world, see J. C. D. Clark, *English Society 1660–1832: Religion, Ideology and Politics During the Ancien Regime* (rev. ed.; Cambridge: Cambridge University Press, 2000).

Earlier, Mother notes the poor example of the Israelites who doubted God when Pharaoh did not immediately let the people go: "They had already seen sufficient to convince them, that GOD was able to perform his promise, and the History of their Forefathers, Abraham, Isaac, and Jacob, abounded with instances of his loving-kindness towards those who put their trust in him; therefore it was a great Crime in them to doubt" (p. 225). The duty of the Israelites was faith in God who was clearly revealed to them, so, Mother implies, the duty of humans today is also faith in God, who is still clearly revealed to all.

In her introduction to reading Scripture, Trimmer argued for the existence of God as the designer of the natural world and benefactor of humans, from the evidence of the observable natural world. Trimmer saw the Bible as God's revelation to humans so they would better know the character of God and their duties toward God. Trimmer's choice of introductions to the Bible informed the way she interpreted Scripture, and the way she taught others to read and understand it.

Trimmer's introductory work expects that readers will continue to read and learn more from the Bible. At the end of the first edition of *An Easy Introduction*, Mother discusses the first three chapters of Genesis with Charlotte, with the understanding that the two will continue to read and discuss the Bible together. Mother does link the reading of Gen 1 to the discussions of the natural world she and the children previously had, but does not highlight the lessons from nature as she explains these three chapters to Charlotte. Once Mother makes the shift from the works of God seen in the world to the word of God found in the Bible, her focus is on the biblical text, and understanding that text.

There are two key instances of Mother asking Charlotte to reflect on her own experience to aid in her understanding of the material in Gen 1–3. First, Mother clarifies the idea that humans are made in the image of God:

> You must not suppose, my dear, that the Almighty has, like us, bodily parts.—If that were the case, he could not be as he is, in all places at all times; what we mean by speaking of God's hands, &c. is only this; that he can converse with us the same as if he had a Tongue or Mouth; can discern all that we do or say, as perfectly as if he had Eyes and Ears; can reach us as well as if he had Hands and Feet.—We can neither describe nor conceive the perfections of the Supreme Being; we are therefore obliged to make use of such expressions as these, when we would speak of his power. (pp. 237–38)

Here Mother clarifies the metaphorical language of the Bible so that Charlotte would not think that being in the image of God meant looking like God. Charlotte's experience of the world might lead to an improper understanding of the Bible in this case. In the second case, Mother asks

Charlotte to think of her own decisions and ability to act to explain the concept of free will. Here Charlotte's experience of the world assists her understanding of the idea of obeying or disobeying the command of God:

> Before I say any thing farther concerning the Tree of Knowledge, let me, Charlotte, ask you a question. Do not you find that you can chuse [*sic*] whether you will speak Truth or Falshood [*sic*]? Whether you will be kind or unkind to other People? Whether you will obey your Papa and me, or not? And in short in every action of your Life, that you have a *choice* whether you will do Good or Ill, and take the consequences?— This power of the Mind is called *free Will*. Adam and Eve were endued with it, and the whole race of Mankind, that is all the Men and Women who have ever been in the World, inherit it from them. (pp. 242–43)

Mother's reliance on Charlotte's experience of nature on their walks to build an argument for God's existence is extended so that Charlotte's experiences are called upon to aid her understanding of the Bible and theological concepts that arise as she and Mother read together. Drawing connections between the concrete world of Charlotte's experience and the biblical text assists Mother in teaching abstract theological concepts about the invisible God.

Trimmer's second work, *Sacred History*, can be understood as an expansion of the final lesson on Genesis, particularly as this lesson was not included in any edition of *An Easy Introduction* after the first. In *Sacred History* Trimmer's primary concern was theological: she wanted her readers to know God. Knowledge of God would then lead to proper behavior and worship. The natural world provided Trimmer with her argument for the existence of God; it also provided her with her argument for the importance of the Bible. Nature did not tell Trimmer her duty toward her creator, but the Bible did. Trimmer built on this understanding of the Bible in her second work, intended to give her readers an understanding of God as revealed in the metanarrative of Scripture.

Recovering Trimmer

Many scholars have read Trimmer primarily as a children's author, not as a theologian or biblical interpreter; thus, Trimmer's *Easy Introduction* is treated as an early science textbook for children, or as an example of early environmental education.[23] In this light, Trimmer is compared to

---

23. See both Marsden, "Book of Nature," and Sylvia Bowerbank, *Speaking for Nature: Women and Ecologies of Early Modern England* (Baltimore, Md.: The Johns Hopkins University Press, 2004).

many other women, but seldom men, who wrote books on nature.[24]
Donelle Ruwe does compare Trimmer's *An Easy Introduction* to Jean-
Jacques Rousseau's *Emile* (1762), and calls Trimmer's work a "marvel-
ous corrective to Rousseau's explicit misogyny."[25]

Trimmer's works are not primarily studied by theologians or biblical
scholars, thus the theology and interpretations of the Bible they contain
are often downplayed or misunderstood. For example, in her study of
women writing on nature, Sylvia Bowerbank implies that cruelty to
animals was one of Trimmer's major concerns, and that preventing it
motivated her work.[26] Bowerbank overstates the case; certainly Trimmer
often mentioned animal cruelty in her works, but the motivation for her
body of work came not from her concern for animals, but from her
religious concern for the souls of people with and for whom she worked.
Bowerbank observes a link between the knowledge that texts written by
women gave, and the action that this knowledge was expected to bring
about. "Women's educational texts thus have the dual aim of informing
and transforming children. So strong is the moralizing tendency in these
texts that they can be said to resemble conduct books more than books of
natural philosophy."[27] Trimmer, like her contemporaries, expected that
knowledge of nature would transform her readers. She was, however, not
most interested in the transformation that a knowledge of nature would
bring her audience, but in the transformation brought about by knowing
God through nature and the Bible. Trimmer's emphasis was less on

---

24. See Ann B. Shteir, *Cultivating Women, Cultivating Science: Flora's Daughters and Botany in England, 1760–1860* (Baltimore, Md.: The Johns Hopkins
University Press, 1996), 69. For the effect of feminist criticism on the study of
children's literature, see Lissa Paul, "From Sex-Role Stereotyping to Subjectivity,"
in *Understanding Children's Literature* (ed. Peter Hunt; London: Routledge, 1999),
112–23.

25. "Not unlike Trimmer's Henry and Charlotte, Emile learns first from nature
through his tutor's manipulations of his natural curiosity. Unlike the tutor, however,
who has an almost sinister ability to educate Emile through anticipating his questions and controlling his environment, Trimmer's mother is direct in her instructions,
and her interpretations are explicit rather than manipulative. It is a marvelous corrective to Rousseau's explicit misogyny that, in Trimmer's woman-centered narrative,
little Henry is the one incapable of comprehending the Bible. He can participate in
the nature walks, but only his sister is mature enough for theological and biblical
lessons" (Donelle Ruwe, "Guarding the British Bible from Rousseau: Sarah Trimmer, William Godwin, and the Pedagogical Periodical," *Children's Literature* 29
[2001]: 1–17 [10]). Trimmer did not mention Rousseau at all in *An Easy Introduction*, so I am not certain she meant it to be read as a corrective to Rousseau.

26. Bowerbank, *Speaking for Nature*, 149.

27. Ibid., 142.

moral action and more on the knowledge of God. For scholars such as Bowerbank and Shteir, who are not theologians, it may be easier to analyze Trimmer's call for moral action than her theology; Trimmer's theology and knowledge of the Bible, though, should be examined by scholars with appropriate expertise.

In *An Easy Introduction* the natural world is not studied as an end in itself, but as an introduction to the Bible. It contains an extended design argument for the existence of God, and so could be compared with works of natural theology like that of Trimmer's contemporary, William Paley (1743–1805).[28] Paley's well-known work, *Natural Theology, or Evidence of the Existence and Attributes of the Deity, collected from the appearances of nature*, was published in 1802, some 22 years after Trimmer's *An Easy Introduction*—which was in its tenth edition in 1799, and continued to be printed into the 1830s. While much has properly been made of the influence of Paley's work, little research has been done into the influence of Trimmer's widely distributed earlier work. Connections might exist between the popularity of Trimmer's work and the later popularity of Paley's work. Possibly adults, who were exposed to *An Easy Introduction* as children, found that *Natural Theology* espoused a position they were already familiar with, and so they more easily assimilated it into their understanding of the world.

Eighteenth- and nineteenth-century religious works written for children have not been studied by biblical scholars or theologians. The example of Trimmer's *An Easy Introduction* suggests that current understanding of popular belief and theology in the late eighteenth century could be substantially enhanced by examining both that work, and other works written for children. A study of children's works would provide scholars with an understanding of what adults thought it was important to teach children, thus accessing ideas of popular theology held by adults. The study could also provide scholars with a glimpse into the way that training children influences the thinking of the next generation of adults. The history of ideas tends to focus on works written for adults; works written for children might also fruitfully contribute to this discipline.

---

28. William Paley, *Natural Theology, or, Evidences of the Existence and Attributes of the Deity: Collected from the Appearances of Nature* (London: R. Faulder, 1802). Both Trimmer and Paley were expressing ideas that were very much a part of the culture of the late eighteenth century. These ideas were earlier expressed in the work of John Ray, *The Wisdom of God Manifested in the Works of the Creation* (London: Samuel Smith, 1691).

Conclusion

Sarah Trimmer's first book, *An Easy Introduction to the Knowledge of Nature and Reading the Holy Scripture*, introduced children to reading the Bible through an exploration of the natural world. Reading nature before reading the Bible influenced the way Trimmer taught her audience to read and understand the Bible. Trimmer's work first argued for the existence of God, using a version of the design argument, then argued for the necessity of further revelation from God, the Bible. Finally, children were allowed to read the Bible, and learned to interpret it and understand it properly. The task of teaching children to read, interpret, and understand the Bible was expanded in Trimmer's second work, the six-volume *Sacred History*. Trimmer's often reprinted first book is noteworthy as it contains a simplified version of the design argument popularized by William Paley 22 years after Trimmer's book was initially published. The existence of Trimmer's work raises questions about the reception of Paley's work, and points to further work to be done in examining the role of books for children in the fields of historical theology, the history of biblical interpretation, and the history of ideas.

ELIZA SMITH'S *THE BATTLES OF THE BIBLE*:
BIBLICAL INTERPRETATION IN SERVICE
OF A CHRISTIAN SOCIAL AGENDA
IN NINETEENTH-CENTURY URBAN SCOTLAND

Bernon Lee

The Battles of the Bible is a book written by Eliza Smith and published in Edinburgh in 1852.[1] Smith wrote under the cloak of anonymity, using the appellation "a clergyman's daughter." She is also the author of *Chapters on the Shorter Catechism* and *Female Examples Selected from the Holy Scriptures*.[2] The former is a volume designed to explain and expound upon the shorter version of the Westminster Catechism for the benefit of children; the latter, as the title suggests, offers meditation and commentary upon the lives of selected women portrayed in the Bible. Beyond information gleaned from the subject matter of Smith's writings, we have scant detail about the author. One might surmise, from her choice of a setting in "one of the mid-land counties of Scotland" in *Chapters on the Shorter Catechism*,[3] that she lived in the Midland Valley of Scotland, perhaps in or proximate to Edinburgh.

The goal of this brief essay is, first, to provide a description of the salient theological features of *The Battles of the Bible*. I seek, as a secondary objective, to explain some of the unique aspects of Smith's thinking on religious matters with reference to her environment. Specifically, I

1. *The Battles of the Bible* (Edinburgh: Paton & Ritchie, 1852).
2. *Chapters on the Shorter Catechism: A Tale for the Instruction of Youth* (2d American ed.; Philadelphia: William S. Martien, n.d.); *Female Examples Selected from the Holy Scriptures* (London: J. Hatchard & Son, 1848). None of Smith's various published works provides dates for her birth and death.
3. Smith, *Chapters*, 1. The household of Mr. Gray, a clergyman in one of the mid-land counties of Scotland, serves as the primary locus for exposition on points of the Shorter Catechism. In support of a working hypothesis of this same region as the geographical locus of the author, it is noteworthy also that two of Smith's major works are published in Edinburgh. This essay shall proceed on this reasoned assumption in its effort to describe the setting for the composition of Smith's book.

shall demonstrate that Smith's interpretation of the Bible reflects the ethos of evangelical Christian expression in nineteenth-century urban Scotland. The result is a particular reading of scripture that emphasizes the virtues of industry and a confidence in divine justice, while eschewing impetuosity and the irresponsible allocation of resources. This essay is a concise survey of the contributions of Smith's book, with an effort to explain some of its unique features with reference to the socio-religious landscape of nineteenth-century urban Scotland.

A Brief Description of the Contents of the Book

The Battles of the Bible is a retelling of stories about military conflict from Genesis to Kings. The setting for the narrative is a visit by three children, Marianne, George, and Johnnie, to the home of their grandfather. Grandfather's launch into an account of battles in the Hebrew Bible is in response to George's complaint that the Bible is a "tiresome book," an endless string of battles unworthy of attention.[4] Grandfather seeks to cultivate an enjoyment of biblical narrative and an appreciation of its religious message. That Smith's thoughts are synonymous with those of Grandfather is evident in the fact that the author, in the preface to the book, mentions the same purposes for the book.[5] For Smith, the motivation for Bible reading must transcend notions of duty. Indeed, one must approach the Bible with the expectation of a profound pleasure to be derived from its pages: readers "must taste its spirit" before they can "know its excellence."[6]

We would, however, be mistaken to assume that attention to aesthetic matters is the sole end to Smith's designs for her book. Her expressed desire is "to lead the young, and those who assist them in studying the Holy Book, to study it with a purpose." That purpose is to pursue a practical lesson from individual passages of the text.[7] The didactic tone of the work is evident in its design. The narrator intrudes upon the conversation between the characters, often in order to relate an incident at Grandfather's house, providing a "springboard" to a new lesson from scripture.[8] In other places, Grandfather directs the children's learning with

---

4. Smith, *Battles*, 4.
5. Ibid., v–vi.
6. Ibid., v.
7. Ibid., vi.
8. The survey of the religious content of the book in the following section of this essay shall provide examples of such digressions from the conversation between characters in the book.

well-formulated questions and suggestions for answers. In the conclusion of each chapter, Smith prods readers to recall the content of such
"lessons" with questions. At these points in the book, the style of writing
assumes the form of catechism. At the end of the chapter on Israel's
conflicts during their wilderness wanderings, for example, Smith asks the
reader to recall the answers she suggests (through Grandfather) to
questions raised in the course of the chapter.[9] She repeats, in terse form,
questions already raised within the chapter. What can one learn from
Caleb's and Joshua's stand against the opinion that Israel ought to abandon any hope of possessing the land promised by God? How is the
conduct of Moses in the face of threats a positive example? What is to be
learned from the defeat of Israel at Hormah? Conscientious readers,
therefore, would be prompted to remember the answers and to search the
chapter for those they have forgotten. The pedagogical intention behind
the composition of Smith's book is evident in these closing segments of
each chapter. Learning about orthodox belief and practice, therefore,
goes hand-in-hand with an appreciation for the aesthetics of the Bible.

Religious Content of the Work

The clarion call of Smith's interpretation of the Bible is to trust in God.
In numerous discursive statements within the book, Smith, through the
words of Grandfather, remarks upon acts of faith with the purpose of
exhortation. Evidence of trust in God is to be seen in a variety of expressions. Abram's disbursement of a tenth of spoils from battle into the
hands of Melchizedek in Gen 14:20–24 is indicative of the patriarch's
belief that God is the author of victory.[10] Joshua's victory at Jericho (Josh
6:1–27) is a lesson for all that faith in God makes up for human deficiency
in military might and strategy.[11] Jonathan's defeat of the Philistines
comes through God's direction because of Jonathan's acknowledgment
of divinity (1 Sam 14:8–10).[12]

But the Bible does not provide only positive examples of a robust trust
in divine character. The accounts of battles in the Bible, according to
Smith, also provide examples of ill consequences for the failure to trust
God. Smith chides the Amalekites for not acknowledging God and assist-
ing the elect (Exod 17:8–16). Their defeat at the hands of the Israelites is

9. Smith, *Battles*, 30–31.
10. Ibid., 8.
11. Ibid., 25, 46.
12. Ibid., 167.

justly deserved.[13] The discouraging report of the spies sent out by Moses (Num 13:27–29) is another instance of infidelity. Their inability to foresee a defeat for the inhabitants of Canaan is particularly abhorrent in light of the success Israel experienced against Egypt with divine assistance.[14]

Brash behavior also is a symptom of infidelity before God. Therefore, she agrees wholeheartedly with the biblical narrator that Saul's resolve to curse anyone under his command who would partake of food before the defeat of the Philistines (1 Sam 14:24) is rash and ill-conceived.[15] Indeed, the curse jeopardizes the life of Saul's own son (1 Sam 14:30–44). In contrast to his father's impetuosity, Jonathan's willingness to submit to the injustice of Saul's judgment is a sign of "composure of spirit which can bear injustice with meekness."[16] The deliverance of Jonathan through an outcry of the people (1 Sam 14:45–46) is indicative of God's pleasure over Jonathan's behavior. This is in accordance with the concern over the cultivation of steadfast belief in God's goodness seen when Joshua set up monuments of stone at the Jordan River (Josh 4:1–11). Smith is concerned that this same virtue be impressed upon youth.[17]

Faith in God flows from a firm understanding of God's character, which must lead to humility. This view is evident in Grandfather's commendation of the Gibeonites for their willingness to accept a humble, even humiliating, position in relation to the Israelites (Josh 9:24–27). In Grandfather's words, "their humility is a pattern to us: it teaches us to seek only for mercy—to ask for life eternal from God; and whatever lot he may assign for us in this world though we may be placed in a very low position."[18] The submissive disposition of the Gibeonites, and that of Jonathan from the earlier example, is encouraged. A similar spirit is seen in Gideon's refusal of kingship (Judg 8:22–24).[19] Gideon's refusal to be king is, in Grandfather's words, "an example of piety and humility"; it is evidence that he "worked for the glory of God and the good of the people." Humble submission to the divine agenda, therefore, is the opposite of impetuosity and vainglory.

Such words of teaching and exhortation characterize much of Grandfather's retelling of stories in the Hebrew Bible. But beyond this main thrust of Smith's book, her work entertains questions regarding theodicy.

13. Ibid., 26.
14. Ibid., 21–22.
15. Ibid., 171.
16. Ibid.
17. Ibid., 43.
18. Ibid., 71.
19. Ibid., 129.

The semblance of vicarious punishment in the execution of Achan's family along with the perpetrator of the transgression is troubling to young Marianne (Josh 7:16–26),[20] as is the savagery of the destruction at Jericho and Ai (Josh 6:1–27; 8:1–35).[21] However, Grandfather, in both cases, is there to quell any course of thinking that might impugn the justice of God. In the former case, he explains that Achan's family bears guilt for their silence concerning their father's transgression. In the latter, God has already demonstrated his forbearance in tolerating the transgressions of Canaan for a long period of time; the Israelites are mere instruments of divine justice. Similar explanations abound for cases where individuals of questionable character triumph over others, such as Ahab's victory over Benhadad (1 Kgs 20:1–42)[22] and Shalmaneser's defeat of the northern kingdom (2 Kgs 17:1–41).[23] In all cases, God's freedom to bring retribution through any agent removes any assumption of favor for the victorious party in a conflict. Smith applies her creativity in constructing the conversations of the book, anticipating problems young readers encounter in the Bible.

A similar dexterity of thought, if biased in favor of the Israelites, is characteristic of Smith's perspectives on deception. In several cases, Smith, through the words of Grandfather, is unwavering in her condemnation of any misrepresentation of truth. Smith, for example, is critical of Jael's deceptive portrayal of herself to Sisera as an ally against the Israelites (Judg 4:18–19), as well as her subsequent betrayal of Sisera's trust by killing him after he had fallen asleep.[24] Smith is steadfast in her conviction despite the heroic Deborah's praise for Jael. She dismisses Deborah's evaluation as a misguided perspective born in the midst of the ecstatic throes of victory. But elsewhere, Smith is careful to discern different aspects of motivation behind deception. Some of these acts of deception are deemed praiseworthy. Rahab's concealment of the spies through deception (Josh 2:4–6) may be despicable, but her desire to seek their deliverance is honorable.[25] Similarly, a redemptive feature of the Gibeonite deception is seen through their humility in accepting terms of servitude (Josh 9:22–27).[26] In both cases, the penchant for deception is a product of Canaanite influence and a lack of knowledge of the true God

20. Ibid., 53.
21. Ibid., 61.
22. Ibid., 243.
23. Ibid., 295.
24. Ibid., 113.
25. Ibid., 39.
26. Ibid., 69.

(Israel's YHWH). But in the midst of that depravity, Smith discerns a spirit of fervor for the worship of the true God that is praiseworthy, albeit misguided to some degree.

The shades of gray that characterize Smith's portrayal of biblical personages are brought to bear upon the issue of deception itself in another of her works. In Smith's *Chapters on the Shorter Catechism*, a more nuanced perspective on the subject may be glimpsed. There, the definition of that which is forbidden in the ninth commandment is any word or deed that might be "prejudicial to truth, or injurious to our own or our neighbor's good name."[27] Smith's further elaboration on the matter of deception would include, within the purview of the prohibition, the upkeep of a promise that ought not to have been given and accurate testimony that is born of intention to cause harm to another.[28] Smith provides an example of the latter in a narrative about a child reporting in accurate detail a sibling's accidental breakage of flower pots in the home, with the sole intention of delighting in the punishment to be meted out to the sibling.[29] The "maintaining and promoting of truth between man and man" is, therefore, no longer a simple matter of the accurate representation and reporting of fact. By Smith's definition, the essence of the catechism on the subject of deception is the promotion of a mind-set free of "evil principles"—the intention to malign another, delight in the suffering of another—that would undermine one of the foundational premises of good Christian society based upon an authentic desire to serve the best interests of one's neighbor. The beginnings of such a nuanced understanding of integrity in speech, I believe, are visible in Grandfather's mixed evaluations of characters in the Hebrew Bible who do depart from telling the truth. Just as truth-telling in *Chapters on the Shorter Catechism* is a virtue under a limited set of conditions, so it is here in *Battles of the Bible*. In the latter, the evaluation of a biblical character's integrity in deception is modified in accordance with the degree of earnestness in service of the divine agenda. A measure of deception in service of God may be tolerated.

Perhaps the most curious characteristic of Smith's work is its attention to industry as a virtue. She pursues this theme in segments of the Bible where it appears marginal to the narrative. For example, Grandfather's comment on Rahab's concealment of the spies amid stalks of flax includes the positive observation that Rahab was an industrious woman

27. Smith, *Chapters*, 228.
28. Ibid., 230–31. Smith does not provide an example of an illegitimate promise.
29. Ibid., 228–30.

(Josh 2:6).[30] The Danites' seeking territory for themselves among the landholdings of Ephraim (Judg 18:1–31) becomes an occasion for an exposition on the ills of sloth, and a predilection for living off the assets of others.[31] When the Danites smite the residents of Laish and the biblical narrator notes the weakness of the victims for their isolation (Judg 18:27), Smith's interpretation, through the voice of Grandfather, is that of an indictment of Laish for the lack of strategic foresight. The inhabitants "had no rulers to control their excesses, so they lived indolent and careless lives." The Danites, according to Grandfather, are able to exploit easily those who "cannot overcome their own passions" in order to better their lot.[32] Further on in Smith's commentary on the latter portion of Judges, the biblical narrator's statement that an elderly man returns from work in the field to encounter a Levite and his concubine in Gibeah (Judg 19:16) becomes, again, occasion for teaching on the same subject. Seizing upon the singular statement about the man's return from the field, Grandfather remarks that "that industrious old man would enjoy the comforts of his home far more than the idle people of the place who did nothing but mischief all day."[33] In Grandfather's words, "rest is pleasant after labor; we cannot know how pleasant it is until we have labored."

Smith's attention to industry as a virtue in reading Judges draws upon elements of marginal import in the stories. An indication of the gravity of the subject for Smith is her willingness to stray far from the central concerns of the narratives in order to attend to it. Through her interpretation, the ethic of industry imposes upon the text of the Bible. In summary, Smith's approach to biblical interpretation in the book is didactic. She holds in high regard the teachings of scripture, and exhorts young readers to adhere to the lessons of the Bible.[34] She is meticulous and creative in her exposition of scripture, and zealous in defending the justice of God. She advocates a deep trust in divine providence, which, in her view, must lead to humility, that is an absence of brashness coupled with a conscientious and balanced perspective in planning, industry, and

---

30. Smith, *Battles*, 38.
31. Ibid., 89.
32. Ibid., 91.
33. Ibid., 94.
34. Smith's high regard for the Bible is evident throughout the book. This disposition finds explicit expression in the Preface to the book: "There is no book like the Bible. From the study of no human composition can the same benefit be derived as from the study of the Word of God. This all acknowledge who believe the Scriptures to be divine" (Smith, *Battles*, v).

submission to God's agenda. The content and posture of Smith's approach to biblical interpretation are amenable to a definable socio-religious ethic of middle-class Christian society in Scotland of the 1800s.

A Socio-Historical Context for Smith's Interpretation of the Bible

The backdrop for the particularities of Smith's interpretation of the Bible is the population explosion in the various urban centers of Scotland and the consequential social pressures that ensued. The forces of industrialization from 1800 onwards favored an urban location for the economies of scale. Between 1830 and 1920, according to Richard Rodgers, the population of Glasgow quadrupled, and that of Paisley doubled between 1801 and 1841.[35] The increase in the population of Edinburgh and Leith for this same period exceeded the accumulated population of previous centuries. A consequence of the rapid growth was the shortage of affordable housing. Flats were re-partitioned to accommodate more residential units. Lodging houses conceived as short-term solutions became permanent fixtures in cities.[36] Overcrowding occurred as tenements increasingly fell into disrepair. Many of the make-shift accommodations lacked water closets within the structures or in their back yards. Human excrement, therefore, poured into gutters or was collected by carts at appointed hours. Under such conditions, disease was rampant. Cholera epidemics occurred in 1832, 1848–49, and 1853–54. Typhus broke out in several parts of the country as well. Infant mortality rates were on the rise between 1860 and 1900; by the time of the Great War, it was still at an alarming level of 122 deaths for every 1000 births.[37] The situation in Scotland's cities was dire.

Richard Finlay, in speaking of living standards in this period, notes that the increased opportunity for employment was the product of expansion in the heavy industries.[38] The reliance of this sector of the

35. Richard Rodgers, "Urban Settlement: 1830–1920," in *The Oxford Companion to Scottish History* (ed. Michael Lynch; Oxford: Oxford University Press, 2001), 620–21.

36. Ibid., 620.

37. Ibid. The response of the emerging professional elite was to flee the inner cities for newly established suburbs. By the latter half of the nineteenth century, as Rodgers observes, a "horizontal" system of socio-economic segregation had emerged in the cities of Scotland, created by movement (away from the center) by those with means to escape the squalor of the inner cities.

38. Richard Finlay, "Living Standards: 1800 Onwards," in Lynch, ed., *The Oxford Companion to Scottish History*, 392–94 (393).

economy on export markets meant that prosperity came in spurts. Periods of unemployment were interspersed with times of demand for labor.[39] Rates of emigration and prostitution rose during periods of downturn. Despair from the filth and squalor of urban settlements was exacerbated by times of financial hardship. Finlay, furthermore, draws a connection between the worst period of economic downturn and increase in alcohol consumption.[40]

The ravages of unchecked industrialization in Scotland's cities met with a pronounced response from church and society, often, according to Maver, with a tinge of millenarian zeal.[41] The dominant expression of millenarian fervor in the early nineteenth century among evangelicals, an emerging and increasingly prominent group in Scottish Christianity, was Premillenialism; this was the belief that the second coming of Jesus Christ would occur prior to a thousand-year reign by him on earth.[42]

39.   The reason for the gravity of the situation in Scotland, according to Finlay, was the paltry numbers constituting the middle class. The bulk of the population was made up of lower-earning unskilled and semi-skilled labor. With few having a significant disposable income, Scotland's cities were unable to capitalize on the spin-off in retail and services generated by industrialization elsewhere in Britain. Sole reliance on an unsteady and insecure export market was the result.

40.   Finlay, "Living Standards," 393. Finlay observes a steady fall in alcohol consumption from 10.8 liters per head to 7.3 liters per year as the ravages of rabid industrialization receded between 1840 and 1910. These figures, for him, suggest escapism through alcohol consumption in Scotland's darkest times. Finlay's observations, however, must be tempered by A. E. Dingle's findings on the same subject ("Drink and Working-Class Living Standards in Britain, 1870–1914," *The Economic History Review* 25 [1972]: 608–22 [619]). Dingle explains the fall in alcohol consumption towards the end of the nineteenth century as the result of a diversification in household expenditures, spurred by a proliferation of goods and services in that period. This is the effect of the "delayed industrial revolution," an increase of cheap mass-produced items engendering a seismic shift in habits of consumption across the country. The precise reasons for the increase or decrease of alcohol consumption, however, need not concern us here. Of greater importance is the perception, by the middle and upper classes, of excessive alcohol consumption as a reason for the socio-economic decrepitude of the working classes. In fact, it is this perception by contemporary middle-class critics and much of later socio-historical scholarship that Dingle's article seeks to modify (ibid., 608). Smith's work, likely, is the product of a sub-culture that would share the possible misconstruction of working-class culture that Dingle points out.

41.   Irene Maver, "Urban Society: 1880 Onwards," in Lynch, ed., *The Oxford Companion to Scottish History*, 627–28 (627).

42.   D. W. Bebbington, *Evangelicalism in Modern Britain: A History from the 1730s to the 1980s* (London: Unwin Hyman, 1989), 81–83; D. W. Bebbington, "Religious Life: Evangelicalism," in Lynch, ed., *The Oxford Companion to Scottish*

According to this view, the Second Advent was imminent, and the task of evangelism was, therefore, urgent. In the evangelical imagination, however, the provision of a remedy to the problems in the inner cities was an integral component of evangelism.[43] Millenarian zeal thus fanned the flames of social action and commentary among evangelicals about the working classes. Vocal and political radicals emerged calling for social change. Such change would demonstrate the moral rectitude and self-sufficiency of the working class and find a remedy for the urban decay of the time.[44] In the wake of this initiative were the temperance movement and a cult of self-improvement emphasizing moral and material advancement, eschewing any activity or ethic that would hamper such advancement. This cultural movement was dubbed "respectable culture."[45] Sobriety and thrift were central values in the cult of "respectable

History, 515–16 (516). This last essay offers a concise description of the rise of evangelicalism and its impact on Scottish Christianity. Evangelicals, in Bebbington's description, placed emphasis on the Bible, the doctrine of atonement, the need for conversion and aggressive participation in spreading the faith through Christian education and social action. Beginning with several revivals in the eighteenth century (e.g. in Cambuslang in 1742, Kilsyth in 1848), the evangelical movement gained strength, rising to form the majority in the General Assembly of the Church of Scotland by 1834. The movement, especially, expressed a unified commitment toward evangelism and schemes for social welfare, despite divisions between Calvinist and Arminian streams of tradition. The movement, in Bebbington's view, was distinguished from traditionalists of the established church, who demanded conformity to church order and inherited doctrine. From the outset, therefore, the movement was pragmatic and deeply concerned with social issues.

43. Bebbington, *Evangelicalism*, 119. By 1825, Thomas Chalmers, an evangelical leading the charge of mission in the inner cities, had set in motion a system of lay visitation aimed at alleviating the problems of the inner cities through counsel.

44. Peter Hillis ("Presbyterianism and Social Class in Mid-Nineteenth Century Glasgow: A Study of Nine Churches," *Journal of Ecclesiastical History* 32 [1981]: 48–49) includes within the working class artisans (engineers, smiths, boiler makers, etc.) and unskilled workers (porters, chimney sweeps, laborers, etc.).

45. Finlay defines "respectable culture" as "the value system which was used by members of the Scottish working class to differentiate themselves from those who were deemed 'unrespectable' or 'rough'" (Richard Finlay, "Respectable Culture," in Lynch, ed., *The Oxford Companion to Scottish History*, 522–23 [522]). Through "temperance, thrift, hard work, religiosity, and self-improvement, members of the respectable working class sought to create a stable social environment for themselves and their families" (p. 522). Bebbington (*Evangelicalism*, 126) concurs: respectability, in his view, was the "kernel of high Victorian values"; "education, religion, virtue, industry, sobriety and frugality" were the hallmarks of that culture. Noteworthy is the close connection between moral and material improvement in both Finlay's and Bebbington's descriptions of the culture.

culture." Idleness and the unproductive use of time and resources were the greatest detriments to progress. Given this context, Smith's unexpected focus on the industry of the fieldworker in the aforementioned story of the Levite and his concubine (Judg 19:16) is hardly strange.

The penchant for self-improvement within the working class was an infusion of middle-class values, which were a result of an upwardly mobile agenda as the middle class sought a share of the privileges that had long been monopolized by the upper classes.[46] Towards this end, the expanding middle class, buoyed by the fruits of recent industrialization, came to espouse an ethic of material improvement through industry and the sound management of resources. Within this perspective, acts of philanthropy that would dampen the incentive to thrift and hard work were anathema.[47] Dependence on charity was to be regarded a greater shame than inertia. Philanthropists sponsored programs promoting "rational recreation," the term designating activities incorporating the values of

46. Maver, "Urban Society," 627. The specifics of the struggle of the middle class against the landed upper class shall be described below. The hierarchy within churches reflects the close connection between the values of industry and managerial acumen and middle (and upper) class society. A study of leadership in nine churches by Peter Hillis ("Presbyterianism and Social Class," 47–64) reveals that social ascendancy was linked closely with election to leadership. While the working class made up the majority of church members, this socio-economic segment had minimal representation in kirk sessions; the leadership was drawn, almost exclusively, from the middle and upper classes. Hillis cites the example of Alexander Gilmour who rose from "grain-weigher and store-keeper" in 1841 to proprietor of his own firm by 1859. Of interest is Gilmour's election to leadership at the United Presbyterian Church in Glasgow as an accompaniment to his rise in social status (Hillis, "Presbyterianism," 51). In speaking of the requirements for election to leadership in the church, the *Christian Journal* (a notable publication of the Relief Church cited by Hillis) states concerning worthy candidates for leadership in the church: "From the manner in which some view the secular affairs of churches, they would deal with them on the same principles as they would any other money affairs, and suppose that anyone qualified to collect and disburse money for any sort of object has the requisite qualification to manage this concern of a church" (Hillis, "Presbyterianism," 53). The sound practice of management, the responsible allocation of resources, thus may be seen to be the common characteristic of value for ascendancy within both church and society. That ascendancy to ecclesiastical leadership often entailed induction to the middle class bespeaks the source of the aforementioned requisite qualities for advancement: the classes already amply represented in church leadership. Finlay goes as far as to suggest that the values of leadership were foisted upon the working class by the middle class in order to create a "pliable and docile workforce" (Finlay, "Respectable Culture," 522). Ironically, the value espoused within working-class reform was one that would carry one beyond the confines of that class.

47. Bebbington, *Evangelicalism*, 121; Finlay, "Respectable Culture," 522–23.

"respectable culture."[48] The pursuit of "rational recreation" fostered the creation of libraries, parks, museums, and athletic facilities. The activities surrounding such venues became counter-measures to the activities of "rough culture": the unabated consumption of alcohol, spirited participation in anti-authoritarian demonstrations, rioting, bare-knuckle boxing, cockfighting, pigeon racing, dog racing, and the gambling that almost always surrounded these sporting events.[49] In place of such activities, "rational recreation" envisioned the inculcation of discipline and spiritual elevation through, among other things, instruction in music and the cultivation of flowers and prize vegetables. Furthermore, the accumulation of knowledge held a position of pride within this ideological framework, and libraries, parks and art galleries were the favored venues of "rational recreation" as opposed to time spent in public houses.[50] Women were encouraged to attend to the details of domestic duty, even as the cleanliness of a home became measure of a household's adherence to the cult of discipline and self-improvement. Within such a vision for self-edification and social advancement, the economic inertia of the hill country of Ephraim (Judg 18:1–31), from the perspective of Smith, would serve well as a negative example.[51] Equally reprehensible are the misdirected interests and indolence of Laish, attitudes which Smith

48. "Rational recreation," the set of activities conceived to express and engender the values of "respectable culture" (see above), these values and activities stands in contradistinction to the activities of "rough culture" (see below).

49. On "rough culture," see W. Hamish Fraser, "Rough Culture," in Lynch, ed., *The Oxford Companion to Scottish History*, 531–32. Apart from fairs and sporting events, the public house was the favored venue for the varied expressions of "rough culture." According to Fraser, the public houses had lost their function as establishments for dining by the 1840s, and become male-dominated places of intemperate behavior and debauchery (Fraser, "Rough Culture," 531). The disorder often spilt out into the streets. Edinburgh (in 1792 and 1796) and Glasgow (in 1819 and 1821) witnessed widespread destruction and rioting. By the early nineteenth century, the context for Smith's book, public opinion held in disdain the multifarious expressions of "rough culture" because of such outbreaks of disorderly conduct. Peter Bailey's study of public policy in Victorian England (*Leisure and Class in Victorian England: Rational Recreation and the Contest for Control, 1830–1885* [London: Routledge & Kegan Paul, 1978], 36) observes similar concerns about English working-class culture in the nineteenth century. While rational recreation stemmed from a basic humanitarian concern, the middle class was concerned also with "the problem of containing the 'dangerous classes', that indeterminate but volatile menace that lurked in the rookeries of the big cities."

50. Maver, "Urban Society," 628.

51. Smith, *Battles*, 89.

thought could lead only to economic hardship.[52] Unlike the culpable parties in these stories, the working class had to realize its responsibility in forging improvement. Smith's interests in reading scripture were in line with those of "respectable culture."

The alliance of ecclesiastical (specifically, evangelical) interests and middle-class values and aspirations was founded on the grip of the land-owning upper class on the election of ministers for the Church of Scotland (the practice of patronage). This espousal of upper-class interests from the pulpit and its promotion in church policy caused great apprehension outside the highest echelons of Scottish society. Beginning in the late seventeenth century, efforts to abolish the practice of patronage ended without enduring success.[53] With the emergence of a robust middle class on the heels of industrialization by the early nineteenth century, the middle class gained the financial and political capital to effect change through political channels. This initiative for change was coupled with the evangelical emphasis on conversion, piety and zealous pastoral ministry among the working class. Promoters of middle-class political aspirations portrayed the land-owning upper class as a barrier to social and economic progress, especially among the working class. In 1834, the General Assembly of the Church of Scotland was persuaded to pass an act to restore the popular right to veto a patron's nomination to fill a parish vacancy.[54] Concern for the plight of the working class became synonymous with the quest to pry the church apart from upper-class interests.[55] While the measure to set limits on the influence of the

52. Ibid., 91.

53. For a concise description of the issue of patronage leading up to disruption in the Church of Scotland in the nineteenth century, see Stewart Brown, "The Disruption," in Lynch, ed., *The Oxford Companion to Scottish History*, 170–72. The festering issue of patronage became the reason for several movements to secede from the Church of Scotland from 1733 onwards (e.g. the Secession Church; the Relief Church). Prior to the formation of the Secession Church and the Relief Church, efforts were made, without success, at the Reformation to abolish patronage. In 1690, zealous Presbyterians were able to persuade the Scottish parliament to remove the practice, and to replace it with a system of election in sessions of the kirk. However, despite protests from the Church of Scotland, the British parliament restored the practice in 1712, and the problem persisted through the eighteenth century (Brown, "The Disruption," 171).

54. Ibid., 171–72.

55. The alienation of the working class from the established practices of many churches could be perceived in the simplest of matters. Hillis ("Presbyterianism," 56–59) cites the financial burdens of church membership (Sabbath collections), expectations of proper dress and the lack of free seating (the practice of charging

upper class in ecclesiastical policy in 1834 was successful, Scotland's Court of Session pronounced the Veto Act illegal in 1839. The evangelicals withdrew from the established church in 1843, and founded the Free Church of Scotland. Within five years, riding the crest of popular support, the new church had over 700 congregations, 500 primary schools, a college, and an active home and foreign mission. The established church, meanwhile, had receded to being a minority establishment, commanding the adherence of a mere third of Scotland's church-going population.[56]

Thus, a growing segment of the church in Scotland, hitched to the particular political interests of the middle class, broke the stronghold of the land-owning upper class upon the church in nineteenth-century Scotland. From the view of evangelicals, the Church of Scotland, with its upper-class interests, was ill equipped to deal with the social problems arising from industrialization. The injustice of a church under the sway of the landed upper class and its neglect of working-class concerns was an easy connection to forge. Patronage and the working-class woes were one and the same problem. The result was a blend of middle-class Liberalism and Presbyterian evangelicalism, a blend which, according to Maver, was a concoction that gave "spiritual credibility" to the advancement of the middle-class social ethic through the construction of public amenities that sponsor the activities consonant with the cult of self-improvement.[57] Within the framework of a reformation in church and

---

rent for the better seats in churches was a common means of financial support for churches) as deterrents to working-class attendance at church. All this, coupled with the fact that the majority of church discipline constituted a middle-class assault upon vices associated with the working class, created a formidable barrier for the working class. The situation was similar in nineteenth-century industrial cities in England (E. R. Wickham, *Church and People in an Industrial City* [London: Lutterworth, 1957], 90–91, 110–11).

56. Brown, "Disruption," 172. Noteworthy is the fact that the seceding churches varied little from the Church of Scotland in theology (I. G. C. Hutchison, *A Political History of Scotland, 1832–1924: Parties, Elections and Issues* [Edinburgh: John Donald, 1986], 16). Evangelical concerns did not extend beyond the matters of patronage and the failures of the established church in countering the socio-economic problems posed by rapid industrialization. In light of the last factor, the energy for reform propounded by evangelicals was strongest in the cities (Hutchison, *Political History*, 16).

57. Maver, "Urban Society," 627–28. Liberalism as a political movement, according to Maver, came to reflect middle-class values, and was closely associated with Presbyterian evangelicalism. In the nineteenth and the twentieth centuries, Liberalism championed women's suffrage, free trade, the establishment of a minimum wage, social insurance, land reform and the abolition of patronage. The lower middle class and the working class were the main beneficiaries of Liberal political

society, the idea of rational recreation was born, a "dualistic ideology
that blended moral redemption with material improvement."[58] Good
theology, founded upon correct biblical interpretation, was to be the
catalyst behind the movement. This view was alien to the interests of the
Church of Scotland under the auspices of the land-owning upper class. If
the church was to be effective in tackling the social issues of urban
Scotland in the nineteenth century, then patronage had to be defeated. In
such manner, the push for a redistribution of power and privilege within
church and society became inextricably linked with orthodox Christian
practice working its way through working-class social reform.

Eliza Smith's book fits well within the increasingly dominant middle-
class, evangelical ethos of the early nineteenth century. Within this
socio-historical framework, Grandfather's propensity for seeking out
models of industry and responsible living in biblical narrative finds its
place. Even the narrative frames around the stories from scripture dwell
upon these themes. An idyllic weekend at Grandfather's house involved
having the children shuttle between domestic duties, garden work, and
catechism.[59] Care of the soul and the environment permeate much of the
narrative outside Grandfather's storytelling. In line with the middle-class
evangelical perspective of the time, the good life is to be found in self-
improvement through productive labor. Through Smith's interpretation,
Bible reading is the beginning of this ethical trajectory.

Conclusion

Eliza Smith's *The Battles of the Bible* emphasizes the Christian virtues of
a firm belief in the goodness and justice of God. Where the stories of the
Bible might suggest a different view of God, she defends the integrity of
God with creative imagination. For Smith, faith in God finds expression
through unwavering adherence to divine direction and courage in the
face of conflict. The products of such steadfast faith are humility, a
disdain for brash action, industry, and patience in the face of persecution.

From our location as readers, the attention to industry as a virtue,
seeking it in places where labor is of marginal import in the biblical text,
is unique. This feature of her work reflects a middle-class evangelical
Christian attitude regarding the ill effects of rapid industrialization on
Scotland's cities in the early nineteenth century. Within this context,

strategy. For a brief description of Liberalism in Scotland, see I. G. C. Hutchison,
"Liberalism," in Lynch, ed., *The Oxford Companion to Scottish History*, 386–87.

58. Maver, "Urban Society," 627–28.

59. Smith, *Battles*, 2–4, 15, 63–64, 314–15, et al.

Smith's high regard for the authority of Scripture, insistence upon fidelity to the Christian God, and attention to industry and self-improvement among Christians find their place. It is nothing less than a thoughtful response to a specific set of circumstances facing the church in urban Scotland.

"MISS GRESWELL HONED OUR HEBREW AT OXFORD": REFLECTIONS ON JOANA J. GRESWELL AND HER BOOK *GRAMMATICAL ANALYSIS OF THE HEBREW PSALTER* (1873)

J. Glen Taylor

Background to Greswell's Grammatical Analysis of the Hebrew Psalter

Introduction

This essay considers Joana Julia Greswell, an accomplished (though marginalized) Oxford Hebraist[1] of the nineteenth century, and her extraordinary book, *Grammatical Analysis of the Hebrew Psalter*.[2] Only through the endorsement of her book by the famous scholar-churchmen J. J. S. Perowne[3] and R. Payne Smith[4] was Greswell's book taken from the shadows of patriarchy and put to use as a textbook of Hebrew for divinity students at Oxford and elsewhere. In writing such a book Greswell joined the distinguished company of her uncle Edward Greswell (1797–1869), a well-known biblical scholar who wrote books on the Gospels and biblical chronology that were similarly used as texts at

---

1. J. J. Greswell's relation to Oxford University was obviously not that of an academic appointee; she resided in Oxford, was the daughter of an Oxford Tutor and Dean, and her book was used in the classrooms of Oxford University.

2. Oxford: James Parker & Co., 1873.

3. J. J. S. Perowne, Canon of Llandaff, is best known for his commentary on the Psalms, often reprinted: J. J. Stewart Perowne, *The Book of Psalms: A New Translation with Introductions and Notes Explanatory and Critical* (London: Bell & Daldy, 1864). Unless otherwise noted, quotations of Perowne in this paper come from the fourth revised edition of 1878, as reprinted by Zondervan. Greswell herself used the second revised edition of 1871 (Greswell, *Grammatical Analysis*, iv).

4. R. Payne Smith (1818–1895) is best known for his *Thesaurus Syriacus* (2 vols.; Oxford: Clarendon, 1879–1901). A condensed English translation of this was prepared after his death by his daughter Jessie (Mrs. Margoliouth) under the title *A Compendious Syriac Dictionary founded upon the Thesaurus Syriacus* (Oxford: Clarendon, 1903).

Oxford.[5] In testimony to its enduring usefulness, Greswell's *Grammatical Analysis* has been downloaded almost 600 times since becoming available online through the University of Toronto in 2006.[6] The words of a recent blogger no doubt resonate with the experience of many students of Hebrew in the late nineteenth century: "Julia Greswell's Grammatical Analysis of the Hebrew Psalter, 1873, has been the perfect companion to my studies...in the Hebrew Psalter."[7]

Biographical Information
Little is known about Julia Greswell. Much more is known of her uncle and grandfather, both famous scholars, and of her father.[8] Many details of her life can nonetheless be inferred from the biographical information on her male relatives and gleaned from other sources, such as census reports.[9]

Joana Julia Greswell was born in 1838 to the Reverend Richard Greswell and to Joana Julia Armetriding. Having the same first name as her mother, the daughter was known as "Julia." She was one of only two children, the other being a younger sister by three years: Helen Margaret Greswell.

The Greswell girls had in their father an ideal tutor, not the least because he himself had been exceptionally well tutored by his own father, the Reverend William Parr Greswell (1756–1854). Of him, Richard Greswell's biographer writes:

> William Parr Greswell was a man of great acquirement and of solid learn-
> ing. A considerable author, too, he was... But his greatest work by far
> was authorship of another kind. It may be questioned whether another
> instance could be found of a father (who beginning life as he did with a

---

5. Edward Greswell's books on these topics (in Latin) include, *Dissertations on the Principles and Arrangement of an Harmony of the Gospels* (Oxford: Oxford University Press, 1830), and *Introduction to the Tables of the Fasti Catholici, Both the General and the Supplementary* (Oxford: Oxford University Press, 1852).

6. "Grammatical Analysis of the Psalter," n.p. (cited August, 2009). Online: http://www.archive.org/details/analysispsalter00gresuoft.

7. Suzanne McCarthy, "Julia Greswell," n.p. (cited August, 2009). Online: http://powerscourt.blogspot.com/2008/04/julia-greswell.html. It is on the basis of such present-day-student endorsements that I have taken license to imagine the similar endorsement contained in the title to the present essay.

8. For a biographical essay on Richard Greswell in which his daughters are mentioned, see John William Burton, *Lives of Twelve Good Men* (2 vols.; London: J. Murray, 1889), 2:93–121.

9. I am indebted to David Horrock, a former student, for drawing my attention to the online resource "UK Census." Online: www.ukcenusonline.com.

miserable pittance of 50£. a year) could yet boast of having trained and sent up to the University, (after in part educating,) five sons, every one of whom achieved high honours, and obtained a Fellowship—viz., at Balliol, at Corpus, at Oriel, at Brasenose, and at Worcester respectively.[10]

It is not hard to imagine Julia's father Richard putting his two girls through paces of learning similar to those he had received at the hands of his own father. Indeed, Richard Greswell's biographer explicitly states that Richard "had himself superintended" the education of Julia and her younger sister.[11] The designation of a census-taker for the year 1851 was probably more true for Julia and Helen than for most if not all other girls at Oxford—"scholar at home"![12]

Information about the girls' father, Richard, also provides important background knowledge on Julia Greswell. Julia's father was born on July 22nd, 1800 in Denton, Lancashire, where his father was perpetual curate. Richard's siblings were such that Julia had on her father's side six uncles and two aunts.[13] Richard was recognized at a young age for his special aptitude for accounting mathematics, but when his two older brothers William and Edward received honors at Oxford, Richard was directed to apply at Worcester College, where he won a fellowship designated for a clergy child. Richard won the fellowship and went on to attain a double-first class (along with a classmate, the later famous biblical scholar Dr. Pusey). Richard Greswell became Assistant Tutor at Worcester in 1822, Full Tutor in 1823 and Dean in 1825.[14] Testimonials of his students attest to his mastery of the Greek of Euclid, to his being an able teacher of rhetoric and ethics, and to his brilliance at mathematics.[15] Richard was by

10. Burton, *Lives of Twelve Good Men*, 2:94. (The last word "respectively" cannot be taken to mean that Richard, who attended Worcester, was the youngest. Burton goes on to clarify that Richard was the fourth among seven brothers.)

11. Ibid., 2:121.

12. Of Julia the census records for the address of 21 Beaumont Street, St. Mary Magdalene, Oxford: "Joana J. Greswell Dau[ghter] Unm[arried] F[emale] [Age] 13 Scholar at Home Oxford." "1851 Census," n.p. (cited August, 2009). Online: http://www.ukcensusonline.com.

13. Richard's older brothers were: Thomas Haemer (1795–1819), who, though young, succeeded his uncle as Master of Chetham Hospital School; William (1796–1876), rector of Kilve and a fellow at Balliol College; and Richard (1797–1867), fellow at Corpus Christi College. Richard's younger brothers were Charles (1802–1844), a physician; Francis Hague (1802–1830), also a fellow at an Oxford College; and Clement (1809–1882), rector of Tortworth and a fellow of Oriel College. Neither of the two daughters is named in my source (Burton, *Lives of Twelve Good Men*, 2:94–95 n. 2).

14. Ibid., 2:96.

15. Ibid., 2:96–98.

nature shy and appeared to be very nervous when teaching, so much so that he seldom if ever preached. One of Richard's professors, the Reverend John Miller, commended Richard for his aptitude as a student, noting his "perseverance, modesty and dutifilness."[16] Other reports on the character of Julia's father consistently mention his "childlike simplicity of character" and his "utter guilelessness of disposition."[17] To this his biographer adds, "at Oxford...this friend ever seemed to me, more than any of his fellows, to stand apart—to stand alone."[18] These character traits no doubt helped Julia and Helen to nurse with untiring dedication a beloved father in his later years, despite his failing mind. He died peacefully at the family home on 39 St Giles Street in Oxford on June 22nd, 1885, his 85th birthday.

Richard Greswell's legacy was to be "the saviour of the cause of Church Education in England," a title that aptly describes his monumental political and benefactory efforts to oppose the secularization of education in England, an endeavor he began at age thirty-five.[19]

Richard Greswell's advocacy to continue the Church of England's influence in English schools raises the matter of the Greswell family's religious outlook. Julia's father and his family were traditional Anglo-Catholic Anglicans, much of whose scholarly and churchly efforts were directed against stemming the tide of theological liberalism in England and abroad. For example, uncle Edward, an Anglican clergyman, defended traditional views about the Bible in the face of perceived opponents such as Renn Dickson Hampden and the Pentateuchal iconoclast Bishop Colenso.[20] Not being a writer, Richard's commitment to preserve the faith came through his classroom teaching, political advocacy and active involvement in the Tractarian movement (up to the time it became no longer exclusively Anglican).[21] Since Richard's weekly attendance at St. Mary's church on Sundays has been recorded, Julia's may be assumed as well.[22]

16. Ibid., 2:95.
17. Ibid., 2:93. Burton notes these traits as widely held; cf. ibid., 2:118–19.
18. Ibid., 2:94.
19. For a description of the situation and Greswell's role in addressing it, see ibid., 2:99–110; for more on the former, see also Richard Brown, *Church and State in Modern Britain, 1700–1850* (London: Routledge, 1991), 259–60.
20. Hampden (1793–1868) was accused of heresy by Tractarians; despite controversy surrounding his theology, he was elected and consecrated bishop of Hereford in 1848. John William Colenso (1814–1888), bishop of Natal, was controversial for his views on biblical criticism.
21. Burton, *Lives of Twelve Good Men*, 99.
22. Ibid., 119.

Julia Greswell's conservative Anglo-Catholic background comes through in her book not by way of making attempts to defend the Psalter against potentially problematic views,[23] but mostly by including in her short introductions to each Psalm the season of the Church Year in which a Psalm is featured.

Several other details help to flesh out the life of one whose own biography should have been written. Julia Greswell's parents were married on April 5th, 1836 at St. Mary Magdalene Church, Oxford. Julia's mother was the daughter of the Reverend James Armitriding (1750–1832). There are hints that the family was well off; Richard Greswell was described as "bountiful...even munificent" and is said to have allocated his entire wages to charity.[24] In support of the notion that the family had wealth, the census of 1851 records the names of a governess and four household servants. In 1854 the family moved to 39 St. Giles, Oxford, where Julia's father resided until his death.[25] It was certainly at the Beaumont Street house that Greswell was taught her languages; such study no doubt continued in the other home as well. (These languages include Hebrew and Greek, of which she had expert knowledge, along with Latin, French, and German; Welsh and Aramaic are quite possible, whereas her knowledge of Sanskrit and Italian is not clear.) Curiously, a census taken in 1871 has Greswell's mother and a sister living in Mathon, Worcestershire. Given that there was a spa nearby at Great Malvern, her mother may have moved there for health reasons, as it was not long after this, in 1875, that her mother died. Two years before her book was published, then, Julia Greswell was living at St. Giles with no sibling and only one parent: her scholar father. Julia continued to live at 39 St. Giles until some time between 1891 and 1901, by which time she lived at 70 Woodstock Road in Oxford. The comment "living on own means" beside her name and address (and that of her sister Helen with whom she lived) in the census both of 1891 and of 1901, implies that she was financially comfortable later in life. Sales from her book may have helped her financially. According to the Registry Office of Headington, Joana Julia Greswell died in 1906. She is likely buried alongside her parents, whose

23. For example, unlike Horsley, she makes no attempt to reconcile the statement at the end of Ps 72, "here end the prayers of David the son of Jesse," with the continuance of Davidic Psalms later in the Psalter. Horsley offers the unlikely explanation that the statement refers only to Ps 72; Samuel Horsley, *The Book of Psalms, translated from the Hebrew, with notes, explanatory and critical* (2 vols.; London: F. C. & J. Rivington, 1815), 2:195.

24. Burton, *Lives of Twelve Good Men*, 98, 114. When possible, R. Greswell secretly gave away money.

25. Ibid., 120.

graves are in the churchyard of St. Mary Magdalene, Oxford, near the Martyr's Memorial.[26]

It is on the last two pages of Richard Greswell's biography that mention is made of Greswell's pride in his daughters, especially Julia. The biographer Burton writes of the daughters,

> [of] whose attainments and graces he was not without reason proud. The elder [daughter] is in fact one of England's learned ladies, being an excellent Greek and Hebrew scholar. Many a time has her father told me with earnest joy which book of the Aeneid, or of the Illiad, 'Julia had finished that morning.' Her Grammatical Analysis was much commended by learned men. Dr. Pusey praised it.[27]

It is perhaps no surprise that Greswell was motivated to write a text that would be of help to students at Oxford, for her uncle had similarly written works of biblical scholarship that were designed (at least in part) to help Anglican ordinands at Oxford.[28] Seeing a need for students to receive help in learning Hebrew, she wrote this practical help on reading the Psalms in Hebrew.

Greswell's Preface to the Volume
Greswell attributes the idea of writing her grammatical analysis of the Hebrew Psalter to S. P. Tregelles, L.L.D., who wrote a similar analysis of the first four chapters of Genesis and the eighth chapter of Proverbs.[29]

---

26. Burton, *Lives of Twelve Good Men*, 2:121.

27. Ibid., 2:120–21.

28. Julia Greswell's uncle was the relatively well-known biblical scholar Edward Greswell (1797–1869). After being schooled at home, Julia's Uncle Edward later attended the Manchester grammar school. His post-secondary education consisted of a B.A., M.A. and a B.D., all earned at Corpus Christi College, Oxford. Corpus Christi College later employed Edward as a tutor, junior dean, the librarian and then vice-president. He later turned down the offer of becoming President so as not to detract him from his scholarship. Julia's Uncle Edward Greswell taught both Latin and Greek at Corpus Christi. Perhaps significant as a source of inspiration for Julia Greswell, her Uncle Edward's books on the chronology of the Bible and on the principles and arrangement of the Gospels (1830) were used as texts at Oxford. Other works of her Uncle Edward include an exposition of the Parables and other parts of the Gospels (six volumes), and a book on the works of John Milton. He was interested also in correlating sacred and "profane" means of measuring time, such as ancient-secular calendars, ante-diluvian and post-diluvian traditions and natural means of reckoning time.

29. Wilhelm Gesenius, *Gesenius's Hebrew and Chaldee Lexicon to the Old Testament Scriptures, Translated, with Additions and Corrections from the Author's Thesaurus and Other Works* (trans. Samuel Prideaux Tregelles; London: Samuel

Unlike Tregelles, though, Greswell did not provide an interlinear translation.[30] She did, however, provide a still-useful index of each word in the Psalter with chapter and verse, with a page reference to the place where she identifies and discusses the word.[31] Regarding her work, she writes:

> Its object is to give an exact grammatical analysis of every word in the Book of Psalms, in accordance with the principles laid down in the most recent Hebrew grammars. To this are added (as far as I have been able to discover them) the cognate words in various languages, i.e. Sanskrit, Greek, Latin, German, Anglo-Saxon, and English. I have in several places noticed the various renderings of the LXX, Vulgate, Chaldee, Arabic, Syriac, and Aethiopic Versions, taken principally from Rogers' Work on the Psalms.[32]

She comments briefly on the introductions she provides to each psalm:

> At the commencement of each Psalm is a short introduction, containing a very brief statement of its subject and of the circumstances under which it was probably composed. In many of the later Psalms I have noticed the Chaldaisms which point to a somewhat late era in the history of the Chosen People.[33]

The only other thing she adds to the introductions are, occasionally, features she finds peculiar or fascinating, such as:

- "Psalms xviii and lxviii contain an unusually large number of ἅπαξ λεγόμενα..."[34]

Bagster & Sons, 1859). Her familiarity with, and implied respect for, S. P. Tregelles, make it that much more likely that, in addition to using Gesenius's three-volume Latin *Thesaurus*, she also consulted the smaller compendium of Gesenius, entitled *Lexicon Manuale*, translated into English (and sanitized of implications of heterodoxy) by Tregelles. Indeed, her use of this shorter English work seems to be confirmed by a clear case in which Greswell draws from Gesenius *as edited by Tregelles*: in Ps 22:17 Greswell states that, to make sense, "like a lion" would be "a very strange ellipsis," an almost word-for-word supplemental comment of *Tragelles* to Gesenius's discussion (Gesenius, *Lexicon*, ccclxxxviii). On the highly complex redactional history of Gesenius's lexicon, see F. W. Danker, *Multipurpose Tools for Bible Study* (2d ed.; Minneapolis: Fortress, 1993), 95–99.

30. In this respect she bucked the trend of not only Tregelles, but of several other sources as well (e.g. Rogers, Jebb, and Horsley).

31. Greswell, *Grammatical Analysis*, 269–92.

32. Ibid., iv. The book to which she refers is that by J. Rogers, M.A. Canon Residentiary of Exeter Cathedral, who wrote ספר תהלים *The Book of Psalms in Hebrew* (Oxford: J. H. Parker, 1848).

33. Greswell, *Grammatical Analysis*, p. iv.

34. The Greek expression "*hapax legomena*" means words that occur only once (in the Old Testament).

- "the word *sabachthani*[35] used by Our Blessed Lord at His Cruci-fixion, is not *the actual* word which occurs in Ps. xxii, but the equiva-lent of it in the Aramaean dialect then in use among the Jews…"
- "Ps. li contains a verse of only *seven* words in the original, but which cannot be rendered in English by less than *one and twenty* or *two and twenty* words…"[36]

These peculiarities being quite pedestrian, they perhaps reflect on Greswell's status as an amateur Hebraist and a lack of depth that often accompanies it. However, while she was an amateur in the technical sense, Greswell divulges philological and exegetical interests of a deeper nature in her grammar. Here, then, she is likely whetting the appetites of her students for the uneasy philological journey upon which they are about to embark.

Finally, Greswell acknowledges the "works which have been most useful to me, and from which I have most largely borrowed": "Perowne, Phillips, Jebb, Bishop Horsley, Kay, Rogers, Coleman, Hengstenberg, Delitzsch, and Bythner."[37] To these commentators she adds the lexico-graphical works of Gesenius and Fürst, the former of which she was right to prefer for explanations of derivation.[38] She also referred to the com-mentary of Hupfeld.[39]

After her Preface, Greswell offers brief "Introductory Remarks" (see pp. vi–vii). In them she discusses the five-book structure of the Psalter, Davidic and other ascriptions, and variations in the occurrence of the words YHWH and Elohim. Unlike several of the introductions to the Psalms in her sources, she has no discussion of parallelism.[40] A one-page list of abbreviations follows.

35.   "Thou hast forsaken me" (from Jesus' famous question from the cross to his Father).

36.   Ibid.

37.   She provides the full bibliographic information for each work in separate footnotes (Greswell, *Grammatical Analysis*, iv). Despite the authors not being listed alphabetically, the order of listing does not appear to reflect the extent of her indebtedness to these sources.

38.   Greswell, *Grammatical Analysis*, v. Fürst's *Schul–Wörterbuch* was never considered authoritative in the manner of Gesenius. It was a (large) pocket-sized book, the mid-nineteenth-century equivalent to Karl Feyerabend's *Langenscheidt's Hebrew/English Dictionary to the Old Testament* (11th ed.; Berlin: Langenscheidt, 1959).

39.   Hermann Hupfeld, *Die Psalmen* (Gotha: F. A. Pethes, 1855–60).

40.   Parallelism was an especial emphasis of Jebb, who thought himself a key player in the discussion of parallelism and whose remarks still repay attention. Discussions of parallelism are especially apropos where, unlike Greswell, an author provides a translation of the Psalms.

The All-Important Endorsements

The first words of Greswell's book are striking and, to present-day sensibilities, painful: "I fear that it will be thought presumptuous in a Lady to undertake to write a work, the professed intention of which is to afford assistance to Beginners in the Study of Hebrew." These words, appearing in an "Advertisement," point not to the presumption of a woman offering formal instruction to men, but to the more base-level inherent unlikelihood of a "Lady" being learned enough to assist even beginners in such a field of study.[41] She continues:

> It is, therefore, in the way of self-defence against any such charge of presumption, that I am induced to prefix to my volume the accompanying Letters, which have been received by my Father, the Rev. Richard Greswell, from two very distinguished Hebrew Scholars, who have been pleased to express their opinion concerning the probable usefulness of my 'Grammatical Analysis of the Hebrew Psalter.'[42]

Whether either of the expressions—"self-defence," "induced"—or that endorsements were sent to her father—go beyond propriety to convey a sense of frustration, humiliation, or injustice is difficult to know from Greswell's other remarks in her apology for the book. In any event, Greswell concludes her Advertisement with her full name—JOANA JULIA GRESWELL—and not just her initials as at the end of the preface.

The two letters of endorsement, which follow the Advertisment in Greswell's book, are from R. Payne Smith, and J. J. Stewart Perowne. Both scholars heartily endorse the book and applaud Greswell's careful work. More specifically, Smith thought the work would "prove a great boon to students preparing for the Divinity Schools at Oxford, and generally to those who wish to learn Hebrew."[43] Not only would Greswell's work assist future Anglican priests, it would also be helpful for anyone

---

41. Of course there was the reality that women had less access to formal education than men, but there is likely more to the comment; as Marion Ann Taylor has shown, there were many women of biblical (and other) learning who obtained an excellent education by informal means, as in the case, for example, of many daughters of professors and clergymen who were schooled at home with their father's library at hand. See, for example, Marion Ann Taylor, "Reading the Psalms through the Eyes of Nineteenth-Century Women," in *Interpreting the Psalms for Teaching and Preaching* (ed. D. Brent Sandy and Herbert Bateman IV; St. Louis: Chalice, forthcoming); idem, "Anglican Women and the Bible in Nineteenth-century Britain," *Anglican & Episcopal History* 75 (2006): 527–52; and Christiana de Groot and Marion Ann Taylor, eds., *Recovering Nineteenth-Century Women Interpreters of the Bible* (Atlanta: Society of Biblical Literature, 2007).

42. Greswell, *Grammatical Analysis*, [a1].

43. Ibid., n.p.

who wished to learn Hebrew. Smith thought that Greswell's book would "make the acquisition of Hebrew so much more easy," that it might induce "a larger proportion of them [students and younger clergy] to study that language in which so large a part of the Scripture is written."[44] Perowne noted that Greswell's work filled a gap in textbooks for those studying Hebrew: "There are, I believe, very few books of the kind. Bythner's Lyra is antiquated. Bishop Ollivant's Analysis of the History of Joseph is out of print; so, too, is Robertson's *Clavis Pentateuchi*; and yet I know of nothing to take the place of these works."[45] Perowne further thought that theology in England would benefit from language study: "Theology in England will grow stronger and richer in proportion as the Old Testament, as well as the New, is studied in the Original."

We may wish now that Greswell could have published her work without thinking it necessary to have it endorsed by scholars like Smith and Perowne. However, these two letters do provide contemporary scholarly reactions to the work, which aid in our assessment of it from the twenty-first century.

Key Issues Pertaining to Pedagogy, Philology, and Interpretation

Pedagogy

Greswell's book was, and continues to be, useful as a tool for learning and improving one's knowledge of Biblical Hebrew and of the Hebrew of the Psalter in particular. Unlike today, when sophisticated Bible software parses a grammatical form with the wave of a cursor, these were times when identifying grammatical forms was a chore. As is still the case with the Brown–Driver–Briggs incarnation of Gesenius's work,[46] words were not listed according to the form in which they appear in the Hebrew text, but under their root. Prior to the advent of Einspahr's Index to BDB in 1976,[47] students could look forward to spending countless hours rummaging through the lexicon, looking for words listed only by their root—so that one already had to know the derivation of a word to find it!

44. Ibid.
45. Ibid.
46. Francis Brown, S. R. Driver, and Charles A. Briggs, eds., *A Hebrew and English Lexicon of the Old Testament* (Oxford: Oxford University Press, 1906 [and many reprints]).
47. Bruce Einspahr, *Index to Brown, Driver & Briggs Hebrew Lexicon* (Chicago: Moody, 1976).

As Payne Smith's endorsing statement, "usually one does not much approve of works intended to save trouble," perhaps intimates, professors whose knowledge of Hebrew has become second nature are not always sympathetic to just how much trouble students can have looking up forms. Greswell seems inherently to have recognized that time could better be spent telling the student what the form was and how they could more readily identify the form next time through her review of grammar. Without such helps as Greswell offered, the correctly parsed form was so elusive a target as to discourage students from remaining with their study of Hebrew long enough to gain competency at it. For all but the sharpest minds, Greswell's book was no doubt a godsend to students of Hebrew; any suspicion that students might simply lift the forms without learning them was far outweighed by the hope that her book brought—that Hebrew could be learned and had rules that could be demonstrated and reinforced.[48]

A few examples from Julia Greswell's Grammatical Analysis serve more specifically to demonstrate its pedagogical merits:

> *Psalm1:1*: הָאִישׁ the-man subst. m. irreg. with the art. א not admitting Dagesh, (ַ) of the art. is lengthened into (ָ); pl. אִישִׁים only found three times, Ps. cxli. 4, Prov. viii. 4, and Is. liii. 3, but instead of it is commonly used אֲנָשִׁים from the obsolete אֱנשׁ. That same word is also used of things without life.[49]

To be sure, some philological errors appear that will be considered below, but none that the time did not own. More to the point being made

48. A review article came to light late in the preparation of the present study that corroborates this view. The reviewer, admonishing clergy to persevere with their Hebrew, writes: "The difficulty will be to get the time every day to make the first mastery. Perhaps only a few moments can be spared, and precious time is lost in turning over the leaves of grammar and dictionary, and hunting out the particular form or meaning wanted, from the middle of a crowded column or page. Just here is where Miss Greswell's little book will be found an invaluable and long-needed help. With this in his hand, and his Hebrew Psalter open before him, the student will need no other book of reference. Special points can be examined with the aid of larger works, as time may serve; but with this alone, a few moments daily will suffice to make known the translation and derivation of every word in every Psalm" (John McDowell Leavitt, Review of Joana Julia Greswell, *Grammatical Analysis of the Hebrew Psalter, American Church Review* [April 26, 1874]: 312–14 [312]).

49. Greswell's abbreviations, used in this article, are as follows: adv. = adverb; art. = article; com. = common (i.e. masculine and feminine); constr. = construct; convers. = conversive; f. = feminine; fut. = future; gen. = gender; Ger. = German; Gr. = Greek; imp. = imperative; inf. = infinitive; irreg. = irregular; Lat. = Latin; m. = masculine; parag. = paragogic; pass. = passive; pl. = plural; pret. = preterite; prop. = properly; R. = root; sing. (or s.) = singular; and subst. = substantive.

here, though, Greswell shows herself to be an apt teacher. For one thing, she takes the time to review the rule of compensatory lengthening of a vowel before the guttural א in the case of "the man" in Ps 1:1; and for another, in the same entry she provides examples of what one would normally expect the plural form of אִישׁ to be.[50] And of course, by going through the Psalter like this she is teaching both inductively and deductively, an ideal accommodation to the different ways students learn.

A different sort of entry in the *Grammatical Analysis* is of value both on pedagogical as well as exegetical grounds. I refer to the way in which Greswell occasionally elaborates on a difficult grammatical form by laying out the different options clearly. Two examples are especially noteworthy.

(1) *The Word* tᵉnâ *in Psalm 8:2.* Greswell mentions four possibilities for the problem posed by this word in this well-known verse: "Oh LORD, our lord, how majestic is your name in all the earth, which *tᵉnâ* your glory above the heavens."

> תְּנָה hast-set, this word is very perplexing; it may be [#1] Kal 2 m. s. imp. with ה parag. from נָתַן (Which Glory of Thine do Thou set, &.c); [#2] according to some, תְּנָה is an irreg. form of the inf. constr. after the analogy of רִדְךָ Gen. xlvi. 3, (Thou, the setting of whose Glory is above the heavens);[51] whilst others [#3], with a change of vowel points, would read תֻּנָּה Hoph. 3 f. s. pret. from נָתַן;[52] others again suppose [#4] תְּנָה to be a defective form for תְּנָה (Thou whose Glory is extended), תנה being supposed to be kindred with תנן and the Indo-Germanic root tan, whence Gr. τείνω, Lat. tendere, tenuis, and Ger. dehnen.[53]

50.   Her concern can hardly be to teach so rare a form as אִישִׁים for any reason other than to remind the student of the expected form, and thereby to assure the student through the existence of this form that what they have learned about masculine plural nouns, now implicitly being reviewed, applies even here.

51.   In this second case, it is interesting to note that Greswell avoids being misleading in the same way as the better-known commentator George Phillips. Phillips claims it likely that we have "the infinitive for the preterite" and goes on to comment: "That the inf. is often used for a finite tense is well known." It seems possible, perhaps even probable, that Greswell was aware that Phillips's claim is true for the infinitive, but only (or at least much more often) for the infinitive *absolute*, which form this was not. See George Phillips, *The Psalms in Hebrew with a Critical, Exegetical, and Philological Commentary* (2 vols.; London: John W. Parker, 1846), 1:55.

52.   Had Greswell been following Delitzsch, she would have rendered it as "pass. of the תְּנָה in Judges v. 11, xi. 40, which belongs to the dialect of Northern Palestine"; see F. Delitzsch, *Psalms* (trans. Francis Bolton; 2d ed.; London: Hodder & Stoughton, 1880), 151.

53.   Greswell, *Grammatical Analysis*, 33. (I differ from Greswell only in not having the Fractur script for the transliteration of German.)

Here, as almost everywhere else, Greswell is truly remarkable for being extraordinarily succinct. However, I see here a rare case in which Greswell has rendered (or condoned) a form incorrectly. In the third case, her explanation of the form as possibly a Hophal perfect (in her terms, a preterite) fails to account for the initial ת (instead of the expected ה). So simple a mistake more likely reflects a slip of the pen than ignorance. The mistake, too (assuming it is her own), is helpful in demonstrating that she was confident in making her own judgments about the identity of grammatical forms.

(2) *The word* w^eshabtî *in Psalm 23:6b.* Regarding *w^eshabtî* in Ps 23, Greswell is especially clear and helpful, more so than any commentary that I have read. Unlike most commentators, she notes the peculiarity of *w^eshabtî* as "and I shall dwell," the problem being that, were this the correct translation, the *yôd* inherent to *yashab*, "to dwell," would normally be present. In her own remarkably succinct way, she offers the following three possible explanations:

> וְשַׁבְתִּי and-I-will-dwell; some consider this as [#1] a Kal inf. constr.from יָשַׁב with suff. I s., שַׁבְתִּי being for שִׁבְתִּי [#2] others take it as a defective writing for יָשַׁבְתִּי Kal I s. pret. from יָשַׁב; [#3] and others again as Kal I s. pret. from שׁוּב.[54]

Greswell's possibilities are all viable. This contrasts, for example, with the erroneous claim of Phillips who states: "שַׁבְתִּי is the inf. from יָשַׁב. The inf. const. is שֶׁבֶת, and with the affixes the points undergo the same mutations as segolate nouns; hence שֶׁבֶת, שִׁבְתִּי as מֶלֶךְ, מַלְכִּי."[55] Greswell's explanation of the problem with taking the form as an infinitive construct is right, namely, שַׁבְתִּי being anomalous for שִׁבְתִּי, whereas Phillips is misguided in comparing the behavior of I-W verbs in the infinitive construct with the behaviour of qatl-segholates with suffixes, that is, as if שֶׁבְתִּי were not anomalous.

Philology

Greswell uses different terms for verbal forms than many grammarians of the time whose nomenclature was more akin to ours today.[56] Thus, what was then and is still today called the "perfect," Greswell calls the "preterite." And what was then and is still often today called the

54. Ibid., 78.
55. Phillips, *The Psalms in Hebrew*, 1:178.
56. The resultant perception of her grammatical incorrectness is itself incorrect. Moreover, the difference in terminology limits the direct usefulness of her work for

"imperfect," Greswell calls the "future."[57] This should not discourage one from using her grammatical aid today, since Greswell does more than parse forms; she also reviews basic grammar in the course of her thorough, yet succinct, discussions, making her work of abiding usefulness for students.

In the interests of facilitating the use of Greswell's Grammatical Analysis by students today (as nothing so helpful exists today for students of the Hebrew of the Psalms), I supply a comparative chart of terms pertaining to the Hebrew "tenses."[58]

Nineteenth Century	Present Day
Perfect/Preterite	Perfect/*qatala* or Suffixed Conjugation[59]
Imperfect[60]/Future/aorist	Imperfect/*yaqtulu*/Prefixed/Non-Perfective[61]
Conversive	Waw Consecutive/Waw Conversive/Waw Inversive[62]
Preterite with Waw Conversive	Perfect with Waw Consecutive/*weqatal*[63]
Future/aorist with Waw Conversive	Waw Consecutive + Preterite /*wayyiqtol*[64]
	(Short) Prefixed/Preterite/*yaqtul*[65]

A few philological oddities come to light in Greswell's entries on Ps 1:2. These peculiarities merit consideration for the insight they provide on

students today. The semantic recalculation nonetheless is very worthwhile, as she not only identifies grammatical forms correctly, but she frequently adds explanations that serve to review basic Hebrew grammar.

57.   Thus, she renders *yehgeh*, "he meditates," in Ps 1:2 as "Kal 3 m.s. fut. from הָגָה."

58.   Perowne summarizes his extended discussion of the difference between the perfect and imperfect as follows: "the perfect expresses the past resolve and conduct of which the effects still abide; the imperfect or aorist, the character as it presents itself at any moment, irrespective of all question of time" (*Psalms*, 4th ed., 111 n a). Greswell regards the imperfect to include "repeated action" (p. 3); both recognize that *wehayah* is a *waw* conversive form meaning "he will be."

59.   Other terms include: *qtl*, *qatal*, and Perfective Conjugation.

60.   "Imperfect" was used, for example, by Hupfeld and Perowne. (The same is true for "perfect.") For Perowne's view of the meaning of Hebrew tenses (which was of possible influence on Greswell), see his discussion of יהגה in Ps 1:2 in the various editions (*Psalms*, 4th ed., 111). Like Greswell, Perowne also (sometimes) uses aorist to describe the imperfect. To Perowne, as well, the present time can be expressed either by the perfect or imperfect.

61.   Sometimes also long-prefixed, *yiqtol* or *yqtl* form.

62.   Sometimes also *waw* of succession, and *waw*-relative.

63.   Sometimes also inverted perfect, *wqtl*, *w-qatalti*, or *we-qatalti*.

64.   Sometimes also inverted future, imperfect with *waw* consecutive, *wyqtl*.

65.   In the nineteenth century this form was not widely recognized in Hebrew.

Greswell's philological judgment and competency. Here is her entry on *yômām*, "daily," in Ps 1:2:

> יוֹמָם day, prop. daily, adv. from יוֹם subst. com. gen. (rarely f.), dual יוֹמַיִם,
> pl. יָמִים (as if from the sing. יָם) const. יְמֵי:, twice יְמוֹת Deut. xxxii. 7 and
> Ps. xc.15. R. prob. יוֹם unused in Heb., apparently signifying heat.

This entry on יוֹמָם proves true Greswell's claim often to have drawn from Gesenius's lexicon. This is where Greswell got the mistaken notion that the Semitic root behind the word for "day" signifies heat. Here is what Gesenius has at the initial point where the root and its derivates are discussed: "[יוֹם an unused root, apparently signifying heat, compare the kindred roots חָמַם, חוֹם, יָחַם, حمي; the ח being by degrees softened into (ה. and) י. Three roots are thus found with the softer letter יוֹם, יָמַם, יָמָה. Hence יוֹם, יָמִים. Thes.]"[66]

Though Greswell was following the authority in her day, it was not long after her book came out[67] that the verbal roots Gesenius associated with יוֹם that allegedly provide the link with "heat" were rightly removed from his lexicon; the argument based on "softening" and the ready transposition of radicals (deemed more fluid when many Semitic roots were thought to be biliteral) are highly dubious. It is not likely that Greswell knew better than Gesenius (otherwise she would not have invoked the "heat" meaning); her omission of the softening argument probably came for the sake of brevity. In any case, the "omission" was fortuitous; as a result, her work escaped appearing more outdated than would otherwise have been the case.

Gresswell differed from Gesenius by not stating, as he did, that יְמוֹת was "poetic";[68] her concern for brevity might have been at play here, but it is possible that she thought it odd that a "poetic" form would find only one attestation in the Psalms. Greswell also omits Gesenius's mention of Aramaic יְמִין, "days," in Dan 12:13; this is consistent with her tendency throughout not to invoke an Aramaic cognate except: (a) when the Hebrew word in question appears to be an Aramaic loanword (e.g. with בַּרְזֶל in Ps 2:9, p. 10); (b) when the Hebrew word is thought to be

---

66. Gesenius, *Lexicon*, cccxl. "Thes." refers to Gesenius's *Thesaurus Linguae Hebraeae*.

67. The 1899 German (13th) edition of Gesenius has removed all references to possible Semitic roots; Frants Buhl, ed., *Wilhelm Gesenius's Hebräisches und Aramäisches Handwörterbuch über das Alte Testamente* (13th ed.; Leipzig: F. C. W. Vogel, 1899), 315.

68. She could be looking at an earlier place on the same page (Gesenius, *Lexicon*, 361), but that would not explain her citation of the form akin to the feminine plural, nor her reference to the two places where it occurs.

vocalized in an Aramaic way (e.g. with גְּבַר in Ps 18:26, p. 64); (c) when
an attractive nuance is attested in Aramaic but not Hebrew (e.g. with
רָגְשׁוּ Ps 2:1, p. 6); (d) when Aramaic helps to explain an obscure word
(e.g. when, following Gesenius, she mentions that the initial vowel and
half-vowel in כָּאֲרִי "they pierced" in Ps 22:17 might be vocalized in the
manner of an Aramaic active participle m. pl., p. 75); or (e) when a
possible root is attested in Aramaic though not in Hebrew (e.g. with תְּנוּר
in Ps 21:10, p. 71). All other references to Aramaic ("Chald.") are to
Aramaic translations, important for establishing the "original" text.
Significantly, then, Greswell seems never to invoke a Semitic cognate
for "show" in her explanations.[69] This succinct, no-nonsense approach
was noted with admiration by one reviewer, who noted that Greswell's
work was marked by "pains-taking accuracy," and which the reviewer
contrasted "with the pretentious and slovenly work of so much that calls
itself scholarship among men [*sic*] to-day."[70]

Interpretation in Relation to Sources

Greswell makes clear in her preface that she has "borrowed" from many
commentators. By today's standards, she would at many points be guilty
of plagiarism, but originality is neither her claim nor her purpose. Nevertheless, in order to assess Greswell, it is important to distinguish her
contribution from that of others. The result is that Greswell's unique
contribution lies in her own thorough knowledge of Hebrew grammar,
her skill at summarizing and presenting complex material with utmost
brevity, her meticulous attention to detail, and her sole motivation to
assist the student rather than to impress. A question that remains undeter-
mined here is the extent to which she is the source for the many (largely
non-Semitic) words to which she invites comparison.[71]

69. The only exception is when she says "compare" and then lists possibly
cognate words from an impressive number of other languages—Ethiopic, Sanskrit,
German, French, Welsh, Latin, Slavonic, Gothic, Armenian, Anglo-Saxon, Indo-
Germanic, Greek, Persian, and English. Greswell does not heavily depend on any of
her usual sources for this information. This may have been largely her own contribution, as she might be implying in her preface when she writes "so far as I have
been able to discover them" (Greswell, *Grammatical Analysis*, iii). In any event, her
citation of these cognates appears tersely at the end of her explanations; she might
have thought them useful for students learning one or more of these other languages.
(See, however, n. 71 below.)
70. Leavitt, "Review of *Grammatical Analysis*," 314.
71. It is likely that Greswell's listing of various Indo-European "cognates" to
Hebrew words is original to Greswell. While this attests to her knowledge and skill
at various languages, it is not to Greswell's credit as a scholar of languages that she

Greswell claims to have relied most heavily upon Rogers for her comments about possible textual variants reflected in translations such as Latin, Syriac, Greek and so on. For this reason, her indebtedness to Rogers will be explored in some detail.

Psalm 69:33 provides an interesting case, suggesting Greswell was somewhat dependent on Rogers for information on versions, but also her completely independent knowledge of Hebrew. The dependence is evident through Greswell following Rogers in noting that the LXX, Vulgate and Arabic read יִרְאוּ (the imperfect of רָאָה, "to see").[72] Greswell similarly follows him in noting that the same sources, plus the Ethiopic, attest to דִּרְשׁוּ (the Qal imperative m. pl. of דָּרַשׁ "to seek").[73] Greswell, however, shows independence in her willingness to add a few more recent versions to the latter; one is "our Prayer-Book Version."[74] She then contrasts this with the "Welsh Version," which follows the Hebrew.[75] Greswell likely invokes these additional sources from her own knowledge base.[76] Moreover, in many places Greswell gives herself freedom not to follow Rogers, but (likely) some other source.[77]

Greswell is in no way dependent upon Rogers for knowledge of Hebrew. Thus, whereas Rogers simply cites the root radicals attested in the versions, Greswell vocalizes his Hebrew and parses דִּרְשׁוּ.[78]

An overview of Greswell's dependence on other sources will help round out the picture of Greswell as a Hebraist. Her claim to follow Jebb

invoked these cognates, as the scholarship that fostered such "cognates" had already for some time (rightly) gone out of fashion.

72. Greswell, *Grammatical Analysis*, 162; cf. Rogers, *The Book of Psalms in Hebrew* [Notes section], 106.

73. Ibid., 224.

74. Greswell, *Grammatical Analysis*, 163.

75. Ibid.

76. Another source Greswell invokes independently of Rogers is Luther's German translation. Psalm 89:51 further demonstrates that Greswell did not follow Rogers slavishly. She does not include the mention by Rogers that there is a "Chaldean" witness that supports a variant reading of ʿabdekā, "your servant," along with the mention they both make of various Hebrew manuscripts and the Syriac in support of this reading. More interestingly, Greswell makes no mention of a clever emendation to the verse that is suggested by Rogers (*The Book of Psalms in Hebrew*, 235) despite there being no textual witnesses in favor of such. Indeed, I am not aware of any case where Greswell mentions any conjectural emendations suggested by her sources. (Contrast this with a reviewer's baseless chauvinistic claim to the contrary cited later in this essay.)

77. Compare, for example, Greswell (*Grammatical Analysis*, 79) and Rogers (*The Book of Psalms in Hebrew*, 94, 181) on the variants in Ps 24:6.

78. Greswell, *Grammatical Analysis*, 162.

appears overly modest; she could not have followed him very much, because he offers only a translation and very occasional short notes. One clear case where she does follow him is in Ps 63:10 (11), where Greswell's literal translation of יְגִירֻהוּ as "They-shall-make-him-run-out (like water)"[79] matches the literal rendition footnoted by Jebb: "They shall make him run out like water..."[80]

The following two cases are typical of the kind of use Greswell feels free to make of her sources. The examples compare Greswell to both Perowne and Horsley.

Perowne comments as follows on "kiss the son" in Ps 2:12: "The interpretation of these words has always been a difficulty. (I.) the Chald. has קבילו אלפנא, 'receive instruction'; LXX. δράξασθε παιδείας. Vulg *apprehendite disciplinam*; בַּר being thus, as in Arabic, 'piety, obedience,' &c." A few sentences later Perowne writes, "Of the older Versions, only the Syriac has ܢܫܩܘ ܒܪܐ ('kiss the Son')..."

This compares with Greswell, for whom the interpretation of this phrase "has always been a difficulty. The Chal. has קבילו אלפנא, 'receive instruction'; LXX. δράξασθε παιδείας. Vulg. *apprehendite disciplinam*." Then follows immediately, "Of the older Versions only the Syr. has 'kiss the Son'."[81] Although she cites the same terms from the Septuagint and Vulgate, she does not cite the Syriac. The comparison of Greswell to Perowne here shows that Greswell follows her source closely. What she omits are elements extraneous to the discussion or references to languages or scripts with which she is not directly familiar.

At other times Greswell will lift a short comment, such as Perowne's statement that Ps 2 "is of the nature of prophecy," and include it in her short introduction to Ps 2.[82] She does the same with Horsley's comments, though she is not likely to do so when Horsley introduces Psalms he considers to be messianic.[83]

Greswell again uses Horsley selectively in her notes on Ps 42:5–6. Horsley writes: "Read with LXX (Alex.), Vulgate, Syriac, and one MS. of Kennicott's[84] פני ואלהי, as in the last verse of this Psalm, and again

---

79. Greswell, *Grammatical Analysis*, 149.

80. A. T. Jebb, *The Book of Psalms* (London: Longman, 1846), 61 n. 4.

81. Greswell, *Grammatical Analysis*, 11.

82. Perowne, *Psalms*, 113 (4th ed.), 116 (2d ed.); cf. Greswell, *Grammatical Analysis*, 5.

83. This is because Greswell was likely influenced by Perowne's distaste for the criteria by which Horsley judged a psalm as messianic and prophetic; see Perowne's discussion of the "Theology of the Psalms," in his *Psalms* (4th ed.), 42–49.

84. Benjamin Kennicott (1718–1783), a Hebrew scholar, made an extensive collection of Hebrew MSS; these are kept in the Bodleian Library at Oxford.

of the 43d [Psalm], and begin the next verse with עֵלִי."[85] Greswell states: "The LXX. (Alex.), Vulg., Syr., and one MS. of Kennicott read פָּנֵי וֵאלֹהָי, and begin the next verse with עֵלִי."[86] Greswell is more succinct than Horsley and she vocalizes the Hebrew. Moreover, regarding Horsley's use of versions in general, she clearly does not invoke all of his references to them and she invokes references to versions where Horsley has none.

There is at least one instance in which Greswell borrows from one of her sources at considerable length. I refer to the ending to Greswell's discussion of Ps 8. The ending is not only unusual for its lengthy borrowing (15 lines of text in her book), but because it is an extremely rare case in which she diverts from grammatical analysis to theological reflection. The reflection is on the possibility that the dominion of humanity in Ps 8 finds its climax in the phenomenon whereby "(man) passeth the paths of the sea." She borrows from Phillips, who in turn quotes Mendelssohn.[87] Even so, she cannot restrain her grammatical self in making a slight change, whereby she vocalizes Mendelssohn's Hebrew![88]

Greswell's Christian Perspective and Its Influence on Her Interpretation

Church history has witnessed a wide range of Christian readings of the Psalter: from maximalists like Augustine, to restrained minimalists like Calvin, to those at some point in between like Luther. Although the Enlightenment was detrimental to Christological readings, the sources drawn from by Greswell indicate that these readings survived both within the ivory tower (with Horsley in full swing on the one side and others like Perowne and Delitzsch making more modest claims on the other) and at the grass roots (as with Spurgeon's *Treasury of David* and Mrs. Thompson's *Practical Illustration of the Book of Psalms*).[89]

---

85. Horsley, *Book of Psalms*, 1:256–57.

86. Greswell, *Grammatical Analysis*, 112. For a further case of a similar amount of borrowing, compare both at Ps 16:5 (Horsley, *Book of Psalms*, 1:35; Greswell, *Grammatical Analysis*, 55).

87. Compare Greswell, *Grammatical Analysis*, 36 with Phillips, *Psalms in Hebrew*, 1:56.

88. Curiously, although Greswell vocalizes the word, she at the same time omits the article. (The word is הַיִּם, "the day.")

89. Horsley, Perowne, and Delitzsch are listed among Greswell's key sources. See p. 92 above, including n. 37. Charles H. Spurgeon, *The Treasury of David: Containing an Original Exposition on the Psalms* (7 vols.; London: Passmore & Alabaster, 1870–85); Mrs. Thompson, *A Practical Illustration of the Book of*

Although Greswell's purpose was grammatical and not theological, she wears her Christian point of reference without embarrassment. This is most evident in her mention of the occasion in the Christian year when a psalm is given particular attention. Her textual notes and comments on individual verses are largely devoid of focus on application to Jesus or other matters Christian, except that in weighing textual variants she grants the New Testament authority over other witnesses.[90] And though too brief to be a strong basis for judgment, her introductions align quite closely with the christological tone of Perowne much more than, say, with Horsley. Three good psalms with which to assess her role as a Christian interpreter are Pss 2, 22, and 45, commonly regarded in popular circles as Messianic psalms:

> *Psalm 2*: This Psalm, which is of the nature of prophecy, is in some MSS. joined to Ps. i. It describes the Kingdom of Christ, and concludes with an exhortation to the kings of the earth to accept it; it is one of the appointed Psalms for Easter Day. Although not entitled a Psalm of David, we are assured in Acts. iv. 25 that it is.[91]

> *Psalm 22*: In this Psalm (which somewhat resembles the sixty-ninth, and which is one of the Proper Psalms for Good Friday) David prays to the Almighty for help in the midst of overwhelming distress and anguish. Independently of the circumstances of David's case, this Psalm is a foreshadowing of the Passion of Christ, and the first words of it were uttered by our Blessed Saviour when he hung upon the cross (see Matt. 27:46), substituting for the Hebrew verb the corresponding word in the Aramaean dialect then in use among the Jews.[92]

> *Psalm 45*: Under the type of the nuptials of a Jewish king (probably Solomon) with a foreign princess—by some supposed to be the daughter of Pharoah, king of Egypt, and by others of Hiram, king of Tyre—is prefigured the marriage of Christ and His Church. Some persons refer the Psalm to the marriage of Ahab with Jezebel, daughter of Ethbaal, king of the Zidonians; whilst others think that Joram, the son of Jehoshaphat, is the king intended, and Athaliah (who was of Tyrian origin and of the royal family of Israel) the queen. Verses 7 and 8 are quoted by St. Paul, Hebr. 1:8, 9. This is one of the Proper Psalms appointed for Christmas Day.[93]

Psalms: By the Author of the Family Commentary on the New Testament (2 vols.; New York: A. Barclay, 1826).

90. For example, of the possible rendering "their line" in Ps 19:5, Greswell (*Grammatical Analysis*, 69) states, "Almost all of the versions read קַוְלָם which has the authority of St. Paul, Rom. x.18."

91. Greswell, *Grammatical Analysis*, 5–6.

92. Ibid., 72–73.

93. Ibid., 116.

Greswell's Christological hermeneutic as applied to these so-called Messianic psalms may be described as moderate. In this respect her interpretation is comparable to that of Perowne, who advocated a typologically prophetic hermeneutic, and before him, Calvin, who, contrary to Luther, read the Psalms only secondarily as pertaining to Christ.

Psalm 50 is different in that Greswell describes the circumstances of the psalm without any mention of Christ, yet clearly intends the Christian reader to hear him echoed in her description:

> *Psalm 50*: In this sublime Psalm, the only one in this Book ascribed to Asaph, the divine Lawgiver, appearing on Zion in glory similar to that of Sinai, summons the whole creation to witness His judgment of His people. With regard to the first table of the Decalogue, He charges them with formalism, losing sight of the purpose of their outward rites, and the spirituality of His worship. With respect to the second, He severely rebukes the hypocrites who professed to serve Him whilst they violated all His moral commands; and He then concludes with a warning and a promise.[94]

The allusive nature of the description is akin to that of Phillips, from whom she perhaps drew inspiration, and whom she outclasses by being far more subtle and far less caustic towards the Jews of the time.[95]

Greswell reflects her Christian stance most consistently and uniquely by stating the place of a given psalm in the Church Year. Moreover, she uses the terms "type" and "prophecy" to signal to the reader her typological and prophetic hermeneutic for reading the Psalms as pertaining to Jesus Christ. In using the terms "type" and "a prophecy" she likely reflects the influence of Perowne[96] and, like him or Calvin, she strongly resists any tendency not to focus on the psalm in its own time and setting. Unlike Hengstenberg, she does not mount a Christian apologetic in her discussion at any point.

On the title page are two verses that intimate a context of Christian piety for this work of great learning by Greswell. The first is from Ecclesiasticus (47:8). Greswell, likely putting herself in the position of the male speaker of the following words, writes: "In all his works he praised the Holy One most high with words of glory; with his whole heart he sung songs, and loved Him that made him." The second is from

---

94. Ibid., 126–27.

95. Compare Phillips, *Psalms*, 1:391–32. (Phillips equates the wicked with "those brought up in the Jewish faith, but who were nevertheless guilty of great impiety, and led scandalous lives." Of these, writes Phillips, God "intimates His intension to abolish them under the new dispensation.")

96. See Perowne, *Psalms*, 45–49.

Ecclesiastes: "Whatsoever thy hand findeth to do, do it with thy might" (9:10). Julia Greswell's hands found their way to writing a pedagogically sensitive grammatical analysis of the Psalms, and from all appearances she wrote it with her "might"—and extraordinary skill.

Conclusion

Although Greswell's concern was Hebraic and exegetical, she could not escape the issue of gender. It was her father and an especially thoughtful mentor, J. J. S. Perowne, who helped her talent bear fruit to the benefit of the kingdom of God. Reviews of her book were at some times fair and affirming, and at other times bigoted and patriarchal. The following review, devoid of truth in all of its cited claims, aptly demonstrates the latter attitude:

> We regret also that Miss G. has adhered so closely to the authorised version; as, for instance, in constantly representing the Hebrew Imperfect by the English Future, where the sense is manifestly Present. It is perhaps well that she has in general abstained from critical and expository elucidation; for, where she does attempt this, she betrays a very feminine preference for fanciful interpretations.[97]

Happily, this review contrasts with an example of the former attitude; here, as if to chastise the reviewer just cited, as well as to recognize in Greswell a careful scholar, another reviewer writes:

> That a work of this character should proceed from the pen of a lady, is an achievement of which the advocates of the higher education of women may fairly be proud, and an encouraging token of the benefits to be looked for from the revival of female scholarship. The extreme modesty and pains-taking accuracy which characterize Miss Greswell's little volume, are in refreshing contrast with the pretentious and slovenly work of so much that calls itself scholarship among men to-day.[98]

If more women like Julia Greswell had been given access to the academy, the wish of both Payne Smith and Perowne that the study of Hebrew would somehow increase in the land would have been much more fully realized. As a Hebraist and a lover of languages, Julia Greswell was very competent. As a pedagogue she was far ahead of the pack, a godsend to students of Hebrew then, and, to judge from 600 downloads and counting, even now.

97. W. G. E., review of Julia Greswell, *Grammatical Analysis*, page unspecified. I can think of no fanciful interpretation offered by Greswell; in fact, at every turn she resists the conjectures in her male-written sources; see, for example, n. 76 above.
    98. Leavitt, "Review of *Grammatical Analysis*," 314.

HARRIET BEECHER STOWE'S INTERPRETATION OF THE VIRGIN MARY: THE SIGNIFICANCE OF MATERNAL IDEOLOGY FOR HOME AND SOCIETY

Nancy Calvert-Koyzis

Introduction

The 1849 cholera epidemic was especially bad in Cincinnati, where Harriet Beecher Stowe and her family lived. Reports from the time indicate that on June 25, 84 people died in their homes or on the sidewalks. During the week of July 4, which was the peak of the epidemic, 1081 bodies were interred in the cemeteries.[1] The demand for coffins was so great that they became difficult to find and any kind of vehicle was used as a hearse.[2] During the epidemic, Harriet wrote letters to her husband Calvin Stowe, who was recuperating from illness in Brattleboro, Vermont. It is apparent from her missives that her son, Charley, who was born the previous year, was taken ill on July 10. She believed he was recovering on July 15, but by July 23 she reports that they had been "watching all day by the dying bed of little Charley, who is gradually sinking." On July 26 she wrote the following letter to Calvin:

> MY DEAR HUSBAND,—At last it is over, and our dear little one is gone from us. He is now among the blessed. My Charley—my beautiful, loving, gladsome baby, so loving, so sweet, so full of life and hope and strength—now lies shrouded, pale and cold, in the room below. Never was he anything to me but a comfort. He has been my pride and joy. Many a heartache has he cured for me. Many an anxious night have I held him to my bosom and felt the sorrow and loneliness pass out of me with the touch of his little warm hands. Yet I have just seen him in his death agony, looked on his imploring face when I could not help nor soothe nor do one thing, not one, to mitigate his cruel suffering, do nothing but pray in my anguish that he might die soon. I write as though there was no

---

1. Forrest Wilson, *Crusader in Crinoline: The Life of Harriet Beecher Stowe* (Westport, Conn.: Greenwood, 1941), 226–29.
2. Ibid., 227.

sorrow like my sorrow, yet there has been in this city, as in the land of
Egypt, scarce a house without its dead. This heart-break, this anguish, has
been everywhere, and when it will end God alone knows.[3]

Although Stowe suffered great anguish at Charley's death, losing him to
cholera was not her only bereavement. Of the seven children she bore,
Eliza (1836–1912), Harriet (1836–1907), Henry (1838–1857), Frederick
(1840–1870?), Georgiana (1843–1890), Samuel Charles (1848–1849),
and Charles Edward (1850–1934), only three survived her. Frederick
succumbed to alcoholism, went to California and was never heard from
again. Georgiana became addicted to morphine and died in her forties.[4]

Perhaps the most traumatic death for Stowe was that of her son Henry
Ellis Stowe, who, at age nineteen, drowned while swimming in the
Connecticut River in Hanover, New Hampshire, at the end of his fresh-
man year at Dartmouth College. In a letter to the Duchess of Sutherland
on August 3, 1857 she wrote: "Before this reaches you, you will have
perhaps learned from other sources of the sad blow which has fallen
upon us—our darling, our good, beautiful boy, snatched away in the
moment of health and happiness!" In the letter she also describes Henry's
subsequent homecoming: "There he lay so calm, so placid, so peaceful,
that I could not believe that he would not smile upon me... There had
always been such a peculiar union, such a tenderness between us. I had
had such power always to call up answering feelings to my own, that it
seemed impossible that he could be silent and unmoved at my grief."[5]

Of course, because she experienced the deaths of Charley and Henry,
by the time she composed her non-fiction works Stowe understood the
pain of those mothers who had lost sons over the centuries, including the
Galilean peasant woman who lost her son, Jesus. In this essay, I will
investigate Stowe's interpretation of the Virgin Mary in her non-fiction
works against the background of her experience of motherhood. Some of
her works of fiction will be alluded to when they illuminate her biblical

    3.   Harriet Beecher Stowe to Calvin Stowe, July 4, 1849; excerpted from Annie
Fields, ed., *Life and Letters of Harriet Beecher Stowe* (Boston: Houghton Mifflin
Company, 1897), 119. See also Marie Caskey on the influence of Charlie's death on
Uncle Tom's Cabin in *Chariot of Fire: Religion and the Beecher Family* (London:
Yale University Press, 1978), 173–75.
    4.   Joan D. Hedrick, *Harriet Beecher Stowe: A Life* (New York: Oxford Uni-
versity Press, 1994), 140.
    5.   Annie Fields, ed., *Life and Letters of Harriet Beecher Stowe* (Boston: Hough-
ton Mifflin, 1897), 238–39; see also Marie Caskey, *Chariot of Fire*, 178–80, 183,
on the influence of Henry's death on Stowe's writing of *The Minister's Wooing*
(New York: Derby & Jackson, 1859).

interpretation. I will then argue that Stowe used her interpretation of Mary to contribute to her larger project of the maternalization of Victorian society.

Nineteenth-Century Idealization of Motherhood and Stowe's Virgin Mary

Beginning in about 1830, members of the white, English-speaking, Protestant middle class believed that the primary role of a married woman was the care of her children and the maintenance of her home.[6] The "woman's life was physically spent within the home and with the family, while the man's was largely outside the home, at work."[7] The ideological justification of this division of labour and activity was often referred to as "the doctrine of the two spheres" or "separate spheres."[8] Within her "proper" sphere, motherhood was central to the identity of women who lived in the Victorian era. How individual women experienced motherhood varied enormously, but the role of mother was idealized, particularly in relationship to her moral and educative influence on her children:

> From the late eighteenth century secular attitudes to the mother–child relationship, which emphasised the importance of childhood as a stage in the life cycle, conjoined with religious discourses which privileged female piety. The consequence was to exalt moral motherhood and to conceive of it primarily in relation to its moral and educative responsibilities to children.[9]

For Stowe, the Virgin Mary offered a particularly poignant example of this idealization of motherhood. Although in the nineteenth century many Protestants saw the veneration of the biblical Mary, the "height of the sin of idolatry," as one of the more offensive Roman Catholic doctrines, Stowe was fascinated with Mary.[10] Her zeal for Mary was

---

6. See Kathryn Kish Sklar, "Victorian Women and Domestic Life: Mary Todd Lincoln, Elizabeth Cady Stanton and Harriet Beecher Stowe," in *The Public and the Private Lincoln: Contemporary Perspectives* (ed. Cullom Davis et al.; Carbondale, Ill.: Southern Illinois University Press, 1979), 229–43 (229).

7. Carl N. Degler, *At Odds: Women and the Family in America from the Revolution to the Present* (New York: Oxford University Press, 1981), 9.

8. Ibid.

9. Eleanor Gordon and Gwyneth Nair, "Domestic Fathers and the Victorian Parental Role," *Women's History Review* 15, no. 4 (2006): 551–59 (551–52).

10. Eileen Razari Elrod, "Exactly Like My Father: Feminist Hermeneutics in Harriet Beecher Stowe's Non-fiction," *JAAR* 63, no. 4 (1995): 695–719 (710).

particularly evident in her collection of Marian art. As John Gatta remarks, "Stowe owned copies of at least...three sacred Madonnas, including the *Holy Family del Divino Amore* and Raphael's *Madonna del Gran Duca*, in addition to secular renderings of the mother and child motif."[11] In 1853, after her first European tour, she installed Raphael's *Sistine Madonna* in her home at Andover, Massachusetts. Even today, at the Harriet Beecher Stowe Centre in Hartford, Connecticut, one can see her copy of Raphael's *Madonna of the Goldfinch* "hanging conspicuously in the front parlor to illustrate her pioneering display of Madonna artefacts among the households of local Protestant gentility."[12]

In fact, in her book *Footsteps of the Master*, Stowe objected to the Roman Catholic view of and the Protestant defamation of Mary: "The views adopted in the Roman Church with respect to this one Woman of women have tended to deprive the rest of the world of a great source of comfort and edification by reason of the opposite extreme to which Protestant reaction has naturally gone."[13] Unlike other Protestants who disparaged Mary because of the devotion of Roman Catholics to her, Stowe focussed on Mary's motherhood. Stowe saw Mary as blessed above all women throughout time, simply because she was Jesus' mother.[14]

Ultimately, for Stowe, Mary symbolized the divine womanhood that was to "displace the monarchical God of...Calvinism with a divine principle of maternal compassion."[15] Stowe channelled the Victorian idealization of motherhood into an "argument for widespread social change" based on maternal values and "rather than segregate maternal ethics into some private domestic realm," she believed that "motherhood—the morality of woman—should be made the ethical and structural model for all of American life."[16] Basically, she was using this maternal ideology to

11. John Gatta, *American Madonna: Images of the Divine Woman in Literary Culture* (New York: Oxford University Press, 1997), 54.

12. Ibid.

13. Harriet Beecher Stowe, *Footsteps of the Master* (New York: J. B. Ford, 1877), 64. To illustrate Protestant defamation of the Virgin, she follows this statement with a story of how John Knox once threw an image of the Virgin overboard after being compelled to kiss it by "Popish" sailors.

14. Ibid. Here she also decries Mary as the "goddess crowned with stars" for "something nobler, purer, fairer, more appreciable"—referring instead to Mary's role as mother. She may be contrasting what she believes is Mary's significance with Anna Jameson's depiction of Mary in *Legends of the Madonna: As Represented in the Fine Arts* (repr.; London: Unit Library, 1903 [1852]).

15. Gatta, *American Madonna*, 54.

16. Elizabeth Ammons, "Stowe's Dream of the Mother-Savior: Uncle Tom's Cabin and American Women Writers Before the 1920s," in *New Essays on Uncle*

argue against the very foundation of Victorian society: father rule. This stress on maternal ideology and its significance for society is found in Stowe's depictions of the Virgin Mary, particularly in her non-fiction works.

The Virgin Mary in Footsteps of the Master

While Stowe is known today primarily for her works of fiction, particularly *Uncle Tom's Cabin* (1852), she also wrote non-fiction volumes such as *Woman in Sacred History: A Series of Sketches Drawn from Scriptural, Historical and Legendary Sources* (1873), in which she commented on biblical texts that featured women. In 1877 she wrote *Footsteps of the Master*, in which she repeated much of what she wrote in *Woman in Sacred History*, although it was written for a different audience.[17] Because she saw all of her writing as a means of religious instruction, she considered her non-fiction works to be of greater importance than her fiction works because in them she could speak directly about matters of religion. In 1876 she wrote to her son, "I would much rather…have written another such book as *Footsteps of the Master*, but all, even the religious papers, are gone mad on serials."[18]

In both *Woman in Sacred History* and *Footsteps of the Master*, Stowe interpreted biblical passages in which the Virgin Mary is found. While many similarities exist in the interpretation of the Virgin Mary expressed in these works, it is in *Footsteps of the Master* that we find Stowe revelling most in Mary's motherhood, and so it is where I will begin.

Stowe used the liturgical calendar as the organizing principle of the book. Her comments on the Virgin Mary as mother generally fell into the section entitled "Christmas," because here she dealt with Jesus' birth and childhood. While *Footsteps of the Master* was not written particularly for women, as *Woman in Sacred History* was, Stowe did highlight qualities of both Mary and Jesus that would have resonated with her female readers.

While Stowe addressed pastoral concerns in the book, one should also note that she used the scholarly tools and insights of her time. For

Tom's Cabin (ed. Eric J. Sundquist; Cambridge: Cambridge University Press, 1986), 155–95 (159).

17. Harriet Beecher Stowe, *Woman in Sacred History: A Series of Sketches Drawn from Scriptural, Historical and Legendary Sources with Twenty-Five Chromo-Lithographs* (New York: J. B. Ford, 1873), and *Footsteps of the Master* (New York: J. B. Ford, 1877).

18. Elrod, "'Exactly Like My Father,'" 696.

Breaking Boundaries

example, she spoke of the problems inherent in Matthew's genealogy of
Jesus, where she cited some of the learned scholars of her day.[19] Marion
Taylor notes that in Stowe's discussion of Jesus' childhood, "[she]
mentions the apocryphal Gospels and follows her husband's position on
the criteria for distinguishing between true and apocryphal Gospels."[20]

One of the elements of idealized motherhood that comes through very
strongly in Stowe's interpretation of the Virgin Mary is the mother as
moral guide and educator. *Godey's Ladies Magazine* summarized well
the belief of the era that: "Women's duties are of a much higher and
holier nature than man's inasmuch as to her is consigned the moral
power of the world."[21] In contrast to the "darkness of the sensuous
nature" represented by men, it was thought that a woman's motherly
piety radiated a civilizing and redeeming influence on her children. In
fact, in her role as mother, a woman's highest calling was realized
because "upon the mother depended both nation and race."[22]

In her conviction that mothers could have a powerful influence on
society, Stowe bore resemblance to her sister, Catherine Beecher, who
believed that the orderly and prosperous household was a patriotic and
religious duty for American Christian women. Through this ordered
domesticity, American woman would extend over the earth the blessed
influences of Christianity in every social, civil, and political institution.[23]
However, as Gillian Brown states, "Stowe recognized the power for
women in the alliance her sister forged, but she also perceived the limits
of women's power in a patriarchal domesticity. She sought a more
radical and extensive power, to be obtained through the replacement of
the market economy by a matriarchal domestic economy."[24] For Stowe in
Footsteps, Jesus became an example of that matriarchal, domestic
economy in the habits that appeared in his public ministry.

19. Stowe, *Footsteps of the Master*, 53–54.

20. Marion Ann Taylor, "Harriet Beecher Stowe and the Mingling of Two
Worlds: The Kitchen and the Study," in *Recovering Nineteenth-Century Women
Interpreters of the Bible* (ed. C. de Groot and M. A. Taylor; SBLSymS 38; Atlanta:
Society of Biblical Literature, 2007), 99–115 (112). See Stowe, *Footsteps of the
Master*, 78, and Calvin Stowe, *The Origin and History of the Books of the Bible*
(Hartford, Conn.: Hartford Publishing, 1868). For more on Calvin Stowe's influence
on Harriet, see Caskey, *Chariot of Fire*, 183.

21. Gayle Kimball, *The Religious Ideas of Harriet Beecher Stowe* (New York:
Edwin Mellen, 1982), 77; see also Elrod, "'Exactly Like My Father,'" 701.

22. Ibid., 79–80, 78.

23. Gillian Brown, *Domestic Individualism: Imagining Self in Nineteenth-
Century America* (Berkeley: University of California Press, 1990), 20.

24. Ibid., 24.

Of course, Jesus learned the values of this economy from his mother. In *Footsteps of the Master* Stowe stated, "The blessedness of Mary was that she was the one human being who had the right of ownership and intimate oneness with the Beloved [Jesus]."[25] This unity was revealed in Jesus' ministry, for example, in his careful domestic habits in which he was methodical and frugal. "The miraculous power he possessed never was used to surround him with any profusion. He would have the fragments of the feast picked up and stored in the baskets, 'that nothing would be lost.'"[26] For Stowe, Jesus' economical ways were based on the habits of a "frugal home."[27] Even Jesus' illustration of the leaven hidden in three measures of meal "gives us to believe that doubtless he had often watched his mother in the homely process of breadmaking."[28] She was also the "first teacher of the child Jesus in the Law and the Prophets" as she prepared him for his ministry because she knew to what end his life would lead.[29]

The domestic habits in which a mother trained her son also appeared in another of Stowe's works. In her previously published novel, *My Wife and I, or Harry Henderson's Story*, one finds a surprising similarity between Jesus' relationship with Mary and Harry's relationship with his mother. In the novel, Harry was raised at home while his sisters studied at the local female seminary. As a result, Harry spent much of his childhood alone with his mother. Concerning these years, Harry states:

> This association with a womanly nature, and this discipline in womanly ways, I hold to have been an invaluable part of my early training. There is no earthly reason which requires a man, in order to be manly, to be unhandy and clumsy in regard to the minutiæ of domestic life; and there are quantities of occasions occurring in the life of every man, in which he will have occasion to be grateful to his mother, if, like mine, she trains him in woman's arts and the secrets of making domestic life agreeable.[30]

For Harry, while women who were of a pious nature shrank from public life, they were yet the "most needed force to be for the good of the State."[31] He further states, "I am persuaded that *it is not till this class of women feel as vital and personal responsibility for the good of the State,*

25. Stowe, *Footsteps of the Master*, 67.
26. Ibid., 68.
27. Ibid.
28. Ibid.
29. Ibid., 72.
30. Harriet Beecher Stowe, *My Wife and I: or, Harry Henderson's History* (New York: AMS, 1967), 38.
31. Ibid., 37.

as they have hitherto felt for that of the family, that we shall gain the final elements of a perfect society.[32] As Marion Taylor points out, this was also a primary argument for the right for women to vote; when they did, the world would change.[33]

But in this influence, mothers were not to be public figures. Harry believed that mothers should follow the model of the fabled nymph Egeria, who was believed to have dictated the laws of Rome to king Numa Pompilius (753–673 B.C.E.) in secret. Harry stated, "No mortal eye saw her. She was not in the forum, or the senate. She did not strive, nor cry, nor lift up her voice in the street, but she made the laws by which Rome ruled the world."[34]

In like manner, in *Footsteps*, Stowe portrayed Mary as instructing Jesus privately. For Stowe, the "retirement and stillness" of the peasant life in Nazareth" was "peculiarly suited to the constitutional taste both of Jesus and his mother." Mary sought "solitude and meditation" and her "thoughts [were] expressed only confidentially to congenial nature."[35] Mary's private instructions to Jesus were also evident in the following extract from her poem, "Mary at the Cross" (1849), which antedates *Footsteps*:

> O highly favored thou in many an hour
> Spent in lone musings with thy wondrous Son,
> When thou didst gaze into that glorious eye,
> And hold that mighty hand within thine own.[36]

In *Footsteps*, Stowe also interpreted Jesus' private ways as being influenced by his mother: "There is every evidence that our Lord's individual and human nature was in this respect peculiarly sympathetic with that of his mother," particularly since Jesus avoided publicity in his ministry and "wrought miracles with the injunctions of secrecy—'See thou tell no man.'"[37]

Yet for Stowe, Mary's unity with Jesus did not stop with these examples. Mary's intimacy of association with Jesus was paramount in Stowe's interpretation of their relationship. She stated, "There was one woman of all women to whom it was given to know him perfectly,

32. Ibid. (italics are Stowe's).

33. Marion A. Taylor, email message to the author, March 9, 2009.

34. Stowe, *My Wife and I*, 39.

35. Stowe, *Footsteps of the Master*, 69.

36. Harriet Beecher Stowe, "Mary at the Cross," in Wikisource, The Free Library, http://www.en.wikisource.org/w/index.php?title=Mary_at_the Cross&oldid=638617 (accessed February 13, 2009); see also Gatta, *American Madonna*, 160 n. 10.

37. Stowe, *Footsteps of the Master*, 69.

entirely, intimately—to whom his nature was knit in the closest possible union and identity. He was bone of her bone and flesh of her flesh—his life grew out of her immortal nature."[38] The imagery of bones and flesh, of course, came from Gen 2:23, where Adam used the phrase at the creation of his partner, Eve. As John Gatta points out, here Stowe used terminology that was often called upon to describe marriage and used it instead to describe parthenogenesis, the birth of Jesus in spite of Mary's virgin status. For Stowe, however, the Virgin Mother was much more "mother" than "virgin."[39]

Stowe rarely mentioned Joseph in her rendition of Mary's motherhood. She explained that the "blessedness of Mary was that she was the one human being who had the right of ownership and intimate oneness with the Beloved."[40] Because Jesus had no mortal father, Stowe reasoned that Jesus was "more purely sympathetic with his mother than any other son of woman" and that "[a]ll that was human in him was her nature; it was the union of the Divine nature with the nature of a pure woman. Hence there was in Jesus more of the pure feminine element than in any other man."[41] Stowe's feminized Christ, which was idiosyncratic in her day, pervaded her other writings as well.

According to Ammons, in *Uncle Tom's Cabin* Stowe depicted Evangeline and Tom as kinds of mother-Christs. Evangeline, or Eva, the self-sacrificial child in the novel who was named for the "mother of the race," was described as having ethereal qualities. Stowe characterized her as having eyes that shone with "deep spiritual gravity" and portrayed Uncle Tom as gazing on this ethereal child who glided, flew, floated and wafted, but never walked. When Tom looked at Eva, he saw "'something almost divine... He half believed that he saw one of the angels stepped out of his New Testament.'"[42] Because Eva represented a kind of female saviour who elevated "pure womanhood to an almost supernatural level," in order to effect change in a world in which male laws and values had failed, she "reconstitute[d] the world along female rather than male lines."[43] In the role of effecting change that was based upon higher, maternal values, and her self-sacrificial death, Eva "personifies for

38. Ibid., 70.
39. Gatta, *American Madonna*, 56–57.
40. Stowe, *Footsteps of the Master*, 67.
41. Ibid., 70.
42. Ammons, "Stowe's Dream," 164–65, where she also quotes from Harriet Beecher Stowe, *Uncle Tom's Cabin or Life Among the Lowly* (New York: Random House, 1938), 180–81.
43. Ammons, "Stowe's Dream," 163.

Stowe the spotless motherly Christ come to redeem the world from the sins of the fathers."[44]

In *Uncle Tom's Cabin*, Stowe also portrayed Tom as having the virtues of Christ through his "piety, his gentleness, his inexhaustible generosity of spirit, his non-violence, [and] his commitment to self-sacrifice[.]"[45] Tom refused to "meet violence with violence...he remain[ed] compassionate, giving, and emotional to the end," and so he embodied the characteristics of the stereotypical Victorian heroine. According to Ammons, while Tom is characterized in a way that "does rely on the antebellum stereotype of blacks," the characterization "contradicts the widespread racist categorizations of blacks as brutes" who are "incapable of emotions and ideas." In essence, Tom became the gentle Mother "as morally irradiating as Christ."[46]

Thus when Stowe depicted a feminized Christ in *Footsteps*, these characters from *Uncle Tom's Cabin* were in the background. When Stowe spoke of Christ as being "more purely sympathetic than any other son of woman," or believed "[a]ll that was human in him was her nature," she was referring to his feminine and motherly qualities. For Stowe, "Christ alone could feel what a mother felt. Her own heart was like his."[47] By these motherly qualities Christ exemplified a higher set of values—maternal values—than those currently held in Stowe's patriarchal world. Of course, this model of motherhood was nowhere more poignant for Stowe than during Jesus' eventual self-sacrifice.

For mothers like Stowe who had lost children, mothering went hand in hand with suffering, and anguish was bitterest when it was summoned at the death of a child.[48] For Stowe, Mary's blessedness and happiness lay in a gift that was not given to any other mother: "She had a security in possessing him such as is not accorded to other mothers. She knew that the child she adored was not to die till he had reached man's estate—she had not fear that accident, or sickness or any of those threatening causes which gave sad hours to so many other mothers, would come between him and her."[49] By interpreting Mary in this way, Stowe called up the sad memories of the death of her sons Henry and Charley through accident

---

44. Ibid., 164.
45. Ibid., 167.
46. Ibid., 167–68.
47. Caskey, *Chariot of Fire*, 187.
48. One reason for her anguish may have been that Stowe bore fewer children than her mother had. Because of this, the loss of children was felt even more keenly. See Sklar, "Victorian Women," 235.
49. Stowe, *Footsteps of the Master*, 64–65.

and sickness.[50] At the publication of *Footsteps of the Master* in 1877, Charley had been dead 28 years and Henry 20 years. For Stowe, although the Virgin Mary would eventually suffer over Jesus' crucifixion and death, she still had the security of knowing her son would live until he reached adulthood.

According to the Gospel accounts, Mary's bitterest suffering came at the end of Jesus' life. She was there at the cross when many others had forsaken him. Stowe states, "the delicacy of woman may cause her to shrink from the bustle of public triumph, but when truth and holiness are brought to public scorn she is there to defend, to suffer, to die."[51] In this scenario Mary stepped outside the boundary of a "proper" woman's sphere according to Victorian society into the "bustle of public triumph." This in itself was a kind of self-sacrifice, but for Stowe, Mary's sacrifice lay in part in witnessing the brutal death of her son, as she stated: "what were the sights, the sounds, the exhibitions of brutality among which Mary and the women friends of Jesus followed him to the Cross!" And in the midst of this, Mary does not "faint" or "sink," even though the "sword had gone through her heart."[52]

According to John Gatta, Stowe "identified with Mary's perseverance in facing keen personal loss."[53] She obviously empathized with other women, as evidenced by her poem "The Sorrows of Mary" (1867), which she dedicated to "mothers who have lost sons in the late [Civil] war."[54] In the poem, she imagined Mary and the disciple, John, mourning as they sit on sackcloth in a chamber below the room in which Herod and Pilate participated in a grand party. Jesus' crown of thorns, which he had worn while he was beaten and crucified, laid on the floor near her. Mary's sorrow was very great, and presaged the sorrow of the mothers to whom Stowe wrote:

> O mourning mothers, so many,
> Weeping o'er sons that are dead,
> Have ye thought of the sorrows of Mary's heart,
> Of the tears that Mary shed?

50. Additionally, her son Fred had been wounded at the Battle of Gettysburg, after which he struggled with severe alcoholism. Harriet had attempted to help him in many ways, but was never successful. He went to California in 1870 and was never heard from again. But the sorrow of these losses obviously remained with Stowe and formed the lenses through which she perceived Mary's blessedness.
51. Stowe, *Footsteps of the Master*, 73.
52. Ibid., 74.
53. Gatta, *American Madonna*, 57.
54. Harriet Beecher Stowe, "V: Fourth Hour: The Sorrows of Mary," in Literature Online, http://www.lion.chadwyck.com (accessed February 18, 2009).

As the poem continues, it is clear that for mothers, just as for Mary, hope lay in their faith in Jesus' resurrection. Just as Mary's anguish disappeared at the resurrection, so the mothers who lost sons in the war should also find hope in the resurrection of their own sons:

> O mourning mothers, so many,
> Weeping in woe and pain,
> Think on the joy of Mary's heart
> In a Son that is risen again.

Presumably, when Stowe spoke of the hope that sorrowing mothers could find in the resurrection, she spoke also to herself. Gatta comments that Stowe was able to draw "mythic power from her own maternal mourning over baby Charley" in her fiction work, and this seems to have held true for her poetry and her biblical interpretation as well.[55]

More of Stowe's understanding of the significance of the Virgin Mary for her society is found in the words of Harry in *My Wife and I*:

> Let us hope in a coming day that not Egeria, but Mary, the mother of Jesus, the great archetype of christian [*sic*] motherhood, shall be felt through all the laws and institutions of society. That Mary, who kept all things and pondered them in her heart—the silent poet, the prophetess, the one confidential friend of Jesus, sweet and retired as evening dew, yet strong to go forth with Christ against the cruel and vulgar mob, and to stand unfainting by the cross where He suffered![56]

Thus Mary was more than the blessed mother of Jesus. Her example was one that spoke not only to women of the day, but also had the power to influence the laws and institutions of Stowe's society. Stowe does not spell out how precisely this was to occur, but it is obvious that the example of Mary was paramount to Stowe's project of the maternalization of her society.

The Virgin Mary in Woman in Sacred History

In *Woman in Sacred History*, Stowe devoted two chapters to the Madonna. Before investigating her interpretation therein, a few words about this volume are necessary. Because Stowe was among those of her era that recognized women were often missing from accounts of history, Stowe attempted to redress history's wrongs by presenting "a history of womanhood under Divine culture."[57] She approached her subjects, she

55. Gatta, *American Madonna*, 57.
56. Stowe, *My Wife and I*, 39.
57. Stowe, *Woman in Sacred History*, 17.

stated, with the "same freedom of inquiry as the characters of any other history." According to Marion Taylor, in order to present women in biblical history, Stowe "appropriates the tools of contemporary biblical scholars… This approach allows her to set aside traditional theological categories, to reinterpret stories in fresh ways, to criticize traditional readings of texts (even those in the New Testament), and to write for a broad audience."[58] In essence, she used what could be called the "male" world of the academy and the church and combined it with her own particular female reading of the text in order to produce "readings that sometimes challenge traditional interpretations of texts and women's roles."[59]

In this volume, Stowe primarily presented women who had power and authority. The lithographs that accompanied her prose "heightened the mystery, power and sensuous womanliness of her subjects."[60] But, according to Caskey, what was particularly noteworthy in the volume were the prophetesses who "were shown excelling in their domestic attachments and finding exaltation in the cycle of conception, parturition, nursing and nurture…"[61] Above all of these was Mary, the ideal mother.

In her chapter entitled "Mary the Mythical Madonna," Stowe commented on Mary from the standpoint of art history. She saw that while Mary had been shown to observers to be a mythical goddess, she was different from portrayals of goddesses of classical antiquity who had been "worshiped for beauty, for grace, [and] for power."[62] Mary instead was portrayed as the goddess of poverty, sorrow, pity, and mercy who had "numbered her adorers in every land and climate and nation" because she could identify with human sorrow, which was particularly true in her role as mother.[63]

In the bulk of the chapter, Stowe spoke of ancient traditions about Mary: the annunciation of her birth to her mother Anna; her reception at the temple and the declaration of her high destiny; the divine revelation of her future husband, Joseph; the Annunciation; the stories about Jesus' birth in the Bible; and the stories of Jesus' crucifixion and death which are found in art, representations that "celebrate the memory of that mother's sorrows."[64] Stowe gave precedence to another tradition, in

58. Taylor, "Harriet Beecher Stowe," 107.
59. Ibid., 111.
60. Caskey, *Chariot of Fire*, 204.
61. Ibid.
62. Stowe, *Woman in Sacred History*, 169.
63. Ibid.
64. Ibid., 172.

which Christ, "after his resurrection, appeared first to his mother,—she, who had his last cares for anything earthly, was first to welcome his victory over death."[65] This was, Stowe believed, because "He, who loved his own unto the end, did not forget his mother in her hour of deepest anguish."[66] She ended her survey of traditions with the story of Mary's Assumption into heaven and her position as "mother of the Christian Church."[67]

But Stowe was not comfortable with many of these legends that, as she noted, were drawn from "the apocryphal books of the New Testament."[68] She opined that the worship of Mary as divine mother surpassed the worship of her Son over the centuries. Here Stowe refers to leading male scholars of her day, in this case Dr. Pusey, who, in his "Eirenicon," "traces the march of mariolatry through all the countries of the world."[69] Pusey, she stated, showed Mary as "represented commanding her son in heaven with the authority of a mother" and as one who was "identified with him in all that he says and does."[70] In order to correct these misapprehensions, she turned to an article by Reverend F. Meyrick in *Smith's Dictionary of the Bible* entitled "Mary" where she found that the origin of the cultus of Mariolatry was not found in Christian writings from the first to fifth centuries.[71] In fact, the Christian fathers of the first three or four centuries freely criticized Mary, particularly her "unbelief," and her "excessive ambition and foolish arrogance and vain glory, in wishing to speak with Jesus while engaged in public ministries." Stowe believed that Mary's character "ha[d] suffered by reaction from the idolatrous and fulsome adoration which has been bestowed on her" by Roman Catholics but "unjust depreciation" on the part of Protestants who

---

65. Ibid.
66. Ibid.
67. Ibid., 173.
68. Ibid., 174.
69. Ibid., 175. Edward Bouverie Pusey (22 August 1800–16 September 1882), was an English churchman and Regius Professor of Hebrew at Christ Church, Oxford. He was one of the leaders of the Oxford Movement. He was an Anglican who, in pursuing reunion with the Roman Catholic Church, wrote his "Eirenicon" in 1865. It offended Catholics particularly by its handling of the traditions about Mary. See William Barry, "Pusey and Puseyism, *Catholic Encyclopedia* (1913), in Wikisource, The Free Library, http://www.en.wikisource.org/wiki/Catholic_ Encyclopedia_(1913)/Pusey_and_ Puseyism (accessed February 19, 2009).
70. Stowe, *Woman in Sacred History*, 175.
71. Ibid.; Reverend F. Meyrick, Stowe states, "was one of her Majesty's inspectors of schools, late fellow and tutor of Trinity College, Oxford" (ibid.).

wanted to "make up for the unscriptural excesses…"[72] It is in response to this misunderstanding of Mary's motherhood that Stowe writes her chapter entitled "Mary the Mother of Jesus."

Much of this second chapter on Mary's motherhood is similar to her comments on Mary in *Footsteps of the Master*. Mary is the educator and most intimate friend of Jesus; she is known for a serious, calm, and balanced nature; she and Jesus have a close, intimate knowledge of one another; she suffers greatly at his crucifixion and death; and her influence on him is private, secret, and noble.[73] Stowe lauds Mary for living and acting in her son and not in herself: "Like a true mother she passed out of self into her son, and the life that she lived was in him; and in this sacred self-abnegation she must forever remain, the one ideal type of perfect motherhood."[74]

In her interpretation of Mary's ancestry, Stowe again used the work of contemporary scholars. Using Lightfoot as her guide, Stowe asserted that Jesus' Davidic ancestry came through Mary's genealogy, not Joseph's, which was the traditional interpretation of Jesus' ancestry found in Matt 1:15–16 and Luke 3:23.[75] Gatta comments, "While granting Mary exalted status, Stowe denies Joseph even his traditional singularity as Jesus' only genealogical link to the messianic kingship of David; she endorsed a curious exegesis of Luke 3:23–38, whereby Mary, too, stands by birth within the house of David."[76]

This characterization of Mary's exalted ancestry is in accord with Stowe's interpretation of Mary in this chapter as the true Victorian lady. In contrast to *Footsteps*, described above, here Stowe depicted Mary as the "offspring and flower of a race…from the finest physical stock of the world…trained and cultured by Divine oversight."[77] Mary was of "royal lineage," and, with her husband, remained "in, but not of, the sordid and vulgar world of Nazareth, living their life of faith and prayer, of mournful memories of past glory, and longing hopes for the future."[78] In other words, she was a member of the upper classes.

72. Ibid., 176.
73. Stowe, *Woman in Sacred History*, 181, 185, 193, 197, 198.
74. Ibid., 198.
75. Ibid., 185; J. B. Lightfoot (1828–1889) was a celebrated theologian and New Testament scholar. Among other honours, such as becoming the Lady Margaret's Professor of Divinity at Cambridge University, he was Bishop of Durham and chaplain to Queen Victoria.
76. Gatta, *American Madonna*, 57.
77. Stowe, *Woman in Sacred History*, 182.
78. Ibid., 183–84.

In accord with the Victorian expectations of women in Stowe's day, Mary had remarkable control over her emotions. She exhibited a "serious, calm and balanced nature," "practical good sense," and did not "faint or fall" while she stood by the cross where her son was crucified.[79] And, like Victorian women who were expected to influence their surroundings through private communications, she was remarkable for her silence in the face of all the miraculous events that attended Jesus birth, and pondered "them in her heart."[80] Thus Mary became a model of Victorian motherhood.

As in *Footsteps*, Stowe portrayed Mary's anguish at the crucifixion and death of her son in *Woman in Sacred History* in a way that would speak to her female readers. Mary stands by Jesus' cross "silent [and] firm" with the conviction that even though "the whole world turn against him, though God himself seems to forsake him, she will stand by him, she will love him, she will adore him till death, and after, and forever!"[81] She was the one who entered into his sufferings in the last hour. Stowe continues, "Never has sorrow presented itself in a form so venerable. Here is a depth of anguish which inspires awe as well as tenderness."[82]

At the end of this chapter, Stowe specifically outlines how it was that Mary was the "one ideal type of perfect motherhood." Although Mary felt deeply, she tempered her emotions by an "equable balance of the intellect." Although she may have had a "public mission," her powers were all "concentrated in the nobler, yet secret mission of the mother," wherein she never sought "to present herself as a public teacher."[83] In short, Stowe states, "Mary is presented to us as the mother, and the mother alone, seeking no other sphere. Like a true mother she passed out of self into her son, and the life that she lived was in him; and in this sacred self-abnegation she must forever remain, the one ideal of perfect motherhood."[84]

Thus, for Stowe, Mary's entire absence of self-seeking and self-assertion were the crowning perfection of her character. She saw these attributes, along with Mary's steadiness and silence, as in accordance with God's will, which her readers were to take reverently to their own bosoms in emulation. Thus as in *Footsteps*, readers were to follow the

79. Ibid., 185, 186, 197.
80. Ibid., 188.
81. Ibid., 197.
82. Ibid.
83. Ibid., 198.
84. Ibid.

example of Mary in *Woman in Sacred History*, but the focus was neither on how much she influenced Jesus, nor as clearly on how she acted as an example of the maternalization of Victorian society.

Conclusion:
The Significance of Stowe's Virgin Mary for Home and Society

The Virgin Mary loomed large in Harriet Beecher Stowe's understanding of what it meant to be the ideal Victorian mother. She was the moral educator and guide for Jesus in their private domestic sphere and she ran a frugal, orderly, and prosperous household. She taught Jesus in private because she eschewed teaching in public and she preferred privacy and solitude as befit her womanly sphere. She was trained and cultured and was from the upper classes. She was pious, emotionally stable, and loyal. She had a close relationship with her son and her thoughts and actions were on behalf of his welfare, not hers. Like Stowe and many of her readers, Mary knew what it was to suffer at the death of her beloved offspring.

Mary's motherly qualities lay the groundwork for many of Jesus' characteristics. Mary's domestic frugality and methodical ways influenced his ministry when he did not waste food when feeding the 5000. His illustration of the leaven hidden in three measures of meal was taken from watching his mother as she made bread. She taught him the Law and the Prophets in order that he might be prepared for his ministry. Because of their intimate relationship and the absence of his father, Stowe portrayed Jesus as a man with feminine, motherly qualities, and his self-sacrifice became the essence of the motherly characters Eva and Tom from *Uncle Tom's Cabin.*

In Stowe's eyes, Mary was blessed because she knew that her son would eventually reach adulthood in contrast to mothers of the Victorian era who had no such assurance. For Stowe, who lost Charley and Henry before they reached adulthood, this would have been a remarkable gift. Yet Mary was perhaps the best example of motherhood when she was depicted in anguish next to the cross of her dying son. By this example in particular Stowe saw Mary as "the great archetype of christian [*sic*] motherhood," that "shall be felt through all the laws and institutions of society."[85]

85. Stowe, *My Wife and I*, 39.

Thus for Stowe, the Virgin Mary was the ideal model for the maternalization of society. Her influence over her son that led to his feminine, motherly ways was a template for how she hoped this maternalization would spread in her society. Dorothy Berksen describes Stowe's maternalistic society in this way:

> She does not call for a matriarchy in which women literally will rule over men; instead she calls for a reversal of social and political values in which the traditionally "feminine" values will be infused into political and social institutions. If there is to be a millennial society, she suggests, then both men and women must be guided by the principles traditionally reserved for the domestic, feminine sphere, and shared by the "feminine" Christ of the New Testament. The new society that will result from this wedding of Christian and feminine virtues…will be communal, anti-materialistic, non-competitive, racially tolerant and essentially classless. It will be a society governed by the same principles that govern the loving, well-ordered family.[86]

Thus, for Stowe, the Virgin Mary was a figure of incredible influence, not only in her example for mothers of Stowe's time, but also in regard to the reformation of her society. As Stowe stated in *Woman in Sacred History*, "In Mary, womanhood in its highest and tenderest development of the MOTHER has been the object of worship. Motherhood with large capacities of sorrow, with the memory of bitter sufferings, with sympathies large enough to embrace every anguish of humanity!—such an object of veneration has inconceivable power."[87]

---

86. Dorothy Berkson, "Millennial Politics and the Feminine Fiction of Harriet Beecher Stowe," in *Critical Essays on Harriet Beecher Stowe* (ed. Elizabeth Ammons; Boston: G. K. Hall, 1980), 244–58 (245).
87. Stowe, *Woman in Sacred History*, 169.

OLYMPIA BROWN:
READING THE BIBLE AS A UNIVERSALIST MINISTER
AND PRAGMATIC SUFFRAGIST

Beth Bidlack

Introduction

In one of her last sermons, preached on September 12, 1920 at the Universalist Church in Racine, Wisconsin, and just a few days after women voted for the first time in the United States, Olympia Brown preached on Ps 24:7—"Lift up your head, O ye gates; and be ye lift up, ye everlasting doors; and the King of glory shall come in" (KJV). In this sermon she compared the recently won women's vote to the lifting of the gates:

> It is now nearly thirty years since I resigned my pastorate in this church. That is a long time and many things have happened, but the grandest thing has been the lifting up of the gates and the opening of the doors to the women of America, giving liberty to twenty-seven million women, thus opening to them a new and larger life and a higher ideal. The future opens before them, fraught with great possibilities of noble achievement. It is worth a lifetime to behold the victory.[1]

Throughout her career as a minister and later as a suffragist, Olympia Brown used the Bible to support her arguments for women's rights. Her understanding of Scripture was greatly influenced by her educational experiences and Universalist theology. This essay will explore her understanding and use of Scripture by (1) providing a biographical sketch of Brown; (2) outlining briefly Universalism in the early nineteenth century, including Hosea Ballou's influence on Brown and her family; (3) describing how Brown's educational experiences influenced her

---

1. "The Opening Doors," Olympia Brown Papers (OBP), Schlesinger Library (SL), Radcliffe Institute, Harvard University, folder 36; reprinted in Dorothy May Emerson, ed., *Standing Before Us: Unitarian Universalist Women and Social Reform 1776–1936* (Boston: Skinner Books, 2000), 460.

understanding of the Bible; and (4) demonstrating how she used Scripture in her struggle for woman's suffrage, as illustrated in three of her speeches. In order to appreciate more fully her understanding and use of Scripture, it is helpful to begin with a short sketch of Brown's life, including her earliest exposure to religion. As will become apparent throughout this essay, her early liberal religious upbringing greatly influenced her educational pursuits, her understanding of ministry, and her struggle for women's rights, including the right to vote.

1. *Brief Biographical Sketch*

Olympia Brown's parents were both born in Plymouth, Vermont, an area that Brown describes in her autobiography as a place that "had produced a class of pioneers and patriots as powerful and rugged as their hills."[2] "The Republic of the Green Mountain" was known for being an early promoter of abolition and the Revolutionary War hero Ethan Allen. Brown's father, Asa Brown (1808–1887), was born in "Plymouth Union," and her mother, Lephia Olympia Brown (1811–1900), was born in a nearby area known as "Plymouth Notch."[3] Olympia Brown described her parents and other residents of Plymouth as being "truly educated" by the study and love of good books and by intelligent conversation and reflection.[4] Shortly after they were married in 1834, Lephia and Asa Brown traveled west, following a group from nearby Ludlow, Vermont to the small town of Schoolcraft, Michigan. They purchased a little farm and log house three miles north of the town in an area called Prairie Ronde.

---

2. Gwendolen B. Willis, ed., *Olympia Brown: An Autobiography* (Racine, Wisc.: G. Willis, 1960), 1. For additional biographical information, see Olympia Brown, *Acquaintances, Old and New, Among Reformers* (Milwaukee: S.E. Tate Printing, 1911); Charlotte Coté, *Olympia Brown: The Battle for Equality* (Racine, Wisc.: Mother Courage Press, 1988); Dana Greene, *Suffrage and Religious Principle: Speeches and Writings of Olympia Brown* (Metuchen, N.J.: Scarecrow, 1983), 1–17; Beverly Zink-Sawyer, *From Preachers to Suffragists: Woman's Rights and Religious Conviction in the Lives of Three Nineteenth-Century American Clergywomen* (Louisville, Ky.: Westminster John Knox, 2003); Catherine R. Hitchings, "Olympia Brown," in *Universalist and Unitarian Woman Ministers* (2d ed.; Boston: Universalist Historical Society, 1983), 30–31; and Laurie Carter Noble, "Olympia Brown," http://www25.uua.org/uuhs/duub/articles/olympiabrown.html (accessed November 11, 2008).

3. Brown, *Acquaintances*, 1.

4. Ibid., 2.

Shortly after their arrival in Michigan, on January 5, 1835, Olympia Brown was born, followed two years later by her sister Oella. At that point, her father built a larger house for the growing family. In 1839, another sister, Marcia, was born, and in 1843, a brother, Arthur, followed. Oella, her closest sibling, married and moved to Chicago. She became a schoolteacher and eventually settled in Everett, Washington. Marcia married and raised her family in Kansas. After finishing law school at the University of Michigan, Arthur moved to Salt Lake City and later became a United States Senator.

Education played an important role within the family. Brown referred to her mother as the earliest reformer that she ever knew.[5] Even though there were many household responsibilities on the farm in Michigan, "she yet seized every opportunity to read and her mind was well stored with knowledge."[6] Years later, Brown would affirm that her mother's "reading was extensive and her judgment of and taste for literature was remarkable."[7] Evening readings were an important time in the Brown household and included not only standard books of the time, but also Horace Greeley's *New York Weekly Tribune*, "the farmer's authority for everything from grains and soils to religion and reform."[8] It was in the *Tribune* that Brown read about the Woman's Rights Convention in Worcester, Massachusetts, held on October 22 and 23, 1850: "The speeches stirred my soul, the names of the participants loomed up before me as the names of great heroes often inspire young boys. They seemed to me like prophets of a better time; not only the participants in that meeting but all the great reformers of that day had a fascination for me."[9] In the *Tribune*, Brown also read about Antoinette Brown (no relation) who had been ordained to the Christian ministry in 1853 by a congregation in South Butler, New York. She later recounted her feelings at the time: "My imagination was all afloat, my ambition was stirred. Antoinette Brown! How many times I repeated the name! Antoinette!! Antoinette!! It seemed to stand for everything that was beautiful and exalted."[10] Thus, the seeds of ministry were planted firmly in Olympia Brown.

In addition to evening readings, Brown's father built a schoolhouse on his land. He visited the neighboring families, asking them to contribute

5. Ibid., 7.
6. Ibid.
7. Ibid., 8.
8. Ibid.
9. Ibid., 9.
10. Ibid.

to a modest salary and board for a teacher. Eventually, the funds were raised, and the Brown children began their formal schooling, encouraged by their mother who "made it a rule that if any child was studying, she need not be called on for housework."[11] Once Olympia and her sister Oella outgrew the small schoolhouse, they were sent to the public school in nearby Schoolcraft. At age fifteen, Olympia began to teach school.[12] Shortly thereafter when Brown's mother learned about Mary Lyon's Mt. Holyoke Female Seminary, she "determined that her two older daughters should now go to this school." Her father, on the other hand, thought such an idea "an absurdity."[13] Because her father controlled the household funds, Brown set about trying to persuade her father of the importance of women's education, a commitment that she and her mother shared. Eventually, her father conceded, and Brown and her sister busied themselves with their studies, hoping to shorten the usual Mt. Holyoke course of study from three years to two.

In September of 1854, Brown, her sister, and their friend Mary Allen arrived at Mt. Holyoke in South Hadley, Massachusetts.[14] Upon their arrival, they were greeted with a list of rules: "young ladies are not allowed to stand on the portico, young ladies are not allowed to stand in the doorways, young ladies are not allowed to linger in the halls, and so on for forty rules daily, more or less!"[15] This was quite a change from their home in Michigan where Brown and her sister had studied for nearly a year in preparation for Mt. Holyoke. Here, they were told, "we never examine young ladies in algebra, we never examine young ladies in Latin."[16] Mary Lyon, the founder, had died in 1849, but when Brown arrived Mt. Holyoke's curriculum had generally remained unchanged. Brown faced larger challenges at Mt. Holyoke, which will be described in more detail below.

After one academic year, Brown left Mt. Holyoke in bitter disappointment. She recounted that her father empathized so much with her experiences there that he told her she could go to any school of her choosing. She was determined to attend a "real college." At the time, there were only two colleges that would admit women—Oberlin and Antioch. Brown learned that although Oberlin admitted women, it restricted their full participation in the educational process. Lucy Stone and Antoinette

11. Willis, *Autobiography*, 5–6.
12. Ibid., 7–8.
13. Ibid., 9.
14. Ibid.
15. Ibid., 10.
16. Ibid.

Brown both completed courses of study at Oberlin, but were not allowed to participate in the public speaking opportunities open to the male students. As a result, in 1856, Brown chose to attend Horace Mann's Antioch College in Yellow Springs, Ohio. She later recounted her excitement about Antioch: "I was not disappointed. Although the college was new and poor, and lacked most of the equipment thought necessary in a college even then, I found the intellectual atmosphere most congenial."[17] In order to be close to the Brown children who also attended Antioch, her parents moved from Michigan to Yellow Springs. Once all four had graduated, the family moved back to Michigan, this time to Kalamazoo.[18]

During the winter of 1860–61, Brown participated for the first time in a petition drive for woman's property rights while staying in Cleveland, Ohio with the family of Antioch classmate, Mattie Tilden. The point of the petition was to allow married women control over their inherited property and earnings and the right of guardianship of their children. At that time, inherited property and earnings were transferred to the husband upon marriage. In addition, children born as a result of the marriage were under the guardianship of their father, not their mother.[19] Brown was so successful in getting signatures that she was invited to help present the petition to the Ohio legislature.[20] That petition helped Ohio women gain property rights and inspired Brown to continue working for woman's rights.

After she graduated in 1860, Brown looked for a theological seminary that would admit women because she intended to pursue ordination. She again dismissed Oberlin as an option because of Antoinette Brown Blackwell's[21] experiences there and settled, instead, on the Canton Theological Seminary at St. Lawrence University, the Universalist seminary in New York, where she studied from 1861 to 1863. In 1863, she graduated from Canton and was ordained by the Northern Universalist Association.[22] Her

17. Ibid., 13.
18. Ibid., 22.
19. See Brown, *Acquaintances*, 19–25, for Brown's account of her first petition drive.
20. Coté, *Olympia Brown*, 50.
21. In 1856, Antoinette Brown married Samuel Charles Blackwell and became known as Antoinette Brown Blackwell.
22. Brown knew that Antoinette Brown Blackwell had not been ordained by a denomination: "I had always greatly admired Antoinette Brown... She was the only woman I knew of who was preaching, and I doubt not that my admiration for her had some influence in my determination to enter the ministry. Yet even she had not had official ordination from any denomination, and therefore did not have the authority or influence which ordination should give" (Willis, *Autobiography*, 18). Some

graduation and ordination did not occur without a great deal of struggle. When she appeared before the ordaining council of the Northern Universalist Association at its annual meeting, she discovered that there was a delegate from Huvelton, New York where she had preached the previous week. Although there was much discussion and some opposition, the council was persuaded by the Huvelton delegate and voted in favor of her ordination. After ordination, she served churches in Vermont (1863), Weymouth, Massachusetts (1864–70), Bridgeport, Connecticut (1870–76), and Racine, Wisconsin (1878–87). She was serving the Weymouth congregation when President Lincoln was assassinated. A meeting of all the Weymouth ministers was scheduled so that together they might plan a memorial service; however, some of the men were opposed to her

scholars believe that Lydia Ann Moulton Jenkins, not Olympia Brown, may have been the first woman to be ordained by a denomination, the Universalists, in 1860, but Brown herself seemed to be unaware of this claim, as she noted: "This was the first time that the Universalists, or indeed any denomination had formally ordained any woman as a preacher. They took that stand, a remarkable one for the day, which shows the courage of those men" (Willis, *Autobiography*, 21). Several scholars have affirmed Brown as being the first woman ordained by a denomination (e.g. Catherine F. Hitchings, *Universalist and Unitarian*, 30; Greene, *Suffrage and Religious Principle*, 13; and Zink-Sawyer, *From Preachers to Suffragists*, 52). Mrs. E. R. Hanson, author of *Our Woman Workers: Biographical Sketches of Women in the Universalist Church for Literary, Philanthropic and Christian Work* (2d ed.; Chicago: The Star and Covenant Office, 1882), 426, also affirmed this status for Brown and claimed that Jenkins was not ordained: "Lydia A. Jenkins, who was one of our earliest preachers or evangelists, laid no claim to the title 'Rev.,' as she was never ordained." Hitchings does not even include an entry for Jenkins in her collection of short biographical sketches on Unitarian and Universalist women ministers (*Universalist and Unitarian*). David Robinson claims that "Olympia Brown...was *one* of the first women ordained to the ministry by an American denomination (1863)" (*The Unitarians and the Universalists* [Westport, Conn.: Greenwood, 1985], 223). In his biographical sketch of Lydia Jenkins, Robinson cites the Universalist scholar Russell E. Miller who referred to Jenkins as "the first woman to be regularly fellowshipped as a Universalist preacher" (*The Larger Hope* [Boston: Unitarian Universalist Association, 1979–85], 1:547). More evidence is needed to determine if being in fellowship was the same as being ordained at that time. Charles Semowich is one of the few to assert that Jenkins, not Brown, was the first woman ordained by a denomination in the United States ("Lydia Ann Jenkins: Women's Rights Activist, Physician, and First Recognized Woman Minister in the United States," *Yesteryears* [1985]: 40–54). Robinson refers to the work of Charles Semowich (p. 199 n. 33), as does Charles A. Howe, "Lydia Ann Jenkins," n.p. (cited November 10, 2008). Online: http://www25.uua.org/uuhs/duub/articles/lydiaannjenkins.html. Jenkins's ordination is difficult to verify because the records of the Association that ordained her do not seem to exist. Additional research in this area is needed.

participation so she held a separate service at her own church in Wey-mouth and later recalled, "I preached as good a memorial sermon as I could, and when the day was over all my church joined in approving my efforts."[23]

In the summer of 1867, at the request of Lucy Stone and her suffragist husband Henry Blackwell, Olympia was very active in the "Kansas Campaign." That year, the citizens of Kansas were to vote on a state suffrage amendment. In the midst of the summer heat, Brown gave hundreds of speeches on behalf of the woman's suffrage movement. Susan B. Anthony praised Brown's efforts in Kansas, in spite of the defeat of the ballot measure: "Never was defeat so glorious a victory. My dear Olympia, if ever any money gets in to my power to control, you shall have evidence that I appreciate the herculean work you have done here in Kansas the past four long months."[24] Elizabeth Cady Stanton joined Anthony in her praise of Brown:

> Chief among the women who labored in Kansas in 1867, are Olympia Brown and Viola Hutchinson,—the one speaking and preaching, the other singing, her sweet songs of freedom, in churches, school-houses, depots, barns, and the open air. Olympia Brown…is the most promising young woman now speaking in this cause. She is small, delicately organized, and has a most pleasing personnel. She is a graceful, fluent speaker, with wonderful powers of continuity and concentration, and is oblivious to everything but the idea she wishes to utter. While in Kansas she spoke every day for four months, twice and three times, Sundays not excepted. She is a close, clear reasoner and able debater. The Kansas politicians all feared to meet her. One prominent judge in the State encountered her in debate, on one occasion, to the utter discomfiture of himself and his compeers… She followed him, using his own words, illustrations, and arguments, to show the importance of suffrage for woman, much to his chagrin, and the amusement of the audience, who cheered her from beginning to end. At the close of the meeting a rising, vote was taken, of those in favor of woman's suffrage. All the audience arose, except the judge, and he looked as if he would have given anything if consistence would have permitted him to rise also.[25]

23. Willis, *Autobiography*, 24.

24. Brown, *Acquaintances*, 73–74. For more on the Kansas campaign, see Brown, *Acquaintances*, 55–74 and Brown's account in Elizabeth Cady Stanton, Susan B. Anthony, and Matilda Joslyn Gage, eds., *History of Woman Suffrage* (6 vols.; repr., Salem, N.H.: Ayer Co., 1985 [1881–1922]), 2:259–61.

25. Elizabeth Cady Stanton, "The Woman's Rights Movement and Its Champions in the United States," in *Eminent Women of the Age: Being Narratives of the Lives and Deeds of the Most Prominent Women of the Present Generation* (ed. James Parton et al.; Hartford: S. M. Betts, 1868), 402–3.

Brown was a charter member of the American Equal Rights Association, which was founded in 1866. When it dissolved in 1869, she supported both the National Woman Suffrage Association (NWSA) and the American Woman Suffrage Association (AWSA). Brown was careful not to favor one organization over the other in spite of their differences, but she did serve as a Vice-President-at-Large of the NWSA.[26] When the two merged in 1890, she supported the newly formed National American Woman Suffrage Association, but in 1902, founded the Federal Suffrage Association, which advocated the passage of a federal law providing for the enfranchisement of women.[27] In 1868, she helped found the New England Woman's Suffrage Association.[28] In 1887, after nearly twenty-five years of ministry, she left the parish and began working full time for woman's suffrage. For nearly thirty years, she was the President of the Wisconsin State Woman's Suffrage Association.[29]

26.   Willis, *Autobiography*, 46; see Stanton, *History of Woman Suffrage*, 3:955–57, for the NWSA Constitution, which lists Brown as a Vice President. Dana Greene notes that when the NWSA and AWSA were formed in 1869, "Brown walked a narrow line between them, supporting both the Stanton–Anthony faction, with whom she felt stronger sympathy, as well as Lucy Stone and the Boston women. She frequently attended the conventions of these associations and later served as Vice-President of the National Woman Suffrage Association" (Greene, *Suffrage and Religious Principle*, 3). The NWSA and AWSA were both founded in 1869, due to a dispute over the Fifteenth Amendment to the United States Constitution. The Fifteenth Amendment states that "[t]he right of citizens of the United States to vote shall not be denied or abridged by the United States or by any state on account of race, color, or previous condition of servitude" (U.S. Constitution, amend. 15, sec. 1). The NWSA, founded by Susan B. Anthony and Elizabeth Cady Stanton, opposed the Amendment because it did not include *sex*, along with race, color, or previous condition of servitude. Membership in the NWSA was open only to women, whereas membership in the AWSA was open to both women and men. The AWSA, founded by Lucy Stone, Henry Blackwell, and Julia Ward Howe, supported the Fifteenth Amendment and believed that woman suffrage could best be obtained by state-by-state campaigns. The NWSA, on the other hand, believed woman suffrage could only be obtained via a federal Constitutional amendment. In 1890, both groups realized a unified voice was needed regarding woman suffrage, and thus the National American Woman Suffrage Association (NAWSA) was formed. For more on the AWSA, see Stanton, *History of Woman Suffrage*, 2:756–862. For more on the formation of the NAWSA, see Stanton, *History of Woman Suffrage*, 4:164 and 5:3–22. For more on the Federal Suffrage Association, see Stanton, *History of Woman Suffrage*, 5:656–59.

27.   Greene, *Suffrage and Religious Principle*, 5.

28.   For more on the founding of the New England Woman's Suffrage Association, see Brown, *Acquaintances*, 75–79.

29.   For more on Brown's role in the Wisconsin State Woman's Suffrage Association, see Brown, *Acquaintances*, 100–115.

In spite of protests from her mother and some of her friends that marriage would interfere with her preaching, in April 1873, she wed John Henry Willis (1825–1893), also a Universalist and a member of the Bridgeport church. John and Olympia agreed that she, following the example of Lucy Stone, would keep her "maiden" name, but many would later refer to her as Mrs. Willis.[30] In her autobiography, Olympia recalled John's support of her very fondly: "I thought that with a husband so entirely in sympathy with my work marriage could not interfere, but rather assist. And so it proved, for I could have married no better man. He shared in all my undertakings, and always stood for the right."[31] Willis owned a small business in Bridgeport, and later managed the *Racine Daily Times*. When he died unexpectedly in 1893, Brown wrote, "Endless sorrow has fallen upon my heart... He was one of the truest and best men that ever lived, firm in his religious convictions, loyal to every right principle, strictly honest and upright in his life."[32] John and Olympia had a son, Henry Parker Willis (1874–1937), who completed a Ph.D. at the University of Chicago and became a well-known economist who taught at Columbia University, and a daughter Gwendolen Brown Willis (1876–1969), who completed a Ph.D. in Classics at Bryn Mawr College, where she also taught. During her later years Olympia Brown spent winters with her daughter in Baltimore and summers at her home in Racine. Brown was one of the few early pioneers who lived to vote in the 1920 election. She died in Baltimore on October 23, 1926. After her death, her daughter played an instrumental role in organizing her papers and giving them to the Schlesinger Library at Radcliffe College.

2. *Universalism and Hosea Ballou*

Growing up in rural Michigan, Olympia did not attend church or Sunday School; however, her mother, who "cherished the teachings of the Reverend Hosea Ballou of Vermont, one of the founders of Universalism," gave Olympia and her siblings their religious instruction.[33] Although John Murray, with his message of "not Hell, but hope," is considered the

30. For a brief account of Brown's conversation with Lucy Stone regarding "Miss," "Mrs.," and married names, see Brown, *Acquaintances*, 38.

31. Willis, *Autobiography*, 26.

32. Ibid., 27.

33. Ibid., 12. For more on Universalism in America, see Ann Lee Bressler, *The Universalist Movement in America: 1770–1880* (New York: Oxford University Press, 2001); Richard Eddy, *Universalism in America* (2 vols.; Boston, 1886); Russell Miller, *The Larger Hope* (2 vols.; Boston: Unitarian Universalist Association, 1979–85).

Father of American Universalism, Hosea Ballou (1771–1852) also played a very important role in the history of the denomination. From 1802 to 1809, Ballou had a circuit-rider ministry in Vermont, where Olympia's family lived prior to moving to Michigan. During this time, he wrote *A Treatise on Atonement*, in which he emphasized the love, not the judgment, of God and the "brotherhood of man." He believed that everyone will experience God's salvation. Along with early Unitarians, he advocated the use of reason in interpreting Scripture. He quickly rose to leadership within Universalism, moving to Portsmouth, New Hampshire in 1809, then to Boston in 1817, where he served as minister of the Second Universalist Society until his retirement in 1845.

In 1803, the General Convention of Universalists approved the following Profession of Belief, commonly known as the Winchester Profession, which served Universalism until its consolidation with Unitarianism in 1961. Ballou's theology greatly influenced this statement of faith, which in turn influenced his *Treatise on Atonement*:[34]

> Article I. We believe that the Holy Scriptures of the Old and New Testaments contain a revelation of the character of God, and of the duty, interest and final destination of mankind.
>
> Article II. We believe that there is one God, whose nature is Love, revealed in one Lord Jesus Christ, by one Holy Spirit of Grace, who will finally restore the whole family of mankind to holiness and happiness.
>
> Article III. We believe that holiness and true happiness are inseparably connected, and that believers ought to be careful to maintain order, and practice good works; for these things are good and profitable to men.

As their denomination grew, Universalists recognized that their commitment to "practice good works" applied not only to daily individual life, but also to society at large. One way they sought to affect society was to advocate for a public education system because they felt that "most of the private schools were promoting orthodox religious beliefs; hence, they welcomed the idea of public schools, which operated under the principle of church–state separation, where no religious instruction would be permitted."[35]

---

34. Ernest Cassara, ed., *Universalism in America: A Documentary History of a Liberal Faith* (3d ed.; Boston: Skinner House Books, 1997), 110. See also Charles A. Howe, *The Larger Faith: A Short History of American Universalism* (Boston: Skinner House Books, 1993), 20–21. The statement of faith is known as the Winchester Profession because it was adopted in Winchester, New Hampshire.

35. Howe, *Larger Faith*, 40–41.

3. *More on Brown's Educational Experiences*

As noted above, Brown faced many day-to-day challenges at Mt. Holyoke, but perhaps her biggest challenge was her encounter with "orthodox" theology. Not only were students expected to spend half an hour each day alone in prayer,[36] but an evangelist also visited the school regularly. Brown recounted one such visit as follows:

> At one time a distinguished preacher from Boston came and stayed for several weeks, his duty among us being to inquire into our "state of mind," and to hold daily services with the purpose of converting any waverers... My sister and I were considered suitable objects for this zealous missionary, and we were invited to evening meetings at which we were confronted with embarrassing questions as to our religious convictions, which we were not prepared to answer... However, even this proved profitable to us for we were now obliged to study our Bibles, and to read and investigate in order to form our own opinions. We managed to evade the religious persecution, privately sent to Boston for books, and set to work to find out for ourselves whether we were to believe in such uncongenial doctrines, and if not, how to give reasons for our non-belief. Through my private studies I became thoroughly imbued with the doctrines of Divine Love, the Fatherhood of God, and the Brotherhood of Man, which have ever since been the joy of my life.[37]

Having faced this theological challenge, Brown chose not to return to Mt. Holyoke, but to attend to Antioch College, where she again challenged the status quo. When she asked the administration to include women in the school's lecture program, she was told there were no women comparable to the invited speakers (e.g. Horace Greeley, Wendell Phillips, and Ralph Waldo Emerson). In response, she and her fellow female students raised the funds necessary to invite Antoinette Brown Blackwell to speak on a Saturday evening and preach the following morning in a local church.[38] This was another life-changing event for Olympia, who later recounted, "It was the first time I had heard

36. Willis, *Autobiography*, 11.
37. Ibid., 12.
38. Brown Blackwell was ordained on September 15, 1853 at a congregational church in South Butler, New York. She resigned just ten months into her ministry and later joined the Unitarian Church. Regarding Brown Blackwell's ordination, Brown noted, "Her ordination was not by any ecclesiastical authority or in accordance with the requirements or usages of any of the denominations, and therefore did not establish a precedent or open a way for other women to enter the ministry except as her example served as a stimulus and inspiration for others and thus led them to try to open the doors so long sealed against them" (Brown, *Acquaintances*, 17).

a woman preach, and the sense of the victory lifted me up. I felt as though the Kingdom of Heaven were at hand."[39] Her passion for women's rights was rekindled further at Antioch, when Frances "Aunt Fanny" Gage (1808–1884), a journalist and novelist, who was an outspoken advocate of women's rights, temperance, and abolition, came to give a lecture on women's rights. Olympia recalled that Gage "opened the work of the evening by reading the description of the virtuous woman in the last chapter of Proverbs. It has been a favorite chapter with me and I often read it at Suffrage meetings as it really contains the gist of the whole matter. 'Give her of the fruit of her hands and let her own works praise her in the gates.' That is just what the advocates of Woman's Suffrage ask."[40]

These positive educational experiences at Antioch are in sharp contrast to another experience she had there. As Olympia recounted, Professor Craig of the faculty spoke to the male students of Antioch one Sunday and to the female students the following Sunday:

> On the first Sunday he took for his subject two characters from the Bible "Samson and Samuel." Samuel, he said, represented the spiritual life of Israel, but Samson represented the physical strength. He made two long sermons on these, one in the morning, the other in the afternoon, eulogizing both characters. On the following Sunday, he preached two very short sermons to the women, taking "Ruth and Esther" as his subjects. Ruth, he said "represented the plain prose of woman's life. She did not go about trying to get her name into the papers. She followed Boaz. She followed him to the field. She married Boaz, and that there was all there was of it. That was the plain prose of woman's life." In the afternoon he spoke on Esther. He said "Esther represented the poetry of woman's life. She wanted to save her people. She was willing to put herself in peril to accomplish this. She said 'if I perish, I will perish, but I will go before the King.' And she went to make her plea, which was successful." The women students were indignant at these sermons, as most of them were thinking of some work or position outside the common field society had assigned to women, and the idea that the plain prose of woman's life was simply to marry Boaz, was repugnant to us, and especially the very peculiar way of getting a husband.[41]

Brown was determined to become a preacher. Given her experiences at Mt. Holyoke, she had become "anxious to tell people the truth about the doctrine of endless punishment. I vainly supposed that if people could only be told that there was no such thing as everlasting punishment as it

39. Willis, *Autobiography*, 15.
40. Brown, *Acquaintances*, 10.
41. Willis, *Autobiography*, 16.

was then literally preached they would be rejoiced… I was determined to seek ordination."[42] Thus, upon graduating from Antioch, she looked for a theological school where she could continue her education. In her *Autobiography*, she recounted that when she wrote to the Theological Seminary at St. Lawrence University,

> Mr. Ebenezer Fisher, the President, replied that I would be admitted and would have all the opportunities that the school afforded, but he felt called upon to state that he did not think women were called to the ministry. But, he said, "I leave that between you and the Great Head of the Church." This, I thought, was just where it should be left, and I could not ask anything better. But when I arrived I was told that I had not been expected, and that Mr. Fisher had said that I would not come as he had written so discouragingly to me, I had supposed this discouragement was my encouragement, and I went with high hope and great expectation. I determined, at any rate, to make the best of it and to like everybody and everything.[43]

In spite of her positive attitude, Brown faced much discrimination at St. Lawrence. She recounted one such event in which several young men harshly critiqued her sermons:

> Every Wednesday we read before the class sermons which we had composed and each was invited to criticise [*sic*]. The young men usually indulged in very derogatory remarks about my sermons, which I found hard to bear. The mildest of these criticisms was this frequent one: "Well, it was very good, but I should hardly call it a sermon." There were two young men who prided themselves on devising various petty forms of annoyance, like getting under my windows and mimicking my voice which they thought peculiar… I tried not to notice these disagreeable things, realizing that it was the first time in this country that a woman had undertaken this task, and wishing that others who would come after me might not experience the same treatment.[44]

4. *Use of Scripture in the Struggle for Woman's Suffrage*

Beginning at Antioch and throughout her parish ministry, Brown worked for woman's suffrage. Susan B. Anthony, a well-known leader of the woman's suffragist movement, had long encouraged her to take the world for her "pastoral charge."[45] In 1887, almost twenty years after

42. Ibid., 18.
43. Ibid.
44. Ibid., 19.
45. OBP, SL, folder 129, Susan B. Anthony to Olympia Brown, "Take the world for your pastoral charge," March 12, 1868.

138   *Breaking Boundaries*

Anthony's plea, Brown left full-time parish ministry for full-time suffrage work, bringing along her Universalist theology and educational experiences, which would greatly influence her work.[46] Three of her speeches, in particular, reveal the influence of her theology and education on her suffrage work: (1) "Address on Woman Suffrage"; (2) "Why the Church Should Demand the Ballot for Women"; and (3) "Woman's Place in the Church."

First, in her "Address on Woman Suffrage" (undated), Brown concluded that "[w]oman Suffrage is the only possible salvation for this country."[47] In order to make this assertion, she built her argument as follows. First, as support of her claim that "[t]he Christian Religion teaches the lesson of service, [and] mutual helpfulness," she began by paraphrasing relevant biblical passages, including "Do as you will be done by" (Matt 7:12); "By love serve one another" (Gal 5:13); and "If one member suffers all the members suffer with it. If one member rejoices, all the members rejoice with it" (1 Cor 12:26).[48] She continued by arguing that the founders of this country were "men inspired by a great idea, that of the equality of the human race and the worth of the human being and they aimed to found a great Christian Republic in which there should be 'neither Jew nor Greek, nor bond nor free, nor male nore [sic] female'" (Gal 3:28). Here and elsewhere there are allusions to the Winchester Profession, as in the following excerpt: "A Christian democracy such as we claim to be here is the outgrowth of this Christian ideal of the worth of man and the duty of all men to work together, cooperating for the common good." Brown also made a more pragmatic argument by noting that both men and women have contributed financially to this country, and, therefore, they should both contribute with the ballot as well. In this speech, Brown made a case that women have a different moral outlook, perhaps even a superior morality, than men:

---

46. The passage of the Wisconsin "School Suffrage Law" in 1855, prompted her resignation: "This law gave rise to much discussion and being interpreted as giving women full right to vote, necessitated a thorough canvass of the state in order that the women might be instructed in regard to their rights. The consequence of this was at length the resignation of my ministerial work in Racine, which occurred in 1887." Brown continued preaching part-time for "four years in Mukwonago, Wisconsin; two in Columbus, and one in Neenah at different subsequent periods" (Willis, *Autobiography*, 29).

47. OBP, SL, folder 49.

48. For the most part, Brown does not include the citation for the biblical verses she uses in her sermons and speeches. Often, she paraphrased verses rather than quoting them exactly.

Men and women view subjects from different standpoints. Woman is interested first of all in the home and in the children and in the social life around her. She, naturally, thinks first of the Philanthropies and all those instrumentalities which go to make the home secure and which tend to a better development of child life. Men, on the other hand, are interested in business. The questions which appeal to them are financial questions. They are questions of money. Our Legislators give their attention very largely to purely money questions... Now when we have the business side represented and the home and the Philanthropies represented we may look for a good government. But the effect of having only the money side presented has been to place an undue value upon material things and has given rise to what we call the materialism of our time. We attach such great importance to the money power, we bow down before the Golden Calf. We allow ourselves to be governed by a dozen men who control the finances of the whole country. A great many people today are complaining of the supremacy of the wealthy classes and of their control in our Government and our politics. And yet this is the direct result of a masculine government in which the feminine influence has not been felt. The result is indeed disastrous... [E]mancipation can only come by giving the ballot to all the people, by securing the influence of women in favor of the great Philanthropies, in favor of those things that tend to building up purity and truth in our communities.[49]

In her autobiography, Brown argued that the differences between the nature of men and women make women well suited for ministry: "There is certainly room for women in the ministry. It is often said of a preacher 'he is a good preacher but no pastor. He does not call upon his people.' This is because one man cannot do everything, and the same person is not usually suited to both pastoral work and pulpit service. Many of the larger churches now have two ministers for this reason. One of these should be a woman."[50] Yet Brown did not state which aspect of ministry women are best suited for—pastoral work or the pulpit. She herself seemed able to do both successfully. It was her desire to preach that led her to pursue ordination, but her pastoral nature also increased church membership and helped her congregations to work together (e.g. for capital improvements to their churches).[51]

49. OBP, SL, folder 49.
50. Willis, *Autobiography*, 29.
51. In her speech "Woman's Place in the Church" she stated that women have the qualities needed in the Church: "It is my own opinion, as a woman of seven years' experience in the ministry, that the work of the minister is peculiarly suited to woman, that the great need of the present time is women in the clerical profession. Just what we want to give life to our churches, and awaken the people to effort, is the enthusiasm and the heart which earnest, devoted, educated women could bring to

In the second speech under examination, "Why the Church Should
Demand the Ballot for Women" (undated), Brown drew on Gal 3:28
once again, but she extended her argument by asserting that women have
had a unique and prominent role in the life of the church from the very
beginning: "Women from the very first have been the very life of the
Church. The Master revealed Himself spcially [*sic*] to women. The first
miracle was wrought at the request of a woman. They were last at the
cross and first at the sepulchre, and when he rose from the dead he
revealed himself first of all to a woman and bade her go and proclaim the
risen Lord."[52] She also maintained that within the early church, "Christianity broke down the old barriers and admitted women to the public
assemblies, recognized their right to speak as they were moved and to
bear their testimony in the great congregation, and from that day to this
Christianity and the Christian Church have been upheld, inspired, sustained and honored by the work of women and a very large proportion of
the membership is composed of women."[53]

In this speech, Brown also appealed to the common sense of justice of
her audience: "The Church is composed in considerable part of women…
Should not this large body of church members express an opinion on
questions pertaining to the common good? The Church is the repository
of Christian truth; it stands for honesty and purity and it aims at the
highest things; should not its whole influence be felt at the ballot box?"[54]
Thus, the Church owed women its support regarding suffrage because
women had worked so hard for the Church. This is somewhat reminiscent of her argument in her "Address on Woman Suffrage" that because
both women and men contribute financially to society, both should have
the right to vote. In fact, Brown portrays the Church as unable to fulfill
its potential as a powerful force in society because it "…is hampered,
crippled, weakened by the disfranchisement of the majority of its members… Society today needs the votes of the church women in settling the
great moral problems of our time… [T]he Church if it would maintain
the dignity and self-respect that belong to such an organization, if it
would do its grandest work, must secure the ballot for its women."[55]
Brown believed that only when women have secured the right to vote can

the work" (OBP, SL, folder 25; reprinted in Greene, *Suffrage and Religious
Principle*, 70–78).
   52. OBP, SL, folder 49; reprinted in Greene, *Suffrage and Religious Principle*,
141. The speech is reprinted in Greene, *Suffrage and Religious Principle*, 139–43.
   53. OBP, SL, folder 49; reprinted in Greene, *Suffrage and Religious Principle*,
141.
   54. Greene, *Suffrage and Religious Principle*, 139.
   55. Ibid., 141–42.

the ideals of Christ be made manifest in society. This sentiment was also reflected in her sermon "The Opening Doors," mentioned at the beginning of this essay.

In the third speech under investigation, "Woman's Place in the Church" (May 10, 1869), Brown touched upon themes that are also found in her second speech. She described the unique role women played in Christianity, being the last at the cross and the first at the tomb, as well as the ones who were first commissioned to "preach the risen Saviour."[56] The first disciples were chosen not because they were men, but because they were "earnest and loyal to the truth, and filled with the Holy Spirit."[57] Phoebe, for instance, embodied these same qualities and serves as an example of the role that women played in the early church (Rom 16:1–2). In this speech, Brown expanded on the role of women by claiming that Christianity itself was the first religion to contain a *feminine* element: "It was for Christ, first in the history of the world, to recognize woman as worthy of the respect, the liberty, and the obligations that belong to a human being. He saw her capability of grasping those great principles which lie at the basis of the absolute religion, and of applying those principles to the needs of the world."[58] Brown claimed that whereas other religions "took note of strong, able, and *free* men, Christianity cared for the humble, the poor, and the oppressed. It broke the shackles which the old barbarous law of might makes right had imposed upon woman. It recognized the feminine element in human society and made it a power for good."[59]

Adopting a typological approach to scripture, Brown noted that Old Testament prophecies foreshadow "a society of gentleness, charity and peace, when the lion and the lamb shall lie down together, and a little

56. OBP, SL, folder 25; reprinted in Greene, *Suffrage and Religious Principle*, 70–78.

57. OBP, SL, folder 25; reprinted in Greene, *Suffrage and Religious Principle*, 72.

58. OBP, SL, folder 25; reprinted in Greene, *Suffrage and Religious Principle*, 70. As Beverly Zink-Sawyer notes, "In this essay, Brown foreshadowed what would become a major theme in her suffrage rhetoric: the uniqueness of the Christian faith in transcending all other systems of belief in its concern for 'the humble, the poor, and the oppressed' and in breaking 'the shackles which the old barbarous law of might makes right had imposed upon woman.' Christianity represented a new way of organizing society and shaping human relationships, and those who claimed to live under its principles would be recognized by their embrace of new ideals and redefined human qualities" (*From Preachers to Suffragists*, 91).

59. OBP, SL, folder 25; reprinted in Greene, *Suffrage and Religious Principle*, 70.

child shall lead them" (Isa 11:6) and a time in which God will "pour out [God's] spirit upon all flesh, and your sons and your daughters shall prophesy" (Joel 2:28). Recalling her days at Antioch and the speech of Frances Gage, in this address Brown harkened back to Prov 31:10–31: "And I recall, too, that grand prophecy contained in the last chapter of Proverbs, a description, I believe, yet to be realized, when the Christian woman, free, enlightened, endowed with all rights of the citizen, shall take her place in the Master's vineyard, girded with strength and honor, her mouth filled with words of wisdom and her own works praising her in the gates." Brown also paraphrased and conflated the Eden story (Gen 3:15) and the ancestral promise (Gen 22:18 to Abraham; 26:4 to Isaac) when she stated the following: "The seed of the woman shall bruise the serpent's head. In her shall all the nations of the earth be blest."[60]

Conclusion

Olympia Brown spent her life advocating for women's rights, including equal educational and vocational opportunities, as well as the right to vote.[61] Her experiences of discrimination at Mt. Holyoke, Antioch College, and St. Lawrence University were in direct opposition to her understanding of Universalism. Her theology—her belief in an all-loving God and the worth of every human being—and her commitment to the betterment of society greatly influenced her use of Scripture in her suffrage speeches. In the three speeches discussed in this paper, Brown paraphrased and, at times, conflated Scripture; recounted the role of women in the Gospels and the early church; argued for the moral superiority of women in society during the nineteenth century; and asserted that Christianity was the first religion to include a feminine element— that of caring for the weak, poor, and humble. Like her adversaries, she was selective in her use of Scripture, citing texts that embodied her Universalist theology and political ideology. She did not directly appeal to scriptural authority, but rather to the moral sensibilities of her audience. As this study has shown, Brown's use of Scripture is not scholarly

60.   OBP, SL, folder 25; reprinted in Greene, *Suffrage and Religious Principle*, 78.

61.   "Female Education" OBP, SL, folder 38; reprinted in Greene, *Suffrage and Religious Principle*, 21–34. See also her "The Higher Education of Women," *The Repository: A Magazine for the Christian Home* 51 (February 1874): 81–86; reprinted in Greene, *Suffrage and Religious Principle*, 89–98, and Dorothy May Emerson, *Standing Before Us: Unitarian Universalist Women and Social Reform 1776–1936* (Boston: Skinner House Books, 2000), 246–51.

and technical, but rather is pragmatic, based on her experiences, and employed to make her argument for the inclusion of women in broader societal roles.[62] As her daughter, Gwendolen B. Willis, noted in the preface to Brown's autobiography, she was a pioneer in the work for the admission of women to the Christian ministry: "...[T]he ministry was the first objective in her life, since in her youthful enthusiasm she believed that freedom of religious thought and a liberal church would supply the groundwork for all other freedoms. Her difficulties and disillusionments in this field were numerous. That she could rise superior to such difficulties and disillusionments was the consequence of the hopefulness and courage with which she was richly endowed."[63] It was with this hope and courage that Brown embodied her roles as both a Universalist minister and a suffragist.

62. Brown's approach is in contrast to that of Antoinette Brown Blackwell's more careful, scholarly approach to Scripture ("Exegesis of I Corinthians XIV, 34, 35; and II Timothy, 11, 12," *Oberlin Quarterly Review* 4 [July 1849]: 358–73).

63. Willis, *Autobiography*, unnumbered preface.

LEAVING EDEN:
RESURRECTING THE WORK OF KATHARINE BUSHNELL AND LEE ANNA STARR

Kristin Kobes Du Mez

Time after time, the historical record reveals how the feminist biblical interpretation of one generation quietly slips into obscurity and is all but lost to future generations. The neglect of historical women's theologies, however, comes at a cost, as it skews our understanding of history and robs the present generation of a potentially "usable past." This essay considers the theological writings of Katharine Bushnell (1855–1946) and Lee Anna Starr (1853–1937). Through their retranslation and reinterpretation of the first chapters of Genesis, these two American Protestant women sought to provide a basis for a profound re-visioning of Christian theology and thereby challenge the Victorian social order in which they lived.

Like many other women's rights activists of the late nineteenth and early twentieth centuries, Bushnell and Starr believed that traditional Christianity bore substantial responsibility for the social, political, and legal inequalities women had suffered throughout Western history.[1] In many ways their intentions to address the theological foundations of women's oppression were similar to those of Elizabeth Cady Stanton, whose efforts to expose the masculine bias of the Scriptures and offer a new *Woman's Bible* are now well known to historians and feminists alike.[2] But unlike Stanton, Bushnell and Starr worked within the orthodox Protestant fold. They adhered to the inspired and even infallible nature of the word of God. Whereas Stanton felt free simply to toss aside any passage she found disagreeable—an approach which led to a serious backlash against her work and the project of women's theology more

---

1. Bushnell and Starr both published their major works in the 1920s, but they developed their theologies over the course of several decades.
2. See Kathi Kern, *Mrs. Stanton's Bible* (Ithaca, N.Y.: Cornell University Press, 2001).

generally—Bushnell and Starr considered each word of the Scriptures sacred. Bushnell, for example, pointedly eschewed the aid of higher critical methods in her effort to demonstrate the liberating effects of the Christian gospel for women. She insisted that her work "assumes that the Bible is all that it claims for itself"—that it is "inspired," "infallible," and "inviolable."[3] She criticized the work of "destructive higher critics" who manipulated the text beyond what was acceptable. Although she found higher criticism "both tempting and fascinating," allowing for "brilliant guesses" as to the meaning of particular passages, she preferred to leave the text unaltered, even if at times the meaning remained obscure.[4] Starr also parted ways with what she termed "modern destructive criticism." As she presented the issue, "the Bible is, or is not, the inspired word of God. If it be the former, we may forego human emendations; if the latter, it cannot speak to us with authority on any question."[5]

And yet, despite the conservative interpretive methods to which they adhered, Bushnell and Starr were able to construct extensive, proto-feminist revisions. They were able to accomplish this in part because of their knowledge of the biblical languages. Trained in Hebrew and Greek, they developed sweeping retranslations as well as reinterpretations of the Scriptures. Although they believed that the Scriptures contained the inspired word of God, they considered only the original words of the Scriptures—in the original languages—to be inspired. All later translations reflected the inevitable prejudice of male translators and interpreters. "Turn to the Title Page of your Bible," Bushnell instructed her readers. Both the Authorized and Revised Versions claimed they were "translated out of the original tongues, diligently compared and revised." But "these assurances do not hold good," she argued, at least not "where the status and welfare of one-half the human race is directly and vitally

3. Katharine C. Bushnell, *God's Word to Women: One Hundred Bible Studies on Woman's Place in the Divine Economy* (repr.; Mossville, Ill.: God's Word to Women Publishers, n.d. [1923]), paragraph 2. (Bushnell organized her book into numbered paragraphs; all following citations from *God's Word* refer to these paragraph numbers rather than to page numbers.) Bushnell cited 2 Tim 3:16 on the inspired nature of the Bible, Isa 40:8 on its infallibility, and John 10:35 on its inviolability. In paragraph 5 she clarified that when she spoke of the Bible as inspired, infallible, and inviolable, she did not refer to the English version, "or any mere version, but to the original text."

4. Bushnell, *God's Word*, 11. Comparing the higher critical method to cut glass and her own lower method to uncut diamond, she concluded that she preferred the unaltered text "to a pretty setting forth of mere sentiment."

5. Lee Anna Starr, *The Bible Status of Woman* (repr.; Zarephath, N.J.: Pillar of Fire, 1955 [1926]), 56–57.

concerned."[6] Men would find what they wanted to find in the Scriptures, and ignore any evidence to the contrary. For this reason, it was essential that women translate and interpret the Bible as well.

Social Reform and Theological Change

In order to understand the source of their theological critique, it is essential to locate Bushnell and Starr in their historical and social contexts. Like many other Protestant women of their time, both Bushnell and Starr were active in social reform, and throughout their careers their theology would remain intimately connected to their social activism.

Lee Anna Starr was an early pioneer in the Woman's Christian Temperance Union (WCTU), serving a brief stint in prison for her participation in the Woman's Crusade of 1873–74.[7] Her experiences in temperance reform convinced her that righteousness might at times contradict law and respectability, a conviction that would shape her future biblical studies. After graduating from Allegheny Seminary in 1893—the first woman to do so—she became ordained in the Methodist Protestant Church and served as pastor of a number of small, Midwestern churches.[8] Through her study of Scripture she became convinced that faulty translations and misguided interpretations had long fostered the subordination of women, and she set out to reassess the theological foundations of Christian views of womanhood. In 1900 she published *The Ministry of Woman*, a booklet articulating a biblical justification for women's right to preach, and she also developed a biblical defense of woman's suffrage, traveling the country to lecture on the topic for the WCTU.[9] Later in her career she worked to advance women's rights in the Methodist Protestant denomination, and in 1926 she published *The Bible Status of Woman*, a meticulous examination of Old and New Testament passages concerning women.[10]

6.   Bushnell, *God's Word*, 144. And, she added, "the highest good of the other half" was "just as vitally concerned, if even more remotely and less visibly."

7.   On Starr's life, see June Greene, "First Woman," *The Pittsburgh Press* (July 31, 1939).

8.   Allegheny Seminary is now Pittsburgh Theological Seminary of the Presbyterian Church, U.S.A. Starr was following in the footsteps of Anna Howard Shaw, who in 1880 became the first woman to be ordained in the Methodist Protestant Church after having been refused ordination in the Methodist Episcopal Church.

9.   Lee Anna Starr, *The Ministry of Women* (Chicago: Skeen, Aitken, 1900).

10.   Lyman Davis, *Democratic Methodism in America: A Topical Survey of the Methodist Protestant Church* (New York: Fleming H. Revell, 1921), 78–79, measured Starr's importance among the women of the church second only to Anna Howard Shaw.

Katharine Bushnell's theological writing was also rooted in her social activism. After studying classics and medicine at Northwestern University, Bushnell served for three years as a medical missionary for the Methodist Episcopal Church in China.[11] By observing the oppression of women in Chinese society, she came to understand that Western women, too, suffered from a tradition of subjugation. Most significantly, she came to realize that the Christian Scriptures—wrongly translated and interpreted—helped to perpetuate this oppression. She came to this conclusion after bringing what she perceived to be a "sex-biased" translation of the Chinese Scriptures to the attention of male missionaries. Her colleagues assured her that the Scriptures had been so rendered in order not to offend the "pagan prejudice against the ministry of women" among the Chinese.[12] To Bushnell, this blatant manipulation of God's word was a startling revelation. It was not long before she began to wonder if a similar bias against women might have shaped English translations; comparing her English Bible to Hebrew and Greek texts, she soon uncovered ample evidence to confirm this suspicion.

After returning to the United States in 1882, Bushnell began working for the social purity department of the WCTU.[13] Her social purity work revealed to her the effects of flawed biblical teachings on the lives of women as she observed first-hand the harsh effects of a sexual double standard which held women to far higher standards of purity than men. She became nationally and then internationally known for her investigations of prostitution in the lumber camps of northern Michigan and Wisconsin, and then in the British brothels in India and China. In the course of her purity work she repeatedly confronted the fact that "respectable" Christian citizens and government officials could engage in such

11. For a biography of Bushnell, see Dana Hardwick's *Oh Thou Woman that Bringest Good Tidings* (Kearney, N.E.: Morris Publishing, published by Christians for Biblical Equality, 1995).

12. Katharine C. Bushnell, *Dr. Katharine C. Bushnell: A Brief Sketch of Her Life Work* (Hertford: Rose & Sons, 1932), 20.

13. Reflecting Frances Willard's "Do-Everything" policy for the WCTU, the social purity department led efforts to raise the age of consent laws in several states, shut down brothels, assist "fallen women," and shift blame from prostitutes to the men they believed "seduced" or entrapped women into prostitution. On the social purity movement, see David J. Pivar's *Purity Crusade: Sexual Morality and Social Control, 1868–1900* (Westport, Conn.: Greenwood, 1973), and Brian Donovan's *White Slave Crusades: Race, Gender, and Anti-Vice Activism, 1887–1917* (Urbana: University of Illinois Press, 2006). Donovan argues that the purity campaigns helped to construct and maintain racial boundaries during a time in which constructions of race were particularly volatile.

reprehensible actions toward women.[14] She found the source of such hypocrisy in a male-dominated tradition of biblical interpretation.

After delving into biblical studies, Bushnell began a correspondence course for women. Beginning in 1910 she periodically published portions of her work, and in 1923 her studies culminated in the publication of *God's Word to Women*.[15] Although Bushnell and Starr do not seem to have collaborated in person on their biblical studies, they were both members of the Association of Women Preachers (International Association of Women Ministers) in the 1920s, and by that point in time they had become familiar with one another's work. Their projects were similar in scope and aim, and Starr cited Bushnell frequently in her *Bible Status of Woman*. Although Starr's book went beyond Bushnell's in certain ways, it contains a more accessible version of many of Bushnell's central arguments.[16]

14. Bushnell, *Brief Sketch*, 22.

15. For a detailed publication history of Bushnell's numerous editions of this work, see Hardwick, *O Thou Woman*, 86–87.

16. Jessie Penn-Lewis's *The "Magna Charta" of Woman According to the Scriptures* (Bournemouth: The Overcomer Book Room, 1919), also contained a more accessible, abridged version of Bushnell's work. Both *God's Word* and Starr's *Bible Status* contain dense argumentation and are heavily footnoted. Bushnell's work in particular suffers from a lack of organization. These factors may have contributed to the limited popular reception of both books. M. Madeline Southard, president of the Association of Woman Preachers, admired the work of both Bushnell and Starr, but when she wanted to ensure that modern biblical translations did not "perpetuate certain injustices to women," she passed along Starr's *Bible Status* to the American Standard Bible translation committee. Luther Weigle, the chair of the translation committee, claimed that he, along with James Moffatt, Millar Burrows, and several other members of the committee, had found Starr's book to be "of real value," and assured Southard that they were "doing [their] best to guard against the sort of unfairness of which she writes" (Madeline Southard, letter to Luther Weigle, 18 October 1940; and Luther Weigle, letter to Madeleine Southard, 25 July 1941, Madeline Southard Papers [99-M26], Schlesinger Library, Carton 1). Responding to Southard's suggestion, he wrote that he "had not thought of asking a woman scholar to read the manuscript before publication, but that probably is an excellent idea," and that he thought he would propose it to the committee at their next meeting. Weigle's apparent enthusiasm for the idea is questionable, however. I have found no record in the minutes of the Standard Bible Committee of this proposal taking place, and have found no mention of Starr's book in the "List of Books Used by the Bible Revision Committee, 1939–51, 1968" in the papers of the Standard Bible Committee at Yale Divinity School. In a letter sent to Moffatt, presumably from Weigle's secretary, the writer expressed that Weigle had requested that a copy of *The Bible Status of Woman* be sent to Moffatt. "He feels that it is a matter that the Committee will have to deal with some time, and he would like you to look it over" (Luther A. Weigle,

In the Beginning...

Bushnell's and Starr's revised translations of the first chapters of Genesis not only reveal the theological foundation from which they hoped to advance profound social change, but also demonstrate the radical potential of their seemingly conservative methods. The traditional interpretation of the Genesis narrative depicted an inferior Eve seducing Adam into tasting the forbidden fruit, leading to humanity's fall into sin and their expulsion from the garden. But Bushnell and Starr offered a dramatically different account.

Both Bushnell and Starr began their projects by asserting the original equality of man and woman at creation; in doing so they contested a number of traditional arguments for male supremacy. Man's creation before woman did not establish his superiority, they argued; rather, the order of creation appeared to be ascending rather than descending. "If priority of creation is a proof of superiority," Starr wrote, "the monkey has advantage over man," for, after all, "the monkey was on the scene first."[17] Bushnell concurred, noting that "every man has a mother who was made before himself, and yet she is held to be his inferior"; even more pointedly, she suggested that according to the logic of traditional interpretations, since "cows were made before men—even before theologians,—men must be subordinated to cows."[18]

They also rejected the "inane fable" of Eve's formation from Adam's rib, which had long been used to justify women's inferior status; they suggested that rather than implying woman's inferiority, that passage, too, might suggest the opposite.[19] After the account of Adam's creation

letter to James Moffatt [March 27, 1941], Luther Allan Weigle Papers, Sterling Memorial Library, Yale University, Box 4). I am particularly grateful for the assistance of Lynda Leahy at the Schlesinger Library and for a Schlesinger Library Research Support Grant that made this investigation possible.

17. Starr, *Bible Status*, 22. Starr noted that the substance of the male body came from inorganic matter, while woman "was built of organic substance." Additionally, she argued that "man physically is of coarser mold. The beard and hirsute cuticle ally him, in appearance at least, more closely to certain members of the animal kingdom." She noted that "Mr Darwin himself incautiously admits that 'hairiness denotes a low stage of development." While she assured readers that she herself attached "no importance to these incidentals," she mentioned them only "to show that claimants for the superiority of man by no means occupy an unassailable position."

18. Bushnell, *God's Word*, 346.

19. Gen 2:21–22. See Bushnell, *God's Word*, 43, and Starr, *Bible Status*, 22–23. The "rib story" was just one piece in a misogynistic pattern of Christian thought that perpetuated the subjugation of women, Bushnell and Starr contended. But its harm was not limited to its detrimental effect on women. More recently, the story of the

in ch. 1, they noted, "God saw everything that He had made, and, behold, it was very good." However, by the next chapter God declared that it was "not good that the man should be alone" (Gen 1:31; 2:18 [KJV]). To understand how the "very good" state of humanity became "not good," Bushnell suggested that the Hebrew expression traditionally translated as "alone" could also mean "in-his-separation." Adam, then, may have become separated from God, falling slightly from his original perfection even before the Serpent's tempting. In order to redeem the stumbling Adam, she explained, God created a helpmeet for him, taking Eve out of Adam.[20] Both Bushnell and Starr pointed out that traditional interpretations of helpmeet as an inferior assistant or mere afterthought could not be legitimated in this context. They noted that the Hebrew word translated "help" occurred twenty-one times in the Old Testament, and twenty of those times it connoted a superior form of help—in sixteen cases referring in fact to divine assistance.[21] If anything, they argued, the passage suggests that Eve was created to offer a higher form of assistance.

Bushnell and Starr also contested the supposed fact that man had been given the power to name both the animals and, importantly, woman, as a basis for women's subordination. Both Bushnell and Starr, for instance, called attention to the fact that it was Eve who named her offspring, a detail many expositors apparently had found inconsequential.[22] And as for Adam naming Eve, Bushnell argued that although the man called his helpmeet "Woman," a closer examination of the text revealed that "it was not Adam, but the Word of God itself" that declared woman "*the mother of all living*." Adam simply affirmed this fact in calling his wife "Eve," which in Hebrew resembles the word "living."[23] Starr, too, found this change important. As she noted, the first woman's name was changed from *Isha*, which meant "Female man," to *Havvah*, signifying "Life,"

---

rib had been held up as an example of the implausible passages of the Bible that precluded belief for many rational people. Bushnell reminded her readers that when they heard "a rationalist ridiculing the 'rib' story of 'creation,'" they should keep in mind that the rationalist was not "in reality ridiculing the Bible, though he may think he is. He is holding up to contempt a stupid mistranslation" (Bushnell, *God's Word*, 39).

20. Bushnell, *God's Word*, 35; Starr, *Bible Status*, 23.

21. Starr, *Bible Status*, 24. See also Bushnell, *God's Word*, 34.

22. Starr, *Bible Status*, 24. See also Bushnell, *God's Word*, 477.

23. Bushnell, *God's Word*, 83. Bushnell here was referring to Gen 3:15, where God tells Eve that her seed will crush the serpent's head. She cited John Monro Gibson, who defined the "seed of woman" as those who are spiritually her children, those who are "on the side of good, the side of God and righteousness" in the drama of redemption (*The Ages before Moses: A Series of Lectures on the Book of Genesis* [New York: Anson D. F. Randolph & Company, 1879], 122).

since Eve was to be the "mother of all life." Far from seeing woman's new name as a symbol of her subordination to man, Bushnell and Starr both considered this designation a significant affirmation of her status, one that "uninspired men" never would have allowed.[24] Moreover, Bushnell also observed that Christ, who was "born of a woman," was also "fittingly named by woman." Responding to the promise of a redeemer, Eve herself "bestowed upon Him the title 'Lord'" (Gen 4:1). Hannah, another Old Testament woman, "first called Him 'The Anointed,' that is, 'Christ'" (1 Sam 2:10). And the Virgin Mary, she wrote, "was instructed to name Him, before He was born, 'Jesus'" (Luke 1:31). Thus, Bushnell concluded, "that name which is above every name, THE LORD JESUS CHRIST, at which 'every knee shall bow, of things in heaven, and things in earth, and things under the earth,'" was in fact bestowed upon the redeemer by three individual women, three "prophetesses of God."[25] Bushnell and Starr found no biblical evidence to suggest that God created women to be subordinated to men, but ample evidence to the contrary.

After establishing the equality of men and women at creation, Bushnell and Starr turned their attention to the story of humanity's fall into sin found in Gen 3. According to traditional interpretations, God punished Adam for eating the forbidden fruit by cursing the ground so it would produce food only through Adam's painful toil; God then cursed Eve by greatly increasing her pains in childbearing, and by commanding that she "desire" her husband and that her husband should rule over her (Gen 3:16–19). Both Bushnell and Starr recognized that this passage had profoundly influenced the status of women over the course of human history; indeed, Gen 3:16 had long been referenced as a key to women's identity and the justification for women's subjection.[26] But they pointed

24. Starr, *Bible Status*, 54–55.
25. Bushnell, *God's Word*, 81. In her sweeping rereading of Genesis, Bushnell turned many negative Christian stereotypes of women on their head. She depicted Eve and Mary not as opposites, but as sisters. Eve was the mother of all (spiritually) living, while the Virgin Mary gave birth to Christ, to the "Seed" which would crush Satan's head (Gen 3:15) and bring about fulfillment of God's prophecy concerning womanhood and humanity (ibid., 76). In fact, Eve was so inspired by God's promise that her seed would "crush the serpent's head," that she wrongly anticipated the birth of her first child, Cain, as the fulfillment of that promise, naming him in Gen 4:1 "the Coming one" (for a detailed discussion of this passage, see paragraphs 77–81).
26. "No passage of Scripture has claimed a larger place in the thought of mankind," lamented Starr, "than Genesis 3:16" (Starr, *Bible Status*, 27). Gen 3:16 (KJV) reads: "Unto the woman He said, I will greatly multiply thy sorrow and thy conception: in sorrow thou shalt bring forth children; and thy desire shall be to thy

out that theologians who looked to Gen 3:16 to understand God's will for women looked elsewhere to discern man's destiny. Man's commissioning in Gen 1:28—which Starr noted was addressed to Eve as well as Adam—was a popular choice for establishing God's will for man, as were New Testament discussions of Christ's atonement.[27] Bushnell and Starr, however, claimed that finding woman's destiny in a "curse" but man's destiny in Christ's atonement was not only patently unjust, but it also established a theological double standard that effectively denied the power of Christ's atonement for half of the world's population.[28] If Christ atoned for men's sin, then the same must be true for women, they argued. If not, Starr explained, "we face the appalling fact that the Almighty— one of whose attributes is Love—'in His inscrutable wisdom,' and 'for His own glory' brought into being a human creature with full intent to 'greatly multiply' her 'sorrow and conception'; to rack her with birth-pangs, and to subject her to the dominion of her husband." Such teaching was reprehensible. "Away with such dogma!" she exclaimed, accusing men who propounded such doctrine of being "afflicted with mental and moral myopia."[29]

Not only did Bushnell and Starr refuse to locate God's will for women in Gen 3:16, but they went on to question whether Eve had ever, in fact, been cursed by God. By reassessing Eve's sin and the subsequent curse, they established the foundations for a profoundly different biblical narrative and a new vision for the social order.[30] Bushnell began by examining the presumed sin of both Adam and Eve. Although popular Christian

---

husband, and he shall rule over thee." As Starr explained, "Mankind has never over-looked it"; it was "one of the great, outstanding passages of the Bible," holding "a large place in the world's thought" (ibid., 49). "It is astounding," Starr wrote, "that translators, revisers, and compilers, requisition Genesis 3:16 whenever the Divine intent concerning woman is under discussion." The verse could be found "on the margin of every reference Bible. Exegetes and commentators seize upon it with avidity as their favorite proof-text" (ibid., 19).

27. Starr, *Bible Status*, 18–19, 49. Starr noted that men look to Gen 1:28 as their heritage, while they "generously point woman to Genesis 3:16 as her allotment." Jesus Christ, however, when addressing the loose divorce laws of his age, pointed not to Gen 3:16, but to "*the beginning.*" Starr observed that Gen 3:16 "has received a thousand-fold more attention than Genesis 3:17–19, where God addressed man after the fall."

28. Bushnell, *God's Word*, 363.

29. Starr, *Bible Status*, 20.

30. Bushnell and Starr knew that they were embarking on an innovative theological endeavor. But they maintained that women needed to "hew a hermeneutical and exegetical road for ourselves" since traditional theology pointed "no other way for women" but "into a 'curse'" (Bushnell, *God's Word*, 102).

tradition generally blamed Eve for the fall into sin, Bushnell pointed out that the New Testament actually taught that Adam, not Eve, was "the one who brought sin into the world, and death through sin." New Testament passages twice referred to Eve as having been deceived, and thereby brought into the transgression, but the Apostle Paul declared eight times that "one person" alone was accountable for the Fall. Twice he named that person as Adam, who, he noted, was not deceived.[31] Eve's greater culpability for the fall, Bushnell concluded, was thoroughly unbiblical and "*taught by tradition only.*"[32] Paul held Adam accountable for the fall, she explained, because Adam's sin was far more serious than Eve's. Turning back to the Genesis account, she noted a striking difference in the way Adam and Eve responded to God after they had eaten the forbidden fruit. Eve confessed, "The *Serpent* beguiled me, and I did eat." Adam, too, confessed, but then added, "The woman whom *Thou* gavest to be with me, *she* gave me of the tree, and I did eat."[33] Both admitted that they had eaten of the forbidden tree, Bushnell assessed, and both told truthfully of "the *immediate* influence that led to the eating"; in that they were equal. However, rather than assigning the remote cause of his sin to Satan, Adam instead "accuses God to His face of being Himself that remote cause."[34] As Starr noted, Adam responded to God's question with a startling counter-charge, posing himself as the aggrieved one.[35]

31. 1 Tim 2:14 states that "Adam was not deceived, but the woman being deceived was [literally, 'became'] in the transgression," or, as rendered by the British New Testament scholar Richard Weymouth, according to Bushnell, the woman "was thoroughly deceived, and so became involved…" 2 Cor 11:3 reads, "the serpent beguiled [literally, 'thoroughly deceived'] Eve through his subtlety"; 1 Cor 15:22 reads "In Adam all die…" Other passages blaming one person (Adam) for the fall into sin can be found in Rom 5:12–19. See ibid., 91.

32. Ibid., 92. Eve's presumed greater culpability, and a misunderstanding of "the curse," had had tangible effects on the sexes down through the centuries, Starr argued. "We find man doing his utmost to evade the penalty imposed upon him; he has invented all kinds of machinery to lighten his toil; his insistent demand has been for shorter hours of labor; he has sought for himself the easy places, and unless man-written history belies him, as often as otherwise he has impressed the 'weaker sex' to do the sweating for him." But "from the hour of his apostasy man felt it incumbent upon him to supervise woman; to see that she underwent in fullest measure the penalty imposed upon her. He rebuked every attempted evasion as rebellion against the Almighty. It is recorded that when anaesthetics were first discovered and used in cases of severe suffering at maternity, some clergymen preached against it, declaring that 'such relief from pain was contrary to Scripture, since pain at maternity was a part of the curse'" (Starr, *Bible Status*, 48).

33. Bushnell, *God's Word*, 68. See also Starr, *Bible Status*, 45.

34. Bushnell, *God's Word*, 69.

35. Starr, *Bible Status*, 45.

By "becoming a false accuser of God," then, Adam "advanced to the side of the serpent." But Eve, by exposing "the character of Satan before his very face, created an enmity between herself and him."[36] But then why would Adam's arrogance be "rewarded with sex supremacy," with man given the power to rule over woman, Starr wondered.[37] Both Starr and Bushnell concluded that the "curse" that had traditionally been understood as God's punishment of Eve, was in fact *Satan's* spiteful curse on women. Indeed, in Gen 3:15, a verse traditionally pointed to as the first promise of Christ's coming, God addresses Satan, saying: "And I will put enmity between thee and the woman, and between thy seed and her seed; it shall bruise thy head, and thou shalt bruise His heel" (Gen 3:15). Here God widened the breach already opened by Eve's blaming the serpent, Bushnell explained.[38] Satan would naturally wish to cripple woman, his enemy, to inhibit her from carrying out that destiny; the most logical way for Satan to do so would relate to her childbearing, since it would be through childbearing that she would bring into the world the seed that would crush the Serpent's head.[39] What "common sense tells us Satan would *most certainly* wish to do"—that is, increase woman's pain of childbearing—most theologians told us God did, Bushnell explained.[40] They would have people believe that after God exalted Eve as the progenitor of Christ and put enmity between her and Satan, God suddenly turned and pronounced several curses upon her. This seemed both inconsistent and illogical; indeed, it would be an unprecedented occasion where God and Satan were working on the same side, for the same result.[41]

To work out an alternative reading, one that did not contradict her sense of God's righteousness or her understanding of Christ's own view of womanhood, Bushnell turned to the original Hebrew. Rather than "I will greatly multiply thy sorrow," she contended that v. 16 should read, "Unto the woman He said. A snare hath increased thy sorrow." The difference in the original Hebrew between the two translations lies wholly in the interlinear vowel-signs, which, as Bushnell explained, were

36. Bushnell, *God's Word*, 71.
37. Starr, *Bible Status*, 45.
38. Bushnell, *God's Word*, 99. Here Bushnell noted that "despite the popular cry regarding the 'universal Fatherhood of God, and the universal brotherhood of man,' which is in part true, we who accept the Scriptures as authority must not forget that Satan, as well as God, has his children—moral and spiritual delinquents—among men" (p. 73).
39. Bushnell, *God's Word*, 99. See also Starr, *Bible Status*, 56–57.
40. Bushnell, *God's Word*, 100.
41. Ibid.

later additions and ought not to be considered inerrant.[42] Bushnell also took issue with the translation of the Hebrew *HRJWN* as "conception," in "I will multiply thy sorrow and thy conception." Wrongly translated, this phrase had "wrought terrible havoc with the health and happiness of wives," Bushnell argued, "because, so read, it has been understood to rob woman of the right to determine when she should become a mother, and to place that right outside her will and in abeyance to the will of her husband." The word in question was actually two letters short of spelling the Hebrew word for conception, Bushnell attested, as "all Hebrew scholars know." "Our highest lexical authorities," she reported, "call it a 'contraction, or erroneous.'"[43] "Indeed!" exclaimed Bushnell; "and is one-half the human family to be placed at the mercy of the other half on such a flimsy claim as this!" Here she turned a commitment to the literal interpretation of the Bible to the defense of women: "We stand for our rights, as women, on the assurance of our Lord, that *no word* in Divine law has lost any of its consonants, or angles of a consonant; and on our Lord's promise we demand a very different rendering of the word." For an alternative reading she consulted the Septuagint, which translated the word in question as "thy sighing." Accordingly, the sentence reads: "A snare hath increased thy sorrow and thy sighing."[44] Both Bushnell and Starr considered this a significant revision, particularly when combined with what followed.

The last part of v. 16, "thy desire shall be to thy husband, and he shall rule over thee," had played a central role in the subjugation of women in Christian tradition, both Bushnell and Starr agreed. Particularly when "desire" (the Hebrew *teshuqa*) was translated "lust," the verse had "been the cause of much degradation, unhappiness and suffering to women," and had instigated "much immorality among men, in the cruelty and oppression they have inflicted upon their wives." It in fact composed "the very keystone of an arch of doctrine subordinating woman to man." Since all of the Apostle Paul's pronouncements on the "woman question" were routinely interpreted through this verse, Bushnell determined that it stood as the ultimate foundation of Christian views of womanhood, and as such it deserved careful scrutiny.[45]

42. Ibid., 117; 5–16. See also Starr, *Bible Status*, 43.
43. The "highest lexical authorities" she referred to are Francis Brown, S. R. Driver, and Charles Augustus Briggs. G. J. Spurrell commented, "It is an abnormal formation, which occurs nowhere else in the Old Testament." See Bushnell, *God's Word*, 121; and Starr, *Bible Status*, 43–44. Here and in the examples that follow I have preserved Bushnell's transliterations of the Hebrew and Greek text.
44. Bushnell, *God's Word*, 121. See also Starr, *Bible Status*, 44.
45. Bushnell, *God's Word*, 139.

In her analysis of *teshuqa*, Bushnell rejected both of the traditional renderings. "Desire" and, to a greater degree, "lust," implied woman's subordinated status, her "morbid sensuality," and her confinement to the domestic realm. But Bushnell argued that both terms were faulty translations of the original Hebrew. Having studied several ancient texts and scholarly commentaries, she concluded that the Hebrew *teshuqa* should be more accurately rendered "turning away." A more reliable translation of "Thy *desire* shall be to thy husband," or "Thy lust shall pertayne to thy husband," would be: "Thou art turning away to thy husband."[46] Bushnell's translation of the passage erased any hint of a cursed female sensuality, a crucial step in rehabilitating the legacy of Eve. Moreover, her translation of the passage would lead to a profound redefinition of what constituted sin for women and for men.

Bushnell and Starr accused men everywhere of following in Adam's footsteps by oppressing women, but they did not hold women altogether guiltless in their fate. Eve had not sinned grievously by blaming God for her own disobedience, as had Adam, but she had committed another mistake that would bring about a grave result. Rightly translated, Gen 3:16 records God's prophecy; upon seeing that Eve was "inclining to turn away from Himself to her husband," God warned Eve that for this she would suffer appalling consequences.[47] Here Bushnell again departed radically from Christian tradition by suggesting that only Adam, and not Eve, had been evicted from the garden after the Fall. Bushnell reminded her readers that immediately after her confession of guilt, Eve had been named the "mother of all *living*." If Eve were indeed spiritually living, Bushnell reasoned, then "we see no reason why Eve should have found a 'flaming sword' between herself and the tree of life."[48] But further reading finds Eve outside of the garden. Here the immediate consequences of the prophecy found in Gen 3:16 are evident. As God had foretold and subsequent history unfailingly demonstrated, Eve eventually made the disastrous, sinful choice to turn to her husband and follow him out of Eden.[49]

Bushnell, then, did not exonerate women from all sin. But she did dramatically redefine what constituted sin for women. Based on her

---

46. Indeed, a number of ancient texts strongly supported this rendition of the passage. Neither the KJV nor the RV, however, had construed the meaning correctly. For Bushnell's full analysis of *teshuqa*, see *God's Word*, 122–45. See also Starr, *Bible Status*, 28.

47. Bushnell, *God's Word*, 124.

48. Ibid., 96–97.

49. Ibid., 122.

rereading of Genesis, Bushnell maintained that conventional conceptions of sin—associated with pride—remained appropriate when applied to men. But, over the course of history from the time of the fall, women had been far more likely to commit the sin of inappropriate humility. As they ate from the tree of knowledge of good and evil, both Adam and Eve had wanted to be "as God." The sin of Eden, then, was the sin of pride. But while Eve repented, Adam continued in his rebellion. Since that time, Bushnell explained, a dispute had raged between God and man for control of the throne. And what role, she asked, would God have women play in this dispute? According to a tradition shaped by male expositors—males, Bushnell claimed, continued to participate in this struggle for the throne—women were to "show their humility, their willingness to take a lowly place." Women were to "show they owe no allegiance but to MAN ALONE," not even to God's angels.[50] But by doing so, they would be acting as accomplices in man's rebellion against God. "What madness for women to do this!" she exclaimed, "and call it 'humility!'" Within Bushnell's framework, male authority over women was nothing other than the fruit of man's original sin. And men's injunctions for women to be silent, submissive, and "womanly" contradicted God's will and reflected man's original rebellion against God.[51] Women continued to sin the sin of Eve when they submitted to men rather than to God, and men sinned the sin of Adam in dominating and subordinating women.

Both Bushnell and Starr agreed, then, that the concluding words of Gen 3:16, "…and he shall rule over you," should be read as a prophecy rather than as a penalty. Starr envisioned God standing in the garden with Adam and Eve, looking down through the ages and foreseeing the "awful outcome of their sin," and the awful subjection of women that would follow.[52] It was not God who subordinated "Eve to Adam, and all women to their husbands, as has been claimed by the Church throughout many centuries." Instead, it was "man" who "gradually brought about that subordination to himself."[53] The effects of this subordination were undeniable. Indeed, human history provided a clear record of the prophecy's fulfillment. "Did the entrance of sin bring about the dethronement of woman?" Starr asked. "Has her sorrow and her conception been multiplied? Did her turning away to her husband result in her subjugation?

---

50. Ibid., 390. Here Bushnell quoted Arthur Penryn Stanley, Dean of Westminster.

51. Ibid., 391. Bushnell added that "Satan knew very well how to clothe an insult to God in the garments of "humility" and "womanliness."

52. See Starr, *Bible Status*, 44–45.

53. Bushnell, *God's Word*, 418.

Yes—a thousand times, Yes!"[54] With the advent of sin into the world, women became the ultimate victims. "The historian has never lived," Starr intoned, "who could chronicle all her wrongs or tabulate half her woes." Since Eden, her path had led precipitously downward. She had become chattel, "a toy or slave, subject to every whim of her lord and master"; she had no value in her own right, useful only to stand at the side of some masculine figure, enhancing his value.[55] But such degradation contradicted the will of God, both Bushnell and Starr agreed, and women's redemption could only come through a proper understanding of the Scriptures.

Contesting Victorianism: Female Virtue and Woman's Sphere

Bushnell and Starr hoped that their theological writings would bring about comprehensive social change. Indeed, their biblical revisions directly challenged key components of the Victorian social order. According to Victorian ideals, "true women" exhibited purity, passivity, and an innate religiosity.[56] A woman's special virtue, combined with her delicate weakness, equipped her for her role as wife and mother, placing her at the center of the Victorian family—which, in turn, served as the basis for Victorian society. She occupied the private sphere of the home, where her virtue was protected from the evils of the public sphere, and where she could influence her husband and sons to be godly men and good citizens.[57] Women who failed to live up to these exalted standards

54. Starr, *Bible Status*, 29. Bushnell also concluded that "as a prophecy it has been abundantly fulfilled in the manner in which man rules over women," and this was particularly true, she argued, in countries where the Christian gospel has not taken hold (*God's Word*, 127).

55. Starr, *Bible Status*, 29.

56. On Victorian ideals of womanhood, see Barbara Welter, "The Cult of True Womanhood: 1820–1860," *AQ* 18 (1966): 151–74; Kathryn Kish Sklar, *Catherine Beecher: A Study in American Domesticity* (New Haven: Yale University Press, 1973); and Barbara Epstein, *The Politics of Domesticity: Women, Evangelism, and Temperance in Nineteenth-Century America* (Middletown, Conn.: Wesleyan University Press, 1981), along with Nancy F. Cott, *The Bonds of Womanhood* (New Haven: Yale University Press, 1977), and Linda K. Kerber, *Women of the Republic: Intellect and Ideology in Revolutionary America* (Chapel Hill: University of North Carolina Press, 1980).

57. As Methodists, Bushnell and Starr were perhaps particularly attuned to the significance of true womanhood and the domestic ideal for the lives of American women. As Gregory Schneider discusses in *The Way of the Cross Leads Home: The Domestication of American Methodism* (Bloomington: Indiana University Press,

of womanhood—by demonstrating an unwomanly assertiveness or questionable purity—suffered under the harsh condemnation of respectable society.[58] But Bushnell and Starr contended that the notion of female virtue celebrated in Victorian culture was not only unhealthy—leaving women unable to exhibit the strength and courage necessary to protect themselves—but unbiblical as well. Women were being taught from Christian pulpits to be weak, submissive, and "feminine," when, in order to be truly virtuous, they needed to "be strong, in body, mind and spirit."[59]

As Bushnell argued, a proper reading of Genesis demonstrated that Eve had sinned when she submissively followed Adam out of Eden; she and Starr insisted that further examination of the Scriptures provided additional evidence that God had never intended for women to exhibit passivity or to be subordinated to the will of men. Generations of male translation and interpretation, however, had warped this truth into a defense of women's oppression. Bushnell, for example, found evidence of male bias contributing to faulty ideals of Victorian womanhood in her examination of the Hebrew word *cha-yil*. In the over two-hundred times that *cha-yil* appeared in the Hebrew Bible, it had always connoted "force, strength, or ability," variously translated into English as "army, war, host, forces, might, power, goods, riches, substance, wealth, or valiant." Bushnell identified four exceptions to this rule, however (Ruth 3:11; Prov 12:4; 31:10, 29). "In every case where it referred specifically to a woman," translators had assigned a different meaning: "'virtue'— i.e. chastity."[60] This translation helped to bolster Victorian ideals of womanhood, but Bushnell insisted that "women prefer to know what the Bible *says*, rather than to be merely reminded of a favorite axiom among men."[61]

When she turned her attention to the New Testament, Bushnell found a similar pattern of gendered mistranslations. The Greek word *sophron*, for example, was an adjective occurring four times in the New Testament. In the King James Version it appeared twice as "sober" and once

---

1993), nineteenth-century Methodist literature was saturated with references to the central role the Christian home played in the Methodist faith, and to its importance in structuring the broader culture according to the will of God. It was perhaps no coincidence that what became known as the "Methodist Age" in American religious history was concurrent with the rise of American domesticity.

58. Women of color and lower-class women, for example, were largely excluded from "true womanhood."

59. Bushnell, *God's Word*, 633.

60. Ibid., 624, 633.

61. Ibid., 631.

as "temperate"; but when referring to women only (Tit 2:5), it was rendered "discreet."[62] This "sex-bias" in translation was not accidental, Bushnell contended, citing a Greek commentary written by Henry Alford, Dean of Canterbury, to illustrate her point. Having established the meaning of *sophron* in its noun form as "self-restraint," Alford insisted that "discreet" "certainly applies better to women than 'self-restraint.'" For "self-restraint" implies effort, Alford explained, "which destroys the spontaneity, and brushes off, so to speak, the bloom of this best of female graces." Bushnell understood that this interpretation reflected common Victorian understandings of womanhood rather than biblical truth. She sardonically thanked Alford "for thinking that women can practice self-restraint without effort," but on behalf of all Christian women she added, "when we are reading our Bibles we prefer to know *precisely* what the Holy Ghost addresses to us, instead of finding between its pages the opinion of even the most excellent uninspired man."[63]

Bushnell detected another illustration of "sex-bias" in the English translation of the Greek word *exousia*. There seemed to be no disagreement on its connoting "power," Bushnell contended; "its meaning is patent; there is no mystery about the word." The word appeared 103 times in the New Testament; 69 times it was rendered "power," 29 times "authority," two times "right," and once each "liberty," "jurisdiction," and "strength." "But," Bushnell explained, "in one single instance it happens to be used exclusively of woman's power" (1 Cor 11:10). And "here at once its sense is called into question." Indeed, Bushnell described how the conundrum of women's power caused the translators to pen the longest note in the entire Authorized Version of the Bible to explain "how Paul means that this 'power' must be abdicated by woman, in order that her *husband* may assume it instead." Bushnell's frustration was evident upon realizing that, for such translators, "it cannot be possible that women should have power!"[64]

Bushnell found additional examples of bias in other New Testament passages. The Greek word *kosmios* or example, was translated "well

---

62. Bushnell, *God's Word*, 639.

63. Ibid. See also 640.

64. Ibid., 641. Bushnell examined 1 Cor 11:1–16 in detail in paragraphs 216–39. She reported how translators and commentators had added a number of words to the original text in order to procure the meaning that a woman was to yield her authority to her husband, rather than wield authority herself. The Bible, and St. Paul, Bushnell purported, "says nothing of this sort, but the Marginal Note, and the Bible Commentators teach it." She could not resist noting the suspicious nature of this alteration, as it was "*husbands*, not wives," who have "discovered this extraordinary meaning for St. Paul's words" (ibid., 218).

ordered, in both outward deportment and inner life," except when referring to women's dress (1 Tim 2:9), where it was rendered "modest."[65]
And *hagnos*, a term meaning "holy," according to Bushnell, was
translated "pure" or "clear" five times, but "chaste" in the three instances
where it qualified a noun of the feminine gender. Given this pattern,
Bushnell wondered why men should not also be taught chastity. "These
may be straws," she concluded, "yet they all point in the same direction."[66]

Perhaps the most significant biblical text to which Bushnell turned in
order to challenge the Victorian idealization of female virtue and to
dismantle the notion of a sexual double standard was the well-known
New Testament story of a woman caught in adultery (John 8:1–11). This
portion of the Scriptures, which Bushnell referred to as the *pericope de
adultera*, recounted the story of an adulterous woman taken by a group
of religious authorities to Jesus for punishment. Jesus, however, refused
to condemn the woman, inviting those among her accusers without sin to
cast the first stone. Bushnell was alarmed to find that modern critics
doubted the authenticity of the passage, and she turned to ancient texts to
construct a textual and historical defense of the narrative.[67] In her opinion, it should not be surprising that a number of male scholars had come
to question the authenticity of the pericope. Far more remarkable was the
fact that these verses had survived centuries of male bias to be available,
in any form, to the present generation. She suggested that the most persuasive argument for the validity of the pericope might come not through
the scrutiny of ancient texts, but rather through an examination of the
unique message of the narrative itself. In fact, the persistent opposition
to the teaching of the pericope might provide some of the strongest
evidence for its authenticity. Given the record of mistranslations and
manipulations Bushnell had unearthed when it came to women's virtue
in the rest of the Scriptures, she claimed that the pericope must be
authentic. No man, she insisted, would ever have invented it, or have
allowed it in the canon, had there been any intimation that there was any
question as to its authenticity.[68] "Where ever has existed the man in

65. Ibid., 644. *Kosmios* is an adjective related to *kosmos*, meaning "orderly,"
according to LSJ *s.v.* "κόσμιος," I,2. Interestingly enough, in BDAG it is translated
as "appropriate for winning approval," or "modest," *s.v.* "κόσμιος," 2.

66. Bushnell, *God's Word*, 644. Bushnell does not identify the passages where
hagnos was translated "chaste," but she is presumably referring to 2 Cor 11:2; Tit
2:5, and 1 Pet 3:2.

67. Bushnell patterned her defense of the pericope on the work of John Burgon,
Dean of Chichester. See Bushnell, *God's Word*, 677–81.

68. Ibid., 682.

ancient times or modern," Bushnell challenged, "so jealous for the rights of women, so skilful in drawing a picture of *absolute justice*, and yet so unscrupulous in character, and so influential, as to have foisted this story upon the credulity of the Church[?]" And how, she demanded, could "the ecclesiastical authorities," who lived "so far beneath its principles of justice in dealing with fallen woman," have allowed the story to persist, not daring to "wipe it out of existence." "No stronger proof than this is needed that it is a true incident in the life of our Saviour."[69]

For both Bushnell and Starr, the historicity of the pericope was of utmost importance. The story not only dismantled any notion of a sexual double standard that had proved so damaging to women, but it also demonstrated Christ's compassion for women. As Starr reflected on his response to the woman taken in adultery, she noted that "He never by word or deed, lent encouragement to the disparagement of woman."[70] Dismissing traditional fears that the pericope condoned sin and moral laxity, Bushnell instead argued that it encouraged repentance and culti- vated *true* virtue. The story would not "suit the views of men who are over-careful as to the prudent conduct of their wives, while loose in their own morals," Bushnell acknowledged, but it would bring hope to "the fallen girl," and to "the victim of society's cruel injustices." The basic principle of morality was not women's purity, she insisted, but rather justice. And "there is nothing which destroys morality out of the human heart so effectually and quickly as injustice."[71] Therefore, "no good was ever done, and no good can ever be done," she claimed, "by legal enact- ments for the benefit of society, which, for reasons of 'prudence' omit principles of justice." In fact, she added, "Here is where the great mistake is being made on the 'woman question.' Is it 'prudent' to allow women to do thus and so?—men ask themselves at every step of woman's progress." But, Bushnell asserted, "The only question that should be asked is: Does justice demand this? If so, 'let justice be done though the heavens fall'; anything short of justice is mere mischief-making."[72]

69. Ibid., 684. See also 685.
70. Starr, *Bible Status*, 175. Starr added that "[Jesus] set at naught every man- imposed restriction on woman. He recognized no double standard: with Him there was no such thing as a preferred sex. He stood woman side by side with man, and addressed her as a member of the human family... No wonder when He walked the Dolorous Way to Calvary, women followed Him and 'bewailed and lamented Him; But Jesus, turning unto them, said, Daughters of Jerusalem, weep not for Me, but weep for yourselves and your children'" (ibid., 176).
71. Bushnell, *God's Word*, 688, 690.
72. Ibid., 690.

Bushnell and Starr further challenged the foundations of the Victorian social order by developing a fascinating critique of patriarchy based on an examination of Old and New Testament texts on marriage. Rather than celebrating women's roles as dutiful wives and sacrificial mothers, they asserted that the marriage bond constituted one of the greatest sources of woman's subjection to man. "From the Stone Age to the present age," Starr wrote, the wife "has been the chief sufferer from man's mania to dominate woman… Law-books have been weighted with enactments calling for her subjugation; religion has spoken in almost every tongue and commanded that she obey her husband; custom has decreed that she take a back seat in the affairs of life. Mankind has ever been intolerant of self-assertion on the part of the wife." From the time of Eve women had suffered in their marital relationships, Starr and Bushnell claimed, and women continued to repeat the sin of Eve by turning to their husbands rather than to God.[73]

Drawing on the work of modern anthropologists, both Bushnell and Starr traced the development of patriarchy following humanity's fall into sin.[74] But Bushnell and Starr took issue with leading anthropologists who adhered to an evolutionary teleology and considered patriarchy the culmination of human progress. Instead, they argued that the development of patriarchy reflected man's rebellion against God and Eve's tragic decision to turn away from God and submit to man. To substantiate this claim, they drew attention to Gen 2:24, where God established the law of marriage immediately after separating Eve out of Adam, declaring, "Therefore shall a man leave his father and his mother, and shall cleave unto his wife." Bushnell emphasized that this was a "most interesting" interjection in the account of "ancient history" set forth by Moses, where God seemingly stepped forth "to address humanity directly and impressively." Here God promulgated "for all time the duty of husband to wife, not of wife to husband"; God's ordinance for marriage clearly supported

---

73. Starr, *Bible Status*, 82. Marriage ceremonies evidenced this pattern, powerfully symbolizing "the wife's obsequious relation to her husband." Starr pointed out that in Christian cultures a woman's status was ritualized by a bride approaching the hymeneal altar, "leaning on the arm of her father, who 'gives this woman away' as transferred property to the man she meekly vows to 'serve, to honor and obey.'"

74. Bushnell, for example, cites J. J. Bachofen's *Das Mutterecht* (1861), J. F. McLennan's *Primitive Marriage* (1865) and *Studies in Ancient History* (1886), and John Lubbock's *Marriage Totemism and Religion* (1911), along with the work of W. Roberson Smith, Herbert Spencer, E. B. Tylor, E. A. Westermarck, and James Frazer. Starr, too, cited McLennan, Smith, and Spencer, along with Eliza Burt Gamble's *The Sexes in Science and History* (1916).

a matriarchal rather than a patriarchal system.[75] But in leaving the garden, Eve foreshadowed the reversal of this fundamental law of marriage—which God had instituted for the protection of women—leaving all women vulnerable to the abuse of men.

To challenge the existing patriarchal gender relations, Starr and Bushnell also turned their attention to New Testament passages that seemed to support male headship and wifely submission. Starr, who dealt in detail with each Pauline pronouncement regarding women (1 Cor 11:3; Eph 5:21–33; Col 3:18–19; 1 Tim 5:14), contested the undue importance ascribed to these passages over the centuries. "Opponents in particular," she noted, had "exalted these writings to first place in every discussion of the subject"; they had elevated the Apostle Paul "to the position of supreme arbiter of every mooted question." Together with Gen 3:16, the Pauline epistles had become "the 'stock in trade' of such as seek to stay woman from the path of progress, and to perpetuate her age long restrainment." "Down through the centuries," Starr explained, the Christian church—and Protestants in particular—had clothed the Apostle Paul with infallibility, while Paul himself never made such a claim.[76] In fact, the authority of Paul often seemed to trump the authority of Christ himself. Expositors had found the need to "tug and wrench" at the words of Jesus in order to bring them in accord with the writings of Paul. "Why not reverse the process?" Starr inquired.[77] Instead, centuries of theologians had interpreted the Pauline pronouncements to effect "the perpetual tutelage of woman," using the Scriptures to argue that a woman "must ever be the ward of man."[78]

But, as Bushnell explained, it was "neither [a woman's] duty nor her privilege to *give herself* away to any human being,—in marriage or in any other way." A woman could be neither a useful instrument in God's hands nor "an efficient servant of His Church," Bushnell claimed, "until she comes to understand that 'she is not her own; she is bought [by Christ] with a price.'"[79] Women should not trust men and sacrifice their own selves to the point that their surrender to God alone is vitiated, she warned, adding in mock horror: "What! A woman not trust her husband!"

75. Bushnell, *God's Word*, 44.

76. Starr, *Bible Status*, 232, 235.

77. Ibid., 235, 239.

78. Ibid., 241. See also ibid., 251.

79. Bushnell, *God's Word*, 344. "There is no social redemption for woman until the chain that binds her to the lusts of her own, and of man's flesh is broken," Bushnell wrote, "and she maintains the inviolability of free-will, as her sustained attitude towards every human being, including her husband."

Bushnell was well aware of the fact that conventional views of the ideal marriage relationship seemed to suggest that "every husband *loves* a trusting wife," and that a wife should lean all her weight upon her husband. Anything less than this ideal, "any less trust than this," it was assumed, "will bring discord into the family." Bushnell conceded the possibility for discord, admitting that quarrels might well ensue when a wife failed to trust her husband to "this idolatrous extent." But she reminded her readers that Christ himself said, "I came not to send peace, but a sword." She believed that family concord could be best preserved without a wife's idolatry of her husband; "but if not, let discord prevail."[80]

By challenging traditional understandings of marriage, Bushnell and Starr disrupted conventional notions of women's domesticity and the Victorian celebration of a woman's sphere. The very concept of a "woman's sphere," they insisted, was utterly unbiblical. Male expositors had manipulated biblical texts to support their own prejudiced belief that women ought to be restricted to a limited sphere of activities, while men remained at liberty to define their own "sphere." Any passage that seemed to support their view of "woman's sphere" they exaggerated in the English translation, and those which would contradict their "masculine preconception" they toned down in translation. "This making use of 'diverse weights and measures is an abomination in the sight of God," Bushnell averred.[81] She was convinced that a careful reading of the Scriptures "would lead to remarkable revisions in the commonly-accepted ideas of woman's 'sphere.'"[82]

Starr agreed that false biblical exegesis and male prejudice had long worked to convince women that their God-ordained sphere was the home. So much had been said in the past about "woman's sphere," she informed her readers, that it had become a "trite saying that 'Woman's sphere is home.'" But Starr vigorously rejected this notion. "Woman's

---

80. Ibid., 392. Her own experiences had convinced her that "to be humble and obey God alone will surely bring tribulation to any human being, sooner or later." It would only be a question of time before one encountered a human law that contravened God's laws. "We are often told that the days of persecution are past and ended," Bushnell noted. But they have ended only because people have accepted "man's laws as God's whole will." National laws and social customs, however, such as the assumption that "the laws of a husband must be met by unquestioning obedience by the wife," should not be confused with the will of God. "It is as true to-day as it ever was that 'traditions,' i.e., man-made laws, ever 'make void the commandments of God' at all inconvenient points, and it ever will be so" (ibid., 397).

81. Ibid., 370. See also 616–44.

82. Ibid., 468.

God-given sphere," she wrote, "is as wide as the earth's circumference, as high as the firmament and as deep as the sea." The thought that women could inappropriately or rebelliously transgress the boundaries of their "sphere" was ridiculous, she argued. "Talk about a woman getting out of her sphere! She would have to get off the earth in order to do that. Every foot of this globe has been deeded to her as much as to man." Those who said otherwise sinned not only against women, but against God.[83]

Bushnell and Starr understood that in challenging the very foundations of the Victorian social order they would not be unopposed.[84] But they were convinced that they stood upon solid biblical ground, and were confident that truth could not be "wounded unto death by false exegesis. Though crucified, consigned to a rock-hewn tomb, and sealed with seven seals, it will have its Easter morn."[85]

For a variety of reasons, however, their ideas never achieved the broader influence they had sought. By the time they published their major works, Bushnell and Starr were increasingly out of step with pre-vailing trends within American Protestantism, and within the women's movement. Rejecting traditional Christianity as male dominated but upholding the authority of the Scriptures, Bushnell and Starr did not fit securely within either the conservative or the liberal factions of an increasingly polarized faith. In the face of modernist advances, many conservatives embraced a staunch literalist interpretation of the Bible and grew increasingly suspicious of modern translations. At the same time, they resisted calls for women's rights, associating the emancipation of women with the evils of modernism, and choosing instead to reify Victorian gender arrangements as the God-ordained foundation for an orderly society. Meanwhile, liberal Protestants largely embraced the tools of higher criticism and abandoned traditional notions of biblical authority; they downplayed the importance of theology as a basis for social reform, and turned instead to the promise of modern science. In doing so, liberal Protestants had little use for the careful biblical revision work of Bushnell and Starr.

---

83.   Starr, *Bible Status*, 21.

84.   If a man or woman determines "to wholly follow the Lord," trouble is sure to brew, Bushnell wrote, since following God would inevitably bring one up against "all sham customs and wicked human legislation" (*God's Word*, 398). Citing William Lecky's *History of European Morals from Augustus to Charlemagne* (New York: Appleton, 1873), she reminded her readers that "the peculiar animosity" expressed towards the early Christians was due in part to "the constant interference with domestic life" that ensued upon women converting to Christianity (p. 319).

85.   Starr, *Bible Status*, 122.

In a similar manner, leaders in the women's movement increasingly abandoned theology as a basis for women's rights, embracing instead the authority that modern science and professionalization could offer their cause. In the wake of the backlash that Stanton's *Woman's Bible* unleashed, many leading women's rights activists concluded that it would be advantageous to avoid the entanglements of religious debate. Indeed, many historians have been unaware that a rigorous defense of women's rights continued within some circles of American Protestantism well into the twentieth century.

Bushnell and Starr had been well aware of trends to diminish the authority of the Scriptures, but they insisted that the Bible remained central in shaping people's understanding of women's roles in society. Even in the 1920s, Starr contended that "The Bible holds [an] enlarged place in the thought of mankind—not a jot or tittle has been surrendered. 'What saith the Scripture?' 'Thus saith the Scripture,' and 'It is written' more than ever determine the beliefs of the race."[86] Subsequent history would bear out this conviction. Few prognosticators in the 1920s would have predicted the resilience of conservative Protestantism into the twenty-first century. The continuing vitality of conservative Christianity is particularly evident when one considers the astounding growth of the church in the global South over the past several decades.[87] As scholars have pointed out, Christians in the global South are more likely than their Western counterparts to believe in the inspired nature of the Scriptures and to uphold literal interpretations. They regard the Old Testament as authoritative as the New, and look to the Bible for a guide to social issues, including questions of gender, family, and sexuality.[88] Given this context, it is perhaps not surprising that Katharine Bushnell's writings are finding a new audience. Women from Kenya to Pakistan are rediscovering Bushnell's work, and finding within it the foundations for a

86. Ibid., 17. As Elizabeth Cady Stanton had noted at the end of the nineteenth century, "So long as tens of thousands of Bibles are printed every year, and circulated over the whole habitable globe, and the masses in all English-speaking nations revere it as the word of God, it is vain to belittle its influence." Although Stanton herself had long abandoned any sense of the Bible as "the word of God," having through reason "repudiated its divine authority," even she acknowledged "sentimental feelings" that persisted for things one once believed sacred (Stanton, *The Woman's Bible* [repr.; New York: Arno, 1972 (1895–98)], 11–12).

87. See, for example, Andrew F. Walls, "Christian Scholarship in Africa in the Twenty-first Century," *Journal of African Christian Thought* 4, no. 2 (2001): 44–52 (46), and Philip Jenkins, *The New Faces of Christianity* (New York: Oxford University Press, 2006), 9.

88. Jenkins, *The New Faces of Christianity*, 4, 15–16.

biblical critique of patriarchy.[89] The work of Bushnell and Starr, then, not only deserves a place in histories of female biblical interpretation, but it also has the potential to shape a new generation of Christians who share a commitment to biblical authority with a desire for a more liberating theology of gender.

89. Information on the global reach of Bushnell's teachings can be found on the website "God's Word to Women," http://www.godswordtowomen.org. Constructed in the 1990s by three American women (Barbara Collins, Patricia Joyce, and Gay Anderson), the site contains information on women and men promoting Bushnell's teachings in Kenya and Pakistan. See, in particular, Gladys Nyanchama Nyakweba, "GWTW Missions: Kenya," n.p. [cited June 25, 2009]. http://www. godswordtowomen. org/mission_kenya.htm. I am also grateful to Gladys Masore, who has generously shared with me her efforts to bring the teachings of Bushnell to women throughout Kenya.

ELIZABETH MARY MACDONALD: AN EARLY CANADIAN CONTRIBUTION TO THE STUDY OF WOMEN IN THE ANCIENT NEAR EAST

Rebecca G. S. Idestrom

Introduction

Throughout history, women have studied and interpreted the Bible, and many of their studies have been published. However, until more recently, awareness and knowledge of women's writings on Scripture have often been lost or largely ignored by the academic community. Therefore it is important to recover these lost voices and their writings if we want a more complete and better understanding of the history of biblical interpretation.[1] When the door finally opened for women to study at universities towards the end of the nineteenth century, few women entered the academic world to pursue doctorates in biblical studies. In the early twentieth century, however, one Canadian woman did. In this essay, I will explore the contribution of one of the early foremothers of Canadian biblical studies, Elizabeth Mary MacDonald (1897–1984). MacDonald was a woman who not only interpreted the Bible, the Old Testament in particular, but who also had an interest in the role of women in Old Testament Law and in the ancient Near East.[2] Her doctoral dissertation,

---

1. The important work of recovering women biblical interpreters throughout history is being done by Professor Marion Taylor at Wycliffe College, University of Toronto, as well as by many of her friends and colleagues. Several special sessions have been held at the Canadian Society of Biblical Studies as well as at the Society of Biblical Literature Annual Meeting on the history of women interpreters of Scripture. See Marion Ann Taylor and Heather E. Weir, eds., *Let Her Speak for Herself: Women Writing on Women of Genesis* (Waco, Tex.: Baylor University Press, 2006); Christiana de Groot and Marion Ann Taylor, eds., *Recovering Nineteenth-Century Women Interpreters of the Bible* (SBLSymS; Atlanta: Society of Biblical Literature, 2007). Marion Taylor is presently editing a *Dictionary of Women Interpreters of the Bible* (Grand Rapids: Baker Academic, forthcoming).

2. An earlier version of this paper was presented at the Canadian Society of Biblical Studies annual conference, May 2003 at Dalhousie University, Halifax,

entitled *The Position of Women as Reflected in Semitic Codes of Law* (1931), was an important study of women in the ancient Near East, in which MacDonald compared the status of women as reflected in the Babylonian, Assyrian, and Israelite codes of law.[3] Elizabeth MacDonald is also an important figure in that she played a significant role in terms of the history of women at the University of Toronto. She was one of a handful of women who completed doctoral degrees from the University in the early days of granting doctorates and allowing women to study at the University. We will briefly look at her life, the context in which she was found, and then analyze her study of women in Semitic codes of law. We will also consider some of the factors that influenced her work and her importance to biblical studies in Canada.

Her Life

Elizabeth Mary MacDonald was born in Wolfville, Nova Scotia on December 2, 1897.[4] She was the only daughter of Christina Margaret Logan and Peter MacLaren MacDonald. Her father was a Presbyterian minister, who became a United Church minister upon the creation of the United Church of Canada in 1925. He served churches in Wolfville and Truro, Nova Scotia before coming to Toronto in 1904. There Elizabeth's father pastored a number of Presbyterian and United Churches before retiring in 1946.[5]

After finishing high school at Westminster Ladies College in Toronto, Elizabeth MacDonald enrolled at the University of Toronto in 1917, in the Faculty of Arts at University College, and completed her B.A. in 1921, her M.A. in 1923, and her Ph.D. in 1928. During this time she met her future husband, Matthew Truran Newby, who also studied at University College beginning in 1922, majoring in Greek and Hebrew. Both

Nova Scotia. In the essay I use the terms Old Testament and Hebrew codes, rather than Hebrew Bible, because these are the terms that MacDonald used. When she spoke of the Hebrew codes, she was referring to the Old Testament laws, and when she used Old Testament she meant all of the Hebrew Bible including the laws.

3. Elizabeth Mary MacDonald, *The Position of Women as Reflected in Semitic Codes of Law* (University of Toronto Studies; Oriental Series 1; Toronto: The University of Toronto Press, 1931).

4. She went by the name Beth.

5. In Toronto, he pastored Cowan Avenue Church and St. Paul's Presbyterian Church, Bathurst Street United Church and was assistant Minister at Timothy Eaton Memorial Church (1941–46) just before he retired. "With Churches in Toronto for 40 Years," Obituary of P. M. MacDonald, February 12, 1960, *Canadian Obituaries 1957–1962* (University of Toronto Library Archives, Toronto).

MacDonald and Newby were students of Professor William Robert Taylor, who was the head of the department of Oriental Languages at the time (from 1914 to 1951).[6] Since MacDonald was very good at languages, Professor Taylor suggested that she tutor Matthew Newby in German. This is how they met and became better acquainted.[7] Newby was born August 21, 1901 in Pittsburgh, Pennsylvania, but his family moved to Canada in 1911 when he was ten years old. After completing his B.A. in 1926 and M.A. in 1927 at the University of Toronto, he studied theology for three years at Wycliffe College and became an ordained Anglican priest in 1930. MacDonald and Newby were married on June 27, 1934. They served at St. Matthew's Anglican in Toronto, then St. George's-on-the-Hill, Islington, and later, in 1953, Newby became Canon at St. James Cathedral in Toronto. At the same time, Newby continued his academic career, by becoming Teaching Fellow at University College (1929–31; 1936–40) and Lecturer in Introductory Greek at Wycliffe College (1940–49). He was appointed Associate Professor of Oriental Languages at Trinity College in 1947, full professor and acting head of the department of Oriental Languages in 1950, and finally head of the department until his retirement in 1971.[8] Elizabeth MacDonald and Matthew Newby had one daughter, Margaret Frances, born May 28, 1936.

This background demonstrates the significant place that the Church played in Elizabeth MacDonald's life, both in terms of being raised in a minister's home as well as marrying a minister. Her church experience included attending the Presbyterian Church, the United Church of Canada, and the Anglican Church. This heritage probably had some influence on her choice of what to study in university and her desire to pursue biblical studies. She came to the academic study of the Bible from a Christian background rooted in the mainline Churches of Canada. Education was also very important to her family, so it is not surprising

6. Elizabeth MacDonald studied with Professor William Taylor from 1917 to 1928 and Matthew Newby studied with him from 1922 to 1927.

7. Margaret Frances Newby McMullin (daughter to Elizabeth and Matthew Newby), telephone interview with author, July 2003.

8. In 1968, Wycliffe College honored Newby by conferring on him the degree of Doctor of Divinity. See Fred V. Winnett and W. Stewart McCullough, "A Brief History of the Department of Near Eastern Studies (formerly Oriental Languages) in the University of Toronto to 1976–1977" (unpublished essay, University of Toronto Library Archives, Toronto), 54, 56; "Matthew Truran Newby," *The Anglican* (December 1978).

that she pursued a Ph.D. and married an academic whose interests in biblical studies and biblical languages mirrored her own.[9]

Elizabeth MacDonald is a significant figure when we consider the history of women at the University of Toronto. Women were first allowed to enroll as students at the University of Toronto in 1884.[10] The Ph.D. degree was first introduced at the University in 1897; the first two women to receive a doctorate were Clara Cynthia Benson and Emma Sophia Baker in 1903.[11] MacDonald was the sixteenth woman to get a Ph.D. from the University,[12] and she was the very first woman to receive a doctorate in the department of Near and Middle Eastern Studies (then known as the department of Oriental Languages; it was renamed the Near Eastern Studies department in 1956; in 1996 it was renamed as the Department of Near and Middle Eastern Civilizations). In terms of the history of the department, Elizabeth MacDonald was the eleventh person to receive her Ph.D.[13] As the first woman to earn a doctorate in the department of Oriental Languages she broke new ground, in a field that was dominated by male scholars.

The significance of MacDonald's achievement is further highlighted when we consider that it was another 43 years until another woman received her doctorate in Near Eastern Studies: Donna Runnels in 1971, followed by Eva Esther Dessen and Libby Ruth Mandel Garshowitz, both in 1974.[14] Thus, out of the 36 Ph.D. degrees that were completed in

9. Her father encouraged her to go to university. Professor Robert Taylor, her dissertation supervisor, was very impressed by her and encouraged her to pursue a Ph.D. (McMullin, telephone interview).

10. Martin L. Friedland, *The University of Toronto: A History* (Toronto: University of Toronto Press, 2002), 91–92. Friedland has a whole chapter on the Admission of Women at the University (Chapter 9).

11. Anne Rochon Ford, *A Path Not Strewn with Roses: One Hundred Years of Women at the University of Toronto, 1884–1984* (Toronto: University of Toronto Press, 1985), 46.

12. Jill McBryde, "Early Graduates and Academic Women at the University of Toronto" (unpublished essay, April 1979, University of Toronto Library Archives, Toronto). The other doctorates were in chemistry, philosophy, biology, physics, classics, geology, mathematics, and botany (according to McBryde's list of women Ph.D. graduates up to 1930).

13. The first two people to get a Ph.D. in the department of Oriental Languages were Richard Davidson and Ross George Murison, both in 1902.

14. Donna Runnals, "Hebrew and Greek Sources in the Speeches of Jospehus' *Jewish Wars*" (Ph.D. diss., University of Toronto, 1971); Eva E. Dessen, "A Commentary of R. Menahem Ben Simon of Posquieres on Jeremiah" (Ph.D. diss., University of Toronto, 1974); Libby Garshowitz, "Shem Tov ben Isaac Ibn Shaprut's

the Near Eastern Studies department between 1902 and 1975, only four were earned by women.[15] What also makes MacDonald stand out when one compares her with her female contemporaries at the University of Toronto is that she pursued her studies in an unusual subject area. Most of the women studying at the university at the time were studying English and modern languages, preparing for a teaching career. Instead, MacDonald chose to study Hebrew and Greek and pursue biblical studies and ancient Near Eastern literature in particular.

Elizabeth MacDonald was also a pioneer in that her Ph.D. dissertation was published as the first volume in the Oriental Series of the University of Toronto Studies, which was a new series offered by the University of Toronto Press. This in itself testifies to the importance of her work and the recognition that it received by the professors in the department. Besides her dissertation supervisor Professor W. R. Taylor (1882–1951), J. A. Craig (1854–1932), W. A. Irwin (1884–1967), and T. J. Meek (1881–1966) taught in the department during her tenure as a student.[16] In his review of MacDonald's published dissertation, W. A. Irwin's appreciation for her work is reflected in his view that she had set the bar high for the series. He wrote: "It is to be hoped the 'Toronto Oriental Series' will announce further numbers on this same level of excellence."[17]

Touchstone (Even bohan) Chapters 2–10, Based on Ms. Plut. 2.17 (Florence, Biblioteca Medicea Laurenziana), with Collations from Other Manuscripts" (Ph.D. diss., University of Toronto, 1974).

15. Judy Mills and Irene Dombra, *University of Toronto Doctoral Theses, 1897–1967* (Toronto: University of Toronto Press, 1968), 86–87; *University of Toronto Doctoral Theses, 1968–1975: A Bibliography* (Toronto: University of Toronto Press, 1977), 88–89.

16. Jacob Maier Hirschfelder (1819–1902) and James Frederick McCurdy (1847–1935) were previous professors in the department, McCurdy being the most influential in shaping the department at the time. William Robert Taylor, having completed his Ph.D. in the department in 1910, first came to teach there in 1911 to fill a one-year post. In 1913 he returned for another one-year appointment but then became full professor and head of the department in 1914 (when McCurdy retired), a position he held until 1951. James Alexander Craig taught in the department from 1914 to 1922, William Andrew Irwin taught there from 1919 to 1930, and Theophile James Meek was there from 1923 to 1952 (Winnett and McCullough, "A Brief History," 1, 7, 18–27).

17. W. A. Irwin, "Women among Berbers and Semites: II. Semites," *American Journal of Semitic Languages and Literature* 49 (1933): 267–68. Although Irwin was at the University of Chicago at the time of writing this book review, he had been part of the faculty in the department from 1919 until 1930 and had known MacDonald as a student.

In the descriptions of graduates in the University of Toronto archives, MacDonald was described in the following way: "Instead of the fiery temper habitually accompanying burnished copper hair, Beth is most amicable. She is sincere to a degree and incomparable as a friend."[18] Along with this write-up, the quotation cited under her photograph was from William Shakespeare's play *Twelfth Night*. It read: "I have one heart, one bosom, and one truth, and that no man has; nor never none shall master be of it, save I alone."[19]

Upon graduating with her doctorate, she was offered a job at the Royal Ontario Museum in Toronto. Unfortunately, she had to decline the position because her mother was ill at the time and needed care. MacDonald ended up looking after her mother and as a result was never able to pursue a career where she could apply her studies and research skills.[20] When she married Matthew Newby in 1934, she became a wife, mother, and clergy spouse and in these roles she supported her husband in his parish ministry and academic pursuits.[21]

MacDonald's Doctoral Dissertation

Although she never became an academic, Elizabeth MacDonald did make an important contribution to biblical studies, as well as to women's studies. In this way, she is an important foremother to Canadian women who have since pursued biblical and ancient Near Eastern studies at the doctoral level. MacDonald's Ph.D. dissertation, *The Position of Women as Reflected in Semitic Codes of Law*, was completed in 1928 and published in 1931 by University of Toronto Press.[22] It is interesting to note that her dissertation, being 79 pages in length, was significantly longer than other dissertations in the department. For example, the doctoral dissertations completed before MacDonald's were between eleven and

18. MacDonald, Elizabeth Mary, A 1973–0026/260 (76), University of Toronto Library Archives, Toronto.

19. Ibid.

20. The fact that her father did not believe that it was suitable for a woman to work outside the home did not help the matter (McMullin, telephone interview).

21. Their daughter Frances McMullin shared that her mother often helped her father in his work; they would discuss it together. Elizabeth and Matthew also kept up their languages, by speaking and writing to each other in different languages, including ancient Semitic languages. For example, one year they wrote each other Christmas cards in Aramaic. Between them, they knew thirteen languages. In this way, Elizabeth was able to make some use of all the languages she had studied, and she was able to support her husband in his work (McMullin, telephone interview).

22. It cost $1.00 Canadian to purchase her book at the time.

fifty-one pages in length, and after hers, between 23 and 64 pages. The Ph.D. dissertations did not become 200–300 pages until 1936 (the one exception was E. J. Pratt's dissertation in 1917, which was 203 pages long).[23] Thus her doctoral dissertation was a larger, more substantial piece of work than that of her colleagues at the time. Her bibliography of 68 sources also demonstrates that she had done a lot of research, setting an example of someone who had thoroughly engaged the scholarly literature in the field. Her bibliography was up-to-date, including the latest publications on the topic.[24] In this way, she raised the bar by setting a high standard for others doing doctoral work.

In her research, MacDonald chose to compare the position or status of women as reflected and outlined in the Babylonian, Assyrian, and Israelite codes of law. For each law code, she systematically examined the position women held in these societies in terms of being a daughter, wife, mother, and widow, and in terms of their roles in the economic and religious life of each community. In doing so, she wanted to see the advances made by women as well as the privileges lost with the emergence of patriarchy, in comparison with the status of women in a primitive, nomadic society which she assumed was matriarchal.[25] She also traced the development of patriarchy and its impact on women by comparing earlier Babylonian and Assyrian law codes with the later Hebrew code. In her study, MacDonald concluded that both advantages and disadvantages accompanied the emergence of patriarchy, and this was demonstrated in all three Semitic codes. She also argued that "the

23. *University of Toronto Doctoral Theses, 1897–1967*, 86–87. Although E. J. Pratt eventually became a famous Canadian poet and a professor of English Literature at Victoria College at the University of Toronto, he began his studies in theology and completed a Ph.D. dissertation in the department of Oriental Languages in 1917, writing on "Studies in Pauline Eschatology and its Background." E. J. Pratt, "Studies in Pauline Eschatology and its Background" (Ph.D. diss., University of Toronto, 1917).

24. In reality, she used more than 68 sources, because when she used a work only once, she would mention it in a footnote instead of putting it in her bibliography. Of the sixty-eight sources in her bibliography, eight were in French, twenty-eight were in German, and thirty-two were in English. She also shows evidence of having worked with the Hebrew and the Akkadian texts. Thus, in her research, she consulted more works in other foreign languages than she did English sources. Her thorough interaction with other scholars in the field is also demonstrated in the number of footnotes she used and in her discussion in those footnotes. Although the footnotes reach 266 in number, in reality she had more footnotes because whenever she was reusing a work she often would list the same footnote number more than once.

25. MacDonald, *The Position of Women*, 5.

highest ideals of womanhood" were being aimed for in the Hebrew laws in comparison to the Babylonian and Assyrian laws.[26]

Before turning to the particular law codes, MacDonald began her study by briefly describing the position of women in primitive Semitic life, so that she could determine what advances women had made or privileges they had lost over time. She identified this primitive period in human history as the time before the dispersion (when the human race divided, according to Gen 11). She admitted that this section of her study was more speculative because of the lack of sources, but that one could draw some conclusions, by analogy, with the life and customs of nomads who had lived on the Arabian Peninsula. Here she drew on the work of anthropologists and sociologists.[27] Her main observation was that the primitive Semites were matriarchal or matronymic (the line of descent going through the mother), thus giving women more independence. She had the right to divorce, which was an advantage, since women would later lose this right. At the same time, the moral standards of women were lower in this system, since, for example, a woman could have more than one husband at the same time (called polyandry). However, after the dispersion, MacDonald noted that *baal* marriages began to emerge and this development became a step downward for women as they began to lose freedom and legally became mere possessions. As women moved from more nomadic lifestyles to settled communities, they received a definite place in the social and religious order in a more patriarchal society.[28] Patriarchy then emerged as the dominant organizational framework of Semitic society. Having begun by describing the status of women in primitive Semitic life, MacDonald then proceeded to look at the status of women in the three Semitic codes. She began with the code of Hammurabi, since it was the oldest of the three law codes.

In this code, women appeared in all spheres of ancient Babylonian life—domestic, economic and religious—revealing that they had more independence than in the later Semitic codes.[29] She argued that there

26. Ibid., 73.

27. Ibid., 5. Here she drew on the work of G. A. Barton, *A Sketch of Semitic Origins* (1902).

28. MacDonald, *The Position of Women*, 5–10. In this chapter, she acknowledged the influence of W. Robertson Smith, *Kinship and Marriage in Early Arabia* (1885), and A. Jaussen, *Les coutumes des Arabes* (1908) on her thought.

29. Ibid., 11. MacDonald dated the Code of Hammurabi to 2004 B.C.E. MacDonald interacted a lot with the following scholars' work on the code: C. Edwards, *The Hammurabi Code* (1921); A. H. Sayce, *Babylonians and Assyrians* (1899); S. Landersdorfer, *Die Kultur der Babylonier und Assyrier* (1925); P. Koschaker, *Rechtsvergleichende Studien zur Gesetzgebung Hammurabis* (1917); M. Jastrow Jr.,

were echoes of the matronymic system in the code of Hammurabi (e.g. a woman had more freedom to choose whom to marry, she could inherit, etc., although she had no rights in the case of divorce). MacDonald believed that this independence demonstrated that woman "was no piece of property in Babylon."[30] The only right the husband had over his wife was that he could sell her to serve three years for a debt he owed, but after three years she would be free again. He could not sell her for any other reason, since she was not merely his property.[31] MacDonald noted "an atmosphere of partnership in marriage which is incompatible with a wife being a mere possession."[32] There was also no levirate marriage in the code, which MacDonald saw as positive, yet the widow would be provided for.[33] In comparing the advantages and disadvantages for a Babylonian woman in that society, she concluded that, "on the whole, speaking of the free-woman, her position was remarkably favourable and far from being servile. Her father, or husband had not the power of life and death over her, nor the power to punish her at will. She was not an object of sale in marriage" even though there was a business contract involved.[34] She concluded that the advantages outweighed the disadvantages.[35]

When she examined the Assyrian code, MacDonald discovered that women did not fare as well in comparison to the laws in the code of Hammurabi.[36] The father had almost complete power over his daughter; for example, by choosing her husband for her, or selling her into service indefinitely if he owed a debt. She was "clearly a marketable object"[37]

An Assyrian Law Code (1921); idem, *The Religion of Babylonia and Assyria* (1898); idem, *Die Religion Babyloniens und Assyriens* (1905); B. Landsberger, *Zu den Frauenklassen des Kodex Hammurabi* (1915–16); D. G. Lyon, *The Consecrated Women of the Hammurabi Code* (1912); E. Cuq, *Etudes sur le Droit Babylonien* (1929).

30. MacDonald, *The Position of Women*, 16.
31. Ibid., 17.
32. Ibid.
33. Ibid., 23–24.
34. Ibid., 31.
35. Ibid., 32.
36. MacDonald dated the Assyrian code to 1300 B.C.E. In this section, she interacted a lot with the following scholars' work on the Assyrian code: M. Jastrow, *An Assyrian Law Code* (1921); E. Cuq, *Etudes sur le Droit Babylonien* (1929); idem, *Un recueil de lois assyriennes* (1922); V. Scheil, *Receuil des Lois Assyriennes* (1921); I. M. Price, *The So-Called Levirate-Marriage in Hittite and Assyrian Laws* (1926); K. L. Tallqvist, *Old Assyrian Laws* (1921); H. Ehelolf, *Ein altassyrisches Rechtsbuch* (1922); P. Cruveilhier, *Le droit de la Femme* (1927).
37. MacDonald, *The Position of Women*, 33.

and seen as a man's possession, indicated by the veil she was required to wear.[38] The divorce laws also did not favor the woman, for the husband could divorce his wife for any reason at all, since no grounds were necessary for a divorce.[39] If the father or husband were displeased with her, they could punish her as they wished, but in some cases the laws stipulated that she be brutally punished with mutilation or death.[40]

After analyzing the Assyrian code, MacDonald concluded that

> The Assyrian woman does not appear from AC [the Assyrian code] to have enjoyed as favourable a position in society as the Babylonian woman. Her advantages are soon summed up. She was not sold in marriage, rather, the same contract system as in CH [the code of Hammurabi] prevailed. She had greater freedom as a widow. The state saw that she did not suffer if her husband was absent in its interests. But to her disadvantage, she was under her father's powerful control; he could punish her as he chose. Her husband was chosen for her, and as a prospective wife she had to submit to the Levirate system even to the inclusion of her father-in-law, or her dead fiancé's son.[41]

Women were clearly disadvantaged in the Assyrian laws. MacDonald did note remnants of the matronymic system in Assyrian law in that it was common for the wife to live in her father's house and not with her husband, making it necessary for her husband to visit her there. "Although she was expected to be faithful to him, she was not subject to [her husband's] authority."[42] This was an echo of the matriarchal system.

When MacDonald analyzed the status of women in the Hebrew codes of the Old Testament, she looked at four codes, dividing the law according to the historical-critical source theory of J, D, E, P (although the order and dating of the sources differed from the more accepted order and dating of JEDP), dating the J code from the ninth century, D from the eighth, E from the seventh, and P from the sixth.[43] She argued that there was a development in the role of women as one analyzed these

---

38. Ibid., 37, 48.

39. Ibid., 40.

40. Ibid., 38, 40.

41. Ibid., 48. Only if there were no eligible men in her husband's family was she officially recognized as a widow and free to remarry.

42. Ibid., 39.

43. Ibid., 50. It is possible that her ordering and dating of the sources was simply a mistake of switching the order of D and E, since later she wrote that D came from the seventh century and not the eighth century as she originally suggested (ibid., 63). She referred to these sources as codes rather than as sources, and argued that they were based on even older codes, perhaps even the code of Hammurabi and the Assyrian code (ibid., 50).

codes, the later codes being more favorable to women where a higher conception of woman was developed.[44] In her study, MacDonald also relied on the biblical narratives to supplement her knowledge of women's position in ancient Israel since the law codes represented the ideal rather than what may have been practiced in reality.[45] Since the Hebrew codes were primarily concerned with Yahwistic religion, she stated that they were "[c]haracterized throughout by religion and the additional plea of the prophets for humanity, mercy and justice, [and that] we find at times a softness that is not there in the other codes."[46]

Although it was unlikely that an Israelite woman could choose her own husband (with the exception of the later code P, in Num 36:6 where she could marry whom she chose provided that it was within her own tribe), the fact that women had freedom to tend flocks or go to wells where they could become acquainted with men led MacDonald to conclude that there may have been Hebrew marriages resulting from choice. As evidence for this, she gave examples of men and women meeting at wells (Gen 24:15; 29:9; Exod 2:16) and added that "there are many examples of affectionate couples in the OT."[47] Although there were references to gifts given when entering into marriage, MacDonald argued that "the Hebrew woman's position as a wife and mother argue against actual purchase marriages."[48] She admitted that others would disagree with her and have argued that the wife was simply one of the husband's possessions, a mere chattel. In her response to them and to verses which seem to lend support to this conclusion (like the Tenth Commandment in Exod 20:17; Deut 5:21), she wrote: "But these things, except children, constituted all the material things that a man could have in life and what more natural than that his wife should be mentioned in this connection as

44. Ibid., 51. In her analysis of the Hebrew codes, she interacted a number of times with the following scholars: G. Beer, *Die soziale und religiöse Stellung der Frau im israelitischen Altertums* (1919); E. B. Cross, *The Hebrew Family* (1927); T. Engert, *Ehe und Familienrecht der Hebräer* (1905); P. Cruveilhier, *Le droit de la Femme* (1927); A. Eberharter, *Ehe und Familienrecht der Hebräer* (1914); E. Ring, *Israel's Rechtsleben* (1926); E. Day, *The Social Life of the Hebrews* (1907); A. Bertholet, *A History of Hebrew Civilization* (1926); C. M. Breyfolge, *The Religious Status of Woman in the Old Testament* (1910); I. J. Peritz, *Woman in the Ancient Hebrew Cult* (1898); S. R. Driver, *The Book of Genesis* (n.d.); J. Benzinger, *Hebräische Archäologie* (1894); D. W. Amram, *The Jewish Law of Divorce* (1896); H. Schaeffer, *The Social Legislation of the Primitive Semites* (1915).

45. MacDonald, *The Position of Women*, 50.

46. Ibid.

47. Ibid., 51. Unfortunately, she did not give specific examples of the "affectionate couples" she had observed in Scripture.

48. Ibid., 53.

in all probability she was what he valued the most."[49] While the order of coveting one's neighbor's house being listed before coveting the wife in Exod 20:17 might suggest that the house was more valuable than the wife in view of property, this understanding did not last because the order was reversed by the Deuteronomic writers "who were interested in raising woman's status."[50] MacDonald believed that the status of women improved in the Deuteronomic code.

MacDonald argued that in general the Old Testament codes of law revealed that

> the position of woman varied greatly. In one case she might be in subjection to, and in another case apparently on equal terms with her husband... Admittedly her legal status was below her husband's but a legal status is one thing, and common practice another. From her position as a mother, and from the fact that she was not excluded from participation in the religious life, we may conclude that as a wife she could not have held a greatly inferior position. She was often the stronger character (Gen. 16:18, I Sam. 25, II Ki. 4:8–10) and did not allow herself to be subjugated by a husband or by fear of consequences. Under subjugation, her initiative would have disappeared, but it is difficult to find an OT reference where a wife was at a loss, while indications of her resourcefulness and instances where she had the upper hand are numerous. A cowed, slave-like race of women would have afforded none of these. Love in marriage, moreover, was a common thing among the Hebrews... The fact that woman's influence was feared by the writers of the earliest code (Ex. 34:16) as well as later (*e.g.*, Deut. 7:3, 1 Ki. 11:3, Ez. 9:2, Neh. 13:25) shows that she was a force to be reckoned with and no mere chattel.[51]

Interestingly, MacDonald's view here was more influenced by the Old Testament narratives than the law codes, since she believed that the narratives reflected more the realities of life at the time.

When it came to the Hebrew laws on divorce, even though the right to divorce lay with the man and not the woman, MacDonald saw the divorce laws in Deuteronomy as positive, safeguarding the woman from being divorced at the whim of her husband. Several laws protected the woman by making it difficult for the husband to divorce his wife, such as the requirement of a bill of divorce or the proving of charges against her in court.[52] In comparison with Babylonian and Assyrian laws, MacDonald saw this as more favorable for Hebrew women.[53] The stress on the virtue

49. Ibid., 56.
50. Ibid.
51. Ibid., 57–58.
52. Ibid., 58.
53. Ibid., 60.

of Hebrew women in comparison to Babylonian and Assyrian women was also seen as positive, since this led to less immorality and emphasized faithfulness in marriage.[54] MacDonald also argued that the wife and mother could not have had "a servile position in relation to her husband in her home," or she would not have been respected by her children if she was "treated as a creature of his will."[55] She noted that more frequently the woman named her children and she influenced the children when it came to religion.[56]

Religiously, women participated fully in the worship of the Lord, even though they could not be priests. This did not bother MacDonald because of her view of the *nature* of women. She wrote: "Even if woman's ritual uncleanness had not excluded her from the office she was by nature unfitted for the sacrificing priesthood. The slaughtering of animals is contrary to her nature."[57] Here MacDonald's dislike of killing animals seemed to influence her view of what was natural for women. Thus she saw no problem in women being excluded from the Israelite priesthood. Instead, in this context she highlighted that women could be prophetesses, which she viewed as a much more positive role.[58]

MacDonald concluded that the Hebrew codes had both positive and negative effects on the status of women. But in comparison to women in Babylonian and Assyrian laws, "a more exalted idea of womanhood had developed among the Hebrews, and her virtue and faithfulness was valued for their own sake. Bigamy and polygamy with their attendant evils were giving place to monogamy."[59]

In MacDonald's concluding chapter she reviewed and summarized the similarities and differences between the three Semitic nations and their codes as they related to the status of woman. One observation she made was that

> the change from the nomadic to the settled life was doubtless what made woman more of an individual and won for her in the eastern Semitic world her economic independence. A settled abode and the necessity for all to unite against an outside enemy tended to break down tribal distinctions and this in itself gave woman more freedom.[60]

54. Ibid.
55. Ibid., 63.
56. Ibid. She gave the following examples of mothers naming their children (Gen 4:1; 29:32–35; 30:6–13, 17–24).
57. Ibid., 67.
58. Ibid.
59. Ibid., 69.
60. Ibid., 70.

She also believed that the settled life was one of the contributing factors that led to the change from the matriarchal or matronymic system to the patriarchal system.[61] "With the settled condition and the acquiring of property (plus a sense of personal property rights) a man could support a wife by himself, and with wealth, more than one: so the patronymic system and the patriarchate were due to economic conditions."[62] With the change came both positive and negative effects. In fact, MacDonald did not see patriarchy as entirely evil; there were both drawbacks and improvements for women with patriarchy. For example, she believed that the fact that the power to divorce (with all three nations) lay with the man alone was a negative effect of patriarchy. However, the notion that the woman was the man's property also led to the emphasis on her faithfulness which MacDonald saw as positive. "Yet the old idea that the wife was her husband's property still clung in connection with the matter of her faithfulness, and for that, if not for ethical reasons, virtue was demanded of her. That it was demanded at all was an advance and this was one favourable result of the patriarchal system."[63]

In comparing the Babylonian, Assyrian, and Hebrew codes, MacDonald claimed that one of the reasons for the differences between the three nations and their laws about women was rooted in the character of each nation. As a people group, the Assyrians were more inherently cruel by nature, whereas the Babylonians were "a milder people interested in art and culture, and the Hebrews were interested primarily in religion."[64] This would explain some of the differences in their laws. The Assyrians were more abusive of their women than the others, as reflected in their code. In comparison, women fared better in the Babylonian and Hebrew codes.[65]

In her final assessment of the Babylonian, Assyrian, and Hebrew codes, MacDonald concluded that the Hebrew codes revealed that the "highest ideals of womanhood were being striven for. Despite the evils in connection with divorce and debt, she attained an independence and self-reliance and an opportunity for further development to which she would never have attained so long as the primitive conditions flourished."[66] Thus the status of women improved with the Israelite religion and law. She concluded that

61. Ibid., 71.
62. Ibid.
63. Ibid.
64. Ibid., 72.
65. Ibid., 72–73.
66. Ibid., 73.

Conjectures on the basis of data furnished by law codes can be only relatively true. Legal regulations are one thing, actual practice another. Women's legal status is one thing, her actual position another... Life is never wholly determined by the letter of the law. If in some instances the lot of the Semitic woman was even less bearable than the codes indicate, it is no doubt equally true that there were many instances in which personal factors and the human element enabled her to rise to a higher position in society than is indicated in the codes.[67]

This statement reveals one of the reasons why MacDonald relied so much on Old Testament narratives in her study, allowing them to influence her interpretation of the Hebrew codes. For her, the narratives in the Bible reflected more the reality of what actually happened, how laws were put into practice in ancient Israel, whereas the laws presented the ideal, whether practiced or not.[68] It was a question of the ideal or theoretical vs. reality. Thus the biblical narratives became the hermeneutical key or lens for her reading of the Old Testament law codes. In her opinion, the biblical narratives presented a more positive view of the status and role of women in ancient Israel in general than if one's understanding was based solely upon how they were presented in the Old Testament laws. This factor played a role in her study.[69]

MacDonald's approach to the ancient Near East laws and the status of women was also influenced by the nineteenth-century evolutionary notion

67. Ibid.

68. In introducing the Hebrew codes, MacDonald wrote: "Since in these more or less idealistic codes, parallels for a great many references in CH and AC are lacking, it is necessary to have recourse to the narratives to augment our knowledge of women's position. The latter are composite, and as a result, are in places contradictory" (ibid., 50). G. R. Driver, one of the reviewers of her book, was critical of her approach because he argued that her work was "based on a literal acceptance of the text." Although she recognized the composite and sometimes seemingly contradictory nature of the Old Testament narratives, her conclusions did demonstrate that she believed that the narratives reflected the reality of what happened in ancient Israel (in contrast to the laws that were more theoretical and ideal). G. R. Driver, Review of Elizabeth Mary MacDonald, *The Position of Women as Reflected in Semitic Codes of Law*, *Journal of Theological Studies* 34 (1933): 187–88.

69. In his review of her book, A. G. Barrois wondered why MacDonald had not examined legal judgments and contracts made in the Babylonian and Assyrian cultures in order to see how the laws from Hammurabi and the Assyrian code were being put into practice. Barrois too believed that these law codes were theoretical whereas the legal contracts revealed historical reality. MacDonald had only applied this approach to the Old Testament. A. G. Barrois, Review of Elizabeth Mary MacDonald, *The Position of Women as Reflected in Semitic Codes of Law*, *Revue Biblique* 42 (1933): 459–60.

of developmentalism—that is, that as the human race naturally develops over time, it improves. This evolutionary framework of seeing development from a more primitive and nomadic world to a more sophisticated and settled society shaped her interpretation, and caused her to see the later Hebrew codes on a higher level than the earlier Babylonian and Assyrian codes. In the Hebrew codes the lot of women had improved in comparison.

It is also possible to argue that her Christian background had an effect on her more positive view of how women were treated in the Old Testament and Israelite law, in comparison to the other ancient Near Eastern laws. Her Christian view of morality and the importance of fidelity in marriage also led her to evaluate some aspects of patriarchy as positive in the Old Testament.

In her study of the status of women in the three Semitic codes, MacDonald used a comparative religions approach to study the topic. With more archaeological discoveries being made in ancient Mesopotamia, comparative studies were becoming increasingly popular within biblical studies at the time. While MacDonald was a student at the University of Toronto, the department of Oriental Languages introduced courses on the History of the ancient Near East as part of the curriculum in 1925, believing that this subject was important for understanding the biblical world.[70] At the time, the department also hired T. J. Meek in 1923, who had a strong interest in the ancient Near Eastern languages and literature. He had been Professor of Semitic Languages at Bryn Mawr College and had written his Ph.D. dissertation on the "Old Babylonian Business and Legal Documents."[71] Alongside Meek, W. A. Irwin also did a lot to popularize courses in Oriental History and Literature.[72] In this intellectual milieu where both the faculty and curriculum emphasized the study of ancient Near Eastern history and its literature, it is not surprising that MacDonald chose a topic and an approach in which

70. Winnett and McCullough, "A Brief History," 21.

71. Ibid., 19, 26; T. J. Meek, "Old Babylonian Business and Legal Documents" (Ph.D. diss., University of Chicago, 1915). Meek's more important works were published after MacDonald's doctoral dissertation and therefore are not reflected in her bibliography. These were *Old Akkadian, Sumerian and Cappadocian Texts from Nuzi* (Cambridge: Cambridge University Press, 1935), and his translation of Mesopotamian legal documents, including the Code of Hammurabi for the publication *Ancient Near Eastern Texts Relating to the Old Testament* (ed. J. B. Pritchard; Princeton: Princeton University Press, 1950). Nevertheless, Meek's presence in the department and his keen interest in the subject matter was probably an inspiration to many, including MacDonald.

72. Winnett and McCullough, "A Brief History," 19–20.

she compared the legal texts of the ancient Near East. She was simply following the scholarly trend at this time.

MacDonald's work also demonstrated her acceptance of the source-critical approach to studying the Bible. At the end of the nineteenth century, a dramatic paradigm shift had occurred within biblical scholarship with the emergence of historical criticism as an accepted approach to the Bible in many academic circles. This approach had made inroads into the University of Toronto under James Frederick McCurdy (1847–1935), one of the founding fathers of the department of Near Eastern Studies.[73] Thus, Elizabeth MacDonald was thoroughly familiar with the historical-critical approach and adopted a source-critical perspective in analyzing the biblical data in her study. In her bibliography one sees the names of such historical critics as Julius Wellhausen and W. Robertson Smith, among others.[74] Although one could argue that her view of the documentary hypothesis as reflected in JEDP was somewhat simplistic and lacked the complexities of later source-critical theories, she did not question the approach but rather embraced it as a way of interpreting the biblical text.[75] She also adopted the results of anthropological and sociological studies at the time, and incorporated them into her study.[76] MacDonald's dissertation also reveals that she had studied German, French, Hebrew, and Akkadian, as well as the other ancient languages necessary to do her study of the Babylonian and Assyrian codes. She worked meticulously with the primary sources. Her academic training had prepared her well to do her research.

How do we evaluate MacDonald's work within the history of biblical scholarship? Although she never pursued an academic career as a biblical scholar, she did break ground in a male-dominated field for other women. Not only was she the first woman in the department of Oriental Studies to complete a doctorate, in her scholarly work she addressed a topic that related to women. In this way, she is important in the history of

73. J. F. McCurdy succeeded J. M. Hirschfelder (1819–1902) as head of the department of Oriental languages in 1889. He retired in 1914 (ibid., 7–8, 17).

74. J. Wellhausen, *Reste des arabischen Heidentums* (1897); W. R. Smith, *Kinship and Marriage in Early Arabia* (1885); S. R. Driver, *The Book of Genesis* (n.d.), is also mentioned in n. 222 on p. 57.

75. In his review of her book, A. G. Barrois argued that her understanding and dating of the sources JEDP was a simplification of the Documentary Hypothesis. This is also the critique of G. R. Driver. See Barrois, Review of MacDonald, 459–60; Driver, Review of MacDonald, 188.

76. This was especially evident in her first chapter where she analyzed primitive society according to anthropological and sociological studies done on nomadic societies.

women's studies. Although other scholars had studied the topic of women in biblical and ancient Near Eastern laws (as reflected in her bibliography), MacDonald was one of the first women to do an academic and scholarly study of the topic.[77] She broke ground by publishing a major scholarly work on the topic (in an academic series by a university press), at a time when there were few women academics engaged in scholarly publications on the Bible.[78]

How do we assess MacDonald's work in light of later feminist interpretations of the Bible? In approaching this question, we acknowledge that feminists are not a homogenous and monolithic group, and that there is a whole range of varied interpretations and approaches taken by feminists today. Although MacDonald adopted certain views in her study that would differ from positions taken by more recent feminist scholars, her work also anticipated the conclusions of some feminist biblical scholarship of today. For example, she argued that the status of women improved in the Deuteronomic code in comparison to the earlier codes.[79] Although there are those who argue against this view, many scholars today have come to the same conclusion.[80]

MacDonald's assertion that women's position improved with the move from nomadic to settled life fit with her evolutionary framework. A number of feminist scholars today would argue that women actually fared better in the earlier period in an agrarian society (during the time of the tribal confederation), rather than in the later monarchic period.[81]

77. In her bibliography we see only studies done by male scholars listed. Although there may have been other women who had done a similar scholarly work on this specific topic, MacDonald was certainly the first woman in Canada to do so.

78. See Dorothy Bass's discussion of the history of women's involvement within the Society of Biblical Literature in the United States and the challenges and publishing barriers women faced in the early days of being part of the Society. The first woman to become a member in SBL was in 1894. MacDonald was never a member of SBL. Dorothy C. Bass, "Women's Studies and Biblical Studies: An Historical Perspective," *JSOT* 22 (1982): 6–12.

79. MacDonald, *The Position of Women*, 56.

80. Eckart Otto has come to the same conclusion as MacDonald. Eckart Otto, "False Weights in the Scales of Biblical Justice? Different Views of Women from Patriarchal Hierarchy to Religious Equality in the Book of Deuteronomy," in *Gender and Law in the Hebrew Bible and the Ancient Near East* (ed. Victor H. Matthews, Bernard M. Levison, and Tikva Frymer-Kensky; JSOTSup 262; Sheffield: Sheffield Academic Press, 1998), 128–46. For someone who disagrees with this conclusion, see Carolyn Pressler, *The View of Women Found in the Deuteronomic Family Laws* (BZAW 216; Berlin: de Gruyter, 1993), 105–14.

81. See Carol Meyers's work on this topic: *Discovering Eve: Ancient Israelite Women in Context* (New York: Oxford University Press, 1988), and "Everyday Life:

However, when MacDonald spoke of improvement for women when they moved to the settled life, she did not make a clear distinction between the monarchic period and the pre-monarchic period (as later feminist scholars do). She simply spoke of the improved situation for women with the emergence of settled communities.

MacDonald had a positive view of the concept of matriarchy, and made the argument that in the primitive society of the Semites, including the Israelites, matriarchy or a matronymic system existed before the development of patriarchy and then later alongside patriarchy. She said that there were remnants or echoes of this in all the law codes she analyzed.[82] Even though she recognized that this was a minority view, she still made a case for it and saw it as something positive.[83] Although there are scholars who have argued that matriarchy existed in the ancient Near East, there is no agreement on whether it was ever practiced in ancient Israel.[84] For example, in W. A. Irwin's otherwise positive review of her book, he criticized MacDonald on this point. He wrote: "The existence of matriarchal society in Israel (p. 56) is very uncertain."[85] I would have to agree with him. Here she was clearly influenced by the notion of a primitive matriarchy in the ancient world, a view popular in the nineteenth century.[86] Biblical scholars today are less certain about this; a number of scholars would argue against it ever having existed.[87]

Women in the Period of the Hebrew Bible," in *Women's Bible Commentary: Expanded Edition* (ed. Carol A. Newsom and Sharon H. Ringe; Louisville: Westminster John Knox, 1998), 251–59.

82. MacDonald, *The Position of Women*, 5–10, 56, 71.

83. She acknowledged those who questioned this view. See ibid., 5 n. 3.

84. See Roland de Vaux's discussion of different views on matriarchy in the ancient Near East and in ancient Israel. He outlines W. Robertson Smith's position in *Kinship and Marriage in Early Arabia* (1885), who had advocated for the existence of matriarchy among the earliest Semites. De Vaux finds that Robertson Smith's arguments for a matriarchy are not conclusive. Instead, de Vaux (*Ancient Israel: Its Life and Institutions* [trans. John McHugh; Grand Rapids: Eerdmans, 1961, 1997], 20) argues that "Prehistoric Israel is to us a closed book; but whatever may be true of that epoch, there is no doubt that from the time of our oldest documents, at any rate, the Israelite family is *patriarchal*."

85. Irwin, "Women among Berbers," 268.

86. In taking this position, she had been influenced by work of W. Robertson Smith in *Kinship and Marriage in Early Arabia* (1885), as she acknowledged on p. 10 n. 6.

87. Carol Meyers (*Discovering Eve*, 30) writes, "Although some feminist anthropologists might insist that they can identify a few societies in which women were equal or even dominant, the overwhelming consensus is that no society truly egalitarian with respect to gender has ever existed. Furthermore, the notion that a

Some people today may struggle with the fact that women were excluded from the Israelite priesthood in biblical times. This reality was not a concern for MacDonald. She did not advocate that women should have been allowed to become priests in ancient Israel. Her view was not based on theological concerns, but rather was based on her belief that the priestly practice of slaughtering animals in order to sacrifice them went against women's nature. It seems to me that she overlooked the fact that in an agrarian society women would have killed animals regularly for food. Her position was influenced by a particular view of women's nature as gentle and not prone to killing animals.

Although MacDonald acknowledged that there were many disadvantages with patriarchy, the fact that she concluded that there were some positive aspects or advantages with the emergence of patriarchy would be problematic for many today. Those who are engaged in feminist hermeneutics try to reveal what is perceived as a patriarchal bias in Scripture, a perspective seen as negative and oppressive to women. Mary Ann Tolbert writes that feminism is committed to critiquing "all oppressive cultural structures" and to exposing the oppressive structures of patriarchal society.[88] MacDonald, however, did not adopt such a feminist hermeneutic in her approach. Therefore she did not reject patriarchy outright as something completely oppressive to women, but rather adopted a stance where she could see some advantages in a patriarchal society. MacDonald's views, however, were not unusual at the time, but reflected the time period and culture in which she lived and worked.

primitive matriarchy, popular at one time among nineteenth-century evolutionists and their intellectual heirs, has been shown to be dubious at best." MacDonald was one of the "intellectual heirs" who had adopted the popular view at the time. If she had lived today, she may have taken a different position.

88.   Mary Ann Tolbert, "Defining the Problem: The Bible and Feminist Hermeneutics," *Semeia* 28 (1983): 113–26 (114, 119). In her article, she outlines various approaches that feminists have taken to Scripture as they wrestle with the concept of patriarchy and its influence. Tolbert speaks of the irony, tension, and paradox of feminist hermeneutics when she acknowledges that: "So, one must struggle against God as enemy assisted by God as helper, or one must defeat the Bible as patriarchal authority by using the Bible as liberator" (ibid., 120). Rosemary Radford Ruether writes, "The feminist critical principle thus demands that women stand outside of and in judgment upon this patriarchal bias of the scriptures." Rosemary Radford Ruether, "Feminist Interpretation: A Method of Correlation," in *Feminist Interpretation of the Bible* (ed. Letty M. Russell; Oxford: Blackwell, 1985), 111–24 (116). Ruether also advocates that one should adopt the prophetic critique of injustice in the Bible, proclaiming "the good news of liberation from patriarchy" (ibid., 124).

Conclusion

Elizabeth MacDonald is an important figure in the history of women at the University of Toronto, as well as in the history of women in biblical studies in Canada. She is also significant in that her work reflects an important early contribution to the study of women in the biblical world that is still cited by scholars studying this field today.[89] This fact alone demonstrates the lasting value of her research. Even though MacDonald and her study are not widely known today (probably because she did not publish other scholarly works and she never held an academic post),[90] nevertheless her research is a valuable contribution to the study of women's status and roles in the ancient world, especially in terms of the impact of patriarchy on women. Although she came to certain conclusions that would differ from those of some feminists today, this does not negate the value of her work and her pioneering efforts. Her views should be understood in light of the cultural and intellectual milieu in which she was found, that of the early twentieth century. She was influenced by concepts and ideas popular within biblical scholarship at the time. In her context, she was a pioneer who broke new ground. For that she should be remembered.

89. Roland de Vaux, Phyllis Bird, and William Webb refer to her book in their writings. See de Vaux, *Ancient Israel*, 522; Phyllis A. Bird, "The Place of Women in the Israelite Cultus," in *Missing Persons and Mistaken Identities: Women and Gender in Ancient Israel* (Minneapolis: Fortress, 1997), 81–102 (82 n. 7); William J. Webb, S*laves, Women and Homosexuals: Exploring the Hermeneutics of Cultural Analysis* (Downers Grove: InterVarsity, 2001), 285.

90. She is not mentioned in John S. Moir's important book, *A History of Biblical Studies in Canada: A Sense of Proportion* (Chico, Calif.: Scholars Press, 1982).

READY TO SACRIFICE ALL:
THE REPENTANT MAGDALENE IN THE WORK
OF HARRIET BEECHER STOWE

Nancy Calvert-Koyzis

Introduction

Mary Magdalene captured the imagination of nineteenth-century British and American Christians. Biblical scholars, preachers, and rescue workers all proclaimed Mary as the repentant prostitute and regenerate saint. Harriet Beecher Stowe also interpreted Mary in her lesser-known works of non-fiction in imaginative ways that reflected her own upbringing and culture. In this essay I will consider Stowe's interpretations of Mary Magdalene against the background of her social and ideological contexts and in comparison with the work of her contemporaries, Elizabeth Rundle Charles and Sarah Towne Martyn.

Stowe's Early Life and Its Influences

Born in Litchfield, Connecticut in 1811, Harriet Beecher Stowe was the seventh child of Lyman and Roxana Beecher. Lyman Beecher was a pastor who entered the ministry during a time of evangelistic revival that is known as the Second Great Awakening (c. 1800–1840). His zealousness for his ministry meant that he was often away from home. He was an inordinately active man and has been described as moving "through life at full speed, in many ways a driven man, reckless of consequence and fired with belief."[1] He had energetically brought Roxana into the Calvinist fold during their courtship and after their marriage he said, "She entered into my character entirely." To Lyman, this was her greatest virtue.[2]

---

1. Kathryn Kish Sklar, *Catherine Beecher: A Study in American Domesticity* (New Haven: Yale University Press, 1973), 4.
2. Ibid., 5.

Roxana Beecher came from a prominent family that was part of "the town's privileged group of educated and professional families." She was well educated: she spoke French fluently, enjoyed ancient history and devoured books, sometimes by tying those by the best French authors to her distaff to study as she spun.[3] She was used to being a member of the leisured class.

After she married Lyman Beecher, however, Roxana's life changed a great deal. While they lived in Litchfield, not only did she eventually become the mother of several children, but her household also included as many as seventeen boarders from local academic institutions, bond servants, and relatives who visited for lengthy periods of time. Added to this were her social responsibilities as the community minister's wife. Because Lyman was so often away from home, she had to contend with all of this on her own. She died after seventeen years of marriage at age forty-one of tuberculosis, which was most probably brought on by exhaustion.[4]

After her death, the family accorded Roxana Beecher a kind of sainthood. Stowe comments in a letter on the "deep interest and veneration" that her mother inspired in all who had known her, meaning that Harriet constantly heard reminiscences.[5] Roxana was remembered for events that exemplified her pious and submissive nature, such as her inability to speak in company or before strangers without blushing.[6] In these ways she appears to have lived up to the nineteenth-century ideal of true womanhood. Her mother's example of self-denial impacted Harriet's understanding of women and eventually would play a role in her characterization of women not only in her works of fiction, but also in her non-fiction works as well.

According to Harriet's son Charles Edward Stowe, when Roxana died the incident stayed with Harriet "as the tenderest, saddest, and most sacred memory of her childhood."[7] Harriet herself wrote that the following passage in *Uncle Tom's Cabin*, in which Augustine St. Clare described his mother's influence on his life, was a reproduction of her own mother's influence:[8]

3. Joan D. Hedrick, *Harriet Beecher Stowe: A Life* (New York: Oxford University Press, 1994), 5.

4. Ibid., 7.

5. Annie Fields, ed., *Life and Letters of Harriet Beecher Stowe* (New York: Houghton Mifflin, 1897), 11.

6. Ibid., 13.

7. Charles Edward Stowe, *Life of Harriet Beecher Stowe Compiled from her Letters and Journals* (London: Sampson, Low, Marston, Searle & Rivington, 1889), 2.

8. Ibid., 5.

"My mother," said St. Clare, getting up and walking to a picture at the end of the room, and gazing upward with a face fervent with veneration, "she was divine!... She probably was of mortal birth; but, as far as ever I could observe, there was no trace of any human weakness or error about her; and everybody that lives to remember her, whether bond or free, servant, acquaintance, relation, all say the same... Why, cousin, that mother has been all that has stood between me and utter unbelief for years. She was a direct embodiment and personification of the New Testament, — a living fact, to be accounted for, and to be accounted for in no other way than by its truth. O, mother! mother!?" said St. Clare, clasping his hands, in a sort of transport.[9]

As St. Clair's reminiscences indicate, the virtue of a woman was of paramount importance. This womanly virtue was believed by many to be central to the peace and sanctity of the household of which she was the moral guardian. As we shall see, for Stowe, this virtue was found in a woman's willingness to suffer and sacrifice herself after the example of the sorrowing Christ.[10] Like her character, Mr. St. Claire, Stowe had exalted her mother to the pinnacle of moral and spiritual perfection.[11]

Stowe's emphasis on the self-sacrifice of women is particularly evident in her novel *The Minister's Wooing* (1859) in the character of Mary Scudder, who is willing to sacrifice her soul for that of her agnostic cousin James:

How many days and nights have been one prayer for you! If I could take my hopes of heaven out of my own heart and give them to you, I would... Dr. Hopkins preached last Sunday on the text, "I could wish myself accursed from Christ for my brethren, my kinsmen"; and he went on to show how we must be willing to give up even our own salvation, if necessary, for the good of others. People said it was a hard doctrine, but I would feel my way through it very well. Yes, I would give my soul for yours; I wish I could.[12]

While Stowe is known primarily for her works of fiction, particularly *Uncle Tom's Cabin* (1852), she also wrote works of non-fiction, such as *Woman in Sacred History* (1873) in which she commented on biblical

9.   Harriet Beecher Stowe, *Uncle Tom's Cabin or Life Among the Lowly* (repr.; New York: Random House, 1938 [1852]), 277.

10.   Ann-Janine Morey, "American Myth and Biblical Interpretation in the Fiction of Harriet Beecher Stowe and Mary E. Wilkins Freeman," *JAAR* 55, no. 4 (1987): 741–63 (749).

11.   See also John Gatta, *American Madonna: Images of the Divine Woman in Literary Culture* (New York: Oxford University Press, 1997), 53, who also comments on the influence of Roxana Beecher on Stowe's writing.

12.   Harriet Beecher Stowe, *The Minister's Wooing* (repr.; New York: AMS, 1967 [1859]), 27.

texts in which women were prominent. In 1877 she wrote *Footsteps of the Master* in which she repeated much of what she wrote in *Woman in Sacred History*.[13] As I will show in my essay on Stowe's interpretation of the Virgin Mary later in the present volume, because she saw all of her writing as a means of religious instruction, she considered her non-fiction works to be of greater importance than her fiction works because in them she could speak directly about matters of religion. Keeping this in mind, I now turn to Stowe's interpretation of Mary Magdalene in these influential works.

Stowe's Interpretation of Mary Magdalene in
Woman in Sacred History

Because Stowe's interpretations of Mary Magdalene in her 1873 work entitled *Woman in Sacred History* and her later book *Footsteps of the Master* (1877) are so similar, I will focus on *Woman in Sacred History*, where her remarks are also more extensive. It will be obvious to biblical scholars that Stowe did not approach the New Testament from what today would be considered a critical standpoint. However, she did appropriate the methods of nineteenth-century biblical scholars when she followed the "modern fashion of treating the personages of sacred story with the same freedom of inquiry as the characters of any other history."[14] As she re-fashioned Mary Magdalene, it is obvious that she used nineteenth-century ideas of what it meant to be a middle-class woman.

   Stowe begins *Woman in Sacred History* by stating: "The object of the following pages will be to show, in a series of biographical sketches, a history of WOMANHOOD UNDER DIVINE CULTURE, tending toward the development of that high ideal of woman which we find in modern Christian countries."[15] This "high ideal of woman" has been

13. Harriet Beecher Stowe, *Footsteps of the Master* (New York: J. B. Ford, 1877); *Woman in Sacred History* (repr.; New York: Portland House, 1990 [1873]); *Woman in Sacred History* (New York: J. B. Ford, 1873). In this essay, I use both the 1873 and 1990 (repr.) editions of *Woman in Sacred History*. I will distinguish between the two by citing the date of publication after the titles.

14. Stowe, *Woman in Sacred History* (1873), 12; see Marion Ann Taylor, "Harriet Beecher Stowe and the Mingling of Two Worlds: The Kitchen and the Study," in *Recovering Nineteenth-Century Women Interpreters of the Bible* (ed. Christiana de Groot and Marion Ann Taylor; SBLSymS 38; Atlanta: Scholars Press, 2007), 99–115 (107).

15. Stowe, *Woman in Sacred History* (1873), 17. While one might disagree with Stowe's idealization of "modern Christian countries," it is a view that was popular during her lifetime.

called the "cult of the true woman" or "domestic Christianity," in which women, particularly mothers, were seen as those who redeemed the rest of culture. The appropriate characteristics for such women were purity, piety, domesticity, submission, and silence, and their sphere of influence was confined to the home.[16] The true woman was often thought of as the angel in the house who was above passion and self-interest. Sexual disinterest was, in fact, seen to be a noble quality in women. In her book *The Religious Ideas of Harriet Beecher Stowe: Her Gospel of Womanhood*, Gayle Kimball states, "As idealized priestess of the home, woman was stripped of human sexual passion and supposed to submit passively to the male passion of her spouse."[17] In fact, in a letter to her husband Calvin, Stowe explained that one of the reasons that women were so saintly was because they did not have the sexual temptations that men had, and took her case to be the norm, saying that she herself had no sexual passion.[18]

In her account of Mary Magdalene, Stowe cast Mary Magdalene, who is mentioned in Luke 8:2, as the repentant sinner of Luke 7:36–50.[19] According to this passage, Jesus was eating in the home of Simon the Pharisee when an unnamed sinful woman entered. After she had washed Jesus' feet with her tears and wiped his feet with her hair, she kissed and anointed them with ointment. While the Pharisee judged the woman harshly, Jesus told a parable in which it was clear that he forgave the woman because of her great love for him.

Stowe's interpretation of the penitent Mary was not without historical precedent. One of the earliest figures of the Western Christianity to suggest that Mary Magdalene was a repentant sinner was Pope Gregory the Great in a homily he preached at the basilica of San Clemente in Rome in 591 C.E. While speaking about the sinful woman in Luke 7:36–50, he equated her with Mary of Bethany and Mary Magdalene from whom seven demons had gone out (Luke 8:2) and thus depicted Mary Magdalene as a former prostitute.[20] Whether or not Pope Gregory was ultimately responsible for the interpretation, for centuries this tradition was continued in commentaries on the Gospels, church traditions and

16. Eileen Razari Elrod, "Exactly Like My Father: Feminist Hermeneutics in Harriet Beecher Stowe's Non-fiction," *JAAR* 63, no. 4 (1995): 695–719 (698).

17. Gayle Kimball, *The Religious Ideas of Harriet Beecher Stowe: Her Gospel of Womanhood* (SWR 8; New York: Edwin Mellen, 1982), 84.

18. Ibid., 72.

19. See also Stowe, *Footsteps of the Master*, 151–52.

20. J.-P. Migne, ed., *Patrologiae cursus completus: Series Latina* (Paris, 1878), 76:1239.

liturgies. This is in contrast to another scholar of the West, Hippolytus (c. 180–236 C.E.), who earlier called Mary Magdalene the "apostle of the apostles" in his commentary on the Song of Solomon.[21] However, by the nineteenth century the tradition of the penitent Magdalene had become most prevalent and her apostleship was rarely recognized in the Western Church.

For example, in his commentary on Luke, J. J. Van Oosterzee believed that one should assume the sinful woman was Mary Magdalene even if she was not mentioned in Luke 7, but later in Luke 8:2. For Oosterzee, Mary Magdalene had a sin of "voluptuousness."[22] J. P. Lange, whose work was popular at the time, also viewed the sinful woman as Mary Magdalene. He believed that the seven spirits that were reportedly cast out of the Magdalene in Luke 8:2 (cf. Mark 16:9) should be seen as symbolic expressions of ethical misbehavior rather than actual demons. In this case, Mary fit very well the role of the sinful woman (Luke 7:36–50), whose relations were not very ethical.[23]

However, there were scholars who did not believe Mary was the sinful woman, among them Heinrich Meyer, who disagreed with Lange and others, and who believed that a great injustice had been done to her memory.[24] Stowe entered the debate about Mary when she stated, "Some commentators seem to think that the dreadful demoniacal possession which was spoken of in Mary Magdalene proves her not to have been identical with the [sinful] woman of St. Luke. But on the contrary, it

21. Gerard Garitte, ed., *Traite d'Hippolyte sur David et Goliath, sur le Cantique des cantiques et sur l'ante'christ* (CSCO 263; Louvain: Secretariat du CSCO, 1965), 24–26, as translated in Leonard Swidler, *Biblical Affirmations of Woman* (Philadelphia: Westminster, 1979), 210; see also the translation in Ann Graham Brock, *Mary Magdalene, the First Apostle: The Struggle for Authority* (HTS 51; Cambridge, Mass.: Harvard University Press, 2003), 1–2.

22. J. J. Van Oosterzee, *The Gospel According to Luke* (ed. P. Lange; trans. J. P. Lange and Charles C. Starbuck; A Commentary on the Holy Scriptures: Critical, Doctrinal and Homiletical 8; New York: Scribner's, 1865), 121.

23. J. P. Lange, *The Life of the Lord Jesus Christ: A Complete Critical Examination of the Origin, Contents and Connection of the Gospels* (4 vols.; repr.; Grand Rapids, Mich.: Zondervan, 1958 [1872]), 1:441.

24. Heinrich Meyer, *A Critical and Exegetical Hand-book to the Gospels of Mark and Luke* (New York: Funk & Wagnalls, 1884), 349, cf. 357; John J. Owen, *A Commentary, Critical, Expository, and Practical, on the Gospel of Luke* (New York: Leavitt & Allen, 1859), 101. See also F. Godet, *A Commentary on the Gospel of St. Luke* (trans. E. W. Shalders and M. D. Cusin; New York: Funk & Wagnalls, 1887), 233.

would seem exactly to account for actions of a strange and unaccountable wickedness..."[25]

Because prostitution was not specifically mentioned as the reason that the woman in Luke 7 is called a "sinner" in the biblical text, and brcause the woman was not identified by name, scholars today dispute this characterization of Mary Magdalene.[26] However, many biblical interpreters, both in centuries past and in more recent decades, have understood "sinner" as referring to a prostitute or an adulteress, and it is apparent that Stowe shared this view.[27]

While Stowe briefly mentioned the medieval mythology in which Mary Magdalene was portrayed as a missionary and preacher of the gospel, it is clear that for Stowe the significance of Mary Magdalene laid in her repentance and self-sacrificing love.[28] She commented upon a painting of the Magdalene by Batoni that was found in *Woman in Sacred History* in which she believed Mary was shown to be particularly noble:

> Batoni...seems...to set before us one of the highest, noblest class of women,—a creature so calm, so high, so pure, that we ask involuntarily, How could such a woman have fallen? The answer is ready. There is a class of women who fall through what is highest in them, through the noblest capability of a human being—utter self-sacrificing love... Many fall through the weakness of self-indulgent passion, many from love of luxury, many from vanity and pride, too many from the mere coercion of hard necessity; but among the sad, unblest crowd there is a class who are the victims of a power of self-forgetting love, which is one of the most angelic capabilities of our nature.[29]

For Stowe, Mary's descent into a licentious lifestyle was not as a result of weakened morals on her part. After all, she was neither sexually self-indulgent nor did she gain materially from her fallenness, nor was her state because of vanity, pride or financial distress. In fact, her fallenness

25. Stowe, *Woman in Sacred History* (1990), 211.

26. Joseph A. Fitzmyer, *The Gospel According to Luke 1–9* (AB 28; New York: Doubleday, 1981), 688–89; Gail Corrington Streete, "Women as Sources of Redemption and Knowledge in Early Christian Traditions," in *Women and Christian Origins* (ed. Ross Shepard Kraemer and Mary Rose D'Angelo; New York: Oxford University Press, 1999), 330–54 (342–43).

27. H. K. Luce, *The Gospel According to St. Luke* (Cambridge: Cambridge University Press, 1933), 161; I. Howard Marshall, *Commentary on Luke* (NIGTC; Grand Rapids, Mich.: Eerdmans, 1978), 308; John Nolland, *Luke 1–9:20* (WBC 35A; Dallas, Tex.: Word, 1989), 353.

28. Stowe, *Woman in Sacred History* (1990), 211; see also *Footsteps of the Master*, 150.

29. Stowe, *Women in Sacred History* (1990), 207–8.

was because of her virtue—the self-sacrificing love of the true woman, or, as Stowe also portrayed it, an "inconsiderate prodigality of love."[30] Like the prevailing depictions of women of Stowe's time, her Mary Magdalene was not sexually passionate, though she did submit to the passions of a male and so sacrificed herself as a true angelic woman should.

What is also apparent from Stowe's account is that Mary was not from the lower classes, her ruin being based upon factors other than financial need. In the nineteenth century, most women became prostitutes because of dire circumstances, such as alcoholism, abuse and homelessness, or poverty-stricken single-parenthood due to the death of or abandonment by a spouse. Many were immigrants and most were under twenty-five.[31] Some women supplemented their meagre earnings as servants or seamstresses through prostitution. Many of them became prostitutes because their families could not or would not support them.[32] Others entered the profession by sacrificing their "virtue" to a man they loved.[33]

There were also prostitutes who preferred to remain in their profession than marry. According to William Sanger's 1858 survey of prostitutes in New York, some prostitutes resorted to prostitution in order to gratify their sexual desires.[34] Others found their profession attractive because it gave them financial autonomy. In fact, a New York prostitute named Helen Jewett was known for the luxurious lifestyle she had established when she was murdered in 1935.[35]

It seems, then, that Stowe's Magdalene entered her sinful state for the only acceptable reason: self-sacrificial love. Stowe's Magdalene was not portrayed as a Victorian prostitute who practiced her trade out of economic necessity, or as one who sold herself for luxuries or sexual gratification; rather, she was portrayed as a "true woman" and a member of the growing middle class.[36]

---

30. Ibid., 211, and *Footsteps of the Master*, 152–53.
31. Catherine Clinton and Christine Lunardini, eds., *The Columbia Guide to American Women in the Nineteenth Century* (New York: Columbia University Press, 2000), 108–9.
32. E. O. Hellerstein, ed., *Victorian Women: A Documentary Account of Women's Lives in Nineteenth-Century England, France and the United States* (Stanford, Calif.: Stanford University Press, 1981), 415.
33. Ibid., 417.
34. Ibid., 415.
35. Tracy Fessenden, "The Convent, the Brothel, and the Protestant Woman's Sphere," *Signs: Journal of Women in Culture and Society* 25, no. 2 (2000): 451–78 (467).
36. Kimball, *Religious Ideas*, 82–83.

In her chapter on Mary Magdalene in *Woman in Sacred History*, Stowe also used the occasion of Mary's penitence in Luke 7:36–50 to argue that Jesus treated women as equal to men in contrast to the treatment of women in the nineteenth century. Stowe stated that one of the most decided steps in Jesus' early ministry was "his practical and authoritative assertion of the principle, that fallen woman is as capable of restoration through penitence as fallen man, and that repentance should do for a fallen woman whatever it might do for fallen man."[37] For Stowe, Jesus' treatment of women as equals was a sign of his divinity, particularly in the story of the woman caught in adultery (John 7:53–8:11), when Jesus did not condemn her to being stoned but treated her sins like those of any other, proving that "repentant love [was] entitled to equal forgiveness."[38]

Although she was treated as an equal, Stowe's Mary Magdalene still bore female qualities appropriate to the nineteenth century: Mary's ardent, self-sacrificing nature was the basis for her salvation. She found the way to the feet of Jesus through "the uncalculating self-sacrifice and self-abandon of one of those natures which when they move, move with a rush of undivided impulse which, when they love, trust all, believe all, and are ready to sacrifice all."[39] As Mary came to Jesus in repentance, he received her as a penitent sister and absolved and purified her, "and henceforth there was for her a full scope for that ardent, self-devoting power of her nature which had been her ruin, and was now to become her salvation."[40]

Stowe was not the only one of her era to cast Mary Magdalene into the role of a repentant sinner who was not from the lower class. Patricia S. Kruppa writes that, for Victorians, "The scriptural Magdalene may or may not have been a harlot; but to her Victorian interpreters, her poise, grace, and presence were proof of her upper-class origins."[41] One reason for the assumption that Mary was of the upper class is that she is said in Luke to be among the women who followed Jesus and supported him out of their financial means (Luke 8:1–3). Fictional accounts of the life of Mary Magdalene, Kruppa states, "drew freely from *The Golden Legend*, which was a collection of the lives of the saints compiled in the thirteenth century by Jacobus de Varagine, to support the idea that she was a

37. Stowe, *Woman in Sacred History* (1990), 208, and *Footsteps of the Master*, 148.
38. Stowe, *Woman in Sacred History* (1990), 209.
39. Ibid., 212, and *Footsteps of the Master*, 153.
40. Stowe, *Woman in Sacred History* (1990), 211.
41. Patricia S. Kruppa, "'More sweet and liquid than any other': Victorian Images of Mary Magdalene," in *Religion and Irreligion in Victorian Society* (ed. R. W. Davis and R. J. Helmstadter, London: Routledge, 1992), 117–32 (117).

prostitute, but one of the highest social class."[42] In fact, in her section on Mary Magdalene in *Woman in Sacred History*, Stowe begins with a poem by H. W. Longfellow entitled "The Tower of Magdala" in which Mary was confined in a tower where she wore fine clothing and her fingers were covered with rings of pearls, amethysts, emeralds and jasper.[43]

The theme of the repentant Magdalene was so deeply embedded in Victorian thought that her "metamorphosis from harlot to saint was an inspiration to many earnest Victorian men and women of all creeds who were engaged in rescue work."[44] They believed that, if Mary Magdalene could experience rebirth, prostitutes of their time could find the same kind of transformation. Preachers often expounded on the salvation that prostitutes could receive after the example of Magdalene. For example, Charles Haddon Spurgeon, a well-known Baptist preacher of the time who was based in London, told his congregation that one of his sermons on Mary Magdalene had saved a harlot who had stepped inside the church from throwing herself off a bridge to her death.[45] In fact, mission agencies that reached out to prostitutes sometimes called themselves "Magdalen Associations."[46]

In *Woman in Sacred History*, Stowe included poetry by Felicia Hemans (1793–1835) in her chapter on Mary Magdalene. Hemans, an Englishwoman, also associated Mary Magdalene with the sinful woman of Luke 7:36–50, as evidenced by her poem "The Penitent's Offering" where she described the tears and confession that accompanied Mary's ministrations to Jesus. Ultimately, for Hemans, it was not the ointment and tears that restored Mary, but the "blest sacrifice" of her heart:

> No, not by these restored
> Unto thy Father's board,
> Thy peace that kindled joy in heaven was made;
> But costlier in his eyes
> By thy blest sacrifice,
> Thy heart, thy full deep heart before him laid.[47]

42. Ibid., 119.
43. Stowe, *Woman in Sacred History* (1873), 305.
44. Kruppa, "Victorian Images of Mary Magdalene," 125.
45. Spurgeon, "Conversion," in *The New Park Street Pulpit* (Grand Rapids, Mich.: Zondervan, 1963), 344; from Kruppa, "Victorian Images of Mary Magdalene," 125–26. These Magdalene associations were found both in nineteenth-century England and the United States. See Steven Ruggles, "The Inmates of the Magdalen Society Asylum of Philadelphia, 1836–1908," *Journal of Social History* 16, no. 4 (1983): 65–82.
46. Kruppa, "Victorian Images of Mary Magdalene," 126.
47. Stowe, *Woman in Sacred History* (1873), 314–15.

While Mary's participation in the latter scenes of the Gospels was not central to her, Stowe briefly mentioned Mary's part at the cross during Jesus crucifixion, her weeping at the tomb, and her preaching after his death and resurrection. Stowe saw even these events through the lens of one who was "loved much because she was forgiven much."[48] The theme of the penitent "fallen women" colored Stowe's understanding of Mary throughout the Gospel narratives.

Thus, both Hemans and Stowe portrayed Mary Magdalene as the penitent woman who came to Jesus, washing his feet with her tears and wiping them with her hair, and whose nature was defined by self-sacrifice. For Hemans, this sacrifice brought restoration with God. For Stowe, Mary's fall was not because of passion, love of luxury, or financial need, but because of her self-sacrifice. However, not all female writers of the time portrayed Mary Magdalene in the same way Stowe and Hemans did. It is to two of these writers that I now turn.

Mary Magdalene According to Elizabeth Rundle Charles and Sarah Towne Martyn

Englishwoman Elizabeth Rundle Charles (1828–1896) was a prolific nineteenth-century interpreter of the Bible. She was born in Devon and was the daughter of John Rundle, who was a Member of Parliament, and his wife Barbara Gill. According to Taylor and Weir, she was "educated at home and began writing at a young age."[49]

In two of her books, *By thy Glorious Resurrection and Ascension* (1888) and *Sketches of the Women of Christendom* (1880), Charles discussed Mary Magdalene. Because the two accounts are very similar and the fullest portrayal of the Magdalene occurs in *By Thy Glorious Resurrection and Ascension*, I will focus on it. As suggested by the title of her book, in the chapter on Mary Magdalene, Charles is not as interested in the penitent Magdalene as she is in Jesus' post-resurrection appearance to her.[50] She does speak about the tradition of the penitent Magdalene in this way:

---

48. Stowe, *Woman in Sacred History* (1990), 212; cf. *Footsteps of the Master*, 288–89.

49. Marion Ann Taylor and Heather E. Weir, eds., *Let Her Speak for Herself: Nineteenth-Century Women Writing on the Women of Genesis* (Waco, Tex.: Baylor University Press, 2006), 77.

50. In her discussion of Mary and Jesus' post-resurrection appearance to her, Stowe does not mention Mary's declaration of Jesus' resurrection to the disciples. See Stowe, *Footsteps*, 211, 288, and *Woman in Sacred History* (1873), 302.

A general though not universal tradition in the Western Church has woven into one the stories of "the woman who was a sinner," Mary of Bethany and...Mary Magdalene... Our own church, originally [accepted] the Western tradition which identifies the Magdalene with "the woman who was a sinner...[and] popular language continues the tradition, so that the name of the Magdalene is the expression of Christian hope for the most fallen, of the great Christian truth that the Church, like her Lord, admits of no outcast class, or creature, in the world. And whatever conclusion may be reached as to the gathering of the three narratives into one...the Magdalene...abides with us for ever as a type of the grace which restores as the witness for ever that those who have fallen to the lowest depths may rise to the most glorious heights of love and service..."[51]

Although she was somewhat skeptical, Charles espoused the popular idea of the time that Mary Magdalene was the sinful woman who had fallen prior to her relationship with Jesus. Like Stowe, Charles saw Mary as one who was restored to right standing before God through her repentance, although she expressed some doubt as to whether the Western Christian tradition is correct in identifying Mary Magdalene with the "sinful" woman of Luke 7:36–50.

Actually, the Eastern Greek fathers did not conflate Mary Magdalene with the sinful woman, but saw Mary Magdalene, Mary of Bethany, and the sinful woman of Luke 7:36–50 as three different women.[52] In their tradition, Mary Magdalene was deemed to be equal to the apostles, which was a term "reserved for holy men and women who evangelized a whole people."[53]

In much of her other work, Charles, like Stowe, placed a high value on the qualities of the true woman: purity, submissiveness, and domesticity.[54] But unlike Stowe, Charles did not portray Mary Magdalene as having a surfeit of the characteristics of the true woman. In *By Thy Glorious Resurrection and Ascension*, Charles also said that the Magdalene was a woman "of a powerful nature, with the terrible as well as the glorious possibilities of a strong character."[55] Although she was "no weak demonstrative creature, of easy tears and hysterical emotions...[she was] strong to endure as well as to dare; to control emotion, when that

51. Elizabeth Rundle Charles, *By Thy Glorious Resurrection and Ascension* (London: SPCK, 1888), 34–36; cf. *Sketches of Women in Christendom* (London: SPCK, 1880), 49.

52. Susan Haskins, *Mary Magdalene: Myth and Metaphor* (New York: Riverhead Books, 1993), 23; Brock, *Mary Magdalene, the First Apostle*, 169.

53. C. B. Tkacz, "Singing Women's Words as Sacramental Mimesis," *Recherches de Théologie et Philosophie Médiévales* 70, no. 2 (2003): 275–328.

54. Taylor and Weir, eds., *Let Her Speak for Herself*, 3.

55. Charles, *By Thy Glorious Resurrection*, 33–34.

was the service love demanded" as she walked with Jesus "along the rough roads and mountain paths, listening to the Divine teaching, and taking her woman's part of ministering to the earthly wants of all…"[56] Contrary to the characteristics of the true woman, Charles's Magdalene was active in public life, and was strong, daring, and perseverant. However, like the true woman, she seems to have known her place, and to have controlled emotion "when that was the service love demanded" and to have taken care of the disciples' physical needs.

Charles also commented to a much greater extent than did Stowe about Mary Magdalene's activities during Jesus' last week. While Charles's major thrust in her interpretation of the biblical text was Mary's sorrow after Jesus' death and her emotional encounter with him in the garden, Charles also showed that Mary's actions were significant: she was at the cross "[w]hen the Twelve, or at least eleven of the Twelve, had forsaken and fled, and one had denied"; she found the empty tomb but she did not run away as the other women did; she "watched as He was laid to rest" and saw the sepulchre safely closed; she told the disciples of Jesus' disappearance from the tomb; she was the first to see Jesus after his resurrection and to take "the first Easter message" to the disciples.[57]

Because Charles alludes to the significance of some of Mary's actions, her work suggests themes later elaborated upon by biblical scholars. For example, in her "Excellent Women: Female Witness to the Resurrection," Claudia Setzer argues that one of the major reasons Mary Magdalene is significant in the Synoptic Gospels is that she is the key witness to the crucifixion, Jesus' burial, and the empty tomb. While other characters shift in the narratives, Mary Magdalene is the only one who sees Jesus' death and burial and discovers the empty tomb in all three of the Synoptic Gospels. Setzer states, "So the assurance of the correct tomb and the correct body hangs on the reliability and testimony of one woman."[58]

In the biblical record, Mary Magdalene and another Mary, presumably Mary the mother of James (cf. Matt 27:56), were the first to see the resurrected Christ, who instructed them to go and tell the male disciples that he would meet them in Galilee (Matt 28:9). Although Mary was not clearly a witness to Jesus' burial in John's Gospel, she was the first to find the empty tomb and the first to see the risen Jesus (John 20:11–18).[59] In the longer ending of the Gospel of Mark, which is generally considered

---

56. Ibid.

57. Ibid., 34, 30–31, 36–37, 42–47, respectively.

58. Claudia Setzer, "Excellent Women: Female Witness to the Resurrection," *JBL* 116 (1997): 259–72.

59. Ibid., 263.

to be a later addition to the Mark than the shorter ending, Jesus appeared to her after his resurrection. While this last scene is not in the earliest, most reliable text, it does point to the continued significance this tradition played for the members of early Christian communities.

Charles believed that Jesus' commission to Mary "with that first Easter message" to the disciples was momentous: it sounded a great, eternal "peal of victory" and ushered in "that new life which began the new Creation for the whole world."[60] Charles finally summarized her chapter on Mary Magdalene by asserting that the reason Mary received the commission was that the degradation of her former life meant she was one of those who needed to hear its message most of all.[61] Thus Charles believed that Mary Magdalene needed to repent for her former sinful life, but it was not her focus, as it was in Stowe's writing. For Charles, Mary's significance was found in her being part of the major events during Jesus' last week, in particular her being the "Firstborn among many brethren" who told the disciples about the resurrection of the "Firstborn from the dead."[62] Charles's views were in contrast to the many commentators of the time who briefly mentioned Mary's actions during Jesus' last week and her report of his resurrection and ascension to the disciples, but did not consider their remarkable significance.[63]

Charles's work also suggests themes that contemporary biblical scholars have elaborated upon. In her work *Mary Magdalene, the First Apostle: The Struggle for Authority*, Ann Graham Brock has shown how Mary as depicted in the Gospels fits the characteristics of an apostle as defined by Paul: one who witnessed an appearance of the risen Christ and who received a divine call or commission to proclaim Christ's message (1 Cor 15:3, 5–8; cf. Gal 1:15–16).[64] According to Brock, Mary's apostleship is particularly apparent in John's Gospel, where Mary sees

60. Charles, *By Thy Glorious Resurrection*, 47.
61. Ibid., 49.
62. Ibid., 47.
63. John J. Owen, *A Commentary*, 376–79; Meyer, *A Critical and Exegetical Hand-book to the Gospels of Mark and Luke*, 574; idem, *A Critical and Exegetical Hand-book to the Gospel of Matthew* (trans. Peter Christie; New York: Funk & Wagnalls, 1890), 520; Godet, *A Commentary on the Gospel of St. Luke*, 504–5; Frederick D. Maurice, *The Gospel of the Kingdom of Heaven: A Course of Lectures on the Gospel of St. Luke* (London: Macmillan, 1893), 358–62; F. Godet, *Commentary on the Gospel of St. John with a Critical Introduction* (trans. S. Taylor and M. D. Cusin; Clark's Foreign Theological Library 56; Edinburgh: T. & T. Clark, 1889), 3:315–18; Heinrich Meyer, *Critical and Exegetical Handbook to the Gospel of John* (New York: Funk & Wagnalls, 1884), 530–33.
64. Brock, *Mary Magdalene, the First Apostle*, 6–9.

the risen Christ when she is alone and he commissions her to go and tell the disciples of his ascension (John 20:14–18).[65] Instead of seeing the resurrection appearance to Mary Magdalene as a minor, private and personal encounter between Mary and Jesus before his official meeting with the disciples, as many interpreters have previously done, Schaberg has shown how "women were the—or a—primary source of the resurrection faith."[66] Bart Ehrman has gone so far as to state: "She [Mary Magdalene] is portrayed as the first witness to proclaim Jesus' resurrection. If this is true historically, it is hard to deny or underplay her importance. In some sense, you could argue that Mary started Christianity."[67]

An American nineteenth-century female biblical interpreter, Sarah Towne Martyn (1805–1870) wrote about Mary Magdalene in her book *Women of the Bible*.[68] Born in New Hampshire, Martyn was the daughter of Congregational minister, Reverend Ethan Smith and she was educated at home. She married Reverend Job H. Martyn, also a Congregational minister and they had four children. Besides editing a number of religious and women's magazines, she published at least twenty books, many of which were "historical fiction set around the time of the Reformation."[69] Although her interpretations were marked by a romanticized approach to biblical women, she sometimes interpreted biblical texts in ways that could be called "feminist" in comparison with the traditional biblical interpretation her contemporaries used. For example, according to Taylor and Weir, in her interpretation of the narrative of what Christians often call the Fall of humanity in Genesis, Martyn's "purpose was to redeem Eve [in the Genesis account]. She acknowledged Eve's sin, but emphasized *both* Adam and Eve as fallen. She avoided the use of the term 'helpmeet' [for Eve]" and called on her readers "to regard Eve with 'tenderness and veneration.'"[70] Martyn's interpretation is in contrast to those interpreters of Genesis throughout history who have often blamed Eve for humanity's fall into sin and who have often seen her as Adam's "helpmeet," whose sole purpose was to assist Adam.[71]

    65. Ibid., 55–60.
    66. Jane Schaberg, *The Resurrection of Mary Magdalene: Legends, Apocrypha, and the Christian Testament* (New York: Continuum, 2005), 298.
    67. Bart D. Ehrman, *Peter, Paul and Mary Magdalene: The Followers of Jesus in History and Legend* (New York: Oxford University Press, 2006), 186.
    68. Sarah Towne Martyn, *Women of the Bible* (New York: American Tract Society, 1868).
    69. Taylor and Weir, eds., *Let Her Speak for Herself*, 71.
    70. Ibid., 72, italics mine.
    71. John Calvin, *Commentaries on The First Book of Moses Called Genesis* (trans. Rev. John King; repr.; Grand Rapids, Mich.: Baker Book House, 1984),

Contrary to Stowe in particular, Martyn did not connect Mary Magdalene with the sinful woman of Luke 7 at all. In her book *Women of the Bible*, she stated that Mary "has often been most erroneously confounded with the woman mentioned in Luke 7:37–50, who washed the Saviour's feet with her tears, and wiped them with the hair of her head, and who is there described as a *sinner*."[72] Martyn believed that although Mary was subject to possession by demons before Jesus cast them out (Luke 8:2), "she was a woman of spotless character and high social standing. From the period of her cure, she seems to have devoted herself to the service of her great Deliverer with a strength and earnestness of affection proportioned to the benefits she had received."[73] Thus Martyn did not agree with Stowe's depiction of Mary Magdalene as the repentant sinner, but did concur with her depiction of Mary's high social standing. She also echoed some of the concerns of Victorian true womanhood: Mary had "spotless character" and devoted herself to Jesus' "service" with "earnestness of affection."

Like Charles, Martyn focused upon Mary's actions during Jesus' last week. Mary and the other women did not forsake Jesus when he stood among his enemies, but, unlike the male disciples, they followed him "through all those hours of insult and agony, though every pang endured by the august Sufferer must have fallen on their hearts with a weight of intolerable anguish."[74] Martyn also described Mary and her associates as following him to the location of his crucifixion, watching him hang upon the cross, watching the body being prepared for burial, attending the remains to the new tomb, and seeing the body deposited in the new tomb.[75] However, when it came to Mary viewing the empty tomb, Martyn portrayed her as being alone. With all the pathos of nineteenth-century style, Martyn then described Mary meeting Jesus at the tomb, and his command to her to "hasten to my brethren, and say to them, I ascend to my Father and your Father, to my God and your God."[76] Mary was obedient and departed "to carry the good news to her brethren," even though her words were ultimately "in vain" because the disciples did not believe her report until they saw Jesus for themselves (cf. Luke 24:11).[77]

129–31, 151–52; Reverend Canon H. D. M. Spence and Reverend Joseph S. Exell, *The Pulpit Commentary: Genesis* (New York: Anson D. F. Randolph, 1892), 61–62, 50, respectively.

72. Martyn, *Women of the Bible*, 275.
73. Ibid.
74. Ibid., 276.
75. Ibid., 275–77.
76. Ibid., 280.
77. Ibid., 280–81.

Martyn stated that Mary Magdalene and her companions later "were among the five hundred to whom the Saviour showed himself in Galilee; and whether their days were more or less prolonged after his ascension, we cannot doubt that they were spent in the service of their glorified Lord."[78] When she includes Mary among the "five-hundred," Martyn here refers to an account in 1 Cor 15:6 where Paul reported that Jesus appeared to 500 "brothers and sisters." Because for Paul an apostle was one who had seen an appearance of Jesus and had received a divine commission, Martyn actually portrayed Mary Magdalene as having both of the necessary qualifications for apostleship. Though she never actually says that Mary was an apostle, she certainly lays the groundwork for such a conclusion.

Stowe Among her Contemporaries

As noted in the introduction to this essay, Victorian biblical scholars, preachers, and rescue workers found Mary Magdalene to be a captivating figure. She was often viewed at that time as the fallen woman who was redeemed through her repentance and her love for her Saviour. In comparison to Elizabeth Rundle Charles and Sarah Towne Martyn, Harriet Beecher Stowe was particularly affected by this traditional interpretation. For her, the essence of Mary Magdalene was her self-sacrifice, which was the reason for both her fall into prostitution and her redemption through repentance. Stowe saw Mary Magdalene as an example of the true woman: she sacrificed herself after the model of Christ's sacrifice, she was not sexually self-indulgent, and she was among the middle class. Stowe did not see Mary's activities during Jesus' last week as defining her identity; even when she did mention these activities, they were seen through the lens of one who had "loved much because she had been forgiven much."[79]

However, Elizabeth Rundle Charles and Sarah Towne Martyn either questioned or disagreed with the interpretation of Mary as repentant sinner. Charles was skeptical of the tradition of Mary as the repentant sinner because of the differences in the way Luke 7:36–50 had been interpreted in Western and Eastern Christian traditions. Charles did, however, see Mary as a true woman who was moral, middle (or upper) class, and knew her place as she served Jesus and the disciples. In the works of both Charles and Martyn, Mary Magdalene was known for her appearances at significant events during Jesus last week

78. Ibid., 281.
79. Stowe, *Women in Sacred History* (1873), 217.

and the importance of her witness to those events. In this respect both Charles and Martyn come close to the work of feminist biblical interpreters of the twentieth and twenty-first centuries. Both Charles and Martyn also capitalized on Jesus' post-resurrection appearance to Mary and her commission to tell the news of the resurrection and the ascension to the disciples. While Martyn focussed on the account in Luke where the disciples view Mary's report as an "idle tale" (Luke 24:11), Charles focussed instead on John 20 where Mary's report is not greeted with derision.

It is obvious that, even though Stowe, Charles, and Martyn all wrote between 1868 and 1888, Stowe appears to be the one who was most influenced by Victorian cultural understandings of Mary Magdalene. She concurred with biblical scholarship of the day that supported cultural understandings of Mary as the repentant sinner in contrast to scholars who did not support such a view. As has been shown above, the focus of her interpretation was on Mary's self-sacrifice in accord with the model of the Victorian true woman who was to sacrifice herself after the model of Jesus Christ. Given the fact that Stowe's primary model for self-sacrifice was most probably her mother, her interpretation of Mary Magdalene was probably most influenced by Roxana. Elizabeth Ammons believes that Stowe's deep intellectual commitment to nineteenth-century maternal ideology "was rooted in a mother love that she feared she had missed (her own mother died when she was five)—a yearning, in turn, everywhere reinforced by the pervasive ideal of angelic motherhood dominant in Victorian America."[80]

The voices of female biblical interpreters Stowe, Charles, and Martyn have been ignored until only recently. Only in the twentieth and twenty-first centuries, when women became *bona fide* members of the academy, have nineteenth-century female interpreters' voices been heard. Particularly in the biblical interpretations by Charles and Martyn was the groundwork for later feminist interpretations of the biblical text laid out—but no one was listening. It behoves us to continue to listen to them and others like them, so that their voices will be heard not only in whispers in rare book rooms, but loudly and clearly in the lectures and publications of those who specialize in biblical interpretation.

80. Elizabeth Ammons, "Stowe's Dream of the Mother-Savior: *Uncle Tom's Cabin* and American Women Writers Before the 1920s," in *New Essays on* Uncle Tom's Cabin (ed. Eric J. Sundquist; Cambridge: Cambridge University Press, 1986), 155–95.

INDEXES

INDEX OF REFERENCES

INDEX OF AUTHORS

Recent efforts to create a European Central Bank (ECB) have stimulated debate on new topics for research into the political economy of the European Community's institutions. These include the exact division of responsibilities of national governments and the ECB – especially concerning exchange rate policy; the need for and design of constraints on national fiscal policies; and the nature of the transition from adjustable parities and national monetary policies to irrevocably fixed parities and a single European monetary policy.

This volume, derived from a joint conference held by the Centre for Economic Policy Research, the Center for German and European Studies at Georgetown University and the International Monetary Fund, in Washington DC, in May 1991, examines these issues and the choices facing policy-makers. It considers the role of a common currency in facilitating transactions and the likely success of the ECB in achieving price stability. It compares the option of strengthening the existing European Monetary System with existing national currencies to the planned creation of a full monetary union. The book draws heavily on the historical experience of the US to identify the problems that may emerge if there is no clear agreement over responsibility for monetary policy, if the ECB does not take responsibility for the stability of the financial system, or if a system of fiscal federalism does not accompany monetary union. The book also considers the implications of EMU for the international monetary system – for the use of the ECU as a reserve currency and for policy coordination among the G-7 countries. The volume thus provides a comprehensive examination of the issues that will be decisive for Europe in its choice of monetary institutions.

Establishing a central bank: issues in Europe and lessons from the US

The Center for German and European Studies

The Center for German and European Studies of Georgetown University, Washington, DC, was founded in 1990 with generous support of the German government. Its purpose is the promotion of scholarship and teaching on domestic and international topics relating to Germany and Europe in general. It offers a two-year degree program leading to the Master of Arts in German and European Studies; students may also be enrolled simultaneously in PhD programs in the departments of Government, History, Economics and German. Financial aid is available on a competitive basis. The Center hosts at least two postdoctoral scholars each year as well as short-term visitors, speakers, and conferences and symposia. The Center's Director is Professor Samuel H Barnes. Professor Gregory Flynn is Director of Programs.

The International Monetary Fund

The IMF is a cooperative intergovernmental monetary and financial institution. The Fund is unique among intergovernmental organizations in its combination of regulatory, consultative and financial functions, which derive from the purposes for which it was established: to facilitate the balanced growth of international trade, promote exchange rate stability, and assist in the establishment of a multilateral system of payments; to provide financial resources to enable its members to correct payments imbalances; and to provide a forum for consultation and collaboration on international monetary problems.

Managing Director
Michel Camdessus
Deputy Managing Director
Richard Erb
Director of Research and Economic Counsellor
Michael Mussa

Establishing a central bank: issues in Europe and lessons from the US

Edited by

MATTHEW B. CANZONERI
VITTORIO GRILLI

and

PAUL R. MASSON

CAMBRIDGE
UNIVERSITY PRESS

Published by the Press Syndicate of the University of Cambridge
The Pitt Building, Trumpington Street, Cambridge CB2 1RP
40 West 20th Street, New York, NY 10011–4211, USA
10 Stamford Road, Oakleigh, Victoria 3166, Australia

First published 1992

A catalogue record for this book is available from the British Library

Library of Congress cataloging in publication data

Establishing a central bank: issues in Europe and lessons from the US / edited by Matthew B. Canzoneri, Vittorio Grilli, and Paul R. Masson.
  p. cm.
  Papers presented at the conference: 'Designing a central bank', held 1–2 May, 1991 at Georgetown University and sponsored by the Centre for Economic Policy Research, the Center for German and European Studies at Georgetown University, and the International Monetary Fund.
  Includes index.
  ISBN 0 521 42098 9 (hardback)
1. Banks and banking, Central – European Economic Community countries – Congresses.
2. Banks and banking, Central – United States – Congresses.
3. Fiscal policy – European Economic Community countries – Congresses.
I. Canzoneri, Matthew B.   II. Grilli, Vittorio.
III. Masson, Paul R.   IV. Centre for Economic Policy Research (Great Britain)
V. Georgetown University. Center for German and European Studies.
VI. International Monetary Fund.
HG2980.5.A7E84   1992
332.1'1'094 – dc20   91–46674   CIP

ISBN 0 521 42098 9 hardback

m.R.

Printed and bound in Great Britain by
Butler & Tanner Ltd, Frome and London

Contents

ix

Figures

Tables

Preface

This book is the outcome of a conference, 'Designing a Central Bank', that was held on May first and second, 1991, at Georgetown University, and sponsored by the Centre for Economic Policy Research, the Center for German and European Studies at Georgetown University, and the International Monetary Fund. The conference was made possible by grants from the Commission of the European Communities under its SPES programme to support the CEPR's research programme on 'Financial and Monetary Integration in Europe', from the Ford and Alfred P. Sloan Foundations as part of their support for CEPR's International Macroeconomics programme, and from the government of the Federal Republic of Germany to the Center for German and European Studies.

The conferences also included a panel discussion on the problems of central bank design for EMU, which served as a progress report on the state of negotiations at the intergovernmental conference, and after-dinner remarks presented by Michel Camdessus, Managing Director of the International Monetary Fund.

We would like to thank Brad Billings of Georgetown University and his staff for organizing the conference, Kate Millward at CEPR for guiding the present volume to press, and John Black of the University of Exeter for his work as Production Editor.

Matthew B. Canzoneri
Vittorio Grilli   November 1991
Paul R. Masson

Conference participants

Alberto Alesina *Harvard University and CEPR*
Samuel Barnes *CGES, Georgetown University*
Bradley Billings *Georgetown University*
Graham Bishop *Salomon Brothers*
Peter Bofinger *Landeszentralbank in Baden-Württemberg, Stuttgart, and CEPR*
Antonio Borges *Banco de Portugal*
William Branson *Princeton University and CEPR*
Guillermo Calvo *IMF*
Michel Camdessus *IMF*
Matthew Canzoneri *Georgetown University*
Alessandra Casella *University of California at Berkeley and CEPR*
David Currie *London Business School and CEPR*
Behzad Diba *Georgetown University*
Barry Eichengreen *University of California at Berkeley and CEPR*
David Folkerts-Landau *IMF*
Peter Garber *Brown University*
Francesco Giavazzi *Università Bocconi and CEPR*
Alberto Giovannini *Columbia University and CEPR*
Morris Goldstein *IMF*
Vittorio Grilli *Birkbeck College, London, and CEPR*
Dale Henderson *Board of Governors of the Federal Reserve System*
Andrew Hughes Hallett *University of Strathclyde and CEPR*
Mervyn King *Bank of England, London School of Economics and CEPR*
Jeroen Kremers *Ministry of Finance, The Netherlands*
Peter Krogh *Georgetown University*
Paul Masson *IMF*
Bennett T McCallum *Carnegie-Mellon University*
John Pattison *Canadian Imperial Bank of Commerce*
Torsten Persson *Institute for International Economic Studies, Stockholm, and CEPR*
Richard Portes *CEPR and Birkbeck College, London*
Massimo Russo *IMF*
Xavier Sala-i-Martín *Yale University*
Luigi Spaventa *Università degli Studi di Roma, 'La Sapienza', and CEPR*
Richard Sweeney *Georgetown University*
Vito Tanzi *IMF*
Eugene White *Rutgers University*
Geoffrey Woglom *Amherst College*

1 Introduction

MATTHEW B. CANZONERI, VITTORIO
GRILLI and PAUL R. MASSON

This book treats a number of themes relevant to the design of new monetary institutions in Europe.

It is important to situate the conference relative to events taking place in Europe. Two years before, in April 1989, the Delors Committee had made public recommendations for economic and monetary union (EMU) in Europe, and in December 1990 the EC member countries had convened two intergovernmental conferences, one on EMU and the other on political union. The intergovernmental conference on EMU was intended to lead to agreement concerning the form and pace of monetary union, including necessary amendments to the Treaty of Rome and the statutes of a central bank that would be created to carry out EC monetary policy.

The Georgetown conference thus was held at the very time that politicians, government officials, and central bankers were wrestling with these issues. Though draft statutes for the European Central Bank had been sent to EC ministers in November 1990, a number of issues remained unresolved. These included the exact division of responsibilities of national governments and the central bank – especially concerning exchange rate policy; the need for constraints on national fiscal policies, and how to design them; and the nature of the transition from a system of adjustable parities and a single European monetary policy. The papers of the conference apply the techniques of economics to the practical questions facing policy-makers, and serve both to inform their choices and to help us to understand how EMU, should it be created, will function. The book considers the role of a common currency in facilitating transactions and the likely success of a European central bank in achieving price stability and it compares the option of strengthening the existing European Monetary System without abandoning national currencies to the planned creation of a full monetary union. The book draws on the experience of other countries, in particular the United States, to identify problems that may emerge, for instance, if there is no clear understanding

1

concerning responsibility for monetary policy, if the European central bank does not manage the payments system, or if a system of fiscal federalism does not accompany monetary union. The book also considers the implications of EMU for the international monetary system – for the use of the ECU as a reserve currency and for Group of Seven (G-7) policy coordination. The volume thus provides a comprehensive examination of issues that will be decisive for Europe in its choice of monetary institutions.

1   The design of a central bank

A folk theorem in the theory of international finance asserts that the EC cannot simultaneously have (1) fixed exchange rates, (2) free capital mobility, and (3) independent national monetary policies. During the transition to EMU, monetary policy will be left in the hands of the national central banks. It remains to be seen whether existing mechanisms for policy coordination will be sufficient to preserve the Exchange Rate Mechanism now that capital controls have been virtually eliminated. And the problem will remain even if EMU is eventually achieved. The draft statutes for the new European Central Bank call for a federation of the existing central banks, modeled after the Bundesbank and the Federal Reserve System. The working relationship between the banks and control of the system as a whole are issues that are currently being debated. **Barry Eichengreen**'s paper draws on early US experience with the Federal Reserve System to warn against leaving the issue of policy coordination unresolved.

Eichengreen provides a concise history of the evolution of decision-making within the Federal Reserve System. In the early years, individual District Banks issued their own notes and controlled their own discount policies. Decision-making reflected regional preferences that were often conflicting. It took two decades for decision-making to be centralized around the Federal Reserve Board and the Federal Open Market Committee. Eichengreen uses a game-theoretic model to describe the behaviour of District Banks before decision-making was centralized. In his model, each bank has targets for its bond portfolio and for national income; decentralized decision-making results in too little stabilization effort. Eichengreen uses the model to analyse five episodes of policy conflict between the District Banks. He concludes that the early history of the Federal Reserve System serves as a cautionary tale for the EC, illustrating the importance of explicit and unambiguous coordination of national central bank policies during the transition to EMU and once EMU is achieved.

Bennett McCallum thought that Eichengreen's discussion of the Federal Reserve System's early operations was both useful and alarming. However, he had some difficulties with Eichengreen's model and was disappointed that Eichengreen's implications for the EC were not more specific. He also noted that the responsibilities of central banks have changed since the founding of the Federal Reserve System and that Eichengreen's account did indeed serve as a cautionary tale for the EC. However, he argued that the faulty design of the Federal Reserve System reflected problems in the US banking structure at the turn of the century and that a poor theoretical framework for policy-making may have played a role in the US experience. He suggested that US history also provides a cautionary tale in the centralization of banking supervision and regulation.

The EMS has been characterized as an asymmetric structure, dominated by the Bundesbank, that has nevertheless performed rather well in recent years in controlling inflation. Current proposals for EMU envisage a more symmetric decision-making process, and two questions naturally arise. Will the new process really reflect the preferences of European citizens? And what kind of monetary policy will result? The paper by **Alberto Alesina** and **Vittorio Grilli** examines the draft statute for the European Central Bank with these two questions in mind.

Alesina and Grilli begin by extending a well known inflation bias model to a median voter setting. In their model, the median voter would choose a central bank governor who is more conservative (or inflation-conscious) than he is himself; in this way, the electorate commits itself to a low inflation policy. Alesina and Grilli note that the central bank governor must not be subject to political pressure or recall if the commitment is to be binding, and they go on to examine the independence of the proposed ECB, as embodied in the draft statutes. Using an index of central bank independence (that is developed in a separate paper), Alesina and Grilli argue that the ECB should be as independent as the Bundesbank.

The second part of Alesina and Grilli's paper focuses on the economic and political diversity that exists in Europe today. Using an extension of their earlier model, Alesina and Grilli argue that a country that is lacking inflation credibility is more likely to gain from EMU, while a country whose output has a high variance and a low correlation with European output is less likely to gain. Economic and political differences are likely to lead to differences in opinion about monetary policy. So, finally, Alesina and Grilli ask whether the voting mechanism described in the draft statutes would lead to a policy that reflects the preferences of European voters. They find a problem that is common to 'district' systems. Using the results of the last general elections in the twelve EC countries, Alesina and Grilli find that the median European voter is currently well to the left of the median of the European Council. They go on to argue that the appointment and voting procedures described in the draft statute of the ECB would result in a monetary policy that could be very different from the preferences of the median European voter.

Peter Bofinger doubted that a low inflation policy could be guaranteed by simply endowing the ECB with the Bundesbank's charter. He thought that the Bundesbank gave price stability because that was what the German people wanted, and he doubted that the median European voter would have the same preferences. **Luigi Spaventa** complimented the paper for its logical rigor, but he contended that the analysis provided no answer for perhaps the most important question of all: what is there in EMU for the Germans?

Much of the public debate on the creation of a European Central Bank, as well its proposed statute, have focused on the price stability objective of this institution. In their chapter, **David Folkerts-Landau** and **Peter Garber** argue that similar attention should be devoted to the other main objective that central banks have traditionally pursued, that is the maintenance of a stable and efficient financial and payment system. They argue that a central bank is not simply a monetary rule; it is also the lender of last resort and the supervisory agency of the financial system. Folkerts-Landau and Garber assert that the importance of these additional objectives depends on the degree of securitization of the financial markets. The higher the degree of securitization, the higher the probability of liquidity crises and thus the more crucial is the existence of a lender of last resort. In highly securitized financial systems a major share of the market transactions is generated by a large number of non-bank intermediaries, several of which are underdiversified, highly leveraged and vulnerable to failure. Folkerts-Landau and Garber contend that the smooth functioning of this type of market rests on the existence of a well functioning payment system, able to support the large turnover in securities needed for liquidity. The larger the number of participants, the more complex the payment system and the greater the likelihood that the system may become gridlocked. In order to prevent liquidity crises, it is necessary for the central bank to monitor the system and inject liquidity in times of emergency. Folkerts-Landau and Garber argue that this systemic risk is much smaller in financial markets with a low degree of securitization, where there are just a small number of large universal banks and payments are cleared internally in these institutions. They conclude that, unless the ECB statue is revised to include basic banking functions, such as lender-of-last-resort, the financial markets in the Community will have to develop into a predominately bank-intermediated system. This will be incompatible with the recent development in some member countries, e.g. the UK and France.

John Pattison, in his discussion, disagrees with the authors' conclusion that the need for a lender-of-last-resort is greater in a highly securitized system. He argues that higher securitization implies that financial intermediaries can dispose quickly of large amount of assets without noticeable variations in their prices. This reduces the need for financial intermediaries to have recourse to central bank liquidity. Pattison suggests that the need for liquidity in the US financial markets is not a consequence of the degree of securitization, but of other institutional factors, like the restrictions on nationwide branch banking.

2   Transition from national central banks to a common central bank

David Currie's chapter sketches the elements of a cost-benefit assessment of EMU against specific alternatives. The current EMS, with infrequent realignments and preponderant influence of the Bundesbank on monetary policies of Exchange Rate Mechansim (ERM) countries, is probably unsustainable without further institutional development, because otherwise pressures for realignment may eventually become too strong to resist. The case for EMU presented in the Delors Report is based on this view. An alternative is simply to continue to strengthen the ERM of the EMS by increasing monetary policy coordination and instituting formal rules concerning the time between realignments and their size (for instance that they be inframarginal, i.e. within existing bands). Another is the UK proposal to introduce a parallel currency, the Hard-ECU, in order to discipline monetary policies of member countries; this might provide an evolutionary alternative to an administered EMU.

Currie argues that there are appreciable risks and uncertainties in moving towards EMU. Though non-German ERM countries would benefit from having a more symmetric system, since they would have a greater say in European monetary policy, these benefits may be lost if the European central bank does not have the inflation discipline of the Bundesbank. Currie questions the commitment to price stability of other EC countries, and stresses the importance of *de facto* independence for the European central bank and its need to establish a reputation for conservative monetary policies. At the very least, a difficult task of institution building is in prospect, and Currie favours building on the successes of the ERM, reinforcing it in the direction of making the Bundesbank more responsive to European-wide considerations, and possibly using a 'hard-basket' version of the existing ECU in which the stronger currencies get increasing weight to enhance monetary policy coordination.

Andrew Hughes Hallett, in his comments, agrees with Currie's general conclusion; in fact, he would go further in criticizing EMU. He argues that both EMU and the Hard-ERM are 'accident prone', requiring greater coordination of both monetary and fiscal policies to make them work. He suggests that the rigidity of EMU is not a good framework for enhanced coordination, which ideally should take a more general and more flexible form.

The theoretical analysis of the costs and benefits of a monetary union has focused on the trade-off between output stability and price stability objectives. It is argued that, even if the ability to stabilize the economy in the face of country-specific shocks will be reduced, a monetary union will provide gains in terms of the credibility of monetary policies. This type of analysis, however, fails to explain why countries that already have independent central banks will have any interest in joining a monetary union. Some other ingredients must be added to the analysis to answer this question, for example the reduction of transaction costs obtained by switching from a twelve-currency to a one-currency system. **Alessandra Casella** proceeds in this direction and shows that in this framework both high and low inflation countries may find it beneficial to join a monetary union. More interestingly, the support for a monetary union is not only a function of inflation performance, but also of the level of development of the economy. Moreover, the stablishment of a monetary union will induce changes in the relative size of domestic and international markets and this, in turn, will generate redistributional effects that will impact on the support for the union. Casella shows that countries characterized by a relatively high level of inflation will find a monetary union more attractive at a low level of economic development, while the opposite is true for low inflation countries. She concludes, therefore, that the international support for a monetary union is likely to be different not only across countries, but also at different points in time, depending on the level of development of the member countries. Today's support for a monetary union could vanish in the future.

Torsten Persson concurs with the basic thrust of Casella's argument, but he questions the robustness of some of her specific conclusions. Using a different setup, Persson also finds that support for a monetary union depends on particular market configuration in the various countries, but not necessarily in the way predicted by Casella's model. Moreover, he argues that the ultilitarian policy-making process assumed by Casella may not be the most plausible to adopt. Persson suggests, as an alternative, a majoritarian policy-making approach and shows that the results would be different in this case.

3   Fiscal policy requirements of a common currency area

The literature on optimal currency areas suggests that the benefits of a common currency have to be weighed against the loss of an important tool for macroeconomic stabilization. Regional imbalances that are caused by inflexibility of nominal prices may be alleviated by a change in exchange rates, accompanied perhaps by a change in regional monetary policy. In a monetary union, this is no longer possible, and, it is asserted, more of the burden for regional adjustment must fall on fiscal policy. Most monetary unions are complemented by a federal fiscal structure that performs this regional stabilization automatically. By comparison, the federal budget of the EC is very small. The paper by **Xavier Sala-i-Martín** and **Jeffrey Sachs** tries to evaluate the importance of the regional stabilizers that are built into the US federal fiscal system.

Sala-i-Martín and Sachs divide the US into nine regions (defined by the US Bureau of the Census) and use regression analysis to estimate the elasticities of federal tax payments and transfers to changes in regional income. They then use the elasticities to assess the importance of the fiscal structure to regional stabilization. They find that 'a one-dollar reduction in a region's per capita personal income triggers a decrease in federal taxes of about 34 cents and an increase in federal transfers of about 6 cents.' So, the one-dollar reduction in regional income only results in a 60 cent decrease in disposable income, with the tax structure providing most of the effect. Sala-i-Martín and Sachs also make some rough estimates for the EC. They calculate that a one-dollar decrease in a European region's income would only decrease its tax payments to the EC by about one half of one cent, a far cry from the 34 cents in the US system.

Both the paper and the comments of **Behzad Diba** and **Alberto Giovannini** questioned the Keynesian analysis behind the worries about macroeconomic stabilization and whether national fiscal authorities or private capital markets would provide the necessary income insurance in any case. Diba noted that the EC has managed rather well in recent years without major exchange rate realignments, but he also noted that if the road to EMU involves constraints on national fiscal policies, the past may be a poor guide to the EC's ability to cope with future regional disturbances. Giovannini noted that national governments in the EC are already providing automatic stabilizers roughly the size of those in the US. But he also noted that the regional approach to fiscal stabilization requires the running of regional fiscal deficits. Like Diba, he worried that constraints on national fiscal policy might prevent some EC governments from continuing these stabilization efforts.

The relationship between monetary institutions and monetary policies has been the subject of intense research, including several chapters of this book, and it is now relatively well understood. Much more uncertain, however, are the channels of transmission between fiscal policies and monetary policies. Much of the current political debate on the future monetary union is focused on the design of measures that will prevent fiscal distress in some member countries from spilling over to the rest of the Community, thus endangering European monetary discipline. According to some, to break the connection between national fiscal conduct and European monetary policies it is sufficient to create an independent European central bank with a statutory prohibition on providing lines of credit to national governments or Community agencies and to accessing primary markets for national public debt. Others believe this measure to be insufficient, doubting the irrevocability of such statutory clauses. Instead, they propose the introduction of fiscal rules that will require member countries to reduce their fiscal imbalance before joining the monetary union, and to maintain their public deficit within present limits as a condition of remaining in the monetary union.

A third point of view is that fiscal rules are unnecessary, since financial markets by themselves impose sufficient discipline on fiscal authorities by changing the cost of borrowing. **Morris Goldstein** and **Geoffrey Woglom**'s chapter analyses the validity of this market-based fiscal discipline by studying the recent experience in the United States. This case is relevant since the US is an important example of a monetary union among states which have a considerable amount of fiscal independence. Importantly, the monetary union has been successful without resorting to federally imposed fiscal rules on member states, just by preventing state governments from having access to central bank financing. It is true, however, that the success of the monetary union may be also due to the fact that state governments have displayed considerable fiscal discipline compared to some European countries. Goldstein and Wolgom investigate if this fiscal discipline can be the result of the constraints imposed by private financial markets. By using a set of survey data on the yields of state general obligation bonds that covers 39 states from 1973 to 1991, they test whether the cost of borrowing has been related to state debts and deficits. Their conclusion is that states with larger stocks of debt and larger fiscal deficits are associated with larger risk premia. Interestingly, however, they also find that states with more stringent, self-imposed, constitutional limits on the amount of borrowing, face a lower cost of borrowing.

Vito Tanzi commented that the existence of larger risk premia on bonds of states with larger debts and deficits does not yet prove the market discipline hypothesis. In fact, for the argument to be complete, it must also be proved that higher interest rates induce governments to reduce their borrowing. The paper, however, does not shed light on this second aspect. Vito Tanzi also noted that fundamental differences exist between the United States and Europe, that make the applicability of this results to the current debate problematic. Possibly the most crucial difference is the level of credibility of the United States union compared to that of a future European union.

4 Global implications of a European central bank

The chapter by **George Alogoskoufis** and **Richard Portes** looks beyond the creation of a European central bank and considers the implications for the international monetary system of the creation of EMU and the replacement of 12 national currencies by the ECU. The international demand for the ECU is likely to be greater than for the national currencies it replaces. It seems likely that EMU will thus hasten the relative decline in the international use of the dollar, but the experience of sterling suggests that reserve currency use changes very slowly. In any case, the quantitative significance for the EC of increased international seigniorage would be limited. Another aspect of EMU is the effect on international monetary policy coordination, currently conducted among the G-7 and in other forums, of having Europe 'speak with one voice' in monetary matters. It may lead to a more symmetric system in which the United States, Japan, and Europe constitute roughly equal poles. Will this stabilize or destabilize the international economy? The authors conclude that EMU is unlikely to undermine the evolution towards greater nominal exchange rate stability among major currencies.

Jeroen Kremers, in his comments, is not troubled by the conclusion of Alogoskoufis and Portes that the international implications – and potential gains to Europe – of EMU are quite modest. He stresses that the advantages of a common, stable currency are mainly *domestic* ones, and are related to those that will result from the creation of a European single market.

Part I The design of a central bank

2 Designing a central bank for Europe: a cautionary tale from the early years of the Federal Reserve System

BARRY EICHENGREEN

1 Introduction

Important questions concerning the structure and operation of a European central bank (ECB) remain to be answered. How much independence should national central banks retain during the transition to a single currency? What voting or mediation rules should be used to resolve conflicts among the national representatives on the ECB's governing council? What role should be played by existing central banks in implementing pan-European policies once the ECB comes into operation?

The Delors Report and the provisional statutes of the ECB, drafted by the governors of European Community central banks in Basel in November 1990, provide clearer answers to some of these questions than others. According to the Delors Report, during the transition to a single central bank ('Stage 2' of the process of monetary unification in the language of Brussels), national central banks will retain full nominal independence in the sense of continuing to issue their own national currencies and to intervene in domestic financial markets, but little real autonomy in that exchange rates will become immutably fixed and hence money supplies and interest rates will be determined by market forces. According to the draft statutes of the ECB, the policies of the new institution will be decided by votes cast by members of the bank's council, consisting of the 12 governors of the existing central banks and 6 executive directors appointed by the European Council. Voting will be by simple majority.[1] Governors and executive directors will be forbidden to accept instructions from national governments or from the European Parliament and Council. Once the ECB comes into operation, national central banks will forsake their remaining autonomy and become mere branch offices of the new institution.

13

Although there exists no precedent for the process of institution-building in which the European Community is currently engaged, the founding and early operation of the Federal Reserve System in the United States provides a suggestive parallel with ongoing developments in Europe. In the early years of the Fed, the individual reserve banks, while issuing bank notes that traded at fixed exchange rates vis-à-vis one another, essentially controlled their own discount policies. As American officials came to appreciate the problems posed by this arrangement, control over policy was gradually transferred to Washington, D.C. The stance of policy came to be determined by the Federal Reserve Board and an Open Market Investment Committee dominated by representatives of the 12 district reserve banks, just as representatives of the 12 European nations are envisaged as sitting on the council of the ECB. Implementation, especially of open market purchases, remained a matter for the individual reserve banks, however. Shifting authority to Washington D.C. did not eliminate regional conflicts in and of itself; neither did it resolve problems of policy implementation so long as individual reserve banks could opt out of System transactions. Only after authority was definitively centralized in the hands of the Board of Governors and the Federal Open Market Committee did the new institution finally come to operate smoothly.

The early history of the Federal Reserve System thus should be read as a cautionary tale.[2] It suggests that Stage 2 of the Delors Plan contains potential sources of instability. It provides an argument for a direct transition from Stage 1 (national monetary autonomy) to Stage 3 (complete centralization of authority).[3] It suggests the need for more thought about the voting and mediation procedures to be used to reconcile and aggregate national interests. It points to the advisability of reducing existing European central banks to mere branch offices of the ECB or of eliminating them entirely.

2   Institutions for decision-making in the early years of the Fed

In the early years of the Federal Reserve System, authority was much more decentralized and disputed than is suggested by many histories of the US central bank.[4] Decentralization created problems not anticipated by the framers of the Federal Reserve Act. In response to those problems, the institutional arrangements initially envisaged were gradually reformed. The first 22 years of the Federal Reserve System's existence (from the Federal Reserve Act of 1913 to the Banking Act of 1935) thus can be characterized as a trial-and-error process leading ultimately to the effective centralization of authority.

2.1 The consequences of the Federal Reserve Act

It seems remarkable, given the extent of decentralization and confusion over the locus of authority, that the newly-created Federal Reserve System succeeded in operating at all. Two factors were responsible for the peculiar state of affairs in which the Federal Reserve Board and the reserve bank Governors found themselves. First, the framers of the 1913 Act, while sensitive to the scope for regional conflict, finessed the issue by creating a federal structure but essentially declining to address the question of how it should operate. Second, the framers inadequately anticipated the problems with which the new institution would be confronted and the instruments with which those problems would be addressed.

The Federal Reserve System was created to provide an 'elastic currency' – that is, one which would be available in the quantities required by the changing needs of commerce and industry. Notes issued by the reserve banks had to be backed with gold to the extent of 40 per cent. The remainder of the collateral could take the form of eligible paper (commercial, agricultural and industrial paper and bankers acceptances), but insofar as eligible paper fell short of 60 per cent, gold had to make up the difference. These regulations applied by federal reserve district. Insofar as a reserve bank possessed gold in excess of that required, it could inject additional notes into circulation.

The framers anticipated that discount policy would be the principal instrument through which elasticity would be lent to American credit markets. When demands for credit rose, for seasonal or other reasons, member banks would discount commercial paper with reserve banks. The volume of discounts provided by the latter could be regulated by adjusting reserve bank discount rates. Discount policy was buttressed by a separate rate charged by each reserve bank for advances on acceptances and government securities.

The Federal Reserve Act was ambiguous about the role of the reserve banks and the Federal Reserve Board in determining the rates charged for discounts and advances. The 1913 Act stated only that 'Every Federal reserve bank shall have the power ... to establish from time to time, *subject to review and determination of the Federal Reserve Board*, rates of discount to be charged by the Federal reserve bank for each class of paper, which shall be fixed with a view of accommodating commerce and business.'[5] A possible interpretation of this passage is that the initiative to alter discount rates lay with the reserve banks but that the Board possessed veto power. Another is that the Board, using its power of 'determination,' might order a change in prevailing discount rates.

As early as January 1915, reserve bank Governors began to complain that the Federal Reserve Board was exceeding its authority in the specificity and scope of its instructions regarding discount policy. They established the Governors Conference as a venue in which to meet and defend their independence.[6] At its second meeting, a number of Governors asserted that the Board had no legal right to impose restrictions on the type of acceptances that could be purchased by reserve banks. Rolla Wells, Governor of the St. Louis Fed, complained that the Board's practice of suggesting discount rates infringed on the prerogatives of the reserve banks. Benjamin Strong, the influential Governor of the Federal Reserve Bank of New York, shared this opinion.[7] Toward the end of 1915 the Governors Conference adopted a resolution criticizing the Federal Reserve Board for its 'exercise of pressure.'[8] The Board's response was to demand that the Governors Conference be discontinued and to insist that the Governors should meet only when called by the Board.[9] Thus, the question of whether the Board or the reserve banks had the final say over discount policy remained far from resolution.

Even more problematic was that the framers of the Federal Reserve Act, having failed to anticipate the importance of open market operations, said even less about the conduct of security transactions than about discount policy. Other than stating that the Federal Reserve Board could issue regulations governing the types of securities the reserve banks might buy and sell, the 1913 Act had made virtually no mention of them. Between 1915 and 1923, the Board made no effort to do significantly more than this.[10]

In particular, the 1913 Act made no provision for coordinating the security sales and purchases of the individual reserve banks. The assumption was that each reserve bank would conduct such purchases and sales independently.[11] Insofar as there existed financial markets outside of New York in which municipal warrants and Treasury securities were traded, there arose the prospect that reserve banks would bid against one another when entering the market. It might seem perplexing that Fed officials worried that competitive open market purchases would have put undue upward pressure on bond prices (downward pressure on interest rates), especially if one assumes that the purpose of open market purchases was to lower interest rates. But in fact, in the early years of the Federal Reserve System, the main purpose of open market purchases was not to lend elasticity to the currency or to otherwise contribute to the conduct of what we would now call monetary policy. Rather, it was simply to enable the reserve banks to accumulate a portfolio of earning assets out of which to pay their expenses. Only after 1922, when the case for open market operations as an instrument for controlling commercial bank reserves had been articulated by W. Randolph Burgess, among others, did the technique begin to come into systematic use.

The approach to the conduct of open market operations agreed by the members of the Governors Conference was to establish maximum and minimum prices at which transactions would take place. In practice, the reserve banks repeatedly violated the agreement when it threatened to prevent them from acquiring the earning assets needed to meet their expenses.[12]

The consequences of these arrangements were highlighted during the business cycle downturn that began in 1920. As a result of the decline in economic activity, the volume of rediscounts fell off, eroding the interest income of the reserve banks. To restore their earnings, they purchased considerable quantities of government securities.[13] The Treasury and the Federal Reserve Board objected that the reserve banks were bidding against one another in the execution of orders and destabilizing the prices of government bonds.

2.2   Formation of the Open Market Investment Committee

In response, in May 1922 there was created on the recommendation of the Governors Conference a committee, comprised of the Governors of the New York, Boston, Philadelphia and Chicago reserve banks, to centralize the execution of orders for purchases and sales of securities.[14] At first, this was just a mechanism to prevent the reserve banks from bidding against one another for earning assets. But in October of the same year the Governors Conference voted to give the committee power to 'make recommendations' to the reserve banks regarding purchases and sales of government securities.[15] Whether their recommendations were binding and whether reserve banks retained the right to conduct open market operations on their individual initiative was left unclear.

These ambiguities were addressed in March 1923, following an extended study of open market operations by the Federal Reserve Board. This study came at the end of protracted dispute between the Board and the reserve banks, led by the New York Fed. Treasury officials objected that reserve bank transactions in government securities were disrupting their debt management operations, and insisted that the Board force the reserve banks to divest their portfolios of government bonds.[16] Adolph Miller, the economist on the Board, presented to his colleagues a proposal that the Board assert its control over the open market policies of the reserve banks. Learning of Miller's plan, the reserve banks rebelled. Governor W. P. G. Harding of the Federal Reserve Bank of Boston denied that the Board possessed more than 'broad supervisory power' and questioned whether it could do more than regulate the type of securities in which the reserve banks could transact.[17] On behalf of the Board, Miller responded that Washington possessed the power to dictate both the volume and composition of the open market transactions of the reserve banks.

A resolution approved by the Board on March 22nd asserted that the Board possessed the authority to 'limit and otherwise determine the securities and investments purchased by Federal Reserve banks.'[18] It added to the committee comprised of 4 reserve bank governors a fifth member, to be appointed by the Federal Reserve Bank of Cleveland, and named the body the Open Market Investment Committee (OMIC). According to the March 22nd resolution, the new committee came 'under the general supervision of the Federal Reserve Board.' This reorganization can be read as an attempt to assert the authority of the Board over the New York Fed in the conduct of open market operations. A separate Federal Reserve System open market investment account, operated by the New York Fed but under the supervision of the OMIC, was established to free the other banks from having to maintain accounts with the New York bank.[19]

The thrust of this resolution was that, while the OMIC would recommend open market purchases and sales to the reserve banks, its recommendations would be subject to approval by the Federal Reserve Board.[20] In practice, the OMIC almost exclusively recommended purchases and sales of bankers acceptances and short-term government securities. Actual purchases and sales were still delegated to the New York Fed and on occasion to other reserve banks.

The critical variables determining the volume of acceptances purchased by the reserve banks were their acceptance rates, which determined the quantity of acceptances offered. In turn, the most important acceptance rate was that of the Federal Reserve Bank of New York, since far and away the largest acceptance market was New York City. In light of this asymmetry among reserve banks, procedures were adopted to redistribute acceptances from New York to other Federal Reserve districts. As acceptances came into the New York Fed, they were allocated to the other reserve banks in proportions set by the OMIC. Open market purchases of government securities, when undertaken by the New York Fed on instructions issued by the OMIC, were then apportioned to the other reserve banks in agreed percentages.

In principle, an OMIC decision to conduct open market purchases not only had to be approved by the Federal Reserve Board but also had to be submitted to the individual reserve banks, which could decline to participate. Similarly, reserve banks had the option of refusing to take their share of the securities accepted by the New York Fed, even though the shares were established by the OMIC. On occasions when this occurred in the 1920s, the New York bank absorbed the residual.[21]

The reserve banks did not concede the Board's right to dictate their open market operations.[22] The 1923 resolutions of the Federal Reserve Board left the reserve banks the right to opt out of open market operations recommended by the OMIC and the Board. More controversial was whether reserve banks were also entitled to conduct open market operations of which the Board did not approve. Some reserve bank officials asserted that this was the case.[23] They threatened to enter the market on their own volition even if the Board disapproved.[24] It appears that they did so on more than one occasion in the 1920s.[25]

These disagreements were aired in meetings of the OMIC and in its dealings with the Board. As early as April 1923 the Board instructed the OMIC to conduct large-scale open market sales, for the purpose of liquidating reserve bank holdings of government securities.[26] The OMIC first voted that maturing Treasury certificates should not be replaced, and then, under Federal Reserve Board and Treasury pressure, agreed to $50 million of sales from reserve bank portfolios. This was not enough for several members of the Board, however, who chastised the head of the OMIC, J. H. Case (chairing the Committee in Strong's absence), for not carrying out the Board's instructions. Case complained that the Board had exceeded its authority by ordering security sales. In his view, the limits on the Board's authority were the same as those which had prevailed prior to the March 1923 resolutions. Ultimately, the OMIC bowed to Washington's pressure, selling a second $50 million of government securities, and thereby reducing its holdings from more than $200 million in April to less than $100 million in July.

2.3 Establishment of the Open Market Policy Conference

By the end of the 1920s, complaints about the growing influence of the Federal Reserve Board and OMIC were widespread in the Southern and Western United States, regions whose reserve banks were not represented on the five-member OMIC. Representatives of these districts argued that the excessive expansion of credit in 1927–29, which supposedly had led to the stock market boom and crash, was the fault of the reserve banks beholden to Wall Street interests that dominated the OMIC. They criticized the latter as a power-hungry, extra-legal body not provided for by the Federal Reserve Act.[27]

Such criticisms were largely responsible for the Federal Reserve Board's decision to dissolve the OMIC in March 1930 and to replace it with a new committee, the Open Market Policy Conference, or OMPC. All 12 reserve banks were represented on the OMPC. The Board endowed it with an executive committee, once again limited to representatives of 5 reserve banks. This time, however, the executive committee was responsible only for executing, not initiating, policy.[28] Substantive policy decisions were to be made instead in regular meetings of the OMPC, with representatives of all 12 reserve banks present. Nothing ensured the leadership or even participation of the Governor of the New York Fed on the executive committee. Thus, the reorganization of the OMIC into the OMPC was seen as an attempt to 'curtail the control exercised by the New York Reserve Bank.'[29]

The establishment of the OMPC significantly clarified lines of authority and control. Once again, however, ambiguities remained. The 1930 resolution was less than clear about who possessed the final say about the conduct of open market operations. It stated that 'The conclusions and/or recommendations of the Open Market Policy Conference, when approved by the Federal Reserve Board, shall be submitted to each Federal Reserve bank for determination as to whether it will participate in any purchases or sales recommended; any Federal Reserve bank dissenting from the proposed policy shall be expected to acquaint the Federal Reserve Board and the chairman of the executive committee for the reasons for its dissent.'[30] Apparently reserve banks could still decline to engage in open market operations recommended by the OMPC.

2.4   The Banking Acts of 1933 and 1935

The Federal Reserve Board at last acquired definitive control over open market operations as part of the Banking Act of 1933. The Open Market Policy Conference was renamed the Federal Open Market Committee (FOMC) and finally given legal standing. In keeping with practice since 1930, it was composed of one representative from each of the 12 reserve banks. At last it was explicitly stated that 'no Federal Reserve bank shall engage in open-market operations under section 14 of this Act except in accordance with regulations adopted by the Federal Reserve Board.' If a reserve bank wished to purchase or sell government securities for its own account, it was now required to first obtain the consent of the Board. Rates of interest and discount on acceptances and bills of exchange had to conform to the regulations of the Board. Final authority over these matters now clearly rested with the Board in Washington, D.C.

The individual reserve banks still retained limited autonomy under the 1933 Act. While prohibited from initiating open market transactions on their own, they had the right to refuse to participate in open market operations recommended by the Board. Moreover, individual reserve banks were still permitted to buy government securities in an emergency as needed to afford relief to banking institutions in their districts.[31]

The 1933 Banking Act contained two revealing provisions. It specified that no officer or other representative of a federal reserve bank was permitted to negotiate with a foreign bank except with the Board's permission. It asserted that the Board was entitled to be represented in all such negotiations and that it had the right to oversee all relations with foreign central banks. This clause was a reaction to a controversy which had arisen in 1927, when Benjamin Strong, the Governor of the Federal Reserve Bank of New York, had initiated negotiations with a group of foreign central bankers and failed to keep the Board apprised.[32] Another provision of the 1933 Act authorized the Federal Reserve Board to fix for each federal reserve district the percentage of member bank loans secured by stock or bond collateral. This clause was an outgrowth of the Board's attempt in 1929 to utilize a policy of 'direct pressure' to ration stock market speculators out of the loan market, a tactic whose implementation was resisted by the New York Fed.[33]

These reforms were consolidated by the Banking Act of 1935.[34] The Federal Reserve Board's name was changed to the Board of Governors of the Federal Reserve System. The composition of the FOMC was changed so that it was now composed of the 7 members of the Board of Governors plus 5 representatives of the reserve banks. The 5 reserve bank appointees were to represent all parts of the country, not just the Northeast and Middle West, as had been the case in the 1920s with the OMIC. Thus, the dominance of Washington, D.C. over the formulation of monetary policy was ensured as much by reducing the influence of the reserve banks of the Northeast and Midwest as by elevating the influence of the Board. Finally, decisions of the FOMC were made binding. Reserve banks were prohibited from engaging in, or (for the first time) declining to engage in, open market operations mandated by the FOMC.

3   Impact on policy

To analyse the impact on policy of the conflicts that arose in the early years of the Federal Reserve System over the control of open market operations and of the different institutional arrangements used to resolve them, I first specify a simple analytical model with which these issues can be addressed. I then use this model to structure my discussions of five critical episodes from the early history of the Fed.

3.1   An analytical model

The model utilized here is an adaptation of that in Eichengreen (1985). I use it in this case to analyse the incentives facing district reserve banks in a national setting, instead of the more familiar problem of the incentives facing national central banks in an international setting. The parallels will be obvious.

Consider the interaction of two reserve banks, referred to as 'New York' and 'Chicago' for reasons that will become evident in Section 3.2.2 below.[35] Each reserve bank minimizes a loss function L. The loss increases as earnings on its bond portfolio deviate from their desired level and as output deviates from its target.

$$L = [(B - \bar{B})^2 + a(Y - \bar{Y})^2] \qquad L^* = [(B^* - \bar{B}^*)^2 + a^*(Y - \bar{Y})^2]$$
(1)

Variables with asterisks refer to the Chicago bank, those without them to New York. B (B^*) denotes bonds in the reserve bank's portfolio, $\bar{B}$ the corresponding target number of bonds. Y is nominal income in the economy, $\bar{Y}$ its corresponding target level.[36] a (a^*) is the weight attached to income deviations relative to earnings deviations in the loss function.

$\bar{B}$ can be thought of as the bond portfolio that optimally trades off current interest earnings (which increase with B) against future lender-of-last-resort capacity (which is a decreasing function of B, since additional lending requires open market purchases which are constrained by gold cover restrictions). Similarly, Y can be thought of as indexing not only the current level of income but also the current stability of the banking system.

Y is an increasing function of the (cumulated) open market purchases of the two central banks. The simplest possible specification makes that function linear and additive:

$$Y = B + B^*$$
(2)

Expansionary open market operations can raise nominal income by increasing the monetary base (Friedman and Schwartz, 1963) or by countering disintermediation and debt deflation (Bernanke, 1983). In the historical context at hand, I have in mind expansionary open market operations as a means of providing liquidity to a banking system unable to restore its liquidity itself because of asymmetric information about the quality of bank assets and problems of adverse selections.[37]

Each central bank possesses one instrument (open market operations) with which to minimize its loss function.[38] Consider first the simple case in which the two reserve banks are identical in all respects, so that $a^* = a$. Substituting (2) into (1) and minimizing the loss subject to the assumption that the policy of the other reserve bank is given yields the reaction functions for the two banks:

$$\partial L/\partial B = [a/(1 + a)] B^* - [1/(1 + a)]\bar{B} - [a/(1 + a)] \bar{Y} + B = 0$$
(3a)

$$\partial L^*/\partial B^* = [a/(1 + a)] B - [1/(1 + a)] \bar{B} - [a/(1 + a)] \bar{Y} + B^* = 0$$
(3b)

The reaction functions are depicted in Figure 2.1 B and B^* are lower at the Nash solution N, where the two reaction functions intersect, than at the cooperative solution C, the point where the indifference contours of the two reserve banks are tangent.[39] Each central bank has two objectives: stabilizing the level of output and the banking system, and holding lender-of-last-resort capacity in reserve for the future. Since future lender-of-last-resort capacity depends only on its own bond portfolio, while output economywide depends not only on its own bond portfolio (the larger its bond portfolio, the greater its expansionary open market operations and hence the higher the level of output) but also on the bond portfolio of its counterpart, each reserve bank holds a smaller bond portfolio and engages in fewer expansionary open market operations when it behaves non-cooperatively than when it cooperates. Each reserve bank derives only some of the benefits of open market purchases; the rest accrue as a positive externality to the other bank. At N, it does too little to stabilize output and the banking system currently. Cooperation, were it to be forced on the two central banks by the Board of Governors, is a way of internalizing this externality. Note, however, that starting from the cooperative point C, each reserve bank has the option of reverting to its reaction function so long as it retains the alternative of opting out from cooperative actions mandated by the Board.

What is the effect of introducing asymmetries into the model? Assume for example that $a > a^*$. There are a number of rationales for such an assumption. One can imagine that, compared to Chicago, New York better appreciates the impact of open market operations on macroeconomic stability or attaches a higher weight to economic stability itself. Alternatively, if Y is interpreted as proxying not only for the level of income but also for the stability of the banking system today, Wheelock's (1988) evidence for the 1920s and 1930s that open market purchases, by whatever Federal Reserve bank they were initiated, disproportionately increased the reserves of member banks in the New York district provides a further rationale for the assumption. In this case, open market purchases can be seen as enhancing the stability of the New York Fed's client banks to a greater extent than it enhances the stability of the member banks of the Chicago district, thereby justifying the assumption that $a > a^*$.

This situation is depicted in Figure 2.2. Chicago's reaction function is flatter than New York's. New York is more inclined than Chicago to respond to open market purchases by the other reserve bank with open

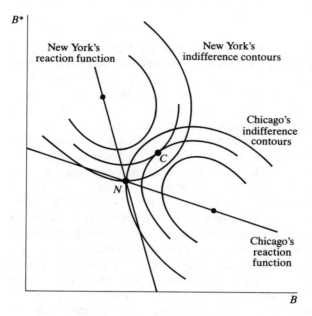

Figure 2.1   New York and Chicago's reaction functions: the symmetric case

market sales of its own, since New York attaches greater weight to the stock of bonds held outside the Federal Reserve System, upon which the level of economic activity depends. By comparison, Chicago is less inclined to respond to New York's open market sales with open market purchases of its own, since member banks in New York benefit more than member banks in Chicago from an increase in the stock of bonds held outside the Federal Reserve System.

Again, current stabilization is underprovided. Both reserve banks hold smaller stocks of earning assets and do less to stabilize output and the banking system at the Nash solution than would be the case if they cooperated.

In summary, the decentralization of control over open market operations for most of the interwar years is likely to have led the stabilization function to be undersupplied. Moreover, reserve banks such as New York whose member banks benefit most from stabilization are likely to have borne a disproportionate share of the burden of supplying it. How important this was for policy can only be determined through the examination of particular historical episodes.

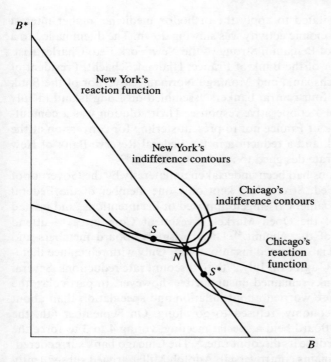

New York's
reaction function

New York's
indifference contours

Chicago's
indifference contours

Chicago's
reaction
function

B^*

S

N

S^*

B

Figure 2.2   New York and Chicago's reaction fuctions: the asymmetric case

3.2   Case studies

Case studies provide a second approach to analysing the impact of
differences and conflicts over policy within the Federal Reserve System.
They illustrate how the Board's failure to properly impose cooperative
behavior on the reserve banks led the stabilization function to be undersupplied. They show how disputes between the Board and the reserve
banks led to delays that caused intervention to be provided at inappropriate times, and how differences of opinion between the Board and the
reserve banks sometimes led the banks to provide even less of the stabilization function than they would have wished.

3.2.1 The 1927 discount rate reductions

The first episode of controversy occurred in 1927. The economy was in a
short-lived recession, popularly attributed to Henry Ford's decision to
shut down his assembly lines for six months to shift over from the Model
T to the Model A. Great Britain and Germany were experiencing gold

outflows, yet hesitated to apply the orthodox medicine, higher interest rates, because economic activity was slowing down. The dilemma led to a famous meeting of Benjamin Strong of the New York Fed, Charles Rist, Deputy Governor of the Bank of France, Hjalmar Schacht, President of the German Reichsbank, and Montagu Norman, Governor of the Bank of England. The four central bankers assembled on Long Island in July 1927 to negotiate a cooperative response. Their solution was a commitment by the Bank of France not to present sterling for conversion at the Bank of England, and a reduction in the Federal Reserve Bank of New York's discount rate designed to repel gold inflows.[40]

These negotiations had been undertaken unilaterally by the Governor of the New York Fed. Strong had kept only one member of the Federal Reserve Board, Daniel Crissinger, apprised of his intentions, and invited only members of the Open Market Investment Committee to attend formal sessions of the summit.[41] Unsurprisingly, Board members and reserve bank officials resented his initiative.[42] Only with reluctance therefore did the OMIC agree on July 27th to discount rate reductions. Several of the reserve banks remained unsupportive, however. In particular, the Chicago Fed, more worried about inflation and speculation than about the weakening economy, refused to go along. On September 6th, the Federal Reserve Board held a special meeting, voting 4 to 3 to force the Chicago Fed to reduce its discount rate.[43] The Chicago bank surrendered.

This decision remains controversial. Adolph Miller argued subsequently that the decision to lower discount rates set the stage for the excessive speculation of the Wall Street boom and ultimately for the crash that inaugurated the Great Depression.[44] I have argued elsewhere that this view is misleading.[45] The 1927 cut in discount rates actually helped to abbreviate the 1927 recession, and there is no evidence that it was in fact responsible for the stock market boom and crash.

In terms of the theoretical model of Section 3.1, this episode can be thought of as an early instance in which the Board compelled the individual reserve banks, principally New York and Chicago, to move from a point like N to one like C. The Board's authority to do so remained disputed, however. Indeed, the controversy provoked by its action inhibited it from taking similar steps in 1928–29.

3.2.2 The Fed's response to the great bull market
A second episode of controversy over authority and control swirled around the restrictive monetary measures taken in response to the 1928–29 stock market boom. The Fed's decision to tighten in order to restrain the rise of the stock market is now regarded as a grave policy error that set the stage for the Great Depression.[46] The impetus to do so

came not from the Board, however, but from the Chicago Fed, the same reserve bank that had opposed discount rate reductions in 1927 on the grounds that they encouraged speculation. In January 1928 the directors of the Chicago bank voted to increase its discount rate. This can be thought as an attempt by Chicago to defect from the cooperative solution – that is, to move from C, the equilibrium imposed on the reserve banks by the Federal Reserve Board in September 1927, to a point directly below it on the Chicago bank's reaction function.

This time Chicago's decision was reluctantly accepted by the Federal Reserve Board, which, according to Wicker, wished to avoid repeating the episode of the previous September in which it had embarrassed the Chicago Fed.[47] Only two Board members, Edmund Platt and George James, actually favored the Chicago Fed's proposal to raise the cost of credit. Others worried about seeing 'business penalized for the excesses in the stock market' but yielded on grounds of reserve bank autonomy.[48]

The Chicago Fed's position, that increases in discount and acceptance rates were needed to contain stock market speculation, spread to other parts of the Federal Reserve System in 1928. This is a prediction of the model: once the cooperative solution C cannot be sustained and one reserve bank defects, the other reserve banks will also revert to their reaction functions, raising discount rates and/or reducing open market purchases until the Nash solution at N is reached.

Yet some opposition to higher discount rates remained. Governor Roy Young of the Board continued to oppose rate increases on the grounds that they would injure industry and trade.[49] Young protested when on January 3, 1929 the directors of the New York Fed voted to raise the buying rate on acceptances. He asserted that the action required the prior approval of the Board, a position which George Harrison, the new Governor of the New York Fed, disputed.[50]

This controversy can be understood in terms of two fundamental disagreements within the Federal Reserve System. One concerned the best way to contain speculation on Wall Street without doing damage to business and trade. Members of the Federal Reserve Board, including a reluctant Young, preferred a policy of 'direct pressure' – moral suasion to deter member banks from extending brokers loans and other credits that might be used for speculative purposes. Direct pressure was intended to ration speculators out of financial markets without disrupting the access to credit of legitimate borrowers. The New York Fed preferred discount rate increases, both because it doubted the effectiveness or direct pressure given the fungibility of funds, and because it did not wish to discriminate against its Wall Street clientele.

The second fundamental disagreement concerned reserve bank autonomy.

At the first meetings of the OMIC following Benjamin Strong's death in 1928, the Board submitted to the reserve bank governors a proposal to revise procedures for conducting open market operations. It proposed expanding the size of the OMIC from 5 to 12 members in order to eliminate the dominance of the 5 reserve bank governors from the Northeast and Midwest. No immediate action was taken, however.[51] Two weeks later the Board for the first time vetoed a recommendation forwarded by the OMIC.[52] Both actions were intended to assert the Board's authority over the OMIC, and to signal that henceforth the Board would oversee even the smallest decisions of the latter.

On February 14, 1929, the directors of the New York Fed voted unanimously to increase the discount rate and telephoned the Board to obtain confirmation. When the Board instructed the New York bank to hold off until the Board considered the matter the following day, the directors in New York informed the Board that they would not leave the bank premises until they received a response from Washington, D.C. To assert their dominance, the Board then voted unanimously to veto New York's decision.[53]

This sequence of events repeated itself 10 times over the subsequent 4 months. The directors of the New York Fed voted repeatedly to raise the discount rate; the Board repeatedly vetoed their action. While 'no one questioned the legal right of the Federal Reserve Board to veto our rate increases,' in Harrison's words, continued refusal was 'seriously disturbing to both the officers and directors of the several Federal reserve banks.'[54]

Several of the New York directors threatened resignation on the grounds that their powers had been usurped. The directors were invited to Washington to confer with the Board. Finally in August of 1929 the New York Fed was allowed to raise its discount rate.

In terms of the model, these events are best understood as an attempt by the Board to reassert its authority over the reserve banks in the wake of its loss of influence in 1928. Ironically, that reassertion, while it should have had beneficial consequences in the long run (by facilitating cooperative solutions to the policy game), had adverse consequences in the short run. The conflict delayed the New York Fed's efforts to raise its discount rate to the point that, when the increase finally came, it was no longer timely. But New York's desire to assert its autonomy encouraged it to go through with the increase anyway. By August, when the discount rate increase finally came, industrial production in the United States had already begun to decline. Discount rate increases lent further impetus to the downward spiral of activity.

3.2.3 The Fed's response to the 1929 crash

A third conflict occurred in the aftermath of the October 1929 Wall Street crash. The crash created a liquidity crisis in New York. Brokers who had borrowed from New York banks, pledging stock as collateral, found themselves unable to repay. Almost half of the loans of central reserve city member banks in New York were collateralized by securities; a third were extended directly to stock brokers and dealers in New York City. Immediately following the crash, banks in the interior of the country which had placed money at call in New York repatriated their funds. The New York Fed, seeing its member banks placed at risk, intervened by purchasing $100 million of government securities on the open market.

In terms of the model of Section 3.1, the crash can be thought of as shifting New York's reaction function to the right. This induced open market purchases by the New York Fed (a rise in *B*) and, given the flatness of their reaction functions, little response by the other reserve banks.

New York's action was undertaken without prior approval by the Federal Reserve Board. Indeed, Harrison authorized this intervention even without consulting all of his own bank's directors.[55] Officials in Washington, DC were torn. The majority of Board members approved in principle of providing additional liquidity to financial markets in distress, but they were alarmed by the precedent represented by New York's unauthorized, unilateral action.[56] Harrison was called on the carpet. He protested that the 1923 agreement between the Board and the reserve banks permitted the latter to purchase securities for their own account. If doing so was ever justified, this was the case in extraordinary circumstances like those of October 1929. Once again the Board disagreed. Open market operations, its members asserted, were at the Board's volition and its volition alone. Governor Young of the Board noted that the Board 'had been given most extraordinarily wide powers [and] that so long as the Board had those powers, they would feel free to exercise them.'[57] Having repeatedly vetoed the New York Fed's attempts to alter its discount rate, the Board threatened to do so again unless the New York bank promised to refrain from engaging in further unauthorized open market purchases. The Board authorized the Governor, should the Board not be immediately available, to act on its behalf in the event of an emergency.

For the moment, the controversy remained unresolved. So long as it persisted, the dispute continued to disrupt the Federal Reserve system's attempt to engineer a concerted response to the economic slump. On October 1st the OMIC had been authorized by the Board to purchase short-term government securities in amounts not to exceed $25 million a week. On November 12th the OMIC, led by Harrison, recommended that the ceiling be raised. The Board vetoed its decision on the grounds that 'the general situation is not sufficiently clarified for the system to formulate and adopt a permanent open market policy at this time.'[58] A bargain was hammered out under which the New York Fed agreed to refrain from further open market purchases for its own account, at least until their legality had been determined, in return for the Board's approval of the OMIC's recommendation. On November 25th the Board confirmed this deal by a narrow margin.[59]

3.2.4 Open market operations in 1932

A fourth conflict concerned the use of open market operations in 1932. Until the Glass-Steagall Act came into effect at the end of February, open market purchases were constrained by the availability of free gold. Glass-Steagall eliminated the constraint and allowed the Fed to inject additional notes into circulation by purchasing government securities.[60]

The Governors of the 12 reserve banks were divided on the efficacy of doing so, however. The majority apparently believed that, in light of the deflation and depressed business conditions that by early 1932 had persisted for almost 2½ years, open market purchases could not hurt and might actually stimulate recovery. A vocal minority, led by the Governors of the Chicago and Boston banks, warned that open market purchases would only provoke another round of inflation and unhealthy stock market speculation.[61] Since money was already plentiful, they argued, open market purchases would serve no useful purpose. It was better, as this view was articulated by James McDougal, Governor of the Chicago Fed, for the Fed to hold its note-issuing capacity in reserve for some future time when it would be of greater value.[62]

Thus, the dispute within the Federal Reserve System is typically portrayed as a disagreement over doctrine.[63] Epstein and Ferguson (1984) suggest, however, that the Chicago and Boston reserve banks had ulterior motives. Member banks in their districts held or were acquiring short-term securities in disproportionate numbers. The earnings of those banks would suffer if open market purchases were initiated and interest rates were reduced. This prompted the Boston and Chicago reserve banks to intervene on their members' behalf by opposing open market purchases.[64]

With the majority of Governors nonetheless supporting open market operations, Harrison attempted to push a purchase program through the OMPC and the Board. On April 12th, 1932, the OMPC approved by a vote of 10 to 1 Harrison's resolution authorizing an additional $500 million of open market purchases to be undertaken as soon as possible. Only Roy Young, now Governor of the Boston Fed, voted no, although McDougal of Chicago warned that this inflationary policy might undermine public confidence.[65] The OMPC purchased $100 million of securities weekly before exhausting its authorization. At that point the OMPC approved an additional $500 million of purchases, despite negative votes by Young and McDougal.[66]

So far there is nothing exceptional about this episode. A difference of opinion existed among the members of the OMPC, and policy was determined by majority vote. The story gets interesting when one observes that the Chicago and Boston reserve banks, and the former in particular, could and did increase the cost to the other reserve banks of carrying out the policy. Chicago and Boston threatened to sit on the sidelines while the other reserve banks purchased securities. Since gold backing restrictions on notes applied individually to each reserve bank, this raised the danger that the cover ratio of the New York Fed or another reserve bank would fall below the legal minimum.[67]

By the end of the June, the gold cover ratio of the New York bank had fallen to 50 per cent, while Chicago's was still 75 per cent.[68] If the New York Fed continued to purchase securities without Chicago's support, its capacity to provide future lender-of-last-resort facilities to banks in its district would be eliminated.[69] In principle, the Board could have forced Chicago to rediscount on behalf of New York, transferring some of its gold there, but officials within the System viewed this step as undesirable on the grounds that it would reveal the depth of division within the Federal Reserve system and therefore demoralize the markets. By June, Harrison himself was questioning the advisability of continuing the program of open market purchases unless Chicago and Boston agreed to participate. As he put it, 'I do not see how this bank [New York] can continue to carry so much more than its share of the load.'[70]

Harrison's efforts to win over officials in Chicago and Boston proved unavailing. Nor did his efforts to get his acquaintances in the Chicago banking and business community to pressure the Chicago Fed bear any fruit. Mounting gold losses compelled the OMPC and the Board to halt open market operations in August.[71] Thus, resistance by a minority of reserve banks, notably Chicago, increased the cost to the others of providing the stabilization function, forcing open market purchases to be abandoned sooner than would have otherwise been the case. In terms of the model of Section 3.1, inadequate cooperation led the stabilization function to be undersupplied.

3.2.5 The 1933 banking crisis

A fifth conflict (the final one considered here) arose out of the banking panic with which Franklin Delano Roosevelt was greeted upon taking office.[72] Panic surfaced first in Michigan in February 1933; by early

March bank runs had spread to virtually every state of the union. The question is why the Fed did not do more to stabilize the banking system. Officials throughout the Federal Reserve System recognized the banking system's need for liquidity. By early March, however, the gold cover ratio System-wide had fallen to 45 per cent. The provision of additional liquidity threatened to violate this most basic provision of the gold standard and, in the prevailing view, to further demoralize financial markets.

Gold losses were borne unevenly by reserve banks, with New York experiencing far and away the greatest pressure. Foreigners, fearing a possible devaluation of the dollar, scrambled to get their money out of the country in order to avoid the capital losses that would result.[73] Since the vast majority of foreign deposits was held by New York banks, gold was drained from the coffers of The New York Fed. In addition, difficulties in Michigan and throughout the interior prompted the liquidation of correspondent balances in New York. In the three weeks ending on March 8th, 1933, New York suffered more than 100 per cent of the gold losses of the Federal Reserve System.[74] On March 4th, when US monetary gold reserves were 44 per cent of the note and deposit liabilities of the Federal Reserve system, the gold backing of the notes of the New York Fed had fallen to the 40 per cent statutory minimum.[75] In terms of the model of Section 3.1 above, this is an example of the situation in which New York was forced to bear a disproportionate share of the stabilization function.

As in 1932, the Chicago Fed was the principal repository of the System's excess gold reserves. At the beginning of March 1933, the Chicago bank's gold reserve was still 65 per cent. In principle, the New York Fed might have obtained additional gold from Chicago. On March 1st, the Chicago Fed lent $105 million to its New York counterpart by purchasing a matching amount of New York's government securities and acceptances under a repurchase agreement. On March 3rd, however, Chicago withdrew its cooperation.[76] Spokesmen for member banks in Chicago were skeptical that the New York banks would be significantly strengthened by the transfer of funds, but they were convinced that their own position would be weakened. They pressured the Chicago Fed to withdraw its support for New York.

On March 4th the Federal Reserve Board considered the situation but declined to compel the Chicago Fed to aid New York.[77] The New York Fed was forced to curtail its lender-of-last-resort activities.[78] the New York Stock Exchange and other exchanges nationwide suspended operations the same day. The bank holiday followed immediately. This can be thought of as the situation at point S^* in the analytical model, where Chicago acts as a Stackelberg leader. Chicago was aware of New

York's commitment to support its member banks and the stock exchange. It could reduce its contribution to stabilizing financial markets in anticipation of New York taking up a part of the slack. Chicago's refusal to provide part of the stabilization function forced New York to shoulder a disproportionate share of the burden. Since the cost to New York of additional lender-of-last-resort activities eventually proved prohibitive, less of the stabilization function was provided than would have been the case had the Board forced the reserve banks to cooperate.

On March 7th the Federal Reserve Board finally compelled Chicago and the other reserve banks to resume interdistrict rediscounting on behalf of the New York Fed. This allowed the latter to resume discounting on behalf of member banks. It became possible to gradually reopen the commercial banks whose operations had been suspended by the bank holiday. The stage was set for reconstruction of the American financial system.

4   Implications for a European Central Bank

While the particulars of this history will not carry over to Europe in the 1990s, some general lessons are certain to apply. In this conclusion I emphasize four implications of the early history of the Federal Reserve System for the design of a European Central Bank.

The first implication is the importance of close coordination among national central banks once monetary unification is achieved. Any attempt to decentralize monetary control at the level of national central banks creates the danger that their stabilization function will be underprovided. Since stabilization has the character of an international public good, no national central bank has the incentive to internalize all of the international spillovers created by its actions. Efficiency requires transnational control.[79] The dangers raised by its absence are acute whether goal of stabilization policy is output or price stability. European policymakers have clearly stated the need to centralize control once a European central bank comes into operation. But the point applies equally well to Stage 2 of the monetary unification process, when exchange rates are immutably fixed but national central banks may retain a considerable degree of autonomy. From this point of view, the current approach to Stage 2 poses considerable dangers.

A second implication is the importance of resolving in advance controversies over the locus of control. If residual uncertainty remains, it is likely that monetary unification will be followed by a period in which national central banks test the limits of their autonomy and take independent action as a way of demonstrating to the newly-established European central bank that some such autonomy remains. This is likely to evoke a strong response by the ECB designed to demonstrate authority. In the early history of the Fed, this process of thrust and parry led to disastrous delays.

A third implication is that, to prevent such controversies from arising, issues of autonomy and control should be addressed explicitly. The same point applies, of course, to the managerial hierarchy of any enterprise, not just to a central bank. But it is in the public sector, where questions of authority and control become politically charged, that the temptation to circumvent them is greatest. Given the politically-charged nature of these issues, the framers of the Federal Reserve Act sought to avoid them. This led to the disputes which disrupted policy for fully two decades. The draft statutes of the European central bank, in their current form, leave open substantial questions of authority and control. The early history of the Fed underscores the need to provide definitive answers before the new institution comes into operation.

The fourth and final implication of this cautionary tale is the importance of endowing any new institution with a model of the central banking function that is coherent and pertinent. In the case of the Fed, this model was missing; hence the centralization of authority in the 1930s was a mixed blessing. On the one hand it permitted the emergence of an institutional structure capable of internalizing the interregional externalities that characterize monetary policy and resolved the disputes over authority and control that had created extended policy deadlocks. On the other hand it enhanced the influence of factions within the Federal Reserve System who least appreciated the role for monetary policy in countering the Great Depression, and undermined the position of others, notably officials of the Federal Reserve Bank of New York, who were most aware of the need for offsetting action. According to the draft statute of the Eurofed, the model of the central banking function is one in which monetary policy should be targeted first and foremost at price stability. Imagine that at some future date the problem is not inflation but, say, bank insolvencies or another potential source of financial instability. Then it is not clear that concentrating the central banking function in a single entity with this charge is the best way of ensuring that policy is adapted to new imperatives.

Nor is it obvious that the adoption of explicit rules and restrictions on operating procedures will be helpful in the long run. In the US case, the failure of the Fed's architects to anticipate the importance of open market operations and the problems created by the free gold constraint graphically illustrate the point. The Great Depression that resulted in part from difficulties thereby created should serve as the ultimate warning to European policymakers.

NOTES

I thank Sonali Vepa and Glenn Yamagata for assistance; the Library of Congress, Columbia University and the Federal Reserve Bank of New York for permission to cite documents in their possession; and Matt Canzoneri and David Wheelock, along with my conference discussants, Bennett McCallum and Eugene White, for helpful comments.

 1 Weighted voting is foreseen for financial matters, such as paying in capital and allocating profits, though the weights remain to be determined. See Committee of Governors (1990), p. 11.
 2 At least two authors (Thygesen, 1989; Miron, 1989) have analysed this tale previously. Neither, however, takes the methodological approaches that I adopt here.
 3 In this paper I do not address the more fundamental question of the advisability of monetary unification. See however Eichengreen (1990). Rather, I assume that it will take place and inquire into the operation of European monetary policy thereafter.
 4 This statement does not apply uniformly, and it certainly is not applicable to all early analyses of Federal Reserve policy. Two excellent accounts of the controversies, upon which I draw heavily, are Clark (1935) and Harris (1933).
 5 Emphasis added.
 6 The Governors Conference, comprised of the 12 reserve bank governors, was an outgrowth of a meeting of reserve bank officials held in Washington on 20–1 October, 1914. It met in December 1914, four times in 1915, four times in 1916 and once in 1917.
 7 US Congress (1971), p. 13; Chandler (1957), p. 70.
 8 The resolution was then forwarded to the Board. US Congress (1971), p. 14; Chandler (1957), p. 73.
 9 US Congress (1971), p. 15. In the event, the Board managed to secure only a suspension of Governors Conference meetings until the end of World War I.
10 Clark (1935), p. 162.
11 Several reserve banks found themselves incapable of doing so owing to the lack of an organized market in the relevant securities within their districts. The only significant market in US government securities in the early decades of the twentieth century was that in New York. Hence at the second meeting of the Governors Conference in January 1915, the other reserve banks appointed the New York Fed as their agent for purchasing securities on the open market. The New York bank not only purchased securities on the instructions of other reserve banks but also resold to them securities already held in its portfolio.
12 Chandler (1957), p. 78.
13 Annual Report of the Federal Reserve Board, 1923, p. 13; Stabilization Hearings on HR. 7895, 1926, p. 863.
14 Stabilization Hearings on HR. 7895, 1926, p. 863.
15 Harrison Papers, Governors Conference, vol. I. 10–12 October 1922, p. 12; Stabilization Hearings on HR. 7895, 1926, pp. 310–11.
16 Chandler (1957), pp. 222–3.
17 Chandler (1957), p. 225.
18 Stabilization Hearings on HR. 7895, 1926, p. 865.
19 Burgess (1936), p. 218.
20 Stabilization Hearings on HR. 7895, 1926, pp. 865–6.

21 Clark (1935), p. 169.
22 Governor Strong, in letters to J. H. Case written in the spring of 1923, complained that the Board had exceeded its authority. Chandler (1957), p. 228.
23 Stabilization Hearings on HR. 7895, 1926, pp. 866–867; Stabilization Hearings on HR. 11806, 1928, p. 403.
24 US Congress (1971), p. 102; Stabilization Hearings on HR. 7895, 1026, p. 866.
25 Chandler (1957), p. 229.
26 The remainder of this paragraph draws in Chandler (1957), pp. 229–32.
27 Kemmerer (1938), pp. 203–4.
28 Friedman and Schwartz (1963), p. 368.
29 Clark (1935), p. 176.
30 Hearings on Banking Systems, 1931, p. 158.
31 Thus, even had the 1933 Banking Act been in effect in 1929, the New York Fed might well have had the option of intervening on behalf of New York banks embarrassed by the liquidation of brokers loans, even without Federal Reserve Board approval. On this 1929 episode, see below, pp. 29–30.
32 For an account of this episode, see below, p. 26.
33 On the 1929 policy of direct pressure, see below, pp. 27–8.
34 A source for this is the testimony of Eccles in Hearings Before the Senate Committee on Banking and Currency, 4 March 1935, 74th Congress, First sessions, pp. 179ff.
35 Obviously, nothing of substance is affected by the convenience of reducing the number of players from 12 to 2.
36 I let Y denote nominal rather than real income or output in order to link it to monetary policy in a particularly simple fashion. Since price and output changes were positively correlated in the critical period considered here, nothing of substance is affected by this assumption.
37 On this 'fire' sale' problem, see Bentson et al. (1986). Stabilizing the banking system would stabilize output through the channels emphasized by both Bernanke and Friedman and Schwartz. Thus, to accept the rest of the analysis it is not necessary to buy into a particular model of the monetary transmission mechanism.
38 It is straightforward to reformulate the model so that the discount rate rather than open market operations is the policy instrument. See Eichengreen (1985) for an example. In applying the model to case studies in Section 3.1 below, I refer to open market purchases and discount rate reductions interchangeably.
39 I have selected a particular point of tangency along the contract curve, that at which the losses of the two banks are equal, on the grounds that they are symmetrical in all respects.
40 The authoritative account of these meetings is Moreau (1954).
41 Wicker (1966), pp. 110–11.
42 Hamlin Diaries (Library of Congress), XIV, pp. 12–13, July 25.
43 Hamlin Diaries, XIV, p. 29.
44 Hearings on Banking Systems, 1931, (Part VII), p. 132 and *passim*.
45 Eichengreen (1992), chapter 8.
46 For two recent statements of the view, see Field (1984) and Hamilton (1987).
47 Wicker (1966), p. 118. In terms of the model, this can be thought of as an instance where the cooperative solution C is too costly to sustain.
48 Goldenweiser Papers (Library of Congress), memorandum of 28 January 1928.

49 The Governor of the Federal Reserve Board was the 1920s equivalent of what is known today as the Chairman.

50 Harrison cited the fact the New York Fed had for many years changed its buying rate for bills 'without any question or disapproval by the Board'. Young retorted that 'he did not intend any longer to be a rubber stamp.' Harrison Papers, Conversations, vol. 1, memorandum of January 25, 1929, p. 3.

51 Recommendations of the Federal Advisory Council to the Federal Reserve Board, 28 September 1928, printed in *Annual Report of the Federal Reserve Board for 1928*, p. 229.

52 Harrison Papers, Open Market, Vol. 1, Letter from Roy Young to Gates W. McGarrah, Acting Chairman, Open Market Investment Committee, November 27, 1928.

53 Not only was this an attempt to force the hand of the Board, but Harrison noted that the commercial bankers who served as directors of the New York Fed would be placed in an embarrassing position if the Board held its decision overnight and the bankers were then to conduct securities transactions with the inside information that the New York Fed's rate might be raised subsequently. Hamlin Diary, XV, February 14, 1929, pp. 169–70; Harrison, Conversations, Vol. 1, memorandum of February 14, 1929.

54 Harrison Papers, Conversations, Vol. 1, memorandum of April 25, 1929, p. 1.

55 He reached a few of them by telephone at 3:00 in the morning. Stabilization of Commodity Prices, U.S. House Banking and Currency Committee, Subcommittee, hearings (72:1) (April 13, 1932), p. 475.

56 Hamlin Diaries, XVI, pp. 186–89, November 4–9, 1929.

57 Harrison Papers, Conversations, vol. 1, memorandum of November 15, 1929, p. 6.

58 Harrison Papers, Open Market, vol. 1, Letter from R. A. Young to George Harrison, November 13, 1929.

59 Harrison Papers, Miscellaneous, vol. 1, letter, November 25, 1929. For a more detailed account of this episode, see Friedman and Schwartz (1963), pp. 366–67.

60 In arguing that free gold mattered, I follow Wicker (1966) and Epstein and Ferguson (1984) but dissent from Friedman and Schwartz (1963). The free gold problem arose from the fact the Federal Reserve notes had to be collateralized with either gold or eligible (commercial) paper. Treasury securities did not qualify. Insofar as eligible paper fell below 60 per cent of Federal Reserve notes, the remaining share had to be backed with gold. The Fed's free gold fell to less than $400 million in late 1931 and early 1932, limiting the open market purchases that were feasible.

61 Those who had indulged in speculative excesses, in this view, should now be made to pay the price. Additional open market purchases would only reward and encourage the reckless, thereby setting the stage for another round of speculative excesses and leading eventually to another crash and an even more catastrophic slump. On the genesis of the liquidationist view, see DeLong (1990).

62 Harrison Papers, Discussion Notes, Meeting of the Board of Directors, 14 July 1932, pp. 273–4; Friedman and Schwartz (1963), p. 371.

63 See for example Wheelock (1988) for a recent statement of this view.

64 In terms of the analytical model of Section 3.1, this situation can be thought of

38   Barry Eichengreen

as one in which open market purchases have a large (and costly) impact on the first argument of the Chicago Fed's loss function ($B - \bar{B}$).

65 Harrison, Open Market, vol. II, minutes of meeting, April 12, 1932.
66 Harrison, Open Market, vol. II, minutes of meetings, May 17 and June 16, 1932.
67 Harrison, Open Market, vol. II, minutes of meetings, July 14, 1932 reported veiled threats by Boston and, especially, Chicago. Glass-Steagall had only eliminated restrictions on the 60 per cent of the backing that now could be made up of government securities as well as eligible bills, without eliminating the 40 per cent gold cover restriction that remained in place until Roosevelt suspended the gold standard in 1933.
68 Friedman and Schwartz (1963), p. 387.
69 In terms of the analytical model in Section 3.1, this can be thought of as forcing New York to accept a large value of $\bar{B}$, insofar as $\bar{B}$ can proxy not only for interest earnings but also for lender-of-last-resort capacity held in reserve.
70 Harrison, Discussion Notes, vol. II, Meeting of the Board of Directors, June 30, p. 252; Meeting of the Executive Committee, 5 July 1932, p. 257.
71 Harrison, Discussion Notes, Meeting of the Board of Directors, July 7, 1932, p. 265. Eichengreen (1992), chapter 10.
72 The account of the 1933 banking panic presented here draws on Eichengreen (1991), chapter 11.
73 This is the explanation for the 1933 banking crisis emphasized by Wigmore (1987), Temin (1989) and Eichengreen (1991) alike.
74 Wigmore (1987), Table 2.
75 New York was not the only reserve bank forced to limit its purchases of bills because of its low level of reserves. Chandler (1971, p. 219) mentions Philadelphia, Cleveland, Richmond, Atlanta, Kansas City and Dallas as other reserve banks all of which suffered from the same problem.
76 Wigmore (1987), p. 747.
77 James (1938), pp. 1062–3.
78 Wigmore (1987), p. 748.
79 Essentially the same point, in a somewhat different context, is made by Casella and Feinstein (1989). A similar point – that monetary policies have international spillovers that create inefficiencies when they are not taken into account – also applies, of course, in a situation in which nations have independent currencies. See for example the contributions to Buiter and Marston (1985). But one can argue that, so long as nations have independent currencies and retain the option of changing the exchange rate, they are better able to insulate themselves from these spillovers.

REFERENCES

Bentson, G., R. A. Eisenbeis, P. M. Horovitz, E. J. Kane and G. S. Kaufman (1986), *Perspectives on Safe and Sound Banking*, Cambridge, Mass.: MIT Press.
Bernanke, B. (1983), 'Nonmonetary Effects of the Financial Crisis in the Propagation of the Great Depression', *American Economic Review* **73**, 257–76.
Buiter, Willem and Richard Marston, eds. (1985), *International Economic Policy*

Coordination, Cambridge: Cambridge University Press.

Burgess, W. Randolph (1936), *The Reserve Banks and the Money Market*, New York: Harper & Brothers, revised edition.

Casella, Alessandra and Jonathan Feinstein (1989), 'Management of a Common Currency', in Marcello de Cecco and Alberto Giovannini (eds.), *A European Central Bank?*, Cambridge: Cambridge University Press, pp. 131–55.

Chandler, Lester V. (1957), *Benjamin Strong, Central Banker*, Washington, DC: Brookings Institution.

(1971), *American Monetary Policy, 1928–1941*, New York: Harper and Row.

Clark, Lawrence E. (1935), *Central Banking Under the Federal Reserve System*, New York: Macmillan.

Committee of Governors of the Central Banks of the Member States of the European Economic Community (1990), 'Draft Statute of the European System of Central Banks and of the European Central Bank', manuscript, 27 November.

DeLong, J. Bradford (1990), 'Liquidation' Cycles: Old-Fashioned Real Business Cycle Theory and the Great Depression', unpublished manuscript, Harvard University.

Eichengreen, Barry (1985), 'International Policy Coordination in Historical Perspective: A View from the Interwar Years', in Willem Buiter and Richard Marston (eds.), *International Economic Policy Coordination*, Cambridge: Cambridge University Press, pp. 139–78.

(1990), 'Couts et avantages de l'unification monetaire de l'Europe', in Pierre Beregovoy (ed.), *Vers l'union economique et monetaire europeenne*, Paris: Ministere de l'Economie des Finances et du Budget.

(1992), *Golden Fetters: The Gold Standard and the Great Depression, 1919–1939*, New York: Oxford University Press.

Epstein, Gerald and Thomas Ferguson (1984), 'Monetary Policy, Loan Liquidation, and Industrial Conflict: The Federal Reserve and the Open Market Operations of 1932', *Journal of Economic History* **44**, 957–84.

Field, Alexander J. (1984), 'Asset Exchanges and the Transactions Demand for Money, 1919–29', *American Economic Review* **74**, 43–59.

Friedman, Milton and Anna J. Schwartz (1963), *A Monetary History of the United States 1867–1960*, Princeton: Princeton University Press.

Hamilton, James (1987), 'Monetary Factors in the Great Depression', *Journal of Monetary Economics* **13**, 1–25.

Harris, S. E. (1933), *Twenty Years of Federal Reserve Policy*, Cambridge, Mass.: Harvard University Press.

James, F. Cyril (1938), *The Growth of Chicago Banks*, New York: Harper and Brothers.

Kemmerer, Walter (1938), *The ABC of the Federal Reserve System*, Princeton: Princeton University Press (11th edition).

Miron, Jeffrey (1989), 'The Founding of the Fed and the Destabilization of the Post-1914 U.S. Economy', in Marcello de Cecco and Alberto Giovannini (eds.), *A European Central Bank?* Cambridge: Cambridge University Press, pp. 290–327.

Moreau, Emile (1954), *Souvenirs d'un Gouverneur de la Banque de France*, Paris: M. T. Genin.

Temin, Peter (1989), *Lessons from the Great Depression*, Cambridge, Mass.: MIT Press.

Thygesen, Nils (1989), 'Decentralization and Accountability within the Central Bank: Any Lessons from the U.S. Experience for the Potential Organization of a European Central Banking Institution?' in Paul De Grauwe and Theo Peeters (eds.), *The EMU and European Monetary Integration*, London: Macmillan, pp. 91–114.

United States Congress, Committee on Banking and Currency of the House of Representatives, Subcommittee on Domestic Finance (1971), *Federal Reserve Structure and the Development of Monetary Policy, 1915–1935*, 92d Congress, First Session, staff report, Washington, DC: GPO.

Wheelock, David C. (1988), 'Interregional Reserve Flows and the Fed's Reluctance to use Open-Market Operations During the Great Depression', unpublished manuscript, University of Texas at Austin.

Wicker, Elmus (1966), *Federal Reserve Monetary Policy 1917–1933*, New York: Random House.

Wigmore, Barrie (1987), 'Was the Bank Holiday of 1933 Caused by a Run on the Dollar?' *Journal of Economic History* **47**, 839–56.

Discussion

BENNETT T. McCALLUM

Barry Eichengreen's paper provides a useful and authoritative account of operational difficulties generated in the early years of the Federal Reserve system by certain decentralized aspects of that organization's design. In particular, the failure to specify a single decision-making entity with unambiguous control of open market operations led on several occasions to courses of action that appear in retrospect to have been decidedly undesirable. In part the problem stemmed from decentralization *per se* and in part from the absence of clear and well-specified procedures, according to the paper, an absence that left the way open for regional reserve banks and the Washington-dominated Board (in its several manifestations) to take positions designed to gain power vis-à-vis each other, even at the expense of overall system policy objectives.

Eichengreen's historical account impresses me as interesting and of considerable importance. I have no major disagreement with the general outline of his story or his conclusions, but I do have a pair of reservations concerning the paper that are significant enough to warrant discussion.[1] The first of these concerns the 'analytical model' put forth in Section 3.1. In particular, it is unclear to me that this model provides a reliable vehicle for analysis of the type being undertaken. One weakness of the setup is that it is exceedingly static; it involves no explicit consideration of conditions expected to prevail in the future. But the main weakness involves the relationship between the reserve banks' loss function (1) and those of society, i.e., individual members of the economy's population. The expressions in (1) evidently represent objectives of the reserve banks, not society's, for the $(B - \bar{B})^2$ terms would not appear in an objective function designed to reflect the preferences of typical individuals. But then it is unclear what normative meaning can be given to the target levels of nominal income, $\bar{Y}$. The latter could differ from the level that is socially optimal and could do so in either direction. Thus it does not follow that outcomes in which $Y < \bar{Y}$ in the model actually imply policy stances that are too restrictive in terms of individuals' preferences.

My other main reservation can be expressed as a desire for additional help from the paper in understanding just how the early history of the Fed system relates to today's consideration and planning for a European central bank. In his concluding section, Eichengreen mentions four lessons or implications of the historical episodes for the design of a decentralized central bank, but consider what these four lessons are said to be. The first is 'the importance of close coordination among national central banks once monetary unification is achieved. Any attempt to decentralize monetary control ... creates the danger that their stabilization function will be under-provided' (p. 33).[2] Then the second implication 'is the importance of resolving in advance controversies over the focus of the control' (p. 33) and the third is that 'issues of autonomy and control should be addressed explicitly' (p. 34). Finally, the fourth implication 'is the importance of endowing any new institution with a model of the central banking function that is coherent and pertinent' (p. 34). The problem that I see with these lessons is not that they are unwise or incorrect, but rather that they are nonspecific and somewhat platitudinous. The second and third points, in particular, would seem to pertain to *any* central bank, centralized as well as decentralized – and also to any automobile producer, or economic research centre, or organization of almost any kind. Much the same could be said for the fourth lesson, moreover, if the words 'the central banking' were replaced with 'its.'[3] Admittedly the first of the four lessons does pertain specifically to a central banking entity, but even in this case it is unclear just how to develop the connection between the early Fed and the proposed European institution. One major problem is that these are central banks with very different responsibilities. Specifically, one of the most essential duties of the European central bank will be to prevent ongoing inflation – in other words, to provide a nominal anchor for the European price level.

But it was not a responsibility of the Fed's in the 1920s and 1930s to make basic decisions of this type, for the nominal anchor was provided by the gold-standard obligations that the Fed was legally charged to maintain. There are certainly additional duties of importance for central banks in today's regime of fiat money, but this function of controlling the average inflation rate is arguably the primary responsibility. So it is not the case that one can straightforwardly draw conclusions about the European central bank's committee design, its voting rules, or other critical constitutional provisions on the basis of the Fed's early experiences.

In conclusion, I would like to depart somewhat from the specifics of Eichengreen's paper in order to present an argument pertaining generally to the importance of central banking arrangements. In particular, I want to call attention to an argument first outlined in McCallum (1990, pp. 984–5) regarding the relationship between monetary and fiscal authorities. On this subject it is almost certainly true that the most fre-quently-cited publication of the last 15 to 20 years is the Sargent and Wallace (1981) paper entitled 'Some Unpleasant Monetarist Arithmetic.' As most readers will know, that paper included a few technical novelties, but its basic message was the suggestion that an economy's monetary authority cannot prevent inflation, by its own control of base money cre-ation, if an uncooperative fiscal authority adopts a course of action that implies a continuing stream of basic deficits. Formally, the paper empha-sizes that time paths of base money and fiscal (tax & spending) variables are unavoidably related via the government's budget identity, and points out that the relationship makes noninflationary money creation inconsis-tent with ongoing basic deficits.[4] Whether the central bank has control over inflation thus apparently depends upon, in the words of Sargent and Wallace, 'which authority moves first, the monetary authority or the fiscal authority? In other words, who imposes discipline on whom?' (1981, p. 7). Having posed the problem in this way, the Sargent-Wallace paper then goes on to suggest that it might well be the fiscal authority that dominates the outcome. In fact, the paper's analysis proceeds by simply assuming that the fiscal authority dominates, an assumption that is implemented by conducting the analysis with an exogenously given path of basic deficits. In this way the paper seems to suggest that even a determined central bank could be forced by a fiscal authority to create money along a different path than the one desired.

But is this actually possible? It is of course true that fiscal authorities may be able to bring *political* pressure to bear on central banks in ways that are difficult to resist. But the Sargent-Wallace analysis is not devel-oped along political lines; instead it seems to invite the reader to imagine that a politically independent central bank could be dominated in some sort of *technical* sense by a stubborn fiscal authority.

But a bit of thought about the hypothetical experiment indicates that such a conclusion is entirely unwarranted. The point is that an independent central bank is technically able to control its own path of base money creation, but fiscal authorities cannot directly control their own basic deficit magnitudes. For deficits are measures of spending in excess of tax collections; so if a fiscal authority embarks on a tax and spending plan that is inconsistent with the central bank's noninflationary creation of base money, it is the fiscal authority that will have to yield – because it does not have the purchasing power to carry out the planned expenditure. The fiscal authority does not have actual control over the instrument (the deficit) that it is presumed to control in the Sargent-Wallace experiment. Thus a truly determined monetary authority can always have its way, technically speaking, in monetary versus fiscal conflicts. This simple point implies that the design of a central bank's constitution is a matter of utmost importance, just as the existence of this conference volume would suggest.

NOTES

1 At the time of the conference, I had additional objections concerning (i) some econometric evidence pertaining to policy shifts occurring at times of organizational change and (ii) a sixth case study involving post-World War I inflation. Neither of these subsections appears, however, in the present version of the paper.
2 Eichengreen's language seems to associate underprovision of base money (relative to B) with 'underprovision of the stabilization function.' That usage seems unfortunate, since in actual economies an underprovision of stabilization might reflect a situation in which policy is excessively expansive.
3 Thus this lesson pertains to central banking only as a matter of syntax, not as a result of the logic of the discussion.
4 This result pertains to basic deficits, i.e., deficits measured exclusive of interest payments, but not to deficits measured in the conventional interest-inclusive manner (McCallum, 1984).

REFERENCES

McCallum, Bennett T. (1984), 'Are Bond-Financed Deficits Inflationary? A Ricardian Analysis', *Journal of Political Economy* **92**, 123–35.
(1990), 'Inflation: Theory and Evidence', in B. M. Friedman and F. H. Hahn (eds.), *Handbook of Monetary Economics*, Vol. II, Amsterdam: North-Holland Publishing Co.

Sargent, Thomas J., and Neil Wallace (1981), 'Some Unpleasant Monetarist Arithmetic', Federal Reserve Bank of Minneapolis *Quarterly Review* 5, 1–17.

EUGENE N. WHITE

The development of a European federal state by existing national governments represents an extraordinary political achievement. One of the few historical parallels is the formation and evolution of the United States. The operation of the American federal state has been the subject of experiment for over two hundred years, producing a large catalog of mistakes to be avoided. To analyze the dangers hiding in the stepwise formation of a European Central Bank, Barry Eichengreen draws upon the history of the Federal Reserve System – a federal central bank *par excellence* – to provide a cautionary tale for European policy makers. Although the institutional details are different, Eichengreen carefully extracts some key lessons from history to argue that federalized monetary control may be destabilizing. No one who reads the history of the Fed's early years of internecine strife can walk away without some concern for how the European Central Bank's Stage 2 will operate.

In this comment, I would like to suggest three qualifications to the concerns raised by Eichengreen's essay. First, the faulty design of the American federal bank was, in large part, the product of the nations' banking structure at the turn of the century. As Europe's banking structure is not as flawed, the centrifugal forces may not be as great. Secondly, while errors in the design of the Federal Reserve deserve attention, the role of a poor theoretical framework for policy should not be ignored. Lastly, in addition to monetary problems, federalizing the regulation and supervision of banking may create new problems, for which American history also provides a cautionary tale.

While the reasons for adopting a federal structure for a European central bank may be obvious, why the US chose a federal structure and why it had persistent problems is less well known. The Federal Reserve was not designed to accommodate any pre-existing monetary authority of the states. Its origins lie in the reform movement that followed the panic of

1907. The original architects – Senator Nelson Aldrich and his Wall Street advisors – felt that the greatest weakness of the banking system was the absence of a central bank. But, they were astute enough to realize that an institution patterned after European central banks would not be politically acceptable in the US because of the fear of domination by either Washington or New York.

To succeed in Congress, a central bank would have to be acceptable to the majority of banks, which numbered over 20,000 in 1913. No other industry was as well represented in every Congressional district as banking. To make the idea of a central bank palatable to bankers, Aldrich and his advisors proposed multiple reserve banks modelled after the clearing houses. The clearing houses were institutions familiar to all banks, which in addition to clearing and collecting checks had in times of panic helped to modestly expand liquidity. The Federal reserve banks thus seemed to bankers to be only improved private institutions (see West, 1977).

While the Federal Reserve system was ultimately more than an association of clearing houses, it was politically necessary to endow the bankers with considerable control in order to secure passage of the Federal Reserve Act. Consequently, the Board in Washington was appointed by the President, but the officials of the Federal Reserve banks were elected by member banks. The struggle for control persisted for two decades largely because the bankers had no desire to cede their share of control. It is noteworthy that the problem of governance was only eliminated when the banks were themselves crushed by the depression, permitting the passage of legislation to centralize power.

While most discussions of the Fed in the 1930s usually blame poor policy for its mistakes, Eichengreen focuses on structural flaws in governance as the source of the Fed's problems. The dispute over the control of policy between the Board and the Federal reserve banks certainly tarnished the Fed's public image, but it is hard to determine whether the structure of governance or incorrect theory were behind the Fed's mistakes. Although it is difficult to distinguish which of these two factors was more important, the crucial years 1929–33 are instructive.

Here the appropriate counterfactual to ask is what if authority over central banking functions had been wholly delegated to the Board of Governors and the reserve banks had acted as obedient branches. The outcome might have been worse because the Board followed misguided policies, which were only briefly offset by the New York Fed. When the stock market crashed in 1929, the New York Fed stepped in to ensure that liquidity did not dry up in the money markets. However, the bank took this step without the approval of the Board. The Board regarded this move as an act of insubordination with some members disapproving of the action itself. Had the Board been in complete charge, the Fed probably would not have quickly performed its duty as lender of last resort, permitting the crash to have much graver consequences for the economy. Throughout the depression, the New York Fed was more inclined to take what we would regard as the correct policy actions, in contrast to the Board and other Federal reserve banks. Centralization of authority could very well have worsened the Fed's performance.

The cautionary tale provided by Barry Eichengreen is a tale about monetary policy. However, it is important not to lose sight of the other functions of a central bank: the regulation, examination and supervision of banks. According to the current draft of the statues of the European Central Bank, monetary policy in Stage 3 will be completely centralized, but the other functions will be largely left to the national central banks. Each 'branch' will have the power to regulate, examine and supervise its own banks at home and their operations abroad. While monetary policy is clearly the premier task of a central bank, leaving these other functions to the new 'branches' of the European Central bank is not simply giving them an unimportant sop. The history of American banking regulation provides another cautionary tale about the dangers of multiple agencies. The history suggests that without centralized control the central bank 'branch' with the minimal regulatory and supervisory practices will set the standards for the Community.

The unfortunate history of the American regulation of banking can be briefly described. Until the Civil War, states chartered and regulated their own banks. The partial collapse of the banking system during the war led to the creation of a new federal agency of Office of the Comptroller of the Currency, which charters national banks. To crush the state banks, Congress placed a heavy tax on state bank notes, forcing most to close their doors or accept a national charter by 1870. The federal banking regulations were, however, far from minimal and states found it attractive to redesign their banking codes with weaker regulations. Over the next 25 years, the number of state banks grew rapidly; and by 1895 the number of state banks exceeded the number of national banks. Seeing federal preeminence slip away, Congress lowered the minimum capital reserve and other regulations for national banks in the Gold Standard Act of 1900 and the Federal Reserve Act of 1913 (see White, 1983). The competition between federal and state regulators thus relaxed banking regulations.

The creation of the Federal Reserve and later the Federal Deposit Insurance Corporation made matters more complicated. A commercial bank had the 'choice' of three federal regulators. The Comptroller of the Currency was the primary regulator for national banks, the Federal

Reserve for state member banks and the FDIC for non-member state banks. Each agency conducted its own examination and supervision of banks to ensure compliance with federal law and their own guidelines and regulations. Each agency jealously guarded its autonomy and regarded itself as the best. This divided authority posed no serious problems in the heyday of the New Deal banking system when banks activities were narrowly circumscribed. But in the 1960s, when innovation, competition and inflation began to erode the New Deal regime, the absence of any centralized banking regulator was a source of trouble. In this decade, American commercial banks began to seek expanded powers to offer more products and services. As banks were regulated by separate authorities, which possessed considerable autonomy and discretion, new powers were haphazardly granted to banks, creating a very uneven playing field.

Although the three federal agencies regulating commercial banks – the Federal Reserve, the OCC and the FDIC were all supposed to be operating with the same policy objectives, there were substantial differences in their practices. After a long and public dispute over whether to have frequent surprise call reports, President Johnson intervened, ordering the agencies to settle their differences. In 1964, the first Interagency Coordinating Committee was established. Yet this group only discussed issues, and it did not serve to coordinate practices (White, 1991). Each agency developed and maintained its own separate systems for rating bank loans and its own computerized analysis to detect liquidity and solvency problems. This minimal interagency cooperation sank to an all time low in the early 1970s when personal differences between the heads of the three agencies loomed large.

Effective efforts to coordinate these agencies came only when crises arose. After several large bank failures and a widespread weakening of the banking system, the Federal Financial Institutions Examination Council (FFIEC) was created in 1978 to promote uniformity in the supervision of banks. It was charged with producing uniform examination report forms, reporting systems, and common schools for examiners (Golembe and Holland, 1986). But FFIEC ran into each agency's ingrained view of its sovereignty and superiority. Although it increased uniformity, the council remained a collegial body where cooperation effectively required unanimity.

Maintaining different regulations for each class of banks is difficult. The weakest set of regulations tends to dominate the rest because banks can switch regulators by switching their affiliation, which in turn puts pressure on regulators to alter their rules. Attempting to attract jobs and capital, many states also get into the act, by altering banking regulations. In one notable example, South Dakota eliminated usury rates on consumer loans so that Citicorp and others would set up banks to handle their national credit card operations. Maintaining effective examination and supervision is also a problem. One salient example occurred when the United National Bank of Tennessee effectively gave the Comptroller the slip when it switched to a state charter and put itself under the FDIC's authority, only to have a spectacular failure later.

Given that the European central banks will have considerable autonomy and discretion in regulating their 'home' banks, American history should worry European policy makers. If a German bank opens offices in Italy, what will be the response of the Bank of Italy to complaints that German banks have a competitive advantage because of differences in accounting rules, examination practices and other regulations? What will happen if someday, an Italian bank decides to move its domicile from Italy to Germany to take advantage of the different regulations? Even if there is no centralized regulatory and supervisory authority, what sort of organization should be set up to coordinate policy?

In sum, while coordination problems for monetary policy may loom large, they can be eliminated by a more rapid transition to Stage 3 of the European Central Bank plan. Much more consideration needs, however, to be given to the proposed federal structure of banking regulation – or Europe may face some of the perils of American banking.

REFERENCES

Golembe, Carter H. and David S. Holland (1986), *Federal Regulation of Banking, 1986–87*, Washington, DC: Golembe Associates, Inc., pp. 34–37.

West, Robert Craig (1977), *Banking Reform and the Federal Reserve, 1863–1923*, Ithaca: Cornell University Press.

White, Eugene Nelson (1983), *The Regulation and Reform of the American Banking System, 1900–1929*, Princeton: Princeton University Press, Chapter 1.

(1991), *The Comptroller of the Currency and the Revolution in Banking, 1960–1990*, Washington, DC: Office of the Comptroller of the Currency, Chapter 1.

3 The European Central Bank: reshaping monetary politics in Europe

ALBERTO ALESINA and VITTORIO GRILLI

1 Introduction

One of the most challenging tasks in the process of European integration is the creation of new institutions, such as the European Central Bank (ECB). Important and difficult questions need to be addressed in this process, such as: how independent should the European Central Bank be from political institutions? What voting rules should be adopted by the governing board of the ECB, when deciding about European monetary policy? How do we ensure that the preferences of European citizens will be reflected in the choice of policies of the ECB?

The governors of the twelve central banks of the EEC countries have recently proposed a statute for the ECB which provides some answers to these questions. The purpose of this paper is to address these issues and evaluate the proposed statute from the point of view offered by recent politico-economic models of monetary policy. In particular, we focus upon the trade-off between the objectives of low inflation and output stabilization.[1]

We begin by considering, as a benchmark, the situation in which the political integration of Europe has been completed, so that one can think of a 'European nation' with its legislature and executive. Following Rogoff (1985), we show that the legislature (universally elected in this new 'European nation'), has an incentive to set up an independent Central Bank, and to appoint a governor who is more 'inflation-averse' than the European median voter.

The proposed statute does indeed guarantee a very high level of independence to the ECB. Using the index of independence recently developed by Grilli *et al.* (1991), we show that the ECB, according to this statute, would be as independent as the Bundesbank currently is from the German government. In fact, the proposed institutional structure of the ECB will be very similar to the current one of the Bundesbank.

We then proceed to consider the more realistic situation in which the political integration of Europe is not complete. Different country members of the union and different groups within each country may have substantially different preferences over the conduct of monetary policy. We analyse how different voting rules for the appointment of the ECB board may lead to different policy outcomes. The proposed statute takes as given the fact that political integration in Europe is not complete. In fact, according to the statute, the executive committee of the ECB, including the President, will be appointed by the European Council, i.e. by the committee of the twelve Prime Ministers, and not by the European Parliament, i.e. a truly 'European' legislative body. Different voting rules, assigning different weights to the member countries, may lead to very different outcomes. We suggest that it is not at all clear that the proposed rules to appoint the board of the ECB and the voting rules within the board, will accurately represent the preferences of the European median voter.

The paper is organized as follows. In Section 2 we consider the choice of a Central Banker in a completely integrated, (politically and economically) Europe; we review Rogoff's (1985) argument which highlights the benefit of an 'independent' and 'conservative' Central Bank. In Section 3 we analyse in detail the proposed institutional structure of the ECB and, in particular, its degree of independence. In Section 4, we consider the situation in which Europe is not completely integrated economically and politically, so that different countries have different preferences over the conduct of monetary policy. In Section 5 we analyse how these different views of the EEC members can be aggregated in various voting schemes; we argue that the preferences of the European median voter may not be well captured by the decision process leading to the formulation of monetary policy, as proposed in the statute. The last section offers concluding comments.

2   The ECB in a politically unified Europe

2.1   Monetary policies in a political union

We first consider the situation in which Europe has achieved political unity so that the European Central Bank can be considered like the national central bank of a country called 'Europe'. Thus, this central bank will pursue goals and implement policies which are truly 'European' in nature. In this section we ignore issues such as the voting rules within the ECB board and the procedures to appoint the latter. We simply assume, for the moment, that in this hypothetical 'European nation', the legislature has appointed a board and a president of the ECB with preferences given below in equation (1). In specifying the economic framework and the Central Bank preferences we follow closely the analysis of Kydland and Prescott (1977), Barro and Gordon (1983) and Rogoff (1985). The preferences of the ECB president and board are given by:

$$\mathscr{L}_E = \tfrac{1}{2}\,\mathscr{E}[\pi_E^2 + b(x_E - \bar{x}_E)^2] \tag{1}$$

where $\mathscr{L}_E$ is the loss function, which depends upon the European inflation rate, π_E, and upon the deviation of European output, x_E, from a given level, $\bar{x}_E$. $\mathscr{E}(.)$ is the expectation operator. Output is determined according to the standard expectational Phillips curve relation:

$$x_E = (\pi_E - \pi_E^e) + \epsilon \tag{2}$$

where π_E^e is the expected rate of European inflation. In (2) we have assumed, without loss of generality, that the 'natural' level of output is zero, and we have set equal to 1 the partial derivative of output with respect to unexpected inflation. ϵ is a random shock with mean zero and variance equal to σ_ϵ^2. It is important to emphasize that the ECB, as well as society, has a target level of output $\bar{x}_E$ which is greater than what would be achieved by the economy without any unexpected inflationary shocks. This wedge between the market-generated, 'natural', level of output (i.e. zero), and the target level $\bar{x}_E$ can be justified by the existence of various distortions in the labour market, such as income taxation or trade unions. These distortions keep the level of employment and output below the level which would be achieved in a non-distorted economy. Thus, the policy-makers have an incentive to circumvent these distortions by generating unexpected inflation which raises the level of economic activity.[2]

The timing of events in this model is as follows: at the beginning of each period, wage contracts are set and, more generally, expectations about inflation are formed. Then, the shock ϵ is realized and observed by the ECB which sets the inflation rate based upon this information.[3] By assumption, wage contracts cannot be contingent on the realization of the shock, nor can they be indexed. Henceforth, to simplify notation, we drop the time subscripts. The time-consistent inflation policy in this set-up is given by:

$$\pi_E = b\bar{x}_E - \frac{b}{1+b}\,\epsilon \tag{3}$$

and the corresponding output level is:

$$x_E = \frac{1}{1+b}\,\epsilon \tag{4}$$

Equation (3) is obtained by substituting (2) into (1), taking the first-order conditions with respect to π_E and then imposing the condition of rationality of expectations.

Equations (3) and (4) highlight the well known time-consistency problem in this model. The term $b\bar{x}_E$ in (3) implies that the average inflation rate is above zero – its target value according to (1) – without any benefits in terms of average or variance of output.

The first-best policy, which would eliminate the inflation bias introduced by the term $b\bar{x}_E$, without reducing the extent of output stabilization, would instead be:

$$\pi_E^{\cdot} = -\frac{b}{1+b}\,\epsilon \qquad (3')$$

This is the inflation rule that the ECB would follow if it could make an irrevocable, and thus credible, commitment. The problem is, of course, that such a policy is time-inconsistent, thus not credible, because of the bank's incentive to generate unexpected inflation in an attempt to increase the average level of output.[4]

The crucial parameter which characterizes this trade-off between average inflation and variance of output is b. The lower this parameter in the Central Banker's objectives, the lower is the average rate of inflation, but the higher is the variance of output, which is given by

$$\sigma_x^2 = \frac{\sigma_\epsilon^2}{(1+b)^2}$$

If $b = 0$ the inflation bias is completely eliminated, but no stabilization is achieved. In this case, in fact, $\sigma_x = \sigma_\epsilon$, i.e. the variance of the shock is completely transmitted to output. A very important question is, then what 'b' should 'society' choose for the Central Bank? It is worthwhile to emphasize that throughout our discussion we disregard as unrealistic the possibility of making the first-best rule, $(3')$, credible, thus implementable. One important point that our stylized model captures is that the first-best rule may be reasonably complicated, i.e. it may go beyond a simple monetarist rule with a constant rate of money growth. For example, in our model the first-best rule is contingent upon the realization of a random shock; in reality more than one contingency might be relevant. One way of making a rule like $(3')$ credible is to write it into the Central Bank's statute or, perhaps, into the country's constitution. However, it is not realistic to assume that a contingent, reasonably complex monetary rule can be inserted in an unchangeable statute. Obvious problems of supervision and enforcement, particularly if the economic shocks on which the rule is contingent are not easily observable, would make such an institutional arrangement ineffective, if not counterproductive.[5] In what follows we pursue, instead, the idea of choosing an agent with appropriate preferences, to whom the conduct of monetary policy is delegated.

2.2 The optimal ECB in a political union

Suppose now that European citizens vote upon what 'governor' to appoint. By assumption, each possible governor is associated with a different 'b' in his objective function. Thus, the voters in fact vote on what 'b' the Central Bank should have in its objective function. After this parameter (i.e. a governor) is chosen, the Central Bank is independent, that is, the governor can freely implement his desired policy; there is no possibility of recall, or of replacing the governor.[6] The voters differ only with respect to the relative weight which they assign to inflation and stabilization. For example, individual j has preferences given by:

$$\mathcal{L}_E^j = \tfrac{1}{2}\,\mathcal{E}[\pi_E^2 + b^j(x_E - \bar{x}_E)^2] \tag{5}$$

We assume that the voters will choose by majority rule the central banker, i.e. b. The chosen central banker, b is such that there is no other individual, b^i, preferred to b by a majority of voters in a pair-wise comparison. In this set up, majority voting on a pair-wise comparisons results in the selection of the governor most preferred by the voter with the median b in his utility function, i.e. b^m.[7]

Let us determine, therefore, which is the governor most preferred by the median voter. The median voter will prefer the governor who will implement the policy which minimizes his loss. Therefore the governor preferred by the median voter is obtained by solving the following problem:

$$\min_b \tfrac{1}{2}\,\mathcal{E}[\pi_E^2 + b^m(x_E - \bar{x}_E)^2]$$

If a Central Banker of 'type b' is appointed, he follows the policy rule given in (3) which leads to output level given in (4). Thus, using (3) and (4), we obtain:

$$\min_b \tfrac{1}{2}\,\mathcal{E}[(b\bar{x}_E - \frac{b}{1+b}\,\epsilon)^2 + b^m(\frac{1}{1+b}\,\epsilon - \bar{x}_E)^2] \tag{6}$$

The first-order condition implicitly defining the choice of b is given by:

$$b\bar{x}_E^2 - \frac{\sigma_\epsilon^2}{(1+b)^3}\,(b^m - b) = 0 \tag{7}$$

From this condition we notice that, since at $b = b^m$ the left hand side of (7) is positive, b must be less than b^m. Similarly, since at $b = 0$ the left hand side of (7) is negative, the optimal b must be positive. Therefore, the appointed ECB governor will be more 'conservative' than the median European voter, (i.e. he will value fighting inflation more than the median voter) but not a totally conservative one, i.e. $b > 0$. This argument generalizes to an explicit voting model a point originally made by Rogoff (1985); he showed that society's welfare is maximized if the conduct of monetary policy is delegated to an independent and 'moderately conservative' Central Banker.[8] By taking the total differential of (7) we can also show that:

$$\frac{\partial b}{\partial \sigma_\epsilon^2} = \frac{(b^m - b)}{(1+b)^3 \left\{ \bar{x}^2 + \sigma_\epsilon^2 \dfrac{[1 + b^m + 2(b^m - b)]}{(1+b)^4} \right\}} > 0 \tag{8}$$

since $b^m > b$, and

$$\frac{\partial b}{\partial b^m} = \frac{\sigma_\epsilon^2}{(1+b)^3 \left\{ \bar{x}^2 + \sigma_\epsilon^2 \dfrac{[1 + b^m + 2(b^m - b)]}{(1+b)^4} \right\}} > 0 \tag{9}$$

Thus, the more the median voter is concerned with output (i.e. the higher is b^m) and the more volatile is output (i.e. the higher is σ_ϵ^2) the less conservative is the Central Banker which would be chosen in equilibrium by majority rule.

Finally, it should be stressed that in order to delegate monetary policy to an agent with preferences which are different from those of the majority of the voters, the agent must be independent. Otherwise, the median voter would want to 'recall' the Central Banker when the latter is trying to implement the conservative monetary rule. Therefore, it is important that delegation to the Central Bank is credible. Thus, we now turn to an analysis of the degree of independence of the ECB, according to the proposed statute.

3   The independence of the ECB

Measurement of the degree of autonomy of a Central Bank is far from straightforward, since there does not exist a single indicator that can properly take into account all the different aspects which are relevant in this respect. We have chosen to follow the criteria proposed by Grilli, Masciandaro and Tabellini (1991), where a distinction is introduced between political independence and economic independence of a monetary institution.[9]

3.1 Political independence of the ECB

Political independence is defined as the ability of a Central Bank to choose its economic policy objectives autonomously, without constraints or influence from the government. First, an important element protecting the autonomy of a Central Bank is the guarantee for the governor and for the board of directors of a sufficiently long term of office. Short terms of office could make the directorate of the bank more vulnerable to political opportunistic pressures because of the almost constant uncertainty about their reappointment.[10] In addition, short appointments increase the likelihood that every government (even a short-lived one) appoints a new Central Banker; this would increase the volatility in the conduct of monetary policy (Alesina, 1989). The proposed statute of the ECB sets the term of office for the President at eight years (Art. 11.2), the same as for the Bundesbank. For all the other Central Banks with a specific duration at the President's office, the term is shorter; for example, in the UK it is five years and in Spain it is four years. In Italy, France and Denmark, the governor's mandate does not have an explicit duration. This, however, does not imply a life appointment. On the contrary, as has happened in the past, this could facilitate sudden dismissal of the governor.

Turning now to the board of the ECB, we first notice that the statute of the ECB envisages the creation of two different decision-making bodies: the Council and the Executive Committee, which is a subset of the Council. The Executive Committee is supposed to be elected by the European Council of Prime Ministers for an eight-year term. The other members of the Council are the twelve governors of the EEC national central banks. The duration of their mandate, therefore, will depend on the various national regulations. However, the ECB stature prescribes (Art. 14) a minimum term of five years for all the Council's members. This will require changes in the statutes of the banks of Greece and Spain for which the current term of the governor is four years. The eight-year term of the ECB board is identical to the term of the board of the Bundesbank, and is longer than that of any other European country. For example, in France it is six years, in the UK it is four and in Italy it is three.

A second important factor determining the autonomy of a central bank from political pressures is whether the statute of the bank prescribes an explicit participation of the government in monetary policy decisions. This participation could be in the form of the requirement of a formal approval by the government of monetary policy and/or in the form of the presence of government officials on the central bank board. The proposed statute of the ECB explicitly forbids any representative of the European Council to be part of the ECB's Council (Art. 15.1). The statute only allows the passive presence, i.e. without vote, of a small number of EEC officials at the Board meetings. Moreover, the statute does not require approval of monetary policy either by the EEC institutions, or by national governments. In fact, it explicitly forbids (Art. 7) the members of the ECB's Board to receive any instructions from either community or national political institutions. These regulations are very similar to those of the Bundesbank, and are much stricter than most of the other EEC Central Banks. For example, both in France and in the UK, government representatives are part of the respective Central Bank boards, and monetary policy must be explicitly approved by the government.

In addition, the ability of a Central Bank to pursue its own objectives without political interference is enhanced if these objectives are explicitly stated in the Central Bank statute and thus cannot be easily and arbitrarily changed by the particular government in power. Article 2.1 of the ECB statute states that the main objective of the ECB is price stability. Again, the similarity between the proposed ECB and the Bundesbank is evident. Amongst the EEC countries, only the Central Banks of Denmark and the Netherlands, in addition to the Bundesbank, have the objective of price stability explicitly stated in their statutes. The statement of general price stability objective in the statute of the ECB, although important, is far from a guarantee that the first-best, i.e. the zero average inflation policy given in (3'), becomes enforceable. In our opinion, the statement of price stability as a 'main objective' should be interpreted simply as a measure to protect the ECB board against unavoidable political pressures to pursue short-run expansionary policies, particularly in times of economic distress. It is therefore a way of increasing the independence of the ECB but, by itself, cannot eliminate the time-consistency problem. If credibility problems could be avoided, and first-best policies implemented, by simply writing general objectives into Central Bank statutes, we would not observe so much discussion on monetary institutions and monetary controls.

3.2   Economic independence of the ECB

The second dimension of autonomy of a Central Bank is its economic independence, that is, the ability to use without restrictions monetary policy instruments to pursue monetary policy goals. Specifically, the most important and common constraint to the daily management of monetary policy derives from the Central Bank's obligation to finance public deficits. This constraint is particularly important for countries with high levels of public debt, like Belgium, Ireland and Italy. The similarity between the ECB and the Bundesbank, in this respect also, is quite

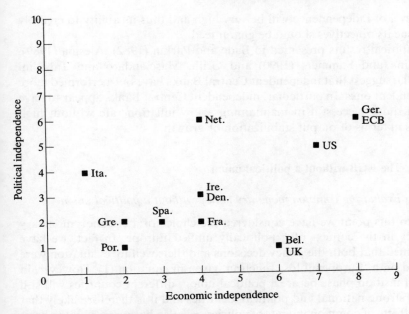

Figure 3.1   **Central bank autonomy in Europe**

striking. In particular, Article 21.1 forbids the ECB to open lines of credit to community or national public institutions, even on a temporary basis. The same article bans the ECB from participating in the primary market for national government bonds. The ECB is allowed to participate only in secondary markets for government bonds to implement 'open market operations.' This arrangement is very different from the situation in France and Italy, for example, where the Central Banks are allowed to grant credit facilities to their Finance Ministries.

Tables 3A.1 and 3A.2 in the Appendix summarize the political and economic independence of the ECB and compare it to that of the other EEC central banks and the US Federal Reserve. The results of these tables are plotted in Figure 3.1. As already mentioned at the beginning of this section, these indexes must be interpreted with caution. For example, while from the tables the Bundesbank and the Federal Reserve may appear to be highly independent, they are still subject to political inter-ference. As it should be clear from the discussion above, however, the similarities between ECB and the Bundesbank are pervasive. In fact, according to our classification, they practically coincide, and they are far more independent than any other EEC central bank.

In conclusion, if the ECB is created according to this proposed statute, its level of independence will be very high and thus its ability to credibly pursue its objectives should be guaranteed.

Empirical results presented in Bade and Parkin (1982), Alesina (1989), Alesina and Summers (1990) and Grilli, Masciandaro and Tabellini (1991), suggest that independent Central Banks have out-performed more dependent ones. In particular, independent Central Banks appear to have been quite successful in maintaining a low inflation rate without high costs in terms of output stabilization or growth.

4   The ECB without a political union

4.1   Evaluating common monetary policy without a political union

Up to this point we have considered the choice of a common monetary policy in the context of a politically unified Europe. In fact, we have assumed that both the policy decisions and their welfare evaluation were based on a 'European' loss function, given in equation (1). However, in the transition phase before a political union, different countries will still have strong national and political identities and it is therefore likely that the effects of common monetary policies will also be assessed on the basis of national welfare and preferences. In other words, while monetary policy will be set at the European level, thus following (1) and (2), each country will evaluate the consequence of the policy according to its national welfare function, which can be represented by:

$$\mathcal{L}^i = \tfrac{1}{2}\,\mathscr{E}[\pi_E^2 + \beta_i\,(y_i - \bar{y}_i)^2] \tag{10}$$

where

$$y_i = (\pi_E - \pi_E^e) + \mu_i \tag{11}$$

y_i is the output level of country i and μ_i is a country-specific stochastic shock. Notice that, being in a common currency world, we have assumed that inflation is the same in all countries, equal to the European level π_E.[11] Substituting the ECB-time consistent policy given by (3) into (11) and (10) we obtain:

$$\mathcal{L}^i = \tfrac{1}{2}\,\mathscr{E}[(b\bar{x}_E - \frac{b}{1+b}\,\epsilon)^2 + \beta_i\,(\mu_i - \frac{b}{1+b}\,\epsilon - \bar{y}_i)^2] \tag{12}$$

which represents the welfare level achieved by country i when monetary policy is decided at the European level, according to the rule given in (3). We can compare (12) with the loss that would be suffered if, instead, monetary policies were to remain under national control. Following a procedure identical to the one employed to derive (3), we obtain that, in this case, the time-consistent inflation policy for country i is:

$$\pi_i = \beta_i \bar{y}_i - \frac{\beta_i}{1 + \beta_i} \mu_i \tag{13}$$

Output would then be given by:

$$y_i = \frac{1}{1 + \beta_i} \mu_i \tag{14}$$

Therefore, the loss in this scenario is given by:

$$\mathscr{L}_N^i = \tfrac{1}{2} \mathscr{E}\left[\left(\beta_i \bar{y}_i - \frac{\beta_i}{1 + \beta_i} \mu_i \right)^2 + \beta_i \left(\frac{1}{1 + \beta_i} \mu_i - \bar{y}_i \right)^2 \right] \tag{15}$$

Subtracting (15) from (12) we obtain the difference in welfare between a monetary union and a world in which monetary policies are set at the national level:[12]

$$\mathscr{L}^i - \mathscr{L}_N^i = \tfrac{1}{2} \left[\bar{x}^2 (b^2 - \beta_i^2) + (1 + \beta_i) \left\{ \left(\frac{b}{1 + b} \right)^2 \sigma_\epsilon^2 - \left(\frac{\beta_i}{1 + \beta_i} \right)^2 \sigma_\mu^2 \right\} \right.$$
$$\left. - 2\beta_i \left\{ \left(\frac{b}{1 + b} \right) \sigma_{\epsilon\mu} - \left(\frac{\beta_i}{1 + \beta_i} \right) \sigma_\mu^2 \right\} \right] \tag{16}$$

where σ_μ^2 is the variance of μ_i and $\sigma_{\epsilon\mu}$ the covariance between μ_i and ϵ. Notice that, to economize notation, we dropped the subscript i on σ_μ. For simplicity, we have also assumed $\bar{x}_E = \bar{y}_i \equiv \bar{x}$.

4.2 Country-specific costs of common monetary policies

Equation (16) highlights two distinct components of the difference in welfare under a monetary union instead of deciding monetary policy independently. The first component depends on political divergencies, i.e. differences in preferences as represented by differences between b and β_i. The second component depends on economic dissimilarities as summarized by σ_ϵ, σ_μ and $\sigma_{\epsilon\mu}$.

Consider first the political differences, and to better focus on them let us eliminate the economic differences by assuming $\mu_i = \epsilon$ in all states of the world, so that $\sigma_\mu^2 = \sigma_\epsilon^2 = \sigma_{\epsilon\mu} \equiv \sigma^2$. Then (16) becomes:

$$\mathscr{L}^i - \mathscr{L}_N^i = \tfrac{1}{2} \left[\bar{x}^2 (b^2 - \beta_i^2) + \sigma^2 \left(\frac{b}{1 + b} - \frac{\beta_i}{1 + \beta_i} \right) \left(\frac{1 + \beta_i}{1 + b} b - \beta_i \right) \right] \tag{17}$$

Equation (17) reveals that participation in a monetary union can improve welfare if the ECB preferences are more conservative than the national preferences, i.e. $b < \beta_i$. This is a restatement of the result of Section 2. A monetary union can be beneficial if it allows countries to 'buy' credibility for anti-inflationary policies. Therefore, the countries that have more to gain from a monetary union, in this respect, are the one with higher inflation biases.

We now turn to the economic differences. Assume, therefore, the absence of political differences, i.e. $\beta_i = b$ (and $\bar{x}_E = \bar{y}_i$ as before). Then, (16) reduces to:

$$\mathcal{L}^i - \mathcal{L}^i_N = \tfrac{1}{2}\left[\frac{b^2}{1+b}(\sigma_\epsilon^2 + \sigma_\mu^2 - 2\rho_i\sigma_\epsilon\sigma_\mu)\right] \tag{18}$$

where ρ_i is the correlation coefficient between μ_i and ϵ. Consider first the case in which the two shocks are perfectly positively correlated, i.e. $\rho_i = 1$. Then (18) becomes:

$$\mathcal{L}^i - \mathcal{L}^i_N = \tfrac{1}{2}\left[\frac{b^2}{1+b}(\sigma_\epsilon - \sigma_\mu)^2\right] \tag{19}$$

Therefore, if there are differences between the variance of national and European output, the welfare of the country will be lower in a monetary union. The intuition is clear; if $\sigma_\epsilon > \sigma_\mu$ then the ECB will be stabilizing too much from the perspective of country i while if $\sigma_\epsilon < \sigma_\mu$ the ECB will not be stabilizing enough.

Consider now the case in which European and national output have the same variability, but are not necessarily perfectly correlated, i.e. $\sigma_\mu^2 = \sigma_\epsilon^2 = \sigma^2$, but $\rho_i \neq 1$. In this case, (18) reduces to:

$$\mathcal{L}^i - \mathcal{L}^i_N = \tfrac{1}{2}\left[\frac{b^2}{1+b}\sigma_\epsilon^2(1-\rho_i)\right] \tag{20}$$

Therefore, the smaller is the correlation between μ_i and ϵ the worse off country i is made by its participation in the monetary union. This is because, if ρ_i is low, the ECB will be constantly either over or under stabilizing from the point of view of country i. For example, in the extreme case of perfect negative correlation the ECB would be, contracting when country i experiences a recession, and expanding when country i experiences a boom.

Summarizing, the costs of joining a monetary union depend on the differences in behaviour between national and European output. The larger the differences in output variances and the lower the correlation between domestic and European output, the higher is the potential cost of being part of a monetary union.

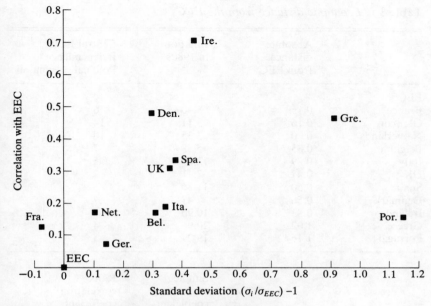

Figure 3.2   Economic distance from the EEC, 1970–89

Following this line of argument, in Figure 3.2 we measure the 'economic distance' from the EEC of the twelve EEC countries according to the standard deviations and the correlation coefficients of the growth rate of their outputs.

Some caution is necessary when inspecting Figure 3.2, since the output series that we observe are the result of national monetary policy which should be excluded from analysis. In fact, output variances and correlations reflect the type and degree of intervention that the national monetary authorities have exerted over the last 20 years.

Figure 3.2 shows that the countries which have more to lose from a monetary union, from a stabilization point of view, are the countries at the periphery of Europe: Greece, Portugal and Ireland, while the least affected will be France, Germany and The Netherlands.

This conclusion, however, does not take into account the 'credibility gains,' discussed above, that can result from a participation in the union, which could compensate for the 'economic distance' from the EEC.[13] In Table 3.1 we report, for each country, our index of 'economic distance' from the EEC, together with the degree of independence of its central bank and its inflation performance during the 1980s. From this table emerges the interesting fact that the countries that have more to lose from

Table 3.1. *Economic distance from the EEC*

	Absolute distance from EEC[a]	Inflation in 1980s %	Central Bank Independence Political + economic
EEC			14
France	0.15	8.40	6
Germany	0.16	3.11	14
Netherlands	0.20	3.35	10
Belgium	0.35	5.58	7
Italy	0.39	12.80	5
UK	0.47	7.71	7
Spain	0.50	11.36	5
Denmark	0.56	7.47	7
Ireland	0.83	10.90	7
Greece	1.02	20.96	4
Portugal	1.16	19.27	3

	Simple correlation coefficient	Rank correlation coefficient
Distance, inflation	0.86	0.69
Distance, independence	−0.66	−0.66
Inflation, independence	−0.82	−9.93

Note: [a] Computed as: $\left[\left(\dfrac{\sigma_i}{\sigma_{EEC}}\right)^2 + (1 - \rho_i)^2\right]^{1/2}$

the stabilization point of view are also the ones that could gain more in terms of credibility of their monetary policies. For example, Portugal, Greece, Ireland and Spain are among the countries with the largest distance from the EEC and, at the same time, the countries with the most dependent central banks and highest inflation. The simple correlation coefficient between distance and inflation is 0.86, and between distance and central bank independence is −0.66. An important question which can be raised regarding this 'credibility gains' explanation of the monetary union is why the countries who do not need credibility, i.e. the 'low β' countries would want to join the union. Even though, according to Table 3.1, the 'low β' are also those more correlated with Europe, thus have less to lose, it is not clear why they would want to engage in this process. The answer has to be that they gain on other grounds, such as the reduction of transaction costs and monetary uncertainty (see Casella, 1991) or the gain from cooperation in monetary policy, which are not explicitly modelled here. More generally, a widely shared view (see Krugman, 1989, for instance) of the process of European economic integration, is that the economic gains are only one part of the story and, perhaps, not the most important. Long-run political gains resulting from the creation of a 'European nation' may be important considerations.

4.3 Appointing the EBC Council without a political union

In the analysis above we have assumed that the characteristic of the ECB (i.e. b) is exogenously given. However, the ECB policy will be decided by a Council that is composed by the national central bank governors. Therefore, each country has the opportunity to participate and affect the policy choice through its central bank governor. Through the choice of the central bank governor, therefore, each country has the opportunity to compensate for its 'economic distance' from the EEC by appointing a governor with appropriate preferences. Given that the ECB Council decisions are taken under majority rule, the policy that will be implemented is the one that is (*ex-post*) preferred by the 'median' Council member. Therefore, the intensity of preference of each governor does not matter for the policy decision and, thus, a country does not have any strategic incentive to misrepresent its own preferences (in addition to the reasons discussed above). Consequently, the optimal appointment of governor for country i is formally obtained by selecting a governor with a b that minimizes (12). The first-order condition determining this choice is given by:

$$b\bar{x}_E^2 + (1 + \beta_i)\frac{b}{(1 + b)^3}\sigma_\epsilon^2 - \frac{\beta_i}{(1 + b)^2}\sigma_{\epsilon\mu} = 0 \qquad (21)$$

Taking the total differential of (21) it can be shown that:

$$\frac{\partial b}{\partial \sigma_\mu} = \frac{\beta_i\rho_i\sigma_\epsilon}{(1 + b)\{(1 + 3b)\bar{x}^2 + (1 + \beta_i)\sigma_\epsilon^2/(1 + b)^3\}} > 0 \qquad (22)$$

$$\frac{\partial b}{\partial \rho_i} = \frac{\beta_i\sigma_\epsilon\sigma_\mu}{(1 + b)\{(1 + 3b)\bar{x}^2 + (1 + \beta_i)\sigma_\epsilon^2/(1 + b)^3\}} > 0 \qquad (23)$$

Therefore, the smaller the variance of domestic output, and the smaller the correlation between domestic and European output, the more conservative will be the representative chosen for the ECB Council. This is because, if the correlation is low, country i would prefer an ECB which does not stabilize much, since the latter would often stabilize in the wrong direction from the point of view of country i.

We now turn to examine how the objective function of the ECB will be determined, according to the proposed procedures.

5   Voting on European monetary policy

The proposed rules concerning the appointment and voting procedures of the board of the ECB are as follows. The Board is composed of 18 members: the 12 governors of the national central banks plus six members, including the Governor of the ECB, who are appointed by the European Council. These six members also form the Executive Committee of the ECB. The Board votes by majority rule, one person one vote. The Governor's vote has a tie-breaking power. The only exception to the 'one person one vote' rule concerns decisions over the allocation of the seigniorage across countries.

The draft of the statute (at least the version which has been made public), does not specify explicitly the voting rule which has to be adopted by the European Council in choosing the six members which form the Executive Committee of the ECB. Presumably, this voting rule will reflect the relative size of the members of the EEC.[14] The European Council usually deliberates using a qualified majority rule, in which a proposal needs more than 70 per cent of the votes to be approved. The weights are designed so that the four biggest countries alone (Germany, France, United Kingdom and Italy) do not have the required 70 percent majority.

The proposed composition of board clearly reflects that the authors of the statute had two goals in mind. On one hand, they intended to guarantee a 'voice' to every country, even the smallest ones, by including every governor of the national central banks. On the other hand, if the board were composed only by these 12 central bankers, the smaller countries would be overrepresented. The six members, including the Governor, reequilibrate the weights.

An important question can then be asked: how successful will this system of appointments and voting rules be in representing the views of the European voters? The following simple example suggests that such rules may be quite unsuccessful in reflecting the preferences of the European voters. Suppose, for the sake of simplicity, and no loss of generality, that the twelve countries were of equal size. Suppose that in each country there were two parties, 'left' (L) and 'right' (R). In seven countries R has a 51% plurality and holds the position of Prime Minister. In five countries L has a 55% plurality and the Prime Minister. In this case, in a politically unified Europe, L would have a majority. With the proposed rules, instead, the governor and the executive board would be elected by an R majority in the European Council of Prime Ministers. This is of course, a well known problem in the context of election of legislatures with a district system.[15]

In order to emphasize how different outcomes may result from differing voting rules, we have considered, as an example, the results of the last general elections in the twelve EEC countries. We proceeded as follows. In each country we have divided the political parties into five groups: (1) 'extreme left' (EL) which includes communist parties, other minor extremists groups and radical 'green' parties; (2) 'left' (L) which includes socialists and social democratic parties; (3) 'Christian Democrats' (CD) which includes Christian Democratic parties and other centre parties; (4) 'right' (R) which includes conservative parties; and (5) 'extreme right', which includes all the right wing extremist groups.

An important assumption in the discussion which follows, is that parties can be 'aggregated' across nations; that is, for instance, we assume that all the socialist parties in the twelve countries are relatively similar to each other. It should be emphasized that parties aggregate themselves in groups in the European Parliament. In our classification we followed, whenever applicable, this European Parliament grouping.

Clearly, some 'judgment calls' are needed to make our classification, but none of these judgment calls affect the qualitative nature of the issues which we raise. In Table 3A.3 in the Appendix we illustrate our classification for the twelve countries, and we report the percentage of votes and of seats obtained in the last election.

Consider for example the case of Italy, in which the last general elections were held in June 1987. These were the results:

		% Shares	Seats
EL:	Communists, DP, Greens	30.8	138
L:	Socialists, Radical Party, Social Democratic Party, Republican Party	23.6	143
CD:	Christian Democrats, Sud Tirol Party	35.7	237
R:	Liberal Party	2.1	11
ER:	MSI	5.9	35

(Vote shares add to less than 100% due to minor unclassified parties)

We then identify the 'median voter'. In terms of shares, the median is such that on the left of the median we have EL + 82% of L; on the right of the median we have 18% of L + CD + R + ER. We indicate this median in terms of *shares* (m(sh)) with L19, which indicates that the median lies

Table 3.2. *'Median voters' in Europe*

	m(sh)[1]	m(seats)[2]	PM[3]	Population weights[4]
Belgium	CD 48	CD 35	CD	3.1
Denmark	CD 57	CD 66	R	1.6
France	L 4	L 23	L	17.2
Germany	CD 90	CD 91	CD	18.8
Greece	L 5	R 100	R	3.1
Ireland	R 78	R 89	R	1.1
Italy	L 19	L 20	CD	17.7
Luxembourg	CD 70	CD 69	CD	0.1
Netherlands	CD 66	CD 66	CD	4.5
Portugal	CD 91	CD 84	CD	3.2
Spain	L 20	L 20	L	12.0
UK	CD 15	R 85	R	17.6
EU	CD 80	CD 56[5] CD 33/15[6]		

Notes:
1 m(sh) = median in shares. See text for the definition.
2 m(seats) = median in seats. See text for the definition.
3 PM = political orientation of the current (March 1991) Prime Minister.
4 Population weights = percentage shares of the population of each country in 1988. *Source*: IMF, *IFS*. We do not consider former East Germany since the electoral results considered are pre-German unification.
5 Weighted median.
6 Unweighted median. Since there is an even number of members the median is given by the fourth and fifth CD members, counting from the left.

within the L group with 19 per cent of it on the right of the median. the analogous procedure applied to seats leads to a median in *seats* (m(seats)) equal to L20. The fact that the two medians are basically identical underlines the high degree of proportionality of the Italian electoral system.

The first two columns of Table 3.2 report our computations of m(sh) and m(seats) for the twelve countries. These calculations are derived from the information provided in Table 3A.3 in the Appendix. The third column identifies the political orientation of the Prime Minister of the twelve countries. The last column reports the share, in percentage, of the population. As an illustration consider m(sh) of Denmark and The Netherlands. The former is CD57, indicating that 57 percent of CD parties are on the right of the median. This indicates a more right wing median than that of The Netherlands in which 66 percent of CD parties are on the right of the median.

The last line of the Table reports the European median in shares, obtained by computing (using the population weights given in the last column of the Table) the shares of different parties; the third column in this line reports the median for the case of a 'one person one vote' rule in the European Council of the Prime Ministers, and for the case of a vote weighted by the population shares.[16]

The picture emerging from Table 3.2 is quite interesting. The European median in vote shares, m(sh), is significantly on the left of the median of the European council, particularly for the case of unweighted votes. The median in terms of shares is close to the extreme left of the CD group, while the weighted median of the council of Prime Minister is around the middle of the CD group and the unweighted median is on the right of the CD group. In different words, the EL and L combined have about 44 percent of European votes (see Table 3A.3) but less than 30 percent in a weighted vote of the Prime Ministers and 15 percent in an unweighted vote in the European Council.

Let us now consider the Board of the ECB, and let us assume (with a wisp of faith) that the governors of the national Central Banks somehow reflect the preferences of the Prime Minister of their countries. Since this Council votes with a 'one man one vote' rule, the share of the 'left' will be somewhere between the 15 percent unweighted share and the 30 percent weighted share. It would be 15 percent if only national governors were in the Board; 30 percent if all the members of the board were appointed by a weighted vote in the European Council.

The possibility of large discrepancies between medians is even more emphasized by the following hypothetical example. Suppose that an election were held in France and the Socialists fell from the current 49 to say, 43 percent of the vote, leading to a victory of conservative bloc, which gains the Prime Minister position.[17] With everything else unchanged, this would imply that the European Left (EL and L) would now have about 42 percent of the popular vote, less than 12 percent of a weighted vote, and less than 10 percent in an unweighted vote of the European Council, since only Spain would have a 'L' prime minister. With this change in France the last line of Table 3.2 would read: CD 77; CD 18 and CD 15 respectively. This difference is remarkable: in terms of shares only one-fifth of CD would be needed to achieve a left wing majority, in terms of Prime Ministers only a sixth of the CD votes would be needed to achieve a right wing majority.[18] In any way one looks at this situation, it is clear that the almost 50 percent of left voters would be vastly underrepresented in the Board of the ECB.

Two important caveats, however, mitigate the extent of these observations. First, the strong Socialist minorities in countries where the Prime

Minister is non-Socialist, have some influence on policy-making. In one country (Italy) the Socialists are a powerful member of the coalition government and clearly influence the Prime Minister's behaviour in the European Council. More generally, governing parties cannot completely ignore opposition views, particularly if the opposition is strong.

Second, the ideological distance between parties, say Socialists and Conservatives, may be declining, and may be less important than 'national' differences of interests regarding monetary policy. If this is the case, what really matters is the allocation of voting rights between countries, regardless of who is the Prime Minister. However, results by Alesina and Roubini (1990) suggest that partisan differences on economic policies remain significant in several OECD economies.[19]

In summary, this section has highlighted a very simple but important point. The current decision-making rules for the European Community, including the appointment of the executive committee of the ECB, are such that the allocation of 'power' between parties may depart substantially from the relative plurality at the European level of the same parties. This is a feature which is not uncommon in district systems, but the specific nature of the European Council composed in a sense by only 12 'districts,' is more likely to create large discrepancies between the division of 'seats' in the board of the ECB and the shares of popular votes in Europe. In the example which we examined based on current electoral results, the left was disadvantaged. This does not mean, at all, that there is an anti-left bias in the rules. In fact, we would have found the opposite bias, if we had looked at the situation in the late seventies. Thus, it would be incorrect to argue that these voting rules achieve the 'conservative bias' which may be desirable for monetary policies.

This problem occurs, obviously, because the political integration of Europe is far from complete, so that a 'European' government is not formed within a European Parliament with a true legislative function and elected in universal European ballots. Note that we are not necessarily advocating that the truly empowered European Parliament should be elected with a proportional system, in which case the above mentioned discrepancies between medians would disappear by definition. However, even if, say, an English style district system were to be adopted, one certainly would not choose to have 12 districts coinciding with the current twelve country members of the EEC. In other words, there is a tension between a completely unified monetary policy and voting rules over monetary policy which appear dictated by the present European reality of politically independent member states.

6   Conclusions

In a politically unified Europe, the ECB should be an independent 'agent' to whom the European government delegates the conduct of monetary policy. The governor of the ECB should be appointed by the European Parliament and should be chosen such that his preferences are more anti-inflationary than the European median voter. In fact the median voter would vote for a Central Banker more 'conservative' than himself. The appointment process, by virtue of a universally and directly elected European Parliament would ensure that the preferences of European voters would be reflected in the conduct of monetary policy.

We have examined how the ECB as described by the proposed statute will conform to this ideal. We can summarize our argument in three basic points.

First, the proposed statute will guarantee a substantial amount of political independence to the ECB. We concluded that the ECB, according to this statute, will be as independent from national and European political institutions as the Bundesbank. In fact, the proposed statute is in many respects quite similar to that of Bundesbank. Certainly, it is much more similar to the latter than to any other Central Bank in EEC countries.

Second, we emphasized that in a situation in which the EEC is not completely unified economically and politically, different member countries may have substantially different preferences over the conduct of monetary policy. For example, we argued that countries at the periphery of Europe, such as Greece, Ireland and Portugal may have to pay the highest costs of giving up their monetary independence. However, these are also countries which will obtain high benefits in terms of 'credibility' of anti-inflationary policies. In addition, different parties within each country, in general will disagree over the conduct of the European monetary policy.

Third, we argued that the proposed system of appointment of the ECB Board and the voting rules within the Board, may lead to decisions which could be quite far from the preferences of the European median voter. For example, using the last election results in the twelve countries, we showed that the European left would be vastly under-represented in the ECB Board, relative to the proportion of votes received by the left in national elections. These discrepancies, which can be quite substantial, occur because the Board is not appointed by a legislative body elected in European elections. Instead, according to the proposed statute, the monetary policy decisions will be taken using a certain system of weights attributed to the representatives of each country. The reason why the proposed statute of the ECB ignores the European Parliament is, of course, that this body does not have any real legislative power, since a politically united 'European nation' does not exist. However, these voting rules based on a 'non-politically-unified-Europe' may misrepresent the preferences of the European voters.

It has been argued with good reasons (see Krugman, 1989, for instance) that a complete monetary union in Europe is an important intermediate step toward political union. In this paper, on the other hand, we highlighted several reasons why the working of a monetary union will depend crucially on the future political structure the European Community.

Appendix   Common monetary policy with different inflation rates

It is likely that, even if a monetary union is implemented, the rate of inflation will not be equalized across the member countries. Consider, therefore, the case in which inflation in country i is given by:

$$\pi_i = \pi_E + \delta_i \tag{A1}$$

where δ_i is a random shock with mean zero and variance σ_δ^2. In this case, equations (10) and (11) in the text become:

$$\mathcal{L}^{i'} = \tfrac{1}{2}E\,[\pi_i^2 + \beta_i\,(y_i - \bar{y}_i)^2] \tag{A2}$$

and

$$y_i = (\pi_i - \pi_i^e) + \mu_i \tag{A3}$$

respectively. Consequently, the expected welfare of country i in the union is now given by:

$$\mathcal{L}^{i'} = \tfrac{1}{2}\mathcal{E}\left[\left(b\bar{x}_E - \frac{b}{1+b}\,\epsilon + \delta_i\right)^2 + \beta_i\left(\mu_i + \delta_i - \frac{b}{1+b}\,\epsilon - \bar{y}_i\right)^2\right] \tag{A4}$$

Subtracting equation (15) from (A4), we obtain:

$$\mathcal{L}^{i'} - \mathcal{L}_N^i = \tfrac{1}{2}\left[\bar{x}^2(b^2 - \beta_i^2) + (1+\beta_i)\left\{\left(\frac{b}{1+b}\right)^2\sigma_\epsilon^2 - \left(\frac{\beta_i}{1+\beta_i}\right)^2\sigma_\mu^2\right\}\right.$$
$$\left. - 2\beta_i\left\{\left(\frac{b}{1+b}\right)\sigma_{\epsilon\mu} - \left(\frac{\beta_i}{1+\beta_i}\right)\sigma_\mu^2\right\} + \beta_i\{\sigma_\delta^2 + 2\rho_{\delta\mu}\sigma_\delta\sigma_\mu\}\right] \tag{A5}$$

$$= [\mathcal{L}^i - \mathcal{L}_N^i] + \beta_i\{\sigma_\delta^2 + 2\rho_{\delta\mu}\sigma_\delta\sigma_\mu\}$$

where $\rho_{\delta\mu}$ is the correlation coefficient between δ_i and μ_i, and we have assumed that δ_i and ϵ are independent. Therefore, unless $\rho_{\delta\mu}$ is sufficiently negative to compensate for σ_δ^2, the results are now less favourable to a monetary union than in the case discussed in the text. The rest of the analysis of Section 4, however, remains unchanged.

Data Appendix

Table 3A.1. *Political independence of central banks*[20]

	Appointments				Relationship with government		Constitution		Index of political independence
	1	2	3	4	5	6	7	8	9
Belgium			*						1
Denmark	*						*	*	3
France	*	*							2
Germany	*	*	*		*		*	*	6
Greece		*						*	2
Ireland	*					*		*	3
Italy	*	*	*		*				4
Netherlands	*	*	*		*		*	*	6
Portugal					*				1
Spain			*	*					2
UK					*				1
US			*	*	*		*	*	5
ECB		*		*	*	*	*	*	6

Notes
1 = Governor not appointed by government.
2 = Governor appointed for > 5 years.
3 = Board not appointed by government.
4 = Board appointed for > 5 years.
5 = No mandatory participation of government representative in the Board.
6 = No government approval of monetary policy is required.
7 = Statutory requirements that central bank pursues monetary stability.
8 = Explicit conflicts between bank and government are possible.
9 = Overall index of political independence, constructed as the number of asterisks in each row.

Comments on the European Central Bank
1 = President appointed by European Council (Art. 11.2).
2 = President appointed for 8 years (Art. 11.2).
3 = Council members: 6 Members of Executive Board: appointed by European Council (Art. 11.3). 12 Governors of National Central Banks: appointed according to their national rules, thus mostly by national governments.
4 = Council members: 6 Members of Executive Board: appointed for 8 years (Art. 11.3). 12 Governors of National Central Banks: appointed for at least 5 years (Art. 14).

Table 3A.1 (*cont.*)

5 = Council of European Communities representative and/or European Commission representtive may attend meetings of the Council, but they are not part of the Council itself, and thus they cannot vote (Art. 15.1).
6 = Neither the ECB, nor the national central banks, nor the other members of the Council may seek or take any instruction from Community institutions, governments of Member States or any other body (Art. 7).
7 = The primary objective of the System shall be to maintain price stability (Art. 2.1).
8 = Explicit conflicts between bank and government are possible (Art. 2.2 and Art. 7).
Source: Data for the eleven national Central Banks are from Grilli *et al.* (1991).

Table 3A.2. *Economic independence of central banks*

	Monetary financing of budget deficit					Monetary instruments			Index of economic independence
	1	2	3	4	5	6	7	8	9
Belgium		*	*	*	*	*		*	6
Denmark		*			*	*	*		4
France			*	*		*	*		4
Germany	*	*	*	*	*	*	*	*	8
Greece				*		*			2
Ireland		*	*	*		*			4
Italy				*					1
Netherlands			*	*		*	*		4
Portugal				*		*			2
Spain				*	*			*	3
UK	*	*	*	*		*	*		6
US	*	*	*	*		*	*	*	7
ECB	*	*	*	*	*	*	*	*	8

Notes
1 = Direct credit facility: not automatic.
2 = Direct credit facility: market interest rate.
3 = Direct credit facility: temporary.
4 = Direct credit facility: limited amount.
5 = Central bank does not participate in primary market for public debt.
6 = Discount rate set by central bank.
7 = No portfolio constraints in place since 1980.
8 = No bank loan ceilings in place since 1980.
9 = Overall index of economic independence (being the number of asterisks in columns 1–8).

Comments on the European Central Bank
1 = No Direct credit facility (Art. 21.1).
2 = Purchase of Treasury bonds only on secondary market, thus at market rate (Art. 21.1).
3 = Credit facility never allowed, not even on a temporary basis (Art. 21.1).
4 = Zero amount (Art. 21.1).
5 = Central bank does not participate in primary market for public debt (Art. 21.1).
6 = The Council shall formulate decisions relating to intermediate monetary objectives, key interest rates and supply of reserves (Art. 12.1).
7 = Portfolio constraints are not part of the list of functions the ECB can perform (Art. 18 & Commentary page 10).
8 = The imposition of bank loan ceilings is not part of the list of functions the ECB can perform (Art. 18 & Commentary page 10).
Source: Data for the eleven national Central Banks are from Grilli, Masciandaro and Tabellini (1991).

Table 3A.3. *Electoral data*

	% Shares	Seats
Belgium: Election date 12/87.		
EL: Communist Parties;	0.6	0
L: Socialists (SP and PS);	30.6	72
CD Christian Democrats (CSP and PSC);	35.5	79
R: Party for Freedom and Progress (PVV), Liberal Reformists (PRL);	20.9	48
ER: Flemish Bloc.	1.9	1
Denmark: Election date 5/88.		
EL: Communist Party, Left Socialist Party;	1.4	0
L: Socialist People's Party, Social Democratic Party;	42.9	79
CD Christian Democrats Radical Liberal;	12.3	23
R: Conservative Party, Liberal Party;	31.1	57
ER: Progress Party	10.9	16
France: Election date 6/88.[*]		
EL: Communist Party;	3.4	27
L: Socialist Party and various affiliates;	48.7	276
CD Rally for Republic; ⎫		
R: Union for French Democracy; ⎬	46.8[**]	178
various conservative groups; ⎭		
ER: National Front	1.1	1

[*]   Second Ballot.
[**] In the computations we classified this center/right coalition of parties as R. This is, however, inessential for our results since the median is within L.

Table 3A.3 (*cont.*)

Germany: Election date 1/87.

EL:	Greens;	8.3	42
L:	Social Democrats;	37.0	186
CD:	Christian Democrats (CDU/CSU);	44.3	223
R:	FDP;	9.1	42

Greece: Election date 11/89.

EL:	Communist Parties and various left wing affiliates;	12.5	21
L:	Socialists (PASOK);	40.7	128
CD:			
R:	New Democracy.	46.2	148

Ireland: Election date 6/83.

EL:	Workers' Party;	5.0	7
L:	Labour Party;	9.5	15
CD:	Fine Gael;	27.1	51
R:	Fianna Fail, Progressive Democrats.	56.0	95

Italy: Election date 6/87.

EL:	Communists, DP, Greens;	30.8	198
L:	Socialists, Social Democrats, Republicans; Radicals.	23.6	145
CD:	Christian Democrats, Sud Tirol Party;	35.7	237
R:	Liberals;	2.1	11
ER:	Social Movement.	5.9	35

Luxembourg: Election date 6/89.

EL:	Communist Party; Green Parties.	13.4	4
L:	Socialists;	27.2	18
CD:	Christian Democrats;	31.7	22
R:	Democratic Party (PD).	16.2	11
ER:			

Netherlands: Election date 3/89.

EL:	Left wing group (Groen Links);	4.1	6
L:	Socialists;	34.2	52
CD:	Christian Democrats;	37.6	54
R:	People's Party for Freedom and Progress, Democrat 66.	20.8	31

Portugal: Election date 7/87.

EL:	Communist Party;	12.1	31
L:	Socialist Party Democratic Renewal Party;	27.1	67
CD:	Social Democratic Party;	50.2	148
R:	Democratic Social Culture.	4.4	4

Spain: Election date 6/86.[*]

EL:	Communists, Bascs;	6.1	13
L:	Socialists;	44.3	184
CD:	Center Parties (PP, CIV, CDS).	40.5	142

[*]   An election was held in October 1989 followed by disputes about allocations of seats due to alleged irregularities. Since complete results for the 1989 elections were not immediately available in this draft we used the 1986 election results.

** Since the median is within the Socialist Party, it is irrelevant for our analysis how we classify this group of parties in the R or CD categories.

United Kingdom: Election date 6/87.

L:	Labour Party;	30.8	229
CD:	Liberals;	22.6	22
R:	Conservatives.	42.3	375

Note: Vote shares add to less than 100% due to minor unclassified parties.

NOTES

Alesina gratefully acknowledges financial support from the Sloan Foundation. We thank our discussants Peter Bofinger and Luigi Spaventa, Matt Canzoneri, several conference participants, James Alt, Howard Rosenthal, Kenneth Shepsle and participants at the NBER macro and international seminars for helpful comments, and Gerald Cohen and Raiko Mancini for research assistance.

 1 We do not intend to examine all the many macroeconomic issues relevant for the process of European monetary integration. For instance, we do not address the important problem of fiscal convergence. We believe that the simple model focusing on inflation and output stabilization is sufficiently rich to highlight our basic message.
 2 See Persson and Tabellini (1990a) for an in depth discussion of this model and for a survey of the releant literature.
 3 We could assume, more realistically, that the ECB controls money supply rather than inflation, and add a 'quantity equation' to close the model. This more general specification complicates the algebra without providing any additional insights.
 4 In fact, if the ECB 'announces' the rule (3') and the public believes such an announcement and expects then the ECB has an incentive to deviate from (3') and implement a policy with a positive average inflation rate.
 5 See Canzoneri (1985) for a discussion of monetary rules with asymmetric information over the realization of shocks.
 6 A similar problem in the context of capital taxation is studied in Persson and Tabellini (1990b).
 7 This is because the preferences which have postulated are of the 'intermediate' type as defined by Grandmont (1978). That is, even though two issues are considered (inflation and output stabilization) voters' preferences differ only in one parameter, *b*. As a result preferences are single-peaked.
 8 Lohmann (1991) has recently extended Rogoff's framework by showing that it is optimal to set a high but finite cost of 'firing' the governor. By choosing a finite cost of 'firing' the governor, society can ensure that in case of 'really bad' realizations of the output shock, the governor will take into account society's preferences for more 'accommodation', for fear of being fired. This argument is not pursued here.
 9 The classification proposed by Grilli *et al* (1990) extends and improves upon earlier work by Bade and Parkin (1982).
10 For an insightful discussion of the effects of the 'reappointment incentive' for governors of central banks, see Alt (1991).

11 In the appendix we analyse the case in which inflation is not equalized across the member countries of the monetary union. The results, however, are not qualitatively different from those discussed above.

12 In pursuing this comparision we are assuming, somewhat unrealistically, that the country shocks (μ_i) are the same under independent policy-making and monetary union.

13 For a discussion of the 'credibility' gains of joining a common currency area see Giavazzi and Giovannini (1989).

14 The weights usually adopted in the European Council are as follows: 10 votes each for Germany, France, Italy and the United Kingdom; 8 votes for Spain; 5 votes for Belgium, Greece, the Netherlands and Portugal; 3 votes for Denmark and Ireland and 2 votes for Luxembourg.

15 For an excellent overview of the issues on the theory of elections of legislatures in a district system see Austen-Smith (1987) and the references cited therein.

16 In computing the 'European median' we ignored, on purpose, the results for the election of the European Parliament. At least until now, this legislative body has been virtually powerless. There is evidence that European voters have used European elections to send 'signals' to their national governments or expressed 'protest votes.' It is very likely that the allocation of seats and shares in the European Parliament could be substantially different if such a body had a legislative authority. Note that the proposed statute of the ECB completely ignores the European Parliament by not granting to this body any role in the appointment or supervision of the board.

17 In what follows, we classify as R the Prime Minister emerging from this hypothetical Socialist loss in France.

18 To be precise, with a 'one person one vote rule' one-sixth of CD (i.e. one vote) would lead to a tie, since there would be 5R, 1CD against 1L, 5CD.

19 These results are consistent with earlier findings by Alt (1985), Paldam (1989a,b) and Alesina (1989).

REFERENCES

Alesina, Alberto (1989): 'Politics and Business Cycles in Industrial Democracies', *Economic Policy* 4, (8), 55–98.

Alesina, Alberto and Nouriel Roubini (1990). 'Political Cycles in OECD Economies', NBER Working Paper No. 3478.

Alesina, Alberto and Larry Summers (1990): 'Central Bank independence and economic performance: Some comparative evidence', unpublished.

Alt, James (1985): 'Political Parties, World Demand, and Unemployment: Domestic and International Sources of Economic Activity', *American Political Science Review* 79, 1016–40.

(1991). 'Leaning into the wind or ducking out of the storm', forthcoming in Alberto Alesina and Geoffrey Carliner (Eds), *Politics and Economics in the 1980s*, University of Chicago Press and NBER.

Austen-Smith David (1987): 'Parties, Districts and the Spatial Theory of Elections', *Social Choice and Welfare*, 4, 9–23.

Bade, R. and M. Parkin (1982), 'Central Bank Laws and Inflation – A Comparative Analysis,' mimeo, University of Western Ontario.

Barro, Robert and David Gordon (1983). 'Rules, Discretion, and Reputation in a Model of Monetary Policy', *Journal of Monetary Economics* **12**, 101–22.

Canzoneri, Matthew (1985): 'Monetary Policy Games and the Role of Private Information', *American Economic Review* **75**, 1056–70.

Casella, Alessandra (1991): 'The Impact of Monetary Unification on the Composition of Markets', unpublished.

Giavazzi, Francesco and Alberto Giovannini (1989). *Limiting Exchange Rate Flexibility: The European Monetary System*, M.I.T. Press.

Grandmont, Jean Michel (1978): 'Intermediate Preferences and the Majority Rule' *Econometrica*, **50**, 317–30.

Grilli, Vittorio, Donato Masciandaro, and Guido Tabellini (1991): 'Political and Monetary Institutions and Public Finance Policies in the Industrial Democracies', *Economic Policy* **6**, (13), forthcoming.

International Monetary Fund. *'International Financial Statistics'*, various issues.

Krugman, Paul (1989): 'Policy Problems of a Monetary Union', unpublished.

Kydland, Finn and Edward Prescott (1977): 'Rules Rather Than Discretion: The Inconsistency of Optimal Plans', *Journal of Political Economy* **85**, 473–90.

Lohmann, Suzanne, (1991): 'Optimal Commitment in Monetary Policy: Credibility vs. Flexibility,' *American Economic Review*, forthcoming.

Paldam, Martin (1989a): 'Politics Matter after all: Testing Hibbs' Theory of Partisan Cycles,' Aarhus University Working Paper.

Persson, Torsten and Guido Tabellini (1990a). *Macroeconomic Policy, Credibility and Politics,'* Harwood Academic Publishers.

(1990b): 'Capital Taxation and Representative Democracy', manuscript.

Rogoff, Kenneth (1985): 'The Optimal Degree of Commitment to an Intermediate Monetary Target', *The Quarterly Journal of Economics* **100**, 1169–90.

Discussion

PETER BOFINGER

This paper by Alberto Alesina and Vittorio Grilli is an important theoretical contribution to the debate on the establishment of a European Central Bank, which is very much dominated by political considerations. Its main innovations are the application of the time-inconsistency model and of the median-voter model to this issue.

Their approach raises three questions:

– Is it really necessary and in the interest of monetary policy that the division of 'seats' on the board of the ECB coincides with the shares of popular votes in Europe?

– Is the loss function, on which the time-inconsistency literature is based, really the loss function of a rational voter?
– Is it sufficient to copy the model of the Bundesbank Act at the European level if one wants to guarantee price stability in Europe?

The answer to the first question depends crucially on the overall approach to the design of a European Central Bank. In this respect the paper offers two different propositions:

– In Section 3 it presents the widely accepted notion that a central bank has to be designed as a politically independent institution, which is mainly committed to the target of price stability.
– In Section 5 a completely different view is adopted. Here the authors regard a central bank as an institution which should minimize the loss function of the European median voter as far as possible, an assignment which includes not only price stability but also an output target above the natural rate. According to this approach the authors come to the result that – in contrast to the ECB's draft statute – the members of the ECB board should not be appointed by the European Parliament.

It is obvious that the two alternative approaches lead to quite different statutes for the ECB. In this regard it is astonishing that the authors address only the relatively minor point of the appointment process of the ECB Board. If one adopted their idea of a central bank, which has to minimize the loss function of the median voter, in a consistent way, the future ECB would have to be entirely different from its present outline:
– the target of price stability would have to be abandoned as it might be incompatible with the preferences of the median voter,
– the terms of the members of the Board should not be longer than or identical with the terms of the European Parliament – otherwise an even greater under-representation of some parties might occur,
– instead of a federatively structured ECB, which will give national governments of small countries too great an influence on the nomination process of the members of the ECB Council, a strongly centralized system should be adopted.

These examples may suffice. It is evident that the Alesina-Grilli critique, if one takes it seriously, cannot be limited to the nomination procedure alone. It would require an ECB which has not very much in common with the blueprint which the authors accept in Section 3.

This inconsistency leads to an interesting question: how can it be that the outline of the ECB, which was drafted by the European Central Bank Governors in 1990, leads to an institution which does not minimize the loss function of the European median voter? The answer requires a more detailed analysis of the model of Barro and Gordon (1983) that underlies the first main part of the paper. Above all one has to ask whether the voters' loss function is adequately described by this model. As the paper shows, the inflationary bias of central banks depends on the existence of a target value for output which is above the natural rate. Although this loss function is widely accepted in the literature, it cannot be regarded as an adequate representation of the loss function of private individuals. By assumption the natural rate of output is obtained in an optimization process of the individuals reflecting all distortions of the economy. From their perspective a level of output above the natural rate is identical with a real wage rate which is lower than the disutility of their work. Thus, the target output level of a rational voter should always be identical with the natural rate. If one would formulate the social loss function in this way, one could easily recognize that the inflationary bias of monetary policy would vanish. In other words, a central bank which was committed to the target of price stability would always represent the preferences of the European median voter. This is supported by the empirical evidence which shows that countries with low (and predictable) inflation rates experienced higher real growth rates than other countries.

Thus, at least for rational voters, it is possible to solve the contradiction between a politically independent central bank committed to the target of price stability and a central bank which tries to minimize the loss function of the median voter. With such voters both approaches are identical. The design of an ECB would be more or less irrelevant.

In reality, however, most voters, especially outside Germany are familiar neither with the empirical evidence nor with the theoretical literature. Thus, one comes to the not very democratic solution that it is in the interest of the population to shield monetary policy as far as possible from political influences even if this implies that some parties are not adequately represented in the nomination process. The democratic legitimacy of such 'hands-tying' rests on the fact that the statutes of the ECB have to be ratified by the parliaments of all EC member countries. If they accept this approach there is no room left for the Alesina-Grilli critique.

As a final point, one has to ask whether the Bundesbank Act would provide an adequate legal framework for the ECB. As the paper mentions, there are in fact many similarities between the ECB draft statute and the Bundesbank Act. However, one should not overlook that it has also many in common with the predecessor of the Bundesbank, the 'Bank deutscher Länder'. This post-war monetary system of West Germany was established by the Military Governments of the three West Zones in 1948. It was characterized by legally independent Land Central Banks ('Landeszentralbanken') and a central institution, the 'Bank deutscher Länder', which was a common subsidiary of the Land Central Banks. Exactly this legal arrangement is now envisaged for Europe.

A second issue which is not adequately discussed in the present debate concerns the target of price stability, which is mentioned in the Bundesbank Act in a somewhat vague form. The draft statute of the ECB, however, is very precise on this point. The question is whether such a stipulation, which even in its rather unclear form was successful in Germany, will suffice to guarantee price stability in Europe. From a public choice perspective the answer would be negative. Central bankers who maximize their private utility function will only pursue price stability if this improves their public influence and their prestige. In a country like Germany, where their public has a strong preference for price stability, such microeconomic incentives lead to the intended macroeconomic outcome. In Europe, where the public has a much less pronounced preference for price stability, these microeconomic incentives for the members of the ECB Council would be much less stringent. Thus, it may not be sufficient to copy the Bundesbank Act at the European level, if one wants to achieve a low inflation rate in the European Monetary Union. The microeconomic incentives for price stability could be easily enhanced if the members of the ECB Council were given a high, but nominally fixed income over their whole term of office.

REFERENCE

Barro, Robert and David Gordon (1983), 'Rules, Discretion, and Reputation in a Model of Monetary Policy', *Journal of Monetary Economics* 12, 101–22.

LUIGI SPAVENTA

The project of a European Central Bank (ECB) has great policy relevance, but is hardly a promising subject for theory. A major merit of this paper is that good theory and neat modelling are put to excellent use for discussing the requirements and the implications of the new institution. More than a great deal of literature on the same issue, this paper provides food for thought and, owing to its analytical rigour, allows problems to be set in precise terms: some of these problems, which the paper leaves unsolved, account, as I shall argue, for the difficulties met by a rapid transition to European monetary integration. Let me first summarize briefly the main points made in the paper, and also the more relevant in view of later discussion.

The framework is the time-consistency problem facing monetary authorities which, though disliking inflation, target a level of output greater than the equilibrium rate. The known outcome is higher inflation than in the first-best solution, without any output gain. The higher the value of the parameter expressing the preference for the output target, the higher the inflation rate, but, if the economy is subject to random shocks, the lower the output variance. In the authors' views the ECB will not escape this time-consistency predicament.

In a politically unified Europe, the (directly or indirectly) elected ECB governor would (given a simple structure of preferences) be the one preferred by the European median voter. The latter – it is shown – would choose a 'Rogoff governor': one caring less for output than he does, hence more conservative than he is, and delivering as a result a lower inflation rate. Such a central banker, however, needs independence to fulfil his role and not be subject to pressures to change his policy. The (draft) statute is satisfactory in this respect as it appears to grant the ECB a high degree of independence – at least as high as that of the Bundesbank.

Without political union, a common inflation rate will coexist with different national preferences regarding the trade-off between inflation and output, as well as with the occurrence of country-specific shocks. The paper provides an illuminating analysis of how joining the union and losing monetary independence affects an individual country's welfare. Disregarding country-specific shocks, the union delivers credibility gains or losses, according to whether a country's inflation bias (given by its output parameter) is greater or less than that appearing in the ECB's loss function. Disregarding political differences, economic losses will be greater, the greater the variance of domestic output relative to European output and the smaller its correlation with European output. Considering the situation and the past record of prospective members of the union it turns out 'that the countries that have more to lose from the stabilization point of view' (because of the greater variance and/or the smaller correlation of their output relative to the EC average) 'are also the ones that could gain more in terms of credibility of their monetary policy' (because of their inflation record and of the lack of independence of their central banks).

Let me now state the basic problem arising from, but not solved by, this analysis, if we accept the authors' contention that a credible implementation of the first-best rule on the part of the ECB is an unrealistic possibility to be disregarded. Why should, in this case, a low inflation country (call it Germany) ever agree to join the union?

Consider first the most favourable case, where political unification occurs at the time of full monetary integration. The authors make political unification coincide with the disappearance of differences of national preferences and welfare functions, and hence of differences of national inflation biases in the output-inflation trade-off. This is indeed a very strong assumption: the implied irrelevance of the regional composition of the electorate would be hard to accept even within the existing nation states. If this assumption is relaxed, while still letting the ECB governor be elected by European citizens rather than by national prime ministers, the European median voter will not coincide with, and will probably be less conservative than, the German median voter: in this case the inflation rate set by the ECB will be higher than that which the German central bank would independently set. Even disregarding this possibility, and hence allowing national preferences to converge to German preferences as a result of political unification, it is hard to assume on top, as the authors do,[1] that political union equalizes the distortions existing in labour markets across different countries. It is the existence of such distortions which, in the authors' view, justifies a target level of output higher than the natural level. As long as differences persist, however, 'natural' rates of unemployment will differ across countries (as they differ across regions of more unified national labour markets), so that the wedges between target levels and natural levels are likely to differ. The ECB target level of output is bound to reflect such divergences and is therefore likely to be higher than that of countries with low natural unemployment: the resulting common inflation rate will therefore be higher than that of the latter.

Without a political union, and with the explicit modelling of different national preferences, the problem becomes immediately evident. While a number of high inflation countries would bear economic losses (because of the higher variance of their output), but obtain high credibility gains and hence lower inflation, Germany would stand to lose on all counts. In addition to some (albeit small) economic losses (see Figure 3.2), there would be high credibility losses, as the output parameter, on which the inflation rate depends, is lower for Germany than for Europe. In terms of the rigorous analysis provided by Alesina and Grilli it turns out that the project of monetary union, with a European central bank setting the common monetary policy and the common rate of inflation, is not incentive-compatible when all countries are considered.

The authors consider this problem in passing (pp. 62–3). Their answer is that countries with a lower concern for output, and lower inflation, must be gaining on other grounds: the reduction of transaction costs and monetary uncertainty; or the gain from cooperation of monetary policy; or, more generally (and more vaguely) the 'long-run political gains resulting from the creation of a "European nation"'. There may well be such gains, and I am the last to require that all factors leading to eminently political decisions be susceptible of accurate modelling. Still, I find the authors' answer far less than satisfactory, especially because it conceals the true bone of contention in the long-drawn negotiations on whether, when and how to begin the process towards monetary union. Whatever the other (unmodelled) gains, they would affect all countries; if anything, they would be lower for Germany (as for transaction costs, monetary uncertainty, and especially monetary cooperation, which the leading country of an asymmetric system has no reason to desire). It will then still be the case that Germany bears more losses and obtains less benefits than a number of other countries: it is not surprising that a quick transition to full union is advocated by the latter countries, but resisted by Germany.

The relevant question then becomes whether there is a remedy for this lack of incentive-compatibility.[2] The German solution is to wait for convergence to occur before setting up a European central bank responsible for a common monetary policy. The implicit assumption is that inflation convergence would signal that national inflation biases have also converged to the lowest (German) denominator, as indeed has been the case for the smaller Northern European countries and possibly for France. This may however, take a long time, as the high inflation countries would lose the additional credibility to be obtained from participation to the union. More importantly, the process may be unstable and result in a permanent, two-speed outcome.

The alternative is to minimize German losses by tightening the monetary constitution of the system. Consider the limiting case in which the ECB, while not setting the output coefficient equal to zero (which would increase output variability), were able to make the first-best solution credible: the inflation rate would then depend only on the realized value of a shock and not be affected by the output target. It can be easily shown that in this case: (i) in a politically unified Europe the chosen governor would be as conservative as the median voter and his preferences would be independent of output variability; (ii) in a politically fragmented Europe each country's governor would exactly reflect national preferences; (iii) most importantly, in the latter case, whether a country gains or loses from the union would no longer depend on the difference between its own and the ECB's inflation bias. As a result, and especially as a result of (iii), the major disincentive for Germany to join would be eliminated.

The authors, as recalled above, disregard the possibility of implementing the first-best rule as unrealistic. Their arguments (p. 52) are that it may be complicated, going beyond setting a given rate of money growth, and that to insert a complex and contingent rule in an unchangeable statute would be both unreasonable and ineffective. The explicit statement of the objective of price stability in article 2.1 of the statute helps to protect the ECB against political pressures, but is by itself unable to eliminate the time-consistency problem (p. 56). I fail to consider such objections as conclusive, if for no other reason than because they stem from what is a most useful, but nonetheless hypersimplified model. One may well wonder if central banks tempted to indulge in inflation surprises with a view to a temporary climb along a short-run Phillips curve really belong to the EMS Europe we have known in the past decade. But apart from this, it may be questioned that a credible anti-inflationary commitment must necessarily be enshrined in a 'simple monetarist rule with a constant rate of money growth' to be written in the bank's statute or in a country's constitution (p. 52). Price stability, it has been argued,[3] – does not require unnecessary inflexibility if the medium-term commitment is credible. Perfection is not of this world, but the Bundesbank is deemed to provide the nearest approximation to it: and the Bundesbank has often shown how short-run flexibility can be reconciled with commitment to price stability.[4] In this vein, the strong opposition of the Bundesbank to proposals that the exchange rate policy of the union be left in the hands of finance ministers can be understood, as that would potentially pre-empt the priority of the ECB's anti-inflation commitment.

A major contribution of Alesina and Grilli is thus to highlight a problem to which they provide no solution. Their analysis allows us to understand the true obstacles on the way to monetary union: for some countries the economic benefits are hard to find, while the potential costs can be easily identified. The political desirability of monetary union as a first step towards political integration may be an important but hardly a sufficient incentive. The unanswered question is whether a sufficiently rigorous design can allay the fears which motivate the resistance against an early start or whether we have to wait until a long and uncertain process of convergence is completed.

NOTES

1 By normalizing to zero natural output for all countries and by equalizing for all countries the target levels of output, they also equalize the 'wedge between the market generated, "natural", level of output . . . and the target level'.
2 This question is addressed in Begg et al. (1991).

3 Begg *et al.*, section 2.2
4 Ibid.

REFERENCE

Begg, D., F. Giavazzi, L. Spaventa and G. Wyplosz (1991), 'European Monetary
    Integration – the Macro Issues', in *Monitoring European Integration: The
    Making of Monetary Union*, London: Centre for Economic Policy Research.

4 The ECB: a bank or a monetary policy rule?

DAVID FOLKERTS-LANDAU and PETER M. GARBER

1 Introduction

It is generally agreed that a European central banking institution will be an essential feature of the final stage of the European Economic and Monetary Union (EMU). To this end the EC Committee of Central Bank Governors has recently produced a Draft Statute of the European System of Central Banks and of the European Central Bank.[1] Although differences of views among governments of member states have meant that the Draft Statute remains incomplete in a number of areas, the most fundamental and consequential omission is the lack of a clear mandate for the ECB to undertake traditional banking functions in support of the financial sector.

Central banks have traditionally had two major objectives. First, central banks have sought to maintain a stable and efficient financial and payments system. This has generally required performing certain banking functions for the financial sector, such as providing an ultimate source of liquidity (i.e., a discount window), participating in the payments system, and regulating and supervising key sectors of the financial system. Second, central banks have sought to stabilize the price level and general economic activity by carrying out monetary functions such as open market operations, foreign exchange operations, and the establishment of minimum reserve requirements.

The draft Statute mandates the maintenance of price stability as the explicit primary objective of the ECB,[2] and the necessary monetary functions and operations of the system are defined in accordance with standard practice. The maintenance of a stable financial and payments system, however, is not an explicit objective of the ECB, and only limited banking functions are admitted as one of the system's five tasks. In particular, the system is authorized only 'to participate as necessary in the formulation, coordination and execution of policies relating to prudential supervision and the stability of the financial system,' which falls notably short of being mandated 'to formulate, coordinate, and execute such policies.'[3] There is no obligation for the ECB to initiate support of the banking or payments system. Furthermore, Article 18.2[4] enables the ECB to restrict the scope for, and set the terms of, all open market and credit operations carried out by national central banks to stabilize local financial or payment systems.

The draft Statute thus clearly subscribes to a 'narrow' concept of the System of Central Banks with a single objective – monetary stability – rather than a 'broad' concept with the additional objective of financial-market stability. In this paper we examine the consequences of a 'narrow' central banking system for Community financial markets.

We conclude that in the absence of such banking functions it will be necessary to slow, or even prevent, the ongoing development of Community-wide liquid, securitized financial markets, supported by a large-volume wholesale payments system. Instead, the historically prevalent bank-intermediated financial system will have to be maintained to lower the likelihood of liquidity crises that demand central bank intervention.

In the remainder of this paper, we first examine the relation between securitization and financial crises (Section 2). We then discuss the role payments systems play in securitized financial markets and the involvement of central banks in payments systems (Section 3). In Section 4 we define the central bank's basic choice problem in establishing the extent of its banking functions, and in Section 5 we establish the need for central banks to supervise financial markets. Section 6 concludes the paper.

2   Securitization and liquidity crises

2.1   Securitization[5]

The accelerating securitization of credit claims, ownership claims, and derivative contracts is a fundamental phenomenon in the evolution of financial markets and market institutions. Securitization induces the establishment of new institutions, drives developments in market mechanisms, payments mechanisms, and other institutional arrangements, and above all spurs an increased demand for liquidity. In this section, we shall show that the extent of securitization of credit and ownership claims is a determining factor in defining a central bank's role as lender-of-last-resort. The more securitized are credit, ownership, and derivative contracts, the greater the likelihood of liquidity problems.

As financial systems mature, there has been a general tendency to substitute securitized credit for bank credit, and equity shares for nontradable

Table 4.1. *Domestic and international commercial paper markets, 1986–90. (Amounts outstanding at end-year, in billions of US dollars[1].)*

	Market opening	1986	1987	1988	1989	1990
United States	pre-1960	325.9	373.6	451.6	521.9	557.8
Japan	end-1987	–	13.8	73.8	91.1	117.3
France	end-1985	3.7	7.6	10.4	22.3	31.0
Canada	pre-1960	11.9	14.9	21.0	25.5	26.8
Sweden	1983	3.7	7.8	9.5	15.9	22.3
Australia[2]	mid-1970s	4.1	7.5	7.9	11.1	10.9
United Kingdom	1986	0.8	3.8	5.7	5.7	9.1
Spain[3]	1982	2.5	2.8	3.1	4.2	8.4
Finland	mid-1986	0.4	2.5	4.9	6.9	8.3
Norway	end-1984	0.9	2.1	1.7	2.0	2.6
Netherlands	1986	0.1	0.9	1.0	0.8	2.0
Total		354.0	437.3	590.6	707.4	796.5
ECP	mid-1980s	13.9	33.3	50.6	58.4	70.4
memo-other Euro-notes[4]		15.1	16.9	13.5	11.1	19.1
Grand Total		367.9	470.6	641.2	765.8	866.9

Source: Bank for International Settlements, *International Banking and Financial Market Developments*, August, 1991.
Notes:
1 Converted at end-year exchange rates, except for Australia.
2 End-June of each year converted at end-June exchange rates.
3 Partial coverage.
4 Short-term notes only.

ownership interests.[6] Better known corporations have increasingly obtained credit in the bond market directly. In some countries, most notably in Germany, there has been a significant increase in the number of initial public equity offerings by mid-sized industrial companies. An important form of securitization had been the growth of negotiable high-quality short-term non-bank corporate and bank obligations, i.e., commercial paper and certificates of deposit, (see Table 4.1) and the growth of exchange-traded derivative products such as interest rate futures. Finally, a substantial part of illiquid bank assets had been securitized through the repackaging of bank assets into tradable securities, most notably in the mortgage market.

The extent of securitization is relatively more advanced in some industrial countries, e.g., the United States, the United Kingdom, and France than in others, such as Germany (see Table 4.1 and Figure 4.1). However, an improved ability to circumvent existing restrictions on securitization

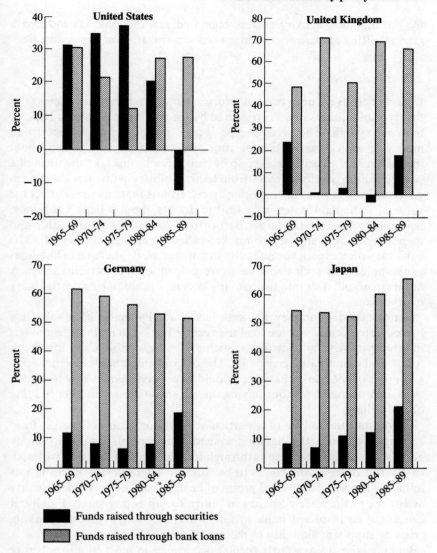

Figure 4.1 Indirect versus securitized funding. (Percent of total business funds raised through securities and bank loans, 1965–89.)
Source: Frankel and Montgomery (1991)

by shifting such activity to less regulated jurisdictions has induced a gradual lifting of existing restrictions on securitization in most countries.[7]

2.2 Liquidity crises

Liquidity crises occur in two basic forms in modern financial systems. The first type of liquidity crisis is triggered by the traditional run on a bank or banking system. The second type relates to illiquidity in securitized money or capital markets. Bank runs result from investor doubts about the solvency of a bank, or a group of banks. Such runs take the form of a sudden shift in portfolios away from bank liabilities in favor of short-term government securities or corporate assets. Events that adversely affect the value of some bank assets may lead to doubts about a bank's solvency, particularly because the larger part of bank assets are nontradable and therefore are not subjected to market-valuation at regular intervals. The bank may then experience difficulty in refinancing its short-term liabilities as the holders of such liabilities make precautionary portfolio shifts. A failure may spill over into the banking system, thus requiring central bank intervention.

Securitization of money markets has generally made it possible for banks, in particular wholesale money centre banks, to finance their assets in large part with bought funds, such as the negotiable CDs, interbank funds, and repurchase agreements. The risk of being unable to refinance a great part of the bank's liabilities would have been significantly less if the bank had operated without relying on wholesale money market funding of its liabilities.

To forestall the failure of a particular bank, or group of banks, from spilling over onto the banking system, the central bank can supply liquidity to the affected banks through its discount facilities and will wish to do so if it deems the banks to be solvent. Alternatively, it can use its influence to induce a selected group of healthy banks to provide liquidity assistance to the affected banks in return for an equity stake. Finally, it can allow an insolvent bank to fail, while avoiding a general banking crisis by supplying liquidity to the rest of the banking system.

Banking crises were a fairly regular occurrence in most countries before the 1940s, leading at times to severe contractions of the money stock with significant negative effects on economic activity.[8] Since then, however, central banks have learned to avoid general bank liquidity crises by providing emergency assistance to the banking system during times of crises. Some typical recent examples of such crises in the UK have been the failure of some large secondary banks in 1973, and the Johnson Matthey Bankers crises in 1984. Both required official support operations. The US Continental Illinois Bank crisis in 1984 also required large scale central bank intervention to prevent contagion to the banking system. Concern about the stability of the banking system led the German Bundesbank in 1983 to request a group of German banks to assist the failing Schroeder, Munchmeyer, Hengst & Co. Bank.[9]

The second type of liquidity crisis – illiquidity in key money or capital markets – occurs as the direct consequence of increased securitization. In securitized money and capital markets, banks are relied upon to supply liquidity to non-bank participants. For example, corporate issuers of money market instruments generally arrange credit lines with banks to assure access to funds on maturity in case problems occur in rolling over the securities. Non-bank financial intermediaries, such as broker/dealers also rely on banks. While they actively supply liquidity to short- and long-term markets as market-makers, dealers also must arrange bank lines of credit to be able to offer this service. Likewise, participants on organized futures and options markets, the heart of the last decade's development in financial engineering, make intensive use of bank lines because of the requirement of nearly instantaneous delivery of cash needed to satisfy margin calls. Credit lines to banks are the only practicable method of assuring such delivery.[10]

A smoothly functioning dealer effectively provides the service of swapping one security for another. The swaps fund the dealer's operation, allowing the dealer to provide liquidity while avoiding the tapping of the dealer's bank line of credit. Nevertheless, only when dealing in very liquid instruments can dealers almost always avoid funding through banks. Dealers maintain credit lines in good funds and securities to finance peak load inventory acquisition or short positions.[11] Low capitalization and high leverage are the essential characteristics of dealers in securities. They therefore tend to be undiversified, highly leveraged, and vulnerable to failure.[12]

The failure of a major money market borrower or dealer may precipitate a liquidity crisis in a money market, such as the commercial paper market. The failure of a borrower can undermine investor confidence and make it difficult for other money market borrowers to roll-over their outstanding obligations, forcing them to draw on their bank lines. The banking system may not be willing to meet this sudden increase for short-term commercial credit because of concern about credit risk.[13] Banks may also be unwilling to continue to finance some dealers because of doubts about their solvency. The banking system may also be unable to generate sufficient funding as the illiquidity or collapse of the CD dealer network may have spread to the CD market because of a lack of invenstor confidence. The ensuing failure among money market borrowers unable to roll-over their obligations, or among dealers unable to fund their positions, will further undermine confidence.

The potential systemic nature of such a situation invites central bank liquidity intervention. An example was the liquidity crisis in the US commercial paper market in 1970, triggered by the Penn Central bankruptcy, as well as the liquidity crisis caused by the October 1987 stock market crash. Both crises required Federal Reserve intervention.[14]

Sudden increases in price volatility in a securitized capital markets are signs of illiquidity that, in turn, can cause precipitous declines in prices and result in bankruptcies among market participants. In capital markets, trading strategies such as stop-loss sales or portfolio insurance rely on market liquidity for their success. For any one small player, the assumption of a liquid market with price continuity is probably reasonable. When all of the selling strategies are triggered simultaneously, however, they have proved to be infeasible. The rest of the market participants may have no knowledge of the existence of such traders because their sell orders lie buried in the future. They will come to the market only if triggered by the proper contingency. When the time comes for these massive sales to occur, the sellers may find no buyers prepared to take the other side of the market at the last reported price, and the price may suddenly collapse. A lack of liquidity in the market may cause a snowballing of sell orders. If the price falls dramatically below its fundamental value due to these liquidity problems, further sales may be triggered. Banks may make margin calls on their loans to security holders and dealers, and cancel lines of credit. This may either bankrupt the holders and dealers or force a sale of their stock, further depressing prices. Hence, working to market, the essence of securitized markets can precipitate bankruptcy from illiquidity among dealers, eliminating dealer networks and inducing a permanent illiquidity and lower prices on securities involved. The spread of insolvencies resulting from price declines and inability to meet margin calls may ultimately affect the banking system as defaults on bank loans mount.

Central bank intervention can prevent liquidity crises caused by large price movements from becoming systemic. The central bank can supply emergency liquidity assistance to the banking system or induce the banking system to supply liquidity to the non-bank market makers. The welfare gain arises from preventing the transformation of liquid into illiquid securities and needless bankruptcies among dealers, and ultimately among banking institutions. If such events are pure liquidity events, then intervention is costless in terms of central bank resources and price level stability.

Alternatively, if the central bank mistakes a fundamental decline of asset prices for a temporary liquidity problem and intervenes, it will either have to (1) weaken the capital of the banking system; (2) countenance price inflation; or (3) absorb some loss itself. By erroneously adding liquidity to a market when the price of the security is higher than its ultimate level, the central bank expands reserves and pressures banks to lend against the securities. If the security price eventually falls as central bank liquidity is withdrawn, market makers will go bankrupt, leaving bad loans on the books of the banks and reducing bank capital. Depositors' confidence in banks will furthermore diminish, and banks will be less able to provide liquidity services in the future. To reduce the damage to the banks of this mistake, the central bank may decide not to contract reserves to their normal level. This leads to a permanent expansion in the money stock and to a rise in the price level.

2.3 Banking markets and liquidity crises

In a financial system without a securitized money market, short-term funding and liquidity management must occur through bank balance sheets, and banks also act as the major brokers and dealers for money. In such a system, there has generally been a small number of large bank players in the market for wholesale funds. Clearing of payments is effectively done internally to banking organizations or among a small group of tightly connected banks.

Few occasions will arise when funds are demanded on a large scale for unexpected settlements. The central bank, therefore, will not often be called upon to provide credit. Alternatively stated, placing most short-term funding on bank balance sheets means that financial markets create few liquid claims, so liquidity problems emerge infrequently.

In addition, a central bank that limits short-term funding to the banking system can make minimum reserve requirements binding and thereby impose a tax on the entire financial system in the form of higher yields and lower prices (liquidity haircuts in the prices) of relatively illiquid securities. Since financial markets would be prohibited from supplying close substitutes to bank products, banks cannot shrink their balance sheets and reserves to a nonbinding level and conduct their liquidity business primarily off their balance sheets.

Thus, financial systems with securitized money and capital markets are more likely to be subjected to liquidity crises than a financial system dominated by the banking market.

2.4   Stifling securitized money markets taxes illiquid issuers

With restricted money markets, large and high quality short-term credits must be carried on bank balance sheets. If a central bank permits large-scale, liquid, and securitized money markets, large institutions that are potential issuers of liquid, short-term securities tend to remove themselves from bank balance sheets, thereby reducing the demand for bank reserves. The price of accessing bank liquidity, therefore, falls for less liquid issuers of securities. A policy of permitting a liquid, securitized money market favors issuers of liquid and illiquid securities by allowing them to access capital more cheaply. If illiquid issues are concentrated among the smaller, riskier firms, the structure of investment by type of firm and type of activity is altered. Alternatively a highly restricted money market will raise the cost of capital to less liquid firms, channeling capital to the larger, lower risk firms.

3   Liquidity and the payments system

The liquidity of financial markets (money, capital, and derivative), as well as the pace of securitization of financial markets, hinges on the ability to settle payments and to move cash.[15] A wholesale payments system capable of processing a large volume of intra-day payment orders is imperative to support the large turnover in securities markets needed for liquidity, the rapidly changing dealer positions financed with repurchase agreements, and margin requirements arising in futures and options markets. In contrast, in a system that lacks such markets, rapidity of payment processing is less crucial since such a large gross turnover and net settlement does not emerge among the numerous entities that are not members of a limited-entry clearing arrangement.

Most wholesale payments systems consist of a central bank that settles payments among a group of clearing banks via their reserve accounts (such as the Fedwire system in the United States) and various private clearinghouse arrangements among subgroups of banks (such as CHIPS for international dollar payments, regional or giro clearing systems in Germany, and netting schemes such as FXNET for foreign exchange transactions).[16] Banks are typically the central participants in wholesale payments systems because of their direct access to 'good funds' (central bank liabilities) for payments, which gives them a comparative advantage in establishing efficient payment arrangements. Good funds constitute the core of any payments system because they are available at full nominal value to make payments under all market conditions (including market crises).

The role of the central bank in a payments system is dictated by the fundamental nature of payments systems: the more effective wholesale payments systems are in supporting securitized money and capital markets, the greater is the credit risk generated within the settlements system, and thus the greater the likelihood of liquidity crises.

In a system of *continuous settlement*, each payment message from one bank to another is accompanied by the good funds specified in the message. As long as the sending bank has sufficient reserves on hand, payments messages are processed without delay. In continuous settlements, receiving banks bear no credit risk from participating in the payment mechanism. This is because the payment must be blocked when the amount of payment exceeds the good funds on hand until more funds are received. If numerous banks face a similar situation, the payments system can become gridlocked. Banks wish to make large payments to each other but cannot send payments because they have not received payments. Thus, a system of continuous settlement on the one hand eliminates credit risk among banks from the day's payments. On the other hand, it does so by reducing the potential speed of transmitting payments. This reduction of liquidity increases the cost of financial activity.

The gridlock problem can be reduced by banks' increasing their reserve holdings. This would involve selling loans to other investors in return for good funds. Bank customers would have to pass-through a higher cost of reserves as the price of increasing processing speed.

To avoid large reserve positions, banks usually engage in *net settlement*.[17] They pay the difference between total payments and total receipts at the end of the day, through a clearinghouse formed for the purpose of executing the net settlement. Good funds held by banks are transferred to the clearinghouse to collateralize partially bank payment orders. Banks can execute delivery of good funds without increasing their total reserves because the individual members of the clearinghouse and their customers believe that net due to positions accumulating during the day are covered by delivery of good funds at settlement.[18]

Credit risk in payment systems arises from the possibility that any of the parties in the chain of intra-day transactions may default on its payment obligations at the time of settlement. If the clearinghouse operates under settlement finality, then the credit risk of the sending bank is distributed over the receiving banks according to the loss-sharing formula adopted by the clearinghouse.[19]

Systemic risk occurs as an outgrowth of settlement risk. The failure of one participant to settle deprives other institutions of expected funds and prevents these institutions from settling in their turn. Thus, although a participant may conduct no business directly with a failed institution, chains of obligation may make it suffer because of the impact that the failed institution has on a participant's ability to settle – that is, the cost of settlement failure reaches beyond the exposure of credited banks to the failing bank.

Settlement at the end of the day is a way for the market to test periodically the liquidity and solvency of the clearing banks. Failure of an institution to settle will either result in an unwinding of all intra-day payments instructions; or under settlement finality, its obligations will be covered by a clearinghouse reserve, or by central bank lending to the clearinghouse or to its members. An unwinding of transactions or failure to fully cover intraday payments made for the delinquent institutions out of clearinghouse reserves will impair the ability of other banks to make payments and hence may produce a systemic liquidity crisis in the absence of central bank intervention.

The failure of an institution to settle can easily be transmitted over the payments system and it could precipitate multiple failures of otherwise healthy financial institutions.[20] As a result, major central banks have played an important role in managing the payments system, including supplying liquidity. For example, the Bank of New York, a major clearing bank in the US payments system, experienced a computer breakdown on November 21, 1985, which led the US Federal Reserve to make an overnight loan of $22.6 billion from the discount window, collateralized by $36 billion in securities. The sheer size of average *daily* payments flows through the domestic and international US dollar wholesale payments system – $1.4 trillion in 1988 – and the difficulties experienced in settling trades and payments following a computer breakdown at the Bank of New York and during the October 1987 equity price downturn have shown that wholesale payments system are a source of systemic risk. In fact, some observers believe 'that the greatest threat to the stability of the financial system as a whole during the October stock market crash was the danger of a major default in one of the clearing and settlement systems.'[21]

A gross or continuous payments system with payment finality and intra-settlement period overdraft facilities, such as the US fedwire system, avoids systemic liquidity crises arising from settlement failures since its payments are final.[22] However, only a central bank has the ability to create a payments system with absolute settlement finality.

In Fedwire payments, the Federal Reserve guarantees unconditionally that a bank payment message sent over Fedwire will be honored as good funds at settlement. If a bank fails to deliver good funds, the Fed supplies the funds without assessing other banks for the deficit in reserves resulting from the failure. Thus, over the course of any day, the Fed insures the market in wholesale payments. Hence, the Fed significantly increases liquidity in the money markets and the efficiency of the payments mechanism. As a result, however, it assumes the risk of making payments for a bank in default. The revenue on reserves deposited with the Fed serves as a compensation for the risk it bears, but it may or may not represent sufficient compensation. There may be more efficient means of charging for this risk-bearing, since in taxing the Fed's net revenues, the Treasury ultimately bears the risk of operating the payment system.

Concerns about the intra-day credit exposure in net-settlement payments systems with payment finality led the Federal Reserve to introduce caps on debit positions with Fedwire and CHIPS, and to propose interest charges on such debit positions. The presence of a cap on the debit position that an individual bank is allowed to run with Fedwire effectively limits the loss that could be incurred by the Federal Reserve as a result of payments instructions sent out over the Fedwire by a failing bank. However, in a situation where investors have lost confidence in a large money centre bank and fail to renew short-term funds, such as maturing certificates of deposit and repurchase agreements, the bank would quickly reach its net debit limit and might then be unable to repay its short-term creditors. As a result, the central bank could be faced with the need to provide funds to the bank through the discount window and hence be subject to the credit risk inherent in the bank asset used as collateral.[23]

In contrast, financial systems with a limited extent of securitization have in practice a small number of large universal banks in the market for wholesale funds. Wholesale payments and securities transactions are cleared internally in these organizations. The risk of nonsettlement is small due to the lack of significant exposure to non-bank financial institutions and an increased ability to work out unexpected problems quickly among the small number of players. Hence, although the clearing banks ultimately clear on the books of the central bank, there is little need for the central bank to provide intra-day credit or stand ready to act as lender-of-last-resort to the clearinghouse to ensure the payments settlement.

3.1 The role of the ECB in the payments system

Although the draft Statute empowers the ECB to issue regulations governing the clearing and payments systems in the Community, it does not mandate the ECB to play an active part in the payments system by providing intra-day credit or to extend lender-of-last-resort guarantees to a clearinghouse.

Current practices regarding clearing and settlement of payments vary widely across member countries. Since mandatory reserves would be held at the ECB, the final settlement of payments among clearing banks would have to occur on the books of the ECB.[24] It will thus be necessary to define clearly the ECB's support for the payments system; whether it will support a gross or continuous settlement system with daylight good funds or it will support a private clearinghouse arrangement by supplying liquidity if the clearinghouse fails to settle.

Such support will be necessary if the ECB wishes to facilitate growth in money market trading volume and development of derivative markets.[25] Failure to support actively the payments surplus in the interest of achieving the efficiency gains from liquid money and capital markets will ensure that the US dollar will continue to act as a vehicle currency for a significant volume of Community financial markets transactions. The dollar clearing facilities currently available, together with strong Federal Reserve (and Treasury) liquidity support, will continue to maintain the US dollar's pre-eminent role in international transactions.

4   The central bank's choice problem

In Section 2, we showed that financial systems with liquid, securitized money and capital markets are more likely to experience liquidity crises than bank-intermediated financial systems. Hence, such financial systems have a greater need for a central bank with a lender-of-last-resort function. In Section 3, we indicated that the greater the extent of securitization, the greater the demands on the wholesale payments system and the greater the need for the central bank to provide daylight credit or to act as a lender-of-last-resort in cases of settlement failure. The elements of a central bank policy role regarding the extent of the central bank's banking functions thus emerges clearly as a *balancing of the cost of lender-of-last-resort operations with the benefits flowing from liquid, securitized financial markets*.

The role and functions of central banks in the major industrial countries emerged during the 19th and early 20th century largely in response to the need to centralize interbank clearing and the holding of reserves. In addition, most central banks also served to monopolize the issue of bank notes and acted as the Government's bank. Central banks supplied liquidity in times of crises (elastic supply of currency) to financial markets and to individual institutions, first in conjunction with their clearinghouse role and then with their note issuance role, by discounting various types of commercial paper.[26] [27]

These microeconomic or banking functions were in most instances combined with the monetary function of supporting a metallic standard or fixed parities under the Bretton Woods system, through an appropriate discount policy. With the monetary and economic catastrophes of the 1920s and the 1930s, and the consequent ascendancy of macroeconomics as a separate discipline in economics, the policy objectives of central banks became ever more defined in terms of the macroeconomic goals of economic stabilization, including price level stabilization. The banking role of central banks became intellectually secondary to the monetary role.[28] In practice, however, the new macroeconomic policy operations were only superimposed on, rather than taking the place of, the pre-existing banking operations of the pre-war central banks, which continued to operate fully as banking entities. Although 'operating instruments' such as short-term interest rates were used as levers, whose manipulation might effect the ultimate goals, they simultaneously were used as the central banks' traditional instruments for influencing banking and financial market activity.[29]

Current central banking practices in the major industrial countries tend to support the hypothesis that liquid, securitized financial markets need to be supported by a central bank with broad banking functions – lender-of-last-resort, involvement in the payments system, and the supervision and regulation of the banking system. In particular, central banks in the large industrial countries with highly securitized and liquid financial markets, such as the United States and the United Kingdom, have a clear objective to secure stable banking and financial markets, in addition to their monetary policy objective. The central banks in these countries have repeatedly demonstrated their willingness to act as lender-of-last-resort to the financial system as a whole, as well as to individual institutions,[30] while at the same time imposing a supervisory and regulatory framework to minimize the occurrence of such crises.

On the other hand, central banks in financial systems with predominantly bank-intermediated credit, such as Germany, have not found it necessary to act as lender-of-last-resort. Consistent with the tradition of its early predecessor the 19th century Reichsbank, the German Bundesbank lacks a mandate to act as a lender-of-last-resort, and has only limited supervisory and regulatory responsibilities.[31]

The welfare loss of liquidity crises can be partly offset by a central bank acting as lender-of-last-resort to the financial system or to individual institutions. However, in any credit operation that it undertakes in the lender-of-last-resort role, a central bank will incur the credit risk and potential losses, associated with the claims it acquires when expanding its liabilities to supply liquidity. Such losses will occur when the market value of the collateral is less than the amount of the loan or advance to the banks concerned.[32] As a remuneration for such credit risk, the central bank receives income from holding the reserve balances of the banking system.

While the monetary effects of the liquidity operations can be sterilized, the central bank's losses on acquired bank assets fall ultimately to the taxpayers. In effect, the taxpayer has assumed the credit risk inherent in bank assets that serve as collateral for central bank lending. Such losses will have to be balanced against the benefits derived from liquid, securitized financial markets with an efficient payments system. Furthermore, the moral hazard generated by the presence of a lender-of-last-resort will have to be mitigated by supervision and prudential regulation of the financial system by the central bank.

4.1   Policy choice

To reduce the expected cost to the public sector arising from the central bank's lending operations undertaken to stabilize financial markets, the central bank can restrict the extent to which financial markets are securitized, it can eliminate payments system risk by requiring continuous settlement with payment finality, and it can impose supervisory and prudential requirements on the banking system. These restrictions will reduce the likelihood of liquidity crises and may reduce the loss to the central bank if a crisis occurs. Such policies, however, tend to restrict the activities of banking firms, limit the range of available instruments, increase the cost of operating the payments system, and generally reduce liquidity in financial markets, all of which will increase the total cost of the financial transactions supporting a given volume of real activities.[33] In the extreme, the central bank can restrict the financial system to operate largely through bank intermediation.

In practice, central banks have, for historical reasons or otherwise, chosen different positions along the credit risk – financial market efficiency trade-off ranging from the highly liquid securitized capital markets in the United States to the predominately bank-intermediated financial system in Germany. The draft Statute for the ECB would seem to leave very little room for the ECB actively to stabilize Community financial markets. Implicitly therefore, the Statute foresees a bank-intermediated financial system without any significant further securitization of finance.

It will then not only be necessary to restrict the further development of liquid, securitized financial markets and large volume wholesale payments systems in the Community financial system, but it will also be necessary to scale-back such developments in the UK and French financial markets.

An important reason why banking functions, in particular lender-of-last-resort operations, cannot be undertaken by national central banks is that such operations may have monetary effects and may be costly in terms of central bank resources. It will be more difficult for national central banks to resist calls to come to the assistance of a local banking system than for a multi-national ECB. Thus, even if the monetary effects of a liquidity operation by a national central bank could be undone by the ECB, it is nevertheless advisable to control banking operations from the centre. Nor could the ECB rely on its ability to avoid a systemic crisis by financing a group of European banks to form a 'lifeboat' to assist a bank or a group of banks in need of liquidity. The diversity of banks across member countries and the lack of cohesion among these banks rules out such operations.

It has been argued that an announced commitment of a central bank to serve as a lender-of-last-resort in a liquidity crisis leads to moral hazard. Knowing the contingencies under which the central bank will support asset prices, market participants will take positions that make liquidity problems and therefore central bank interventions more likely. Rather, the argument goes, the central bank should make no announcement of its responsibility to provide liquidity to financial markets. Implicitly, it would be well known that it would serve as lender-of-last-resort, however. If market participants think that a lack of explicit commitment reduces the set of contingencies in which the central bank will support asset prices, they will be less likely to take positions in which intervention is required. These are exactly the arguments that we have made throughout the paper about how financial markets develop in the presence of central bank liquidity support. It does not follow, however, that implicit liquidity support is superior to explicitly announced support – implicit support is simply an alternative name for a policy of fostering illiquid financial markets. Of course, lack of an explicit liquidity announcement need not reduce the set of contingencies in which market participants believe that the central bank will intervene. The public may in fact believe that the central bank intends to intervene more than it would under an explicit announcement, and market participants may assume positions that make a liquidity crisis even more likely.

5   Supervision and regulation of banking systems

In addition to restricting the extent of securitization of financial interme-diation, central banks can reduce the credit risk incurred during liquidity operations through an appropriate regulatory and supervisory regime on financial systems (not exclusively on banking systems). The regime would be designed to limit the expected losses on bank assets acquired during a liquidity operation to a desired level. In particular, regulations can be designed so that disturbances from the activities of banks other than those relating to payments and liquidity do not spill over into the payments system and become systemic.[34] Such regulations include risk-related capital requirements, separation of investment banking activity from payments activity, position limits, and frequent assessment of the solvency of the bank through examination of its balance sheet. The more restrictive the regulatory and supervisory regimes, however, the greater the total cost of financial transactions, specifically the cost of making payments.

The draft Statute does not envisage an active role for the ECB in the prudential supervision of financial institutions,[35] which is consistent with the limited banking functions mandated in the draft Statute for the ECB. As long as the ECB does not intend to supply liquidity as a lender-of-last-resort to stabilize Community financial markets, it will not be necessary to restrict the amount of credit risk it might assume under such operations through supervisory and regulatory policies.[36]

If, however, the ECB does assume a lender-of-last-resort role, then it will also have to assume a supervisory and regulatory role at the centre of the Community financial system, rather than leave such activities to the national central banks or other agencies. This is because the assignment of responsibility for the supervision of the banking system should avoid inter-agency conflict of interest. Such conflict would arise if the central bank puts its resources at stake, while another agency is responsible for establishing the solvency of central bank debtors. For example, the supervision of the banking system, i.e., the assessment of the market value of banking assets, could be subject to intense political pressure leading to a delay in corrective measures. An independent central bank with its own resources at stake is more likely to assess the solvency of potential borrowers sufficiently accurately to protect its own resources. Thus, as long as there is any potential for central bank lending to credit institutions, the central bank should be responsible for supervising the banking system.

A second argument in favor of centralizing the responsibility for bank supervision in the central bank relates to the central bank's first-hand involvement in liquidity support operations. To reduce credit risk to a minimum and in order to establish the modalities of its intervention (e.g., open market operations versus discount window) the ECB will have to establish quickly whether it is facing a pure liquidity crisis or an insolvency crisis. The initial problem will most likely have become apparent at the time payments are settled, and hence speed is of the essence if a systemic payments crisis is to be avoided. The expertise and information necessary to conduct a successful liquidity operation at minimal credit risk requires the intimate involvement of the central bank with the banking system. During the October 1987 stock market crash, for example, the successful intervention by the Federal Reserve required a knowledge of dealer obligations to the banking system, of the potential magnitude of margin calls, and of the position of the money centre banks. It is unlikely that such expertise can be developed and retained outside the ECB.

6   Conclusions

The draft Statute for a System of European Central Banks, the centre-piece of EMU, defines a 'narrow' ECB – a central bank shirking basic banking functions such as lender-of-last-resort to financial markets and the payments system, and supervision and regulation of banking markets. In this paper, we have demonstrated that this choice will also determine the future structure of the Community financial system. In particular, an ECB eschewing any substantive banking function will have to guide the development of Community financial markets in the direction of a predo-minately bank-intermediated financial system, avoiding any significant degree of liquid, securitized markets, including markets for short-term corporate obligations, bank liabilities, repurchase agreements, derivative instruments, and equity products.

Alternatively, if Community financial markets are to develop further towards liquid, securitized financial markets with a high-volume wholesale payments system, then it will be essential for the ECB to assume a well-defined lender-of-last-resort function, as well as supervisory and regulatory responsibilities.

A policy choice in favor of a bank-intermediated Community financial system, which would inevitably result in a higher cost of financial trans-actions supporting a given volume of real transactions, would imply that a significant portion of intra-Community financial transactions would continue to use the dollar-based financial system.

NOTES

The views expressed are the authors' alone and do not necessarily represent the views of the International Monetary Fund.
  1 Sent to the EC Ministers on November 19, 1990, and amended on April 11, 1991. The proposed European System of Central Banks ('System') is to consist of a central institution, the European Central Bank (ECB), and of partici-pating central banks of the Member States of the Community ('national central banks').

2 '*Article 2 – Objectives*
   2.1 The primary objective of the system shall be to maintain price stability.
   2.2 Without prejudice to the objective of price stability, the system shall
       support the general economic policy of the Community.'
3 See Article 3. Further references to the banking functions of the System are
  equally restrictive. In particular, Article 18.1 enables the System to 'conduct
  credit operations with credit institutions and other market participants' but
  only to achieve the limited monetary objectives of the System. Article 22
  enables the System to 'provide facilities ... and issue regulations to ensure
  efficient and sound clearing and payments systems', but it does not enable the
  system to extend credit or liquidity support to the payments system. Article
  25.1 enables the ECB only to 'offer advice and to be consulted in the interpretation and implementation of Community legislation relating to the prudential
  supervision of credit and of the financial institutions'. Article 25.2 offers the
  possibility of designating the ECB as a competent supervisory authority but
  such a transferal of competence must be specified by further Community
  legislation.
4 'Article 18.2. The ECB shall establish general principles for open market and
  credit operations carried out by itself or the national central banks, including
  the announcement of conditions under which they stand ready to enter into
  such transactions'.
5 The term 'securitization' has frequently been used in the financial press to
  describe the creation of high-quality negotiable, liquid securities by setting
  aside illiquid claims, such as mortgage obligations, consumer receivables, etc.
  to fund such securities. We employ the term here to describe a broader
  phenomenon, namely, the creation of any credit, ownership, or derivative
  claims that are publicly tradable, either in an organized market or over-the-
  counter, and whose prices are, therefore, determined at frequent intervals in an
  open market. Thus, commercial paper and negotiable certificates of deposit
  are securitized instruments, while the interbank market in central bank liabilities, such as the US Federal Funds market, is not securitized. The most
  important quantitative example of securitization involves disintermediation
  from the banking system.
6 To the extent that it existed, the historical comparative advantage of banking
  institutions in assessing credit risk, in monitoring borrower behaviour, and in
  dealing with nonperforming debtors is being eroded by, inter alia, advances in
  information technology, innovations in credit-worthiness signalling
  mechanisms, and improvements in the legal system. Furthermore, financial
  intermediaries, acting as agents rather than as principals, such as investment
  banks, have been increasingly innovative in designing techniques and instruments to bring borrowers and non-bank lenders together. The growth of
  institutional investors, such as pension funds and insurance companies, has
  also created growing demand for securitized debt and equity. Finally, a
  growing stock of outstanding tradable financial instruments increases the
  scope for financial institutions to make a market in these instruments, thus
  increasing liquidity and reducing transaction costs.
7 Folkerts-Landau and Mathieson (1988).
8 The ability to create currency through the open market purchase of securities
  or direct lending against eligible collateral has allowed central banks to supply
  liquidity in times of crisis and thereby guarantee the exchange rate between

bank deposits and currency. In fact, during the period from 1793 to 1933 the United States experienced at least 17 banking crises, while none have occurred since 1933, the beginning of active Federal Reserve intervention. Thus, the systemic financial instability in banking and payment systems was eliminated through the introduction of the central bank clearinghouse where banks would hold their clearing balances and that stood ready to assist banks to convert bank deposit liabilities into currency by taking bank assets as collateral (Schwartz, 1988).

9 During the secondary banking crises in 1973 in the UK the Bank of England organized a 'lifeboat,' a group of primary clearing banks that provided liquidity to the affected banks. The failure of several of the secondary banks is estimated to have resulted in significant losses ($234 million) for the Bank of England, as well as for the lifeboat ($117 million). The Bank of England also arranged a lifeboat for Johnson Matthey Bankers to prevent the failure of the bank from having systemic consequences. The final cost of the operation is yet to be determined.

   The Federal Reserve Bank of Chicago advance $3.5 billion to Continental Illinois Bank during a run on the bank, and the FDIC extended full coverage to all depositors (see US Treasury, 1991).

10 The payment of fees for the use of such credit lines serves as compensation to banks for maintaining reserves and for satisfying regulatory capital require-ments and other restrictions necessary to access their lines of credit to a central bank. Such payments are reflected in the market yields of money market instruments. Securities whose dealers or issuers rarely expect to draw on bank lines of credit to provide liquidity are most liquid, and this is expressed in relatively low market yields. Securities whose dealers expect frequently to use bank lines are relatively less liquid, and the higher probability of having to incur the costs of using the reserves of the banking system manifests itself in a relatively higher yield, or equivalently in the haircut in price, for such securities (Garber and Weisbrod, 1990).

   A liquid, securitized money market provides perfect substitutes for both bank liabilities and assets. It, therefore, allows a banking system to shrink or to expand its balance sheet so that reserve requirements are nonbinding – that is, banks hold the amount of reserves that they want to minimize the total costs of effecting end-of-day net settlement of all the payments generated from inside and outside the banking system, including from the money markets.

11 For a discussion of the impact of available dealer liquid resources on securities market spreads, see Grossman and Miller (1988).

12 For US dealers in securities, the SEC requires 'net capital' of $6\frac{2}{3}$ percent of liabilities where net capital is defined as net worth plus subordinated debt and adjusted for a haircut reflecting the volatility of securities positions.

13 For example, during a recent period in August 1991 securities dealers in the US securities market were forced to draw on their lines of credit with the money centre banks after the rate on repurchase agreements – their traditional source of funding inventories – had unexpectedly risen to levels that could have impaired the solvency of some of the dealers. The sudden increased demand for funds sent banks into the Fed Funds market, which drove the Fed Funds rate to above 30 percent and induced the Federal Reserve to lend in excess of $3 billion through the discount window in order to preserve orderly markets.

14 The Federal Reserve actively supplied liquidity to the banking system through the discount window, and it encouraged the banking system to maintain and extend credit lines to dealers and other market makers so as to avoid a chain of bankruptcies.

15 By cash, we mean 'good funds' – that is, central bank deposits that can shift rapidly through a system of settlement.

16 See Folkerts-Landau (1991).

17 The Swiss payments system is an important exception, in that it is a gross settlement system without intra-day credit extension.

18 In settling net positions, the clearinghouse makes a claim that in the event that one member is in bankruptcy, it has the right to offset payments due from that member with payments due to that member. The clearinghouse makes prior claims over all other creditors to the bankrupt member's liabilities to the clearinghouse to the extent that they are offset by that member's claims on the clearinghouse. Much of the security the clearinghouse adds to the payments mechanism is derived from liability rules. Reserve requirements protect the payments mechanism in a similar fashion. They are assets of the several member banks, but the clearinghouse has prior claim to them in the event of bankruptcy.

19 The US Federal Reserve is an example of a clearinghouse that bears the risk of settlement failure. Reserves of individual banks serve as a guarantee to the Fed of the delivery of good funds against end-of-day net due to positions, but the Fed is covered against a bank's nonsettlement only by that bank's reserve deposits. CHIPS now also operates as a collateralized clearing corporation with settlement finality for payments generated in the Eurodollar and foreign exchange markets.

20 Some of these concerns have been discussed in recent conferences and symposia. For example, the Group of Thirty Symposium on Clearance and Settlement Issues in the Global Securities Markets in London in March 1988; and the International Symposium on Banking and Payment Services, sponsored by the Board of Governors of the Federal Reserve System, June 7–9, 1989; and the Williamsburg Payments System Symposium of the Federal Reserve Bank of Richmond, May 20, 1988.

21 Greenspan (1989)

22 The US Fedwire system is the Federal Reserve's nationwide wire system for transferring funds and US Government securities among foreign and domestic depository institutions operating in the United States. Fedwire is the world's largest wholesale payments settlement mechanism, with an average daily value of transactions of $700 billion (excluding CHIPS net settlement) in 1989. Fedwire payments are made by debiting and crediting reserve accounts maintained by depository institutions at their Federal Reserve banks. The Fedwire payment is finally and irrevocably paid when a reserve bank sends a payment message to a receiving depository institution. The Federal Reserve Bank will execute the payments instruction even if it leads to a debit balance. If the sending bank failed while in overdraft, the risk would be borne by the Federal Reserve Bank. Such an overdraft must, however, be settled by the end of the day, hence the term 'daylight overdraft.'

23 A large proportion of the assets of money centre or clearing banks is financed by short-term funds – certificates of deposit, repurchase agreements, interbank loans – and it is possible that a loss of such funding could make it necessary for

the bank to discount assets other than the eligible government securities. In this case the central bank would be exposed to the private credit risk inherent in such assets.

24 In the Federal Reserve system, each district Federal Reserve Bank has a formal identity, and member banks formally maintain deposit accounts with their district Federal Reserve Bank. Funds move instantly from one member to another, however, even though they have accounts with different district Federal Reserve Banks. There is no central Federal Reserve Bank like an ECB, however, where the district Feds keep funds for interdistrict settlement. Settlement across district Feds occurs through a manipulation under the direction of the Open Market Committee, which reallocates Treasury securities on the balance sheets of the district Federal Reserve Banks.

25 The only Community-wide payments system currently operating is the ECU Clearing and Settlement System. The 45 participating clearing banks, located in 10 EC countries, use SWIFT as netting center, and settle final clearing balances in sight deposits accounts they maintain at the BIS. Such accounts are not allowed to show a debit balance. Clearing banks with a debit position have to obtain ECU funds from creditor banks through bilateral operations. If a clearing bank has insufficient funds in its ECU account to cover its end-of-day settlement obligations, then all intra-day payments instructions will be unwound and those pertaining to the debtor bank will be eliminated. The new clearing balances will be established and added to the clearing for the following day. In securitized financial systems, with high-volume wholesale payments flows among clearing banks, such as unwinding is very likely to cause illiquidity in several other participating institutions (Humphrey, 1984). For this reason, the CHIPS system adopted settlement finality with explicit loss-sharing arrangements in 1990.

26 The German Reichsbank, founded in 1875, was the only major exception; although it supplied liquidity to the financial system during crises by purchasing prime bills on the open market, it did not act as a lender-of-last-resort to individual banks. The risk that a bank failure might lead to generalized illiquidities in the banking system was perceived to be negligible, and the Reichsbank stood aside in a number of bankruptcies among the largest banks. As a result, it also was able to avoid any role in supervising or regulating commercial banks. It appears that the structure of bank liquidity of German commercial banks made such an aloof position vis-à-vis individual banks possible. In particular, the ratio of cash to banks' sight deposits was relatively high and the ratio of bank capital to bank deposits was also comparatively high and, therefore, the risk of contagion among banks was relatively smaller. Thus, individual bank failures were unlikely to spill-over, and generalized liquidity shortages could be met with open-market purchases of bills and supervision and regulation of banks could be performed by a separate agency. In short, liquidity problems were unlikely because all markets, including banking markets, were kept notably illiquid. See National Monetary Commission (1910a), and Goodhart (1988).

27 See Goodhart (1988); Bagehot (1922); Willis (1923); Smith (1936); Sprague (1910); National Monetary Commission (1910a, b, c, d, e, f).

28 This change is especially noticeable in the evolution of post-World War II textbooks on money and banking. These became essentially second-rate macroeconomics texts, reflecting the view of central banking prevalent in

macroeconomics, in which the role of central banks was economic stabilization and the role of banks was purely a mechanistic balance sheet activity of producing deposits that formed a key part of the controllable money supply.

29 The rapid collapse of the main schools of thought in macroeconomics, and the fracturing of macroeconomics itself as a coherent discipline, in the 1980s has engendered an understanding that a central bank cannot play an activist role in stabilizing real economic activity, leaving the attainment of price stability as the main macroeconomic goal. The only consideration of central banking policy as a banking rather than as a monetary policy in the recent academic macroeconomics literature is Sargent and Wallace's (1982) paper on the real bills doctrine vs. price level stability. Sargent and Wallace show that a policy based on a real bills doctrine is welfare maximizing when capital markets are constrained. The result is tainted, however, by its being reached in the context of an overlapping generations model of money demand.

30 The experience of the US Federal Reserve System is the most relevant as a model for the new European system of central banks and the ECB. The Fed's view were clearly formulated by Chairman Volcker in 1983: 'A basic continuing responsibility of any central bank – and the principal reason for the founding of the Federal Reserve – is to assure stable and smoothly-functioning financial and payments systems. These are prerequisites for, and complementary to, the central bank's responsibility for conducting monetary policy as it is more narrowly conceived.

To these ends, the Congress has over the last 70 years authorized the Federal Reserve (a) to be a major participant in the nation's payments mechanism, (b) to lend at the discount window as the ultimate source of liquidity for the economy, and (c) to regulate and supervise key sectors of the financial markets, both domestic and international. These functions are in addition to, and largely predate, the more purely "monetary" functions of engaging in open market and foreign exchange operations and setting reserve requirements; historically, in fact, the "monetary" functions were largely grafted on to the "supervisory" functions, not the reverse' (Federal Reserve System, 1984).

31 The Bundesbank's experience undoubtedly served to form views about the role of the ECB. For example, Dr. H. Tietmayer, member of the Board of the Bundesbank, made the case for a narrow ECB. '... if too many tasks were to be assigned to the European Central Bank this could complicate the conduct of monetary policy. The ECBS should be free, therefore, from responsibilities other than those for monetary policy. In particular, banking supervision should not be assigned to the ECBS, but should be left with national authorities, if only to prevent the ECBS from being forced into a "lender of last resort" function that would not be compatible with its task of safeguarding the currency ...' (Deutsche Bundesbank, 1991).

32 For example, in a wholesale payments system with daylight credit and settlement finality, such as Fedwire, it may be possible for a bank to send a sufficient volume of payments messages to exceed the value of its assets.

33 For example, the absence of extensive derivative markets raises the cost of hedging operations. It is a general proposition that any restrictions on the number and type of instruments that make financial markets less complete lead to inefficient resource allocation.

34 Garber and Weisbrod (1990) have established elsewhere that banks have a comparative advantage in supplying liquidity, hence it is efficient to restrict

those activities of banks that do not relate to the payment system or supplying liquidity.
35 Article 25.2 holds out the possibility of designating the ECB as a complete supervisory authority but such a transfer of competence would have to be specified by Community legislation.
36 Germany is the only major industrial country with a central bank that does not have a substantial supervisory function.

REFERENCES

Bagehot, W. (1922), *Lombard Street*, London: Kegan, Paul & Co.
Deutsche Bundesbank (1991), Auszuge aus Presseartikeln, 11 November.
Federal Reserve System (1984), 'The Federal Reserve Position on Restructuring of Financial Regulation Responsibilities,' *Federal Reserve Bulletin*.
Folkerts-Landau, D. (1991), 'Systemic Financial Risk in Payment Systems', IMF Occasional Paper No. 77.
Folkerts-Landau, D. and Donald J. Mathieson (1988), 'Innovation, Institutional Change, and Regulatory Response in International Financial Markets', in William S. Haraf and Rose Marie Kushmeider (eds.), *Restructuring Banking and Financial Services in America*, Washington, DC: American Enterprise Institute for Public Policy Research, pp. 392–423.
Frankel, Allen B., and John D. Montgomery (1991), 'Financial Structure: An International Perspective', *Brookings Papers on Economic Activity* 1, 257–309.
Garber, P. M., and Steven R. Weisbrod (1990), 'Banks in the Market for Liquidity', NBER Working Paper No. 3381.
Goodhart, Charles Albert Eric (1988), *The Evolution of Central Banks*, Cambridge, MA: MIT Press.
Greenspan, A. (1989), 'International Payment System Developments', speech before the International Symposium on Banking and Payment Services, Washington: Federal Reserve Press Release.
Grossman, S., and M. Miller (1988), 'Liquidity and Market Structure', *The Journal of Finance* 43, 617–34.
Humphrey, David B. (1984), *The US Payments System: Cost, Pricing, Competition and Risk*. Monograph Series in Finance and Economics, Salomon Brothers Center for the Study of Financial Institutions.
National Monetary Commission (1910a), *The Reichsbank and Renewal of its Charter*, Vol. X, Washington, DC: Government Printing Office.
(1910b), *Articles on German Banking and German Banking Laws*, Vol. XI, Washington, DC: Government Printing Office.
(1910c), *The German Inquiry of 1908* (Stenographic Reports), Vol. XII, Part 1 and Vol. XIII, Part 2, Washington, DC: Government Printing Office.
(1910d), *The Great German Banks*, Vol. XIV, Washington, DC: Government Printing Office.
(1910e), *Banking in France and the French Bourse*, Vol. XV, Washington, DC: Government Printing Office.
(1910f), *Banking in Italy, Russia, Austro-Hungary and Japan*, vol. XVIII, Washington, DC: Government Printing Office.
Sargent, T., and N. Wallace (1982), 'The Real Bills Doctrine vs. The Quantity Theory: A Reconsideration,' *Journal of Political Economy* 90, 1212–36.

Schwartz, Anna J. (1988), 'Financial Stability and the Federal Safety Net', in William S. Haraf and Rose Marie Kushmeider (eds.), *Restructing Banking and Financial Services in America*, Washington, DC: American Enterprise Institute for Public Policy Research, pp. 34–63.

Smith, Vera (1936), *The Rationale of Central Banking*, London: P. S. King & Son Ltd.

Sprague, O. M. W. (1910), *History of Crises Under the National Banking System*, National Monetary Commission, 61st Congress, 2nd Session, Senate Doc. No. 538, Washington, DC: Government Printing Office

U.S. Department of the Treasury (1991), *Modernizing the Financial System*, Washington, DC: February.

Willis, Henry Parker (1923), *The Federal Reserve System*, New York: The Ronald Press.

Discussion

JOHN C. PATTISON

1   Introduction

The issue addressed in the paper by Folkerts-Landau and Garber is whether the 'Draft Statute of the European Central Banks and the European Central Bank' erred in limiting the European Central Bank ('ECB') to a monetary role rather than including responsibility for financial stability. One could rephrase this by saying, should the ECB be a Federal Reserve system or a Bundesbank? Clearly the authors have decided that Europe needs an ECB modelled on Federal Reserve lines.

I am going to respond by looking at three major building blocks on which their conclusion rests. These are of broad interest to commercial bankers and central bankers, bank regulators and ultimately those in the political system who give direction to the framework of bank operations and regulation.

These three foundations are: first, the assumption that central banks should have a broad mandate to deal with what are bank solvency, supervisory and regulatory matters; second, that the extent of securitization, rather than simply bank creditworthiness, increases the need for a central bank to be a lender of last resort; and third, that well functioning payments systems require central banks to take private sector credit risk.

Before proceeding it should be fully appreciated that these are very important economic and financial issues. They are rendered even more significant by the difficulties experienced by bank and non-bank financial intermediaries in many countries and by the opaqueness of many of the financial regulatory, supervisory and payment processes to both the public and to academics who have not generally delved into the back-offices of the financial system. This paper makes a particularly worthwhile contribution to these issues in their application to the ECB.

2   Central banks as supervisors

The authors illustrate how central banking evolved from banking institutions to having responsibility for macroeconomic policy superimposed on them. Today many central banks, particularly the US Federal Reserve System and the Bank of England have banking and financial objectives in addition to those of monetary policy. However, no two central banks are the same and the assumption that certain institutional designs provide an argument for the newly proposed European model is insufficient.

The authors are correct in that the differences in scope among central banks are largely explained by differences in the structure of national financial markets. Whereas they identify the most important factor as the relative sizes of securities versus banking markets, I would argue that the most important factor is the probability of a major failure leading to systemic risk. This probably is a function of a much larger number of variables such as the size distribution of banks with direct access to the clearing system. The US experience with a large number of banks and a large number of other financial institutions is rare. Moreover, without nationwide branch banking in the US to provide liquidity to banks, there is a greater onus on the Federal Reserve System to provide liquidity and lender of last resort facilities. As this illustrates there are also a number of policy and political variables which make generalization difficult.

Another point worth greater discussion is the distinction which the authors make between insolvency risk and liquidity risk.[1] I would argue that all central banks are sensitive to liquidity crises such as those stemming from the Penn Central problem or the 1987 stock market crash. Central banks can take liquidity out of the system as quickly as it is injected, thereby not subordinating their goals of monetary control to supervisory type issues. However, in most countries central banks deal with a small number of clearing banks who then make their own credit judgements concerning smaller financial institutions at those difficult moments. In the United States with the large number of banks, credit risk confronts the Federal Reserve directly. To a lesser extent this is also true of the Bank of England. In the latter case, the risk stems from the large number of foreign banks and a number of relatively small merchant banks and accepting houses.

Another factor which deserves comment is that even those central banks which seem to eschew a broad mandate, usually go some way down the road. Even the Bundesbank has a significant regulatory function which involves the supervision of 'approved persons', and the use of the system-wide integration of lending data on individual institutions to assess bank risk. These supervisory functions together with moral suasion and their market clout suffice to reduce or eliminate systemic risk that in other countries might necessitate the provision of liquidity to troubled institutions.

The authors provide a very convincing argument for a broad central bank role in their discussion of the impact of credit risk in payments systems such as Fedwire. As they conclusively illustrate, the more efficient the payments system in a complex financial market, the greater the credit risk internalized within the settlements system. Payments systems that are not irrevocable and final, run the risk that unwinding transactions could cause failures in parties unrelated to those in default.

In the European context, the authors note that the netting of ECU transactions using SWIFT is problematic since all payment instructions for the day will be unwound if a counterparty has insufficient funds at the end-of-day settlement.

In some countries the need for a broader mandate for central banks has been reduced by large banks clearing for small ones, particularly for foreign banks. This shifts the locus for the decision as to whether one is facing a liquidity or an insolvency problem to the large clearing banks from the central bank. Inevitably this leads to a structure where a decision has been made implicitly in the design of the financial system that some institutions are 'too big to fail'.

The authors state that the assignment of responsibility for bank supervision should avoid conflicts of interest among agencies. However, conflicts will occur between the monetary and supervisory functions in a single institution. It could be argued that better decisions will be reached if each agency focuses on its particular goal rather than an individual agency trading them off. This would be because of the specialization of each and the better use of a larger number of better targeted instruments.

3   *Securitization and the role of the central bank*

I disagree with the authors, who assert that the extent of securitization is positively correlated with the need for the central bank to act as a lender of last resort. I speak to this point as someone who has run the domestic funding and treasury operations of a large bank. The extent of securiti-zation does increase the probability of individual failures to settle. In aggregation large banks will find that offsetting transactions reduce the significance of this problem. Since most countries have a small number of large banks through which most transactions pass in the clearings this is mainly a problem for the smaller institutions. Even with a 25 percent fall in the Dow Jones Index in October 1987 and greater falls in places such as Sydney and Hong Kong, the remarkable outcome was that the system was not at all imperilled by the danger of the failure of large institutions because their creditworthiness was immediately and sharply reduced by the market fall. The larger problems were that credit judgements had often assumed too little asset coverage for collateral for non-financial customers. In my experience the collateral which banks take for lending to financial institutions such as brokers/dealers and investment banks is government securities and acceptances at major banks, not commercial debt obligations. The latter are usually sold to a large number of end buyers.

Even more favourably, securitization has meant that banks have many types of liquid, short-term securities which can be purchased or sold at little change in price according to day-to-day liquidity needs. In addition, there are many thousands of corporate and government institutions, if not tens of thousands, which place money in the money market every day. Both these factors reduce the probability that major banks will need recourse to central bank liquidity as financial markets are securitized.

4   Payments systems and systemic risk

One of the implicit distinctions in the above discussion is that the risks were clearing risks or credit risks attendant upon the behaviour of an individual bank. One factor which should be clarified is that clearing risks are stochastic processes. Banks must adjust their reserve positions with the central bank according to their expectations as to the magnitudes of expected gains and losses through the clearing system. In my experience this can be easily managed in a large bank as you are dealing with a zero-sum game with a small number of participants, one of whom is the central bank. Even so, every once in a while it is possible to be spectacu-larly wrong in either direction as, for example, oil companies make large payments, other large unanticipated commercial transactions are made, governments shift funds and so forth. However, although these can impact reserve positions they don't affect solvency as funds are on hand; they may simply be invested in short-term securities awaiting settlement on a different date. In support of the authors' thesis, the central banks know enough about the cash positions of all major clearing participants as well as their short-term liquid asset and liability positions to separate liquidity from solvency questions. I should add that this applies in almost all countries with the possible exception of the US system with its large number of banks.

The authors are convincing on two related points. One is the potential threat of systemic problems in the design of the payments system. Second is how this risk is borne, and in particular, on efficient and inefficient ways to run a payments system.

I would conclude that central banking and bank supervisory systems would not have to overlap except for the vital need to control the incidence of credit risk and to stop it cascading through the payments system. Once again, the practical implications depend upon the number of banks in the system and their riskiness. To reiterate an earlier point, the 'too big to fail' concept is not so much a credit judgement as it is designed to keep the payments system from gridlock or worse.

Even so there is nothing that stops a central bank contracting credit advice from bank supervisors the same way that Moody's or Standard & Poor's reports are used by the private sector. However, the authors would contend that the ECB has no mandate to play a role in the payments system on a European wide basis. The risk inherent in settling ECU is an example of a gap that needs to be closed to facilitate the financial integration of Europe. There is no doubt that such matters are important institutional questions for the future of integrated European financial markets.

5   Further implications

I would like to suggest five points for further thought.

First, it is probably not a coincidence that the Draft Statute for the ECB did not lead to a mandate to stabilize European financial markets. Notwithstanding the current macroeconomic issues facing Germany, as Europe becomes more of a DM zone I would expect the private sector to make its own choices in favour of DM assets and liabilities. Why should the Bundesbank propose or support a Draft Statute which could efficiently lead to a parallel central banking regime and a competitive currency to the DM? Moreover, I believe that the long run will show European financial markets developing around a DM base because the marketplace prefers a real currency to a composite one such as the ECU.

Second, there is a large literature on the economic and bureaucratic decision-making processes of central banks. I am a sufficient believer in the rationality of central banks, irrespective of how much one may like the outcome, to suggest that there is a self-interested rationale behind the Draft Statute.

Third, the authors discussed conflicts of interest and moral hazard with one notable exception. This is the conflict between securities regulators, who have responsibility for banks as issuers of securities and for the full, plain and true disclosure of material facts concerning them, and the central bank or banking supervisor who may not want this information disclosed for systemic reasons.

Fourth, the authors are careful to differentiate between a temporay liquidity problem and an underlying reduction in asset prices and credit worthiness. However, while this distinction can sometimes be made quite easily, in some circumstances the central bank could be put in the invidious position of encouraging a credit expansion for the wrong reasons at the wrong time.

Fifth, it seems that the main issue in this paper is but one of a large number of complex issues involving the regulation of financial institutions in Europe, such as deposit insurance for branches using the single license, harmonization of regulation and so forth. These need to be treated in an interdependent fashion rather than as stand-alone issues.

In conclusion, the authors have provided a good and thoughtful paper with implications enough to keep central bankers, commercial banks and governments working for some time to come. While I may disagree about the institutional architecture, I agree with the authors that the issues in their paper require successful treatment by an appropriate agency.

NOTE

1 Another distinction which needs to be kept clear is that between being a provider of liquidity and being a lender of last resort.

RICHARD J. SWEENEY

David Folkerts-Landau and Peter Garber have given us a stimulating and well written paper on a major issue in designing a European central bank. There are many parts of the paper I like a great deal; it would be easy to use my allotted space to praise their paper and to summarize the parts I particularly liked. The discussant's role, however, is to focus on areas of disagreement. The main disagreement is that the authors of this very well written paper do not make their case as clearly as possible. As I read the paper, sometimes between the lines, the authors make a case for an ECB that is involved with the payments system (supervising it or running it, and also insuring it) and with regulating banks. Two conventional justifications for such involvement and regulation are market failure and the danger that expectations, perhaps destabilizing, might cause avoidable damage. The authors do not really argue these justifications as strongly or as clearly as they might. I want to highlight where these issues arise in their analysis.

Their paper considers three types of crises: runs on banks; a stock market crash; and pressure on the payments mechanism. It is useful to consider each in turn.

Bank Runs Bank runs are a classic fear about financial and monetary systems. The fear seems to have (at least) three bases. First, runs might lead to bank failures and thus substantially reduce the money stock, causing deflation and a recession or even depression. Developed country monetary authorities can now offset any money stock effects caused by bank runs even if the authorities allow banks to fail, perhaps in some numbers. There is no need on this score for the central bank to regulate banks or carry out other central bank functions that F-L and G identify.

Second, healthy banks may be forced to 'close their doors.' This provides a justification for a lender of last resort that will discount economically sound assets of the banks. This discounting provides liquidity in the sense that banks do not have to sell their assets on short notice in a jittery market and take prices that are less than could be obtained if sold over a longer time. Liquidity in this sense is inversely related to the amount of time expected or required to sell an asset at its fair market value; one problem with reading the paper is that it is often unclear exactly what the authors have in mind by the term liquidity.

It is not clear that central bank discounting does much on the score of liquidity. The sorts of assets that the central bank (at least the Fed) will discount are those that can be sold very quickly on the open market. Discounting mainly offers a subsidized higher price (by applying a below-market discount rate) than the banks could obtain on the open market. In some few cases the market for such highly liquid assets may not function or the payments system may break down; in such cases central bank discounting replaces the market. This point really has to do with the payments system discussed below. It is not clear how bad 'closing doors' may be. If the bank's assets really are valuable, then over the time required to convert them at reasonable, obtainable prices, depositors and other bank creditors will get back all of their funds plus accrued interest. The cost is doing without the use of the funds for a few days or weeks or conceivably months; even in this case, there should be credit available elsewhere for the bank's creditors to smooth these problems. The securitization that the authors stress helps with the problem by making the asset side of the bank's balance sheet easier to assess, an aspect the authors seem to overlook.[1]

It is puzzling that the F-L and G Paper, an excellent one, omits discussion of two key issues about banks closing their doors. They do not mention federal deposit insurance or the idea that some banks are 'too big to fail.' From recent US economic history the reason there have been no bank runs on federally insured institutions is because of the insurance, not because of the Fed acting a lender of last resort. It would be very useful to know how deposit insurance, absolute up to some large amount of deposits, fits into the authors' scheme. On the one hand, it is not clear that lender-of-last-resort functions particularly improve the market under the circumstances of the past decade in the US. On the other hand, it is clear that deposit insurance is not something lightly to be undertaken; I have some sympathy for the view that deposit insurance is likely to cause major problems for a financial system and the taxpayers who ultimately guarantee it. These problems arise because of bad incentives for bank decision makers; the effects of these bad incentives can be ameliorated by regulation, but this is rather redundant compared to not having bad incentives in the first place. Similarly, the notion that banks are too large to fail adds to the stability of a banking system but at the cost of encouraging bad resource allocation. On this score, it would be good if F-L and G could spell out more institutional details on EC country banks (the paper is in general very good and informative on institutions and their roles). For example, though the authors tell us that the Bundesbank does not regulate German banks, I wonder if the major German banks are too big to fail? And are they somehow regulated in ways that act to reduce the guarantor's risk? So far then, the only activities of central banks that are not done pretty well by financial markets are open-ended deposit insurance and guarantees that some banks are too big to fail, activities that are at the least questionable.

Third, bank failures may be contagious in the form of altering expectations that have real effects on the economy. There is a long history of believing that the credit system is unstable: it is, for example, a thread throughout the work of John Hicks. Other economists view bankruptcy of financial institutions as no different in effect from that of a comparable sized manufacturing firm (Alchian and Allen, 1972). For example, if creditors come to doubt the solvency of a bank, they may run on it. If the bank fails in the sense of closing its doors, creditors of other banks may have their Bayesian beliefs shifted by the failure and start their own runs. One of the goals of founding the Fed was to create an elastic currency supply. The Fed was to provide currency to banks to meet these runs, in return for safe bank assets that were discounted. This arrangement made a good deal of sense: If the demand for base money rises, the only ways of satisfying it are to increase the stock of base money or to let price deflation increase the real stock, a process easily understood from Patinkin (1965). If the Fed were to allow deflation to work its way out, there might be great instability. As one bank fails, there are runs on other banks. Depositors may rationally realize that the process will cause deflation. Further, they may understand that this deflation will cause defaults on banks' assets and hence more bank failures. The system then has an inherent instability, one based on expectations that are rational; this is similar in spirit to Irving Fisher's debt deflation process. The Fed's actions to increase base money see to it that the outcome will not be deflation and hence short circuit the run by destroying its rational basis. Notice, however, that this stabilization is mainly a result of the Fed attempting to prevent deflation, not through it acting as a lender of last resort, even less it acting to save banks that are 'too big to fail.'

In today's world, the elastic supply of currency is not nearly the issue it was. When people flee bank money, they do not turn to base money but rather to high quality debt. There was, for example, a noticable 'flight to quality' in the form of federal government debt at the time of the October 1987 stock market crisis. In such a case, it is not clear what role the central bank should play beyond expanding base money to satisfy whatever vestigial increase in base-money demand might arise.

One might go further and argue that expectations have strong bandwagon effects (and I have some sympathy for this view[2] or that the system is subject to bubbles and that runs on one or a few banks can have destabilizing effects on the whole system. Appropriate central bank action depends on the expectational problem involved. The authors, so admirably clear on so many points, are not clear on what expectations mechanisms they have in mind. Another way of thinking about the expectations issue is to note that in general the case for government action involves some type of market failure. The authors have not spelled out a particular type of market failure; pointing to bad things that might happen to private markets is not the same thing as pointing out market failure. My guess is that the case they have in mind relies on expectations. I am quite willing to entertain this view, since I have evidence that speculative markets driven by expectations often appear to be systematically inefficient to some extent. But we really need to be told the expectations mechanism and how this leads to market failure. We must also consider government failure: in the US federal deposit insurance and the doctrine that some banks are too big to fail have led to substantial social costs.

Stock-Market Crashes F-L and G provide a lucid discussion of how progressive securitization creates vast financial market interdependencies; this is reminiscent of detailed input-output tables for the US economy. The authors' discussion shows that securitization has a symbiotic relationship to liquidity. On the one hand, economic agents buy and sell securities because they believe that they will be able easily and quickly to realize the fair market value of the assets in a short time – the essence of liquidity. On the other hand, the greater the degree of securitization, the more liquid markets become. Securitized assets may not normally be very liquid; for example, many corporate bonds trade relatively infrequently in thin markets (Warga and Welch, 1990; Eberhart and Sweeney, 1991). For this reason it is difficult in the US to mark-to-market the value of financial firms' assets even if the assets are securitized. In less securitized economies where banks are the major intermediaries, it is even harder to assess accurately the value of the banks' assets; on this margin such banks are more liable to runs than if there were greater asset-side securitization.

The dense input-output network of financial relations is put under great stress when the stock market crashes as in October 1987 (or more mildly in October 1989). One agent's ability to make the transactions s/he desires and to carry out his/her economic function is contingent on a vast array of other agents making their desired transactions. Serious failures of this dense network are exactly liquidity crises: agents are unable to realize quickly the fair market values of their assets. The probability of this dense network failing in a serious way is not clear. Neither is it clear what a central bank should do to help. The authors discuss the central bank supplying liquidity and urging banks to supply liquidity. By the central bank supplying liquidity, I presume they mean open market operations that increase the stock of base money, as apparently happened in October 1987. The central bank may also reduce the discount rate or allow banks to borrow more than otherwise at the discount window, or reduce the grade of asset accepted for discounting. It is not clear that any of these is wise as long as the central bank is supplying an adequate amount of base money; given this is so, the other actions would seem to be propping up banks that might be insolvent. It is not clear that propping up insolvent banks is preferable to keeping them running but transferring ownership to creditors. Further, it is not clear how such actions would affect non-bank agents who are experiencing liquidity problems. For example, a leveraged dealer/broker who is caught short and looks like a bad credit risk is not much helped by the Fed injecting base money or by banks having easier access to the discount window. Further, it is not clear how Fed exhortations to banks to provide liquidity are going to help: do such exhortations mean banks should go against their better judgment, or merely that they should calm down and make loans that really are sensible?

The market survived the crash of 1987. During this crash, a number of brokerage houses and dealers went under. Further, at times the market was effectively closed for individual stocks and at other times the futures and cash markets were out of touch with each other because of poor execution. Both of these phenomena showed that the market was less liquid than some sanguine agents thought; there may well be agents who found the markets even more liquid than they would have thought in the circumstances. We do not know whether agents now view the market as more or less liquid than they believed before. It is interesting to note that the circuit breakers desired by the SEC and the NYSE and now in place are designed in effect to limit liquidity and force agents to accumulate and sift information while held temporarily in an illiquid state. The point of raising circuit breakers is not to endorse them – I do not – but to point out that some observers find the costs of temporary illiquidity small enough to make it worthwhile to impose it.

Breakdowns of the network of financial transactions are illiquidity that leads to further illiquidity. To the extent that agents are surprised by the extent of these breakdowns, the agents are less willing later to take open positions. To the extent that illiquidity is an issue, circuit breakers are surely costly, though there may be offsetting gains in giving the market time for reflection.

When there are market breakdowns, they are costly to those who cannot carry out desired transactions. For example, if I am sure the market is going down further, I may want to sell out my positions, presumably to someone on the other side of the market who has differing views. When we cannot make the transaction and the fall in the market that I anticipated occurs, I lose in an opportunity sense and the partner on the other side of the transaction gains by the same amount; overall, this breakdown simply results in a distribution effect. Of course, if I am at all frequently caught in such distribution effects, I will cut back on my market activity and thereby make the market less liquid; this may be the real cost of market breakdowns. It is hard to see what central bank policy can reasonably do about such breakdowns.

Suppose an agent goes bankrupt because of inability to make transactions in a market that is suddenly illiquid. This is, recall, a distribution effect. Of course the value of remaining assets will have to be sorted out and distributed to claimants. My impression is that the settlements after the October 1987 crash were relatively smoothly handled and taken in stride.

The authors do not say it, but I have the impression that they think a crash might snowball, with illiquidity leading to insolvency, to more illiquidity, more insolvencies and a mighty crash in the end. This might happen. The easiest way for this to happen might be through expectations that become more and more gloomy, pushing down market values of many assets in a downward spiral. This possibility has to be spelled out though, particularly the expectations mechanism, for us to evaluate its plausibility and likelihood and to evaluate where there is much a central bank can do beyond changing the stock of base money appropriately. A snowball effect might constitute a case for government doing something to prevent or ameliorate the problem. Another way to invoke the government is to argue that liquidity is an externality provided by the thickness of markets and number of participants, and hence the government might intervene to increase liquidity. It is not clear how the central bank is to do this for non-banks, in general or during crashes.

Clearing Systems The third type of crisis is a breakdown in the clearing systems that banks and other major players use, whether for foreign exchange transactions or federal funds or similar financial transactions. The authors paint a picture of the likelihood of gridlock under a system where a bank must have reserves at the clearing house at every second to cover a claim that is made against the bank. Reasonably, the clearing mechanism may allow for day-end settlement. With this system, if a bank cannot cover its claims, either the clearinghouse must make good out of its reserves, the member banks must be forced to bear the costs by some formula, or the day's transactions must be unwound. Unwinding the transactions is not a good idea – it magnifies the uncertainty beyond the net amount involved (in effect it forces individual banks to face some risks that the system as a whole can diversify). In the long run, if the clearing-house bears the risk, it must charge system users enough to cover costs; whether this is better than allocating any costs *ex post* to members depends on the formulas used in either. It is clear that either system can be made to work.

If the clearinghouse bears the risk, there is always the possibility that it may become insolvent. The authors argue that only a government agency with access to the Treasury can guarantee that the payments system will not run into this problem. I would say, only a government agency that can print money, that is, only the central bank or the part of government that controls the central bank, can make this a credible guarantee. We have much evidence that state governments cannot make credible guarantees;

for example, the nineteenth century saw state defaults on bonds, and the Depression saw city defaults.

Do we want the central bank to guarantee the clearinghouse? This is a cost and benefits issue. What are the costs of reducing to zero the probability of clearinghouse failure? Surely the authors are correct that government guarantees will lead to government regulation. This regulation has a well known set of costs from the industrial organization literature. The benefits are the avoidance of a clearinghouse default. Suppose an unguaranteed clearinghouse could not cover the loss. We are not told how bad this would be. One might be able to construct an externality case that the economy would be wounded in a major way by an unravelling of many transactions networks. On the other hand, it is not clear that this is an externality any more than a major setback is in any industry that figures in the input-output table.

Further, it is not clear that clearinghouse insolvency would lead to any social costs. One scenario is that the major members of the clearinghouse would quickly and with little friction pay in more capital to make the clearinghouse solvent once again. There are, after all, likely a few members that are large enough to act quickly together and are exposed enough to make free-riding an unimportant problem. Other scenarios are possible, but it would seem that it is up to the authors to show why there will be social costs.

Again, one might argue that the visible failure of the clearinghouse, even if new capital is supplied within hours, might so shake expectations that an undesirable evolution is set off. But this is a case for the authors to make.

In sum, this stimulating paper still has a ways to go to make its case. The basic micro route for justifying intervention or regulation is market failure. The authors have not made this case. Nor have they used one of the basic macro routes, that expectations would be destabilizing in the absence of central bank action. This is not to say that the case cannot be made; but the paper does not make it.

NOTES

1 Even on the liabilities side, I think the authors sometimes confuse the effect of securitization. At one point they argue that a system that relies on banks for intermediation rather than on securitization will give banks fewer problems since creditors cannot take away their deposits or other forms of credit to banks on the short notice that wholesale money center banks are subject to in the US. This seems to confuse the maturity of assets with securitization. It is quite possible that banks have many sight liabilities even if banks are the main form of intermediation. The real problem here is a mismatch of assets and liabilities

in terms of maturity and liquidity, and this mismatching can happen under any degree of securitization.
2 Sweeney (1986) and Surajaras and Sweeney (1991) present evidence that technical trading rules make risk-adjusted profits in foreign exchange markets; one possible explanation for these profits is the existence of bandwagons.

REFERENCES

Alchian, A. A. and W. R. Allen (1972), *University Economics*, 3rd ed., Belmont, CA: Wadsworth Press.
Eberhart, A. and R. J. Sweeney (1991), 'Bond Prices as Unbiased Forecasts of Bankruptcy Settlements.' Washington, DC: Georgetown University, School of Business Administration, Working Paper.
Patinkin, D. (1965), *Money, Interest and Prices*. New York, NY: Harper and Row.
Surajaras, P. and R. J. Sweeney (1991), *Profit-Making Speculation in Foreign-Exchange Markets*. Boulder, CO: Westview Press (forthcoming).
Sweeney, R. J. (1986), 'Beating the Foreign Exchange Market,' *Journal of Finance* **41**, 163–82.
Warga, A. and I. Welch (1990), 'Bondholder Losses in Leveraged Buyouts.' Columbia University, Graduate School of Business, Working Paper.

Part II Transition from national central banks to a European Central Bank

5 Hard-ERM, hard ECU and European Monetary Union

DAVID CURRIE

1 Introduction

The vision of Monetary Union in Europe is of long standing. The Werner Report of 1970 advocated the attainment of Monetary Union by 1980, but was buried beneath a soaring oil price and the collapse of Bretton Woods and the move to generalised floating in the early 1970s. The European Community, with some key exceptions, returned to an adjustable peg exchange rate system in 1979 with the launch of the Exchange Rate Mechanism (ERM for short). Helmut Schmidt and Valery Giscard d'Estaing embarked on the ERM against majority technical advice from economists at the time, but despite that the ERM must be judged an appreciable success: much more durable than its critics expected, and much more successful in establishing a credible and stable framework for anti-inflationary policy. Even the British have finally been won round.

In the early years of the ERM, parity realignments were frequent and sometimes large, on occasions requiring the temporary closure of foreign exchange markets while bargaining over the realignment went on. These frequent realignments were necessary because of the diversity of inflation rates between the participating countries. But the gradual convergence of inflation rates, itself a product of the ERM, led over time to smaller and less frequent realignments. This is illustrated in Figure 5.1, which shows realignments of the participating countries against the Deutsche Mark, which over this period did not devalue against any currency. As Figure 5.1 shows, with the exception of Italy, there has been no realignment within the ERM for well over four years. (The Figure depicts the logarithm of the non-German exchange rates, relative to the DM, measured such that the absolute change reflects the proportional change in the exchange rate). Moreover, the Italian devaluation of January 1990 is the

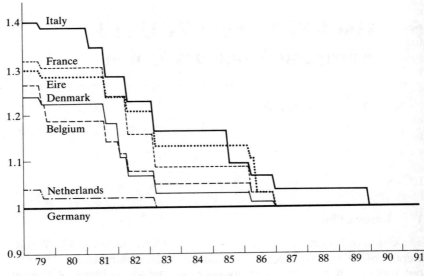

Figure 5.1   Realignments against the DM, 1979–91

exception that proves the rule: the band of variation for the Lira was narrowed at the bottom end of its former broad band, leaving the floor unchanged and requiring a lowering of the central parity and ceiling. This represented a strengthening, not a weakening, of commitment to the ERM by the Banca d'Italia. Thus the evolution of the ERM over the past decade can be represented as an evolution from a soft to a hard form, as European policymakers found the ERM a comfortable framework for conducting anti-inflationary macroeconomic policy.[1] The absence of any realignment over the past year or so, with the double shocks of German union and the Gulf War, is testimony to the durability of the ERM.

The success and durability of the ERM has been an important force in putting EMU back on the agenda. The Heads of State agreed in 1988 to set up a committee to examine possible approaches to EMU, and the Delors Committee reported in 1989 (Committee for the Study of Economic and Monetary Union, 1989). Since then, the agenda has advanced rapidly, with the establishment of an Inter-Governmental Conference on EMU and European central bankers developing their ideas for monetary coordination ahead of EMU. The pace of change has been so rapid that EMU has even forced issues of political union onto the agenda, with Chancellor Kohl explicitly linking the two issues. The present impetus may not be sustained, particularly with German attention diverted to its Eastern domestic problems. Therefore the British Government may well succeed in its aim of slowing the process appreciably, particularly with a tone of moderation, not stridency, that makes it easier for Germany to embrace the UK's position. But the direction of change is likely to be sustained, driven forward by the essential political change in Europe in the 1980s: the switch by France under Mitterrand from a Gaullist to a Communautaire position within Europe.

The creation of the ERM in 1979 did, by contrast, represent a regime change, creating a formal structure of cooperation between the participating central banks, and restricting each country's freedom to alter its exchange rate outside narrow limits by the requirement to secure the agreement of the other member states. By contrast, the evolution of the ERM from its loose, soft form in the early 1980s to its hard form of the past four years or so has taken place without much institutional adaptation. The Basle-Nyborg Agreement of 1987 did increase the availability of the 'very short-term financing facility', which reduced the vulnerability of the ERM system to speculative attack by increasing the funds available to central banks for intervention: it was probably helpful in strengthening the credibility of the ERM in important respects. But there has been little institutional adaptation to reduce the incentive for participating countries to alter their central parities within the system, and realignments represent a real possibility: only last year Karl Otto Pöhl was urging a devaluation on the French, for example, and there are continued calls for a devaluation of sterling. For these reasons, I would characterise the shift from the Soft- to Hard-ERM as a process switch, not a regime change.[2] Because of this, the Hard-ERM cannot be relied upon as a durable system without further institutional development. However, it is not hard to envisage the form that such institutional development might take: it would be straightforward to embody the current near-absence of exchange rate realignments by allowing realignments only after an elapse of years (say, three or four) and insisting that they be intra-marginal (so that the new band overlaps with the old). This would allow central parities to change only very slowly, and would institutionalise the current Hard-ERM arrangement.

This approach of buttressing the advantages of the current Hard-ERM arrangement is not in favour in Europe. Instead the debate focuses on moving forward to monetary union. One possible reason for this is political: the view that moving towards monetary union offers the best means of strengthening the political cohesion of the European Community. But there are also two principal economic reasons: that EMU is a preferable regime, yielding higher net welfare benefits; and that the current Hard-ERM arrangement is not stable. The second argument concerning the stability of the Hard-ERM can be divided further into two parts: that the Hard-ERM is not incentive-compatible for the individual countries participating in it; and that it may be unstable in the dynamic sense, for example, because of the phenomenon of currency substitution.

I wish to discuss the relative benefits of the EMU and Hard-ERM in some detail, together with the issue of incentive-compatibility, which applies as much to EMU as to the Hard-ERM. I deal briefly now with the issue of currency substitution. It is clear that exchange rate stability over prolonged periods will make agents in different countries increasingly indifferent in the choice of currency denomination of money holdings. Thus money demand functions may demonstrate increasing instability. If the monetary authorities choose to attempt to target monetary aggregates, then instability may well result. Currency substitution between DM and non-DM deposits may make the formulation of monetary policy in Germany more difficult, and thus may generate swings in German inflation. Fixed parities will generalise these swings throughout the Community (see Hughes Hallett and Vines, 1991).

My own view is that these worries are exaggerated. Monetary authorities, including the Bundesbank, have increasingly adopted pragmatic methods of monetary control, allowing interest rates to be guided by growth of nominal income in the medium to long term and a variety of indicators in the short term. Financial innovation, which also has also induced instability in monetary aggregates, is likely to increase its impact with harmonisation of financial services regulation after 1992. This will make the pragmatic setting of monetary policy all the more needed. In these circumstances, currency substitution will add somewhat to the problem of interpreting monetary conditions and setting interest rates, but should not induce undue instability.[3] Were the problem more serious than this, it would already have shown up between the stable currencies of the Community, most noticeably between the Dutch Guilder and the DM. Moreover, the switch to a single currency in Europe will throw up exactly the same problems of interpretation of monetary aggregates, at least over an extended transitional period. For these reasons, I do not consider currency substitution to be a serious concern for the current Hard-ERM arrangement.

In analysing the performance of alternative monetary arrangements in Europe, economics has most to offer in analysing the steady-state, systemic properties of the alternative regimes. It is a general characteristic of the methodology of economics that it allows us to say much more about steady states, in which of course I include stochastic steady states, than about the dynamics of transition from one stochastic steady state to another. I do not think that we need to be too apologetic about this, particularly when examining the design of particular regimes. The calculus of discounting may lead us to give weight to the short run at the expense of the long run. But it would be unwise to choose a regime on the basis of its transitional ease rather than its long-run systemic properties. A necessary, but not necessarily sufficient, condition for a desirable regime is that its long-run steady-state and stochastic properties should be satisfactory.

2   The benefits of EMU

In considering the benefits of moving to EMU, the most tangible benefit is that of a single currency in Europe. The resource benefits from eliminating intra-European currency transactions is not large in itself: estimated by the Commission to be in the range ¼–½% of Community GDP.[4] Larger output gains are seen as accruing from the elimination of currency risk, estimated perhaps generously by the Commission at around 2% of Community GDP. Allowing for induced investment and adjustment to a higher capital stock resulting from these efficiency gains applies a multiplier to these gains; and assuming constant returns to capital taken alone, as in the new endogenous growth literature, gives permanent gains to growth. These calculations are pretty soft, and perhaps should not be taken too seriously, but it is clear that the potential benefits could be significant.

What then are the disadvantages? The traditional approach to the issue of monetary union is provided by the literature on optimal currency areas. This suggests that the benefits of eliminating currency exchanges in a monetary union will be larger the greater the degree of intra-union trade; while the costs of abandoning exchange rate flexibility will be smaller the higher the degree of labour mobility, the higher the degree of nominal wage and price flexibility, the more diversified the industrial structures of the constituent economies, and the larger the proportion of common, rather than country-specific, shocks. Applied to Europe, this analysis yields a fairly mixed answer. Labour mobility is clearly rather low in Europe, and much lower than in the United States. But Europe qualifies rather better on the other criteria. An important reason for the progressive abandonment of the nominal exchange rate instrument in Europe in the 1980s is the view that it is an ineffective means of obtaining adjustments in relative competitiveness except in the rather short run: nominal exchange rate changes tend to lead rather quickly to higher inflation, so that over a two to four-year horizon gains in competitiveness are eroded through higher prices and wages. My reading of the optimal currency literature is that it provides a compelling case neither for, nor against, monetary union.

3   The benefits of reputation

However, the answers provided by the optimal currency area literature are limited in one rather crucial respect: they neglect the importance of policy disturbances in choosing between alternative regimes. A change of regime may well involve a change in the institutional structure of policy-making (for example, a move from many monetary authorities to a single one), as well as in the incentive structure facing policy-makers (for example, in the incentives to engage in inflationary policies). These changes can be expected to alter policy, and thereby alter the inefficiencies and shocks to the economy that arise from policy. There is substantial evidence to suggest that policy is an important source of disturbance to the economy, so this neglect matters.

It is for these reasons that the non-German monetary authorities have increasingly sought to 'tie their hands', in the phrase of Giavazzi and Pagano (1988), by fixing their exchange rate against the Deutsche Mark. Against this background, the key question is not the desirability of retaining the exchange rate instrument: that has been largely given up. Rather, it is whether EMU will provide a better or worse framework for delivering low and stable inflation. The Commission takes a predictably positive view of this matter. Using simulations on the IMF's international model, MULTIMOD, they see the evolution of the ERM through to EMU as a steady reduction of inflation and output variability. The document suggests also that EMU will deliver low, as well as stable, inflation, but this need not be so.

One can think of this issue quite straightforwardly in a Barro type world where the only real impact of monetary policy is via monetary surprises. Figure 5.2 shows the familiar one-period trade-off between inflation and output that arises in such a world. A government with reputation will be perceived to resist the temptation to inflate to secure short-term output gains, and so equilibrium will be at a low inflation outcome at the origin O. However, without reputation, the private sector will expect the government to inflate to move to position A. Because this is anticipated, equilibrium will be at a high rate of inflation at point B, where the government has no incentive to spring a monetary surprise.

Although the diagram makes this point in a very simple framework with no nominal inertia that can give rise to short-run Keynesian effects, it is important to stress that the point is valid in a much more general class of models. My colleagues and I have investigated the effect of reputation in a wide class of analytical and empirical models, (see, for example, Currie *et al.*, 1989) and this finding is quite robust. It is not specific to the

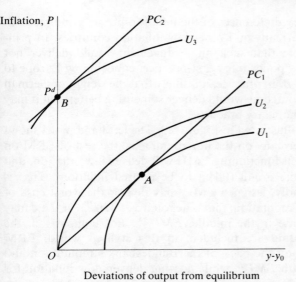

Figure 5.2   Short-run inflation-output trade-off in a Barro world

particular assumptions of the Barro world, which is nonetheless the most convenient framework for exposition.

With flexible exchange rates, Germany enjoys low inflation at the origin O by virtue of the Bundesbank's reputation, while other less fortunate European economies experience high inflation. Within the ERM, the commitment to fix the exchange rate against the Deutsche Mark allows the monetary authorities of these other countries to borrow the reputation of the Bundesbank and enjoy low inflation. What allows them to secure reputation in fixing their exchange rate when they are unable to do so in pursuit of purely domestic objectives is the institutional framework of the ERM: the external commitment to other countries gives the exchange rate objective a credibility that internal objectives alone lack.

4   Will the European Central Bank be independent?

What then is the impact of EMU and the creation of a single European Central Bank? The answer to that question depends rather critically on the structure of decision-making within the new European Central Bank. The proposed structure is one where European monetary policy is set by a committee comprising the governors of the national central banks, supplemented by a few wise experts. With this arrangement, it is clearly possible that the policy preferences of the inflation-prone economies will dominate those of Germany and other low inflation countries. In principle, it is conceivable that such an arrangement would deliver not best-practice monetary policy but worst-practice, condemning Europe to high inflation at point B. In practice, it is likely that the weight of German objections to such an outcome would deliver something better; but it may well not deliver best monetary practice.

The possibilities are illustrated in Figure 5.3. The left hand panel shows inflation rates, for Germany on the horizontal axis, the rest of ERM on the vertical axis. A well-functioning EMU will deliver low inflation, and will therefore be at the origin (taken to be desired inflation). That is marked EMU^B. A badly designed EMU may deliver the worst case of high inflation without reputation: that is denoted as EMU^W. Or there may be an intermediate case in the middle, EMU^{AV}. For comparison, the Hard-ERM and floating are included: in this stylised world, ERM delivers low inflation on the back of the Bundesbank's reputation, and therefore coincides with EMU^B, while floating delivers low inflation for Germany and high inflation for everyone else. The Soft-EMS regime, which gives partial credibility gains to high inflation countries, will lie between the floating and Hard-ERM cases. Taking account of the resource and welfare gains of eliminating residual exchange rate risk and from moving to a single currency, the left hand panel translates into the right hand welfare map: this plots welfare *losses*, so that the aim is to be as close as possible to the origin. Clearly the desirability of EMU relative to Hard-ERM depends crucially on the design of EMU. Progress towards EMU may move us towards low inflation, as the Commission argues; but it may not.

It is clear from this diagram why Germany gains in economic terms from EMU only if the independence of the European Central Bank is assured. The diagram also suggests that the same is true of the other ERM countries. However, our discussion so far has neglected the stabilization issue, and once this is taken into account other ERM countries may prefer EMU even without a strong commitment to price stability. This is because of the asymmetrical character of the ERM, based on German leadership in monetary policy. This means that European monetary policy is set on the basis of essentially German domestic considerations. Consider, for example, a supply shock that impacts asymmetrically between countries, pushing up inflation in Germany but not elsewhere. Under current arrangements, this will lead to a tightening of German monetary policy, and this will have to be followed elsewhere in Europe, despite being inappropriate outside Germany. The result is a loss of welfare for the other ERM countries relative to that of Germany. The

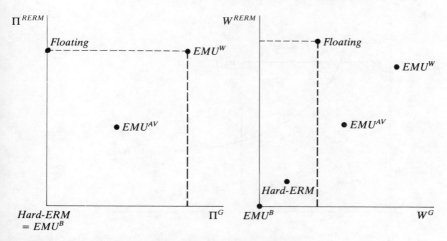

Figure 5.3   Bargaining over ERM versus EMU in a Barro world

benefit that Germany obtains from the Hard-ERM relative to the Soft-ERM or floating derives from this stabilization role: in the face of asymmetrical shocks, the poorer coordination between ERM members under the Soft-ERM imposes a higher cost on Germany, relative to the Hard-ERM case where monetary policy is coordinated largely on German terms. The current shock in Europe resulting from German reunification is an excellent illustration of this point. Under EMU, the sharing of responsibility means that monetary policy will be more directed to European-wide considerations, so that the welfare losses will be more evenly shared. Thus in terms of the right-hand panel, the Hard-ERM point, will tend to move up vertically relative to the others, and may therefore perform worse from the perspective of non-German participants than an indifferent EMU or even the Soft-ERM.

It does not follow from this that the other ERM countries should prefer an indifferent EMU or the Soft-ERM to the Hard-ERM. For there is the alternative that the Bundesbank might soften its position, and pay attention to broader European-wide macroeconomic developments in setting German monetary policy. This is illustrated in Figure 5.4. This plots an indifferent EMU and floating as before. However, the Hard-ERM now becomes a locus of welfare points. This locus plots what happens to welfare as the Bundesbank varies the weight that it puts on non-German policy concerns. With full weight given to German concerns ($a = 1$ at the left hand end of the locus), the welfare loss is low in Germany and high elsewhere: as more weight is given to non-German concerns, welfare losses elsewhere fall, while they rise for Germany. As illustrated, there are

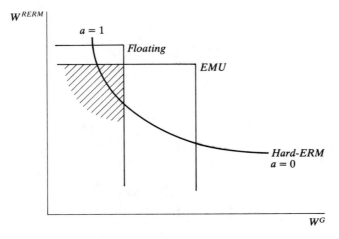

Figure 5.4   Bargaining over ERM versus EMU

a range of values of *a* for which the Hard-ERM is superior to EMU. The hatched zone shows the region in which the Hard-ERM is also superior to floating. As illustrated, the Hard-ERM is incentive-compatible only if the Bundesbank is willing to take some account of European-wide developments in the setting of German monetary policy. Figure 5.4 is hypothetical, but Currie *et al.* (1990) examine this issue formally in a simulation model, with a variety of aggregate supply and demand shocks. The results support the general conclusion: that is, if EMU leads to a loss of reputation in monetary policy, a Hard-ERM arrangement may well be superior; but that the Hard-ERM is unlikely to be incentive-compatible unless the Bundesbank pays regard to European-wide, rather than simply German, macroeconomic developments.

What benefits does Germany derive from the Hard-ERM arrangement relative to either floating or Soft-ERM on the one hand or EMU on the other? In terms of anti-inflation performance, Germany enjoys low inflation under either Hard-ERM or floating. EMU has the major political disadvantage that the ECB may be softer on inflation than the Bundesbank. From the German perspective, the Hard-ERM offers better stabilization of asymmetric shocks, avoiding the coordination problems that arise under either floating or a Soft-ERM. It is an empirical question whether these benefits are large enough for Germany to be willing to consider European-wide stabilization sufficiently to make the Hard-ERM incentive-compatible from the perspective of the other member countries. Thus it is possible that the hatched zone in Figure 5.4 is empty. However Currie *et al.* (1989) find that it is not, and that there is a range over which a Hard-ERM outperforms both EMU and a Soft-ERM or floating.

This case against EMU and in favour of the current Hard-ERM arrangement rests on the possible lack of credibility of a European Central Bank, and this argument is well-recognised. It is usually met by the counter-argument that the need for an independent central bank is generally accepted. The European Commission's document (*European Economy*, 1990) on the benefits of EMU devotes five pages to an analysis of this issue, setting out the conditions for a stable and credible monetary regime. Referring to the proposed European System of Central Banks that will become the European Central Bank or Eurofed, the Delors Report states that 'the System would be committed to the objective of price stability'. This is much more specific than the Bundesbank Act which requires the Bundesbank 'to regulate the amount of money in circulation and credit supplied to the economy, ... with the aim of safeguarding the currency', which leaves open the theoretical ambiguity of whether it is internal purchasing power or the external value against other currencies which is to be stabilised. (See Bofinger, 1990. As an aside, this, of course, means that the Bundesbank is able within its statutes to give some weight to broader European considerations in the interests of preserving the Hard-ERM and exchange rate stability. Whether it wishes to do so, is another question.)

Despite this, there are grounds for doubt. The draft statutes follow the commitment to price stability that I have just quoted by adding 'subject to the foregoing, the System should support the general economic policy set at the Community level by the competent bodies'. This would leave ample scope for acrimonious debate between national finance ministers and the European Central Bank as to whether or not the general economic policy of the Community was consistent with price stability, and should therefore be supported by the Central Bank. It is encouraging that the guidelines for the European Central Bank have been drafted to be more Teutonic than the Bundesbank, and give it considerable independence. But it is significant that an issue within the Intergovernmental Conference is whether or not responsibility for the external exchange rate of the Community should lie with the finance ministers, ECOFIN, or with the European Central Bank, and there are signs that ECOFIN might win out. If fiscal policy is left to be determined by national governments and the extra-European exchange rate is determined by finance ministers, then monetary policy is pinned down. National governments jointly can then determine monetary policy in the medium to longer run, and no careful drafting of statutes for an independent central bank will avoid that. There is, of course, some scope for finance ministers to exert influence over short-run exchange rate policy. But if there is any doubt over the European Central Bank's responsibility in the longer run, its independence will be weakened.

Perhaps more fundamentally, one may question whether it is the statutes and constitution of the Bundesbank that have delivered low inflation, or whether it does not owe rather more to the inflation-aversion of the German people, scarred by the experience of hyperinflation. It is often argued that the credibility of the Bundesbank owes much to the punishment that it would face were it to renege. That punishment in turn depends on the preferences of the society. Of course, German aversion to inflation may have been softened by many years of low inflation, and some other countries, notably France, have themselves developed a commitment to low inflation as a consequence of the experience of the 1970s and early 1980s. Nonetheless, it is clear that, outside a small core of member states, there is a greater tolerance of inflation. If this is so, a European Central Bank will inevitably face less censure from a European public less averse to inflation, and that in turn may mean less credibility. To avoid this requires a constitutional set-up that ensures that the low-inflation vote wins out, but that is a hard trick to pull off.

5   The coordination of fiscal policy

Let me now bring fiscal policy into the discussion. The Delors Report argued two key points about fiscal policy in EMU: first, that the European Central Bank should not finance budget deficits by monetary expansion; and second, that binding fiscal rules would be required to limit the freedom of national governments in fiscal policy. The first of these is generally accepted, but of course it may easily be undermined by the issue of where responsibility for exchange rate policy lies: if finance ministers determine exchange rate policy and national fiscal policy, the European Central Bank will be forced, in effect, to monetise national budget deficits. The second point was widely attacked on a variety of grounds, and has since been softened to the need for 'a system of coordination and self-imposed constraints', but the form that this might take is still open.

To consider the consequences of fiscal coordination in this context, consider the standard Hamada diagram depicted in Figure 5.5 (see Hamada, 1985). On the axes are the fiscal/monetary mix of the two countries: country two on the vertical axis, with a move up representing a looser fiscal/tighter money mix; country one on the horizontal axis. The objective function of country 1 defines a set of indifference curves, connecting points of equal welfare, as perceived by country 1. In the absence of spillovers, these indifference curves would be vertical lines,

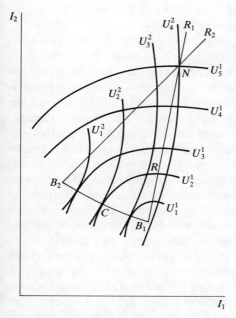

Figure 5.5   Hamada diagram

with the welfare level defined uniquely by the instrument setting I_1. But with spillovers, the instrument setting I_2 influences the welfare of country 1. As a consequence, the indifference curves become curved around the bliss point B_1 (or point of highest welfare) of country 1. Similar indifference curves map out points of equal welfare around the bliss point, B_2, of country 2.

Efficient policies are those for which the indifference curves of the two countries are tangential. These are represented by the contract curve joining B_1, and B_2. These policies are Pareto-efficient, in the sense that one country's welfare can rise only if the other country's welfare falls.

Uncoordinated decision-making need not lead to policies on the efficient contract curve. This may be seen from Figure 5.5 as follows. In the absence of coordination, country 1 will treat country 2's policy as given when deciding upon its own policy. For any I_2 setting, it will therefore choose I_1 to maximize its welfare. Thus it chooses I_1 to give the point of tangency between the indifference curve and the horizontal line corresponding to I_2. Varying I_2 then traces out the reaction function, R_1, of country 1, connecting the horizontal points on its indifference curves. The reaction function, R_2, of country 2 can be defined similarly, depicting the optimal choise of I_2 for given I_1. R_2 connects the points where the indifference curves of country 2 are vertical.

The outcome of uncoordinated decision-making is the Nash point, N, given by the intersection of the two reaction functions. At this Nash outcome, both countries are doing the best they can, given the policies of the other country. But the outcome is inefficient. The Nash point is Pareto-inferior to at least a subset of coordinated policies lying on the contract curve. As depicted, each country would like to be able to engage in expansionary fiscal policy relative to the other: hence the positions of the bliss points, B_1 and B_2. This may arise in a variety of models: it may be for Keynesian reasons to obtain a demand boost without undue interest rate consequences, that may have undesirable supply-side effects; it may also be because this secures a real exchange rate appreciation, facilitating output growth without inflation; it may also occur because an expansionary fiscal policy allows governments to reconcile distributional demands placed on it. Some of these advantages may be short-run in character, but fiscal policy may readily succumb to these pressures. Given this set-up, the uncoordinated outcome will be at the Nash point, N, where the two reaction functions, R_1 and R_2, intersect. Non-coordination leads to an outcome with a lax fiscal/monetary mix and unduly high interest rates. This conclusion is familiar for a world of flexible exchange rates, either floating or the Soft-ERM. And it has applicability to the 1980s, most obviously for the US and Reaganomics, but also to many countries in Europe which saw rising public debt to GDP ratios.

Will EMU contain these pressures? Here there are two starkly contrasted possibilities.[5] If countries can enjoy a fiscal expansion without a rise in the real interest rate that they face, then fixed expansion within EMU may well be attractive: keep demand high, real interest rates low, and inflation controlled by the fixed peg to the DM. In this case tendencies to fiscal expansion will be intensified. By contrast, if risk premia on individual national debt emerge, when governments borrow unduly, then EMU will dampen the tendency to over-expansionary fiscal policy.

The original Delors Report was sceptical about the ability of market-determined risk premia to coordinate fiscal policy in this way, and I think it was right. First, there is the empirical point that this mechanism could have operated under the Soft-ERM, yet there is rather poor evidence for substantial risk premia linked to national over-borrowing. Second, there is the point that expansionary fiscal policies are not necessarily synonymous with debt problems and default, so that risk premia need not emerge, at least on a scale required to moderate borrowing. And finally there will be considerable pressures on a European Central Bank, independent or otherwise, to accommodate fiscal policy, of course in support of (and I quote) 'the general economic policy set at the Community level by the competent bodies.' We see those pressures at work in the case of the US Fed in response to the Savings and Loans fiasco. National default would pose major problems for the Community, and markets might well suppose that the European Central Bank would help out. Moreover, the ECB will be unusual in facing twelve (or more) distinct Treasuries, with possibly no substantial central federal debt. This means that the ECB could undertake this bailing out without altering the stance of its overall monetary policy, by buying-in debt of countries in the course of its open market operations where debt problems are pressing and selling in those countries where they are not. These problems have not arisen in Germany, but I suspect that owes more to the debt-aversion and inflation-aversion of the German public than any specific market mechanism via risk premia.

I therefore conclude that fiscal coordination will be necessary for a well-functioning EMU. But it does not follow that coordination alone will be sufficient. This is because of the problem of credibility of the fiscal authorities. Just because finance ministers get together to coordinate, they will not magically acquire reputation in policy: look for a counter-example to the Community's agricultural ministers. Coordination of fiscal policy without reputation need not help, as Rogoff (1985) has shown for monetary policy. Our preliminary results suggest that it does help, but not much. And the consequences of lack of reputation can be seen in Figure 5.6.

Consider the independent conduct of monetary and fiscal policy, with both set of authorities sharing the same objective function. (This is the set-up relevant to an independent central bank, so that monetary policy is set independently of fiscal policy.) If both have reputation, then their preferences are as shown in the lower left part of the diagram centred around B^R. In this case the monetary authorities set monetary policy on the vertical axis to reach B^R, and the fiscal authorities do likewise with fiscal policy on the horizontal axis.

If both lack reputation, then again the preference maps of the two authorities coincide, but it is as though they are centred around a point to the north-east at B^{NR}: both monetary and fiscal authorities think that a surprise expansion can give rise to a better outcome so that they set policy to achieve B^{NR}. The private sector anticipates this, so the benefits are largely illusory: the distance of B^{NR} from B^R gives some measure of the welfare costs of lack of reputation.

The different positions of the two bliss points, B^R and B^{NR}, in Figure 5.6 reflect the consequences of absence of the reputation in a Barro-type world. A government without reputation considers that it can gain a

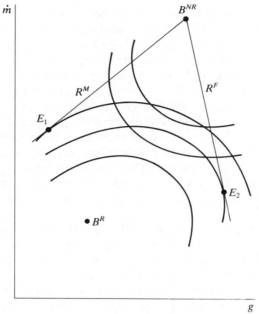

Figure 5.6   The implications of lack of credibility

short-run output advantage by springing an expansionary surprise on the private sector, and therefore chooses to run a more expansionary monetary and fiscal policy. But because the private sector can anticipate this, the expected and therefore actual inflation rate is higher in the absence of reputation. In more general dynamic models, the analysis of the absence of reputation is more complex dynamically, but the same qualitative features arise: the non-reputational outcome is to the north-east of the reputational one, in terms of the axes of Figure 5.6.

Now consider the mixed case where one authority has reputation and the other does not: the most relevant case is where the monetary authorities have reputation, while the fiscal authorities do not. The policy outcome is then determined as a game between the two authorities, with the fiscal authorities as a follower, and the monetary authorities as a leader.[6] The preference map of the monetary authorities is that in the south-west corner centred on B^R; that of the fiscal authorities is in the north-east corner, centred on B^{NR}. The reaction function of the fiscal authorities is R^F, and equilibrium is at E_2, which clearly represents an inefficient outcome. In the short run, the independent European Central Bank may offset the expansion of the fiscal authorities by a more contractionary monetary policy, though the net result may well be a rise in inflation. In the long run it is likely that E_2 will lie somewhat to the north-east of B^R, as shown in Figure 5.6. This means that there is likely to be higher inflation as a consequence of the fiscal authorities' lack of reputation.

What should be done about this? There are, of course, clever debt games that can in principle be played to lock the fiscal authorities into a position where they do not wish to borrow excessively. But one doubts the practicality of these as effective disciplines. Current discussions within the IGC centre on devising simple rules for the conduct of fiscal policy. One suggestion is that medium-term fiscal plans for each member state should be discussed publicly by finance ministers as a form of coordination. This may help, but one doubts whether it would dispose of the problem. I could spend much longer discussing the form of possible simple fiscal rules: my colleagues and I have done much work to devise simple rules that mimic the policy under reputation, and that can be done. But it is not at all simple to devise rules that are sufficiently transparent and intuitive to be incorporated into a draft minute for agreement by Finance Ministers. One simple indicator under consideration – the level of borrowing as a proportion of GDP – does not work well: it varies enormously across member states and is not related in any way to debt sustainability, or to the thrust of fiscal policy. Equally unhelpful is the use of the basic balance as an indicator. Any guidelines for fiscal policy will have to cope with considerable differences in initial positions. Perhaps that is why the Germans, supported by others, are pressing for much more convergence before moving beyond Stage 1 or the strengthened Hard-ERM.

6 Transitional arrangements

If the transition to EMU is to be protracted, the process of transition requires careful management. Otherwise there is a real danger, as Giovannini (1991) argues, that the transition will prove unstable, and the Hard-ERM will revert to floating.

A striking feature of the Delors Report is the lack of substance that it gives to the transitional, Stage 2 of the process towards EMU. It was this gap that the British proposals for an evolutionary approach to EMU were intended to fill. First came a proposal for competing currencies, launched at a meeting of finance ministers in Antibes in September 1989. This was quickly modified to a proposal for competing currencies within the framework of the ERM (H. M. Treasury, 1989), a proposal better understood as competition between monetary policies, rather than currencies (Currie, 1989b). The basic idea was that the removal of barriers to the use of currencies would allow the holders of money to choose freely between alternative currencies: the resulting competition between monetary authorities would impose an anti-inflationary discipline on the individual central banks. Arguably this is close to how the Hard-ERM currently operates (Currie, 1989a). EMU could arise from such competition if one currency becomes predominant: if this were the outcome, then EMU would have occurred as a result of individual consumer choice, and not imposed. Not surprisingly, this vision of EMU resulting from spontaneous choices by individuals was seen by other member states as a formula for putting off EMU indefinitely, an objective that was known to be welcome to the UK government on political grounds.

This British evolutionary approach was then developed further in June 1990 by the proposal for a Hard-Ecu (H. M. Treasury, 1990). The current Ecu is a weighted average of the 12 community currencies. As such, though the weights have changed occasionally, the Ecu has reflected average performance, devaluing against the DM, and appreciating against the lira. The proposal is to create a new Hard-Ecu that at realignments never devalues against any of the Community currencies. There are two ways of doing that:

(1)   Change the weights of the Ecu on realignment, increasing the weight of the hard currencies and reducing that of the weak ones. This we may term the 'Hard-basket'.
(2)   Make the Ecu an independent currency managed by a new institution – this is the British Hard-Ecu. The new institution, called the European Monetary Fund (EMF), would ensure through its open market operations that the Hard-Ecu never devalues.

There are, I think two main reasons why the British favoured of these possibilities the Hard-Ecu rather than the hard-basket. First, the scheme was originally branded as 'competing currencies', and the hard-basket does not fit the competing currency bill. Second, the British government has still not accepted the final goal of the EMU. If parity realignments continue, and the DM continues its track record as a non-depreciating currency, then the DM weight will rise over time, and the hard-basket tends asymptotically to the DM.

The British proposal is then that the Hard-Ecu becomes a common currency, free to be used throughout the Community. Whether it becomes a single currency, displacing existing Community currencies, is a matter of consumer choice – this may or may not occur. If it does, EMU will emerge from an evolutionary, decentralised market process rather than through centralised decision-making in Brussels.

Now interest rates on the Hard-Ecu will have to bear a certain relation with interest rates on the individual Community currencies. There is a view that this means that the European Monetary Fund will have no freedom of manoeuvre. That is incorrect. What is crucial is whether the new institution is a price-taker or can influence interest rates, and that depends on its market power.

Initially one might think that this market power would be quite small. The Hard-Ecu would not appear much more attractive than the DM, and the Bundesbank would very much have the market clout. To be a transitional arrangement, the new institution would have to increase its market influence over time.

The British scheme has a proposal that ensures this. The repurchase provision says that if the new institution raises interest rates on the Hard-ECU and acquires community currencies, the national central banks would have an obligation to repurchase their currencies with hard currencies. To do so, they may well have to borrow Hard-Ecus from the new institution at the higher rate of interest. This provides a powerful mechanism for the new institution to fix interest rates.

On the British proposal, this repurchase arrangement would come into force in Stage 2. Once it does, we have an effective European Central Bank. But in the meantime, we have the basis for an unfortunate power struggle between the European Central Bank and the Bundesbank, which could well follow the messy path of the early years of the Federal Reserve System that Eichengreen (this volume) describes.

It therefore seems more sensible to use a hard-basket, rather than the Hard-Ecu, as the transitional device towards a single currency. Stage 2 then becomes a process in which cooperation between the Community central banks increases, and the structures for cooperation become more formalised and centralised, resulting eventually in an ECB.

A hard-basket could well play an increased role instead of the DM as a reserve currency for the European banking system. As this role increases, so the backing from national currencies could become one-for-one, so that they are fully backed, as for Scottish banknotes. At that point, monetary coordination would be complete. The move to a single currency and the elimination of national currencies could then be a matter of political and administrative convenience.

7   Conclusions

The upshot of my analysis is that there are appreciable risks and uncertainties in moving towards EMU. EMU could work out well; but it could work out rather badly. Given the poor track record of the Community in other fields – agriculture, trade, the Uruguay round, foreign affairs – it would not be surprising if governments wish to move slowly. There is an interesting analogy to be drawn here with Ken Binmore's (1989) analysis of the process of moving towards a social contract; he shows that this involves a series of small, discrete steps, involving the building of trust and credibility between the partners to the social contract.

Those who see the Hard-ERM as unstable will see this gradual approach as non-viable – we either rush forward, or go back to a looser arrangement (Giovannini, 1991). I do not agree. However, to ensure that the Community does not go backwards, there would be advantage in underpinning the Hard-ERM by greater institutional constraints, limiting the frequency and size of any future realignments and possibly moving to tighter bands.

A longer-drawn-out transition to EMU means that substance needs to be given to Stage 2 of the Delors process. It should not be regarded as a stage to skip over, but rather it needs to be designed carefully to avoid the inflationary possibilities of a poorly designed EMU. The British Hard-Ecu scheme is inappropriate: it leaves open appreciable scope for muddle and conflict in Stage 2. An increased role for the Ecu, possibly making it a hard-basket, and strengthening the framework for monetary cooperation in Europe is the right way forward.

NOTES

The support of the Economic and Social Research Council (grant no. W116251003) and the Leverhulme Trust is gratefully acknowledged.
1 This may be for the reputational advantages of 'tying one's hands' noted by Giavazzi and Pagano (1988).
2 Here I use the term 'regime change' to describe shifts in process accompanied by supporting changes in institutions, describing as process switches the case where shifts in the policy processes are unaccompanied by institutional change. For further discussion, see Currie (1992).
3 See Canzoneri and Diba (1991) for the argument that, under plausible assumptions about monetary policy, higher currency substitution may indeed reduce instability.
4 See *European Economy* (1990).
5 For a fuller discussion of the issue, see Bovenberg *et al.* (1991).
6 The sense in which the monetary authorities act as leaders is a little special. Having reputation, they are able to set monetary policy credibly over time, so that the problem of time-inconsistency does not arise. The fiscal authorities lack credibility, and therefore are tempted to adopt an over-expansionary policy in the short run, despite the longer-run problems that this may generate. However, fiscal policy is set period by period against the background of a credible pre-determined medium-term path for monetary policy. In this sense, the fiscal authorities act as followers. For further details, see Currie and Levine (1991).

REFERENCES

Binmore, Kenneth (1989), 'Social Contract I: Harsanyi and Rawls', *Economic Journal* **99**, Supplement, 84–102.

Bofinger, Peter (1990), 'Unresolved Issues on the Road to Economic and Monetary Union in Europe', CEPR Discussion Paper No. 405.

Bovenberg, A. Lans, Jeroen J. M. Kremers and Paul R. Masson (1991), 'Economic and Monetary Union in Europe and Constraints on National Budgetary Policies', *IMF Staff Papers* **38**, 374–98.

Canzoneri, Matthew B. and Behzad T. Diba (1991), 'Currency Substitution and Exchange Rate Volatility in the European Community', mimeo, Georgetown University.

Committee for the Study of Economic and Monetary Union (1989), *Report on Economic and Monetary Union in the European Community*, European Community.

Currie, David (1989a), 'European Monetary Union or Competing Currencies: Which Way for Monetary Integration in Europe?' *Economic Outlook* **14**, 18–24.

(1989b), 'Competition in Policies, not Currencies', *Financial Times*, 15 November.

(1992), 'European Monetary Union: Institutional Structure and Economic Performance', *Economic Journal* (forthcoming).

Currie, David and Paul Levine (1991), 'The International Coordination of Macroeconomic Policy: A Survey', in D. Greenaway, M. Bleaney and I. Stewart, (eds.) *Economics in Perspective*, London: Routledge.

Currie, David, Paul Levine and Joseph Pearlman (1989), 'European Monetary Union or Hard-EMS?', *European Economic Review*, forthcoming.

Eichengreen, Barry (1992), 'Designing a Central Bank for Europe: A Cautionary Tale from the Early Years of the Federal Reserve System', this volume.

European Economy (1990), 'One Market, One Money', **44**, 1–351.

Giavazzi, Francesco and Marco Pagano (1988), 'The Advantages of Tying One's Hands', *European Economic Review* **32**, 1055–82.

Giovannini, Alberto (1991), 'Is Economic and Monetary Union Falling Apart?', *International Economic Outlook* **1**, 36–41.

Hamada, Koichi (1985), *The Political Economy of International Monetary Interdependence*, Cambridge, MA: MIT Press.

H. M. Treasury (1989), *An Evolutionary Approach to Economic and Monetary Union*, HMSO.

(1990), 'Economic and Monetary Union', *Treasury Bulletin*, 14–16.

Hughes Hallett, Andrew and David Vines (1991), 'Adjustment Difficulties within a European Monetary Union: Can They be Reduced?', CEPR Discussion Paper No. 517.

Rogoff, Kenneth (1985), 'Can International Monetary Policy Cooperation be Counterproductive?', *Journal of International Economics* **18**, 199–217.

Discussion

DALE W. HENDERSON

My comment is divided into two sections. Section 1 is a summary and critique of the comparison of three monetary policy regimes, Floating, Hard-ERM, and EMU, contained in Currie's Sections 2–4. Section 2 is a discussion of commitment technologies.

1   Floating, Hard-ERM, and EMU

Using a simple two-region model of Germany and the rest of the ERM (RERM), Currie compares three alternative policy regimes: Floating, Hard-ERM, and EMU.[1] He assumes that different 'commitment technologies' are available under the various regimes. The result he emphasizes most is that a Modified Hard-ERM may be superior to EMU for both Germany and the RERM under his assumptions about commitment technologies.[2]

An inflation bias world   In order to make the logic of his argument clear, Currie begins by analysing a world in which policy-makers face only inflation bias problems. The inflation bias problem faced by a policy-maker in a closed economy is shown in Currie's Figure 5.2. Suppose that the policy-maker's loss (L) rises with squared deviations of output (y) from a desired rate (y^*) above the natural rate (y_o) and with squared deviations of actual inflation (p) from zero:

$$L = (1/2)[a(y - y^*)^2 + p^2] = (1/2)\{a[(y - y_o) - (y^* - y_o)]^2 + p^2\} \tag{1}$$

U_1, U_2, and U_3 in Currie's Figure 5.2 are iso-loss contours representing successively higher levels of loss. The marginal rate of substitution between inflation and the deviation of output from its natural rate is given by the slope of the iso-loss contours:

$$\frac{dp}{d(y - y_o)} = -\left[\frac{\frac{\partial L}{\partial(y - y_o)}}{\frac{\partial L}{\partial p}} \right]_{L=\bar{L}} = -\frac{a[(y - y_o) - (y^* - y_o]}{p} \tag{2}$$

Suppose also that the deviation of output from the natural rate depends positively on the difference between actual and expected inflation:

$$y - y_o = (1/\beta)(p - p^e) \tag{3}$$

which can be arranged as

$$p = p^e + \beta(y - y_o) \tag{4}$$

PC_1 and PC_2 in Figure 5.2 represent this relationship for $p^e = 0$ and p_e equal to its positive equilibrium value, respectively. If the policy-maker cannot commit to deliver zero inflation, the economy will suffer from an inflation bias. That is, equilibrium inflation will be positive even though output is always at its natural rate. The policy-maker minimizes his loss by setting his marginal rate of substitution between inflation and the deviation of output from its natural rate equal to the trade-off between inflation and the deviation of output from its natural rate:

$$-\frac{a[(1/\beta)(p - p^e) - (y^* - y_o)]}{p} = \beta \tag{5}$$

where $y - y_o$ has been eliminated from the marginal rate of substitution using equation (3). In a rational expectations equilibrium the rate of inflation must be positive. Suppose $p^e = 0$ as at point A in Figure 5.2. The policy-maker would have an incentive to choose a positive p because the marginal rate of substitution (slope of U_2) would approach infinity if he chose $p = p_e = 0$, and the trade-off (slope of PC_1) is only β. Only when p^e takes on a high enough positive value does the marginal rate of substitution equal the trade-off when the policymaker chooses $p = p^e$ as at point B in Figure 5.2 where $y - y_o = 0$. Of course, if the policy-maker can commit to deliver zero inflation, the economy will not suffer from an inflation bias. The inflation bias problem faced by the policy-maker in an open economy is the same in most respects.

Currie considers three regimes. First he considers what he calls the Floating regime. Under this regime each policy-maker chooses the value of his own monetary instrument in order to minimize his own loss given the value of the other policy-maker's monetary instrument, and the exchange rate takes on whatever value is implied by the values of the monetary instruments. Under the commitment technology for the Floating regime, the German policy-maker can commit to choose the value of its monetary instrument that yields zero inflation, but the RERM policy-maker cannot. Thus, under Floating the German inflation rate is zero and the RERM has the positive inflation rate implied by the theory of inflation bias.

Next he considers what he calls the Hard-ERM. Under this regime the German policy-maker chooses his monetary instrument to minimize his own loss given that the RERM policy-maker pegs the DM exchange rate, and the RERM policy-maker chooses his monetary instrument to peg the DM exchange rate. Under the commitment technology for the

Hard-ERM, the German policy-maker can commit to choose the value of his monetary instrument that yields zero inflation just as he can under Floating, and although the RERM policy-maker cannot commit to choose the value of his monetary instrument that yields zero inflation, he can commit to choose his monetary instrument to peg the DM exchange rate. Thus, under the Hard-ERM the inflation rate in both Germany and the RERM is zero. The German policy-maker chooses the value of his monetary instrument that yields zero inflation for Germany. In order to peg the DM exchange rate the RERM policy-maker must choose the value of his instrument that yields zero inflation for the RERM.

Finally he considers what he calls the EMU. Under this regime a single European policy-maker minimizes a joint loss function in which the German and RERM loss functions receive equal weight. There may be two currencies or one. If there are two, the single policy-maker chooses the values of the monetary instruments in Germany and the RERM subject to the constraint that the DM exchange rate remains fixed. If there is one, the single policy-maker chooses the value of the monetary instrument for that currency. Under the commitment technology for EMU, the European policy-maker cannot commit to follow the monetary policy that yields zero inflation. Thus, under EMU both Germany and the RERM have the positive inflation rate implied by the theory of inflation bias.

Currie's analysis of an inflation bias world leads to an unambiguous conclusion. Germany is indifferent between Floating and the Hard-ERM, and the RERM prefers the Hard-ERM to Floating and EMU. Therefore, when the interests of both countries are taken into account the Hard-ERM is the preferred regime.[3] Currie extends his analysis in order to establish that the Hard-ERM might be superior to other regimes in more complex settings. He allows for the benefits of moving to one currency under EMU and considers what happens when policy-makers face stabilization problems as well as inflation bias problems.

Currency transactions costs and currency risk Currie recognizes that a comparison of alternative regimes should take account of differences in currency transactions costs and currency risk under the three regimes. He assumes that moving from Floating to Hard-ERM would yield benefits from reduced currency risk, so even Germany would prefer Hard-ERM to Floating.[4] He acknowledges that moving from Hard-ERM to one currency under EMU would yield benefits from reduced transactions costs and currency risk.[5] However, he goes on to argue that both Germany and the RERM may continue to prefer the Hard-ERM to EMU even when these benefits are taken into account because inflation performance may be sufficiently better.

Stabilization problems Currie also recognizes that a comparison of alternative regimes should take account of the stabilization problems faced by policy-makers as a result of disturbances to their economies. In Section 4 he allows for stabilization problems in the Hard-ERM and EMU regimes. It should not be surprising that the Hard-ERM regime may be less attractive for the RERM than the EMU regime when certain stabilization problems are present. Under the Hard-ERM the German policy-maker sets European monetary policy on the basis of German concerns. The interesting shocks to consider are goods demand and supply shocks.[6] For shocks that affect Germany and the RERM in equal but opposite ways (asymmetric shocks) and shocks that affect Germany alone (idiosyncratic German shocks), the change in European monetary policy that makes Germany better off is likely to make the RERM worse off. Only for shocks that affect Germany and the RERM in exactly the same way (symmetric shocks) is it obvious that the interests of Germany and the RERM coincide. Under EMU the European policy-maker sets European monetary policy in a cooperative way. Therefore, for asymmetric and idiosyncratic shocks, Germany is likely to be worse off and the RERM is likely to be better off under EMU than under ERM.

Currie goes on to suggest what I will call a Modified Hard-ERM regime. Under this regime the German policy-maker chooses his monetary instrument to minimize a weighted sum of the German and RERM loss functions where the weight on the German loss function can vary from zero to one and the two weights always sum to one. Currie makes the claim that there are parameter sets for which a Modified Hard-ERM with a weight on the German loss function of about 0.5 is superior to EMU on stabilization grounds alone for a wide variety of shocks. His claim is backed up by the simulation experiments in CLP (forthcoming). It is easy to see why the Modified Hard-ERM might be the same as EMU for both Germany and the RERM on stabilization grounds. It is less easy to see why it can be better. However, CLP show that it can be. No clear explanation of this result is provided by either Currie or CLP. The explanation must be that the German policy-maker's ability to commit himself enables him to achieve better stabilization performance as well as better average inflation performance, but it would be nice to know more.

The result that Currie emphasizes most is that a Modified Hard-ERM regime may be superior to EMU for both Germany and the RERM under his assumptions about commitment technology. The Modified-ERM will yield better average inflation performance for both regions and, provided that Germany gives enough weight to the loss function of the RERM, a stabilization performance that is roughly comparable. The combination of average inflation performance and stabilization performance may be sufficiently better under the Modified Hard-ERM to outweigh the benefits from reduced transactions costs and currency risk under EMU.

Currie's result for the comparison of a Modified Hard-ERM and EMU, is interesting and should be taken seriously. However, a healthy dose of skepticism is in order. The evidence in CLP (forthcoming) that stabilization performance might be comparable under the two regimes comes from a small simulation model with made up coefficients. Even in this model for some shocks it is possible for the German policy-maker to achieve stabilization performance under the Modified Hard-ERM that is roughly comparable to the stabilization performance under EMU only if he puts a weight on RERM loss that is equal to or greater than the weight he puts on his own loss, and it is not clear whether a German policy-maker would be willing or able to behave in this way. In addition, Currie may well be underrating the ability of the European policy-maker to commit himself under EMU.

Currie does not discuss stabilization problems in the Floating regime in Section 4. However, in CLP (forthcoming) it is shown that Floating may be preferred to both the Hard-ERM and EMU by both the German policy-maker and the RERM policy-maker for some shocks because stabilization performance may be sufficiently better. As an example of a shock for which the stabilization outcomes for both Germany and the RERM are best under Floating, CLP present a transient aggregate supply shock in Germany. It is not too surprising that Floating yields a better stabilization outcome than EMU for both Germany and the RERM. Having the European policy-maker act so as to keep the DM exchange rate fixed is worse for both policy-makers than having them keep their monetary policy independence even though they engage in non-cooperative behaviour. It is also not too surprising that Floating yields a better stabilization outcome than Hard-ERM for the RERM.[7] However, it is surprising that Floating yields a better outcome than Hard-ERM for Germany. Having the RERM act so as to keep the DM exchange rate fixed is apparently worse for Germany than having the RERM keep its monetary policy independence and engage in non-cooperative behaviour.[8]

At the conference there was general acknowledgement that floating exchange rates dominate fixed exchange rates on stabilization grounds for some asymmetric and idiosyncratic shocks. However, it was also clear that it was the view of many if not most of the participants that the members of the ERM should continue to keep their exchange rates fixed and that they should eventually adopt a single currency. This view did not seem to be based on firm evidence about what kinds of shocks are most frequent in European countries. Indeed many were willing to concede that the evidence is mixed. Rather the view seemed to be based on the judgment that any possible stabilization benefits of floating exchange rates are more than outweighed by other economic benefits and political benefits of fixed exchange rates and the eventual adoption of a single currency.

2   Commitment technologies

In many games, when it is assumed that players engage in myopic non-cooperative behaviour, the equilibrium payoffs for all players are very low. One way of modifying games so that the players can achieve better equilibrium payoffs is to assume a commitment technology under which some kind of commitment is possible. As stated before, Currie explores two such commitment technologies in his Floating and Hard-ERM regimes.

Many economists, including myself, have resisted exploring commitment technologies like those assumed under Currie's Floating and Hard-ERM regimes because the specification of the commitment technologies is not complete. Under each of these commitment technologies, policy-makers have an incentive to renege on their commitments unless they face harsh enough punishments for doing so. The harsh punishments that Currie's policy-makers will incur if they renege on their commitments are not spelled out in detail. Therefore, it is not clear why the policy-makers should honour their commitments. What is clear is that there is no supranational authority that can impose harsh punishments on policy-makers who break their commitments.

Currie has some discussion of why policy-makers might honour their commitments under the Floating and Hard-ERM regimes. Under Floating and Hard-ERM regimes, the German policy-maker can commit to deliver the value of his monetary instrument that will yield zero inflation. Currie argues that the German policy-maker might keep to this commitment to avoid punishment by the German people, who are particularly sensitive to inflation as a result of having experienced hyperinflation. However, he does not say what the punishment would be. Under Currie's Hard-ERM regime, the RERM policy-maker cannot commit to deliver the value of his monetary instrument that will yield zero inflation but can commit to deliver the value of his monetary instrument that will cause the DM exchange rate to remain fixed. He argues that while the RERM policy-maker might not keep to a commitment to deliver the value of his monetary instrument that will yield zero inflation to avoid punishment by the RERM people, he might keep to a commitment to deliver the value of his monetary instrument that will cause the DM exchange rate to remain fixed in order to avoid the political costs of breaking an international agreement. However, he does not say what these political costs would be. Even though the specification of commitment technologies like those assumed by Currie is not complete, it seems worthwhile to use them. They are one way, if not the only currently available way, of modeling important aspects of some policy regimes that we want to understand better. Of course, it is important to try to improve the specification of commitment technologies and to look for alternative modeling strategies.

If we are prepared to assume commitment technologies under which some kinds of commitment are possible, we can use cooperative game theory to analyse alternative regimes. For example, Klein (1991) uses cooperative game theory to analyse a fixed exchange rate regime in a two-country world that is subject to both money demand and output demand shocks. He finds that for many assumptions about the variances of the shocks there are allocations of adjustment duties between the two policy-makers that are cooperative equilibria.

NOTES

1 These three regimes are also considered in Currie (forthcoming) and Currie, Levine, and Pearlman (forthcoming), hereafter CLP (forthcoming). Currie (forthcoming) provides diagrammatic representations of the regimes. CLP (forthcoming) refer to the Floating and Hard-ERM regimes as the Non-EMS and Hard-EMS regimes and consider a fourth regime which they refer to as Optimal Policy.
2 Currie's derivation of the results in this paper is based on the more formal derivation in CLP (forthcoming).
3 Currie takes one minor shortcut. According to his Figure 5.3, the RERM is indifferent between Floating and EMU, and the text says nothing different. In fact, as is recognized in CLP (forthcoming) the RERM prefers Floating to EMU for the reason first recognized by Rogoff (1985). Under EMU, monetary expansion in the RERM leads to an increase in the RERM CPI only because it leads to an increase in the price of RERM output. The European policy-maker varies the German money supply in order to keep the DM exchange rate fixed. Under Floating, monetary expansion in the RERM leads to a larger increase in the RERM CPI. The RERM CPI rises not only because the price of RERM output increases but also because the RERM currency depreciates against the DM. Since monetary expansion is more inflationary under Floating there is less incentive undertake it. Private agents know this, so under Floating the inflation rate can be lower in the rational expectations equilibrium.
4 In the right hand panel of his Figure 5.3, regimes are ranked taking into account not only loss from inflation but also loss from currency transactions and currency risk. According to this panel Hard-ERM is superior to Floating for Germany. Since German inflation loss is the same under the two regimes, Currie must be assuming that loss from currency risk is lower under Hard-ERM.

5 He cites the Commission estimates of possible benefits from the elimination of intra-European currency transactions and currency risk (1/4 to 1/2% and 2% of Community GDP, respectively) and records some skepticism regarding these estimates but concludes that 'potential gains could be significant.'

6 The German policy-maker can and will offset the effects of any money demand shock in Germany without having any effect on the RERM. The RERM policy-maker must offset the effects of any money demand shock in the RERM as a matter of course in order to keep the DM exchange rate pegged.

7 It is also not too surprising that the Modified Hard-ERM can dominate Floating for the RERM if Germany gives a low enough weight to its own objectives. Apparently, in this case it pays for the RERM to give up the monetary policy independence it has under floating in order to avoid the inefficiency associated with non-cooperative behaviour.

8 The CLP result that Floating is better than the Hard-ERM for Germany in the case of a supply shock in Germany is all the more surprising given a result from Canzoneri and Henderson (1991), hereafter CH. CH consider a shift up in demand for the United States (US) good matched by a shift down in the demand for the rest of the world (ROW) good. For this disturbance floating with non-cooperative behaviour is definitely better for both the US and the ROW than fixing the real exchange rate by making equal and opposite changes in the two money supplies if the policy-makers put a heavy enough weight on employment. However, floating with non-cooperative behaviour is unambiguously worse for the US than a regime that CH call fixed-exchange-rate leadership. Under this regime the US policy-maker chooses his monetary instrument to minimize his own loss, but the ROW policy-maker chooses his monetary instrument so as to keep the real exchange rate fixed. It seems that we need more analysis of regimes in which one policy-maker acts to keep the nominal or real exchange rate fixed.

REFERENCES

Canzoneri, Matthew B. and Dale W. Henderson (1991), *Monetary Policy in Interdependent Economies: A Game-Theoretic Approach*, Cambridge, MA: The MIT Press.

Currie, David (forthcoming), 'European Monetary Union: Institutional Structure and Economic Performance,' *Economic Journal*.

Currie, David, Paul Levine, and Joseph Pearlman (forthcoming), 'European Monetary Union or Hard-EMS?,' *European Economic Review*.

Klein, Martin (1991), 'Bargaining for the Choice of Monetary Instruments in a Simple Stochastic Macro Model,' CEPR Discussion Paper No. 553.

ANDREW J. HUGHES HALLETT

For what is intended to be one of the most far reaching changes in economic organisation this century, there has been extraordinarily little formal analysis of the costs and benefits of monetary union. There have, of course, been many accounts of what the policy-makers intend should happen. But issues of this importance cannot be settled by expectations and intentions (especially if they come from interested parties) unless supported by sufficient analytic evidence. David Currie's paper is therefore a valuable review of his own assessment of monetary policy under EMU and whether it is likely to be an improvement over alternative regimes. In fact he finds EMU is likely to be inferior to other arrangements unless certain additional conditions on increasing the effectiveness of policies within the union can also be met. As that seems improbable in practice, and anyway implies that it is the design of monetary policy rather than monetary union which lies at the heart of better economic performance, I would like to pick out four implications of Currie's analysis.

Explicit coordination and ERM both dominate the more rigid EMU regime.

The most striking result is that optimal cooperative policies and the Soft-ERM regime appear preferable to EMU. Even the Hard-ERM regime is preferable to EMU. These results are shown in Figures 5.3 and 5.4, but are seen more clearly in Figures 5 and 6 of Currie et al. (1990) on which the discussion of pp. 134–8 actually depends. Those results are obtained from a conventional Barro-Gordon model of two inter-dependent economies which are symmetric except in their demand and supply responses to exchange rate movements (the latter innovation to create a 'centre' and a 'periphery' country).[1] It is a pity that the model, preferences, and associated figures are not reproduced, since it is hard to interpret or explain the results without them. Nevertheless the results are:-
(i) Full coordination dominates all other regimes for all values of a (the bargaining power of Germany within ERM/EMU), although it contains adjustable, but not necessarily frequently adjusted, exchange rates. (ii) The Soft-ERM regime effectively dominates EMU, although neither is a full reputation solution. (iii) Soft-ERM also dominates Hard-ERM for $0.4 \leq a \leq 1$, which includes the crucial case of $a = 1$ where German reputation and policy effectively drives the whole system.[2]

These conclusions are consistent with other results (e.g. Hughes Hallett and Vines, 1991, or Masson and Melitz, 1991, with no extra fiscal flexibility), but not with those in *European Economy* (1990) for the reasons which are given in point 2 below. Notice that the 'optimal', 'EMU' and 'Hard-ERM' schemes are all cooperative; the latter two having restrictions on the exchange rate variable, and the former two having fixed values of $a = \frac{1}{2}$ (but why? Currie *et al.*, 1990, p. 11, shows that they are also loci of welfare points). Soft-ERM is a non-cooperative Stackelberg regime where only the leader has reputation. EMU has the extra restriction of no reputation even for Germany. Now if the reputation effects are fairly small (and they seem to be small because the distance of the EMU outcomes, with no reputation at all, from Hard-ERM, with full reputation, is smaller than the distance of the other solutions from Hard-ERM), and if hard is quite hard, then the EMU line (when a is allowed to vary in Figure 4) will converge on the Hard-ERM line as $a \rightarrow 1$. But if $a \rightarrow 0$ the lines will diverge since the German objective function places a penalty 25 times higher on inflation than losses of output compared to other countries (see Currie *et al.*, 1990). Consequently the overall penalty on inflation falls as a falls in both the EMU and Hard-ERM regimes – but it rises on the exchange rate (defined by inflation differentials) term in the ERM case. That means the penalty on inflation falls more slowly in the ERM case than it does in the EMU case. Hence inflation worsens as $a \rightarrow 0$ in both schemes, but it worsens faster under EMU. We therefore get Figure 5A.1 as a general result. In other words, the ERM scheme does indeed dominate EMU for any given a value, because EMU's rigidity is a significant restriction which more than offsets any policy coordination gains which may be implied.

Exchange rate stability does not ensure price stability. Hence the crucial issues are the design of monetary policy and the operation of the central bank, not monetary policy per se.

Like any major change, EMU implies costs as well as benefits. The EC Commission's preferred estimate of those benefits is about 1.5% of GNP, which is very similar to the consensus estimate of the potential gains from policy coordination at the G7 level (Currie *et al.*, 1989). In the policy coordination debate such gains were generally regarded as rather small, being roughly the same size as the range between typical 1-year-ahead growth forecasts made for the OECD countries. It would not take much in the way of costs to overturn the benefits of EMU. It is therefore important to focus, as Currie does, on those costs and on just how much coordination EMU would in fact induce.

A significant degree of price and exchange rate stability has been achieved under the EMS arrangements of the 1980s, as member countries have sought lower inflation and German financial credibility. It is argued

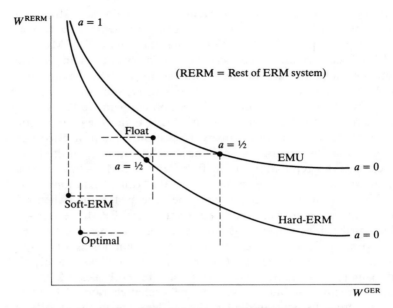

Figure 5A.1   Cooperation versus bargains in an EMU/ERM framework

that a tighter ERM, or EMU itself, would therefore be a better frame-work delivering price stability in the future, although it is important to note that non-member countries actually did just as well, if not better, with similar reductions in inflation and smaller losses in output during the 1980s.

Does this mean that EMU, or a Hard-ERM, can be expected to elimi-nate not only inflation differentials but also inflation itself? And have we found a way of overcoming the conventional trade-off between price stability and higher output? The Commission clearly thinks so, basing their arguments on a series of simulations of their own construction performed on the IMF's MULTIMOD system. Currie's results (as do the results of many other analysts) imply quite the opposite because, although the underlying objectives give 'overwhelming priority to controlling inflation', the floating and EMS regimes dominate most, if not all, of the EMU and Hard-ERM outcomes. That may happen because compromise within EMU effectively neutralises the Bundesbank's reputation as the EMS's lynch-pin, and leads to average rather than best-practice policies. But it is more likely to happen because exchange rate stability cannot guarantee price stability without some price anchor. That would require even tougher monetary controls and greater independence than the

Bundesbank currently supplies (even tougher because the natural convexity of preferences would otherwise lead the central bank to adopt 'poor-practice' monetary policies; see the next paragraph). The new central bank's statutes cannot supply such an anchor. Its independence is intended to be similar to the Bundesbank. But with fiscal policy (and perhaps the ECU exchange rate) under the control of national governments, and a statutory requirement to respect national growth objectives without any obvious mechanism for resolving conflicts between the resulting price and output targets, a new central bank facing 12 self-interested governments is unlikely to be able to exercise the same, let alone stronger, monetary control. An example illustrates the point. Suppose countries A and B are of equal size and structure, but that A suffers a 10% inflation shock (as in the German reunification programme, for instance). Under floating, A's prices rise 10%, B's stay constant and the European price index rises 5%. But under EMU and the same monetary control rules, inflation is spread: prices rise 5% in both A and B. Hence the European price index still rises 5% and nothing has been gained. This happens because under floating, with some attention to the output targets, A's inflation is ultimately accommodated by depreciation against B and the rest of the world. On the other hand, under the EMU regime A's inflation is only partially accommodated (vs. just the rest of the world now) but, because it cannot be localised, twice as many goods suffer the smaller price rises. So the impact on the price index is the same, and removing inflation differentials via EMU does not remove inflation. To do that requires a policy change. That was the point of my work with Vines, and Currie's analysis yields exactly the same conclusion.

Now suppose country B is four times larger than A. Under floating, A's 10% price rise leaves B's prices unaffected and the European price index 2% higher. Under EMU, inflation is equalised so prices rise 2% everywhere. Again there is no gain, except that if people worry more about inflation the higher it gets (i.e. they have convex preferences, and the past year's experience in the UK strongly suggests that they do: 2% inflation hardly matters at all, 10% matters a good deal more than 5 times as much) then the small country will like its gain under EMU more than the large country dislikes its loss. But, by the same token, convexity means that, whereas an individual country will try very hard to rid itself of 10% inflation, the EMU authorities would try much less than proportionately as hard to remove 2% or 5%. Hence we must expect a European central bank to be *less* effective in controlling inflation than an equally constituted Bundesbank. The only way out of this bind, and to give the new central bank the same power to reduce inflation as currently enjoyed by an EMS led by the Bundesbank, is to move to tougher monetary control rules. Simply to change the exchange rate regime will not do.

Hence, I think we are correct to concentrate first on the design of monetary policy and the new central bank – and only then on EMU itself, except that the latter will not bring any extra benefits if monetary policy has been correctly designed in the first place. Confirmation of this proposition comes from investigating why the Commission did not reach the same conclusion. In *European Economy* (1990), EMU is defined as the combination of exchange rate fixity *and* a tougher monetary control rule, so that you cannot tell if the gains are coming from EMU itself or from the change in policy regime. It is easy to show that removing the new control rule (so that the central bank follows the same type of monetary rule under both floating and EMU) makes EMU inferior to floating, while removing the EMU assumption when the stronger monetary control rules are in place scarcely affects the outcomes (Hughes Hallett and Vines, 1991). Evidently what matters is monetary policy, rather than a particular exchange rate regime; and it may well be that institutional changes in the form of a new central bank would be the best outward and visible sign of this new spiritual grace in policy-making.

The Hard-ERM/EMU regimes are accident-prone; greater (fiscal) coordination will be needed to provide policy effectiveness as well as stability in the face of shocks and policy errors.

Other work in this area stresses the importance of fiscal flexibility to compensate for the constraints which a single monetary policy within EMU imposes.[3] Naturally enough, if we deprive countries of one policy instrument they will have to use their remaining (fiscal) instruments more intensively to solve their domestic problems and to smooth the fluctuations which remain in national outputs or prices after the single monetary policy has been used to control the European averages. That has to be done by adjusting each fiscal policy relative to the common monetary policy in such a way as to improve the outcomes for one country without damaging them for another. That inevitably requires a more active coordination of the policy instruments which lie outside the EMU framework as currently defined, and implies that *policy mix* becomes the instrument at the national level.

This explains why it is useful to analyse the underlying policy interactions in the form of the Hamada diagram in Figure 5.5. Currie gets the usual result that non-cooperative policies outside the ERM/EMU framework lead to poorer outcomes because policy makers fail to internalise some of the costs. As drawn, countries prefer fiscal expansions for themselves and end up with unduly lax fiscal policies and overtight money to compensate (a response typical of the US in the 1980s). But if countries

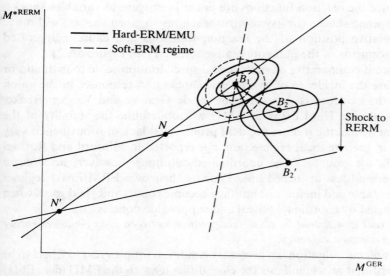

Figure 5A.2   The EMU/ERM regimes are not robust

prefer fiscal discipline at home, the picture reverses (B_1 and B_2 interchange) as in Figure 5A.2 and they end up with unduly restrictive fiscal policies but less monetary contraction. That is the usual European situation. In either case the outcomes are improved with explicit coordination, not only between countries but also between fiscal and monetary interventions.

But Figure 5A.2 implies much more than this. It is easy to show that, as countries move from floating through a loose EMS regime to a Hard-ERM and finally to EMU, currencies become more and more substitutable. That implies increasingly parallel optimal reaction functions because under a Hard-ERM or EMU regime it no longer matters which currency is used to finance fiscal expenditures or to restrict the aggregate money supply.[4] With a virtually fixed link between currencies, the overall impact of fiscal expenditures or money supply changes on any country will be more or less the same whether they are carried out in German Marks or Italian Lire. Narrowing the angle between reactions functions like this implies two things:

(a) The inefficiencies (welfare losses) of a lack of fiscal coordination become more and more marked as the ERM regime is tightened towards EMU. As was clear in Figure 5A.1, it is the coordination of policies, not EMU or ERM *per se*, which matters for delivering a better performance; and

(b) since the reaction functions are linear in exogenous variables/shocks, asymmetric shocks (or asymmetric reactions to given shocks) will move the relative position of the reaction functions and cause exaggerated displacements of the non-cooperative solution (see Figure 5A.2).

Hence if comparative advantage and specialisation serve to maintain or increase the incidence of asymmetric shocks and responses in the union (and the evidence is that they do; see de Grauwe and Vanherverbeke, 1991), then a Hard-ERM or EMU will undermine the stability of the system by making it more accident prone. That lack of robustness is very clear in the empirical regime rankings reported in Minford and Rastogi (1990), for example. The coordinated solutions, however, lie along a shorter and less disturbed line. Thus on their own ERM/EMU regimes are unstable and inefficient; but they become robust and yield gains when supported by coordinated fiscal and supply-side policies.

The real aim should be closer cooperation between policy-makers rather than a common currency.

If greater coordination is a necessary condition for progress to EMU to be successful, it also highlights the chief difficulty with the EMU idea. EMU is a rigid system in which all countries have to behave as if they were identical in structure, preferences and shocks. Hence the calls for 'convergence'. Yet it is clear that countries are not all identical, and it is well known that you get the best out of coordination when you exploit the comparative (policy) advantages of each participant fully. Indeed the gains only flow when you do that, for exactly the same reason that you would never choose to write a book with someone who was identical to yourself in preference to someone whose talents were complementary. So while EMU may capture some of the gains of better coordination, it cannot capture all of them. It is at best a partial coordination device. As we have seen here, a less rigid policy regime would better exploit any comparative advantages in structure or preferences, and therefore yield a better, more coordinated performance. The crucial question is, how much better? On that we have no direct evidence, but one might guess it would be quite a lot better since other studies have shown exchange rate targetting to be a poor substitute for explicit coordination even when it improves on the historical policy choices (Hughes Hallett, 1991).

NOTES

1 The ERM regimes are called EMS regimes in Currie *et al.* (1990).
2 There is some confusion here since Currie's Section 4 claims that Hard-ERM outperforms Soft-ERM, whereas the results being quoted (Currie *et al.* 1990, p. 37) show it to be the other way round when Soft-ERM is their non-EMS

solution. Identifying Soft-ERM with non-EMS appears to be correct since Currie *et al*. (p. 9–11) specify non-EMS to be a German-led Stackelberg regime with floating and EMS reputation for the Bundesbank. An independent float is not consistent with Stackelberg leadership since it necessarily implies that the followers tie themselves to German discipline (within certain limits). Rather than lie between floating and Hard-EMS, such a regime should have better coordination properties in an asymmetric world because it is less rigid (see point 4 below). Hard-EMS has the same form, plus extra penalties on the exchange rate terms and cooperation, with $a \simeq 1$ (hence tighter bands, and outcomes worse for REMS but no better for Germany). An independent float would also imply worse results for an REMS which cannot even borrow a reputation. This is the only interpretation which fits both Figures 5.3 and 5.4 and Currie *et al*. (1990), although no formal definitions of Soft-ERM and floating have been given and nothing in Figure 5A.1 actually turns on identifying soft-ERM with the German-led 'non-EMS' solution.

3 e.g. Masson and Melitz (1991), Begg (1990), Hughes Hallett and Vines (1991).
4 Figure 5A.2 describes policy responses constrained by economic behaviour, inclusive of the exchange rate regime, so that progressively tightening the ERM bands (until EMU is reached) leads to increasingly parallel reactions. If, in addition, EMU also produces convergent preferences (B_1 and B_2 merge) the reaction functions coincide, conforming that two identical countries would always want to react the same way.

REFERENCES

Begg, D. K. H. (1990), 'Alternative Exchange Rate regimes', paper presented at the CEPR International Macro Workshop, Perugia, July, 1990.
Currie, D. A., G. H. Holtham and A. J. Hughes Hallett (1989), 'The Theory and Practice of International Policy coordination: Does Coordination Pay?' in R. Bryant, D. Currie, J. Frenkel, P. Masson and R. Portes (eds), *Macroeconomic Policies in an Interdependent World*, Washington DC: IMF.
Currie, D. A., P. Levine and J. Pearlman (1990), 'European Monetary Union or Hard-EMS?', London Business School Discussion Paper 05–90, forthcoming in *European Economic Review*.
De Grauwe, P. and W. Vanherverbeke (1991), 'Is Europe an Optimal Currency Area? Evidence from regional data', CEPR Discussion Paper No. 555.
The European Economy (1990), 'One Market, One Money', Occasional Paper No. 44, EC Official Publications, Luxembourg, (October).
Hughes Hallett, A. J. (1991), 'Target Zones and International Policy Coordination: The Contrast Between the Necessary and Sufficient Conditions for Success', *European Economic Review* 35, (November).
Hughes Hallett, A. J. and D. Vines (1991), 'Adjustment Difficulties within a European Monetary Union: Can they be reduced?', CEPR Discussion Paper No. 517, and in J. Driffill and M. Beber (eds), *A Currency for Europe*, London: Lothian Foundation Press.
Masson, P. and J. Melitz (1991), 'Fiscal Policy Interdependence in a European Monetary Union', *Open Economies Review* 2, 113–36.
Minford, A. P. L. and A. Rastogi (1990), 'The Price of EMU' in K. O. Pöhl *et al*. (eds), *Britain and EMU*, London: Centre for Economic Performance, London School of Economics.

6 Voting on the adoption of a common currency

ALESSANDRA CASELLA

1 Introduction

The debate over the adoption of a common currency in the European Community has focussed on savings of transaction costs as one of the leading advantages of a monetary union. As international transactions continue to expand, and as they become more complex, the small losses involved in exchanging currencies may grow to sizable fractions of total values, and the savings realized through a common monetary standard may therefore be nonnegligible. The EC has estimated direct, 'mechanical' savings to be of the order of 0.5 per cent of Community-wide GDP (*European Economy*, 1990), with unequal distribution across countries. The belief that transaction costs are one of the main motivations for a common currency is shared by policy-makers and financial journalists (see for example the editorials of *The Economist* in the last two years), by academics (Canzoneri and Rogers, 1990), and, I believe, by public opinion in general.

But if transaction costs are important, they must play a role in determining the composition and the size of the different markets. A common currency would then imply not only lump-sum savings, but a change in the partition of traders between domestic and international activities. This is the view studied in the paper.

Since a monetary union requires a common monetary policy and a common inflation rate, if inflation is distortionary there is a second channel through which monetary unification may affect the formation of markets. The final effect will be a combination of the two forces.

I explore these issues with a simple model where heterogeneous agents belonging to two separate countries sort themselves among markets. For simplicity, I assume that the two countries have identical structure, but that one provides a more stable currency, which is used in all international transactions.

The change in market borders caused by the adoption of a common currency triggers distributional effects, as individuals move between markets, and gain or lose trading partners. The result is disagreement among the citizens of each country over the desirability of the regime. In the model, a referendum is held in each country, asking all citizens to choose between a national money and the creation of the currency union. The results of the referendum generally differ in the two countries, since their initial conditions as high and low inflation economies are different. Still more interesting, the results change with an exogenous development parameter that influences the size and the productivity of markets, suggesting that the adoption of a common currency may be desirable only at particular stages in the evolution of trade.

In particular, the majority of voters in the high inflation country favors monetary unification at lower stages of development, when productivity is low, and transaction costs stemming from the use of the foreign currency in international trade are high relatively to income. In the low inflation country, on the contrary, the creation of a common currency wins the referendum at higher levels of development, when international markets are wide. Providing the international reserve currency then imposes a serious constraint on independent monetary policy. The conclusion is that monetary unification wins a majority of favorable votes in both countries only at intermediate values of the development parameter.

Two aspects of this result deserve to be stressed. First of all, the analysis identifies one reason why the more stable country may eventually favor a common currency. In the current European debate, the German desire to proceed with monetary unification – especially before the reunification of Western and Eastern Germany – is rarely addressed, and most standard formal models are ill-equipped to explain it. Still, the Bundesbank has often expressed concern at the rising international role of the Deutschemark, possibly fearing the lack of flexibility that accompanies the management of an international reserve currency. Several authors believe that such lack of flexibility has been a source of weakness in the past for the dollar and for sterling (see for example Caves, 1968, and Solomon, 1977).

Second, the model ties the choice of monetary regime to the development of markets. By stressing that the attitude towards a common currency changes over time, the model allows us to face explicitly the question of the appropriate moment for the reform. This aspect is again remarkably absent from most discussions of the topic.

The paper proceeds as follows. The next section presents the model. Section 3 characterizes the equilibrium, and Section 4 discusses the results. Section 5 concludes.

2   The model

To study how the size of markets, and therefore individual and aggregate income, responds to the monetary regime, we need a model where monetary policy and transaction costs affect individual decisions on trade.

The framework presented in this paper is borrowed, with few modifications, from Casella and Feinstein (1990b). A continuum of traders is uniformly distributed along a line extending from -1 to 1, and is divided into two halves, representing two identical countries. Each trader's position represents his endowment. Country 1 is formed by agents from -1 to 0, and country 2 by agents from 0 to 1, so that on average the distance between the endowments of traders belonging to the same country is less than the distance between them and foreign endowments. There is no migration.

In each country, some traders belong to a purely domestic market, while the others enter the international market. Once a trader has decided which market to join, he is randomly matched to a partner among those who have selected the same market.

The central assumption of the model is that the return from a transaction, divided equally between the two partners, depends on the two endowments and on an index of monetary discipline. Ignoring taxes, for the moment:

$$y_{ij} = f(x_i, x_j, d)$$

where y_{ij} is each agent's share of the joint return, x_i and x_j are the endowments of agents i and j, and d is the index of monetary discipline, negatively correlated to inflation π:

$$d = d(\pi), \quad d' < 0, \quad d(0) = \bar{d}, \quad d(\bar{\pi}) = 0$$

(the prime sign indicates the first derivative). I assume that inflation is bounded between zero and an upper limit $\bar{\pi}$, so that d reaches the upper bound $\bar{d}$ when inflation equals zero, and zero when inflation equals $\bar{\pi}$.

The assumption that inflation reduces real returns from trade should be seen as a 'reduced form' relationship. In its simpler version, it may represent a delay in converting nominal returns from trade into real assets; in this case, inflation would reduce real returns proportionally. Alternatively, it may arise from more complex links between inflation and markets, summarizing the idea that inflation not only affects the returns from a given set of economic exchanges, but modifies the relative gain from different transactions. The effect of inflation on relative prices, and therefore on real activity, is a recurrent and important point in the literature. It has been extensively documented, and explained with mechanisms ranging from menu costs (Sheshinski and Weiss, 1977) to information imperfections (Lucas, 1973) to thin markets (Casella and Feinstein, 1990a). This is the approach I follow in this paper, and specifically I assume:

$$y_{ij} = 1 + |x_i - x_j|(\beta d - |x_i - x_j|) \tag{1}$$

where 1 is just a scale term, β an exogenous parameter and $|x_i - x_j|$ the distance between the two endowments.[1]

Equation (1) is depicted in Figure 6.1, and has two characteristic features. First, each trader x_i has an ideal partner at distance $\beta d/2$, with the return from trade declining symmetrically as the realized distance falls short of or exceeds the ideal one. Second, the return from all matches is higher the higher is βd.

If inflation were not a concern and βd were very large, the gains from cooperation would increase monotonically the more dissimilar (distant) the two partners were (over the limited support we have assumed). This is a standard assumption on gains from trade: as partners engage in a joint venture, the more diversified are their specific talents and expertise the higher is their potential return. However, the scope for cooperation with a very distant partner is limited by inflation: while inflation reduces the profit from all exchanges, it affects most the transactions between agents with very different endowments, and therefore reduces the distance between ideal partners.

A model where inflation makes the gathering and processing of information more difficult, à la Lucas, can readily provide the background for equation (1). If inflation reduces the ability to monitor the activity of one's partner – to understand the effective market demand for, his good, to read his balance sheets – it is reasonable to believe that this will be more damaging the more distant, and therefore unfamiliar is his type. Thus even if potential gains increase with distance, inflation reduces sharply the return from trading with faraway partners, and effectively constrains the ideal difference between traders' endowments. In this formulation, money is modelled as unit of account, indeed as language, more than as means of payment or story of value. The focus is on the role of the currency used for invoicing.

The parameter β represents the extent to which monetary discipline is essential for trade. Since at higher β the same return can be obtained with a lower d, i.e. with higher inflation, it is appropriate to interpret β as the ability of the economy to prevent distortions brought by inflation. Thus β represents the level of financial development; it will be interpreted more generally as a development parameter. In all cases, however, I will assume that a monetary unit of account is established in both countries.

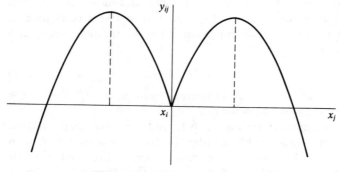

(a) Output as a function of x_i's partner

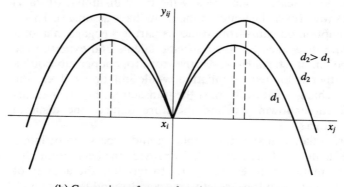

(b) Comparison of output functions for different d

Figure 6.1   The production technology

When traders belonging to the same country are matched, they are assumed to use their national currency; when international traders meet, however, they will conduct their transaction in the more stable of the two currencies at their disposal. The trader who has to exchange between currencies faces transaction costs. Therefore, agent i from country 1, matched with agent j from country 2, will have an after-tax return of:

$$y_{ij} = 1 + |x_i - x_j| \, (\beta \max(d_1, d_2) - |x_i - x_j|) - t_1 - c \qquad (1')$$

where c is positive if $d_2 > d_1$, but equals 0 otherwise (and correspondingly for the trader from country 2). If the two countries share a common currency, this currency is used in all trades, and no transaction costs are incurred.

Inflation is created by a government financing its deficit through money creation. Therefore, for given government expenditure, the index of monetary stability d must be increasing in taxes. If t are per capita lump-sum taxes, I assume:

$$d = F(t) \quad F' > 0, F'' < 0$$

where a double prime indicates the second derivative. The decreasing returns are required for an equilibrium with finite d. Again, this equation is a reduced form stating that the lower is inflation the more difficult becomes reducing its impact on markets even further. For simplicity, F will take the form:[2]

$$d = t^a \quad a = 0.5 \tag{2}$$

This specification will give rise to linear solutions. Nothing substantive will depend on the specific value of a, as long as the parameter is smaller than 1.

In each country taxes are collected from all citizens. If we wanted to stress seigniorage revenues collected from foreigners by the country providing the reserve currency, we could modify equation (2). We could correct the specification so that a given level of d could be obtained with lower direct taxes the larger the circulation of the currency. In general I will ignore this much debated aspect in the present paper. However, when relevant, I will discuss its influence on the results.

Government expenditure is exogenous, and its financing, the trade-off between inflation and direct taxes, is decided so as to maximize the average expected income of all citizens. With national currencies, the policy choice is made separately in the two countries. When the two countries share a common currency, on the other hand, policy decisions must be coordinated and d, the index of monetary stability, must be the same everywhere. Since the two countries are identical, with a common currency it will be assumed that the level of government expenditure is also identical, and the optimal policy will determine d and t so as to maximize the average expected income over the citizens of both countries.

The timing of the model is as follows: first, traders learn their type, then they decide which market to join, finally inflation and taxes are determined. The goal is to characterize a perfect foresight Nash equilibrium, where at d^* – the equilibrium value of d – the composition of markets is optimal, and no trader wants to deviate to a different trading pool. It is then possible to compare the equilibrium under national currencies to the equilibrium with a single money, and to hold a referendum asking the inhabitants of the model to choose between the two regimes. The purpose of the model is to study how the agents' vote differs at different values of the development parameter β.

3   Solution

Consider the problem from the point of view of agent i. Once he enters a market, he is matched randomly with a partner, and his return depends on the distance between the two of them, and on inflation. For a given expected level of inflation, he will therefore join the market where the expected distance between him and a random partner maximizes his expected return. This choice determines the division in trading pools and thus the trade-off between inflation and taxes in the two countries, and finally the inflation rate which in equilibrium was correctly anticipated by all traders.

The properties of this model are discussed in detail in Casella and Feinstein (1990b). The central idea is that, for any given market, each trader's expected distance from a random partner depends on his position on the line. This generates heterogeneous tastes over policy decisions, or, for given policy, different returns from joining a specific market. Exogenous changes that affect market size and composition, for example the establishment of a common currency, are accompanied by distributional effects that are directly correlated to the agents' position on the line. In addition, the impact of a change in regime depends on the value of the parameter β, suggesting the possibility that a reform that would be defeated by popular vote at a certain stage of development may be favored at a different stage.

In this section, I characterize the equilibria in the two monetary regimes when the two countries are divided into three markets; two domestic markets, one in each country, and in international one. With the functional form assumed in equation (1), each market must be formed by a single segment of adjacent traders (see the proof in Casella and Feinstein, 1990b), and therefore the partition of all traders into the three markets must be as depicted in Figure 6.2; the international traders are located on either side of the border between the two countries, while the two domestic markets are formed by agents near the external edges of the two countries. Notice that the average distance between traders in the international market need not be larger than the average distance between domestic traders. From this point of view, the approach differs from traditional international trade analysis based on comparative advantage (à la Heckscher-Ohlin). It is closer to Ricardian models of heterogeneous technologies, or to imperfect competition models of international intraindustry trade (as in Helpman and Krugman, 1985).

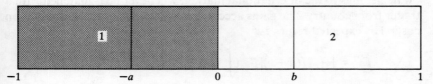

Figure 6.2 The partition into three markets

Consider first the case in which there are two separate national currencies, and two separate monetary policies. Let us call $-a$ the border agent between the domestic and the international market in country 1, and b the similar border agent in country 2. Thus the two domestic markets go from -1 to $-a$ (in country 1) and from b to 1 (in country 2), and the international market from $-a$ to b. We want to determine a and b, d_1 and d_2, and verify that this configuration is indeed an equilibrium.

The first observation is that a symmetric equilibrium with international trade, where $d_1 = d_2$, cannot exist as long as transaction costs are fixed and finite: each country would have an incentive to lower its inflation just ϵ below the other country's level, ensuring the use of its currency in all international exchanges, and saving the transaction costs.[3] Therefore I will assume that country 2 issues the reserve currency, implying $d_2^* > d_1^*$.

Consider $x_i = b$, the trader at the border between the international and the domestic market in country 2. His identity is defined by the condition that he must be indifferent between joining either market. If $d_2 > d_1$, he uses currency 2 in all trades without facing transaction costs. Therefore from his point of view there is no inherent difference in the functioning of the two markets, and he is indifferent between them only if the expected distance from a random partner is the same in both markets: the two markets must have the same size. It follows that:

$$b = (1 - a)/2 \tag{3}$$

The equivalent condition defining the border trader between the domestic and the international market in country 1 is less simple, since a citizen of country 1 uses different currencies when trading with domestic or with foreign partners. Consider agent x_i in country 1. If he belongs to the domestic market, he always uses currency 1, and never pays transaction costs. His expected income is:

$$Ey^D = 1 + 1/(1 - a)[\beta d_1(\int_{-1}^{x_i} (x_i - x_j)dx_j + \int_{x_i}^{-a} (x_j - x_i)dx_j)$$
$$- \int_{-1}^{-a} (x_i - x_j)^2 dx_j] - t_1$$

If he belongs to the international market, whenever he is matched with a trader from country 2 he gains access to currency 2, but faces transaction costs. His expected return is:[4]

$$Ey^I = 1 + 1/(a + b)[\beta d_1(\int_{-a}^{x_i} (x_i - x_j)dx_j + \int_{x_i}^{0} (x_j - x_i)dx_j)$$

$$+ \beta d_2(\int_{0}^{b} (x_j - x_i)dx_j) - \int_{-a}^{b} (x_i - x_j)^2 dx_j - bc] - t_1$$

The marginal trader $x_i = -a$ must be indifferent between joining the domestic or the international market. The value of a is then implicitly determined by the condition:

$$Ey^I|_{x_i = -a} = Ey^D|_{x_i = -a} \qquad \text{where } -a\epsilon[+ 1, 0]$$

or, solving the integrals explicitly, and using equation (3):

$$3\beta d_2(1 + 2a - 3a^2) + 6\beta d_1(3a^2 - 1) + 3(1 + a^3)$$
$$- 7a(1 + a) = 12(1 - a)c \qquad (4)$$

The optimal level of inflation, or equivalently the variable d, is determined in each country so as to maximize the average expected return of the country's citizens.

In country 1, average expected income EY, is:

$$EY_I = \int_{-1}^{-a} Ey^D dx_i + \int_{-a}^{0} Ey^I dx_i$$

and d_1^* is the value of d_1 that maximizes it. Solving explicitly, we find:

$$d_1^* = \frac{\beta}{6}[(1 - a)^2 + \frac{2a^3}{1 + a}] \qquad (5)$$

Exactly the same logic can be applied to country 2. Recalling that traders from country 2 use currency 2 in all transactions, we can derive the expected income in the international and in the domestic market. Integrating with respect to x_i, we obtain expected average income, and a standard maximization with respect to d_2 yields the optimal level of d_2:

$$d_2^* = \frac{\beta}{6}[\frac{2}{1 + a} - \frac{3(1 - a)(2 - a)}{4}] \qquad (6)$$

For given parameter values, equations (3), (4), (5) and (6) form a system of four equations in four unknowns, and can be solved simultaneously to find the equilibrium values of a, b, d_1 and d_2.

We must verify that this solution is indeed an equilibrium, and therefore that no trader would want to change market at the realized values of the endogenous variables. The temptation to deviate is zero for the border traders, since this is the condition defining them. In addition, equilibrium requires that such temptation reach a maximum exactly at the borders. Consider x_i belonging to the domestic market in country 1. The temptation to deviate to the international market, T_i, is:[5]

$$T_i(x_i) = Ey_i^I - Ey_i^D$$

where the expected income in the two markets must be calculated taking into account that x_i belongs to the interval $[-1, -a)$. solving the integrals explicitly, we find that T_i is everywhere concave in x_i, and therefore reaches its maximum at $x_i = -a$ if and only if its first derivative with respect to x_i is nonnegative at $x_i = -a$. This corresponds to the requirement:

$$\beta d_1 + \beta/(a + b)(d_2 b + d_1 a) \le 1 + b \tag{7}$$

In country 2, identical reasoning leads to the condition:

$$2\beta d_2 \le 1 + b \tag{8}$$

Finally, the equations above have been derived for the case:

$$d_2^* > d_1^* \tag{9}$$

We must verify that this inequality is realized.

Summarizing, if the two countries have national currencies and independent policies, there exists an equilibrium where the traders of each country are divided into two groups, one engaged in domestic transactions and the other joining the international market. The borders between markets, $-a$ and b, and the variables d_1^* and d_2^* are determined by equations (3), (4), (5) and (6), and the equilibrium conditions (7), (8) and (9) must be verified.

In this model, a country is defined as a subset of agents who share a common policy, specifically the sources of financing of the government budget. With a common currency and a common policy, therefore, the role of the border between the two countries disappears: international trade is not identified by any characteristic feature that distinguishes it from domestic exchange. In other words, if the world is divided into three markets, but there is a common currency, the only possible equilibrium has the three markets being of identical size, since only in that case would the marginal traders be indifferent between them.

With a common currency, therefore, the international market is formed by agents belonging to the interval $[-1/3, 1/3]$, while the two domestic markets go from -1 to $-1/3$, and from $1/3$ to 1.[6] The three markets are mirror images of each other. If x_i belongs to the international market, his expected income Ey_i^I equals:

$$Ey_i^I = 1 + (\beta/6)d(1 + 9x_i)^2 - x_i^2 - 1/27 - t \tag{10}$$

where d and t are equal across both countries. Since the three markets are identical, the expected income of a domestic trader in country 1 is easily derived from equation (10) by scaling x_i down by 2/3 (i.e. by substituting x_i with $x_i - 2/3$), and similarly for a trader in the domestic market of country 2. Average expected income is the same in each market, and indeed in each country and in the world, and is given by:

$$EY = 1 + (2/9)\beta d - 2/27 - t \tag{11}$$

The optimal value of d is then:

$$d^* = \beta/9 \tag{12}$$

Finally, equilibrium requires that the temptation to deviate be highest at the borders between markets. This corresponds to the condition:

$$\beta d^* \leq 2/3$$

or, substituting (12):

$$\beta^2 \leq 6 \tag{13}$$

The equilibrium with three separate markets exists only when β is not too high. At higher values of β, the size of the markets becomes too small, traders want to be matched with partners at larger distances, and the three markets unite in a single trading pool. This is immediately clear in the case of a common currency, but the same mechanism dictates conditions (7) and (8) when there are two national currencies.[7]

Of course, it is possible to study the switch to a common currency when there is a unique market. However, this begs the question of the impact of the monetary regime on market formation, and is not pursued in this paper.

4   Results

In this section, I present and discuss the impact on market formation, expected income and monetary discipline of the three exogenous factors present in the model: the level of transaction costs, the value of the development parameter β, and the monetary regime. When studying equilibria with national currencies, I will make use of numerical simulations, since no simple analytical solution can be derived.

Consider first the role of transaction costs. By assumption, these costs are present only when the two countries have different currencies, and affect the return from international transactions for those traders whose national currency is weaker. Intuitively, we expect that higher transaction costs, ceteris paribus, must reduce the size of the international market in country 1, while increasing the participation in this market by citizens of country 2 (Recall that b, the border between the two markets in country 2, equals $(1 - a)/2$). The total size of the international market is:

$$a + b = (1 + a)/2$$

and therefore it falls at higher transaction costs.

The impact on monetary stability is also straightforward. In country 1, the larger domestic market requires higher monetary discipline, and d_1 should rise at higher transaction costs. In country 2, d_2 is chosen so as to facilitate trade in two markets, each of which has size $(1 + a)/2$. Since the optimal degree of monetary discipline is an increasing function of market size, d_2 falls as higher transaction costs reduce the value of a. These intuitions were confirmed by numerical analyses. Figure 6.3 depicts the results.

Transaction costs have effects both on average expected income and on its distribution, in both countries. In country 1, average expected income should fall as costs rise, both because of the direct impact of the costs, and because foreign trade is reduced. The reduction in income is not uniform: it affects most those agents still involved in international trade, whereas domestic traders near the border between the two markets actually benefit from the increased number of potential partners. In country 2, higher transaction costs raise average expected income as they reduce the need for monetary discipline. This conclusion would be different at higher values of β, when the marginal return of d is higher, but the values of β required for such reversal are not compatible with an equilibrium with three separate markets.[8] Again, the impact on expected income is not uniform: traders switching from domestic to international transactions benefit most, while domestic traders who now find themselves near the border of the market are hurt by the loss of potential trading partners. Figure 6.4 compares market structure and expected returns for all agents, in the two cases $c = 0.01$ (the dashed line) and $c = 0.05$ (the solid line), with β set equal to 1.

Two observations are in order. First, transaction costs are here discussed as an exogenous parameter, determining markets' composition. If they are affected by regulations or capital controls, then we can think of them as an endogenous policy instrument, and the results on distribution suggest that, as long as foreign trade involves a minority of the population, capital controls could theoretically win a popular referendum.

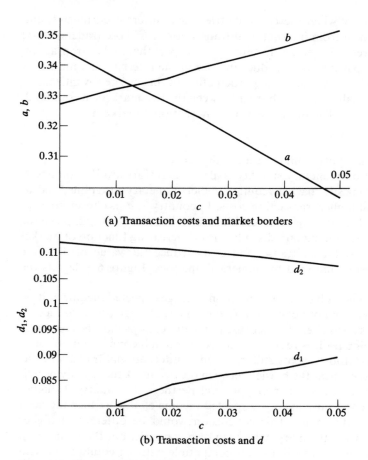

(a) Transaction costs and market borders

(b) Transaction costs and d

Figure 6.3   The role of transaction costs ($\beta = 1$)

Then we would be able to say not only what their effects should be on markets and inflation, but also when they are most likely to be approved. It turns out that in the model discussed so far capital controls, in the form of higher transaction costs, are never approved by a majority of the citizens of country 1. However, part of the result stems from ignoring the tax benefits that capital controls may bestow on the rest of the country.

For example, and this is the second observation, if we consider explicitly the increase in seigniorage revenues stemming from increased use of the national currency, capital controls may be more popular. From the point of view of country 2, the extra seigniorage increases the attractiveness of

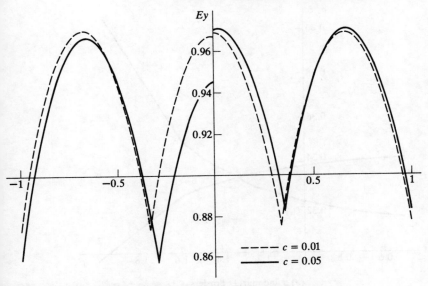

Figure 6.4   Expected individual income and transaction costs ($\beta = 1$)

foreign traders in the international market, and shifts preferences against high transaction costs abroad.

The second exogenous parameter playing an important role in the model is β. Higher values of β increase the return from larger markets, for given d, and at the same time raise the equilibrium value of d: higher development is accompanied by larger markets, and by lower inflation. If the two countries share a common currency, the three markets must be identical, for any β, and thus the composition and the size of the markets are invariant to changes in the parameter. The positive effect of higher β on the variable d and on expected income is then immediately clear from equations (10), (11) and (12). Notice that the impact of β on expected income is largest for those traders near the border between markets, since these are the traders faced with the highest expected distance from a random partner.

If the two countries have two national currencies, changes in β affect the borders between markets. In country 1, higher β and higher returns decrease the importance of the fixed transaction costs, and more traders join the international market. In country 2, some traders close to the border shift from foreign trade to domestic transactions, to compensate for the inflow of agents from country 1 in the international market. The net effect is that the international market and the domestic market in country 2 expand, while the domestic market in country 1 contracts. (Figure 6.5(a)).[9]

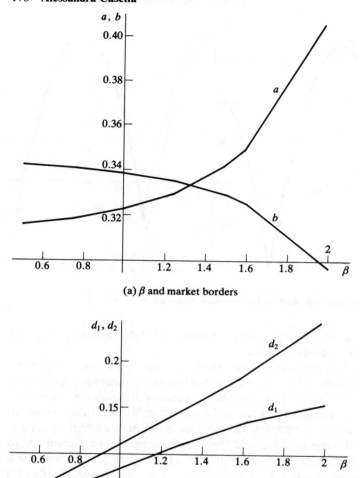

(a) β and market borders

(b) β and d

Figure 6.5   The role of β ($c = 0.025$)

The change in borders also implies that while both d_1 and d_2 rise with β, the increase is smaller in country 1: the use of currency 2 has expanded and the importance of currency 1's stability has decreased. (Figure 6.5(b)).[10]

Finally, at higher β average expected income is higher in both countries. International traders from country 1 are the group benefiting the most, as

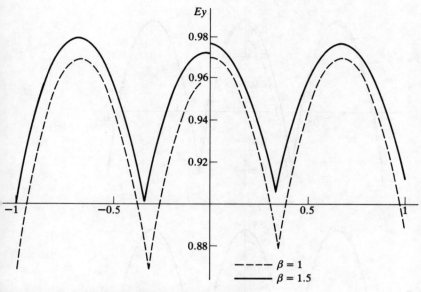

Figure 6.6   Expected individual income and β ($c = 0.025$)

The loss due to the transaction costs is now minor, and the possibility of free-riding on the stability of currency 2 is very valuable. Figure 6.6 depicts expected income for all agents as a function of their location in the two cases $\beta = 1$ (the dashed line) and $\beta = 1.5$ (the solid line), for $c = 0.025$. We are now ready to address the central question of the paper: what is the outcome of a referendum proposing a choice between national currencies and a common money? From the point of view of the citizens of country 1, a common currency has three separate effects: it means zero transaction costs when trading with foreigners; it eliminates the possibility of free-riding on the stability of the foreign currency, and it affects the borders between markets. We know from the analysis above that a reduction in transaction costs, with the accompanying market changes, is advantageous to country 1, but so is free-riding on currency 2. The tradeoff between the two forces depends on the value of the parameter β: at low β transaction costs are high relatively to income, while the value of gaining access to currency 2 is limited, since the international market tends to be smaller and the difference in the stability of the two currencies less pronounced. At high β, the relative strength of the two effects is reversed. Therefore we expect country 1 to be more in favor of a common currency at low β, and change its position later.

The impact of the common currency on country 2 is more subtle, since it

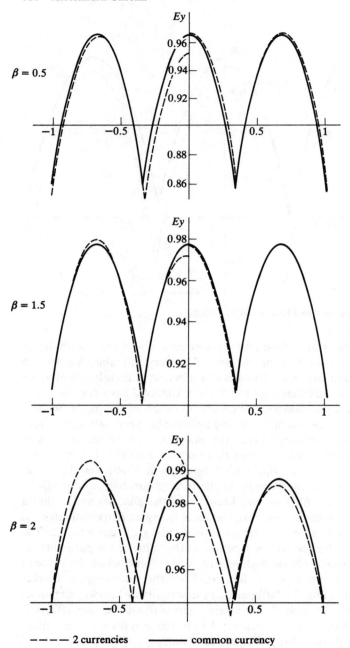

Figure 6.7   Expected individual income and monetary regime

depends only on the influence of the monetary regime on market formation. At low β, national currencies involving transaction costs for citizens of country 1 reduce the size of the international market. This is advantageous for country 2, since it limits the degree of monetary discipline that it must supply. At high β, however, the transaction costs play a small role, and larger numbers of traders from country 1 join the international market. Providing a currency sufficiently stable to sustain the increased volume of international transactions becomes more and more costly. We expect the preference for a common currency to dominate in country 2 when β becomes large enough.

These conclusions are confirmed by numerical analysis, and are shown in Figure 6.7. The expected return for all traders is depicted in the two cases of national currencies (the dashed line) and a common currency (the solid line) for the three different values $\beta = 0.5$, $\beta = 1.5$ and $\beta = 2$ (all for $c = 0.025$). In Figure 6.7, the intermediate value of β is the only one at which a common currency is preferred by a majority of the traders in both countries. More generally, this outcome is consistent with a set of intermediate β values.[11]

As always in this model the distributional effects are important, and emerge clearly in Figure 6.7. The traders most often in disagreement with the majority view are in both countries the domestic traders near the border between the international and the domestic markets. These are the only traders hurt by an expansion of the international market, since such expansion implies for them a loss in potential trading partners. For some parameter values, the result of the referendum can be different from that obtained by comparing average expected income in the two regimes. For example, for $\beta = 1.6$ and $c = 0.025$, a common currency would have only 43% of the votes in country 1, even though it leads to a slightly higher average expected income. However, this is the exception. The popular vote and the aggregate measure are generally in agreement.

Finally, notice that the results of the paper are sensitive to the decision to ignore international seigniorage revenues. If these revenues are important, they move the preferences of the country providing the reserve currency against the common currency, and the preferences of the less stable country in favor of the common currency. However, they do not alter the conclusion that the adoption of a common currency could only occur at intermediate levels of β.

5   Conclusions

Two countries deciding to adopt a common currency must share the same monetary policy and face the same inflation rate. They save on the transaction costs present in international trade when traders have different monetary standards.

In this paper, I have studied the impact of these two factors on the composition of markets. If inflation generates distortions, and if only a fraction of the citizens of a country engages in international trade, then the establishment of a common currency must modify the borders between domestic and international markets. This triggers distributional effects, possibly different in the two countries, and creates disagreement among citizens over the desirability of the currency union.

With the help of a very simple model where the formation of markets is endogenous, I have looked at the result of a referendum asking the citizens of the two countries to choose between national currencies and monetary union. The outcome of the referendum is typically different in the two economies, and changes at different levels of development, suggesting that a common currency will be favored by a majority of traders in both countries only at a particular stage.

In particular, I have assumed that the two countries have identical structures, but that one issues a more stable currency employed in international trade. The high inflation country has to balance the tradeoff between free-riding on the monetary discipline of the foreigners, in the international market, and paying transaction costs. The importance of transaction costs declines at higher productivity, even with growing international exchanges, and therefore preferences move against a common currency at higher stages of development. The low inflation country, on its part, must evaluate the costs of providing monetary stability to all traders in the international market. This becomes increasingly costly as markets expand, and preferences here move towards a common currency at higher levels of development. Only at an intermediate stage may the citizens of the two countries agree on monetary unification.

The analysis highlights two points that deserve more discussion. First, the low inflation country may suffer from the lack of flexibility inherent in being the provider of the international reserve currency. It may then welcome the establishment of a common currency as a more balanced way of sharing responsibility. Second, the desirability of a monetary union may be a function of the intensity of exchanges, and more generally of the development of markets. Thus the prospects for a common European currency may be more favorable now than they have been in the past, and possibly more favorable than they would be in the future.

NOTES

I thank the editors of this volume, Jim Levinsohn, Maurice Obstfeld, Torsten Persson and the participants at the conference for comments and advice. The paper was written at the Hoover Institution, whose hospitality and financial support I acknowledge with gratitude.

1 Notice, however, that the analysis could be conducted under the weaker assumption that inflation reduces real returns proportionally. If a common currency implies a change in inflation rates, it will still affect the formation of markets.

2 The decreasing returns in equation (2) can be encountered either when direct taxes are converted into lower inflation, or at the successive stage when inflation is translated into the 'discipline index' d. As the most straightforward example of the latter case, consider a steady state where at the end of each period each citizen holds one unit of real domestic currency. If G is total government expenditure, T total tax revenues, μ the rate of money creation and M/P the stock of real balances in the economy, then the government's budget constraint is:

$$G = T + \mu M/P$$

or, in per capita terms, using the fact that $\mu = \pi$:

$$g = t + \pi$$

Then d is given by

$$d = (g - \pi)^a = t^a$$

where it is assumed that inflation tax revenues cannot exceed government expenditure.

3 However this policy is not approved by a majority of the citizens, as long as less than half of them are involved in foreign trade. A symmetrical equilibrium exists if the transaction costs are paid by all traders matched with a foreigner, regardless of the currency used in the trade.

4 Notice that an undesirable effect of the random matching is that a trader may well be matched with a partner from the same country, even in the international market.

5 The condition ensuring that no trader wants to deviate to the market closer to his is sufficient to prevent deviations to the third and more distant market.

6 Recall that markets must be formed by unique segments of adjacent traders.

7 An equilibrium with two markets, whose border may or may not coincide with the boundary between the two countries, is also possible as long as $\beta^2 \leq 6$. With $a = 0.5$, the constraint on β necessary to prevent deviation to a neighbouring market is identical independently of the number of markets. When $\beta^2 > 6$, a single market is the unique equilibrium. For a detailed discussion of the transition to larger markets, see Casella and Feinstein (1990b).

8 In this model all equilibria are such that, for given β, the partition with the highest sustainable number of markets always yields the highest average return. In other words, given β, the smaller are the equilibrium markets, and the smaller is d, the higher is expected income. The point is discussed at length in Casella and Feinstein (1990b).

9 Among the citizens of country 2, this mass of traders in the international

market declines as β rises. However, this is an artifact of the assumption that everybody must trade. I conjecture that the result would be different if I had allowed agents with negative expected return from trade to abstain from joining any market.

10 This result deserves more thought. The idea that relatively more unstable currencies are used less as markets expand and trade becomes more international seems at least intuitively appealing. However, in the EC at least, inflation rates have been converging in the last decade.

11 Notice that there are admissible parameter values such that no β exists for which the monetary union wins a majority in both countries.

REFERENCES

Canzoneri, M. and C. Rogers (1990), 'Is the European Community an Optimal Currency Area?', *American Economic Review* **80**, 419–33.

Casella, A. and J. Feinstein (1990a), 'Economic Exchange in Hyperinflation', *Journal of Political Economy* **98**, 1–27.

(1990b), 'Public Goods in Trade: On the Formation of Markets and Political Jurisdictions', NBER Working Paper No. 3554, December.

Caves, R. (1968), *Britain's Economic Prospects*, Brookings Institution, Washington, DC.

Commission of the European Communities (1990), 'One Market, One Money'. *European Economy* **44**, 251–68.

Helpman, E. and P. Krugman (1985), *Market Structure and Foreign Trade*, Cambridge, Ma: MIT Press.

Lucas, R. E. (1973), 'Some International Evidence on Output-Inflation Tradeoffs', *American Economic Review* **63**, 326–34.

Sheshinski, E. and Y. Weiss (1977), 'Inflation and Costs of Price Adjustment', *Review of Economic Studies* **44**, 287–303.

Solomon, R. (1977), *International Monetary System, 1945–76*, New York: Harper and Row.

Discussion

TORSTEN PERSSON

In the debate about monetary unification in Europe, two major economic arguments have been launched by those that favor adopting a common currency. One argument has to do with cementing the credibility gains for low-inflation monetary policy already achieved by the EMS; the other has to do with saving on transactions costs. Academic economists have devoted more attention to the former than to the latter argument. At the same time it is unclear how broad the support is for complete monetary integration – both among policy-makers and among the public – in different countries.

In this light, Alessandra Casella's paper is an interesting and original addition to the theoretical discussion about monetary union. The motivation for the paper runs roughly as follows: if the savings of transaction costs are important enough to constitute a major argument in favor of a common currency, we should expect them to affect economic behaviour; in particular, they should change the economic interaction between agents in different countries. The implied reformation of markets is likely to have asymmetric effects on different agents in a given country. There will thus be distributional effects, the nature of which will shape the degree of political support for monetary unification.

I find this logic and the general approach of the paper convincing. When it comes to the particular approach to modelling the interaction between market formation, policy-making and politics, I am perhaps a little less convinced. The random matching model employed in the analysis is attractive from a theoretical point of view, but it also complicates the analysis a great deal and requires many simplifying assumptions. These assumptions notwithstanding, it is hard to derive analytical results and it becomes necessary to rely on numerical simulations. In the end the reader is left wondering about the robustness of specific results.

What I would like to do in this comment is to suggest an alternative simpler model, which I believe captures the gist of Casella's basic argument, but still lends itself to relatively simple analysis. I will use the model to discuss the issues she takes up in the paper, particularly whether a majority of the public would support adopting a common currency and what characteristics of the economy make such an outcome more likely. I will also use it to discuss some additional issues.

1   An alternative model

There are two countries, each populated by a continuum of individuals. Agent i in a given country has preferences over her private consumption equal to private income y^i and over government consumption g according to

$$u^i = y^i + \tilde{V}(g)$$

where $\tilde{V}(g)$ is a concave function. Private income net of transactions costs depends on whether the agent transacts with foreign citizens in the 'international market' or with domestic citizens in the 'domestic market', such that

$y^i = (1 + \omega) - a(1 - c^i)Min[D(\pi),D(\pi^*)]/\beta$ if i trades in the international market

$y^i = 1 - (1 - c^i)D(\pi)/\beta$ if i trades in the domestic market

These expressions are the counterpart of equation (1′) in Casella's paper. The first term on the right-hand side of each expression is the gross income from transacting in that market: ω thus represents a premium on international transactions. The second term is the cost of transacting in the market. Following Casella, β is a positive parameter measuring the importance of transactions costs in general. In the domestic market, where everyone uses domestic currency, the transactions costs get higher at an increasing rate if domestic inflation π goes up. That is, $D(\pi)$ is an increasing convex function. Transaction costs are continuously distributed in the population according to the idiosyncratic parameter c^i. This parameter has a distribution function $F(c^i)$ with bounded support within the unit interval.

In the international market everyone uses foreign (domestic) currency if the foreign currency is more (less) stable than domestic currency, π^* is lower (higher) than π. The transactions costs in the international market are higher, *ceteris paribus*, even if domestic currency is used (due to $\pi \leq \pi^*$). They are higher still if foreign currency is used (due to $\pi > \pi^*$). That is

$$a = \frac{a^h \text{ if } \pi > \pi^*}{a^l \text{ if } \pi \leq \pi^*,} \quad a^h > a^l > 1$$

Finally, if there is only one common currency, this currency is of course used in all transactions in both countries.

2   Market formation

The single economic decision agent i makes in the model is to maximize her private income by choosing in which market to transact. It is easy to see that only agents with relatively high c^i – that is, with relatively low idiosyncratic transaction costs – will take advantage of the higher return in the international market. But the way agents sort themselves into markets differ somewhat in the low-inflation country and in the high-inflation country.

Consider first the low-inflation country, whose currency is used in international transactions. It is easy to show that the lower bound on c^i, above which agents will sort themselves into the international market can be written as a function of the model's parameters: $C(a^l, \beta, \omega, \pi)$. Anything that decreases the relative net income in the international market makes fewer agents choose to transact in the international market. Thus, C is higher if a^l or π is higher, or if β or ω is lower.

In the high-inflation country there is a similar lower bound: $C^*(a^h, \beta, \omega, \pi, \pi^*)$. Sorting depends on a^h, β and ω in the same way as in the low-inflation country, but since now foreign currency is used in international transactions, it is now a higher π^* which decreases the proportion of domestic agents in the international market, while a *lower* π has the same effect (as long as $\pi > \pi^*$).

With a common currency, sorting in both countries takes place as in the low-inflation country.

3   Policy preferences

Let us next study agents' policy preferences over inflation. Clearly inflation has a cost in the model, since it tends to decrease private income by increasing transactions costs. To introduce a trade-off, I follow Casella and make government spending an increasing function of inflation $g = G(\pi)$. The utility of government consumption can then be written as an increasing and concave function of π: $V(\pi) \equiv \tilde{V}(G(\pi))$. With this assumption, agents' preferences over inflation will be single-peaked, with the preferred inflation rate at the point where the marginal cost of lower private income equals the marginal benefit of higher government consumption.

Since the marginal cost of inflation varies systematically across agents depending on their idiosyncratic transaction costs, their preferred inflation rates, π^i, differ too. Figure 6A.1(a) plots π^i against c^i in the low-inflation country. The figure illustrates how agents with higher c^i and thus lower marginal transaction costs generally prefer a higher π. But the relation between π^i and c^i has a discontinuity at C, because the marginal agent in the international market has higher marginal transactions costs than the marginal agent in the domestic market.

Figure 6A.1(b) plots the analogous relation in the high-inflation country. The qualitative difference relative to the low-inflation case is that π^i is constant above C^*. This is because agents in the international market now use foreign currency when transacting, so that the marginal transaction cost is decided by π^* rather than by π.

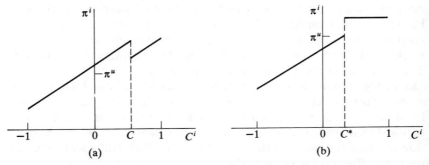

Figure 6A.1   Policy preferences when the majority transacts in the domestic market

4   Utilitarian policy-making

Suppose first we model the policy-making process as in Casella's paper: that is, equilibrium policy – both in the absence and presence of monetary union – is set by a utilitarian planner. The outcome will generally depend, not only on parameters but on functional forms. The following preliminary discussion is based on the assumption that the functions $V(\cdot)$ and $D(\cdot)$ are quadratic and the distribution of c^i is symmetric around its mean of 0 in both countries.

We can then infer from parameter values which of the two countries will have the higher inflation rate in the absence of monetary union. Whichever the initial policy configuration, however, the common inflation rate with a common currency will be a weighted average of the two pre-union rates.

Let us then pose the central question in Casella's paper, namely how a proposal of monetary union would fare in a referendum and how the outcome depends on parameter values. There are a few different cases to consider. Suppose first that the parameter values are such that a majority of the population belongs to the domestic market. (As previously discussed, this will happen when ω or β is high, or when α is low.) Figure 6A.1 (a and b) illustrates the policy preferences in the low-inflation and high-inflation countries, respectively, when C and C^* are both positive – recall that the average and median citizen has $c^i = 0$. It also illustrates the equilibrium pre-union inflation rates with a utilitarian planner, labeled π^u in the figure. The utilitarian inflation rate is below the rate preferred by the average and median citizen in the low-inflation country, but above the rate preferred by the median in the high-inflation country. In both cases, the reason is the discontinuity in policy preferences plus the fact that the planner gives weight to the policy preferences of the minority in the international market in his policy decision.

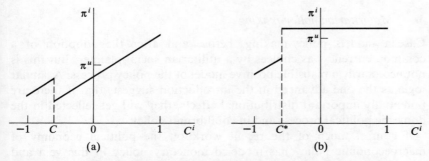

Figure 6A.2   Policy preferences when the majority transacts in the international market

Because individual policy preferences are single-peaked, we know that the median voter will be decisive in a referendum on a common currency. As the figure is drawn, the citizen with $c^i = 0$ is the pivotal voter in both countries (the following argument will hold even if this is not the case). Since the median in the low-inflation country wants a higher inflation rate and the median in the high-inflation country wants a lower inflation rate, moving to a common currency brings the equilibrium rate in the right direction for both of them. Consequently, both the pivotal voters will both vote yes in a referendum, provided that the two countries are not so different that the inflation rate moves too much.

Consider instead a parameter constellation illustrated in Figure 6A.2 (a and b), such that a majority of the population in both countries transacts in the international market. Reversing the previous argument, the pre-union equilibrium inflation rate is now too high for the pivotal citizen in the low-inflation country. From her viewpoint, the planner pays too little attention to transactions costs when weighing in the minority preferences of the citizens in the domestic market. And the inflation rate is too low for the pivotal citizen in the high-inflation country. She is free-riding on the foreign currency, so from her viewpoint the planner pays too much attention to the concerns over domestic inflation of the minority in the domestic market. A proposal of a common currency will now, of course, be voted down in both countries.

At a general level, these preliminary results – and obvious extensions to cases where the pivotal voter is in different markets in the two countries – confirm Casella's conclusion that universal support for a common currency can be expected only for some market constellations. At a specific level, the results are somewhat different, suggesting that her detailed results may not be all that robust. In particular, the present analysis identifies the proportions of citizens who are dependent on international and domestic transactions as determinants of the support for a crucial common currency.

5   *Majoritarian policy-making*

Casella models policy-making, before and after the adoption of a common currency, as choices by a utilitarian social planner. But this is not necessarily a plausible positive model of the policy process. A similar logic as the one advanced in the introduction suggests that if there are potentially important distributional effects, they will get reflected in the domestic political process and in equilibrium policy.

Of course, much of the recent work on the political economy of macroeconomic policy has modeled monetary policy in this vein and has tried to characterize the resulting political distortions. In that light it is interesting to reverse the assumptions in Casella's paper and in the previous section. To do so, assume instead that equilibrium policy, both before and after the adoption of a common currency, reflects majoritarian preferences. And instead pose the normative question how the move to a common currency would affect welfare, once we evaluate the outcome for each country by a social welfare function defined over the utility of its citizens.

For the purposes of this discussion, let us assume that equilibrium policies are determined by majority vote and take the social welfare function to coincide with the objective of a utilitarian social planner. In this case, we get conclusions exactly opposite to those we got under utilitarian policy-making. Suppose that a majority in both countries transact in the domestic market. Then we may just reverse the argument in connection with Figure 6A.1: from the viewpoint of our hypothetical utilitarian social planners, the median voter in the low-inflation country sets too high an inflation rate, while the median voter in the high-inflation country sets too low an inflation rate. Moving to a common currency with a common inflation rate in between the two pre-union rates, thus makes the outcome worse in both countries. But if the majority of the population belongs to the international market, as in Figure 6A.2, a common intermediate inflation rate diminishes the political distortion and increases the utilitarian objective in each country.

The upshot of the preliminary analysis in this section and the previous section is thus that there seems to be an interesting duality between the positive and the normative results: a commitment to adopting a common currency may be particularly valuable precisely in the situation when the move to a common currency is unlikely to gather universal majority support.

6   Concluding comments

Alessandra Casella's analysis of transactions costs and market formation has raised a number of new issues in connection with monetary union and policy-making in Europe. In this comment, I have discussed some of these issues in the context of a model, which is theoretically less appealing than the one in Casella's paper but which permits analytical solutions. One can think of several extensions of the analysis. In this comment, I have briefly dealt with a normative issue: under what circumstances is monetary union desirable given that the equilibrium policy reflects majoritarian rather than utilitarian preferences? It is easy to think of other extensions. For example, Casella mentions the possibility of incorporating the cross-country distribution of the revenues from seigniorage collection in the analysis. I hope that her stimulating paper will stimulate further work on the adoption of a common currency.

Part III Fiscal policy requirements of a common currency area

7 Fiscal federalism and optimum currency areas: evidence for Europe from the United States

XAVIER SALA-I-MARTÍN and JEFFREY SACHS

1 Introduction

1.1 Some background

The issue of the appropriate exchange rate (ER) system for Europe is now hotly debated. Yet the question of whether Europe should have a single currency is not new. It goes back to the very first debates surrounding European economic integration of the late 1940s and the 1950s.[1] From the very beginning people have asked what, in our opinion, is a central question: why do ER problems seem not to exist within some subsets of countries or within a country with a diversity of regions (as, for instance, the United States), while they do exist in the world as a whole? Put differently, why has the 'irrevocably fixed' ER system within the US functioned well, while the Gold Standard and the Bretton Woods systems collapsed? Economists have phrased this question in the following way: what constitutes an optimum (or at least reasonably good) currency area?[2] Different schools have answered this question differently. Classical economists argued that the key variable to exchange rate regimes is transactions costs. Because these transactions costs represent social losses, they should be minimized and the way to do it is to have a single worldwide currency. Thus the entire world is an optimum currency area. J. S. Mill puts it in a very illustrative way:

> '... So much of barbarism, however, still remains in the transactions of most civilized nations, that almost all independent countries choose to assert their nationality by having, to their own inconvenience and that of their neighbors, a peculiar currency of their own.'[3]

Of course, in order to explain the existence of different currencies Mill had to claim a kind of 'barbarism', a view that is not shared by many of his 20th century followers. The New Classical economists claim that one has to weigh the costs of having heterogeneous currencies against the benefits of each country being able to achieve its own optimal rate of money growth. Because they view the process of money supply as essentially a tax on existing money holdings, they see no reason why money growth (or inflation) should not be viewed within the problem of optimal taxation for each country. Hence, they explain the existence of different currencies according to structural differences across countries that lead to different optimal tax rates. For instance, it has been argued that the private technology for evading income taxes in Italy is superior to that in Germany so the optimal inflation tax in Italy may be larger than in Germany. Thus the two countries should enjoy different currencies. See for instance Canzoneri and Rogers (1990).

Another view, associated with Monetarist and Keynesian economists puts the money supply process (and therefore the exchange rate regime) in the context of stabilization policies. Mundell (1961) argued that only regions within which there is relatively high labour mobility should have a unique currency.[4] His (now canonical) example is the following: suppose we have two regions (A and B), each producing one good (a and b respectively) and populated by households who consume a little bit of both goods so that there is interregional trade. Suppose that, starting from a full employment equilibrium position, there is a permanent shift of preferences from good a to good b (ie, at initial relative prices, everybody prefers relatively more of good b and less a). If the relative price between the two goods (the real ER) does not change, there will be a trade imbalance (a deficit for A and a surplus for B). Equilibrium can be restored at the initial relative price by changing the supplied quantities of both a and b. This can be achieved by moving people from region A to region B.

Yet another way to restore equilibrium is by changing the relative price and maintaining the initial quantities. In turn, this can be done through two different channels: the first one involves changing the nominal exchange rate and leaving the nominal prices in the two regions unchanged. This possibility is not present, however, when both regions have the same currency. The second way of moving the real ER is to change the nominal price levels. In the case we are considering, the price level in A has to go down relative to that in B. If prices and wages adjust immediately, the real ER jumps to the new equilibrium level and that is the end of the story. But the economists who support these stories believe that price levels are 'sticky' (possibly due to small menu costs). In this case, the new equilibrium real ER will slowly be reached, but only after a period of 'over-employment' in B and deflation and unemployment in A.

The longer it takes the nominal prices to adjust, the more severe will be the recession in A. Hence, according to this view, if labour is not highly mobile, A and B should have flexible ER so the monetary authorities can stabilize the two regions' output through independent monetary policies.[6] Thus, as mentioned earlier, this view holds that only regions within which there is high labour mobility should have flexible exchange rate systems.

Should Europe have a unique currency? The Keynesian answer, according to what we just have seen, depends importantly on whether the EEC is strongly affected by the type of 'real' shocks we just described or rather by 'monetary shocks' like changes in the demand for money.[7] If we conclude that real shocks are important, then we have to analyze factor mobility among regions (or sectors). The 1992 liberalization will abolish all major constraints on labour mobility, so in principle there seems to be good reason to substitute all individual currencies by a single one. But there are barriers other (and perhaps more important) than legal ones. Europeans have very different cultures and languages, as well as important and well known imperfections in housing markets that stifle mobility even within countries, not to mention between countries. These barriers will still exist after 1992. Hence, under this Keynesian view, if Europe decides to have a common currency, interregional shocks will generate unemployment in some regions and inflation in others. The very survival of the monetary union (and, with it, the political and other forms of unification) could be threatened.[8]

But let us imagine that, for whatever reason, Europeans go ahead and fix their exchange rates forever by creating a unique European currency. What can be done to minimize the possibility of collapse? This can be answered by analysing the regions of the United States. One could think of the US as a collection of regions or states linked by a system, of irrevocably fixed exchange rates. And one can argue that this system has worked reasonably well over the last couple of hundred years. The question is, what did it take?

The first thing to understand is that, even though one might be tempted to think that there are no major interregional shocks requiring large changes in the real exchange rate across regions of the US, this is simply not true. What is true is that, because there are no current account data, policy-makers and journalists do not associate these situations with open economy problems that require large real exchange rate movements. The second point is that, contrary to most people's beliefs, labour mobility across the United States is fairly limited. In a related study Barro and Sala-i-Martín (1991a) found that, ceteris paribus, an increase in a state's per capita personal income by 1% raises net immigration only by enough to raise the state's population growth rate by 0.026% per annum. This slow adjustment through net migration means that population densities do not adjust rapidly to differences in per capita income adjusted for amenities.

1.2   Fiscal federalism and exchange rates

It has been argued that one of the reasons why the US exchange rate system has held up reasonably well is the existence of a 'Federal Fiscal Authority' which insures states against regional shocks.[9] In addition to the mechanisms already mentioned (devaluation, labour movements or recession), there is another way of maintaining a fixed parity without major real imbalances: having a redistribution of income from 'adversely shocked' to 'favorably shocked' regions.[10] After a permanent taste shock like the one proposed by Mundell, we can be closer to full employment without changing the nominal ER or the nominal prices if we tax region B sufficiently and give the proceeds to region A (or reduce tax in A). This will, under some reasonable assumptions about relative demands increase demand for good 'a' and reduce demand for 'b' at the initial relative prices. The tax and transfer policy will mitigate (although not completely eliminate) the initial regional imbalance.

We should note at this point that this interregional public insurance scheme does not even need to be 'conscious': a proportional income tax together with acyclical expenditures and transfers (e.g. unemployment benefits) will automatically work as a tax/transfer system that helps to defend fixed ER parities. Even better, if (as we will see it is the case in the United States) the income tax is progressive and the transfer system is countercyclical, the fraction of the shocks insured by the fiscal system will be even larger.

In addition to this automatic insurance scheme, the federal government may want to have other tools available in order to be able to stabilize large non-stationary shocks such as the S&L crises in the United States or the German unification shock in Europe.

There is set of questions that immediately comes to mind:

(i)   Couldn't the regional governments stabilize output by running countercyclical deficits?

Regional governments (e.g. states within the United States) could try to stabilize regional income by themselves, running budget deficits during regional recessions and surpluses during booms, but such a policy is likely to be much less effective than a federal arrangement. The problem with regional fiscal policy is that budget deficits have to be repaid by higher taxes or lower spending by the same region at some point in the future.

Short-term gains in stabilization may be lost in the future, or even worse, short-run stabilization could be frustrated by Ricardian equivalence if the future taxes are incorporated into consumers' budget constraints. This Ricardian equivalence does not, however, frustrate stabilization when the fiscal policy is carried out by a federal authority, because in that case, the federal arrangement explicitly redistributes the intertemporal tax and spending patterns across regions according to the shocks hitting the regional economies. Lower taxes paid by a region in recession are *not* matched in present value terms by higher future taxes paid by the same region, but rather by higher taxes paid by all regions in the federal area.

Another reason why state and regional governments cannot really smooth income with countercyclical deficits is that, to the extent that factors of production are mobile, they may tend to remain in the state while taxes are low and leave when taxes increase. In other words, when regional governments run large deficits, firms and workers expect future tax increases. Of course that means that they will both tend to leave the region at the time of the tax increases, which will reduce the regional government tax base. Because state governments may fear this reaction, they will choose not to run large state deficits, which substantially reduces the potential role for income-smoothing regional deficits. Recent history shows that regional governments (both in the United States and in Europe) may already be in financial trouble, so further deficits seem like infeasible strategies at this point (see the paper by Goldstein and Woglom in this volume for evidence on this issue).

(ii)   Isn't this insurance scheme infeasible in Europe because the richer countries are already complaining about more redistributional policies to help the South?

No. This paper does not ask whether the federal fiscal system actually promotes long-run income equality.[11] One may want to argue that a federal government is needed to reduce long-run income inequalities through taxes and transfers. But this is not the purpose of the present study and our findings have nothing to do with whether the federal government has other programs to reduce the long-run dispersion of per capita income. In other words, in the federal insurance scheme, the rich countries would not have to pay more than the poor countries.

As an example, let us imagine two countries: R (rich) and P (poor) who decide to create a federal union. Imagine that the rich country has an income of 1,000 Ecus and the poor has an income of 500 Ecus. Suppose that they decide to pay an income tax of 10% to the central government. The government will from then on give a transfer of 100 Ecus a year to R and a transfer of 50 Ecus to P. Note that in the first year there are no net transfers so this program is not designed to redistribute income from Rich to Poor.

Let us imagine that during the following year R suffers an adverse shock that reduces its income by 100 Ecus while P sees its income increased by 100 Ecus. The taxes paid to the Federal Government would still be 10% of income so R would pay 90 Ecus and P 60 Ecus. The transfers received from the central government would still be 100 and 50 Ecus respectively. In effect, therefore, there would be a transfer from P to R by the amount of 10 Ecus. In other words, the insurance scheme we are proposing redistributes income from the country that suffers a favorable shock to the country that suffers an adverse shock, regardless of whether they happen to be Rich or Poor! In particular, it is independent of any other programs the federal governments may want to implement in order to reduce income inequality in the long run.

(iii) Couldn't private insurance markets do the same job?
In principle it is true that an auto worker in Detroit can write a contract with an economics professor in Massachusetts that insures each other's wage against interregional shocks. The problem with this argument is that, due to the practical difficulties in monitoring the wages from people living thousands of miles away, these type of contracts are subject to moral hazard and adverse selection problems that will in practice prevent them from existing.[12] It is shown in Sala-i-Martín (1990) that state GDP and GNP behave very similarly over the periods for which both data are available (which includes the sample considered in the empirical section of this paper). If these contracts were important, the behaviour of GDP and GNP would be very different.

The main goal of this paper is to find out empirically how important is this insurance role of the Federal Fiscal system across the United States' regions. The rest of the paper is organized as follows. In Section 2 we highlight the empirical method used. In Section 3 we describe the data. In Section 4 we report the main empirical results. In Section 5 we quantify the importance of the empirical findings. The last section concludes.

2   Basic method

Our goal is to find by how many cents the disposable income of region i falls when there is a one-dollar adverse shock to that region's income, and when the region belongs to a federal fiscal union. That is we want to see

$$\Delta YD = \Delta Y + \Delta TR - \Delta TX \tag{1}$$

where disposable income – YD – is defined as the sum of $GDP - Y -$ plus transfers from a federal government – TR –, minus taxes paid to the federal government – TX –, with all of the variables to be thought of as discounted present values (note that ΔY in (1) involves only current output however):

Suppose that the tax and transfer system works so that each 1 percent increase in Y produces a β_{TX} percent increase in taxes to the federal government, and a β_{TR} percent increase in transfers from the federal government. In other words,

$$\beta_{TX} = \frac{\Delta TX/TX}{\Delta Y/Y} \text{ and } \beta_{TR} = \frac{\Delta TR/TR}{\Delta Y/Y} \tag{2}$$

Then, combining (1) and (2) we have that

$$\Delta YD = \Delta Y * \lambda \tag{3}$$

where $\lambda = (1 - \beta_{TX}TX/Y + \beta_{TR}TR/Y)$. Procyclical taxes ($\beta_{TX} > 0$) and countercyclical transfers ($\beta_{TR} > 0$) stablilize disposable income in the face of external shocks.

Our empirical strategy will be to estimate the two key elasticities β_{TX} and β_{TR} using United States' state or regional data. The US is a good laboratory because it consists of several economically distinct regions, linked together by a federal government and using an 'irrevocably fixed ER system'. We will divide the United States into nine census regions and try to estimate their federal tax and transfers elasticities (ie their β_{TX} and β_{TR} coefficients). We choose the nine census regions for two convenient reasons. First, the size of the individual regions is then similar to the average size of a member of the European Community. Second, the division we choose is made by the Bureau of the Census to define census region. Thus, we cannot be accused of constructing the regions so as to fit the data better. One could argue that an even more natural unit is the 'state' because states have independent fiscal units (state governments). This is true, but since the ultimate goal of this paper is to apply the results to the European community, the US map with fifty states would look too different from the European one.[13] The regions (as defined by the Bureau of the Census) are described in Table 7.1. To calculate the coefficients β_{TX} and β_{TR}, we will think about the following empirical implementation (which builds on Sala-i-Martín, 1990, Chapter 4):

$$ln(TAX_i) = a_{TX} + \beta_{TX}ln(INCOME_i) + \gamma_{TX}TIME + v_i \tag{4}$$

$$ln(TRANSFER_i) = a_{TR} + \beta_{TR}ln(INCOME_i) + \gamma_{TR}TIME + \epsilon_i \tag{5}$$

where TAX refers to real tax revenue per capita, $INCOME$ is real income per capita and $TRANSFER$ is real value of transfers per capita. The

TIME variable reflects upward/downward trends in relative taxes that are not explained by the relative variations in income. These long-term movements are not cyclically correlated with relative income

The straight implementation of these two equations involves at least three problems. First, we may encounter simultaneity biases. Since higher taxes may depress regional economic activity, simple least squares estimates of equation (4) will have a downward bias. If we think of taxes as being lump-sum, an increase in federal taxes will reduce disposable income and, therefore, aggregate expenditure and output. We should mention here that this is true even if Ricardian Equivalence in the Barro (1974) sense holds. The reason is that people in region A may think that the higher tax rates they are paying now may be used to finance lower taxes in some other regions either now or in the future. Hence, their current human wealth falls with tax increases. Of course we could think of this as being the 'space dimension version' of Blanchard (1985): in his model, people think they can shift taxes to future yet unborn generations which they do not really care about. Here agents think they can shift taxes to people of other regions which they do not really care about either. The discount rates that Blanchard interprets as probability of death can be interpreted here as the 'probability of my taxes being paid by the people of some other state'. If, more realistically, taxes are distortionary rather than lump-sum, there will be additional negative effects on income of a rise in taxes, such as the disincentive to labour supply and investment.

The same type of arguments apply to transfers. Suppose that a decline in activity leads to a rise in transfers, through countercyclical spending programs such as unemployment insurance. If we try to estimate this negative relationship between economic activity and transfers, the estimated coefficient on economic activity will tend to be biased towards zero, since higher lump-sum federal transfers will ceteris paribus tend to increase disposable income and consumption and therefore increase activity in the region. We will try to solve this simultaneity problem by instrumental variables estimation.

The second problem we may encounter is that of endogenous US budget deficits. One can argue that when the overall US suffers a recession, the Federal Government runs a deficit (maybe because optimal tax rates are smooth). If tax rates remain constant and transfers increase or remain constant, the federal government absorbs some of the initial shock. Barro (1979) finds that a one-dollar shock to US income generates an increase in the federal deficit of about 1.8 dollars. In order to make sure that we are not picking up these federal deficit effects, we want to see how the federal taxes and transfers for a specific region change when the regions' income changes by 1% relative to the rest of the nation. That is, we will estimate changes in regional taxes and transfers holding the overall US GNP, taxes and transfers constant. The two modified equations will therefore be the following:

$$ln(RELATIVE\ TAX_i) = a_{TX} + \beta_{TX}\ ln(RELATIVE\ INCOME_i) + \gamma_{TX}TIME + v_i \qquad (4')$$

$$ln(REL.\quad TRANSFER_i) = a_{TR} + \beta_{TR}\ ln(RELAT.\quad INCOME_i) + \gamma_{TR}TIME + \epsilon_i \qquad (5')$$

where relative X refers to the ratio of state i's X to the overall US value of X (where X is either tax revenue, transfers or personal income). Since the relevant variables are not in relative terms, the coefficients β_{TX} and β_{TR} tell us by what percentage the region's taxes and transfers change (relative to the rest of the country federal taxes and transfers) when its income changes by 1% holding constant the changes in US aggregate income.

The third empirical problem we have to deal with involves the error terms. Even though we will start by estimating (4') and (5') with standard ordinary least squares, there is no a priori reason to assume that the error terms are homoscedastic or that they are uncorrelated across regions. Therefore we will estimate the systems of equations allowing for correlation across equations and also allowing for the regional shocks to have different variances in different regions.

3   Data

The data we use are available by state. We aggregate them according to the Bureau of the Census regional definitions which are reported in Table 7.1. The personal income data are net of transfers of taxes and are taken from the Survey of Current Business (SCB). To calculate income per capita we use the population data reported by the SCB.

The lack of a regional or state consumer price index forces us to deflate regional variable by the overall US CPI. This could potentially be a problem if there were large regional relative price movements. Of course, we know that the relative prices will not change in response to nominal or monetary shocks. We tend to think, however, that the response to real shocks (such as productivity changes or consumer preferences shifts) involve changes in relative prices. Internal migration could also have effects on relative prices mostly through changes in the prices of non-tradeables (the most important item of which is probably housing). Given that the data, to the best of our knowledge, do not exist, the best we can do for now is to use aggregate US price data (consumer price index) and hope that these errors are not very large. Sala-i-Martín (1990, Chapter 3) uses city price data for over 30 SMAS to show that these errors are

Table 7.1   *US census regions*

---

(1)   New England (NENG): Connecticut, Maine, Massachusetts, New
       Hampshire, Rhode Island and Vermont.
(2)   Middle Atlantic (MATL): New Jersey, New York and Pennsylvania.
(3)   South Atlantic (SATL): Delaware, Florida, Georgia, Maryland, North
       Carolina, South Carolina, Virginia and West Virginia.
(4)   East North Central (ENC): Illinois, Indiana, Michigan, Ohio and
       Wisconsin.
(5)   East South Central (ESC): Alabama, Kentucky, Mississippi and Tennessee.
(6)   West North Central (WNC): Iowa, Kansas, Minnesota, Missouri,
       Nebraska, North Dakota and South Dakota.
(7)   West South Central (WSC): Arkansas, Louisiana, Oklahoma and Texas.
(8)   Mountains (MTN): Arizona, Colorado, Idaho, Montana, Nevada, New
       Mexico, Utah and Wyoming.
(9)   Pacific (PAC): Alaska, California, Hawaii, Oregon and Washington.

---

probably very small since the largest inflation differential between any
two cities is almost 9% over the last 60 years (which corresponds to an
annual inflation differential of about 0.14%).

Thus, regional nominal income per capita is deflated by US CPI to
create real income per capita. The relative real income per capita data is
the ratio of a region's real income per capita to the overall US real income
per capita.

The tax variable includes personal tax and non-tax payments to the
Federal government as reported by the SCB (which includes individual
and fiduciary income taxes, estate and gift taxes and nontax payments)
plus contributions to social insurance. Of course these are not all the taxes
collected by the Federal Government: in particular we are missing corporate taxes (which, including Federal Reserve Banks, amounted about
10% of total federal receipts in 1986) and indirect taxes and customs
duties (which amounted about 6% of total federal receipts in 1986). The
reason why we are omitting these tax receipts is that the data are not
available at a state level (The Tax Foundation in Washington started
collecting these kind of data in 1981 so we could not find state-disaggre-
gated federal tax receipts before that date). Since we are missing only 17%
of the total, we think that our estimates would not change much if the
missing taxes were included.[14]

We deflate the tax data by the US CPI and we divide by population to
calculate real federal tax payments per capita. Again we divide the
regional variable by the US variable to get relative real federal tax
payments per capita.

Total nominal transfers from the federal government to the state (or region) is the sum of direct transfers to individuals (as reported by the SCB) plus federal transfers to state and local governments. The direct transfer payments to individuals include social security and other retirement plans, income maintenance payments (food stamps, supplementary secondary income for the aged, the disabled and others), veteran benefits payments and payments to nonprofit institutions. Notice that unemployment benefits are not directly included here since unemployment programs are not run by the federal but, rather, by the state governments (although they are indirectly included there to the extent that the federal government increases its transfers to the state government when a state suffers high unemployment). The reason we include transfers to state and local governments is that federal help to region A after a negative shock may involve direct transfers to state and local governments which then either decrease taxes or increase transfers to the private sector (as is the case with unemployment benefits).

A more comprehensive measure of 'federal fiscal help' would include government purchases and project awards. We do not include them in our study for two reasons. First, we did not find time series data on federal purchases by state long enough to match our sample. The Tax Foundation has collected these data since 1981, but the data do not exist before then. Second, these data correspond to 'contracts' not to actual expenditure: the final site of the supercollider will be Texas but this does not mean that all the money will be spent there. Scientists from Massachusetts, workers from Seattle and financial lizards from New York could very well benefit from the money awarded to Texas. Hence, for our purposes, these data are not that useful after all.

There are also other kinds of important transfer payments that are not included in our study up to this point. The federal government transfers involved in shutting down the failed savings and loan institutions would not be picked up the categories of transfer payments we are using, and yet the transfers involved are very large. As an illustration, as of mid-1988, there were 127 FSLIC-insured thrift institutions in Texas with a negative net worth (according to so-called GAAP accounting rules). These institutions had a combined negative net worth of about $151 billion, or about 60 percent of the state's GNP! If Texas were an independent country, these bank failures would produce an extreme financial crisis that would cripple the Texas economy, a large decline in net wealth, and perhaps a significant external debt crisis, to the extent that deposits in the failed institutions were from outside of Texas. Instead, the crisis will produce, at much lower cost, an enormous transfer of income to Texas from the rest of the United States.

We will deflate the transfer data with the US CPI and we will divide by population to calculate real federal transfer receipts per capita. Again we will divide the regional variable by the US variable to get relative real federal transfer receipts per capita.

4   Estimation

4.1   Instruments regressions

As mentioned earlier, the systems (4') and (5') are subject to simultaneity bias problems. To solve this potential problem we will try to find instruments. Candidates for instruments are aggregate variables that may affect different regions in different ways due to the different production structures, etc.

Our list of proposed instruments includes the real price of oil ($ROILP$), US aggregate GNP growth ($DGNP$), and the real value of the US $ ($DOLLAR$). Since regions differ markedly in their natural endowments and product specialization, one may expect that changes in the relative price of oil will affect regions differently. The aggregate growth variable is included on the grounds that different regions will have industrial mixes with different sensitivities to economy-wide business cycle conditions (e.g. services are less cyclical than heavy industry). The real value of the dollar vis-à-vis a basket of foreign currencies is included because different regions have a different mix of tradeables versus nontradeables, and thus will be differentially affected by the extent to which the dollar fluctuates in value versus foreign currencies. There is no good reason to think that these aggregate shocks affect relative taxes and transfers through any channel other than relative income changes. So, in principle, they should be good instruments so long as they are correlated with initial income.

In Table 7.2 we show how well these proposed instruments correlate with relative income. We see that the regressions are highly successful for 8 out of the 9 regions. The exception is the Pacific region (PAC) with an adjusted $\bar{R}^2$ coefficient of about 0.35. The other regions' $\bar{R}^2$ range from 0.65 in WNC to 0.92 in ENC. We can reject the hypothesis that all coefficients are zero for all regions at a 1% significance level (5% for PAC).

Some of the partial correlations in Table 7.2 are interesting. We observe that relative income for NENG is significantly positively correlated with the real value of the dollar ($DOLLAR$) and negatively correlated with the real price of oil ($ROILP$), which reflects the negative wealth effect mentioned above. We also see that when the US grows faster, New England's relative income goes down. The Middle Atlantic region is very similar to

Table 7.2   *Instrumental regressions*

REGIONS	C	TIME	DGNP	ROILP	DOLLAR	$\bar{R}^2$	F-stat
			RHS VARIABLES				
NENG	−0.225	0.020	−0.435	−0.002	0.00099	0.90	42.5
	(−4.19)	(10.5)	(−2.42)	(−2.97)	(5.49)		
MATL	−0.078	0.009	−0.373	−0.001	0.0007	0.84	24.14
	(−2.33)	(7.28)	(−3.34)	(−3.36)	(5.85)		
SATL	−0.140	0.006	−0.071	−0.0008	0.0003	0.65	9.01
	(−3.68)	(4.53)	(−0.60)	(−2.17)	(2.26)		
ENC	0.262	−0.012	0.322	−0.0008	−0.0007	0.93	54.22
	(8.91)	(−11.9)	(3.29)	(−2.42)	(−7.22)		
ESC	−0.13	−0.007	0.273	0.00007	−0.0006	0.82	20.38
	(−5.70)	(−7.67)	(3.43)	(0.26)	(−7.21)		
WNC	0.118	−0.006	0.058	0.000001	−0.0006	0.66	9.21
	(2.88)	(−4.17)	(−0.96)	(−0.34)	(−3.83)		
WSC	−0.219	0.0003	0.228	0.0047	0.00002	0.79	17.15
	(−2.72)	(−0.12)	(−0.84)	(5.58)	(−0.08)		
MTN	−0.027	−0.005	0.150	0.0017	−0.0002	0.79	17.32
	(−0.87)	(−4.62)	(1.47)	(5.30)	(−1.89)		
PAC	0.134	−0.001	−0.020	0.0005	−0.00012	0.37	3.35
	(4.07)	(−0.85)	(−0.18)	(1.50)	(−1.15)		

Note: The dependent variable is per capita real income of each region relative to the US total. The variable *TIME* is a time dummy. *DGNP* is the growth rate of overall US GNP. *ROILP* is the oil price in real terms. *DOLLAR* is the real value of the US dollar (weighted average). The numbers in parenthesis are *t*-statistics. See Table 7.1 for regional definitions. Sample period 1970 to 1988.

NENG. It does very well when the dollar is strong and relatively poorly when oil prices rise. MATL also does poorly when the US as a whole grows faster. The long-run trend in its relative income is positive.

South Atlantic's relative income is also positively correlated with the *DOLLAR* and negatively correlated with *ROILP* and *DGNP*. This later variable, however, is not significant. The long-run trend is positive. East North Central is a very interesting region. Its relative income is very negatively correlated with the *DOLLAR* and the *ROILP*. This region is a major producer of industrial goods (cars) and it is hurt by foreign imports when the dollar is strong. It is also hurt by higher oil prices (as oil is a complementary good for cars). Different from all the above regions, ENC does relatively well when the US as a whole grows faster. The long-run trend is negative.

Fiscal federalism and optimum currency areas   207

East South Central's relative income seems not to be affected by the real oil price (its coefficient is negative but insignificant). This region is hurt in relative terms by a strong dollar and by weak US growth. Its long-run trend is significantly negative. West North Central presents a negative trend and significant relative correlation with the dollar. Its income barely moves when the US GNP growth or the oil price change. West South Central income is very strongly and positively correlated with the real oil price. Given that the states in this region are major producers of oil, this is not surprising. Even though none of the other instruments is significant the remarkable fit ($\bar{R}^2$ of 0.79) shows that this region's relative income is largely determined by oil prices.

The Mountain region is also very positively correlated with oil (some of its states – such as Wyoming – are also major oil producers). The negative correlation between its relative income and the real value of the *DOLLAR* is significant at the 8% level. Finally, the Pacific region is really disappointing. The adjusted R^2 is really low and none of the variables is significant. We have tried eliminating the smaller states (in particular Alaska and Hawaii) but the problem does not seem to come from any of them, but rather, from California. If instead of relative income we regress relative taxes on relative unemployment rates, the coefficients for PAC are very similar to the other regions. This leads us to think that there could be some problem with the Californian income data. In the absence of further work, we should look at the Pacific results with some skepticism.

4.2   Relative taxes equations

We can now proceed to estimate the relative tax and transfers equations (4′) and (5′). The results for the tax equations are displayed in Table 7.3. Each regression has been estimated by three different methods. Columns one and two refer to simple OLS estimates. The first column shows the β_{TX} coefficient and its standard error (the constant and time trend which have been included in the regression are not reported separately[15]). The second column reports the adjusted R^2 and standard error of the regression. Hence, the OLS estimate of β_{TX} for New England is 1.275 (s.e. = 0.0539), the $\bar{R}^2$ is 0.98 and the standard error of the regression is 0.009.

Note that the coefficients for the relative income variable – β_{TX} – reported in Table 7.3 fluctuate around 1.35.[16] The largest OLS estimate corresponds to the South Atlantic (SATL) region – $\beta_{TX} = 1.738$ (s.e. = 0.146) – and the smallest is the Rocky Mountains with $\beta_{TX} = 1.254$ (s.e. = 0.1566). Similar numbers apply for the IV and SUR estimates.

Table 7.3 *Relative taxes versus relative income*

REGION	OLS		IV		SUR	
	β_{TX} (s.e.)	$\bar{R}^2$ [s.e.]	β_{TX} (s.e.)	$\bar{R}^2$ [s.e.]	β_{TX} (s.e.)	$\bar{R}^2$ [s.e.]
NENG	1.275	(0.98)	1.280	(0.98)	1.233	(0.98)
	(0.0539)	[0.0090]	(0.0580)	[0.0089]	(0.0358)	[0.0091]
MATL	1.391	(0.95)	1.434	(0.95)	1.324	(0.95)
	(0.0845)	[0.0094]	(0.0908)	[0.0095]	(0.0563)	[0.0096]
SATL	1.738	(0.89)	1.693	(0.89)	1.688	(0.89)
	(0.1462)	[0.0099]	(0.1834)	[0.0100]	(0.1022)	[0.0100]
ENC	1.370	(0.97)	1.403	(0.97)	1.501	(0.96)
	(0.0938)	[0.0078]	(0.1030)	[0.0078]	(0.0730)	[0.0083]
ESC	1.379	(0.78)	1.336	(0.78)	1.355	(0.78)
	(0.1907)	[0.0141]	(0.2057)	[0.0141]	(0.1328)	[0.0141]
WNC	1.591	(0.62)	1.694	(0.62)	1.658	(0.62)
	(0.2948)	[0.0255]	(0.3443)	[0.0226]	(0.2033)	[0.0225]
WSC	1.323	(0.98)	1.375	(0.98)	1.292	(0.98)
	(0.0537)	[0.0108]	(0.0623)	[0.0111]	(0.0414)	[0.0109]
MTN	1.254	(0.80)	1.260	(0.80)	1.174	(0.80)
	(0.1566)	[0.0134]	(0.1718)	[0.0134]	(0.1046)	[0.0135]
PAC	0.535	(0.37)	0.261	(0.34)	0.6152	(0.36)
	(0.3315)	[0.0166]	(0.5220)	[0.0169]	(0.1920)	[0.0166]
RESTRICTED (1)	1.333	—	1.361	—	1.335	—
	(0.0277)		(0.0321)		(0.0233)	
P-VALUE	0.05		0.08		0.187	
RESTRICTED (2)	1.275	—	1.360	—	1.335	—
	(0.0492)		(0.0318)		(.0233)	
P-VALUE	0.05		0.08		0.05	

Notes: The left hand side of these regressions are the logs of real relative taxes described in the text. The equations have been estimated with a time trend and a constant, not shown separately. The OLS estimates are reported in columns one and two. Each group of four numbers corresponds to the β_{TX} coefficient and its standard error, the adjusted R^2 and the standard error of regression. The restricted (1) systems have been estimated with individual constants and time trends. The p-value corresponds to the test of equality of coefficients across regions. The likelihood ratio statistic follows a chi-square distribution with 8 degrees of freedom. The restricted (2) corrects for heteroscedasticity and allows each region to have its own variance of the error term. The middle two columns reproduce the OLS estimates using instruments reported in Table 7.2. The last two columns refer to seemingly unrelated regressions where the errors are allowed to be correlated across equations. The sample period is 1970–88.

The coefficients reported in columns 3 and 4 refer to the Instrumental Variables regressions. As we argued previously, the reason for using this method is the possible existence of simultaneity bias since higher relative tax rates may reduce relative regional income. Notice that the estimates of β_{TX} are very similar to ones reported for OLS regressions.

Finally in columns 5 and 6 we allow for the regional shocks to relative taxes v_i to be correlated across regions. In order to allow for that we estimate all the regions at the same time in a seemingly unrelated regression estimation system (SUR). Again the estimates are not very different from the OLS ones, suggesting that the correlation of error terms across equations may not be that important.

We are now interested in testing the hypothesis of similar β_{TX} coefficients across regions. If, as we have conjectured, the elasticity coefficient β_{TX} reflects mostly the progressivity of the federal tax system, we should expect these coefficients to be constant across regions. In the last six rows of Table 7.3 we report the β_{TX} coefficients when all regions are constrained to be equal. The constrained OLS coefficient is 1.333 (s.e. = 0.0277). The test for equality of β_{TX} coefficients across regions can barely be rejected at the 5% level (p-value = 0.044). The restricted IV coefficient is 1.361 (s.e. = 0.0321) and the test for equality across regions cannot be rejected at the 5% level (p-value = 0.076). The constrained SUR coefficient is 1.335 (s.e. = 0.0233) and the test for equality across regions cannot be rejected at the 5% level (p-value = 0.177).

The last three rows of Table 7.3 report the restricted β_{TX} coefficients when we estimate the system of regions correcting for heteroscedasticity. The weighting method employed gives more weight to the regions whose standard error of the regression (which is reported in Table 7.3) is smaller. Note that constrained weighted OLS coefficient is 1.275 (s.e. = 0.0492) and p-value 0.05, the constrained weighted IV β_{TX} coefficient is 1.360 (s.e. = 0.0318), and the constrained weighted SUR coefficient is 1.335 (s.e. = 0.0233). We also estimated unconstrained weighted systems which allows us to test the hypothesis of equality of the β_{TX} coefficients across regions. We find that we cannot reject the hypothesis of regional equality at the 5% level in any of the three cases.

In summary, the estimated β_{TX} coefficients fluctuate around 1.35 and we cannot reject the hypothesis that they are equal across regions. This implies that, holding constant the aggregate US variables and adjusting for whatever factors affect the long-run movements in regional taxes, a 1 percent increase in a region's income increases its federal tax payments by 1.35 percent (statistically significantly larger than one). Since there is no 'intentional' reduction in tax rates when a region suffers an adverse shock, these findings just reflect the progressive nature of the US tax system.

Table 7.4   *Average real income, taxes, transfers and disposable income*
($)

REGIONS	*AVG. Y*	*AVG. TX*	*AVG. TR*	*AVG. YD*
NENG	10,960	2,914	1,917	9,963
MATL	10,879	2,936	2,140	10,056
SATL	9,580	2,389	1,746	8,937
ENC	10,282	2,712	1,680	9,250
ESC	7,602	1,880	1,680	7,398
WNC	9,790	2,446	1,707	9,051
WSC	9,162	2,412	1,523	8,273
MTN	9,470	2,330	1,652	8,792
PAC	11,336	2,839	2,026	10,523
US	10,094	2,607	1,811	9,138

Note: The sources of the data are explained in Section 3 in the text. The tax variable has been adjusted for the missing corporate taxes and indirect taxes and custom duties which, as discussed in the text, represent about 20% of federal taxes over the sample period considered.

A simple numerical example will further clarify what the numbers found mean. Consider an economy with an average tax rate of 20% (the average tax rate for our US regions can be calculated to be around 20% from Table 7.4). Suppose further that the average marginal tax rate is about 30%.[17] The β_{TX} coefficient for this economy (which the ratio of marginal to average tax rates) would be exactly 1.5. If the average marginal tax rate were 27%, the β_{TX} coefficient would be 1.35. Hence, our estimates are exactly in the ball park.

4.3   Relative transfers equations

The picture for transfers (Table 7.5) is a bit different. We expected to observe a negative coefficient reflecting the fact that, holding constant US aggregate variables, an increase in regional income would reduce the transfers received from the federal government. The OLS estimates show that, out of nine regions, six are significantly negative, one significantly positive (MATL) and two are not statistically significantly different from zero (one positive point estimate corresponding to ESC, and one negative, corresponding to WSC). The restricted OLS estimate is -0.181 (s.e. $= 0.0409$), but the equality of β_{TR} coefficients across regions can be rejected at the 5% level (p-value $= 0.000$). The instrumental variables

212   **Xavier Sala-i-Martín and Jeffrey Sachs**

Table 7.5   *Relative transfers versus relative income*

REGION	OLS		IV		SUR	
	β_{TR} (s.e.)	$\bar{R}^2$ [s.e.]	β_{TR} (s.e.)	$\bar{R}^2$ [s.e.]	β_{TR} (s.e.)	$\bar{R}^2$ [s.e.]
NENG	−0.230 (0.0818)	(0.54) [0.0136]	−0.212 (0.0883)	(0.54) [0.0136]	−0.262 (0.0629)	(0.53) [0.0137]
MATL	0.246 (0.1259)	(0.37) [0.0140]	0.269 (0.1343)	(0.37) [0.140]	0.222 (0.0649)	(0.37) [0.0140]
SATL	−0.999 (0.1401)	(0.88) [0.0095]	−1.299 (0.2001)	(0.84) [0.0108]	−1.019 (0.0912)	(0.88) [0.0095]
ENC	−0.368 (0.1392)	(0.93) [0.0116]	−0.355 (0.1523)	(0.93) [0.0116]	−0.313 (0.0664)	(0.93) [0.0116]
ESC	0.126 (0.1723)	(0.68) [0.0127]	0.197 (0.1866)	(0.68) [0.0128]	0.053 (0.1129)	(0.68) [0.0128]
WNC	−0.585 (0.0702)	(0.90) [0.0054]	−0.600 (0.0817)	(0.90) [0.0054]	−0.529 (0.0474)	(0.90) [0.0055]
WSC	−0.018 (0.1026)	(0.45) [0.0206]	0.007 (0.1157)	(0.44) [0.0207]	−0.041 (0.0806)	(0.44) [0.0207]
MTN	−0.708 (0.1426)	(0.94) [0.0122]	−0.778 (0.1576)	(0.94) [0.0123]	−0.618 (0.0860)	(0.93) [0.0123]
PAC	−0.591 (0.3808)	(0.38) [0.0190]	−1.418 (0.6725)	(0.88) [0.218]	−0.595 (0.0918)	(0.91) [0.0190]
RESTRICTED (1)	−0.181 (0.0409)	—	−0.171 (0.0458)	—	0.192 (0.0217)	—
P-VALUE	0.00		0.00		0.00	
RESTRICTED (2)	−0.327 (0.0424)	—	−0.306 (0.0472)	—	−0.266 (0.0211)	—
P-VALUE	0.00		0.00		0.10	

Notes: The dependent variable is the log of the real relative transfers from the federal government. See also Notes to Table 7.3.

estimates reported in columns three and four are very similar to the OLS ones (which reflects the fact that we are estimating the relative income regressions in Table 7.2 with high precision). The restricted estimate is −0.171 (s.e. = 0.0458) and can be rejected to be equal across regions at the 5% level (p-value = 0.000).

The results corresponding to the SUR system are reported in columns 5 and 6 of Table 7.5. The restricted SUR estimate is a bit higher than the OLS one although not significantly so (β_{TR} = −0.192, s.e. = 0.0217).

The results for the weighted restricted systems are reported in the last three rows of Table 7.5. The weighted OLS estimate is -0.327 (s.e. = 0.0424). This point estimate is just a weighted average of the OLS estimates above, where the weights are the standard errors of the OLS equations. Notice that, because the regions with positive OLS β_{TR} estimate have relatively high standard errors, the restricted weighted OLS estimate is higher than the unweighted one (where all regions receive the same weight).

Something similar happens with the IV regressions. Because the regions that had positive IV estimates had high standard errors, the weighted estimate is much higher than the unweighted one.

Finally, the results for the weighted SUR system are surprising. When we estimated the unconstrained weighted system (not reported in the Table)[18] we found that ALL the point estimates were negative and significant! The constrained estimate is -0.226 (s.e. = 0.021) and equality across regions cannot be rejected at the 5% level (p-value = 0.1). The better estimates of β_{TR} when we use a weighted SUR system are probably due to the cross-equation interaction of error terms being relatively important for the transfers equations.

Summarizing, the relative transfer coefficients $-\beta_{TR}-$ for a system of nine US regions display some instability if they are estimated giving equal weight to all regions. If we correct for heteroscedasticity, however, the coefficients are much more stable. The restricted unweighted numbers fluctuate around -0.20 while the restricted weighted β's move around -0.30. The apparent instability of the β_{TR} coefficients is not surprising since, unlike taxes, the federal transfer system in the US is not really set as an automatic reaction to personal income.

5   Calculating the federal impact on disposable income

The β coefficients estimated in Section 4 tell us by what percentage the relative taxes and transfers of region i increase when there is a one percent increase in that region's relative income. Looking back to equation (1), we want to ask now, how many cents the federal government actually absorbs when there is a one-dollar shock to the relative per capita income of a region. To do so we can evaluate the estimated elasticities at the average income, tax and transfers. When average income in region i increases by one dollar, the average tax payment increase by $\lambda_{TX} = \beta_{TXi}*TX_i/Y_i$ and the average transfer falls by $\lambda_{TR} = \beta_{TR}*TR_i/Y_i$, where TX_i/Y_i is the average tax rate and TR_i/Y_i is the average transfer for that region. The final disposable income for region i increases by $\lambda = 1 - \lambda_{TX} + \lambda_{TR}$ cents after a one-dollar shock to that region's income.

Table 7.6   *Changes in taxes and transfers due to a 1-dollar shock to income*

Method	λ_{TX} cents	λ_{TR} cents	$\lambda = 100 - \lambda T_X + \lambda_{TR}$ cents
OLS	34	− 3	62
	(35, 33)	(− 5, − 2)	(59, 65)
IV	35	− 3	62
	(36, 34)	(− 5, − 1)	(58, 60)
SUR	34	− 3	62
	(36, 33)	(− 4, − 3)	(60, 64)
WOLS	33	− 6	61
	(35, 30)	(− 7, − 4)	(57, 61 65)
WIV	35	− 6	59
	(37, 33)	(− 7, − 3)	(56, 63)
WSUR	34	− 5	61
	(36, 33)	(− 6, − 4)	(59, 63)

Individual regions' estimates of λ (OLS)

NENG	34	− 4	62
MALT	38	5	67
SATL	43	− 23	38
ENC	36	− 6	58
ESC	34	4	69
WNC	40	− 10	50
WSC	35	− 0	65
MTN	31	− 14	55
PAC	13	− 25	62
AVERAGE	34	− 8	58

Notes: λ_{TX} measures the fall in federal taxes that follows a one-dollar reduction in a region's total income ($\lambda_{TX} = \beta_{TX}*TX/Y$). Thus, 34 means that when a region's income falls by one dollar, the tax payments from that region to the federal government go down by 34 cents. λ_{TR} measures the increase in transfers from the Federal Government that follows a one-dollar increase in a state's income per capita ($\lambda_{TR} = \beta_{TR}*TR/Y$). Thus − 6 means that when a region's income per capita falls by one dollar, transfers from the federal government to that region increase by 6 cents.

The first few rows display the λ's associated with the restricted β's from Tables 7.3 and 7.5. OLS, IV, and SUR correspond to the restristed OLS, IV and SUR systems. WOLS, WIV and WSUR correspond to the restricted weighted OLS, IV and SUR systems. In parenthesis the λ's associated with two standard deviations from the corresponding point estimate for β.

The last few rows display the regional λ's corresponding to the unrestricted unweighted IV systems. The average is the unweighted average of all the λ's above.

In Table 7.6 we use the estimated β coefficients from Tables 7.3 and 7.5 to calculate the corresponding λ's. The first few columns use the restricted estimates. The rows labeled OLS, IV, and SUR display the λ's corresponding to the restricted OLS, IV and SUR estimates of Tables 7.3 and 7.5. The rows labeled WOLS, WIV and WSUR report the λ's corresponding to the restricted weighted OLS, IV, and SUR estimates of Tables 7.3 and 7.5. The numbers in parenthesis refer to the λ's that correspond to two standard deviations away from the point estimates of β. For instance, the restricted OLS numbers suggest that when a typical region in the US suffers a one-dollar adverse shock to its personal income, its average federal tax payments reduce by something between 33 and 35 cents (with a point estimate of 34 cents) and its transfers increase by somewhere between 2 and 5 cents (with a point estimate of 3 cents) so that the disposable income falls by something between 59 and 65 cents (with a point estimate of 62 cents).

Notice that the results for λ_{TX} are very stable across Table 7.6 and move between 34 and 37 cents to the dollar. This stability is due to the stability of the β_{TX} coefficients in Table 7.3. The results for λ_{TR} when we use the weighted estimates are a bit larger than the ones we get by using the unweighted ones: the unweighted λ_{TR} are in the neighborhood of -0.03 while the weighted ones fluctuate around -0.06. Correspondingly the unweighted overall λ's move around 0.62 for the unweighted estimates and around 0.60 for the weighted ones.

The second half of Table 7.6 shows the λ estimates for each of the nine regions. Notice that the estimated λ_{TX}'s are extremely stable (except for the Pacific region). This again is due to our earlier finding that the β_{TX} coefficients are very stable across regions. The average tax response to a dollar shock is 34 cents. The estimated λ_{TR} fluctuate a lot more across regions, and therefore, so do the overall λ's. The average transfer response to a dollar regional shock is 8 cents. The corresponding average total response to a dollar regional shock is 58 cents. Notice that these results are not very far from the ones we got using the restricted estimates.

Taken as a whole, Table 7.6 suggests that when the average region suffers a one-dollar adverse shock to its personal income, its federal tax payments are reduced by something between 33 and 37 cents, the transfers received from the federal government increase by somewhere between one and eight cents so the final disposable income falls by only 56 to 65 cents. Hence, the fraction of the initial shock that is absorbed by the federal fiscal system is between one-third and one-half. Most of the action comes from the tax side which probably reflects the progressive nature of the US federal tax system.

6   Final remarks

We have argued that the US can be viewed as a set of regions tied by an 'irrevocably fixed ER' and that this ER arrangement seems to work effectively. One of the reasons for this reasonably efficient system, could be that the federal fiscal system absorbs a substantial fraction of interregional shocks. This reduces the need for nominal exchange rate realignments.

The existence of this federal fiscal system does not mean that there are no interregional adjustments to be made but, rather, that they are made without devaluations (or major pressures on the one-to-one fixed parities) and without extraordinary recessions.

We tried to estimate empirically the effects of such a federal fiscal system and we found that a one-dollar reduction in a regions' per capita income triggered a decrease in federal taxes in the neighbourhood of 34 cents and an increase in transfers of about 6 cents. The final reduction in disposable per capita income was, therefore, of only 60 cents. That is, between one-third and one-half of the original one-dollar shock is absorbed by the Federal Government.

The much larger reaction of taxes than transfers to these regional imbalances reflects that the main mechanism at work is the progressive federal income tax system which in turn reflects that the stabilization process is automatic rather than discretionary. Our estimates do not include the large one-time transfers that occur when there are large one-time disasters (such as the S&L crises and the huge transfers from the US to the few states involved). Hence, we are underestimating the role of the federal government as a partial insurer against regional shocks.

Some economists may want to argue that this regional insurance scheme provided by the federal government is one of the key reasons why the system of fixed exchange rates within the United States has survived without major problems. And this is a lesson to be learned by the proponents of a unified European currency: the creation of a unified currency without a federal insurance scheme could very well lead the project to an eventual failure.

On the other hand, it could be (rightly) argued that Europe already has a federal system of the type proposed here, insofar as there are European Community taxes. Some simple calculations based on rough estimates show that this is close to negligible: the average VAT tax rate (as a ratio of GDP) for members of the EEC is of the order of 0.5%. Let us assume that the average and marginal tax rates are roughly similar (that is let us assume that tax rate is always constant). This would yield β_{TX} equal to one. The corresponding λ_{TX} would then be about 0.005. That is, if a European region or country suffers a one dollar adverse shock, its tax payments to the European Community will be reduced by half a cent. This contrasts with the 34 cents we found for the United States. Thus, European fiscal federalism has a long way to go.

NOTES

We would like to thank Robert Barro, Willem Buiter, Barça Campió, Behzad Diba, Alberto Giovaninni, and participants at the CEPR/CGES/IMF conference 'Establishing a Central Bank for Europe' at Georgetown University for helpful comments on this and/or on an earlier version that circulated with the title 'Federal Fiscal Policy and Optimum Currency Areas: Lessons for Europe from the United States'.

1 See Hartland (1949), Lerner (1951), Meade (1957).
2 The phrase 'optimum currency area' was coined by Mundell in his classic (1961) paper.
3 John Stuart Mill (1894, p. 176).
4 Although they did not use the phrase 'optimum currency area' the concept of a unique currency for regions with high labour mobility had already been outlined by both Lerner (1951) and Meade (1957). See also Tower and Willett (1976).
5 From a Keynesian perspective, therefore, the question of the appropriate exchange rate regime cannot really be separated from the debate on the importance and causes of nominal rigidities. Of course the existence of nominal rigidities is at the very heart of the current macroeconomic debate. See Blanchard (1990) for a survey.
6 Other criteria mentioned in the literature are 'the degree of openness' (if the marginal propensity to import is very high, a small decrease in income in A and a small increase in B will restore equilibrium); the size of transaction costs (a unique currency reduces transaction and accounting costs); and the extent of financial market integration (high capital mobility would facilitate borrowing and lending; of course that would not help with a permanent shift in preferences but it would certainly be very important if the perturbations were temporary). We will not discuss them because we think that (at least in 1992) Europe will satisfy the two requirements.
  Finally, some economists (Kenen, 1969), argue that open economies should have fixed ER only if they have a variety of exports. If an economy exports only one good, then a single shock may require a major real adjustment.
7 The debate over fixed versus flexible ER does not stop at the analysis of 'what kind of shocks are you more likely to suffer?' Some of the current debate stresses the 'disciplinary' effects of having fixed ER (Giavazzi and Pagano, 1988, Giavazzi and Giovannini, 1989, and Canzoneri and Henderson, 1988). These researchers use a Barro-Gordon (1983) type of model to stress that the existence of fixed ER increases the anti-inflationary reputation of a single government and, therefore, reduces the real costs of a deflationary policy. For a criticism see Obstfeld (1988).
8 The way this problem has been handled up to now in the EMS has been through devaluations. There were 11 episodes of realignment in the first 10 years of the EMS (Giavazzi and Giovannini, 1989).
9 Kenen (1969) was the first to use this kind of argument.

10 Hartland (1949) analysed the implicit interregional transfers within the US. She looked at the treasury fund movements from industralized to agricultural regions in response to the government policy of supporting farm prices in the 1930s. She concluded that 'the most important determinant in the maintenance of regional balance of payments equilibria in this country has been the mobility of productive factors, especially that of capital'. The argument is that the role of the government was not to carry out the actual transfers but to facilitiate private capital movements. See also the Reply by Fels (1950) and Hartland (1950).

11 The issue of convergence across US states and European regions is studied in Sala-i-Martín (1990), Barro and Sala-i-Martín (1991a and b). Sala-i-Martín (1990) also studies the role of the US Federal Government in promoting regional convergence.

12 See Eichengreen (1991) for a discussion of this topic.

13 An even better division would be one based on the 12 Federal Reserve Districts. The tax and transfers coefficients we estimate here, however, are not sensitive to the choice of region. Mulligan and Sala-i-Martín (1991) use 12 Federal Reserve regions in a paper that studies the interplay between money and output in a system of irrevocably fixed exchange rates.

14 The missing proportion is a little larger for the beginning of the sample: about 25%. The income tax receipts have remained more of less constant over the sample.

15 All the systems allow for each region to have its own constant and time trend.

16 The Pacific region is once again an exception with $\beta_{TX} = 0.535$ (s.e. = 0.3315). Its large standard error, however, implies (as we will see in a second) that its OLS estimate is not significantly different from the rest since we cannot reject the hypothesis of equality of β_{TX} across regions.

17 The average marginal tax rate in the United States has fluctuated over the sample. It was 27% in 1970 and progressively increased until it reached a maximum of 38% in 1981. The Reagan tax cuts brought it back down to 34% by 1985. See Barro (1990) for a discussion of these numbers.

18 The results were as follows: NENG = −0.329 (s.e. = 0.052), SATL = −0.202 (s.e. = 0.034), MATL = −0.404 (s.e. = 0.041), ENC = −0.117 (s.e. = 0.032), ESC = −0.770 (s.e. = 0.063), WNC = −0.480 (s.e. = 0.030), WSC = −0.225 (s.e. = 0.037), MTN = −0.210 (s.e. = 0.056), PAC = −0.378 (s.e. = 0.036)

REFERENCES

Barro, R. J. (1974), 'Are Government Bonds Net Wealth?', *Journal of Political Economy* 82, 1095–1117.

(1979), 'On the determination of the public debt', *Journal of Political Economy* 87, 940–71.

(1990), *Macroeconomics*, 3rd edition. Wiley.

Barro, R. J. and R. Gordon (1983), 'Rules, Discretion and Reputation in a Model of Monetary Policy', *Journal of Monetary Economics* 12, 101–21.

Barro, R. J. and X. Sala-i-Martín (1991a) 'Convergence across States and Regions', *Brookings Papers on Economic Activity*.

(1991b), 'Convergence', *Journal of Political Economy* forthcoming.

Blanchard, O. J., (1985) 'Debt, Deficits, and Finite Horizons', *Journal of Political Economy* **93**, 223–47.

Canzoneri, M. and D. Henderson (1988), 'Is Sovereign Policy Bad?', Carnegie-Rochester Conference Series on Public Policy, No. 28.

Canzoneri, M. B. and C. A. Rogers (1990), 'Is the European Community an Optimum Currency Area? Optimal Taxation versus the Cost of Multiple Currencies', *American Economic Review* **80**, 419–33.

Eichengreen, B. (1991), 'Is Europe an Optimum Currency Area?', NBER Working Paper No. 3579, January.

Fels, R. (1950), 'Interregional Payments: A Comment' (on Hartland, 1949), *Quarterly Journal of Economics* **64**.

Giavazzi, F. and A. Giovannini (1989) *Limiting Exchange Rate Flexibility: The European Monetary System*, MIT Press.

Giavazzi, F. and M. Pagano (1988) 'The advantage of typing one's hands: EMS Discipline and Central Bank Credibility', *European Economic Review*, **32**, 1055–75.

Goldstein, M. and G. Woglom (1992) 'Market-Based Fiscal Discipline in Monetary Unions: Evidence from the US Municipal Bond Market', this volume.

Hartland, P. (1949), 'Interregional Payments compared with International Payments', *Quarterly Journal of Economics* **63**.

——— (1950), 'Reply (to Fels)', *Quarterly Journal of Economics* **64**.

Kenen, P. (1969), 'The Theory of Optimum Currency Areas: an Eclectic View, in R. Mundell and A. Swoboda (eds.) *Monetary Problems of the International Economy*, Univ. of Chicago Press.

Lerner, A. (1951), *Economics of Employment*, McGraw Hill, NY.

Meade, J. E. (1957), 'The Balance-of-Payments Problems of a European Free-Trade Area', *Economic Journal* **67**, 379–96.

Mill, J. S. (1894), *Principles of Political Economy*, New York.

Mulligan, C. B. and X. Sala-i-Martín (1991) 'Money and income across the States of the United States', manuscript in progress.

Mundell, R. (1961), 'A Theory of Optimum Currency Areas', *American Economic Review* **51**, 657–65.

Obstfeld, M. (1986), 'Capital Controls, the Dual Exchange Rate and Devaluation', *Journal of International Economics* **20**, 1–20.

——— (1988) 'The Advantage of Tying One's hands: Comment on Giavazzi and Pagano', *European Economic Review* **32**, 1077–82.

Sala-i-Martin, X. (1990), 'On Growth and States', Unpublished PhD Dissertation, Harvard University.

Tower, E. and T. Willett (1976), 'The Theory of Optimum Currency Areas and Exchange-Rate Flexibility', Special Papers in International Economics, Princeton University.

Discussion

BEHZAD T. DIBA

This paper's main text presents some empirical evidence on how federal taxes and transfers serve as a regional insurance scheme in the United States. The authors also argue that the lack of a comparable federal fiscal system in the European Community significantly hinders the EC's prospects as an optimum currency area. They conclude that major fiscal changes in the direction of federalism may be an essential prerequisite for an eventual European Monetary Union.

I find the paper's empirical analysis of US data very interesting. It seems worth emphasizing that Sala-i-Martín and Sachs deliberately abstract from any intertemporal smoothing effects of the overall (Federal State and Local) fiscal system in the US in estimating the interregional smoothing effects of Federal taxes and transfers.

The US fiscal system may affect intertemporal consumption or disposable income both through its effects of the deadweight loss from taxation (as in Neoclassical models) and through the functioning of progressive taxes and entitlement programs as automatic stabilizers (as in Keynesian models). These intertemporal effects, however, should not directly depend on which level of government collects the taxes and undertakes the expenditures.

Sala-i-Martín and Sachs appropriately abstract from the intertemporal effects of the US fiscal system in face of national disturbances; their empirical analysis focuses on the ratios of regional-to-national taxes, transfers, and incomes. Thus, their finding that Federal taxes and transfers attenuate the effect of regional income shocks by about forty percent correctly measures the magnitude of the interregional insurance provided by fiscal federalism *per se*.

Turning to implications of their analysis for the EC, Sala-i-Martín and Sachs draw on two basic premises. The first premise is that government provision of interregional insurance is desirable because financial markets are incomplete and comparable private insurance schemes are not likely to emerge in the absence of government intervention. The second premise is that cultural or linguistic barriers to labour mobility within the EC, in conjunction with regional disturbances, hinder the development of an optimum currency area *because* national price levels are not flexible.

One may, of course, argue about the validity or importance of these premises on several grounds. Moreover, even accepting the two premises (as I am willing to do) would not seem to establish the authors' main argument. The main argument, I think, postulates that the two premises *interact* significantly. That is, the paper seems to claim that the absence of fiscal federalism is a major obstacle to EMU, and that the presence of price rigidities and a common currency would significantly strengthen the case for government provision of regional insurance.

In articulating their argument, Sala-i-Martín and Sachs emphasize the effects of *permanent* changes in preferences for goods produced in different countries. They suggest that, with sticky prices and a common currency, such changes would lead to unemployment in some regions and overemployment in others, and that a federal fiscal system would have the advantage of reducing these regional imbalances. The possibility of permanent shocks may seem relevant because lending and borrowing on EC-wide financial markets may cope with transitory regional shocks (more on this below) but cannot offset permanent shocks.

This emphasis on permanent shocks, however, seems misplaced. In the long run, I presume, the real exchange rate does not depend on the nominal exchange-rate regime or on the empirical significance of short-run price rigidities. Thus, abstracting from transitory shocks (and the transition to new long-run equilibria), the case for or against fiscal federalism in the EC seems independent of the case for or against EMU.

From the long-run perspective, of course, assessing the desirability of government provision of regional insurance in the EC would involve complicated microeconomic considerations (equity, efficiency, market failure, etc.). These considerations, however, pertain to government provision of insurance in general and are conceptually distinct from the macroeconomic issues addressed in the paper. These macroeconomic issues necessarily involve consideration of transitory shocks or of transitions to new long-run equilibria.

Assessing the desirability of a regional insurance scheme during the transition (while price levels adjust) to new long-run equilibria is also complicated. On one hand, such a scheme would make the transition less painful. On the other hand, by the same token, the scheme would probably slow down the requisite quantity and factor-supply responses to permanent shocks.

At any rate, once we focus on transitory shocks or transitions to new long-run equilibria, national fiscal policies within the EC countries would seem to be a close substitute for fiscal federalism in terms of their effect on employment. According to conventional (Keynesian) models of fiscal policy, national governments within the EC should be able to stabilize employment through (discretionary or automatic) changes in taxes and expenditures accompanied by lending and borrowing on EC-wide financial markets.

Sala-i-Martín and Sachs criticize this conventional view on two grounds. First, they argue that Ricardian Equivalence may frustrate any attempt to stabilize employment by changes in regional fiscal policies. Second, they argue that anticipated fluctuations in regional taxes may induce movements in factors of production, eroding the tax-base in regions that must raise their tax rates to retire debt.

I think both of these arguments, to some extent, contradict the basic premises behind the paper. It seems difficult to imagine a world with sticky prices in which Ricardian Equivalence still holds. It also seems difficult to combine high factor mobility in face of regional tax differentials with the basic premise of low labour mobility despite regional employment and income imbalances.

Turning to a more pragmatic point of view, in recent years, the EC seems to have avoided major regional imbalances without quantitatively significant fluctuations in most bilateral exchange rates. Thus, setting aside the possibility of unprecedented regional disturbances, the current fiscal system may be expected to function reasonably well under EMU.

Finally, although I am not convinced that the feasibility of EMU hinges on establishing a federal fiscal system, it may be worth noting that the absence of such a system has implications for policy issues that are peripherally linked to EMU. Specifically, if the path to EMU involves imposing ceilings on national budget deficits and on outstanding amounts of public debt, the flexibility of national fiscal policies may be significantly reduced. In this event, the past performance of national economies may be a poor guide to the likely effects of regional disturbances in the future.

ALBERTO GIOVANNINI

1   Introduction

The paper by Xavier Sala-i-Martín and Jeffrey Sachs takes a position on the issue of European currency integration that I find difficult to interpret. On one side the authors claim that the debate on the desirability of a currency union among European countries has in the past been largely misguided, because it has been too heavily influenced by 'Keynesian' economists. On the other side the paper adopts the most traditional 'Keynesian' views, that in a currency union region-specific shocks cannot be dealt with via the exchange rate, and therefore a system of fiscal transfers needs to be in place.

Despite what seems to me a sort of ideological contradiction, this paper is quite stimulating, and offers important empirical evidence. In my comments I will first discuss the main point of the authors, on the presence of regional automatic fiscal stabilizers in the US and Europe. Then I will relate this discussion to the debates currently being held by European governments and the EC on the appropriate fiscal rules in a European monetary union.

2   Automatic stabilizers in a currency union

Sala-i-Martín and Sachs provide evidence about automatic fiscal stabilizers in the US. Using state data aggregated with the Bureau of Census definition of regions, they estimate the extent to which transfers and taxes respond to region-specific income fluctuations, and the resulting response of disposable per-capita income to fluctuations in output. Their estimates suggest that, in a typical US region, a 1-dollar fall in output leads to a fall of disposable income of only 56 to 65 cents.

This result is explainable, as the authors suggest, by the presence of a progressive federal income tax. A fall in income produces a more-than-proportional fall in taxes, while an increase in income produces a more-than-proportional increase in taxes. In addition, transfers like unemployment compensation are triggered automatically, and automatically shut off, with fluctuations in income and employment. What is the effect of these automatic stabilizers? They redistribute resources from regions experiencing increases in income to regions experiencing income falls. They thus provide a form of insurance against income fluctuations, which might be desirable if individuals' access to financial markets is more limited, or more costly, than the government's.

The authors observe that in Europe a federal income tax is absent, and the size of the EC budget does not indicate that such a system could be put in place soon. They conclude that the conditions for a single currency might not be there. There are two possible objections to this argument. The first is that one should, strictly speaking, indicate precisely the market failures that prevent European citizens from insuring against income fluctuations on their own, in the capital markets. Yet, even in the absence of evidence to the contrary, I am willing to believe that the integration and liberalization of financial markets that is currently under way among European countries will not make automatic fiscal stabilizers irrelevant.

The second objection to Sala-i-Martín and Sachs's conclusion is more serious. The automatic stabilizers already in place in Europe might work better than those in the US. What is the situation in Europe now? Despite the absence of a federal fiscal authority, a system of automatic transfers is already in place. The difference between the system in Europe and that in the US is that, while the latter is internal to the working of a large federal government, the former relies on the market mechanism. An adverse economic shock in one country leads to a more than proportional fall in tax revenues (because the tax system is progressive) and an increase in transfers, thus limiting the fall in disposable income of the private sector. Atkeson and Bayoumi (1991) conclude that in European countries taxes and transfers from national governments insure labour income against specific regional shocks to a similar extent as in the US.

The buffer in European countries, however, is represented by fluctuations in the government budget deficit. To the extent that European governments have access to a single European capital market, countries hit by adverse shocks will be able to borrow in the capital market, and the funds will be provided by countries in surplus, that is by countries hit by favorable shocks.

Thus fiscal deficits in Europe provide as much insurance against asymmetric shocks as the federal fiscal budget in the US. Indeed, the European system might be superior to the US system in that it is subject to market discipline. While transitory deficits by individual European governments need to be financed in an ever-more-integrated capital market, and hence the resource transfers go through a market 'check', in the US such transfers across states are by no means transparent, and are left to the control and discretion of the federal government. The system currently in place in Europe forces countries that are hit be adverse shocks to *pay back* the borrowed funds, while this does not necessarily happen in the US. This in Europe countries are continuously forced to choose between adjustment and financing of adverse shocks. This does not happen to a federal fiscal system, where the decision of adjustment versus financing can be easily avoided.

3   Implications for the debate on excessive budget deficits

In the last few months the debate within the Monetary Committee has concentrated on the disparities in the level of government debt and budget deficits among EC member countries. At the Monetary Committee these disparities are a source of concern for three reasons:

(1) 'Excessive' budget deficits are regarded as a booster of aggregate demand, and high aggregate demand is regarded as a powerful fuel of inflation. Disparities in budget deficits, according to this argument, would therefore impede the convergence in inflation rates that is regarded as a necessary condition for EMU.

(2) 'Excessive' budget deficits are usually associated with high levels of government debt, and they are certainly the cause of them. High government debt raises the spectre of unsustainability, triggered by the debt-deficit spiral.

(3) 'Excessive' budget deficits are regarded as an inefficient absorber or private saving, that crowds out productive investment spending.

Buiter and Kletzer (1991) and Giovannini and Spaventa (1991) discuss the theoretical and empirical underpinnings of these concerns, and I do not want to restate their points here. The important policy question is about the likely effects of the proposed constraints on national budget deficits. In response to the concerns of the effects of deficits listed above, the Monetary Committee has recently proposed three principles designed to identify excessive deficit. These principle are:

- Stocks of public debt must not be so high as to bring a danger of unsustainability.
- Deficits must not be so high in relation to GDP as to threaten price stability.
- Deficits must not exceed expenditure on capital formation.

Reference values have been provided for the first two principles: they are, respectively, 60 percent and 3 percent of GDP. Failure to satisfy the principles above would trigger a procedure whereby the Monetary Committee, with the assistance of the Commission, will present the case to the Council with an opinion (the procedure could be started by the Commission even if these principles were not infringed). If the Council decides that an excessive deficit exists, the country concerned will be in breach of its legal obligations and respect for those obligations will have to be enforced.

Since the principles of excessive deficits and the procedures to deal with them are being discussed as permanent rules, it is important to speculate what would be their effects in the long run. Most likely, the excessive deficits principles will achieve their stated objective, to eliminate budget deficits in the EC countries. The question is whether the elimination of budget deficits will put pressure elsewhere.

In the limit, without considering the limited flexibility provided by the deficits-investments rule, residents of countries hit by adverse shocks will see their disposable income decrease 1-for-1 with the fall in output, because governments will not be able to borrow in the private capital markets in their place. Those individuals with ready access to the capital market will be able to shield part of the negative effects of the shock, via their own borrowing. Those individuals who cannot easily borrow will exercise political pressure for some other form of corrective action.

Where would the pressure go to? the two natural places will be, on one side, the European budget, and in particular structural funds; on the other side, the European central bank, which will be asked to facilitate adjustment to sectoral shocks by lowering interest rates, and by easing its stance of monetary policy, perhaps allowing the ECU to depreciate in foreign exchange markets. In conclusion, eliminating the possibility of budgetary deficits at the national level will make it more difficult for the European central bank to pursue price stability, and will put pressure for an increase in the size of the EC budget. Currently, member countries strongly object to both these outcomes.

The question is then how to establish principles of budgetary discipline – that is, to avoid excessive borrowing by member countries and the ensuing risks of instability of European financial markets – but at the same time preserve a degree of fiscal flexibility to national governments – that is, to avoid pressures on the EC budget and the European central bank. I propose two main avenues:

- The first is to adopt principles of budgetary discipline that utilize business-cycle corrections in the measure of fiscal deficits, and to allow for the occurrence of exceptional circumstances, beyond the control of governments, leading to larger-than-expected budgetary problems.
- The second is to require those countries whose debts and deficits are currently a threat to the stability of financial markets to embark on corrections (possibly including structural measures) that will drastically decrease their debt-GDP ratios over an appropriately short horizon, and to deem those corrections a condition for participation in later stages of EMU.

NOTE

This note is part of a CEPR research program on 'Financial and Monetary Integration in Europe,' supported by a grant from the Commission of the European Communities under its SPES Programme (No. E89300105/RES).

REFERENCES

Atkeson, A. and T. Bayoumi (1991), 'Do Private Capital Markets Insure Against Risk in a Common Currency Area? Evidence from the United States', mimeo, University of Chicago and International Monetary Fund, July.
Buiter, W. H. and K. M. Kletzer (1991), 'Reflections on the Fiscal Implications of a Common Currency', in A. Giovannini and C. Mayer (eds.), *European Financial Integration*, Cambridge: Cambridge University Press.
Giovannini, A. and L. Spaventa (1991), 'Fiscal Rules in the European Monetary Union: A No-Entry Clause,' CEPR Discussion Paper No. 516.

8 Market-based fiscal discipline in monetary unions: evidence from the US municipal bond market

MORRIS GOLDSTEIN and GEOFFREY
WOGLOM

1 Introduction

It is widely accepted that participation in a currency union is inconsistent with independence in the conduct of monetary policy. Indeed, in the ongoing discussions about the path to economic and monetary union (EMU) in Europe, much attention is being devoted both to the establishment of a *central* monetary authority and to securing a mandate for that institution which would give primacy to the goal of price stability. In this sense, there would appear to be an emerging consensus about how to constrain or 'discipline' monetary policy.[1]

Less settled at this stage is what constraints, if any, should be placed on national fiscal policies in a currency union. The debate is influenced by two observations. First, ten years of experience with the European Monetary System (EMS) – during which exchange rate commitments became progressively 'harder' – does not suggest that the exchange rate regime itself will be sufficient to force a convergence around sound fiscal policies. In the words of the Delors Report (1989, paragraph 3):

> the EMS has not fulfilled its potential. ... the lack of sufficient convergence of fiscal policies as reflected in large and persistent budget deficits in certain countries has remained a source of tensions and has put disproportionate burden on monetary policy.

Second, if fiscal policy discipline was not forthcoming in an EMU, then the key objective of the union itself could well be threatened. Specifically, if a member of the union accumulated so much debt that it eventually became unable to service it, there would be pressure either on the central monetary institution to monetize the debt or on other members to bail out the errant borrower. In these circumstances, the central bank would find it difficult to credibly commit itself to price stability and other members would find their own incentives for implementing sound fiscal policies distorted. In time, the private sector would incorporate higher inflation

228

expectations into its wage and interest rate contracts. In the end, the social advantages associated with using one money of stable purchasing power would be forfeited.

Reflecting these concerns, there is strong support for including in any EMU treaty explicit provisions prohibiting monetary financing and bailing out of budget deficits. Still, debate continues on whether such provisions are all that is required to encourage fiscal discipline. At least three separate schools of thought have surfaced.

One view, echoed in the Delors Report (1989), is that binding *fiscal rules* represent the preferred solution to the problem. These rules would impose effective upper limits on budget deficits and on debt stocks of individual member countries, as well as limit recourse to external borrowing in non-member currencies.[2] In brief, the case against rigid fiscal rules is that they are incapable of taking adequate account of differences in the circumstances of members. For example, the same budget deficit (relative to GNP) is apt to be less cause for concern in a country with a high private saving rate, a low stock of debt, a temporarily high unemployment rate, and a good track record on inflation than in one with the opposite characteristics. There are also questions of effectiveness. In this connection, von Hagen (1991) reports a greater tendency for US states with debt limits and stringent balanced budget requirements to substitute unrestricted for restricted debt (by delegating functions and debt-raising power to off-budget entities and local governments).

A second approach, which finds expression in more recent EC Commission reports (see *Economic and Monetary Union*, August 1990, and *One Market, One Money*, October 1990), also calls for constraints on national fiscal policies, but adopts a more discretionary format. Specifically, it proposes that peer group, *multilateral surveillance* be reinforced to discourage errant fiscal policies of individual member countries; in addition, it suggests that the EMU Treaty incorporate the principle that ' . . . excessive budget deficits must be avoided' (EC Commission, 1990a). Suffice to say that this tack too is open to criticism. Multilateral surveillance exercises typically employ a broad set of economic indicators. This sets up the risk that different indicators will send conflicting signals for policy adjustment, thereby allowing an errant fiscal position to continue for too long.[3] Moreover, without previously agreed upon rules available to settle disputes, there is a risk that negotiations, cum pressures for 'solidarity' within the union, could delay unduly the needed fiscal adjustment.

Yet a third – albeit very different – route to fiscal discipline is to entrust private financial markets with that role. Such *market-based fiscal discipline* would take the form of an initially rising default premium on the debt of a member country running excessive deficits. If those deficits persisted, the default premium would increase at an increasing rate, and eventually the offending country would be denied access to additional credit. This increase in the cost of borrowing, along with the threat of reduced availability of credit, would then provide the incentive to correct irresponsible fiscal behaviour. Advocates of the market approach (Bishop *et al.*, 1989) recognize that it will work only if certain conditions are satisfied, namely: (i) capital must be able to move freely, (ii) full information must be available on the sovereign borrower, (iii) the market must be convinced both that there are no implicit or explicit outside guarantees on sovereign debt and that the borrower's debt will not be monetized, and (iv) the financial system must be strong enough to withstand the failure of a 'large' borrower. They do not regard these conditions as unrealistically restrictive. Not surprisingly, those who favor the fiscal rules or surveillance options are less convinced, and point to the developing-country debt crisis of the early 1980s and to the New York City financial crisis of the mid-1970s as graphic illustrations of the limitations of the market's disciplining process.[4] Skeptics also note that high public debts often reflect political polarization or distributional conflicts over the sharing of the fiscal burden – factors that can make fiscal adjustment relatively insensitive to a rise in the cost of borrowing.[5] Presumably, these doubts lie behind the assessments that ' . . . the constraints imposed by market forces might either be too slow and weak or too sudden and disruptive' (Delors Report, 1989, paragraph 30), and that ' . . . the effectiveness of market discipline cannot be taken for granted' (EC Commission, 1990b, p. 100).

In choosing among these alternative mechanisms for achieving greater fiscal discipline, it is natural to seek guidance from the experience of federal states. The experience of the United States is of particular interest for ongoing EMU discussions. For one thing, the viability of the United States as a common currency area is long since firmly established; in operational terms, this implies that one can legitimately disregard expectations of an exchange rate change as contributing to differences in borrowing costs paid by different fiscal jurisdictions. Second, state governments do not have access to central bank financing; as noted above, a similar provision is expected to be included in any EMU treaty. Third, with regard to creditors, US states enjoy immunity from bankruptcy courts, much like a sovereign country does (see English, 1991, and Orth, 1987). Fourth, while many US states have voluntarily imposed their own statutory limits on their deficit-spending and/or borrowing, there are no *federally-imposed* borrowing limits; this provides enough autonomy at the state level to test the market-discipline hypothesis using a cross section of states, while also giving some scope to gauge the influence of fiscal rules on borrowing costs. Fifth, the US capital market is probably closest to the kind of integrated, deep, informationally efficient financial area that Europe seeks to become after 1992. Finally, while individual state and local governments have at times run sizable fiscal deficits, there have been *no* state or municipal defaults on general obligation bonds during the post-World War II period (Davidson, 1990, and Cohen, 1988); (state) fiscal discipline has therefore been more the rule than the exception.

To be sure, there are also significant differences between the United States and Europe that are worthy of explicit mention. As noted by Lamafalussy (1989) and others, in Europe there is a greater concentration of expenditures and, especially, borrowing needs in a few regions; for example, Italy's budget deficit alone – at some 2 percent of EC GDP – is equal to more than half of the aggregate EC deficit. This in turn may mean that a 'no bail-out' pledge will carry less credibility in Europe than in the United States. Another difference is that ratios of debt to total product are much higher – by almost an order of magnitude – in European countries than in American states. Whereas the heavily indebted European countries have (total) debt-to-GNP ratios near and in some cases above 100 percent, their state counterparts in the New England and Pacific regions have ratios on the order of 10 to 20 percent; see Eichengreen (1990).[6] Labour mobility is also much higher in the United States than in Europe[7] – a factor that should make it easier for Americans to discipline higher spending local authorities by fleeing jurisdictions where higher tax burdens are not offset by more generous provisions of public goods.[8] Yet a fourth difference is that the involvement and relative size of the central fiscal authority is much greater in the United States than in Europe. The Community budget is presently about 1 percent of EC GNP and even after creation of the single market, it is not expected to exceed 3 percent; by way of contrast, the federal budget in the United States accounts for roughly a quarter of US GNP. One implication of this difference is that American states do not have as much access (via tax collections) to their residents' incomes as do member countries of the EC; at the same time, region-specific income fluctuations are cushioned to a much greater extent (via variations in tax and transfer payments) in the United States than they are in Europe.[9]

Taken together, these differences imply that the market for EC country debt after EMU may not generate the same default premium for any given risk of default as does the municipal bond market in the United States. But the size of the default premium is not as important as the broader issue of whether changes in the default premium accurately reflect changes in the probability of default, that is, whether interest rates move in response to those aspects of fiscal policy behaviour that alter the probability of default. For if the bond markets do operate in such an informationally efficient manner, then the practical options for leaning more heavily on a 'market-based' approach to fiscal discipline are enhanced. To mention but one possibility, observed relative default premia might be employed as 'indicators' to trigger multilateral surveillance discussions; in this way, the 'incentive' to correct excessive fiscal imbalances could be large even in the face of small increases in the market's cost of borrowing.

The primary purpose of this paper is to provide new empirical evidence on market-based fiscal discipline by estimating the relationship between the cost of borrowing and measures of default risk in the US municipal bond market. Our efforts are aided by access to a set of survey data on yields of state general-obligation bonds that covers 39 states from 1973 to the present.[10] We believe that this survey data, collected by the Chubb Corporation, offers a richer medium for testing the market discipline hypothesis than has been available heretofore; not only is there a much larger sample of observations, but problems of comparability across bonds with different maturities, call provisions, and coupon yields are effectively eliminated by the survey design.[11]

In addition to testing the market discipline hypothesis, the US state data have implications for the first approach to fiscal discipline, binding fiscal rules. The state data contain a variety of self-imposed fiscal rules. Thus we can test whether financial markets perceive these rules to be effective in limiting default risk. While there may be important differences between voluntarily and involuntarily imposed fiscal rules, the state data allow us to test whether it is possible to credibly 'tie one's own hands'.

The rest of the paper is organized along the following lines. Section 2 reviews the theory of default risk in the context of the supply and demand for state borrowing. Section 3 describes in detail the (Chubb) survey data and the other data used, and reviews the specification issues raised by the theory of default risk. The econometric results are presented in Section 4. Anticipating what follows, we do find evidence that states with larger stocks of debt, larger (current) fiscal deficits, and higher trend rates of growth of debt relative to income, pay more to borrow in the municipal bond market than do states with more conservative fiscal-policy track records. Moreover, we also find that, ceteris paribus, states with more stringent, voluntary, constitutional limits on borrowing face a lower cost of borrowing. Concluding remarks are contained in Section 5.

2   The market for state borrowing

2.1   The supply of funds to state borrowers

Theories of the supply of funds to states typically assume that any state's borrowing is a small fraction of total borrowing in the capital markets.[12] Consequently, the market interest rate is assumed to be unaffected by any individual state borrowing. Put another way, states are price takers (with respect to the expected, risk-adjusted interest rate) on credit markets. This does not, however, imply that all states face the same promised interest rate (equivalently, yield to maturity). The promised interest rates on state bonds in fact show considerable variability. It is not atypical for the spread between the lowest and highest yields to be over 100 basis points. This section looks at the theoretical reasons used to explain these spreads in spite of a common, market-determined interest rate. The explanations can be separated into two factors: (i) default risk; (ii) risk premia.

2.1.1 Default risk

Modern capital theory is a theory of the determinants of expected returns. In the case of securities subject to default, the expected return is determined by the stated or promised interest rate and the probability and consequences of default. For example, in the case of a one-period bond on which there is a positive probability of complete default, $(1 - P)$, the relationship between the promised interest rate, R, and the expected interest rate, E, is given by:

$$E = (1 + R)P - 1 \qquad (1)$$
$$= R - (1 - P)(1 + R) < R$$

Because of the probability of default, the expected interest rate is less than the promised rate. Therefore, the promised interest rate on these bonds has to be higher than the interest rate on safe assets, which bear the (after-tax equivalent) risk-free rate, R_T. There are two reasons why the interest rate on loans with the possibility of default are higher than the risk-free rate: default premia and risk premia. Default premia compensate a lender for the expected losses from default. Risk premia compensate a lender for the possible increased riskiness of the total portfolio that results from the possibility of default. Unfortunately, many authors use the terms risk premia and default premia interchangeably in this framework.

Finance theory implies that default premia must be positive for assets subject to default risk, but risk premia may be zero even with default risk. The possibility of a zero risk premium on a loan with default risk occurs when the default risk can be diversified away (i.e., when the default risk is unsystematic). In this case, the lending to one risky borrower does not increase the risk of the total portfolio because of diversification. With diversification, the default risk from one loan is combined with offsetting risks on other loans. To focus initially on the determinants of default risk, we start with the case of no risk premia.

With no risk premia, the expected interest rate on a bond with default risk must equal the risk-free rate, or

$$E = (1 + R)P - 1 = R_T \tag{2}$$

Adding one to both sides of (2) yields:

$$1 + E = (1 + R)P = 1 + R_T \tag{2'}$$

Written in this way, the equality of the expected interest rates implies that the expected repayment of principal and interest on the risky and risk-free securities must be the same. The theory of the promised interest rate on risky debt in this case becomes a theory of the determinants of the risk of default, or, in terms of equation (2), the theory of the determinants of P. The relationship between default risk and the rate on risky state debt can be written explicitly by rearranging (2) to yield:

$$R - R_T = (1 + R_T)(1 - P)/P \tag{3}$$

This equation shows that as the default probability increases, the spread between the interest rate on risky state debt and the after-tax, equivalent risk-free rate also increases.

For our purposes, the most interesting determinants of the probability of default are debt variables and current borrowing. In many different contexts, (e.g., Stiglitz and Weiss, 1981, Eaton and Gersovitz, 1981, Metcalf, 1990, and Capeci, 1990), it has been shown that when current borrowing affects the probability of default, the supply curve can be backward bending, as in Figure 8.1 (a more technical derivation is detailed in the Appendix). At low levels of debt, an increase in borrowing, B, causes the promised rate to rise in order to compensate the lender for the increased probability of default. Notice, however, that the increase in the promised rate, R, also worsens the borrower's financial position by raising the interest expense on new borrowing. Thus, increasing the promised rate, by itself, increases the probability of default.

At some critical interest rate (R_C) and level of borrowing (B_C), the supply curve becomes vertical. At this point with $B = B_C$, any increase in the interest rate would cause the expected rate to *fall* because of the increased probability of default. The only way the promised rate could rise above R_C while fulfilling (2), would be if the level of borrowing fell below B_C; hence the backward bend to the supply curve. Promised rates

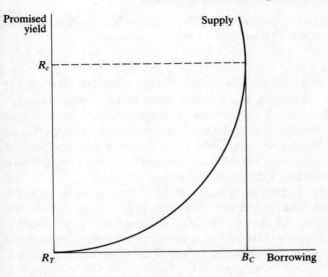

Figure 8.1 The supply curve of borrowing

above R_C, however, are unlikely to be observed in the market for reasons discussed below.

While the supply curve, at least initially, has the normal upward slope, lenders are *not* being induced by higher *expected* rates to increase their supply of credit. Recall that we began the analysis by assuming that the supply of credit to a state was infinitely elastic because any state's borrowing is a small fraction of total borrowing. That assumption is fulfilled in Figure 8.1, in spite of the shape of the supply curve. While the promised rate in Figure 8.1 varies with state borrowing, the expected rate is constant throughout. The slope of the supply curve solely reflects the change in the promised interest rate needed to keep the expected rate constant as the probability of default varies.

While the analysis so far has been very simple, the qualitative results on default risk are more general. For example, while the analysis was done for one-period bonds with the possibility of total default, it generalizes fairly easily for multiperiod bonds and partial defaults. In fact, if the probability of default is constant over time, the analysis immediately generalizes for the case of longer maturity bonds (see Yawitz *et al.*, 1985). In this case, however, one must take account of the fact that only the current deficit must be financed at the current promised rate. As is shown in the Appendix, this complication suggests that the slope of the supply curve increases at an increasing rate the larger the fraction of new borrowing in total borrowing. Thus, positively-valued current deficits may have a strong effect on the cost of state borrowing.

2.1.2 Risk premia

Risk premia complicate the relationship in equation (2) between the interest rate on risky debt, the risk-free rate, and the probability of default. Most theories of risk premia, however, suggest that premia should either be proportional to default risk, or more than proportional to default risk. Thus while equation (3) no longer holds, the interest spread in (3) provides an upward-biased measure of default probabilities, where this bias increases with the probability of default.

Specifying the risk premia associated with state debt requires a specification of planned holding periods. For example, if most lenders are planning to hold state debt to maturity, the only nominal risk is related to the probability of default. Risk premia arise when this default risk cannot be eliminated through diversification (when default risk has a systematic component). In this case, buying risky state bonds would increase the risk on the total portfolio and financial investors would seek to be compensated for their greater exposure to risk by a higher promised yield. While equation (2) no longer holds, the promised yield would still be a positive function of default probabilities.[13]

Many investors, however, either have shorter holding periods, or are concerned for other reasons with the current market value of risky bonds throughout the holding period. A good example of the latter type of investor is a municipal bond mutual fund, which must 'mark to market' each day. In either case, these financial investors are concerned with the volatility of the market value of the state bond throughout its maturity. This volatility will depend on changes in the current interest rate on the bond (i.e., the secondary market yield). Volatility of secondary market yields can result from two causes: (i) cyclical changes in the risk of default, which are independent of debt variables; and (ii) changes in credit ratings. In both cases, these risk premia are likely to be positively related to default risk.

The relationship between debt variables and promised yields is non-linear. As discussed above, as debt variables increase, the promised rate is likely to rise at an increasing rate. This suggests that an exogenous increase in default risk caused by a major recession is likely to have a larger impact on heavily indebted states. Thus, the volatility of yields and the associated risk premia are likely to be increasing functions of default risk. Davidson (1990) presents evidence showing that the spread between municipal bond rated by Moody's as Baa and Aaa is more volatile over time than the spread between the Aa and Aaa rates.[14] This evidence is consistent with the hypothesis that risk premia due to cyclical volatility increase with default risk.

Credit-rating changes are also associated with changes in yields. Rating changes are generally regarded as primarily reflecting unanticipated changes in a state's fiscal position.[15] While one can argue that an Aa state is just as likely to experience either a deterioration or improvement in its fiscal position as a Baa state, risk premia from rating changes still increase with default risk. This relationship results from an important non-linearity between ratings and yields. Many financial intermediaries are prohibited from holding securities rated below investment grade quality (below the Moody's rating Baa, or the S&P rating BBB). With the removal of these large holders, yields would have to rise dramatically to induce the remaining holders to absorb the total supply of debt. Thus, while changes either way in ratings may be equally likely, the *consequences* of a rating downgrade for a Baa state are more severe. An A state, however, faces a greater likelihood of a downgrade below Baa than does a Aaa state. Thus one would expect the risk premia associated with ratings changes to rise with the probability of default.

2.1.3 Conclusions

There are additional factors that affect the interest rates on specific issues of state debt, namely (i) maturity, (ii) callability, (iii) the coupon yield, and (iv) insurance.[16] The complication of these factors, however, can be avoided if interest rates on bonds with identical characteristics with respect to these factors are compared across states. After controlling for these factors, the expected interest rates for all state bonds, after adjusting for risk premia, should be equal to the equivalent after-tax interest rate on Treasuries. The equality of expected interest rates, however, implies that the promised rates, the rates observed directly on financial markets, will differ because of differences in default and credit risk across states. Default and credit risk should be an increasing function of state borrowing.

2.2   The demand for funds by state borrowers

The key issue in the states' demand for funds is whether the quantity demanded is sensitive to the cost of borrowing. If it is, the promised yield could never reach R_C in Figure 8.1. Metcalf (1990) estimates a model of the demand for state borrowing, where states choose between borrowing and tax finance based on demographic factors and the after-tax cost of borrowing. He finds that states do vary their borrowing based on the after-tax cost of borrowing.

This model of the demand for borrowing is important because while states must be price takers with regard to the expected risk-adjusted interest rate, it is implausible to assume that they would be price takers with regard to the *promised* interest rate. The state must recognize that by borrowing more, the promised rate on all new borrowing increases. Specifically, the marginal cost of borrowing one more dollar exceeds the promised rate on this borrowing, and is equal to the promised rate plus the change in the promised rate (which depends on the slope in Figure 8.1) times the volume of new borrowing. But as borrowing approaches B_C, the change in the promised rate is large for small changes in borrowing (i.e., the slope in Figure 8.1 goes to infinity). As a result, the marginal cost of borrowing increases without limit as B approaches B_C, and the state has a strong incentive to keep total borrowing below B_C.

While this model is plausible and receives empirical support, it is not consistent with the credit rationing part of the market approach to fiscal discipline. The credit rationing story can be resurrected, however from different models of state borrowing. For example, Eaton and Gersovitz (1981) develop a model for sovereign country borrowing where a country borrows to smooth its consumption stream. In this model, if the state of nature is adverse enough, a country might wish to borrow above B_C. In this case, the credit markets would limit borrowing to B_C at the promised interest rate R_C. The country is credit-constrained because it would be willing to pay a higher promised rate in order to borrow more, but no lender will lend more. In this model, credit constraints arise out of unforeseen, large shifts in the demand curve.

These two models need not be viewed as mutually exclusive. For example, trend borrowing may be determined by Metcalf's interest-sensitive model, with unanticipated variations around trend being explained by the Eaton and Gersovitz model. The data certainly suggest that there can be unanticipated increases in borrowing. Louisiana's experience during the 1980s provides a dramatic example. In December of 1982, Louisiana was an Aa rated state with promised yields below those of Aaa-rated New Jersey. Five years later, Louisiana was Baa1-rated with yields over 100 basis points higher than New Jersey's. During this time period, deficits in excess of 18 percent of state expenditures were incurred by Louisiana. This suggests that while the trend demand for debt is interest-sensitive, unanticipated increases in demand also occur.

In this paper, we are primarily concerned about estimating the *supply curve* of funds to risky state borrowers. Market-based fiscal discipline can work even with interest-insensitive borrowers via credit rationing. In addition, the simultaneity issues, described below, make estimating the demand curve problematic. For estimating the supply curve, the determinants of the demand for state borrowing are important chiefly because of the identification problem.

3   Data and issues of econometric specification

3.1   Data on market yields

The primary data needed to test for the existence of default premia on state debt are market yields on the obligations of the various state governments. States, however, issue two basic types of bonds: revenue bonds and general obligation bonds. General obligation bonds (GOs) are 'full faith and credit' obligations of the state, whereas revenue bonds are only backed by the revenues of the specific project being financed by the bond. For example, the repayment of interest and principal on a Florida Department of Transportation Bond, a revenue bond, could come from toll revenues. Florida State Board of Education bonds, on the other hand, are financed from the general tax revenues of the state. Given our interest in the fiscal position of state governments, we need yield data on general obligation bonds.

The need for market price data on general obligation bonds, however, raises immediate problems because these bonds are not actively traded. For example, J. P. Morgan tracks the yields on over 75 actively-traded tax exempt bonds in their *Municipal Market Monitor*. Of these bonds, only 5 are state GOs. Surprising as it may seem, information is *not* widely available on the market prices of individual state debt.

As previously noted, however, financial market participants, particularly mutual funds, have a need for current market values. This need is met by brokerage firms (e.g., J. J. Kenny) that place values on bonds issues for a fee. These bond values, however, are not in general transactions prices. Instead, the relationships between the prices on particular issues are specified in what is called a 'pricing matrix'. This matrix uses a relatively small number of transactions prices to infer the values of all the other securities being evaluated. The information that goes into the specification of the pricing matrix is proprietary and not generally available. While it is difficult for an outsider to determine the validity of these matrix prices, it is noteworthy that these pricing services are widely used. In fact, one of the widely-reported municipal bond indices, the Bond Buyer 40, is based on municipal bond 'prices' from these services. Thus, the financial markets' own needs for current market values are not met solely with transactions prices.

Transaction price data and matrix prices suffer from another problem. In addition to default risk, risk premia and tax effects, municipal bond prices and yields are affected by other features that vary by issue. Unless one compares *identical* securities across states, these other features can have a significant impact on yield spreads. For example, a randomly selected issue of J. P. Morgan's *Municipal Market Monitor* (1989) lists the market yields on two Florida State Board of Education Bonds. These market yields are based on the closing bid price at Morgan. On August 24, 1989, the two market yields were 7.05 and 7.27 percent. The bonds were identical, except that the lower yielding bond matured in 2013 as opposed to 2010, was callable at 100 in 1996 as opposed to 102, and bore a coupon of 5 percent instead of 7.25 percent. During the same week, the yield spread between AA and AAA 20-year municipal bonds was reported by Delphis Hanover as 20 basis points. Thus, the yield spread caused by the special features on the two Florida State GOs was wider than the yield spread between two credit-rating categories.

Fortunately, there is a data source that allows us to avoid the problem of comparability on GO bonds, The Chubb Relative Value Study. The Chubb Corporation, an insurance company, has conducted since 1973 a semi-annual survey of 20–25 (sell-side) municipal bond traders. The traders are asked to give the yields on 5, 10 and 20 year maturity GOs for 39 states and Puerto Rico, relative to the yield on a comparable New Jersey state GO. The survey results for December 1989 are reproduced in Table 1. This survey implies that, on average, traders felt that a *comparable* California 20-year GO should have a market yield 14.04 basis points below New Jersey's market yield, while a *comparable* Louisiana 20-year GO should bear a yield 70 basis points higher than New Jersey's. Most important, for our purposes, the Relative Value Study implies that the yield spreads between comparable California and Louisiana 20-year GOs should be 84.04 basis points.[17] Since the bonds being evaluated are comparable across states, the differences in yield spreads can only reflect default risk, risk premia, and tax effects. Thus while the data are not based on transactions prices, they do solve the problem of special features such as call provisions.[18]

As one would expect, these yield spreads vary over the course of the business cycle: over time, the spread for a particular state can vary considerably. For example, during the recession year of 1982, the spread between the highest and lowest rated states of Oklahoma and Michigan was over 170 basis points: in contrast by 1989, the high-low spread fell by a factor of 2 and Michigan was a higher-rated state than Oklahoma (see Table 8.1). These yield spreads behave as one might expect if they, in fact, reflect changes over time in default risk.

Table 8.1. *Chubb relative value study, December 1989. (Basis point spread for a 20-year state GO, relative to a New Jersey 20-year GO.)*

Ranking:		Moody's Rating	Avg. Response	Std. Dev.
1	California	Aaa	−14.04	3.84
2	North Carolina	Aaa	−11.91	4.32
3	Virginia	Aaa	−10.65	4.76
4	Connecticut	Aa1	−9.96	5.09
5	Missouri	Aaa	−8.30	5.28
6	South Carolina	Aaa	−6.74	5.58
7	Georgia	Aaa	−6.39	2.58
8	Maryland	Aaa	−4.65	3.51
9	Tennessee	Aaa	−4.09	5.80
10	New Jersey	Aaa	0.00	0.00
11	Ohio	Aa	1.39	3.41
12	Utah	Aaa	5.57	4.84
13	Maine	Aa1	7.00	4.95
14	Minnesota	Aa	8.13	3.79
15	Montana	Aa	8.39	5.25
16	Delaware	Aa	8.61	4.51
17	Kentucky	Aa	8.70	5.31
18	New Hampshire	Aa1	9.52	3.84
19	Rhode Island	Aa	10.26	3.58
20	Vermont	Aa	11.17	3.56
21	Alabama	Aa	12.09	3.83
22	Wisconsin	Aa	12.13	3.93
23	Pennsylvania	A1	12.91	4.83
24	Mississippi	Aa	13.39	4.49
25	Hawaii	Aa	13.87	3.83
26	Michigan	A1	14.04	4.84
27	New Mexico	Aa	14.48	3.59
28	Illinois	Aaa	14.48	4.67
29	Oregon	A1	16.57	3.59
30	Florida	Aa	17.26	4.11
31	Nevada	Aa	18.74	4.00
32	New York	A1	20.39	4.75
33	Oklahoma	Aa	21.61	7.29
34	Texas	Aa	22.74	5.93
35	North Dakota	Aa	22.83	10.11
36	Washington	A1	24.48	3.05
37	Alaska	Aa	27.39	7.49
38	West Virginia	A1	28.22	5.34
39	Puerto Rico	Baa1	48.09	6.99
40	Massachusetts	Baa1	62.39	11.50
41	Louisiana	Baa1	70.00	12.07

3.2   Other data

To measure state debt, we used data on net, tax-supported debt as reported by Moody's. This debt figure is calculated each time Moody's issues a Credit Report on a new issue. Net tax supported debt includes all debt serviced from state tax revenues even when the state itself was not the issuer (e.g., Massachusetts Bay Transportation Authority bonds in Massachusetts), and deducts from gross debt, obligations that are serviced from non-tax revenues (e.g., Oregon general obligation debt that is backed by mortgage lending). Moody's publishes the latest available numbers for each state annually. These data reflect the most accurate picture of state's fiscal position from the perspective of one of the two major credit rating agencies. Unfortunately, the numbers are not updated at a uniform time during the year. These data are available from 1981 through 1990. To derive measures of the relative size of debt, the nominal debt numbers were deflated by the implicit GNP deflator for the year and divided by trend Gross State Product (based on Department of Commerce, real Gross State Product data). Bond ratings are the Moody's ratings.

Finally, state 'constitutional' debt limitations were measured by an index devised by the Advisory Commission on Intergovernmental Relations (ACIR, 1987). These limitations can vary from a requirement for the governor to submit a balanced budget to a prohibition on the issuance of general obligation debt. The ACIR index tries to measure in one number the restrictiveness of the various provisions adopted by a particular state. The index varies from 0 in Vermont, a Aa-rated state with no restrictions, to the maximum of 10 in 26 states. These 26 states include 8 of the 9 states with no general obligation debt, 7 of the 11 Aaa-rated states, 10 of the 23 Aa-rated states, and West Virginia, an A1 state. For the 5 states (other than West Virginia) rated below Aa, the index ranges from 6 to 3.

The summary statistics for all of our variables are given in Table 8.2. At first glance the data in Table 8.2 seem to indicate that debt levels among the US states are orders of magnitude lower than among the European countries. This conclusion is unwarranted, however, because the Federal government is much larger in the United States than it will be in Europe, at least for the immediate future. As a result, states have less access to the incomes of their residents than do the European countries. Thus it is inappropriate to compare relative debt levels of the US states to the relative debt levels of the European countries. A better comparison of the relative importance of government debt between the US states and the European countries is provided by the fraction of total government expenditures accounted for by interest on the debt. During the 1989 fiscal

Table 8.2. *Summary statistics for major variables*

	Mean	Minimum	Maximum	Std. Dev.
Yield spread	16.5	−28.4	143.5	23.5
Debt	2.3	0.2	7.1	1.4
'Deficit'	0.2	0.0	2.3	0.3
Trend growth in debt	1.5	−11.9	20.6	6.7
ACIR index of debt limitations	7.6	0.0	10.0	2.8

Note: The yield spread is measured in basis points; debt and deficit in percentage points of trend gross state product, and trend growth in debt is percentage points per annum.

year, interest as a fraction of total expenditures ranged between 1.5 and 10 percent (US Census, 1990) for the 50 states. Bishop (1991) reports statistics that suggest the comparable numbers for the European countries range between 5 and 25 percent. Thus, while debt levels are higher in Europe than among the US states, these differences are not as large as the numbers in Table 8.2 might suggest.

3.3   Specification issues

As outlined earlier, our basic aim is to estimate the relationship between the promised interest rate and default risk, where default risk in turn is related, inter alia, to the quantity of debt – or more generally, to a state's past and prospective fiscal policy behaviour. Put in other words, we hope to be able to trace out the supply curve illustrated in Figure 8.1.

The dependent variable in all our regressions is the yield spread on a 20-year state, general obligation bond relative to the yield on a 20-year New Jersey general obligation bond. In a cross-section regression, this implies that the constant term can be thought of as capturing New Jersey's yield.

In contrast to earlier empirical studies, we see four aspects of fiscal policy behaviour as potentially impacting on the probability of default. The first of these is the existing stock of debt (relative to income), which summarizes the scale of the state's past borrowing; ceteris paribus, the higher this ratio, the higher the default probability. Our second fiscal policy indicator is the expected growth of relative debt. This is captured in our regressions by the difference for each state between the trend rate of growth in real debt and trend growth in real state product. A state for which this trend variable is positive will have, on average, a rising relative debt, and thus a larger risk of default over the life of a 20-year general obligation bond.

Recall from Section 2 that the theory of default premia suggests that the slope of the supply curve should increase more rapidly the greater the proportion of new borrowing that must be financed at the current interest rate. If new borrowing causes an increase in the promised yield, then a deficit should affect the yield independently of its effect on total debt outstanding. This provides the rationale for our third fiscal policy variable, namely the increase in debt over the preceding year. We give this variable a value of zero if debt falls and a value equal to the deficit when it is a positive number. The expectation is that the deficit will carry a positive sign in the regressions. Last but not least, we have included the stringency of the state's constitutional debt limitations as also affecting default risk. Here, the argument is that stringent constitutional limitations make it more likely that any deviation from responsible fiscal policy will be corrected before it reaches crisis proportions; as such, we expect the constitutional stringency index to appear in the regressions with a negative sign.

So much for the fiscal variables. Next, we need to consider the likelihood that there are additional factors, particular to each state, that should help to explain default risk. Bond ratings are a discrete measure of all the factors (including fiscal variables) in each state that affect default probabilities. Liu and Thakor (1984) have proposed a two-step regression procedure designed to use the information in these, otherwise omitted state-specific factors. For each year, the rating categories are replaced with the average yield spread for the states in that category. A regression is then run for each year that estimates the numerical value of each state's rating category based on the included fiscal variables (i.e., debt, deficit, trend of the debt-to-income ratio, index of constitutional debt limitations). The *residuals* from these regressions, which we will call the ratings residuals, are an estimate of the quantitative importance of the factors that have *not* been captured by the included fiscal variables. In the second stage, the yield spread is regressed on all the variables employed in stage one plus the ratings residual. This procedure allows one to capture the information that is embedded in bond ratings and that is not already accounted for by the fiscal variables.[19]

Two related specification issues are the non-linearity of the relationship between fiscal variables and promised yields and variations in the risk of default over the business cycle. With regard to the first issue, we assumed that the non-linear supply curve in Figure 8.1 can be approximated by a quadratic function in the debt variables. The problem of the variation in the risk of default with the business cycle was handled with dummy variables. Because the risk of default is higher during a recession year (even with the same debt stock), we included dummies in our regressions to allow the constant term to vary by year. In addition, the non-linearity of the supply curve suggests that the slope may also vary by year. A higher risk of default is likely to change both the location of the supply curve in Figure 8.1 as well as the slope for any value of borrowing. Thus we included slope dummies in our regressions to allow the effect of an increase in the debt variables on yields to vary by year.[20]

The final specification issue is to account for the simultaneity between the promised interest rate and the debt variables. Recall that the issue of simultaneity arises when the states' demand for borrowing is interest-sensitive. The simultaneity problem is therefore likely to be most severe for cross-sectional differences in trend levels of debt. To account for this possibility, we tested our basic pooled equation against a panel model with fixed effects. The fixed-effects model, however, uses deviations from state sample means to estimate the supply equation. As a result, the time-invariant state variables (viz., trend debt growth and debt limitations) must be dropped from this specification.

The fixed effects model has the advantage of controlling for state-specific omitted variables that we cannot measure quantitatively, but which market participants report are important. For example, Delaware is an Aa-rated state, with GO bond yields typically below the average for all Aa-rated states. Yet, Delaware is one of the 4 states with the largest relative debt. Oregon, on the other hand, is an A1-rated state with a well-below average value for its relative debt, about one-fifth the size of Delaware's relative debt. The larger relative debt in Delaware primarily reflects the fact that the municipal government system is much less well developed in Delaware because of its small size. Therefore, the Delaware relative *state* debt is closer to a measure of the relative size of the *state and local* debt for other states.

These unobserved, fixed effects may impart a downward bias to our estimates for the effects of debt on yields. For example, because financial markets know about Delaware's unique state and municipal system, Delaware is able to borrow at relatively low yields (i.e., the supply curve in Figure 8.1 is shifted to the right for Delaware). But given these relatively low yields and an interest-sensitive demand, Delaware has a incentive to borrow more. Our supply curve expects to find a *positive* relationship between cross-section differences in relative debt and yields, but the unobserved, fixed effects impart a *negative* relationship between promised yields and relative debt.

With the fixed-effects model, we avoid having to explain why Delaware has a lower yield than Oregon in spite of the higher relative debt. Instead, we must explain how deviations from the mean in debt. The disadvantage of this approach is that we can only include variables that change over time. Therefore, with this approach, we cannot test for the importance of debt limitations, or for importance of the growth in trend debt.

The fixed-effects model solves the simultaneity problem if mean debt levels are interest-sensitive, while the deviations from the means are not (Hsiao, 1986). It is, of course, possible that deviations from the mean in debt and yield variables are simultaneously determined. Therefore, we also estimated the fixed-effects model with two-stage least squares. The problem here, however, is to find appropriate instruments, variables that affect the demand for borrowing, but are unrelated to supply. Finding appropriate instruments presents a problem because virtually all of the instruments that affect demand also affect the probability of default, and thereby also affect supply. Metcalf (1990) argues that demographic factors, such as the percentage of elderly, and current economic conditions are important exogenous factors in the demand for state borrowing. These same factors, however, are also likely to affect the probability of default. Take for example Metcalf's argument that a large population of elderly in a state can lead to a reliance on debt finance. It seems to us that the same argument implies that that state will have a higher probability of default for any level of borrowing. Default places a heavy burden on a state's residents. Defaulting on a newly issued 20-year state GO, when the bond approaches maturity, however, will not adversely affect the current generation of the elderly. While it is not clear how to solve this simultaneity problem, we experimented with lagged values of debt and economic conditions as instruments.

Table 8.3 presents the basic equation of our pooled regressions along with a priori implications from the discussion of theory and specification issues.

4   Empirical results

Our basic regression results for the yield spread are presented in Table 8.4. These regressions use the largest sample period available with both the Chubb data and the Moody's debt data (i.e., 333 observations).[21] Two versions of our theoretical model are shown. The first one, which we call the full model, includes the current deficit and its squared value, along with all the other determinants of default risk outlined earlier. The second version, which we label the abbreviated model, is identical except that it excludes the deficit variables.

The results in Table 8.4 offer broad support for our theoretical model. The coefficient on relative debt (the ratio of debt to trend state product) is

Table 8.3. *Specification of full model and definitions of variables*

Yield spread = $a_0 + a_1$ Debt + a_2 Deficit + a_3 Debt^2 + a_4 Deficit^2
+ a_5 Trend growth in relative debt + a_6 Debt limit
+ a_7 Ratings residual + a_{8-14} Year dummies
+ a_{15-22} (Year dummies) debt + a_{23-30} (Year dummies) deficit

Yield spread is the basis point value of the spread between the yield on a given state's 20-year GO debt and New Jersey's yield.

Debt is Moody's real net tax supported debt as a fraction of the trend value of real gross state product; $a_1 > 0$, $a_3 > 0$.

Deficit is the change in debt when positive, or zero; $a_2 > 0$, $a_4 > 0$.

Trend debt growth is the difference between trend growth in real tax-supported debt and real gross state product; $a_5 > 0$.

Debt limit is the ACIR index of the restrictiveness of a state's constitutional limitations on debt; $a_6 < 0$.

Ratings residual is the residual from a regression of the moody's rating for each state regressed against the preceding fiscal variables. The rating category is assigned the average value of the yield spreads for the states in that category; $a_7 = 1$.

Year dummies take on the value of 1 for one year between 1983–1989, and zero otherwise; a_{15-22} and a_{23-30} should be larger the greater the default risk in that year (i.e., during a recession).

significant with the expected positive sign, suggesting that debt stocks have a significant influence on borrowing costs. This is a robust finding for our pooled samples, and contradicts Eichengreen's (1990, p. 151) conclusion – based on yield spreads for a single year and on measures of gross state debt – that 'there is weak evidence that higher debt burdens increase the cost of borrowing.' The full model also indicates a significant effect for the current fiscal deficit in increasing a state's promised interest rate. Also, as is suggested by theory, the higher the trend rate of growth of the relative debt, the higher both the default risk and the cost of borrowing. Taken together, these estimates for the debt variables suggest that states which have implemented relatively conservative fiscal policies are perceived by the market as having a lower default probability and thereby reap a market dividend in the form of a lower borrowing cost.

Interestingly enough, the estimated coefficient on our 'constitutional fiscal rule' variable is also significant and with the expected negative sign. Indeed, and somewhat to our surprise, this constitutional debt limitation variable (measured by the ACIR index of fiscal stringency) was the most consistent performer among all the fiscal policy variables, typically emerging as significant with the expected sign not only in the pooled, time-series results but also in the single-year cross-sections. (We also estimated several pooled regressions where the constitutional

Table 8.4. *OLS estimates for the abbreviated and full models*

	Full model (1)	Abbreviated model (2)
Debt	8.26	9.98
	(3.51)	(4.92)
Deficit	23.26	
	(2.37)	
Debt^2	−0.25	−0.40
	(0.86)	(1.55)
Deficit^2	−11.40	
	(2.55)	
Trend debt growth	0.28	0.35
	(2.51)	(3.47)
Debt limits	−1.99	−2.01
	(7.31)	(8.18)
Ratings residual	0.98)	0.99)
	(24.0)	(26.7)
Std. error of est.	12.77	11.94
$\bar{R}^2$	0.70	0.74
Number of observations	333	333

Notes: Sample Period 1982–90; 't' statistics in parentheses. In addition, each regression contained a constant term, year dummies for 1983–90, and slope dummies for the debt variable for 1983–90. Thus the coefficients on debt and the deficit refer to the 1982 coefficients for these variables. The variables are as described in Table 8.3.

debt-limitation variable entered interactively with the debt and deficit variables but the results showed little pattern or reason.)[22]

The implication, for what it is worth, is that states which have voluntarily imposed limitations on their borrowing and debt accumulation are seen by the market as having lower default risk, even after controlling for their past fiscal-policy track records. Using the point estimate in column (1) of Table 8.4, a state with an 'average' set of constitutional limitations (an index value of 7.6) pays 5 basis points more than a state with the most restrictive set of limitations. Presumably, market participants view these fiscal rules as constraining future fiscal adventurism. Because the ACIR index combines a group of rather diverse restrictions (ranging from the requirement that the governor must submit a balanced budget to an absolute dollar ceiling on the amount of general obligation debt), it would be unwise to read too much into this finding. But it does suggest that the benefits of 'tying one's hands' – so emphasized in the literature on the credibility of monetary policy – may be applicable to certain aspects of fiscal policy as well.

This brings us to the ratings residual, which is highly statistically significant with the expected positive sign and with a coefficient that is not significantly different from its expected value of one. Our results do therefore support the notion that credit rating categories contain important information about default risk that is *not* captured by the fiscal variables. It also shows why trying to infer the presence of market discipline from eyeball observations of yield spreads and fiscal policy differences, without attempting to hold 'other things equal' is apt to be misleading. The first-stage regressions that attempt to explain the ratings are not presented, but are qualitatively similar to those estimated in earlier studies.

It would of course be desirable to show not just that default premia increase with looser fiscal policy, but also by how much. This can be calculated – and we in fact do so below – but the estimates, we are afraid, are subject to considerable margins of error. To reflect the theoretically appealing notion that default risk should rise at an increasing rate with higher levels of debt, we attempted to capture the non-linear nature of the supply curve with a quadratic in debt (and in the deficit). Most typically, however, the squared terms appeared in the regressions with the wrong sign and in some cases with a 't' value above 2. This is the case with the estimates for the full model shown in column (1) of Table 8.4: the estimated coefficient on the squared debt stock is negative but insignificant, while that on the squared deficit term is negative with a 't' value in excess of 2. Nevertheless, this imprecision should not overshadow the strong qualitative conclusion implied by our estimates that promised yields increase with the stock of debt.

Earlier on, we also speculated that default risk could vary over time, perhaps on account of the business cycle. Because we have included year-by-year shift and slope dummy variables, the estimated slope coefficients on debt and the deficit refer to 1982. Because 1982 was a recession year, it is not unreasonable to posit that default risk was then at a peak. In fact, the spread between Baa-Aaa municipal bonds was widest for any year in our sample during December of 1982. Thus it is reassuring that the point estimates (the results for the abbreviated model are shown in Table 8.5) for all of the slope dummies on debt are negative and 6 out of the eight are statistically significant. The constant term dummies are primarily positive, but none are statistically significant.

While there is broad support for the theoretical model, our attempt to test for the additional effect of new borrowing was not successful, as is shown by a comparison of the estimates for the full and abbreviated models in Table 8.4. In the results for the abbreviated model in column (2), the relative debt stock, the trend growth of the debt stock, the

Table 8.5. *Time dummies for the abbreviated model (Results for regression of column (2), Table 8.4)*

	1983	1984	1985	1986	1987	1988	1989	1990
Constant term dummy:	4.30	8.54	4.44	7.40	3.63	0.67	−1.40	−5.50
	(0.84)	(1.69)	(0.85)	(1.43)	(0.68)	(0.13)	(0.28)	(1.11)
Coefficient on debt dummy:	−2.58	−3.88	−4.53	−5.97	−4.23	−4.12	−3.97	−1.19
	(1.36)	(2.05)	(2.27)	(3.04)	(2.09)	(2.09)	(2.11)	(0.66)

constitutional debt limitation index, and the ratings residual all appear as statistically significant with the theoretically expected signs. The squared value of the debt stock carries the wrong (negative) sign but has a high standard error.[23] In short, all the same qualitative conclusions apply. It is worth noting that the explanatory power of the abbreviated model (as measured by both the unadjusted and adjusted R-squared) is actually superior to that of the full model.[24] From this, we conclude that our attempts to capture with our deficit variable the additional effects on default risk stemming from new borrowing were unsuccessful (despite the significance of the deficit variable in the regressions for the full model).

Using the estimated coefficients in the abbreviated model, it is possible to calculate some suggestive statistics about the quantitative effect of relative debt on borrowing costs. For example, during the recession year of 1982, relative debt had a mean value of 2.2 percent. An increase in relative debt of one percentage point would have led to an increase in borrowing costs by more than 8 basis points, and the promised yields rise with the relative debt as long as debt was less than 12.3 percent of Gross State Product. The lowest estimates of the effect of debt on yields occurs for 1986, when the slope dummy on debt takes on the largest negative value of −5.97 (from Table 8.5) with a statistically significant 't' value of 3.0. For this year, our estimates imply that an increase in the relative debt by one percentage point (from the mean value of 2.2 percent) would raise borrowing costs by over 2 basis points and promised yields rise with relative debt as long as relative debt is less than 5.0 percent of Gross State Product.

We also estimated the full and abbreviated models on a cross-section of states for single years. Not unexpectedly, estimated coefficients on the fiscal policy variables were typically much less well determined than in the pooled samples, and the sizes – and sometimes even the signs – of the coefficients often changed quite markedly from period to period. For illustrative purposes, we show in Table 8.6 estimates of the abbreviated model for the years 1982, 1987, and 1990. Note in particular how the estimated coefficient on the debt-to-income variable, as well as that on its

Table 8.6. *OLS estimates of the abbreviated model for single years*

	1982	1987	1990
Debt	17.12	3.49	− 3.45
	(2.65)	(0.59)	(1.84)
Debt²	− 1.63	0.06	1.40
	(1.63)	(0.05)	(5.31)
Trend debt growth	0.88	0.32	0.16
	(1.87)	(1.22)	(1.21)
Debt limits	− 3.83	− 1.58	− 2.23
	(3.59)	(2.39)	(6.72)
Ratings residual	0.95	1.03	0.96
	(9.98)	(10.13)	(14.95)
Standard error of estimate	16.96	10.85	5.26
$\bar{R}^2$	0.791	0.762	0.930
Number of observations	37	37	37

Note: The variables are as described in Table 8.3.

squared value, differ across the three years. For example, if one had only the estimates for 1982, it would be concluded that promised yields increased – albeit at a decreasing rate – with the stock of debt, whereas a dramatically different conclusion would emerge from the 1990 results. And if reliance had to be placed on the 1987 estimates, the conclusion would be that there was *no* significant association between promised yields and the stock of debt. In our view, these single-period, cross-section results indicate how constraining it can be to ignore time-series variation in default risk – and even more so – how hazardous it can be to draw conclusions on the market discipline hypothesis from estimates based on a small sample of observations taken at one point in time.

As discussed in Section 3, theory suggests that debt stocks and interest rates should be simultaneously determined. The results discussed so far do not, however, take account of this possible bias. Table 8.7 presents our attempts to account for this simultaneity. The pooled regression of the abbreviated model (from column (2) of Table 8.4) is reproduced in column (1) for comparison. The second column gives OLS estimates of the fixed effects version of the abbreviated model, which are unbiased in the case where mean levels of debt are interest-sensitive, but deviations from the mean are not. The third column gives a two-stage, least-squares estimate of the fixed effects model, where lagged values of debt, debt squared, and the unemployment rate are used as instruments.

The results from Table 8.7 indicate that simultaneity is important, which is what we would expect for interest-sensitive state borrowers. Notice that

Table 8.7. *Accounting for simultaneity in the abbreviated model*

	Pooled OLS (1)	Fixed effects OLS (2)	Fixed effects 2SLS (3)
Debt	9.98	8.53	19.7
	(4.92)	(2.44)	(3.68)
Debt^2	−0.40	0.11	−1.54
	(1.55)	(0.24)	(1.76)
Trend debt growth	0.35	—	—
	(3.47)		
Debt limits	−2.01	—	—
	(8.18)		
Ratings residual	0.99	0.99	1.02
	(26.7)	(24.3)	(22.5)
Std. error of est.	11.94	8.42	8.61
$\bar{R}^2$	0.74	0.68	0.67
Number of observations	333	333	333
Tests of restrictions:			
Test of Col. (2) over col. (1):			$F(34,277) = 8.11$
Test of fixed effects in col (2):			$F(36,277) = 6.88$
Test of time dummies in col (2):			$F(16,277) = 4.61$
Test of fixed effects and time dummies in col (2):			$F(52,277) = 6.30$

Notes: Sample period 1982–90; 't' statistics in parentheses. The regression in column (1) contained a constant term, and each regression also contained year dummies for 1983–90, and slope dummies for the debt variable for 1983–90. Thus the coefficients on debt and the deficit refer to the 1982 coefficients for these variables. The variables are as described in Table 8.3.

in the second column, the squared debt term is still insignificant, but the point estimate is no longer negative. Given the small size of the squared term in the first two columns of Table 8.7, however, the quantitative effects of increases in debt on yields are very similar. The first 'F' test reported at the bottom of Table 8.7 shows that the introduction of 34 extra coefficients in the fixed effects model *does* significantly lower the standard error of the regression over the pooled model of column (1).[25] This result suggests that we must interpret the coefficients on debt limitations and trend debt growth in the pooled sample with care. The significance of these variables in the first column indicates that these variables capture significant information about the cross-state variation in default risk. The rejection of the pooled model in favor of the fixed-effects model, however, indicates (not surprisingly) that there are other cross-state factors that are also relevant. To the extent that debt limitations and trend debt growth are correlated with omitted cross-state factors, the causal effect of these 2 variable on promised yields may be overstated in column (1).

In the third column of Table 8.7, we employ a two-stage, least-squares estimation to account for possible simultaneity between deviations from state mean debt levels and deviations from state mean yields; again, there are substantial changes in our estimates. In this case, the squared debt term reverts to negative, but there is a substantial increase in the size of the positive coefficient on debt. The two-stage, least-squares estimates of the fixed-effects model imply that during 1982 a 1 percentage point increase in relative debt above its mean value of 2.2 percent would lead to an increase in *over* 12 basis points in the promised yield on that state's debt (as opposed to the 8 basis points implied by the OLS estimates in column (1)). Even in 1986 when the slope dummy for debt again takes on its largest negative value, a one percentage point increase in the relative debt would increase the promised yield by almost 7 basis points. Thus, while our attempts to deal with simultaneity have not resolved the anomaly of nonpositive signs on the squared debt terms, they do point to much larger effects of increases in debt on promised yields.

5   Concluding remarks

In the ongoing debate on the need for constraints on national fiscal policies in a monetary union, it is perhaps not surprising that *both* sides have claimed the US experience as supporting their position. Proponents of binding fiscal rules are able, for example, to point to the existence of states' own voluntary constitutional limitations on borrowing as demonstrating their usefulness, as well as to allege lags, overreactions, and inconsistencies in yield spreads across states as arguing against heavy reliance on market forces. Likewise, opponents of fiscal rules can highlight the joint absence of (postwar) defaults by state governments and of federally-imposed fiscal rules; they also regard the observed differences in market yields across states with different fiscal stances as illustrating the sufficiency of 'market-based' discipline. Suffice to say that without some empirical evidence on the link between state fiscal policy and state borrowing costs – while holding other factors constant – it is difficult to choose between these competing claims.

In this paper, we have used survey data on yield spreads for general obligation municipal bonds to get a first fix on the empirical regularities involved. On the whole, we see our empirical results as lending qualified support to the 'first half' of the market-discipline hypothesis. Specifically, we do find evidence that US states which have followed 'more prudent' fiscal policies are perceived by market participants as having lower default risk and therefore are able to reap the benefit of lower borrowing costs. In this context, 'more prudent' fiscal policies encompass not only a lower stock and trend rate of growth of debt relative to income, but also relatively stringent (albeit voluntarily imposed) constitutional limitations on the state's borrowing authority. In this latter connection, however, it remains to be shown whether a fiscal policy rule imposed by a higher level of government would carry the same credibility with the market as one initiated voluntarily by the lower-level borrowing authority itself.

On the basis of our point estimates from the abbreviated model in Table 8.4, we calculate that a (hypothetical) state which has fiscal-policy characteristics that are one standard deviation 'looser' than the mean of our sample would pay roughly 15–20 basis points more on its general obligation bonds than another (hypothetical) state with fiscal policy characteristics one standard deviation 'tighter' than our sample mean.[26] This is in the same ballpark as Capeci's (1990) estimate (for local municipalities in New Jersey) that a one standard-deviation loosening of fiscal policy is associated with an increase in borrowing costs of 22 basis points. In evaluating the size of our fiscal-policy-related default premium, one should keep in mind at least four points. First, there have been *no* defaults on general obligation bonds in the postwar period – a factor that suggests a low probability of default. Second, even if a default did occur, the consequences for borrowers may be much larger than those for creditors. Third, if a state pays say, a 6 percent promised yield on its general obligation bonds, a default premium of say, 20 basis points represents an increase of 3 percent in its nominal cost of borrowing – not necessarily a trivial addition expense. And, as a fraction of its real borrowing costs, the 20 basis point increase would be substantially higher. Fourth, and as noted in the Introduction, it is possible to conceive of (non-market) mechanisms that would magnify the market signal in yield spreads to increase the incentive to discipline errant fiscal policy. But this takes us beyond the scope of this paper and toward the 'second half' of the market-discipline hypothesis, namely, the proposition that authorities faced with increased borrowing costs will rein in their errant fiscal policy behaviour.

Appendix   The supply of state loans

To illustrate the possibility of a backward bending supply curve in the simplest context, assume no risk premia and that the probability, P, of no default is:

$$P = P(Z) \tag{A.1}$$

where $Z = B(1 + R)$; $P(0) = 1$; $P'(0) = 0$; $P' \geq 0$; and P is zero for some large, but finite value of Z.

In this case, equation (2) in the text holds for all risky state borrowers, and the variation in interest rates on risky debt can be determined by totally differentiating (2) by B, and R (using (A.1)):

$$(1 + R)P'[dB(1 + R) + BdR] + dRP = 0 \tag{A.2}$$

which upon rearranging yields:

$$dR/dB = -(1 + R)^2 P'/[P + (1 + R)P'B] \tag{A.3}$$

While the exact, detailed relationship between borrowing and the promised rate depends on higher-order derivatives, two key result follows from (A.3): first, the denominator in (A.3) is initially positive, since $P(0) = 1$ when $B = 0$; second, since P becomes zero for some finite Z, the denominator eventually is nonpositive. The convexity of the supply curve in Figure 8.1, however, does not follow from (A.3) but depends in a complicated way on the second derivative of P.

To illustrate the qualitative nature of the complication of existing debt, consider the case where borrowers have issued some long-term bonds, B, at the rate $\bar{R}$, and only the current (positive valued) deficit, D, is issued at the current rate R. In this case, the end-of-period financial obligations of the borrower are given by:

$$Z = B(1 + \bar{R}) + D(1 + R) \tag{A.4}$$
$$\text{for } D \geq 0.$$

In this case, the analogues to (A.3) are given by:

$$dR/dB = -(1 + R)(1 + \bar{R})P'/[P + (1 + R)P'D]$$
$$dR/dD = -(1 + R)^2 P'/[P + (1 + R)P'D] \tag{A.5}$$

Consequently, the effect of higher debt on the yield differs from the effect of a higher positively valued deficit only to the extent that the current interest rate differs from past interest rates.

While the signs of the second derivatives still depend on P'', one interesting result does follow from (A.5):

$$d^2R/dB^2 = -\{(1 + \bar{R})P'/[P + (1 + R)P'D]\}dR/dB$$
$$\qquad + \text{ other terms proportional to } dR/dB$$
$$d^2R/dD^2 = -2\{(1 + R)P'/[P + (1 + R)P'D]\}dR/dD$$
$$\qquad + \text{ same other terms but proportional to } dR/dD \tag{A.6}$$

The first-terms on the right-hand sides of (A.6) are both positive and the first term for d^2R/dD^2 is larger, as long as $2(1 + R) > (1 + \bar{R})^2$. The remaining terms will be nearly equal as long as R is nearly equal to $\bar{R}$. All this analysis suggests that $d^2R/dD^2 > d^2R/dB^2$.

NOTES

The views expressed are the authors' alone and do not represent the views of the International Monetary Fund. In addition to colleagues in the Research Department of the IMF, the authors are grateful to Tom Barone, John Capeci, R. B. Davidson III, James Dearborn, Peter Garber, Gilbert Metcalf, Michael Mussa, Carmen Reinhart, Lars Svensson, Thomas Swartz, and Irene Walsh for helpful comments on an earlier draft. Ravina Malkani provided much appreciated research assistance.

1 For a discussion of monetary policy issues in an emerging European EMU, see Frenkel and Goldstein (1991).
2 In some proposals, an additional fiscal rule would be that public borrowing would be permissible only to finance investment.
3 For a fuller discussion of this conflicting-signals problem, see Frankel (1990).
4 In the case of the developing-country debt crisis, interest rate spreads on bank loans to developing countries were slow to rise in the mid-to-late 1970s, and the transition to highly restricted access (in the early 1980s) came abruptly. One explanation for the relatively narrow loan spreads is the perception of a bail-out – either of the indebted countries themselves or of the deposit liabilities of the large international banks extending the loans; see Folkerts-Landau (1985). In the case of the New York City financial crisis, it apparently took some time for market participants to realize that New York City was diverting approved funds and pledging future receipts – both earmarked for other purposes – to meet current operating deficits; see Bishop et al. (1989).
5 EC Commission (1990b).
6 The state debt-to-GNP ratios used in this paper are much lower than the figures cited above because we employ a more restrictive measure of state debt that is more closely linked to default risk; see Section 3.
7 Eichengreen (1990). The difference between Europe and United States on the degree of labour mobility is reduced if one only considers mobility across states, since much of US mobility is apparently within states.
8 Obstfeld (1990).
9 Sala-i-Martín and Sachs (1992). It should be noted, however, that estimates of the 'cushioning effect' of the US federal tax and transfer system on region-specific shocks appears to be quite sensitive to the time dimension of the shock – and perhaps also to the level of disaggregation of regions. In this connection, von Hagen (1991) finds a much lower cushioning effect than Sala-i-Martín and Sachs, using a shorter-run definition of shocks and more disaggregated definition of regions.
10 While the municipal bond market includes obligations of cities as well as of states, we consider only the latter in this paper.
11 In a broad survey of the relevance of the US currency union for European Economic and Monetary Union, Eichengreen (1990) estimates the effects of debt variables on yields. Liu and Thakor's (1984) paper is typical of the finance literature on state default risk and fiscal variables. Capeci (1990) provides a broad survey of the municipal bond literature related to default risk.

Most of the studies reviewed, however, are of the local municipal bond market.
12 In credit markets, it is arbitrary on which side of the market the borrowers and lenders are placed. One can talk about the supply and demand for credit, in which case borrowers are on the demand side and lenders on the supply side, or alternatively the supply and demand for debt, which reverses the sides. In this paper, we use the former categories so that lenders supply funds to states and state borrowing leads to a demand for funds.
13 The question of risk premia on sovereign debt is tested empirically in Stone (1990) and Cottarelli and Mecagni (1990).
14 US bonds are given credit ratings principally by Moody's Investor Service and Standard & Poor's. The qualitative description of the Moody's Ratings categories are: Aaa – Best Quality; Aa – High quality; A – Upper medium grade; Baa – Medium grade; Ba – Possess speculative elements; B – Generally lack characteristics of desirable investment; Caa – Poor Standing; may be in default; Ca – Speculative in a high degree; often in default; C – Lowest grade; very poor prospects. In addition to each broad category, a 1, 2, or 3 can be added to the letters to indicate whether the security is in the high, middle, or low end of the ratings category. See Van Horne (1990) for a discussion of the relationship between credit ratings and default risk.
15 The rating agencies, however, try to measure default risk independently of the business cycle. Thus for example, the Baa – Aaa spread widens during a recession instead of the spread remaining constant with fewer Aaa states and more Baa.
16 In principle, the yield on state debt can vary because of taxes. To a state resident, neither federal nor one's own state's securities are subject to state and local taxation. State, general obligation debt, however, is also free of federal taxation, so that the marginal rate of federal taxation for the marginal investor who is indifferent between Treasuries and state debt with appropriate default and risk premia. Various competing theories (summarized in Poterba, 1989) have identified the relevant marginal investor as banks, insurance companies, corporations, or individuals. Poterba (1989) presents empirical evidence in support of the hypothesis that individuals were the indifferent investors during the 1960–88 period, particularly for the case of long-term municipal debt.

In fact, such differences in marginal tax rates are frequently cited for what would otherwise be anomalies in yields across states. For example, Swartz (1989) refers to 'tax related demand' to explain why the yields on Connecticut and California state bonds were consistently among the six lowest during the late 1980s in spite of credit ratings below Aaa. During the same time period, the bonds of at least 5 other Aaa states traded with higher yields. We tested for differences in yields due to differences in average, marginal rates of federal taxation across states, but found anomalous results.
17 The 10 excluded states include the 9 states who have no outstanding GO debt and Arkansas. In addition, we excluded New Jersey, Alaska and Hawaii. The latter 2 states were excluded because of their unique fiscal status.
18 The Chubb Relative Value Survey does not include explicit instructions to evaluate comparable bonds. Tom Swartz of Chubb, however, reports that these instructions are implicit, and that whenever a survey respondent asks they are instructed to evaluate comparable bonds.
19 Cranford and Stover (1988) criticize Liu and Thakor by noting that because the error from the first-stage regression is orthogonal to the fiscal variables, the

point estimates of the fiscal coefficients in the second-stage regression will be identical to an OLS regression of yield on the fiscal variables, omitting the ratings variable. In response, Liu and Thakor point out that while the point estimates will be the same, the standard errors will be lower in the second-stage regression. The question then becomes which are the appropriate standard errors. We believe that the standard errors from Liu and Thakor's procedure are more appropriate for our test. The ratings residual allows us to capture the effects of omitted factors, which if not accounted for would mask the statistical significance of the relationship between fiscal variables and yields.

20 Notice that the ratings variable is also capturing variations in the risk of default over the business cycle. For example, the spread between the numerical values assigned to Baa and Aaa ratings in the recession year of 1982 was 153.6 basis points, whereas the same spread during 1989 was less than half as much at 70.9 basis points.

21 The 333 observations derive from observations on 37 states over the 1982–90 period (9 years).

22 There may well be a problem of multicollinearity here given the preponderance of high values for the debt limitation index.

23 In addition to problems of simultaneity (discussed later in this section), there may also be a multicollinearity problem at work as between the debt and squared-debt variables. In this connection, it is worth noting that when the abbreviated model was re-estimated using *either* the level or the squared value of debt-to-income, the estimated coefficients were significant with the expected positive sign.

24 Note that the ratings residual variable is not the same between the two regressions. In the abbreviated model, whatever information there is in the deficit variable is captured by the ratings variable. This adds to our suspicion that the deficit variable is capturing the increased probability of default from new borrowing.

25 The dependent variables for the regressions in columns (1) and (2) are the yields and deviations from state mean yields, respectively. The latter variable has a smaller variance, which accounts for the lower $\bar{R}^2$ reported in column (2) in addition to the lower standard error.

26 The fiscal-policy characteristics included in this calculation are debt, debt^2, the trend of the debt to income ratio, and the constitutional debt limitation index.

REFERENCES

ACIR (Advisory Commission on Intergovernmental Relations) (1987), *Significant Features of Fiscal Federalism*, Washington, D.C.: US Government Printing Press.

Bishop, Graham, Dirk Damrau, and Michelle Miller (1989), '1992 and Beyond: Market Discipline CAN Work in the EC Monetary Union,' Salomon Brothers, London.

Bishop, Graham (1991), 'The EC Public Debt Disease: Discipline with Credit Spreads and Cure with Price Stability,' Salomon Brothers, London.

Capeci, John (1990), 'Local Fiscal Policies, Default Risk and Municipal Borrowing Costs,' Brandeis University, Department of Economics, No. 259.

Cohen, Natalie R. (1988), 'Municipal Default Patterns,' Enhance Reinsurance Co.

Cottarelli, Carlo, and Mauro Mecagni (1990), 'The Risk Premium on Italian Government Debt, 1976–88,' IMF Working Paper No. 90/38.

Cranford, Brian, and Roger Stover (1988), 'Comment on Interest Yields, Credit Ratings, and Economic Characteristics of State Bonds,' *Journal of Money, Credit, and Banking* **20**, 691–95.

Davidson, R. B. (1990), 'Municipal Market Analysis: A Framework for Analyzing Quality Spreads,' J.P. Morgan, 29 March.

Delors Report (1989), *Report on Economic and Monetary Union in the European Community*, Committee for the Study of Economic and Monetary Union, Brussels: EC Commission.

Eaton, Jonathan, and Mark Gersovitz (1981), 'Debt with Potential Repudiation: A Theoretical and Empirical Analysis,' *Review of Economic Studies* **49**, 289–309.

EC Commission (1990a), 'Economic and Monetary Union: The Economic Rationale and Design of the System', Luxembourg: EC Commission.

    (1990b), 'One Market, One Money – An Evaluation of the Potential Benefits and Costs of Forming an Economic and Monetary Union', *European Economy*.

Eichengreen, Barry (1990), 'One Money for Europe? Lessons from the US Currency Union,' *Economic Policy* **5**, (10), 119–86.

English, William (1991), 'When America Defaulted: American State Debt in the 1840's,' Mimeo, University of Pennsylvania.

Folkerts-Landau, David (1985), 'The Changing Role of International Bank Lending in Development Finance,' *IMF Staff Papers* **32**, 317–63.

Frankel, Jeffery (1990), 'Obstacles to Coordination, and a Consideration of Two Proposals to Overcome Them,' in William Branson, Jacob Frenkel and Morris Goldstein (eds.), *International Policy Coordination and Exchange Rate Fluctuations*, University of Chicago Press for the National Bureau of Economic Research, Chicago, pp. 109–45.

Frenkel, Jacob and Morris Goldstein (1991), 'Monetary Policy in an Emerging European Economic and Monetary Union', *IMF Staff Papers*, forthcoming.

Hsiao, Cheng (1986), *Analysis of Panel Data*, Cambridge: Cambridge University Press.

Lamafalussy, Alexandre (1989), 'Macro-coordination of Fiscal Policies in an Economic and Monetary Union in Europe,' Supplement to Delors Report.

Liu, Pu and Anjan Thakor (1984), 'Interest Yields, Credit Ratings, and Economic Characteristics of State Bonds: An Empirical Analysis,' *Journal of Money, Credit and Banking* **16**, 345–50.

Metcalf, Gilbert (1990), 'Federal Taxation and the Supply of State Debt,' NBER Working Paper No. 3255.

Obstfeld, Maurice (1990), 'Discussion,' *Economic Policy* **5**, (10), 166–69.

Orth, John V. (1987), *The Judicial Power of the United States: The Eleventh Amendment in American History*, New York: Oxford.

Poterba, James (1989), 'Tax Reform and the Market for Tax Exempt Debt,' NBER Working Paper No. 2900.

X. Sala-i-Martín and Jeffrey Sachs (1992), 'Fiscal Federalism and Optimum Currency Areas: Evidence for Europe from the United States', in this volume.

Stiglitz, Joseph and Andrew Weiss (1981), 'Credit Rationing in Markets with Imperfect Information,' *American Economic Review* **73**, 393–410.

Stone, Mark (1990), 'Are Sovereign Debt Secondary Market Returns Sensitive to Macroeconomic Fundamentals?' IMF Research Department Seminar Paper.
Swartz, Thomas (1989), 'State General Obligation Trading Values – Back to the Future,' *Municipal Analysts Forum* 7–10.
Van Horne, James (1990), *Financial Markets Rates and Flows*, 3rd edition, Englewood Cliffs, NJ: Prentice-Hall Inc.
von Hagen, Jurgen (1991), 'Fiscal Arrangements in a Monetary Union: Evidence from the US,' mimeo, School of Business, Indiana University, March.
United States Census (1990), *State Government Finances in 1989*, Washington, D.C.: Department of Commerce.
Yawitz, Jess, Kevin Maloney, and Louis Edderington (1985), 'Texas, Default Risk, and Yield Spreads,' *Journal of Finance* **40**, 1127–40.

Discussion

MERVYN KING

Goldstein and Woglom have provided us with a very timely paper. The question of fiscal discipline is very much a live issue in the Inter-Governmental Conference on monetary union in the European Community. Moreover, whatever provisions emerge in the treaty that is finally signed, the rules on fiscal discipline and excessive deficits are likely to be controversial both in the period running up to entry into monetary union as well as during an eventual union itself. All member countries of the Community recognise that there is a problem of how to deal with excessive deficits in the monetary union. But there is, as yet, less agreement on the set of solutions that have so far been proposed.

Two issues are at the heart of the current negotiations. First, the *trigger mechanism* that brings into play action against an offending country. Second, the *sanctions* that would be taken against a country deemed to have triggered the procedure. The mechanical approach to the trigger mechanism has been discussed in some detail, and three criteria have been at the centre of these proposals. They are:

(1) A debt rule; the debt to GDP ratio in excess of a critical value, say 60%, would be the trigger.
(2) A deficit rule; the deficit to GDP ratio in excess of a critical value, say 3%, would be the trigger.

(3) The permissible deficit would be limited to the amount of public investment – sometimes, rather unfortunately, known as the 'golden rule'.

In addition to the purely arbitrary nature of the critical values that would trigger the procedure, all three criteria raise enormous conceptual and measurement problems. The difficulties of measuring, comparing, and even defining, budget deficits across countries are well known. Differences in the size of publicly owned industries, the financing of public services, the off-budget treatment of pensions and other transfers, the definition of 'government' itself, all suggest that the application of sanctions cannot easily be made the automatic consequence of violating an arbitrary trigger mechanism threshold.

There have, therefore, been suggestions that a better approach be to exploit multilateral surveillance, or peer group pressure. If the trigger mechanism were used merely to invoke a multilateral surveillance programme then the difficulties of definition would create fewer problems. But this approach too will run up against problems if the criteria for excessive deficits are such that, as may well be true in the next year or so, most countries are caught by the criteria. That outcome would devalue the entire process.

So although there is general agreement that we recognise a problem country when we see or visit one on holiday, there is a reluctance to apply automatic sanctions on the basis of arbitrary criteria. This is particularly true when sanctions might take the form of either

(a) fines, or
(b) a suspension of payments from the European Community to the offending country.

Hence it is not surprising that there has been growing interest in the use of market-based sanctions, in which there is no need for an officially agreed set of criteria to trigger a collective mechanism, nor for a collectively administered punishment that would be almost certain to arouse the worst sort of political divisions of which the Community is capable. But there must be a question mark over the effectiveness of market-based sanctions. In the absence of empirical evidence, there is genuine disagreement and uncertainty within the Community on their potential effectiveness. It is important, therefore, that we examine any empirical evidence that might shed light on the effectiveness of market-based sanctions. The Goldstein-Woglom paper is especially interesting in this context.

In order to assess the relevance of the Goldstein-Woglom evidence to the question of monetary union in Europe, it is important to distinguish between two reasons for concern over excessive fiscal deficits. The first is that it is thought that there might be pressure on the European Central Bank to monetise an excessive deficit incurred by a member country if the alternative were for that country to default. In principle, a 'no bail-out' provision would leave the responsibility for debt in the hands of member countries. Some have questioned whether such a provision is really credible in a monetary union. This is, I think, rather too pessimistic a view. The second issue is that excessive deficits – at least in large countries – affect the fiscal stance of the Community as a whole and hence the likely level of interest rates in the monetary union. Of course, these 'externalities' of excessive deficits can occur outside a monetary union as well. But the crucial difference between the two areas of concern is that the former is concerned with the debt ratios for an individual country no matter how large it is and the second is concerned with the increase in total debt issued regardless of how it affects the debt ratios of any one country. The construction of trigger mechanisms and sanctions seems more appropriate to the former than to the latter concern. Hence, even in the absence of sanctions for excessive deficits, the fiscal stance of the larger member countries is likely to be of interest to the monetary authorities even if the trigger criteria have not been violated.

The evidence presented in this paper tests the hypothesis that differences in expected returns on bonds issued by different states in the USA reflect differences in the probability of default. The basic difficulty in testing this hypothesis is obvious. The probability of default is unobservable. Moreover, we cannot use observable frequencies to measure the probability of default because it is such an infrequent event – so infrequent in fact that it has never actually occurred, at least since the Second World War and hence, *a fortiori*, in the sample period used for estimation post-1973. I interpret the results of the paper, therefore, as telling us about correlations between spreads in bond yields and measures of debt to income ratios, deficits and the underlying growth of real debt. And here there is indeed evidence – for thirty-nine states – that differences between spreads, which can vary by 100 basis points or more, are positively correlated with such indicators of 'fiscal indiscipline'. These spreads are small in comparison with those that exist at present within Europe. For example, the spread between Spain and Germany has varied around 500 basis points. How should the correlations found by Goldstein and Woglom be interpreted? There is one point of enormous econometric difficulty concerning *identification*. The aim is to estimate the supply curve of credit to governments, but some of the unobservable variables that affect the supply also affect the demand for such securities. The authors are clearly aware of this problem and use fixed-effects models to deal with the problem but it surely cannot wholly have been removed. Leaving this point to one side, the interpretation of the results must depend upon the model of political behaviour that we believe underlies the decisions that were made in the sample period. Consider two possible models.

The first is a model of an optimising government that attempts to implement an optimal tax schedule over time. With sufficient conditions on the separability of preferences, it can be shown that a government maximising the welfare of a representative agent will choose tax rates such that

(i)   the wedge between consumption and leisure is constant over time, and

(ii) the wedge between consumption in successive periods is zero *ex ante*, but *ex post* will imply a capital levy equal to the innovation in the present discounted value of innovations in government expenditure. This means that deficits will depend on the autoregressive nature of shocks to government expenditures or to the tax base. Countries or states might well differ in this respect, and so the optimal time path of government deficits might well vary across countries. This casts further doubt on the wisdom of specifying arbitrary criteria above which point sanctions are levied.

A second model is one of stochastic shocks to the identity of the government in power, and possibly to the probability of repudiation of a previous administration's debts. These factors are unlikely to be correlated in a simple way with observable variables. Criteria for binding budgetary constraints are a blunt weapon to deal with alleged excessive deficits on the part of a small minority of countries in a population of only twelve members of the community. Market-based discipline does, as the authors point out, enable other influences on default probabilities to be reflected in market default premia.

VITO TANZI

I am happy to comment on a nice paper that deals with an important and topical question and does it clearly and competently. With the help of unpublished and up-to-now unutilized data, the paper reaches interesting conclusions. Given the topic of this conference and the implications of Goldstein and Woglom's paper for the European Monetary Union (EMU), I will focus my discussion on those implications. However, by so doing, I will not do full justice to the authors' work since that work extends well beyond those implications.

It is, by now, widely recognized that, as the authors put it; 'if fiscal discipline was not forthcoming in an EMU, then the very objective of the union itself could well be threatened.' The authors identify three possible approaches to encourage the member countries to promote the required fiscal discipline:

(a) *Binding fiscal rules* as proposed in the Delors Report. Several such rules could be devised relating to the size of the fiscal deficit a country would be allowed to have in a given year; to the level of the public debt; to the change in that level and so forth. A simple example could be a balanced budget rule, or one that requires that the ratio of public debt to gross domestic product does not change. While it is not difficult to think of several such rules, it is difficult to think of rules that are both feasible and good. The experience of countries with laws that require the balancing of the budget, for example, is not very encouraging. These laws have often resulted in a proliferation of extrabudgetary accounts. Furthermore, as the literature of the 1960s emphasized, the fiscal deficit is highly influenced by the behaviour of the economy. Given that cyclical developments influence the performance of the budget, and that these developments are not going to disappear in the future, these rules might require what many economists would consider as highly destabilizing fiscal policies.[1] Going from rules that relate to the behaviour of relevant variables (fiscal deficit, public debt, etc.) in *particular years*, to rules that relate to that behaviour over longer periods (say balancing the budget or stabilizing the ratio of public debt to GDP over the duration of the business cycle) would introduce elements of discretion that might make possible for particular countries to delay taking the needed fiscal actions or might lead to debates over the desirable actions.

(b) *Multilateral surveillance* plus the incorporation in the EMU treaty of the principle that 'excessive budget deficits must be avoided.' The extent of the impact of multilateral surveillance on the policymaking process of some countries is debatable. If the policy-making process were sensitive enough to be significantly influenced by multilateral surveillance, it would probably have avoided the country's getting into fiscal difficulties in the first place. This, of course, does not mean that multilateral surveillance is totally ineffective. It does mean, however, that one must be modest about what can be expected from this process.

(c) *To entrust private financial markets with the role of encouraging fiscal discipline*. In other words, do not impose any specific requirements on the country but put your faith in the market or in God, whichever is relevant, and hope that the market will discipline the countries.

The Goldstein and Woglom paper has an important bearing on the 'put your faith in the market' approach although its relevance may also extend to the fiscal rules approach since they show that the states that have fiscal rules generally followed more conservative fiscal policy. The market approach recognizes that a lax fiscal policy leads to higher (default and premium) risk for those who buy government bonds. This in turn raises the interest rate at which governments can borrow. Higher interest rates presumably discourage additional government borrowing, thus helping restore fiscal discipline.

For this market-related approach to be able to promote fiscal discipline, several conditions, in addition to those mentioned in the Goldstein and Woglom paper, must be satisfied.

First, the default premium in the interest rate must fully and accurately reflect the degree of fiscal discipline. There must not be conceptual or statistical problems which introduce a wedge between the actual fiscal situation and the one reflected, via the default and premium risk, in the interest rate. Given the difficulties that economists have in assessing precisely the fiscal situation of countries, this condition cannot be assumed to be easily met. A few days ago, for example, Professor Modigliani was cited in Italian newspapers to the effect that there is no fiscal problem in Italy, and Professor Eisner has repeatedly stated that the United States has no fiscal problem either. Clearly this is an area where different economists and different investors may see things differently.

Second, and closely related to the first, the relationship between the fiscal situation and the borrowing rate on government bonds must be well-behaved and continuous so that a country's borrowing rate is always a good barometer of that country's fiscal stance. This condition rules out the possibility of sudden changes. No catastrophe theory is applicable here. If the fiscal house falls, it will be smoothly and continuously. This assumption implies that the debt crisis of 1982 in developing countries could not have happened since the lenders would have increased their lending rates and the borrowers would have reduced their borrowing well before the situation reached a critical level.

Third, it requires that the political process within the relevant countries is such that, faced with a significant increase in the cost of borrowing, a well-identified group of policy-makers has the wisdom, the interest, and more importantly, the political power to react in the most desirable way possible by legislating tax increases or cuts in noninterest expenditure.

Furthermore, they will do so immediately regardless of whether the next election is just around the corner or a long time away.

Work on political cycles and on public choice would raise serious questions about this third condition. Also, the experience with fiscal policy in many countries, and the observation of the policy-making process in those countries, make this condition appear even more questionable.[2] The demand for borrowing with respect to changes in the interest rate may be inelastic either because noninterest public expenditure (tied to entitlement or to well-established government programs) is seen as beneficial or productive, or because it would be politically difficult to cut it, or to increase tax revenues, by enough to compensate for the increase in the rate of interest. The junk bond experience of the 1980s may be relevant to countries as well as to enterprises. High interest rates did not prevent excessive borrowing by many enterprises. It is unlikely that they will prevent excessive borrowing by countries. Governments that can remain in power for a while longer by borrowing more and spending more, will be tempted to do so. The additional cost of borrowing would be faced by some other government, and, of course, there is always the possibility that international developments may force down the general interest rates, thus alleviating the fiscal situation.

Goldstein and Woglom estimate the effect of fiscal deterioration on the interest rate. They show that borrowing becomes more expensive when the fiscal situation of the state deteriorates. Thus, at the margin, the cost of government services goes up. However, they do not specifically address the implication of that increase for the servicing of the existing debt in magnifying that effect. Given the existence of large stocks of debt (exceeding 100 percent of GDP in some European countries), it is important to consider the impact of an increase in interest rates not just on the cost of the marginal program but also on the servicing of the existing debt.

The increase in interest rate will have a substitution and an income effect for the government. If the increase in interest rate affected only new borrowing, as would be the case where the existing stock of debt is very low, only the substitution effect would be important. By increasing the cost of borrowing, this effect might induce some reduction in spending. However, if the existing stock of debt is large, an increase in interest rate may not just increase the cost of *net* borrowing but, given the relatively short maturity structure that characterizes the existing debt of many countries, it may quickly translate into a large increase in total interest payments. This can be interpreted as a substantial reduction in the net income of the public sector. The public sector will have less financial resources to finance its non-interest expenditures. In this situation, it will be more difficult to reduce the size of the fiscal deficit since the increase in interest rate will require more borrowing just to service the existing debt. Higher tax revenue or lower noninterest expenditure will be required to maintain the fiscal deficit unchanged. The magnitude of this income effect will depend on the size of the debt-GDP ratio and, in the short run, on the maturity structure of that debt. The obvious conclusion is that it is far easier to be fiscally virtuous in a country that does not have a large public debt to service.

One of the major problems facing the EMU is the initial, highly different, debt-GDP ratios among the member countries. Some of these countries have ratios that, as Goldstein and Woglom put it, are an order of magnitude higher than those of the American states. For this reason the experience of the American states cannot provide much guidance for the European countries. The American states have not had to face the magnitude of the income effect discussed above. It would be nice if the existing public debts would just disappear at the beginning of the European Monetary Union. But, of course, they will not.

Another basic difference touched upon but not discussed in the Goldstein and Woglom paper is the fiscal role played by the federal government in the United States. More than two-thirds of all public spending in the United States is carried out by the federal government which accounts also for about two-thirds of all tax revenue. That role provides powerful fiscal stabilizers to the states. It maintains an expenditure floor when the income of a particular state falls and it reduces the state's disposable income when the state's income rises by more than the average. In Europe there is no central fiscal authority that plays this role and none is planned for the foreseeable future. It may thus be far more difficult for a European country to scale down its public spending. In a monetary union it will also be difficult for countries with large fiscal imbalances to raise the tax level substantially because of the constraint that the harmonization of the tax systems will put on some taxes.[3] Thus, fiscal discipline will require significant expenditure reductions.

Goldstein and Woglom do not have much to say about the states' reaction to the increases in the cost of their borrowing. They limit themselves to assessing the impact of the states' fiscal policy on their cost of borrowing. But this is where the US example could, in spite of the limits mentioned above, have relevance for the European Monetary Union. It is not surprising that lenders prefer to lend to states with sounder fiscal policies. But how quickly have the states responded to the rise in the cost of borrowing? Was the speed and extent of adjustment affected by the size of the stock of debt? Was it affected by the timing of the next elections? By fiscal rules? Have interest rate differentials between fiscally sound and other states persisted over time, or have they been eliminated quickly?

While the experience of the American states can provide some insight for the European Monetary Union, one further fundamental difference between the situation that characterizes the American states and the situation that will characterize at least for some time the European countries must be kept in mind. In spite of their distinct legal identity and their important functions, the American states are integral parts of a whole from which they cannot separate themselves. It is difficult to think of the American states without thinking of the United States of America. When, in the last century, some states tried to break away from the Union, the Union went to war to prevent that. Thus the idea that the United States will remain a united state is never questioned. This idea has acquired full credibility. For the foreseeable future the European countries will retain far more independence. Even after joining the EMU, a country would still have an important separate identity and would still have the option of getting out of the union if, in the judgement of those who determine its policies, the cost of remaining in the Union became too high. It would be naive to think that a commitment to join the Union would be an irreversible action which would not be affected by the perceived economic or political cost of joining and remaining in the Union and which would thus promote the necessary fiscal adjustment.

I have a few comments on the model used by Goldstein and Woglom for the empirical estimations. First, and perhaps of lesser significance, is the fact that the model includes among the independent variables both the current ratio of (net) debt to income and the trend growth of debt relative to income. These two variables are largely the same variable measured in two different ways and I wonder whether they should both be included.

A second comment relates to the way in which the authors have tried to take into account tax effects. Unless I have misunderstood the paper, the authors implicitly assume that the bonds of a given state are largely bought by the residents of that state. They argue that ' ... the [marginal tax rates] in the different states can vary because of differences in the proportion of high-income taxpayers by state. The larger the proportion of high-income taxpayers, the higher the MTR for that state and the lower the yield.' However, in a federation with perfect capital mobility and with full information, there is no reason why the demand for the bonds of a given state should be limited to the residents of that state. As long as the local bonds are tax free, they will attract investors with high marginal tax rates from all over the United States.

A tax aspect that is ignored in the paper is the tax on capital gains. In fact, while the yield on a state or municipal bond is tax free, the capital gains incurred in the sale of that bond are fully taxable and capital losses are deductible. This fact probably influences what the authors call risk premia since it may affect the willingness of investors to buy or sell in the secondary market when capital gains or losses are present.

Finally an aspect of the data used that I found puzzling is the following. If, as they maintain, there has been no default by states since at least World War Two, why is the default premium for some states as large as shown by their Table 8.1? Is this an indication that the market is highly irrational?

In conclusion, this is a rich and interesting paper that has a lot to say about the US municipal bond market. It also has a lot to say about the European monetary system. However, caution is required in extending the US results to the European situation.

NOTES

1 For example, they might require tax increases and/or expenditure cuts in recession years. Only those who believe in an extreme version of Ricardian equivalence would dismiss the potentially destabilizing effects of these policies.
2 For an elaboration of this point see Tanzi (1992).
3 Of course, this does not rule out increases associated with reductions in tax evasion.

REFERENCE

Tanzi, V. (1992), 'The political Economy of Fiscal Deficit Reduction', forthcoming in a World Bank volume, *The Macroeconomics of the Public Sector Deficits*.

Part IV Global implications of a
European Central Bank

9 European Monetary Union and international currencies in a tripolar world

GEORGE ALOGOSKOUFIS and RICHARD PORTES

The European Community countries appear to be locked into a process that may eventually lead their economies to full monetary unification. Although the road to monetary union in the EC is bound to be bumpy, all countries appear committed to the final goal, with the possible exception of Britain. According to plans under negotiation at the inter-governmental conference that started in December 1990, the currencies of twelve European economies, which include a number of leading international currencies such as the Deutschmark, sterling and the French franc, will ultimately be replaced by a new currency, likely to be called the 'ecu'.[1]

European monetary union, when and if it occurs, is bound to have important international implications. The new currency will be issued on behalf of a large economic area, by a new Central Bank which will be responsible for the joint monetary policy of the EC. Other international institutions such as the G-7, the IMF and the OECD will have to adapt (see Alogoskoufis and Portes, 1990), but, more importantly, there will be a major shock to the existing international monetary and exchange rate system. The ecu will be a serious challenger for the role of the US dollar as the dominant international means of payment, unit of account and store of value, and the monetary policies of the new European Central Bank will have far more important international spillovers than those of any of the existing central banks of the EC countries. The extent of these spillovers is likely to affect the process of international policy coordination, and even the exchange rate regime of all the main industrial economies.

The purpose of this paper is to examine the prospective implications of Economic and Monetary Union (EMU) in the EC for the international monetary system. We make a giant leap forward in confining attention to the implications after Stage III, when, according to the time-table first set

273

in the Delors Committee Report, the existing EC currencies will have been replaced by a single currency. Thus, what we compare is the status quo (alias Stage I), in which ten of the twelve EC countries participate in the Exchange Rate Mechanism (ERM) of the European Monetary System (EMS), and two more (the Greek drachma and the Portuguese escudo) are expected to join in the not too distant future, with full monetary union, in which all currencies will be replaced by one. We shall have nothing to say on the transitional Stage II, in which the fluctuation banks for intra-EC exchange rates will be eliminated, but each country will retain its national currency.

We concentrate on two main issues: first on the prospective role of the ecu as an international vehicle and reserve currency, and second on the prospective changes that EMU will imply for the international coordination of monetary and fiscal policies between the USA, the EC and Japan, and the exchange rate regime between the dollar, the ecu and the yen.

1   The international role of the ecu

Like national currencies, international currencies have three major roles. They serve as means of international payments, as units of account and as stores of value. But, there is one major difference between national and international currencies.

Within national borders, the sole use of one currency is usually imposed by government fiat. Thus the question which characteristics make one currency more in demand than another does not usually arise, as market participants have little option but to use the currency designated by the government and supplied by an agency such as the national central bank. It is only in extreme circumstances, such as very rapid inflation, that national currencies are replaced as means of payment, units of account and stores of value by other currencies or commodities.

In the international economy demand factors play a much more important role in the determination of which currencies are being used for these purposes. Since there is no supranational authority that can impose the use of a single currency, these issues are decided in the market place, by the decisions and actions of public and private agents of all countries. Because of the economies of scale in the use of currencies, the externalities involved and the considerable degree of uncertainty and asymmetric information, there is no guarantee that the world will end up with the best monetary system, let alone a single international currency. In addition, there is the possibility of multiple equilibria and considerable instability, as the expectations and beliefs of agents are among the major factors that will determine which equilibrium will prevail.[2]

The history of the international monetary system suggests a series of efforts by the governments of the major economies to coordinate on better equilibria than the ones that would prevail in the international marketplace in the absence of coordination. Since there is no guarantee that the unregulated market will yield a satisfactory international (or indeed national) monetary system, governments have jointly intervened, either in the form of agreeing to implicit rules of the game (as in the classical gold standard), or in the form of designing explicit sets of rules and international institutions (as in Bretton Woods or the EMS) that would ensure that the international monetary equilibrium possessed a minimum of desirable characteristics. In other periods, such as the inter-war period and a large part of the 1970s and early 1980s, international coordination broke down or took a much looser form (e.g. the G-7 summits).

Yet many of the institutions and modes of behaviour from previous regimes do not completely disappear, so there has been considerable continuity to the international monetary system even after the breakdown of coordination and major changes in regime, following shocks to the fundamentals or the preferences of governments. In a world with many equilibria, history and institutions also play a key role in choosing one and may delay the switch from one to another.[3]

EMU can be seen as an important change in the fundamentals of the international monetary system. A sub-set of countries have decided to coordinate on the use of a single currency. The remainder of this section is concerned with the implications of this decision for the currencies that are used as international means of payments, units of account and stores of value.

1.1 The means of payment function

Let us first start with the means of payment function of international currencies. Many seem to think that this function is the most important. For example, according to Cohen (1971), 'An international economy with only national moneys is like a barter economy. . . . Transactions costs are high because of the practical problem of achieving the required double coincidence of wants in the foreign exchange market. However, as in a barter economy, transactions costs can be substantially diminished for an individual if he adapts his own currency mix to that of other individuals, holding for specific use, as international exchange intermediaries, inven-tories of the most widely demanded foreign currencies. These are of

Table 9.1. *% share of national currencies in foreign exchange reserves, all countries*

	1973	1976	1978	1980	1983	1986	1988	1989
US Dollar	84.5	86.7	82.8	68.6	71.4	67.1	64.9	60.2
Pound Sterling	5.9	2.1	1.6	2.9	2.5	2.6	2.8	2.7
Deutsche Mark	6.7	7.3	10.1	14.9	11.8	14.6	15.7	19.3
French Franc	1.2	1.0	1.0	1.7	0.8	0.8	1.0	1.3
Swiss Franc	1.4	1.6	2.1	3.2	2.4	2.0	1.9	1.7
Dutch Guilder	0.4	0.5	0.5	1.3	0.8	1.1	1.1	1.1
Japanese Yen	–	1.2	1.9	4.4	5.0	7.9	7.7	7.9
Major EC curr.	14.2	10.9	13.2	20.8	15.9	19.1	20.6	24.4

Source: IMF *Annual Report* (1990)

course the currencies of the countries that are predominant in world trade – the countries that account for the largest proportion of international transactions' (pp. 25–26). To assess the potential role of the ecu we must look to demand for means of international payments by official bodies and by the private sector.

We begin with the demand by official bodies. As Krugman (1984) among others suggests, 'Probably the most important reason for holding reserves in dollars is that the dollar is an intervention currency' (p. 273).

Table 9.1 presents data on the composition of official international reserves. It demonstrates that the share of the US dollar in official reserves, although declining, is overwhelmingly higher than the share of any other single currency. In fact it is higher than the combined share of all other currencies taken together. The share of major European currencies shows a slow increase, especially since the depreciation of the dollar in 1985–86. It is important to note, however, that these trends are not simply the outcome of revaluations following changes in exchange rates, but also the result of diversification away from the dollar (IMF *Annual Report*, 1990, p. 65).

The data in Table 9.1 probably overstate the position of the dollar, as (after 1979) they add to the SDR value of dollar holdings the SDR value of ECUs issued against dollars, while the SDR value of ECUs issued against gold is not counted as part of exchange rate reserves. If the ECUs issued against dollars are treated as EC reserves, then the share of the dollar for 1989 falls to 52% of the total, and the share of the major European currencies rises to 32.9%. This is more than four times as large as the share of the Japanese yen. But as the IMF *Annual Report* of 1990 comments, 'The overall picture of changes in the trend in the currency

Table 9.2. *% share of national currencies in foreign exchange reserves, industrial economies and LDCs treated separately*

	Indust. Economies			LDCs		
	1980	1984	1989	1980	1984	1989
US Dollar	77.2	73.5	59.4	59.5	66.6	62.1
Pound Sterling	0.8	1.4	1.4	5.1	4.4	5.7
Deutsche Mark	14.3	15.2	22.9	15.4	10.0	11.4
French Franc	0.7	0.1	1.1	2.7	1.5	1.8
Swiss Franc	1.7	1.5	1.5	4.8	2.6	2.4
Dutch Guilder	0.7	0.6	1.2	1.9	0.8	0.8
Japanese Yen	3.3	6.3	8.2	5.4	5.2	7.1
Unspecified	1.3	2.1	4.4	4.8	8.8	8.7
Major EC Curr.	16.5	17.3	26.6	25.1	16.7	19.7

Source: IMF *Annual Report* (1990)

composition of foreign exchange reserves is similar if ECUs ... are treated separately.' (p. 67).

Table 9.2 contains a breakdown of the composition of foreign exchange reserves for industrial economies and LDCs. It suggests a much larger trend decline in the share of US dollars for the industrial economies than for LDCs. In addition, the LDCs seem to have diversified towards the Japanese yen rather than European currencies.

The trend decline in the share of dollar reserves in the portfolios of central banks of industrial economies is likely to be strongly reinforced as a result of the process of EMU. The reduced need for exchange market intervention in dollars by EC central banks that will follow establishment of EMU will entail a significant decline in the use of the dollar as an international means of payment by official bodies. However, this will not make the ecu a major reserve currency outside the EC, unless foreign exchange intervention by non-EC countries is also in ecu. The ecu will substitute for the dollar in the portfolios of non-EC central banks that decide to peg their exchange rate to the ecu. For example, as we show below, the EFTA countries appear to be pegging to the EMS already, although officially most are either floating or pegging to a basket of currencies (Gylfason, 1990, discusses the exchange rate policies of the Nordic countries). In addition, following liberalization in Eastern Europe, Poland and Czechoslovakia have introduced current-account convertibility for residents, and Hungary is not far behind. Convertibility is likely to continue to be a major feature of the economic transformation process in the formerly planned economies (Portes, 1991). That will increase their demand for reserves, in which the ecu is likely to occupy an important position.[4]

Additional demand could arise in case the European Bank for Reconstruction and Development (EBRD) were to conduct a large part of its borrowing and lending in ecu rather than dollars or yen. Such a preference towards the ecu on the part of the EBRD would of course cause an even higher increase in the demand for ecu reserves by the central banks of the Eastern European economies.[5]

In conclusion, EMU is likely to involve potentially significant substitution of ecu for dollars by central banks in the EC. Central banks in other European economies, such as the EFTA countries and the formerly planned economies, are also likely to use the ecu as their principal intervention currency, and the lending policies of the EBRD may further boost its position as an international means of payment. The position of the ecu may be strengthened even further if the worldwide increase in the demand for reserves by central banks continues. Since 1985 policy-makers in the G-7 and elsewhere have been much more positive towards exchange rate management. One expects an increase in the demand for reserves when there is a stronger commitment to defend exchange rates (see Dooley *et al.*, 1989; Black, 1985, however, suggests that the evidence on that is mixed).

We next turn to the means of payment function of international money as it applies to the private sector. Note that whereas international transactions in goods markets are arranged between importers and exporters, eventual payment is intermediated through commercial banks. Thus, what one should look for are the 'thickness' externalities that cause dealers to prefer indirect exchanges through a vehicle currency to direct exchanges of one currency for another. These externalities have to do with transactions costs, and the solution to the problem of double coincidence of wants by the use of money. If there are many dealers prepared to exchange dollars (the dollar market is 'thick'), then a dealer wishing to exchange pesetas for drachmas may find it less costly to go through two exchanges, one of pesetas for dollars and one of dollars for drachmas, than to go through a direct exchange of drachmas for pesetas. However, even when this is not the case, a vehicle currency is still used to finance bilateral trade imbalances (Krugman, 1980).

In a recent article on turnover in the foreign exchange market, the Banca d'Italia *Economic Bulletin* reports on a survey of 21 countries in April 1989. Europe accounted for 50% of the volume of transactions, of which half was in London. The dollar still accounts for 45% of total turnover; the Deutschmark and yen together for slightly over 25%. In Italy (a useful 'representative' case), the dollar and DM account for 39% and 32% of non-lira turnover respectively, and for 54% and 24% of lira turnover. In the forward market the dollar accounts for 40% of transactions against other foreign currencies and 97% of transactions against lire.

The market for ecus will be thicker than the market for any of the current EC currencies. This will make it more likely that the ecu will emerge as a medium of exchange on a par with the dollar in interbank markets. Thus, the fundamentals point towards a potentially large change.

To see this point consider the following example, based on the model of Krugman (1980). Assume that the world consists of three countries, U (whose currency is the dollar), G (whose currency is the DM) and F (whose currency is the FF). Assume that U runs a trade surplus I with F, that F runs a surplus I with G, and that G runs a surplus I with U. Imports of F from U are equal to R, imports of U from G are equal to T, and imports of G from F are equal to S. The structure of payments flows is depicted by arrows in Figure 9.1.[6]

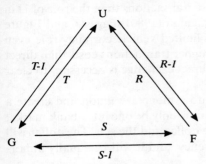

Figure 9.1 The structure of payments between U, F and G

Assuming as in Krugman (1980) that the percentage of transaction costs in the inter-bank market is a negative function of total volume in the market, and that the structure supports the dollar as a vehicle currency, we examine two potential equilibria. The one depicted in Figure 9.2(a) involves partial indirect exchange. The volume of transactions in the DM-FF market is equal to $S-I$, the imports of F from G, while the volume of transactions in the \$-DM and \$-FF markets is equal to T and R respectively. The dollar (\$) is a vehicle currency, as the financing of the trade deficit between G and F is intermediated through dollar markets, but the financing of trade imbalances between G and U and F and U is not intermediated through the DM-FF market. Figure 9.2(b) depicts the second potential equilibrium. This involves total indirect exchange, as all

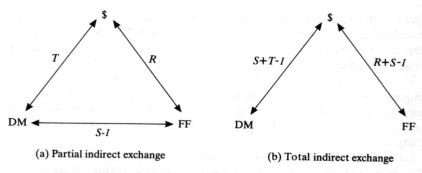

(a) Partial indirect exchange   (b) Total indirect exchange

Figure 9.2   The dollar as a vehicle currency; partial and total indirect exchange

of the financing of trade between F and G is intermediated through dollar markets. This would apply if the economies of scale were so large as to make two exchanges in the dollar markets less costly than one exchange in the DM-FF market. In each of these cases the dollar plays a special role as a vehicle currency as it enters into more transactions than the role of U in world payments justifies itself. As Krugman (1980) suggests, and Figure 9.2(a) makes clear, the $ 'will play a limited vehicle currency role even when roundabout exchange involves higher transactions costs than direct exchange. The reason is that some indirect exchange is necessary to clear the currency markets . . .' (p. 519).

Now suppose the G and F merge into a monetary union and create a common currency, the ecu. There will now only be one inter-bank market for foreign exchange, that between the dollar and the ecu. The dollar will lose its special status as a vehicle currency, and it will be equally important as the ecu.

This example is oversimplified in that it ignores transactions involving countries other than the USA and the EC 12. The dollar's role is important because it also intermediates in the financing of trade between the EC 12 and third countries, as well as trade of third countries among themselves. One of the reasons is again lower transaction costs in the interbank market. Thus, there is no guarantee that the ecu will substitute for the role of the dollar in these other markets. However, the reduction of transaction costs in all markets involving the ecu, vis-à-vis the markets involving the current EC currencies, will make this far more likely than in the absence of EMU.

Table 9.3 serves to highlight the importance of the European Community for world trade. It demonstrates that the EC accounts for a higher percentage of world exports and imports than the USA, even when intra-EC trade is netted out. The average share of the EC in world exports

Table 9.3. *% shares in world exports and imports of US, Japan and EC*

	1974	1979	1984	1989
		Exports		
USA	12.7	12.0	12.2	12.5
Japan	7.2	6.8	9.5	9.4
EC				
Gross	36.1	38.5	34.4	38.9
Net	14.8	13.6	16.6	15.7
		Imports		
USA	20.0	20.3	18.5	16.4
Japan	11.5	10.2	7.4	7.0
EC				
Gross	55.5	56.9	34.5	38.8
Net	25.4	23.4	16.9	16.6

Source: IMF, *Direction of Trade Statistics*, Yearbooks, 1981, 1990.
Note: The 'net share of the EC has been calculated by excluding intra-EC trade from the total trade of the EC. However, to preserve comparability with the other shares intra-EC trade was not subtracted from world trade (the denominator).

in the 1970s was of the order of 14%, as opposed to about 12% for the USA and 7% for Japan. In the 1980s the EC share rose to about 16% and Japan's rose to 9.5%, as opposed to a stagnant share for the USA. A similar position applies with regard to world imports, although the comparison between the 1970s and the 1980s is distorted by the effects of the oil and commodity price shocks of the 1970s that served to swell the share of imports of industrialized countries.

These facts point towards a significant potential for the ecu as a means of payments in international markets. The dollar will certainly be displaced in intra-EC trade as a result of Stage III of monetary union (intra-EC trade was a massive 22% of world trade in 1989), and will also be displaced with a high probability in trade involving the EC and third countries. Thus, the trade fundamentals are very favourable to the ecu.

In all this it is worth keeping in mind a second lesson from the Krugman (1980) model. This is that 'history will matter: once an exchange structure is established, it will persist unless the structure of payments shifts enough to make it untenable, or unless the system experiences a shock large enough to shift it from one equilibrium to another' (p. 523). We feel that EMU is a large enough shock, that will make the current position of the dollar untenable. It is bound to cause an unprecedented upset in the inter-bank market. Even the experience with the replacement of sterling by the US dollar in the inter-war period may not have involved as large and as abrupt a change in the fundamentals of the international monetary system as EMU is likely to bring (see Brown, 1940, for a classic treatment of this episode). However, the exact nature of the new equilibrium is difficult to predict, especially as even the simplest triangular exchange models (as those examined in the Krugman, 1980, paper) have multiple equilibria, and beliefs may play an important role in determining which equilibrium prevails. To paraphrase Newlyn (1962), international money 'falls within that perplexing but fascinating group of phenomena ... affected by self-justifying beliefs. If the members of a community think that money will be generally acceptable, then it will be; otherwise not' (p. 2).

It is also worth noting that for both the interbank market and the non-bank private sector the ecu will not be adopted unless transaction costs are low and banking in it is as cheap as the alternatives. The extent to which this will be the case will also depend on the success of financial deregulation in bringing down the cost of banking in the EC (Giovannini and Mayer, 1991). It will also depend on central bank and regulatory policies determining the costs of using the ecu payments mechanism (Folkerts-Landau and Garber, 1992).

1.2   The unit of account function

We next turn to the unit of account role of international money. This is closely linked to the means of payments role for national economies, although less so in the international monetary system. The unit of account role for an international currency depends first on whether importers and exporters invoice in that particular currency. Black (1985) presents evidence that whereas European firms invoice a very large proportion of their exports in their own currency, the proportion of their imports that is invoiced in other currencies, and especially dollars, is quite significant. On the other hand, Japanese firms invoice mainly in dollars, while more than 70% of LDC exports, 95% of OPEC exports and 85% of Latin American exports are invoiced in dollars. In an update and re-examination of these trends, Black (1989) finds that the share of Japanese exports invoiced in dollars has been falling over time, while the share dominated in yen has been rising. He also reports some indirect evidence that the share of US trade denominated in foreign currencies is rising. At the same time the Japanese and European shares of world exports have also been rising, while the share of US exports seems to have been stagnant (Table 9.3). The consequence seems to be a trend decline in the share of dollar-denominated world trade.[7]

In all probability EMU will result in almost exclusive invoicing in ecu by

EC firms. The only likely exceptions are imports from the US and Japan, and some primary commodities, if invoicing by commodity producers were to continue to be in US dollars. It is also quite possible that the economies of scale created by the substitution of a number of European currencies by a single one will induce firms from other areas that trade mainly with the EC to start invoicing in ecu. This may include the EFTA countries, many Middle Eastern and Mediterranean economies, as well as the newly liberalizing economies of Eastern Europe. It may also induce many multinational Japanese and US firms to follow suit, as they will also benefit from such economies of scale.

To the extent that trade relations become concentrated in regional blocs (e.g. Europe–Africa, Japan–Asia, US–Latin America), we might end up with at least three vehicle cum unit-of-account currencies. But insofar as trade is more uniformly distributed geographically and multilateral, there will still be powerful forces behind the use of a single dominant currency for these roles. In the latter case the change in the fundamentals will favour the ecu, but history (inertia) will favour the dollar. For example, it seems unlikely, although not unthinkable that the OPEC countries and producers of other internationally traded commodities will switch from dollar to ecu invoicing soon after the establishment of EMU. Again any change will depend on the extent and the speed with which the ecu displaces the dollar as a means of payment in international trade. As we suggested above, the fundamentals point towards a big displacement of the dollar as a means of international payments. Displacement of the dollar as an international unit of account is bound to follow at least partially, and possibly at a later stage.

The second aspect of the unit of account role of an international currency is related to whether there are countries that peg their own currency against it. Table 9.4 reports the number of countries that peg their exchange rate to the US dollar and other currencies. This is also a reflection of the importance of a currency as an international unit of account. Of the 55 countries that either pegged their currency or maintained limited flexibility against a single other currency in March 1990 (all these are LDCs), 34 did so against the US dollar, and 14 against the French franc. However all these economies are small, and even jointly they do not amount to much in terms of the world economy. In any case, as we suggested above, pegging against the ECU is on the increase. It is now official policy in Sweden and Finland (and unofficial policy in other EFTA countries), and the ECU is proposed as the unit of account in the payments system to be established between the Soviet Union, Czechoslovakia, Poland and Hungary (see footnote 2), and the lending of the EBRD.

Table 9.4. *Exchange rate arrangements, March 31, 1990: Number of currencies that peg against a single currency*

	Fixed Peg	
US $		30
French Franc		14
Other		5
	Limited Flexibility	
US $		4

Source: IMF *Annual Report* 1990.

Thus, although the ecu has a long way to go in order to become a major international unit of account, a number of factors will favour such a development. One is the momentous changes in Eastern Europe. The East European economies will necessarily have closer trade and financial links with Western Europe than with the United States or Japan. This makes it far more likely that both their firms and their central banks will use the ecu as a unit of account.[8] The process will also depend on the stability of exchange rates between the dollar, the yen and the ecu. If the US dollar were to display high volatility against the yen and the ecu, while their exchange rate was relatively stable, it would boost the chances of the ecu (and the yen) to substitute for the dollar as an international unit of account.

Table 9.5 reports correlation coefficients of dollar exchange rates for a number of currencies, with the DM-dollar rate. It demonstrates the high correlation of the EFTA currencies with the Deutschmark rather than the US dollar, especially since 1987 when EMS realignments stopped. Since January 1987 the correlation coefficient of the EFTA currencies with the DM is much higher than the correlation coefficient of sterling and the Portuguese escudo, let alone the Greek drachma which has been following an independent crawling peg policy, fully accommodating inflation differentials with the rest of the EC. It is also instructive to compare the high EFTA correlations with the low correlation of DM and yen exchange rates, in a period in which the G-7 were supposedly cooperating closely in exchange markets. Thus, exchange rate developments since 1987 suggest that the ecu may be an important unit of account for other economies with strong links with the EC, such as the current EFTA currencies.

Traditionally, the means of payment (international reserve) and unit of account (vehicle currency) functions of money go hand in hand. This was the case with sterling during the gold standard, and with the dollar during

Table 9.5. *Correlation coefficients of exchange rates against the US dollar with the DM/$ rate*

	Currency	Mar 1979–May 1991	Jan 1987–May 1991
EC			
France	Franc	0.718	0.994
Italy	Lira	0.615	0.987
UK	Pound	0.581	0.808
Belgium	Franc	0.858	0.996
Denmark	Krone	0.868	0.992
Greece	Drachma	0.023	0.028
Ireland	Pound	0.727	0.998
Holland	Guilder	0.997	0.999
Portugal	Escudo	0.123	0.793
Spain	Peseta	0.556	0.904
EFTA			
Austria	Schilling	0.999	0.999
Finland	Markka	0.093	0.936
Norway	Krone	0.589	0.954
Sweden	Krona	0.570	0.968
Switzerland	Franc	0.976	0.949
Japan	Yen	0.740	0.185

Note: The correlation coefficients have been calculated from end of month spot exchange rates, from OECD *Main Economic Indicators*, various issues.

the Bretton Woods system and beyond. It is very likely that the ecu will eventually become the dominant unit of account and means of payment in Europe and its immediate vicinity like North Africa and the Middle East. But it is more uncertain whether it will replace the dollar elsewhere. Much will depend on whether the dollar displays weakness because of the persistence of global imbalances, as well as on the attitudes of traders in the inter-bank markets, the Japanese and the LDCs.

1.3 The store of value function

The final issue related to the fundamentals of whether the ecu will become an important international currency has to do with the willingness of private investors to hold ecu assets. Some of the factors that affect the international investor also affect central banks, although central banks have an additional transactions motive as they have to intervene in support of their currencies.

Table 9.6. *Currency structure of the international bond market: total stocks, end of year*

	1982		1988		1989	
	US$bn	%	US$bn	%	US$bn	%
Total	259.1		1,085.4		1,175.7	
US Dollar		56.1		43.3		45.8
Swiss Franc		16.4		12.8		11.2
Japanese Yen		6.4		12.2		10.4
Deutsche Mark		12.1		9.6		7.5
Sterling		1.8		6.7		6.1
ECU		1.2		4.3		3.9
Major EC currencies		15.1		20.6		17.5

Source: BIS *Annual Report* 1990.

As in the case of central bank reserves, US dollar bonds make up a significant proportion of the international bond market. Table 9.6 contains data for selected years. The data suggest a small decline of the role of the US dollar since the early 1980s, and a slight increase in the share of EC currencies, from 15.1% in 1982 to 17.5% in 1989. The small dollar retreat has been accompanied by a sharp rise in the share of Japanese yen-denominated bonds.

Since stocks are slow to change, we also present in Table 9.7 some data on new bond issues. The decline of the dollar in the 1980s is more apparent from these data. Note that in 1990, admittedly a year of dollar weakness, the share of new bond issues in EC currencies exceeded the share of dollar-denominated bonds.

Clearly the fundamentals are related to risk and return, and there are considerable uncertainties both about the fundamentals and about the appropriate model for thinking about international financial investment (see Hall and Miles, 1991). A number of developments may work in the ecu's favour in the longer term. First we may witness a diminution of the so-called 'safe haven' motive for dollar holdings. If the liberalization of the East European economies proves durable and not a forerunner of political instability, and if the EC is successful in 'widening' as well as 'deepening', then Europe may eventually seem a much safer 'haven' than previously. This, together with the liberalization of financial markets in the EC, could increase the attractiveness of ecu-denominated assets. The second factor at work may be the anti-inflationary reputation of the Bundesbank, if it can credibly be transferred to the European Central

Table 9.7. *International issues of bonds, breakdown by currency of issue*

	1971	1976	1981	1986	1987	1988	1989	1990
Total ($ bn)	3.8	15.4	26.5	187.7	140.5	178.9	212.9	179.6
			%					
US dollar	59.7	65.1	80.2	62.9	41.3	41.7	55.2	38.4
Japanese Yen	–	–	1.5	9.9	16.1	8.9	7.3	12.9
EC Currencies	39.9	22.5	12.2	21.1	29.3	35.0	27.1	40.9
Deutsche mark	22.9	18.4	5.2	9.1	10.7	13.2	7.7	10.2
Sterling	1.6	–	2.0	5.6	10.7	13.2	8.7	12.0
French franc	1.3	0.4	2.0	1.9	1.3	1.3	2.1	5.0
Italian lira	–	–	–	0.2	0.5	0.9	1.6	3.0
Dutch guilder	7.1	3.0	1.6	0.5	0.8	0.1	1.1	0.8
ECU*	7.0	0.7	1.4	3.8	5.3	6.3	5.9	9.9
Other Currencies	0.4	12.4	7.6	6.1	13.3	14.4	10.4	7.8

Source: OECD *Financial Statistics Monthly*, various issues.
Note: * Before 1981 European Unit of Account.

Bank. Conversely, if liberalization in Eastern Europe and detente were to stall in the run-up to EMU, or if the economic strains of unification were to raise German inflation significantly, it would be that much more difficult for ecu assets to displace dollar assets in international portfolios.

At this stage, the uncertainties involved are reflected clearly in recent issues of the OECD *Economic Outlook*. In December 1989 it stated that: 'Over a longer period, portfolio diversification considerations point to some factors that could continue to favour the dollar, but others that are unfavourable. On balance, the unfavourable factors could be the stronger' (p. 44). Among such factors the OECD suggests that 'The growing importance of the ECU in financial transactions – notably bond issuance – combined with the creation of the EC single market and progress toward some form of monetary union in Europe, could over the longer-term result in a significant erosion of the status of the dollar as "the" international currency' (pp. 44–5). In December 1990, commenting on the narrowing of the differentials between US long rates and those for Japan and Germany it suggests that: 'What is important about these movements in relative yields is that they may be fundamental rather than temporary ... There is growing evidence that Japanese life insurance companies have reduced investment in foreign securities, while significantly increasing domestic loans. At the same time they have begun to diversify away from US securities towards increased holdings of European and Canadian assets. Similarly there has been less capital outflow from Germany, as domestic investment possibilities have risen significantly following unification.' (p. 11).

On the other hand, the 'thickness externalities' discussed above in respect of trade are not absent from financial transactions. Here, however, worldwide financial integration and globalization seem inexorable, in contrast to the possibility of regional trading blocks. Thus, financial globalization may slightly favour the continued dominance of the US dollar in bond markets.

2   Lessons from the experience of sterling

It is worth considering what history has to teach us about the speed with which EMU will bring about the possible changes in the international monetary system in favour of the ecu that we discussed in the previous section. A shock to the international monetary system such as full monetary union between so many large economies issuing important international currencies is unprecedented. The only historical experience that is remotely relevant is the decline of Britain in the world economy, and the replacement of sterling by the US dollar as an international currency. In this section we try to draw some of the parallels with that experience.

As is well known, before World War I, sterling had no serious rivals in its role as the main international currency, and London was by far the most important financial centre in the world. In the era of the international gold standard sterling convertibility was unquestioned. Britain was the world's principal creditor nation, the greatest exporter of new capital, and trade with Britain was a large part of the international trade of virtually every country in the world. As Cohen (1971) remarks, 'Especially after 1860, sterling came to circulate almost universally as a transactions and quotation currency' (p. 60). Due to the unique position of London as a financial centre, sterling served as a store of value for both private agents and governments, and this gave the Bank of England a leading role in the management of the international gold standard (see Eichengreen, 1987).

World War I brought about many changes in the fundamentals underlying the role of sterling in the international monetary system. The convertibility of sterling into gold became doubtful, Britain's role in international trade diminished and its foreign assets were depleted. New forms of international settlements caused a diminution of the role of London as a clearing house for international trade, and New York and Paris emerged as important financial centres, breaking the virtual monopoly of London. This caused difficulties for monetary management by the Bank of England. The dollar (and to a lesser extent the French franc) emerged as serious competitors for the role of sterling. It is worth noting, however, that even in 1925 sterling still accounted for a larger proportion of international trade and international assets than any other currency.

A landmark in sterling's replacement by the US dollar as the main international currency was the devaluation of 1931, the inconvertibility of the pound, and the creation of the sterling bloc (Cairncross and Eichengreen, 1983, discuss this episode). This was followed by other countries and gave the coup-de-grace both to the attempted restoration of the gold standard in the inter-war period, and to the role of sterling as a major international currency.

However, sterling retained a significant international role, through the creation of the durable sterling bloc, or sterling area as it came to be known after World War II. To quote from Cohen (1971), 'Since 1931 the predominant trend seems to be towards a regionalization of sterling's international status. ... In a sense, before 1931 all of the world was a sterling region. That was the meaning of globalization. But with the suspension of convertibility, sterling's world began to shrink.' (p. 65). By 1971 its functions as an international currency also seem to have shrunk to virtually nothing, both inside and outside the sterling area.

What lessons can one draw about the impact of the creation of the ecu on the international role of the dollar? As we saw in the previous section, there is a slow but identifiable diminution of the international role of the dollar already. The reasons are not yet fully understood, but they must have to do with the reduced importance of the United States for international trade and finance, the emergence of the United States as a net international debtor, exchange rate instability, and a worse record on inflation than countries such as Germany and Japan. Unless these trends are reversed, and we see this as unlikely, EMU may not be more than the 'straw that broke the camel's back'. As the analysis suggested, EMU is likely to be a very large shock to the current international monetary system. It is a change in the fundamentals that is probably greater than the change of the underlying position of Britain in the inter-war period and the further weakening of its international economic position in the aftermath of World War II.

What is likely to emerge in the place of the current international monetary system? Shall we see a trend towards regionalization, as the experience of sterling in the 1930s seems to suggest, or shall we see a new urge for global monetary cooperation, in the spirit of Bretton Woods?

Answers to such questions would be even more speculative than answers in other parts of this paper. The experience of sterling suggests that both routes are possible. The regionalization route involves protectionism and the creation of semi-separate trading and currency blocs. This route was followed in the early 1930s, and according to Nurkse (1944) and Kindleberger (1986) it led to the international propagation and amplification of the Great Depression. The cooperation route was followed in the post-war period. It led to the establishment of the Bretton Woods system with institutions like the IMF, the World Bank, the GATT and others, which have served the interests of the world economy well. The chances are that EMU will serve as a catalyst for closer international cooperation, in the context of a tri-polar international monetary system. The danger of regionalization is serious, however, and it should not be too heavily discounted.

3   Transitional issues

It is also worth examining in somewhat more detail the process by which the ecu could become a major international currency after the establishment of EMU. For this to happen there must be a demand for ecu from the rest of the world, which we have examined, but there must also be a matching supply. Ecus will be supplied at the beginning of the third stage of EMU, by the translation of the stock of financial assets denominated in the current EC currencies into ecu. This will of course include assets held by the rest of the world. However, since one expects a reduction in the dollar holdings of EC countries, new ecu will be accumulated in the rest of the world only if the EC runs a series of balance of payments deficits. Whether the deficits are due to the current or capital account matters only insofar as current account deficits are usually seen as a sign of weakness, and may undermine the credibility of the European Central Bank. If past trends and current fiscal policies are maintained, however, only a sharp fall in private savings (a possible consequence of financial deregulation) or a rise in private investment could lead to the EC running significant current account deficits. Table 9.8 reports current accounts as a percentage of GNP/GDP for the EC, Japan and the USA. This picture may change markedly in the run-up to EMU.

A rapid buildup of ecu balances in the rest of the world would require significant private and official capital outflows. Such outflows will take place, for example, if the liberalization of Eastern Europe continues and creates investment opportunities that attract direct investment from the EC countries. If the EC becomes an important capital exporter to the rest of the world, then the ecu may eventually become a widely held international currency. It was exactly this process that led to the establishment of the international role of sterling in the 19th century and the role of the dollar after World War I. However, one should not discount the possibility of an 'ecu shortage', in the same way as there was a 'dollar shortage'

Table 9.8. *Current balances of EC, Japan and US, % of GNP/GDP*

	1971	1976	1981	1986	1987	1988	1989	1990	1991	1992
EC	0.8	-0.6	-0.7	1.4	0.8	0.3	0.2	0.0	-0.6	-0.4
Japan	2.5	0.7	0.4	4.4	3.6	2.8	2.0	1.2	1.2	1.5
US	-0.1	0.2	0.3	-3.1	-3.2	-2.6	-2.1	-1.8	-0.2	-1.0

Source: OECD *Economic Outlook* (June 1991).

in the 1950s.

Of course, the EC's balance of payments deficit need not correspond to the supply of ecu. Central banks can borrow ecu from financial markets to build up ecu reserves and private financial intermediaries can increase the supply of ecu assets.[9]

What also has to be considered in assessing the prospects of the ecu as an international currency is the willingness of the Europeans to allow it to become one. The European Central Bank may resist the widespread international use of the ecu because of a perceived burden of acting as an international lender of last resort. There are two recent historical examples; the post-war prohibition on the part of the UK of the use of sterling balances for third country credits, which may have been a stimulus to the growth of the Euromarkets; and the Bundesbank's reluctance to allow the DM to be used as an intervention currency in the EMS because this would have led to increased external influences on domestic monetary policy.

If the European Central Bank pursues the opposite route of actively promoting the international use of the ecu, one cannot discount the possibility of a tug of war between the ecu, the incumbent (the dollar) and the major other contender (the yen) for international monetary supremacy. This could be a dangerous development. One might draw this lesson from the interwar experience of the rivalry between sterling and the dollar, with the French franc on the sidelines (Eichengreen, 1987). Even without such a potential rivalry, if EMU results in large-scale substitution of ecu for dollar balances, the tendency for ecu appreciation vis-à-vis the dollar may be a cause for concern. There may well be an increased need for better monetary policy coordination at the international level to cope with such an eventuality.

4 Costs and benefits of EMU in a tripolar world

What are the likely cost and benefits for Europe and the rest of the world? Benefits lie in the generalized reduction in transactions costs for Europeans and possibly for the rest of the world. There may also be benefits if the rise in the ecu and the reduction in the number of players in the international money game cause closer international monetary policy coordination. There may be costs for Europeans in the lender of last resort function of the Central Bank issuing a leading world currency. We have covered some of the issues above; the main new points we introduce here are the possible redistribution of international seigniorage, which we find insignificant, and the possible consequences for policy coordination and the international exchange rate regime, which may be significant indeed, although difficult to assess with precision.

Lender of last resort costs are currently shared between the IMF, the Federal Reserve Board, the Bank of Japan and the Bundesbank. EMU will upset the current sharing of responsibilities, in substituting the European Central Bank for the Bundesbank in an enhanced role. However, it is unlikely that there will be additional costs on that score for the EC as a whole.

The ecu foreign exchange market will be thicker than the markets of individual EC currencies. A thick market is inherently less volatile than thin markets and it may imply lower transactions costs, but it will also be harder to control by official intervention. Even if volatility were to increase, however, costs may be very small. For example, Baxter and Stockman (1989) failed to find any real effects from the higher volatility of real exchange rates under flexible exchange rate regimes, although Kenen and Rodrik (1986) and Peree and Steinherr (1989) have done so.

EMU might redistribute international seigniorage. If the ecu were to become a major international currency, there would be possibilities of raising seigniorage from the rest of the world. What would be the quantitative significance of such seigniorage? A comparison with other international currencies may be instructive. Cohen (1971) estimated that the seigniorage extracted from the fact that sterling was still a major regional currency in the 1950s and 1960s was almost zero. On the other hand, recent estimates by the Fed put the stock of dollar notes and coins held outside the United States at about $130 bn. With treasury bill rates of the order of 8% per annum over the longer run, this amounts to around $10 bn per annum, which is equal to about 0.2% of the 1988 US GNP. Corresponding numbers for the EC would be substantially lower. If they were to rise to one-fifth of the dollar seigniorage (say $2 bn), then international seigniorage would amount to about 0.05% of EC GNP.[10]

We now turn to the implications of EMU for international macroeconomic policy coordination. There are several types of uncertainty that constitute obstacles to successful coordination (see Frankel, 1988). The players may have incomplete or inaccurate knowledge of the initial position – the state of their own economies and those of other players. We may expect EMU and the associated development of intra-EC surveillance to improve this knowledge. On the other hand, it may be more difficult for the Community as a whole to agree on the weights to assign to target variables than for the individual major EC economies that now participate in G-7 coordination.[11] Without formal modelling, however, it is hard to say *a priori* whether coordination is easier with seven players having relatively well-defined objectives than with four, of whom one then speaks with somewhat less clarity. At this stage of our knowledge it is unlikely that we could obtain analytical results for such a problem. Nor is it clear whether the need for (benefit from) coordination is greater or smaller: there is no such need with only one agent, nor with an infinite number of atomistic agents. However, we know very little about how the costs of coordination failures vary between these two extremes.

An important set of issues relates to analytical aspects of the international coordination of monetary policies. Is the reduction in the number of major players in the international monetary arena likely to make coordination of monetary policies easier? Will EMU promote greater exchange rate instability worldwide, i.e., between a European currency and the dollar and yen? Some of the relevant factors can be examined with the help of three-country models. A major prior question is whether the US currently acts as a Stackelberg leader vis-à-vis the G-7. If so, the emergence of another major player (in fact two – the EC and Japan) will transform the nature of the game.

For example, Giavazzi and Giovannini (1989) suggest that more symmetry may generate instability in the international monetary system. If one economy is much larger and more closed than the others, it may be quite happy to act as a Stackelberg leader, using the money supply as its monetary policy instrument, without regard for its nominal exchange rate. One may then have an equilibrium in which the large economy sets its money supply, while the small economies intervene to affect their nominal exchange rates. However, if another major player were to emerge, in the absence of full cooperation, the greater symmetry may lead to instability. Both economies will have an incentive to try to use exchange rate policy, as their bilateral exchange rate vis-à-vis the other large country matters more, and in such a case insability will arise. Thus, in the presence of large shocks we may see both economies trying to manipulate their exchange rates, i.e. use beggar-thy-neighbour monetary policies, in which case there is a reversion to flexible exchange rates. As the authors put it, 'when the size of the Nth country is much larger than that of the other country (or countries), so that bilateral exchange-rate fluctuations do not significantly affect the Nth country's output and real income, a regime of managed rates does not display the instability that characterizes the symmetric case' (p. 208). These results suggest that the greater symmetry that EMU will imply for the international monetary system may result in a reversion to flexible exchange rates internationally.[12]

Our view is that such a conclusion is unwarranted in the circumstances. The international monetary system today is not as asymmetric as (say) the classical gold standard or Bretton Woods. The leadership of the United States has been significantly eroded, and Japan and Germany have been major players for some time now (see Group of Thirty, 1988).[13] Thus, EMU will not result in a qualitative switch from an asymmetric to a symmetric system, as the current system is already symmetric in many ways. In fact, the current arrangements, especially after the meetings at the Plaza in September 1985, can be interpreted as cooperative management of exchange rates and world monetary policy by the G-7. For example, Funabashi (1988) in his wide-ranging assessment of the process from the Plaza to the Louvre suggests that 'One of the achievements of the Plaza strategy was to force consensus despite the existence of ideological obstacles' (p. 229). To the extent that the current international monetary system is already symmetric and cooperative in the setting of monetary polices, there is little scope for EMU to destabilize it. In fact, Germany and France in the Plaza to the Louvre process clearly had the concerns of the EMS in mind. According to Funabashi 'as the EMS factor was vital to the West German Plaza strategy, so it was to that of the French. The Germans sought to avoid a painful schism within the EMS that a free fall of the dollar might cause, while the French wanted to keep the West Germans from taking over the EMS' (p. 125).

Thus, the shift to a more symmetric system as a result of EMU will not be substantial. The current system already seems to be characterized by some cooperative determination of monetary policies with exchange rate targets, although it may be second-best in that there is little use of fiscal policies for stabilization purposes (Alogoskoufis, 1989). In fact, in some ways the system resembles the blueprint of Williamson and Miller (1987), although there is the important difference that the central parities that constitute the targets of the monetary authorities of the G-7 are not publicly announced (see Miller *et al.*, 1989, for theoretical and empirical investigations of alternative blueprints).

In conclusion, EMU is unlikely to undermine the evolution of the international monetary system towards greater nominal exchange rate stability between the dollar, the yen and European currencies. Monetary policies are already being determined in a coordinated manner, and this looks likely to continue insofar as there is no clear 'hegemon' in the system. If anything, more symmetry among the players is likely to increase the need for (benefits from) coordination. An EC currency can unilaterally peg to the Deutschmark (accepting EMU discipline), but the ecu cannot unilaterally peg to the dollar or yen – close and reciprocal monetary policy coordination will be required to maintain exchange rate stability (see Portes, 1990). The implementation of monetary (exchange rate) policy in the EC will naturally be in the domain of the European Central Bank. To the extent that it is independent and non-accommodative it will contribute to price stability both in the EC and internationally (see Alogoskoufis, 1991). However, finance ministers, both in the European Council and the G-7, will ultimately decide the Community's views on the choice of the international exchange rate regime and will also be involved in issues such as (for example) the determination of target zones.

Issues relating to the international coordination of fiscal policies and the adjustment of external imbalances should also be considered. Recent discussions of blueprints for international monetary reform and their associated assignment rules provide an appropriate context.

Nation states will remain sovereign even under EMU. Under the most probable institutional scenarios, and unless the provisions envisaged in the Delors Report are adopted in their most extreme form, it is unlikely that the nature of the fiscal coordination game will change significantly. But fiscal outcomes will condition the Community-wide monetary policy. In addition, without independent national monetary policies, there will be more pressure in individual countries to use fiscal policy for domestic stabilization, as well as incentives to consider incomes policies. On the other hand, EC-level taxation and expenditure cannot be expected to grow markedly relative to national budgets, nor to become significantly more amenable to use as tools of discretionary stabilization policy.

There are a number of ways in which EMU may promote appropriate fiscal adjustments. The first has to do with the rules envisaged in the Delors Report for limits on national budget deficits. It now seems unlikely that such precise limits will be applied, but EMU may well result in more fiscal policy coordination within Europe. On the other hand, to the extent that European fiscal policies are coordinated, the EC may have more bargaining power in international institutions like the G-7, to avoid a repetition of the outcomes of the early 1980s, when disagreements among the Europeans weakened pressure on the US administration to consider the international repercussions of its macroeconomic policy mix. For example, Putnam and Bayne (1987) suggest that since 1981 'the non-American summit participants would be unanimous in complaining about US interest rates, the budget deficit and the strength of the dollar, at least until the dollar turned down in 1985. But there was less unanimity about causes and cures. The simplest remedy, which appealed to the French Socialists, would be for the Americans to loosen their monetary policy. However, the other governments were committed to the path of monetary rectitude embarked upon after the second oil shock, and they were uneasy about recommending the opposite course to the Americans. ... Thus ... the Americans mostly temporized. "Wait a while", was their message in Ottawa; "Let's study it", the approach in Versailles; "Our boom will solve it", the line in Williamsburg; and "After our elections", the promise at London II. Serious action on the dollar and the budget deficit had to wait till 1985.' (pp. 127–8).

The question whether EMU would increase potential coordination gains for the rest of the world and therefore induce the US to be more cooperative does not admit an easy answer. The existing views and the available empirical evidence are mixed. For example, as Currie *et al.* (1989) report in their recent survey (p. 26), the US benefits from coordination in empirical studies appear to be half as large as the benefits for Europe, irrespective of whether one examines coordination between the US and Germany or between the US and the EC. However, such studies do not take into account the major changes in the international monetary system that EMU may bring about. On the other hand, Alogoskoufis and Martin (1991) and Cohen and Wyplosz (1991) suggest that the nature of the international monetary system in the early 1980s was an important constraint on the ability of Europeans to act independently and counteract the fiscal shocks emanating from the United States (Reaganomics). They suggest that EMU will relieve this external constraint on European macroeconomic policy, and would in turn make it more difficult for the US to be uncooperative, as it would not be able to get away with beggar-thy-neighbour policies.

Economic policy coordination is ultimately and essentially political. Distributional issues must be resolved by a political process, both among countries in the EC and between the Community and its partners. Even if policy coordination is expected to bring gains, it will not be implemented unless there is some *ex ante* understanding about the distribution of such gains. The bargaining necessary to reach such an understanding will be easier for the Community as a unit vis-à-vis the US and Japan than for the four major EC countries acting individually in the G-7. On the other hand, *ex post* verification of compliance with an agreement on policies and enforcement of sanctions for non-compliance may be harder for the US and Japan vis-à-vis the EC than in dealing with individual countries. And it will take some time for the EC to establish the credibility in implementing policy commitments that some of its major member countries currently possess.

NOTES

We have benefited from the comments of Paul Masson, and the remarks of participants in workshops at the European Commission and the Georgetown Conference on the European Central Bank, in particular Bill Branson, Guillermo Calvo, Jeroen Kremers and Niels Thygesen. Neither they nor the CEC are in any way responsible for errors or for any aspect of our analysis. Financial support from the Commission of the European Communities and the CEPR FIMIE Project is gratefully acknowledged.

1 Throughout this paper we use 'ecu', with lowercase letters, to refer to the future common currency of the European Community. We use ECU, with uppercase letters, to denote the initials of the European Currency Unit, the existing unit of account of the European Monetary System, which is defined as a weighted average of EC currencies.

2 There is a theoretical literature investigating the emergence of media of exchange when there are more than two traders. Excellent examples ar the models of Jones (1976) and more recently Kiyotaki and Wright (1989) and Matsuyama *et al.* (1991). Typically such models have a multiplicity of equilibria. For example, in the Kiyotaki and Wright model there are equilibria with one money, but also equilibria with more than one.

3 See Yeager (1976) for a comprehensive history of the international monetary system since the 19th century. Kindleberger (1984) provides a history focused on Western Europe.

4 Poland introduced convertibility of the zloty in trade transactions on 1st January 1990, with an adjustable peg for the exchange rate, but it pegged against the dollar. However, according to a recent report 'The central banks of Soviet Union, Czechoslovakia, Poland and Hungary ... pledged support for a new banking payments system for trade among east European nations. The system would use as a common currency the Ecu, the basket of the main west European currencies.' (*Financial Times*, 24 April 1991). In addition, the Polish devaluation of May 1991 was accompanied by a move to a basket peg (trade-weighted).

5 Note that the capital of the EBRD is denominated in ECU. The trend towards the use of the ECU by the central banks of eastern European economies has already started, as the report quoted from the *Financial Times* confirms.

6 Note that although there are bilateral trade imbalances between countries, each country is assumed to be in balance of payments equilibrium, which in this simple model is defined as a zero trade balance.

7 These trends have also been examined in two recent papers by Tavlas (1990) and Tavlas and Ozeki (1991).

8 However, this tendency, which was also mentioned before, will not be unopposed, either at the micro or at the international macro level. A symbolic example is the reported resistance from the United States to the use of the ECU as unit of account for fixing the quotas of the new European Bank for Reconstruction and Development.

9 We are indebted to Paul Masson for this point.

10 The CEC (1990) study, using a different method and assuming a treasury bill rate of 7% arrives at 0.045% of GDP. Both their calculation and ours consider only high-powered ecu, netting out interest-bearing obligations.

11 In Alogoskoufis and Portes (1990) we discuss the changes that EMU will

probably imply for the institutions of macroeconomic policy coordination, such as the G-7. See also Dobson (1991).

12 The results in Kremers and Lane (1990) suggest that it may be easier for a European Central Bank to control the money supply than any of the current national central banks in the EC.

13 In any case, there is a lot of confusion about the definition of leadership in a repeated game. Stackelberg leadership is not an appropriate concept, and even the less precise notion of asymmetry may no longer be appropriate.

REFERENCES

Alogoskoufis G. S. (1989), 'Stabilization Policy, Fixed Exchange Rates and Target, Zones', in M. Miller, B. Eichengreen and R. Portes (eds), *Blueprints for Exchange Rate Management*, London, Academic Press and CEPR.

(1991), 'Monetary Accommodation, Exchange Rate Regimes and Inflation Persistence', CEPR Discussion Paper No. 503, London (forthcoming in *The Economic Journal*).

Alogoskoufis G. S. and C. Martin (1991), 'External Constraints on European Unemployment', in G. S. Alogoskoufis, L. Papademos and R. Portes (eds), *External Constraints on Macroeconomic Policy: The European Experience*, Cambridge, Cambridge University Press and CEPR.

Alogoskoufis G. S. and R. Portes (1990), 'International Costs and Benefits from EMU', CEPR Discussion Paper No. 424, London (forthcoming in *European Economy*).

Baxter M. and A. C. Stockman (1989), 'Business Cycles and the Exchange Rate Regime: Some International Evidence', *Journal of Monetary Economics* **23**: 377–400.

Black S. (1985), 'International Money and International Monetary Arrangements', in Kenen P. B. and R. W. Jones (ed), *Handbook of International Economics*, Volume 2, Amdsterdam, North-Holland.

(1989), 'The International Use of Currencies', in Y. Suzuki, J. Miyake and M. Okabe (eds), *The Evolution of the International Monetary System: How Can Stability and Efficiency be Attained?*, Tokyo, University of Tokyo Press.

Brown, W. A. Jr (1940), *The International Gold Standard Reinterpreted, 1914–1934*, New York, AMS Press and NBER.

Cairncross A. and B. Eichengreen (1983), *Sterling in Decline*, Basil Blackwell, Oxford.

Cohen B. J. (1971), *The Future of Sterling as an International Currency*, London, Macmillan.

Cohen D. and C. Wyplosz (1991), 'France and Germany in the EMS: The Exchange Rate Constraint', in G. S. Alogoskoufis, L. Papademos and R. Portes (eds), *External Constraints on Macroeconomic Policy: The European Experience*, Cambridge, Cambridge University Press and CEPR.

Commission of the European Communities (1990), 'One Market, One Money', *European Economy* **44**: 1–347.

Currie D. A., G. Holtham and A. Hughes Hallett (1989), 'The Theory and Practice of International Policy Coordination: Does Coordination Pay?', in

Bryant R. C., D. A. Currie, J. A. Frenkel, P. R. Masson and R. Portes (eds), *Macroeconomic Policies in an Inderdependent World*, Washington DC, International Monetary Fund.
Dobson W. (1991), *Economic Policy Coordination: Requiem or Prologue?*, Washington DC, Institute for International Economics.
Dooley M. P., J. S. Lizondo and D. J. Mathieson (1989), 'The Currency Composition of Foreign Exchange Reserves', *IMF Staff Papers* **36**: 385–434.
Eichengreen B. (1987), 'Conducting the International Orchestra: Bank of England Leadership under the Classical Gold Standard', *Journal of International Money and Fincance* **6**: 5–29.
Folkerts-Landau D. and P. Garber (1992), 'The ECB: A Bank or a Monetary Policy Rule?', this volume.
Frankel J. (1988), *Obstacles to International Macroeconomic Policy Coordination*, Studies in International Finance No. 64, Princeton University.
Funabashi Y. (1988), *Managing the Dollar: From the Plaza to the Louvre*, Washington DC, Institute for International Economics.
Giavazzi F. and A. Giovannini (1989), 'Monetary Policy Interactions under Managed Exchange Rates', *Economica* **56**: 199–213.
Giovannini A. and C. Mayer (eds) (1991), *European Financial Integration*, Cambridge, Cambridge University Press and CEPR.
Group of Thirty (1988), *International Macroeconomic Policy Coordination*, New York and London, Group of Thirty.
Gylfason T. (1990), 'Exchange Rate Policy, Inflation and Unemployment: The Experience of the Nordic Countries', CEPR Discussion Paper No. 377.
Hall S. and D. Miles (1991), 'An Empirical Study of Recent Trends in World Bond Markets', Discussion Paper in Financial Economics FE-3/91, Birkbeck College, London.
Jones R. A. (1976), 'The Origin and Development of Media of Exchange', *Journal of Political Economy* **84**: 757–75.
Kenen P. B. and D. Rodrik (1986), 'Measuring and Analyzing the Effects of Short Run Volatility in Real Exchange Rates', *Review of Economics and Statistics* **68**: 311–15.
Kindleberger C. (1984), *A Financial History of Western Europe*, Allen and Unwin, London.
(1986), *The World in Depression, 1929–1939*, revised edition, Berkeley, University of California Press.
Kiyotaki N. and R. Wright (1989), 'On Money as a Medium of Exchange', *Journal of Political Economy* **97**: 927–54.
Kremers J. M. and T. Lane (1990), 'Economic and Monetary Integration and the Aggregate Demand for Money in the EMS', *IMF Staff Papers* **37**: 777–805.
Krugman P. (1980), 'Vehicle Currencies and the Structure of International Exchange', *Journal of Money, Credit and Banking* **12**, 513–26.
(1984), 'The International Role of the Dollar: Theory and Prospect', in J. F. O. Bilson and R. C. Marston (ed), *Exchange Rate Theory and Practice*, Chicago, University of Chicago Press (for NBER).
Matsuyama, K., N. Kiyotaki and A. Matsui (1991), 'Toward a Theory of International Currency', Discussion Paper No. 931, Department of Economics, Northwestern University.

Miller M., B. Eichengreen and R. Portes (1989), *Blueprints for Exchange Rate Management*, London, Academic Press and CEPR.

Newlyn W. T. (1962), *Theory of Money*, Oxford, Oxford University Press.

Nurkse R. (1944), *International Currency Experience*, Geneva, League of Nations.

Perree E. and A. Steinherr (1989), 'Exchange Rate Uncertainty and Foreign Trade', *European Economic Review* 33: 1241–64.

Portes R. (1990), 'Macroeconomic Policy Coordination and the European Monetary System', in P. Ferri (ed), *Ten Years of the EMS*, London, Macmillan.

(1991), 'The Transition to Convertibility for Eastern Europe and the USSR', in R. Brunetta (ed), *Economics for a New Europe*, London, Macmillan.

Putnam R. D. and N. Bayne (1987), *Hanging Together: Cooperation and Conflict in the Seven Power Summits*, Revised Edition, Cambridge Mass., Harvard University Press.

Tavlas G. (1990), 'On the International Use of Currencies: The Case of the Deutsche Mark', IMF Working Paper 90/3, Washington DC.

Tavlas G. and Y. Ozeki (1991), 'The Japanese Yen as an International Currency', IMF Working Paper 91/2, Washington DC.

Williamson J. and M. Miller (1987), *Targets and Indicators: A Blueprint for the International Coordination of Economic Policy*, Washington DC, Institute for International Economics.

Yeager L. (1976), *International Monetary Relations*, New York, Harper and Row.

Discussion

JEROEN J. M. KREMERS

This paper examines important aspects of the process of European integration and the role of the ecu in that process. It was born, as indicated by Richard Portes at the Georgetown conference, out of a feeling that the current focus on 'Europe 1992' is turning into intra-European 'navel staring', and that important international monetary aspects are being overlooked. Let me summarize some of the main points, and place a few footnotes. The paper relates to the final stage of EMU, so – with the authors – I abstract from transitional issues and refer to the ecu as the single European currency managed by the European Central Bank (ECB).

The paper examines if, in addition to the expected reduction of transaction costs, an important argument favoring monetary union in Europe might be the increased role of the ecu in the international monetary system. Will a major role for the ecu be *worthwhile* for Europe? It turns out that the benefits may in fact turn out rather modest:

(1)   The ecu foreign exchange market will be thicker than any of the markets currently existing for EC currencies, so there will be less market volatility. However, this benefit has more to do with the increased efficiency of Europe's financial markets more generally (associated with the EC internal market program) than with the international role of the ecu.

(2)   The scope for raising seigniorage from the rest of the world turns out to be quantitatively rather small.

These benefits do not look too impressive. And they may be counterbalanced by significant costs. Just as the Bundesbank has long been reluctant to allow the deutsche mark to play a prominent international role since this could render domestic monetary control in Germany more difficult, the ECB may be cautious on the international role of the ecu. This may be true particularly in the first years of EMU, when the ECB will need to gauge the EC-wide demand for a single European currency. This will be difficult enough even without any promient demand for the ecu from outside the EC.

Thus, the reader is left wondering exactly why anybody in Europe would wish the ecu to enter a tug of war with the dollar and the yen for international monetary supremacy (Section 3). The paper does not indicate precisely who stands to gain.

A related but separate issue addressed in the paper concerns the *potential* international role of the ecu, quite apart from the question of who stands to gain. Several fundamental factors would seem to point to scope for a larger role for the ecu than for the total of the present European currencies:

(1)   The open EC market will lead to more extra-EC trade, hence to an enlarged role for the ecu as a means of payment and unit of account.

(2)   Financial liberalization in the context of the internal market program will enhance the efficiency of ecu markets.

(3)   The EMU will broaden the zone of monetary and price stability in Europe beyond the current 'hard core' of the ERM, which might enhance the role of the ecu as a store of value and, together with enhanced trade links, might entice non-EC countries to peg their currencies to the ecu.

(4)   The authors expect a greater emphasis on exchange rate management in the world, and hence a greater need for ecus in official reserves.

The bottom-line: scope probably exists for a larger international role for the ecu; it remains unclear, however, how soon this might materialize; and it is, moreover, unclear who in Europe stands to gain. My conclusion, therefore, would be that the potential of an increased role for the ecu can hardly be a major argument favoring monetary union in Europe.

Such a conclusion would in my view not be an unhappy one. For in order to appreciate fully the importance of EMU, one ought to step back a bit and remember that the prime rationale for EMU was, and is, to provide a stable financial environment for the free and open EC internal market (to be completed as early as by the end of this year!). Together, the internal market and the EMU are to greatly improve the functioning of market forces in the European economy and the utilization of Europe's resources. This process, which is already well under way, goes a great deal further than the reduction of transaction costs or the ecu being a contender with the dollar in the international market place. Thus I would not consider the focus on EMU and the internal market 'navel staring' – particularly so since, despite much progress so far, a lot of work still remains to be done.

Surely, nevertheless, the paper deals with important issues. Referring to the growing role of Germany, Richard Portes in his welcoming words to the conference mentioned the new slogan: 'Ein Markt, ein Geld, und eine Sprache.' That indeed it remains important to weigh – as in this paper – the pros and cons of European integration also in the international monetary field, is obvious in the light of rumours that, in a variation on Keynes, the logo of the European Central Bank will carry the motto: 'In the long run we are all German anyway'!

Index